Mastering ServiceNow

Conquer ServiceNow by getting to grips with the power behind the platform

Martin Wood

[PACKT] enterprise
PUBLISHING
professional expertise distilled

BIRMINGHAM - MUMBAI

Mastering ServiceNow

First published: May 2015

Production reference: 1260515

Published by Packt Publishing Ltd.
Livery Place
35 Livery Street
Birmingham B3 2PB, UK.

ISBN 978-1-78217-421-9

www.packtpub.com

Cover image by Vivek Sinha (vs@viveksinha.com)

Credits

Author
Martin Wood

Reviewers
Jason Butz
Jonathan Jacob
Ruen D Smith
Matt White

Commissioning Editor
Edward Gordon

Acquisition Editor
Sam Wood

Content Development Editor
Rohit Kumar Singh

Technical Editor
Menza Mathew

Copy Editors
Sonia Michelle Cheema
Jasmine Nadar
Aditya Nair
Merilyn Pereira

Project Coordinator
Mary Alex

Proofreaders
Stephen Copestake
Safis Editing

Indexer
Tejal Daruwale Soni

Graphics
Abhinash Sahu

Production Coordinator
Aparna Bhagat

Cover Work
Aparna Bhagat

About the Author

Martin Wood has spent the last few years spreading the word about ServiceNow. His first exposure to the platform was as one of its first customers in the UK in 2008, when he built a custom ITSM application. He enjoyed the experience so much that he joined the company. Now, he works with a variety of clients, ranging from blue-chip enterprises to SMEs, helping them utilize the power of ServiceNow. Martin is passionate about helping people make an informed choice and enjoys speaking at ServiceNow user conferences.

He lives in the beautiful Berkshire countryside with his wife, Sarah. They both love exploring the world and enjoying good food and great wine!

About the Reviewers

Jason Butz began learning about ServiceNow in 2013, and with the aid of several years of experience with web technology, he quickly started pushing the limits of what the framework could do. He has made numerous customizations and integrations to it to accomplish business goals and increase efficiency. He has since moved on to focus on web application development; however, it remains a valuable resource for people involved in the development of ServiceNow. It also acts as a code reviewer to ensure that quality is maintained.

Jonathan Jacob has been honing his expertise in ITSM since 2011. After being introduced to ServiceNow while working for a large publishing company, He joined a ServiceNow Solutions partner. There, he was able to consult for a number of industries from higher education to telecommunications. He has since returned to his roots in publishing as an architect in ServiceNow at The New York Times Company. Outside the world of ITSM, Jonathan is an avid cook and a hamburger enthusiast.

Ruen D Smith has been using ServiceNow since 2011. He has been a part of several client companies of ServiceNow, such as Deutsche Bank, UBS, National Grid, Gatwick Airport, and Microsoft. He has previously worked for ServiceNow partners, such as Innovise, Focus group, and HCL. He works as an administrator and is a Certified Implementation Specialist.

Matt White is a cloud security architect, with over 13 years of experience in information security. He has a reputation for designing and implementing large-scale security solutions for cloud platforms and service providers since 2011. He is currently building ServiceNow's third-party integrations for security products and enabling security automation for ServiceNow's security operations team. In previous roles with EMC and VMware, he served as the chief security architect for several cloud initiatives, including Mozy Online Backup, Cloud Foundry, and the vCloud Air service.

I'd like to thank Martin Wood and Packt Publishing for the opportunity to review and contribute to the publication of this book. It represents a broad coverage of our cloud platform and is a must-have for any administrator or developer creating business solutions with ServiceNow. I am always amazed and excited to see what innovations customers and partners are implementing with this great product.

Disclaimer

Martin wrote this book in his personal capacity. The views expressed are his own, and do not necessarily reflect that of ServiceNow.

Table of Contents

Preface

Congratulations! You have just become the ServiceNow System Administrator for Gardiner Hotels—one of the most successful chains in the region. The CIO realized that ServiceNow exactly fits his needs; a suite of feature-rich applications built upon a robust platform that makes the process of configuration and customization quick and easy. The SaaS architecture means that installation time is virtually nonexistent, which means that you can concentrate on what you want to do. The single tenancy model gives you power to configure and customize the system as needed, but without worrying about hosting or availability. You are in control of this power!

The simplicity of the basic operation is a little alluring. You can easily log in and start working. However, don't be fooled! Due to the breadth and depth of options, ServiceNow can quickly become overwhelming. Just like any other technology, ServiceNow has its own language, best practices, and idiosyncrasies. This is where this book comes in. By focusing on key areas within the platform, we look beyond the basics, in order to understand exactly what is going on. After reading this book, you should have a much better knowledge of how ServiceNow is best utilized, enabling you to create new custom process applications, and configure and customize built-in functionalities. All the applications you may use are built on top of the ServiceNow platform; by understanding this, you will be able to tackle almost any app.

What is in this book

Each chapter dives deep into the foundations of the platform. The book focuses on the specifics of ServiceNow, not what JavaScript is. We'll look at the hows, but more importantly, the whys. We'll explore options, and there is advice, but always along with justification. By understanding how things work, you will be better equipped to make your own decisions.

In this book, you will be configuring ServiceNow to be more useful to Gardiner Hotels. We'll achieve this by building out a sample Hotel Management application designed to showcase many of the capabilities within ServiceNow.

Chapter 1, ServiceNow Foundations, looks at how ServiceNow is structured from an architectural perspective. We explore how the platform is hosted and then dive into the building block of tables, fields, and building interfaces.

Chapter 2, Server-side Control, shows how you can implement your business logic, and then start to automate, validate, and verify data and processes.

Chapter 3, Client-side Interaction, explores how you can make the life of the people using your application just a little bit better by providing validation, feedback, and quick interaction techniques.

Chapter 4, Getting Things Done with Tasks, the Service Catalog and Service Portfolio looks at some of the base application functionalities in ServiceNow. Understand how a task-driven process system is kickstarted by the Task table, by taking advantage of Graphical Workflow, the Service Catalog and Service Level Management.

Chapter 5, Events, Notifications, and Reporting, introduces another level of interaction with your users, by generating reports and scheduling jobs, and handle incoming and outgoing email. Keep everyone informed about what's happening.

Chapter 6, Exchanging Data – Import Sets, Web Services, and Other Integrations, is about importing data from other systems, integrating ServiceNow in your application landscape. No instance is an island!

Chapter 7, Securing Applications and Data, focuses on the challenges of protecting your most important assets: your information. We make sure the right people have the right data.

Chapter 8, Diagnosing ServiceNow – Knowing What Is Going On, helps you when things go wrong. Troubleshooting and investigation hints and tips are explored, so you can get back to full power quickly.

Chapter 9, Moving Scripts with Clones, Update Sets, and Upgrades, builds on the previous chapters to explore how you can get your hard work in the right place. Understand how upgrades work, and how teams can work together to get stuff done.

Chapter 10, Making ServiceNow Beautiful with CMS and Jelly, focuses on creating a self service portal, but also discusses how the ServiceNow interface is built. Having a good looking, well-designed frontend really enhances adoption.

Chapter 11, Automating Your Data Center, looks at having ServiceNow in charge of your IT. By discovering what is out there, then automating the maintenance and deployment of the new functionality, ServiceNow will become an invaluable part of your business.

What you need for this book

ServiceNow is an enterprise SaaS platform. In order to work with the application, you will need access to a ServiceNow instance, with System Administrator access. The examples in this book are about a custom application, but it is strongly recommended that any work is performed in a subproduction instance.

ServiceNow does offer instances as part of their developer program. You can sign up here: `https://developer.servicenow.com/`. These instances may use a different build and version, which means that some of the examples may not be relevant.

Alternatively, contact your ServiceNow representative and request a temporary sandbox instance.

The examples have all been built with the Eureka version of ServiceNow, released in mid 2015. Both earlier and later versions are likely to work, though some platform and application functionalities will obviously change.

Who this book is for

This book will be most useful to those who understand the basics of IT, web technologies, and computer science. We discuss how ServiceNow implements common design patterns and technologies, enabling you to get a better understanding of how ServiceNow operates.

There is a great deal of functionality in ServiceNow, and it simply isn't possible to cram everything into a single book. ServiceNow has a comprehensive wiki and a popular community forum. The ServiceNow training department has a series of mixed media courses to get you up to speed quickly. We aren't going to replicate these, and the book expects that you have taken the basic admin course as a ServiceNow System Administrator. Two important things to be done are:

- Keep the wiki page open at `https://wiki.servicenow.com/`
- Sign up to the community at `https://community.servicenow.com/`

Every ServiceNow System Administrator needs to have at least a basic understanding of JavaScript. JavaScript underpins the ServiceNow foundations, and, hence, is essential to fully master ServiceNow. An in-depth knowledge of all the intricacies of JavaScript is not needed, since many of the idioms and objects used are ServiceNow-specific. Nonetheless, scripting is part of the product. A review of a good JavaScript manual may be helpful!

We also assume a working knowledge of basic web technologies, such as HTML and CSS, and standard concepts, such as databases and SQL.

Conventions

In this book, you will find a number of text styles that distinguish between different kinds of information. Here are some examples of these styles and an explanation of their meaning.

Code words in text, database table names, folder names, filenames, file extensions, pathnames, dummy URLs, user input, and Twitter handles are shown as follows: "If you remove the `_list` part from the URL, you will be presented with the first record that matches."

A block of code is set as follows:

```
var sa = new SimpleAdd();
sa.increment().increment();
gs.log('Accessing the variable number ' + sa.number)
```

When we wish to draw your attention to a particular part of a code block, the relevant lines or items are set in bold:

```
if (email.subject.indexOf("approve") >= 0)
  current.state = "approved";
if (email.subject.indexOf("reject") >= 0)
  current.state = "rejected";
```

Any command-line input or output is written as follows:

```
ALTER TABLE u_check_in ADD `u_comments` MEDIUMTEXT
```

New terms and **important words** are shown in bold. Words that you see on the screen, for example, in menus or dialog boxes, appear in the text like this: "Create a new field called **Comments**, by double-clicking on **Insert a new row...**"

Warnings or important notes appear in a box like this.

Tips and tricks appear like this.

Reader feedback

Feedback from our readers is always welcome. Let us know what you think about this book—what you liked or disliked. Reader feedback is important for us as it helps us develop titles that you will really get the most out of.

To send us general feedback, simply e-mail `feedback@packtpub.com`, and mention the book's title in the subject of your message.

If there is a topic that you have expertise in and you are interested in either writing or contributing to a book, see our author guide at `www.packtpub.com/authors`.

Customer support

Now that you are the proud owner of a Packt book, we have a number of things to help you to get the most from your purchase.

Downloading the example code

You can download the example code files from your account at `http://www.packtpub.com` for all the Packt Publishing books you have purchased. If you purchased this book elsewhere, you can visit `http://www.packtpub.com/support` and register to have the files e-mailed directly to you.

Errata

Although we have taken every care to ensure the accuracy of our content, mistakes do happen. If you find a mistake in one of our books—maybe a mistake in the text or the code—we would be grateful if you could report this to us. By doing so, you can save other readers from frustration and help us improve subsequent versions of this book. If you find any errata, please report them by visiting `http://www.packtpub.com/submit-errata`, selecting your book, clicking on the **Errata Submission Form** link, and entering the details of your errata. Once your errata are verified, your submission will be accepted and the errata will be uploaded to our website or added to any list of existing errata under the Errata section of that title.

To view the previously submitted errata, go to `https://www.packtpub.com/books/content/support` and enter the name of the book in the search field. The required information will appear under the **Errata** section.

Piracy

Piracy of copyrighted material on the Internet is an ongoing problem across all media. At Packt, we take the protection of our copyright and licenses very seriously. If you come across any illegal copies of our works in any form on the Internet, please provide us with the location address or website name immediately so that we can pursue a remedy.

Please contact us at `copyright@packtpub.com` with a link to the suspected pirated material.

We appreciate your help in protecting our authors and our ability to bring you valuable content.

Questions

If you have a problem with any aspect of this book, you can contact us at `questions@packtpub.com`, and we will do our best to address the problem.

1
ServiceNow Foundations

This opening chapter picks out the most significant foundations of ServiceNow, starting from the bottom up. Understanding the fundamentals of the ServiceNow platform is important. It gives insight into the concepts that underpin how everything else works.

> Although long, the chapter is not exhaustive and does expect a basic familiarity with the ServiceNow interface. Remember to reference the ServiceNow documentation and any training material you may have.

Perhaps you've decided to build a new hotel and you want to ensure it won't fall down. The architect's drawings need to be understood and the right building materials ordered. It's costly (and career limiting!) if it collapses in the week after opening!

In this chapter, we review the blueprints. We understand the important design aspects of ServiceNow so that we can build on them later. The data structure available to us is critical, to enable us to model information and processes in the right way.

In this chapter, we will cover:

- The physical components of the ServiceNow architecture
- How everything you see and do is in the database
- A review of the most important field types
- The magic of reference fields and table inheritance
- Using and building a good interface

Diving into the infrastructure

An **instance** is several things. It is a URL (something like https://<instance>.service-now.com/); it's software running in the cloud; it's your copy of the ServiceNow platform.

ServiceNow provides a platform and suite of applications as a service. They worry about the hardware, Internet connectivity, and operating system security and provide you with the URL. All you need to get going is a web browser.

Being in charge

An instance is an independent implementation of ServiceNow. It is isolated and autonomous, meaning your instance is not shared with other customers. ServiceNow uses a single-tenancy architecture, which means your instance is yours: you can do what you want with it, such as changing logic, updating the UI, and adding fields.

Every customer has several instances; again, all isolated and independent. One instance might be marked out for developing on, another for testing, and one for production. And, because each instance is independent, each one can be running a different release of ServiceNow. The production instance only differs because it has more powerful hardware.

> *Chapter 9, Moving Scripts with Clones, Update Sets, and Upgrades*, discusses how you can use your instances for tasks such as building functionality, testing it, and then making it live.

Changing your instance

A new instance starts with a few ServiceNow applications, some demo configuration, and example data. This is often called the out-of-the-box state. One of the example data elements is the **System Administrator** user. You are able to log in and get going, getting full control immediately.

Everyone makes changes to their instance. Unless the people who will be using the system are called **Beth Anglin** or **David Dan** (some of the default example users), you'll need to load some users at the very least. Some ServiceNow customers configure a lot and some do the bare minimum. You can choose how much you wish to do. Because it is single-tenant, you can alter the configuration and data in almost any way you see fit. Now, it might not always be smart to do that, but you can!

> My favorite analogy, if you haven't guessed it, is a building. ServiceNow gives you an office that is yours. It starts off identical, built to the standard plans, but you can redecorate or remodel as you see fit. Perhaps even knock down a wall! (Let's hope it's not load-bearing.) This is the benefit of single-tenancy.
>
> Multitenancy might be an apartment in a block. It is generally more efficient to pack lots of people together in a single building, and you can build it pretty high. However, you don't have the flexibility that being in control gives you. The landlords of the block won't let you knock down a wall!
>
> The vast majority of customers have their instance hosted by ServiceNow. This means the people who built the house will also look after it, on their land. You get great economies of scale, and the benefit of tools and automation design to perform maintenance and give support fast. All the gardeners and janitors are on site, ready to work—they don't need to travel to help out.

Choosing functionality with plugins

All ServiceNow functionalities are delivered as **plugins**. When an instance is turned on, one of its first tasks is to load all the plugins that are turned on out of the box. There are quite a few of those, over 200 in the Eureka version of ServiceNow. And there are several hundred more that you can turn on if you want. A plugin may provide an app, like Human Resources Management, or provide new platform functionality, like Domain Separation. Each new version of ServiceNow brings new plugins and updates to existing ones.

> *Chapter 9, Moving Scripts with Clones, Update Sets, and Upgrades,* talks about plugins and upgrading ServiceNow in more detail.

When a plugin is turned on, all the data and configuration that the application needs is loaded into the database, meaning that it is ready for work in just a few moments. Many also contain demo data, giving you examples of how it could work.

Digging into hosting

A ServiceNow-hosted instance is split over two physical datacenters, a high-availability pair. Each location runs independently of the other, giving a semiclustered environment. In the event of a catastrophic disaster, with one location being completely unavailable, the other nodes will just pick up the load, with almost no downtime. In fact, the process of switching between locations is used for maintenance procedures, enabling your instance to be well-protected against hardware and other failures.

When you visit your instance, you are directed through several layers:

- By looking up the DNS records, you are directed to the currently active datacenter
- The load balancer, by reading a cookie, directs you to the application server you have your session with
- If you aren't logged in, you get directed to the least-busy application server
- Your application server then uses the database currently determined as active

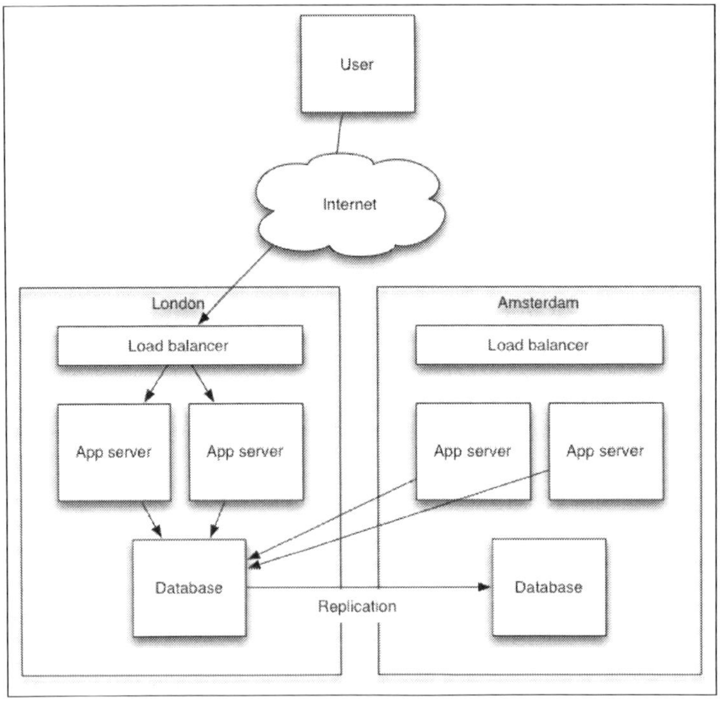

Knowing the nodes

From an architecture perspective, a ServiceNow instance is made up of several application and database servers or nodes. These are generally running on shared hardware, meaning that although your instance is logically separate and independent, it is physically hosted alongside another customer. At each location, there are generally at least two application nodes, each running a copy of the ServiceNow platform, which work together to share load. Additionally, there may be worker nodes installed to process the non-interactive jobs, such as event processing. Even though you'll never directly log in to these worker nodes, they perform some background processing, allowing the interactive application servers to respond more quickly to user requests. For example, a worker instance might send out e-mails or deal with integrations. While there are generally lots of application nodes, there is only one active database server, running on a separate physical server. It does have a redundant pair hosted in the remote datacenter.

> *Chapter 5, Events, Notifications, and Reporting*, explores the concept of event queues in more detail.

Exploring the database

So you've got an instance and have logged in. Great! What can we see? We can see database records.

You may not realize it, but the homepage, the reports, and the menus to the left are all database records:

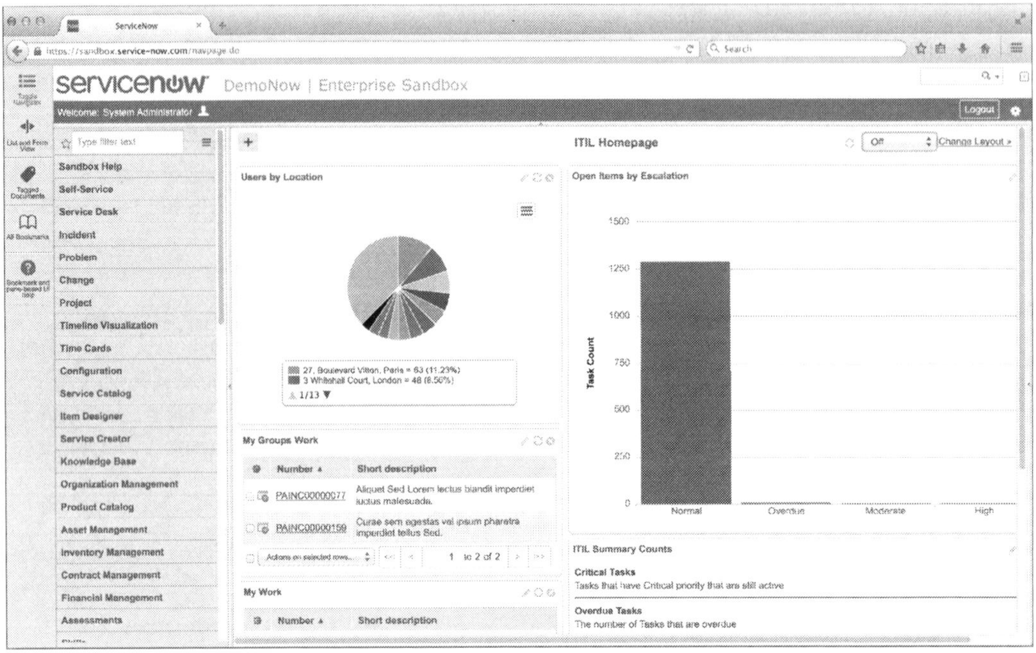

Almost everything in ServiceNow is an entry in a database. When you look at the user interface, virtually everything you see—from the data typed in by a user, to log files, to how the views are structured—is stored in the instance's relational database. Even the scripts you write are kept in a string field in a record, and the files you upload are stored in chunks in the database.

Everything is built on the top of this structure. You don't need to reboot the server to apply new functionality; you are just updating data records. You don't need to reload configuration files—any properties you set will be read on the next operation. Even the database metadata, information about the fields themselves, is stored in another table.

This gives you extraordinary control and ability. You can organize, search, and manage the data in an unprecedented manner. You can find scripts the same way you find users, by searching tables. You can control and secure any data, regardless of what it is, by using Access Control Rules. This means you can focus on designing and building great business applications, since the platform works in a consistent manner.

> ServiceNow may be considered a high-level platform that is based on the concept of *Model-View-Controller*. When building a ServiceNow application, you can first think of the data structure. You determine what information you need to store and how it all links together, creating tables and fields. This is the *model* aspect.
>
> Automatically, you get a simple *view* on this data, with forms and lists showing your information.
>
> And you can build simple ways to manipulate and change the data, through automation and simple manual updates. This is the *controller* aspect.

Introducing the Gardiner Hotel data structure

One of the first things that many people learn how to do in ServiceNow is to add a field. In ServiceNow, this is a straightforward operation—you add the new field to a form or a list using the UI. Under the covers, the ServiceNow platform is performing, among other operations, a simple SQL command to add a column to the table you are manipulating. When you add a field, you add a column to the table. When you remove a field, you are dropping it. There is no magic—the platform interface just makes it easy to do.

> ServiceNow allows you to add fields to every table in the system. If you decide that adding another is a good idea, you have the power to do it!

In order to work through the ServiceNow functionality, we are building a hotel management application for your new employer, Gardiner Hotels. It will involve building a simple data structure, but one that is highly interlinked.

Here is a representation of the tables we will create in this chapter:

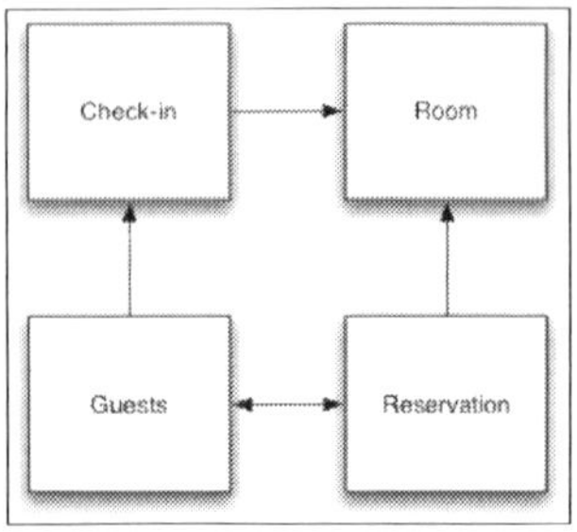

This diagram represents several common activities within a hotel, and their links to each other.

- **Guests**: The reason why Gardiner Hotels exists! Our guests' details are the most important information we have. We definitely need their names, and optionally their e-mail addresses and phone numbers.
- **Room**: This represents where our guests will sleep. We store the room number and the floor it is on.
- **Check-in**: When guests want their room key, they check in. We record who is checking in to a room, when, and who made the entry.

  We will create a link to the **Room** table so we can easily see information about the room, such as what floor it is on.
- **Reservation**: Our guests like staying with Gardiner Hotels, and they often book months in advance.

  One reservation might be for many guests, especially if the whole family is coming. A big family might need a big room. We need to record where exactly they may stay.

> Over the course of the book, we will expand and further develop the application. Its primary use is to show you as much of the capability of ServiceNow as possible, so some of the examples may be done better in other ways.

Creating tables

Firstly, let's create an app to hold our configuration in. Navigate to **System Applications** > **Create Application**. Fill in the following value and click on **Submit**:

- **Name**: `Hotel`

> The convention for navigating through ServiceNow uses the following structure: **Application Menu** > **Module**. For modules with separators, it will be **Application Menu** > **Section** > **Module**. The easiest way to find a particular link is to type it in to the **Application Filter** at the top left of the menu. Make sure you are choosing the right one, though, because some modules are identically named.

Then find the **Tables** Related List, click on **New**, and fill in the following values:

- **Label**: `Check-in`
- **Name**: `u_check_in`

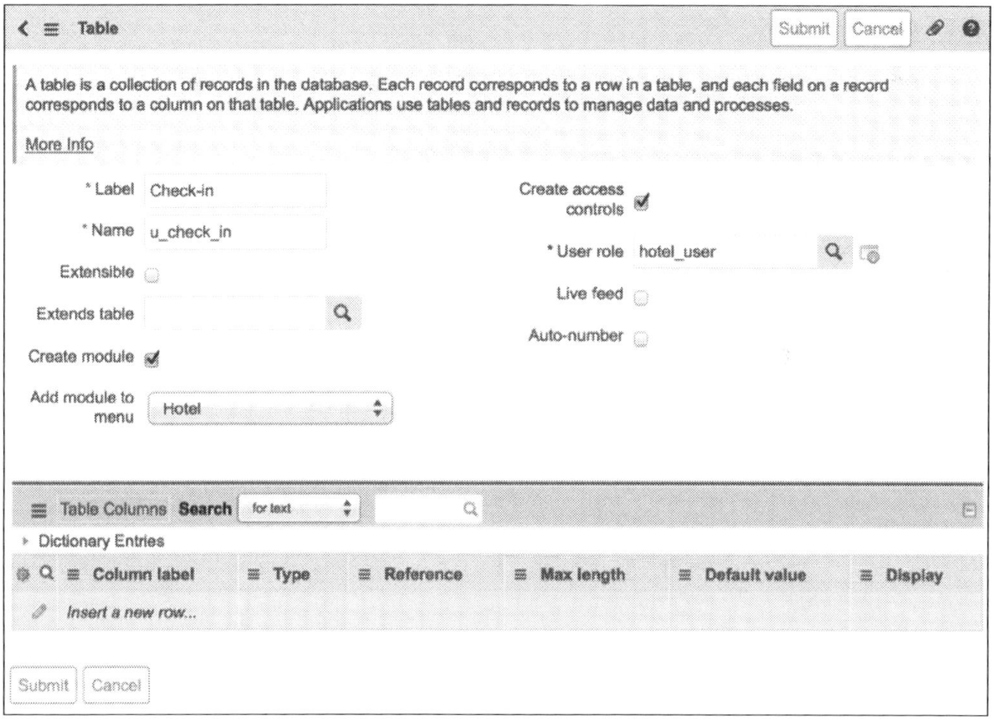

The rest of the default entries should be fine.

> Many technical items in ServiceNow have a label and a database name. In this case, the database table is called `u_check_in`, while an entry in the **Field Labels** [`sys_documentation`] table contains the mapping between the name and the label. I'll use the **Label** [`database_name`] format throughout the book.

When you click on the **Save** button, the application server creates the table in the database.

> I recommend using the **Save** button to commit records to the database, accessible via the 3-line menu icon, or by pressing *Ctrl* + *S*. This ensures that the record is renamed on screen rather than redirecting to the previous page.

Adding fields

When you create a new table, you get some system fields. They include two dates (when a record was created and when it was last updated), two string fields (containing the user ID of who created it and who updated it), a unique GUID called the `sys_id`, and a field that counts the number of updates to the record. They are all updated automatically, and it is generally good practice to leave them alone. They are useful just as they are!

> We'll be discussing the `sys_id` field a lot in just a moment!

The following screenshot shows how the system fields are represented within the tables:

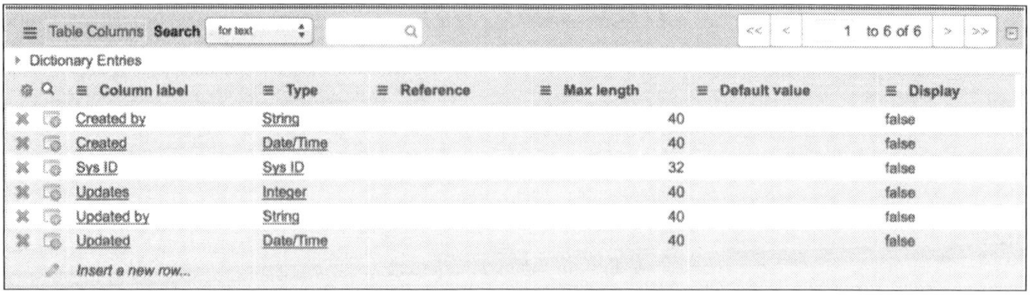

> The autogenerated fields are very helpful to the System Administrator for finding records quickly. I always add the **Updated on** field to my lists, since it makes finding the records I've been working on (such as scripts) much faster.

In addition to these automatic fields, we need to create some of our own. We will need several, but right now, let's create something to store any requests that the guest may have. Perhaps they may have specifically requested a high floor.

Create a new field called **Comments** by double-clicking on **Insert a new row...**. Fill out the row with the following data and then save the record:

- **Column label**: `Comments`
- **Type**: `String`
- **Max length**: `500`

The following screenshot displays how the columns list looks before saving the changes:

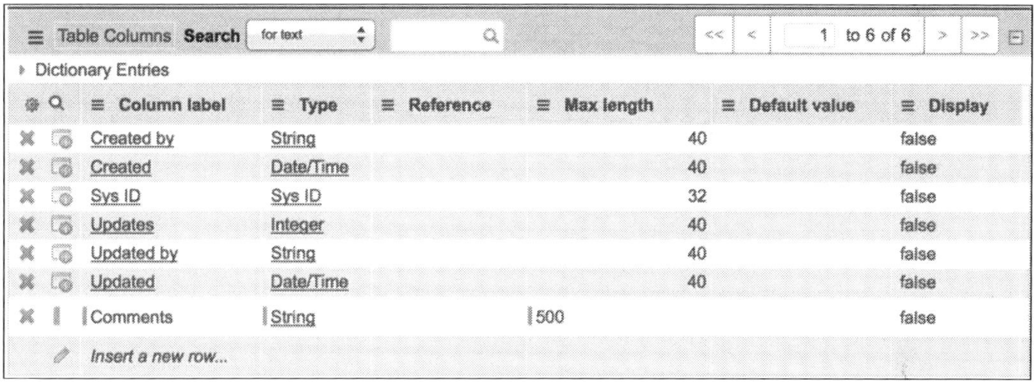

Table Columns Search for text | 1 to 6 of 6

Dictionary Entries

Column label	Type	Reference	Max length	Default value	Display
Created by	String		40		false
Created	Date/Time		40		false
Sys ID	Sys ID		32		false
Updates	Integer		40		false
Updated by	String		40		false
Updated	Date/Time		40		false
Comments	String		500		false
Insert a new row...					

> All the fields and tables that you create will get a `u_` prefix in the name, while the label will stay as is. This helps you (and the upgrade process) to separate them from the out-of-the-box functionality.
>
> Upgrades are discussed in more depth in *Chapter 9, Moving Scripts with Clones, Update Sets, and Upgrades*.

Knowing what's happening

Behind the scenes, the application server is running SQL commands against the database. Specifically, at the time of creating the field, the following was executed:

```
ALTER TABLE u_check_in ADD 'u_comments' MEDIUMTEXT
```

> If you wish to see these commands, navigate to **System Diagnostics** > **Debug SQL**. This will place lots of information at the bottom of the page. Other diagnostic tools like this are discussed in *Chapter 8, Diagnosing ServiceNow – Knowing What Is Going On.*

This demonstrates a key concept. Whenever you perform an action in ServiceNow, it results in a string of database commands. The database is altered and the platform's internal state is updated. These actions are generally carried out quickly, with the whole process completed in about half a second. No downtime is necessary.

Introducing the dictionary

The **dictionary** is a metatable. It describes your table and fields—what their name is, how big they are, along with any special attributes they may have. For example, one field might be dependent upon another. A dictionary entry might also be referred to as an **Element Descriptor**.

The table is represented by an entry in the dictionary with a table value, type of `Collection`, and no column name. When the **Comments** field was added to the **Check-in** table, the platform also made a dictionary entry with the table and a column name. You can view it by navigating to **System Definition** > **Dictionary**.

The options that are available in the dictionary are dependent upon what type of field you are working with. Reference fields, which we will explore in a moment, have extra functionality that is controlled here, such as dynamic creation.

As we work through ServiceNow, we'll spot functionality that is enabled through the dictionary. However, much of it can be achieved in other ways, often in a better manner.

> Older versions of ServiceNow have a read-only tick box available on the dictionary form by default. While it can be included and used in later versions, it is usually a better idea to use security rules instead. Having a field marked as read-only is a binary choice, and giving System Administrators control over data is a good idea. You get that granularity with security rules, which we will explore in *Chapter 7, Securing Applications and Data.*
>
> The easiest way to navigate to a dictionary entry is by right-clicking on the label of the field and choosing **Personalize Dictionary**. You can see some details about a field, such as what table is it in, by choosing the **Show** option on the menu that appears on right-clicking.

The Globally Unique Identifier

The ServiceNow database is a relational database. This means that one bit of data can relate to another. To ensure that every record or row can be referenced easily, every record has a unique identifier: a **primary key**.

In ServiceNow, this primary key is something that isn't related to the data itself. It is a **globally unique identifier** or **GUID**. This GUID is stored as a 32-character string, made of hexadecimal characters (the numbers 0-9, plus the letters a-f). The number of unique GUID values is so large that the probability of two accidently being the same is negligible. This is an example GUID: `5137153cc611227c000bbd1bd8cd2005`.

> This type of identifier is sometimes known as an **OID** or **object identifier**. It has no special significance; it just uniquely identifies a data row. It can also be called a **surrogate key**.

Whenever you create a record in ServiceNow, the platform generates a new GUID. The characters that are generated are random—a mixture of several sources, including the date and time and details specific to the instance, meaning it is not sequential or predictable. The GUID is saved alongside the record, in a special field called `sys_id`. The `sys_id` field is heavily used in the ServiceNow platform—you will start seeing GUIDs everywhere!

As an example of how ServiceNow uses the `sys_id` field, conduct the following experiment. Construct a URL similar to the one that follows, substituting <instance> with the name of your instance, and visit it with your browser: https://<instance>.service-now.com/sys_user.do?sys_id=5137153cc611227c000bbd1bd8cd2005.

In a new instance, you should happen across the user record of **Fred Luddy**. (If the demo data has been removed, you will get a **Record not found** message.)

It is useful to examine the structure of the URL. Firstly, spot the `sys_user` table. Then spot the GUID. With these two items, the instance knows exactly what data it needs to pull up and present to you.

Every record has a `sys_id` field. It is the only field that ServiceNow really cares about. It also looks after itself. You don't need to worry about it during day-to-day operations.

> Reference fields, as we'll see, are very reliant upon the `sys_id` fields. When we get into scripting in *Chapter 2, Server-side Control*, you'll be seeing more of them!

Every other field is non-mandatory and non-unique to the database platform. You can have two records that are otherwise identical but only have a differing `sys_id` field. (It is possible to enforce uniqueness in other fields too, as we'll see later.)

This means that, in general, you can change the value of fields to whatever you like and still maintain referential integrity; no system errors will occur. If you want to rename a user or a group, go ahead. Since everything related to that user will be associated to it via the `sys_id` field, the name of the user is not important.

Many other products do not use surrogate keys; data is linked together using user-provided data. If you change the name of a group, for example, this can remove all group memberships and assignment to tasks. Not in ServiceNow!

> An important exception to this behavior is with roles. Roles are referred to by their name in scripts, so if you change the name, all scripts that use it will need to be altered (though security rules *do* refer to the role through the `sys_id` field.) In general, it is a good idea to keep the name of roles the same.

It is a good idea not to interfere with this flexibility. When you are building functionality, try not to refer to records using their name or `sys_id` in scripts. Instead, use the properties or attributes of the record itself to identify it. So, rather than hardcoding that a particular room in our hotel needs special treatment, create another field and use it as a flag. The VIP flag on the **User** table is a good example of this.

Building hierarchical tables

ServiceNow is built on a relational database. Instances hosted by ServiceNow use MySQL—a popular open source database that is robust, well featured, and scalable. Relational databases are relatively simple to understand, which is one of the reasons why they are most commonly used; data is held in a tabular format with each table storing information about a particular item. Relationships may exist between these items. Our database design described in the previous section has four tables, each relating to the others. For example, the **Check-in** table will relate to the **Guest** table to know who checked in.

> The ServiceNow platform can run on almost any relational database, such as Oracle or SQL Server. But supporting different architectures is difficult, so it is not a standard offering.

Benefiting from an object-oriented design

The simplicity of a relational database means that, on its own, it does not easily represent the data structures used in modern object-oriented programming languages. One particularly useful function of an object-oriented approach is inheritance.

> Inheritance allows one object to build on the functionality of another. Why duplicate effort when you can reuse existing capability?

In ServiceNow, a table can inherit another. The parent table defines the base functionality, while the child table, built on top, can continue to use it. That means that any fields you add to the base table are automatically available to the child too. In fact, almost all functionality you add to the base table is available to the child.

In our **Hotel** application, we want to store information about our guests. We need to know their names, their telephone numbers, and perhaps their addresses. ServiceNow has got a built-in table for storing people—the **User** table. But we want a special type of person—guests. Let's keep staff in the **User** table and guests in a new extension table.

> The **User** table in ServiceNow defines who can log in and use the platform functionality. Sometimes you need a contact database, which stores information about people: their names, phone numbers, location, and who their manager might be. It's tempting to build the contact database as a separate table and keep the two separate, but I recommend using the **User** table as the basis for both. It saves the duplication of data and allows reuse of a special functionality that is built specifically for the built-in table. But do be aware of licensing.

Extending the User table

Let's extend the ServiceNow **User** table in order to have a special class for guests. First, we have to mark the **User** table as extendable. Go to **System Definition** > **Tables** and find the **User** [`sys_user`] table. Make the following change and save once you're done:

- **Extensible**: `<ticked>`

> It is likely you will get a pop-up message asking if you want the **User** table to be included in the **Hotel** application. Click on **Leave Alone**; we want to keep things as they are. We don't want to include the **User** table in our application, only the **Guest** table.

Now, go to our application by navigating to **System Definition** > **Custom Applications** > **Hotel** and create another new table. Use the following data:

- **Label**: `Guest`
- **Name**: `u_guest`
- **Extends table**: `User`

If you look at the fields available on this new table, you'll see lots of fields already, beyond the normal automatic five. These additional fields are those defined on the **User** table.

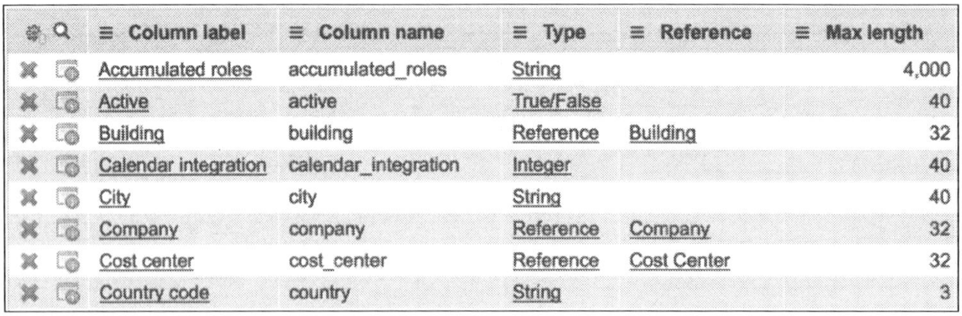

Column label	Column name	Type	Reference	Max length
Accumulated roles	accumulated_roles	String		4,000
Active	active	True/False		40
Building	building	Reference	Building	32
Calendar integration	calendar_integration	Integer		40
City	city	String		40
Company	company	Reference	Company	32
Cost center	cost_center	Reference	Cost Center	32
Country code	country	String		3

What does this mean? The **Guest** table has *inherited* the fields of the **User** table. This is extremely useful; I don't need to create the name, telephone, and e-mail fields – they are already available for me.

Indeed, when you create a table that inherits another, you gain all the functionality of the parent. Most of the scripts, rules, and policies of the parent automatically apply to the new table. But sometimes you want to create the functionality for the child table only. So, ServiceNow lets you place it at the level you need.

> We'll cover how scripts are handled in ServiceNow in the next chapter.

Interacting with hierarchical tables

Our new table is the right place for storing information about our valued customers. While useful fields have been inherited from the **User** table, it doesn't contain everything. Make a new field to store their membership number. For simplicity, create a text field with a Column label named `Membership Number`.

To do this, click on **Design Form** on the **Guest** table record. Find our new field from the left-hand-side list, drag it underneath the **Last name** field in the layout, and click on **Save**:

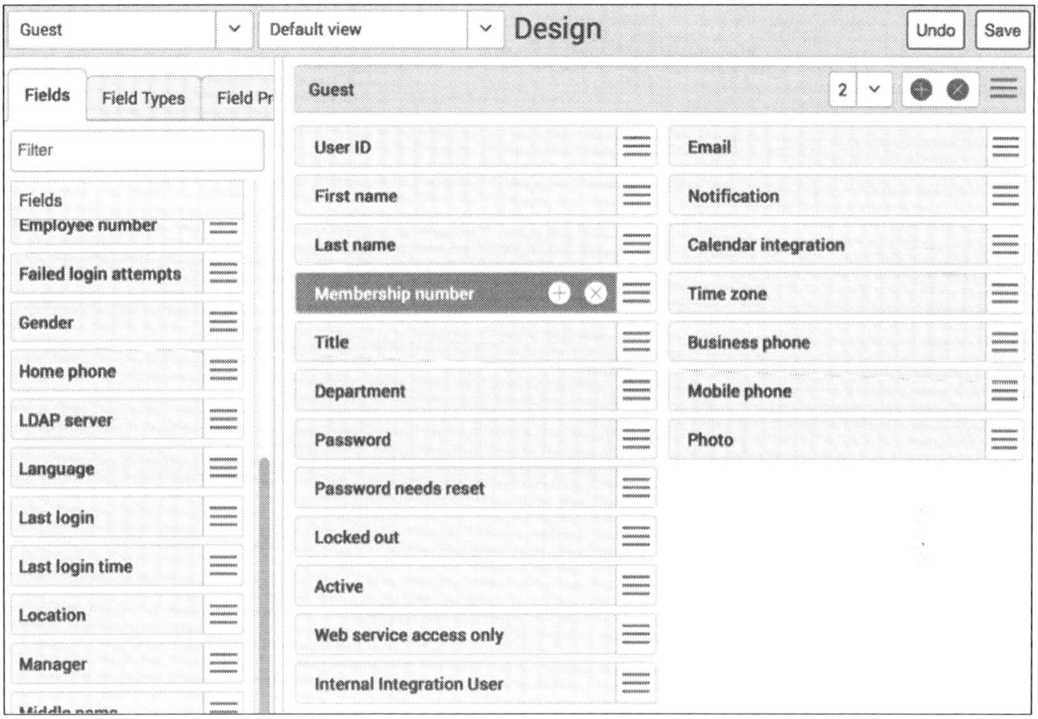

[Check out the wiki if you need help on this step: `http://wiki.servicenow.com/?title=Form_Design`.]

To test, let's create a new guest record. Navigate to **Hotel** > **Guest** and use this data:

- **First name**: `Alice`
- **Last name**: `Richards`
- **Membership number**: `S2E1`

Great! We can enter a membership number fine. And if we look at a standard **User** record such as **Fred Luddy** (**User Administration** > **Users**), the **Membership number** field does not show up.

Viewing hierarchical tables

You may have noticed that our new guest, Alice, showed up when you visited the **User** table. That's because Alice is both a user and a guest. A **Guest** record will be treated just like a **User** record, unless there is something specific that overrides that behavior. In our case, the only difference between a **User** and **Guest** right now is that the latter has an extra field.

> This behavior is called polymorphism, and is a very useful functionality. Use the base or extended functionality, as you need it.

But this gives rise to something that confuses many. If I look at the **Guest** table, I can add, through **Personalize List**, the **Membership number** field.

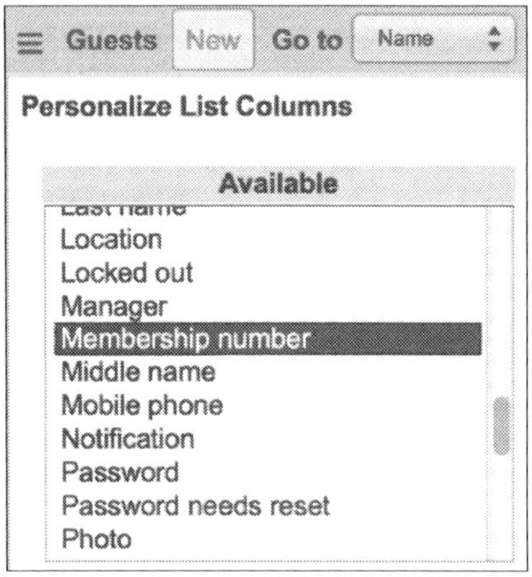

However, if I try to add a **Membership number** on the **User** table, I can't.

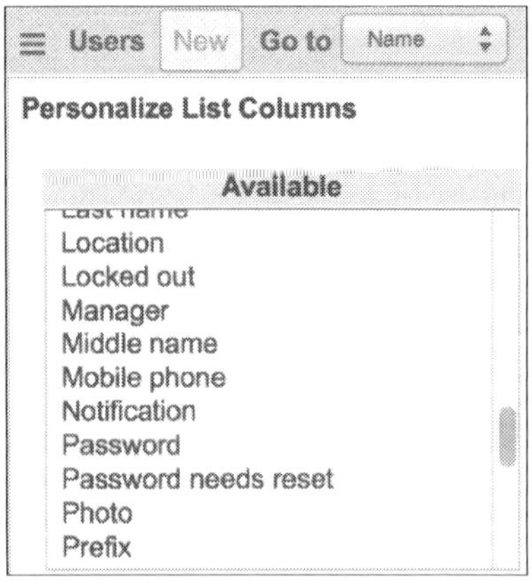

This is because a **User** doesn't have a membership number; only a **Guest** does. Think carefully about where you position fields to ensure they can be seen at the right level.

> You can turn on a property that lets you view inherited fields in the base table. This is discussed more in the *Dot-walking* section in this chapter, as well as the *Reporting* section, in *Chapter 5, Events, Notifications, and Reporting*.

Overriding field properties

Inherited fields allow you to easily reuse functionality. However, sometimes, you want the fields in the extended table to work differently to the base table. This is accomplished with dictionary overrides.

For example, let's change the default time zone for new guests so that it's different to that of the **User** table. The current default for **Users** is the system time zone, and **Guests** inherits this setting.

Navigate to the dictionary entry for the **Time zone** field (perhaps through **System Definition** > **Dictionary** or by right-clicking on the label) and look for the **Dictionary Overrides** tab. Click on **New**. Use the following data:

- **Override default value**: `<ticked>` (tick this option)
- **Default value**: `Europe/London` (or your own choice!)

Now, when you create a new **Guest** record, it sets the default time zone to be `Europe/London`. Any new **User** records will be unaffected.

> You can also change field labels so that they are different for the base and extended tables. Navigate to **System Definition** > **Language File** and create a new entry, populating **Table** with the extended table name (such as `u_guest`). The **Element** field should be the field name.

Understanding the background behavior

You might be wondering how this all works.

A child table is a normal database table. However, it does not recreate all the fields of the parent. Instead, the only columns in that new table are the new fields. For example, if I were to run the `DESCRIBE u_guest` SQL command on the database, I'd only see two fields: `u_membership_number` and `sys_id`.

So, when I look at Alice's record on the **Guest** table, the ServiceNow platform is actually joining the parent table and the child table together, behind the scenes. ServiceNow takes the independent tables and (invisibly) joins them together, creating the illusion of a single, bigger table.

Our friend, the `sys_id` field enables the platform to do this. If you remember, the `sys_id` field uniquely identifies a record. In the case of an extended table, the `sys_id` field is actually stored in two places: on both the parent and child tables. The platform joins both together whenever you query the **Guest** table.

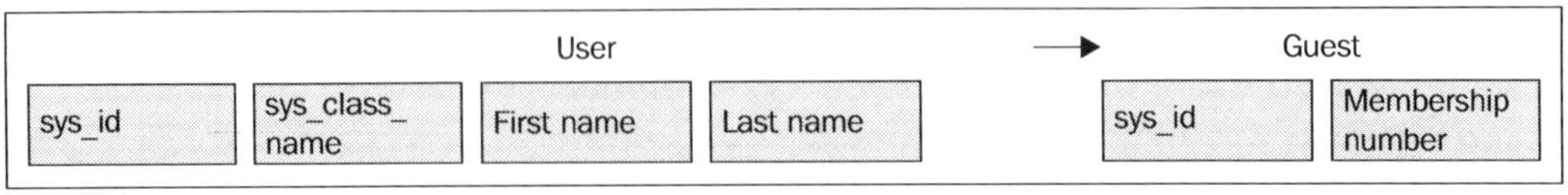

When you mark a table as extendable, you are also adding a second system field: **Class** [`sys_class_name`]. It contains the name of the table that the record represents. For example, the **User** record representing **Fred** would have `sys_user` in the **Class** field, while the **User** record for **Alice** would be `u_guest`. With this information, ServiceNow can join tables if necessary and present you the appropriate data.

> In the Dublin version of ServiceNow, this backend behavior has changed. There are now two models for table extension: hierarchical and flat. The hierarchical method consists of multiple tables that are joined together as needed just as described, while a flat structure consists of one very large table with all the columns of every table. When you make a new table and add a new field, in reality it is simply adding another column to the base table. The platform again hides this from the user. This does not have an impact on how table extension works in ServiceNow and is purely undertaken for performance reasons on larger instances.

The ServiceNow interface knows about this behavior. When you navigate to a record, ServiceNow will always show you its actual class. So, even if I am viewing a list of **Users**, when I click on **Alice**, I will see the **Guest** form, with all of the appropriate attributes. The Schema Map is really helpful to visualize what is going on. Navigate to **System Definition> Tables**, choose the table you are interested in, and then click on **Show Schema Map**. The following screenshot shows the Schema Map of the **Guest** table.

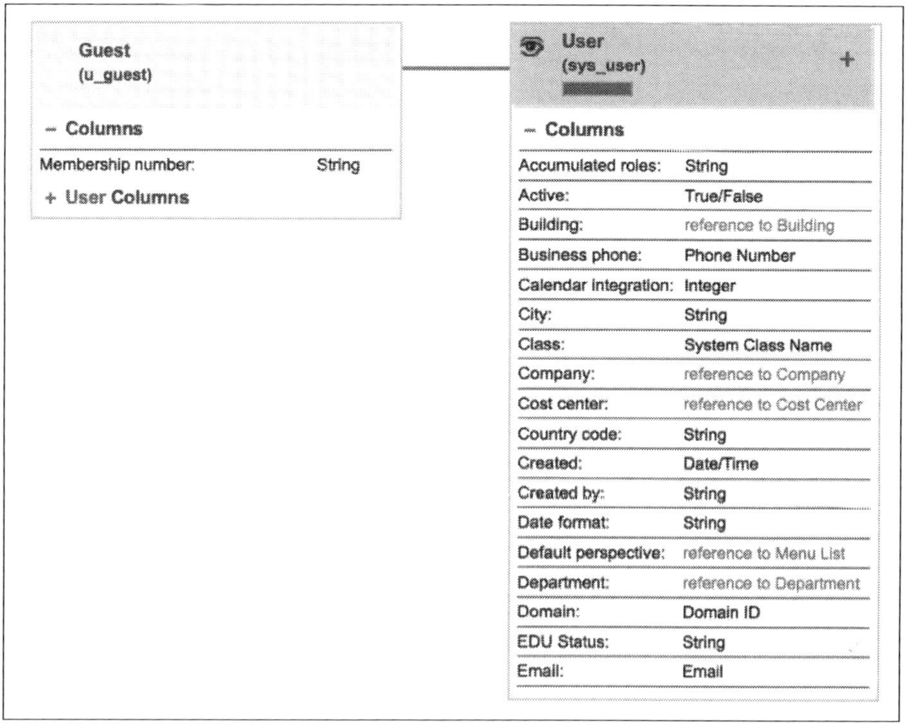

> This wiki article has more information on the Schema Map: `http://wiki.servicenow.com/?title=Schema_Map_for_Tables`.

Changing class

Once a record is stored in a particular table, a neat trick is to move it. If I decide that Alice is actually a user, I can alter the value of the **Class** field. The platform will drop any **Guest**-specific information and start working just like a **User**. The **Class** field can be added to a form or list, and is represented as a choice list. Often, you will want it to be read-only.

> The ability to change the class is a powerful feature and you should be aware of the consequences. It is unusual to reclassify a record, and it may throw off reporting; for example, if you counted ten users and nine guests, and suddenly one switched, you might have an overbooking. It may also clear reference fields, which we are about to discuss.

So far, we've discussed how you can add fields into a specific class, and seen how they are inherited. But this will work with much more than fields! As we work through the chapters, we'll see how functionality such as Business Rules, Access Control Rules, and Import Sets all benefit from hierarchical tables.

Storing data

There are lots of different fields provided by the ServiceNow platform. We will explore some of the simpler ones first, before moving on to the fundamental backbone of the data structure with reference fields:

- **Journal input**: These fields provide an always-empty textbox designed to store notes, but does not store the information in the field on which it's created. Instead, when you enter text into a journal input field, it's saved in the **Journal Entries** [`sys_journal_field`] table.
- **Journal list**: They don't have any entry capabilities at all. Instead, you make it dependent upon a journal input field, and it shows all its entries by querying the **Journal Entries** table automatically. This allows you to have two journal input fields for one journal list. Journal lists are also known as Journal outputs.
- **Journal**: These are a combination of both Journal input and Journal lists, doing both jobs together.
- **Choice**: They are text fields, but rendered as HTML select fields. The value that is stored in the database is plain text. Another table, the **Choices** [`sys_choice`] table, stores the options and labels. This lets the platform convert "wip" in the database to present "**Work in Progress**" to the user. Any values that don't have a label are highlighted in blue in the dropdown.
- **Integer choice**: These fields use numbers instead of text to achieve the same result. They are useful for representing states, since they allow you to use greater than or less than conditions, but have proven difficult to work with since the numbers don't mean much!

> Use caution when dealing with the out-of-the-box integer choice fields, such as **State** on the **Task** table. If you reuse them (which is a good idea), you should always align your states to the existing ones. For example, **3** should represent **Closed**. If you do not align them, then users will be confused when reporting. This is discussed in detail in *Chapter 4, Getting Things Done with Tasks.*

- **Currency**: They are string fields that combine the currency and the amount together. `USD;1000` represents $1,000. The platform uses this information to provide conversions between different currencies. For example, if I prefer to see amounts in GBP, the platform will, if it has the latest currency rates, display £675.
- **Date**: There are several **Date** fields in ServiceNow. The time is stored as UTC in the database, and the appropriate display value is calculated by the user's profile.
- **True/False**: These fields are simple Boolean values in the database. They are rendered as tick boxes.
- **URL**: These fields provide a space to enter a link, which can easily be made clickable.
- **HTML** and **Wikitext**: Other fields, like these, provide different interfaces to manipulate strings. It is tempting to use HTML fields in lots of places, but they do come with overhead, and browsers have different capabilities. For example, Firefox is able to encode an image into a data URI and store it in these fields, while IE is not able to. Test carefully if you want to use capabilities like this.

Attachments

In addition to text, ServiceNow can also store binary data. This means that anything (images, music, or even a multitude of PowerPoint documents), can be saved in ServiceNow. Just like everything else, binary data is stored in the database. However, rather than using a blob field, binary data is split into 4k chunks and saved into the **Attachment Documents** [`sys_attachment_doc`] table. Each chunk of a file refers back to the **Attachments** [`sys_attachment`] table, where the filename, content type and size, and other metadata are stored.

An attachment is always related to another record. Information on this other record is stored with the other metadata in the **Attachments** table. For example, if a **Reservation** record had a PDF of the booking form attached to it, the **Attachment** record would contain the file name of the document, as well as the `sys_id` of the **Reservation** record.

> We'll see in later chapters that there are often better ways than manually adding attachments containing booking information. Why not have the e-mail come directly into ServiceNow? (We'll see how in *Chapter 5, Events, Notifications, and Reporting*.) Or even better, have the guests perform the booking directly with ServiceNow? (*Chapter 10, Making ServiceNow Beautiful with CMS and Jelly*, shows us how to do this.)

Setting properties

One of the simplest ways to control the platform is to set properties. There are lots of things you can change by just clicking on a box or changing a value. And just like everything else in ServiceNow, the configuration properties that you set are stored in a table: the **System Properties** [`sys_properties`] table to be precise.

To see how many options you can choose, type in `Properties` into the filter text of the **Application Navigator**. The many matches are shown, including **System Properties** > **UI Properties**. This collection contains some very useful options, including how forms look and feel, if list editing is enabled, and whether **Insert and Stay** is always available. You may want to take some time to find out what they do.

Some properties are not categorized, but all are accessible via **System Properties** > **All**. This gives a large list—almost 700 in Eureka. This book will guide you to the more relevant ones, but many are documented on the wiki:

`http://wiki.servicenow.com/?title=Available_System_Properties`

> In older versions of the platform, the list is available by typing in `sys_properties.list` in the filter text of the **Application Navigator**.

Reference fields

When designing the data structure for a hotel, you may want to link a guest's record with the room they have checked in to. It won't be good for business if we don't know who has checked in where! This is exactly what a reference field does; it creates a link between two records, one pointing to another.

When we examined the URL for a particular record, it contained two parts: the table and the `sys_id` value of the record. These are the two items needed to reference a record. So when you create a reference field, you need to select which table it should point to. And the contents of the field will be a 32-character string. Sounds familiar? Yep, you will be storing a `sys_id` in that field.

> Reference fields are one of the most important items to understand in ServiceNow. The database sees a string field containing the `sys_id`, a foreign key. However, this is meaningless to a person. Therefore, the platform allows you to pick a field that will be displayed. For a person, this might be their name. Other records might have a user-friendly reference number. This is usually an incremental number; there are scripts that can generate one automatically. You can choose which field to show by ticking the **Display** field in the **Dictionary** entry, but this is only useful to the user. Only the `sys_id` is important to the platform.

Reference fields are used throughout ServiceNow, just like a proper relational system should. Scripting, lists, and forms all understand references fields, as we'll see as we work through the chapters.

Creating a reference field

Let's think about something that the **Hotel** application needs—a room directory. Each room has several attributes that defines it: its room number, how many beds it has, and what floor it is on. We can represent this information as fields in a **Room** record, all stored in a dedicated room table. Once we have this, we can modify the **Check-in** table to record which room has been taken by which guest.

As before, navigate to the **Hotel** record under **Custom Application**, and create a new table with the following data:

- **Label**: `Room`
- **Name**: `u_room`

Create a field to store the room number:

- **Column label**: `Number`

> Don't use the **Auto-number** option, but create a new field using the **Related List**.

And another field to store the floor it is located on:

- **Column label**: `Floor`
- **Type**: `Integer`

The final result should look like this:

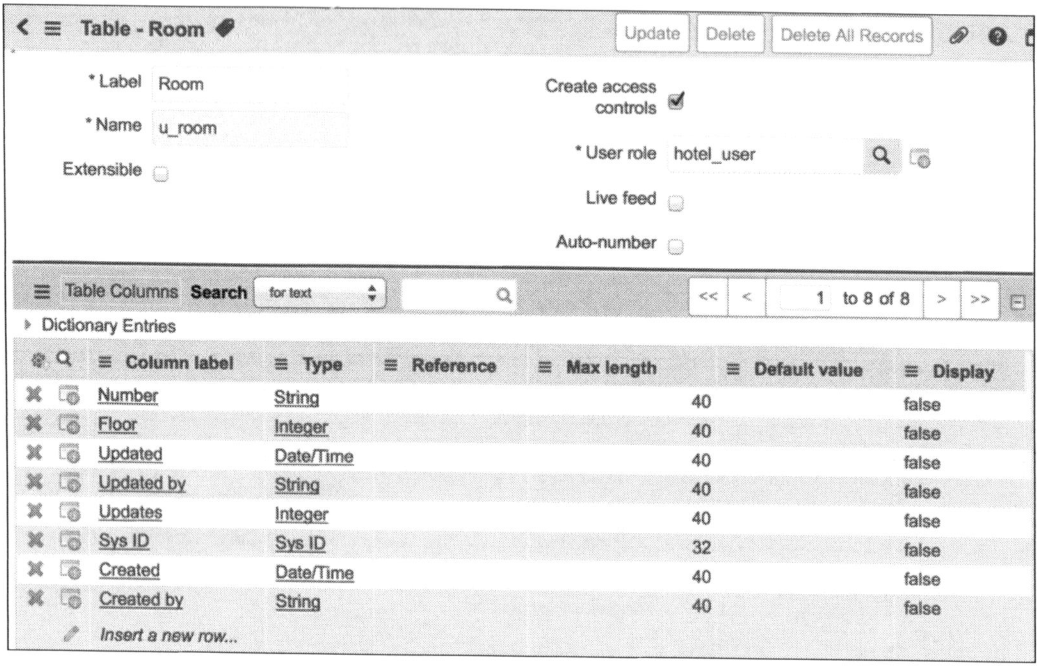

Create a few example records, giving each one a different number. Make several on the same floor. Perhaps one of them might be Room 101 on the first floor.

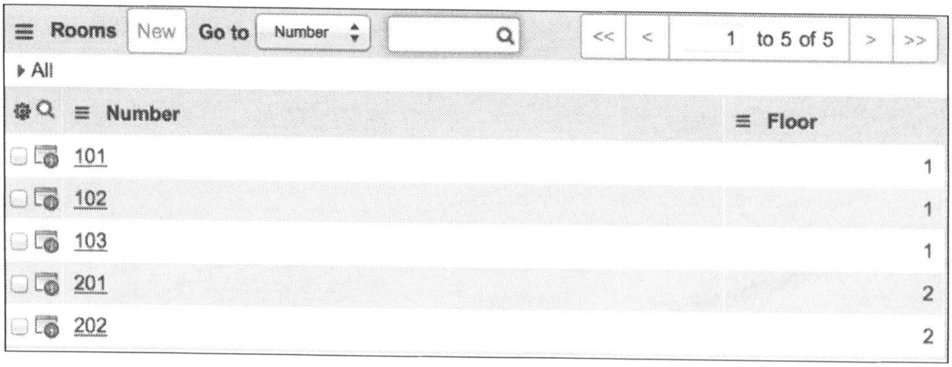

Note that the platform does not force you to choose different numbers for each record. Unless you mark a field as unique, or you create a rule to check, the platform will allow you to create them.

> To mark a field as unique, you can edit the dictionary entry of that field. (You will need to configure the dictionary form and add the **Unique** checkbox.) By ticking that field, you are asking the database to enforce it. It does this by making that field a unique key. This has two impacts. Positively, it creates an index on that field. However, if a user attempts to save a duplicate value, they will get a message saying **Unique Key violation detected by database**. This can be a little jarring for a non-technical user. Try to catch the error with a Business Rule first.

Now that we have a list of rooms, we need to create the link between the **Room** and **Check-in** records.

A reference field can be referred to as a "one-to-many" relationship. Since a room may be checked in to multiple times (one day you have one particular guest, and the next day another may sleep in it after our fabulous cleaners have done their work), but for a single check-in, you can only select one room. You can only sleep in one bed at once!

> A classic example of a one-to-many relationship is between a mother and her children. A child can only have one biological mother, but a mother can have many children.

The following diagram shows the relationship between **Room** and the **Check-in** record:

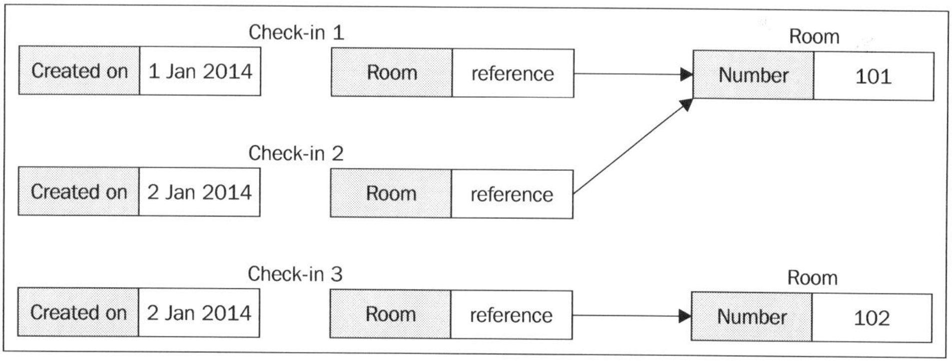

In the **Check-in** table, create two new fields. One for the room, using the following data:

- **Column label**: `Room`
- **Type**: `Reference`
- **Reference**: `Room`

And another for the guest:

- **Column label**: `Guest`
- **Type**: `Reference`
- **Reference**: `Guest`

Now, create a few example **Check-in** records. To simulate someone going into Room 101, create a new entry in the **Check-in** table. You may want to rearrange the form through **Form Design** to make it look a little better.

[Note that when you try to select a guest, only **Alice** is available. Since the reference field is pointing to the **Guest** table, users are not shown.]

You can view the **Room**-to-**Check-in** relationship from both directions. If you are on the **Check-in** form, you can see which room is in use through the reference field. The reference icon is very useful for viewing more details about the record—just hover over it.

[If you hold the *Shift* key on your keyboard while you move your mouse cursor over the reference icon and then into the pop-up window, the information will remain until you click on the Close button. This is quite useful when copying data from that record without losing place.]

You can easily view the relationship from the other perspective too. When you create a reference field, you can add a Related List on to the form or list of the referenced table. This will let you see all the records that are pointing to it.

Click on the reference icon next to the **Room** reference field to go to its record. On the **Room** form, navigate to **Personalize** > **Related Lists**. It will be named in this format: `table->field`; in our case, **Check-in->Room**. Right-click on the list headings and go to **Personalize** > **List Layout** and add the **Guest** field alongside **Created**.

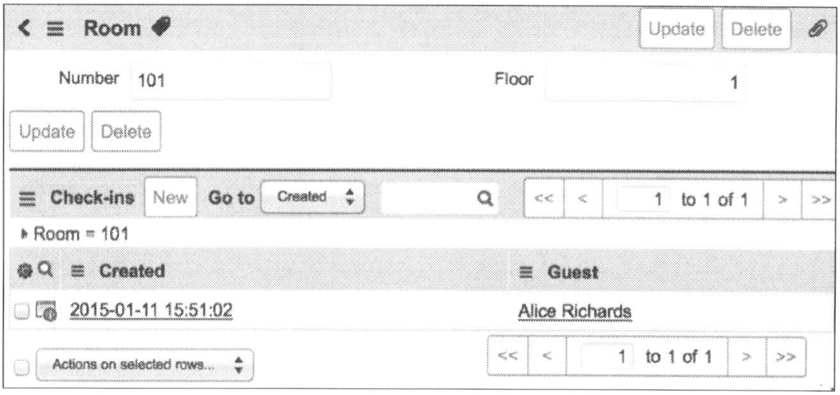

The Related List gives you a **New** button. When you click on this, you will see the **Check-in** form but with the reference field already filled in. So, if we know which room we want to check a guest in to, we can navigate to the **Room** record, click on the **New** button in the **Check-in** Related List, and need not type in the room number again.

Using Reference Qualifiers

By default, a reference field can select from any record on the referenced table. However, often, you want to filter the results. For example, you may want to specify a guest as inactive, perhaps representing someone that won't be visiting Gardiner Hotels any longer. Therefore, let's filter out the inactive guests so they cannot be inadvertently checked in.

Reference Qualifiers allow you to do this. When you edit the dictionary entry of a reference field, you can specify the filter you want to apply. These can be specified in three different ways:

- **Simple**: Lets you specify which records should be returned using a condition builder.

> Simple is the default **Reference Qualifier**. Click on **Advanced view** in **Related Links** to see the other options.

- **Dynamic**: Lets you pick from prebuilt scripts. The choices they give often differ depending on the context of the record or the session. A good example is **Me**, one of the **Dynamic Filter Options**. This will return whoever is currently logged in, meaning that users who look at the same query will have personalized results.

> You can build your own **Dynamic Filter Options** by navigating to **System Definition** > **Dynamic Filter Options**. This is shown in *Chapter 2, Server-side Control*.

- **Advanced**: This is the original way to create **Reference Qualifiers**. It accepts an encoded query. JavaScript can be embedded in these queries, by prefixing it with `javascript:`. Creating a Dynamic Filter Option is the more reusable option.

> An encoded query is a field-operator-value triplet, separated by the caret (^) symbol. This string represents part of the `where` clause of the resulting SQL query. For example, `active=true` specifies all records where the `active` field is true, while `active=true^last_name=Smith` represents `active` being ticked and the contents of the `last_name` field being `Smith`.
>
> One easy way to get an encoded query is to build a filter in the list view, right-click on the result, and choose **Copy Query**.

For our **Hotel** application, let's use a simple **Reference Qualifier**. On the **Check-In** form, right-click on the **Guest** field label, and choose **Personalize Dictionary**. Set the **Reference qual condition** field to `Active - is - true`.

Now, if you mark a guest as inactive, they cannot be selected when checking in, neither through the magnifying glass lookup window and nor using the type ahead functionality.

Dot-walking

Dot-walking is a very important concept in ServiceNow. It means you can access information through reference fields quickly and easily. It can be leveraged throughout ServiceNow—both through the interface and through code.

You've already used dot-walking. When you hover over the reference icon, you can see information from that record. That's the whole concept! We are using the platform's capability to "see through" reference fields and pull out information from that record. And, as we'll see in the next chapter, the same is possible through code.

> By default, extended fields are not available while dot-walking. The **Membership number** field would not be available when dot-walking through a **User reference** field.
>
> The **Allow base table lists to include extended table fields** property in **UI Properties** changes this for the UI. Scripts can use a special syntax when dot-walking. This is discussed in more depth in *Chapter 2, Server-side Control*, and *Chapter 5, Events, Notifications, and Reporting*.

Using derived fields

Dot-walking can be used throughout the user interface. Another example is adding **derived fields** to lists, forms, and queries. A derived field is a field from another record that is found through a reference field.

For example, we could add the floor number of the room as a derived field on the check-in form. The floor number doesn't belong to the check-in record, and if we change the room on the form, the system will dynamically change what floor number is displayed.

> With scripting, you have the option to copy data through the reference field onto the record you are dealing with. That data then becomes part of the record. Derived fields will exist through the link only.
>
> This concept is important to understand. If the referenced record gets deleted or changed, it will then affect our current record. For example, if we delete the room record, the check-in form won't be able to show what floor it was on. If we change the floor value on the room record, our check-in form will show the new value.

The simplest example of information that is derived is the display value, which was mentioned earlier. If the display value of the referenced record changes, you'll see it altered everywhere. Since the `sys_id` is the primary key for a record, you can easily rename groups, alter the names of users, or update virtually any record without penalty.

Navigate to **Personalize** > **Form Layout** on the **Check-in** form. Even though the **Room** field is already added to the form, it is still in the available list. It should have **[+]** as a suffix to the field name, showing it is a reference field that can be dot-walked in to; for example, **Room [+]**. A green plus icon is made available on selecting a reference field. If you click on that icon, you get to see the fields in the **Room** table. Choose the **Floor** field and add it to the form. It should be labeled **Room.Floor**, showing that you are dot-walking. Click on **Save**.

> Derived fields can only be added via **Form Layout** (rather than **Form Design**) as of the Eureka and Fuji versions of ServiceNow.

The **Check-in** form should now have several fields in it: the **Room** reference field, the **Floor** derived field, and a simple **Comments** field.

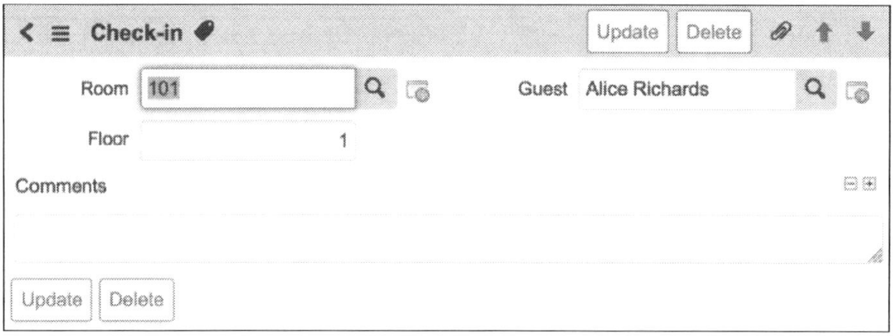

> Note how the **Floor** field is editable. If the value is changed and the **Submit** button is clicked on, it is actually the **Room** record that will be altered.

Dynamic creation

What happens if you try to associate with a record that doesn't exist, such as doing a check-in for a guest that has never been to the hotel before? If you type in the name into the reference field that doesn't match an existing record, then the red background warns the user that the record won't be saved properly. Indeed, if you try, you will get a message saying: **Invalid update**.

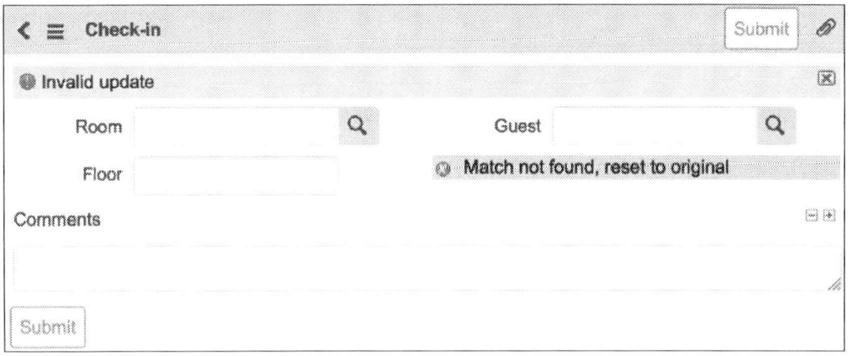

One way to create a record quickly is to use the reference picker and click on the **New** button on the list in the popup window. You then get a form that you can fill out, which comes with a **Save** button. But a faster way is to use **dynamic creation**, which allows you to type the name directly into the reference field.

Go to the dictionary entry of the **Guest** field on the **Check-in** table. Click on **Advanced View Related Link**, tick the **Dynamic creation** checkbox, and then click on **Save**. Now, if the guest doesn't exist, a green background will be present instead. This indicates that the record will be created.

> By default, the new record will have the display value populated. For a **User** record, the display value is a field that is called **Name** that is actually dynamically created from the **First name** and **Last name** fields. The scripts on the user table will organize the data into the most appropriate place.
>
> When you turn on **Dynamic creation**, you'll see an area in the dictionary for scripting a more complex scenario. Sometimes, this is very helpful, if only to flag that this record was dynamically created. Often, you want to track this is happening, since it is very easy to create lots of duplicates with dynamic creation; for example, is it Tom, Thomas, or Tommy?

Deleting records

When you click on the **Delete** button, the platform removes it from the database. But what if there is a reference field value that points to that record? For example, if we delete a **Room** record, what happens to the **Check-in** records? The **Check-in** table has a reference field that points to the **Room** table. What happens?

There are several ways that ServiceNow deals with it. The choice is set on the dictionary entry of a reference field:

- **By default** (or when the choice is set to **Clear**): the platform will empty all reference fields that point to that record. When deleting a **Room** record, all of the **Check-in** records that point to it will have the **Room** field emptied.
- **Delete** or **Cascade**: Any record that pointed to the deleted record is *also* deleted. This means that deleting a room would also delete all the **Check-in** records that pointed to it! **Delete no workflow** is an extension of this; with this option, only directly related records will be deleted (it does not cascade).

> Delete is a useful choice if the related record has no purpose without its referenced record. For example, if you delete a user, then a reservation makes no sense.

- **Restrict**: This option will stop the transaction if there are related records. If there are any records pointing to the deleted record, then abort the deletion. The platform would prevent you from deleting the room. This is the most conservative option, useful for preventing mistakes.

> For instance, once a room has been checked in to, you may not want to delete it. You should first contact the customers staying there and let them know that a wrecking ball may come through their walls!

- **None**: This option will mean that the platform does not alter any related records. Reference fields will stay populated with a `sys_id` that points to an invalid record.

The majority of the time, the default option of clear is the right choice. It does mean, however, that you lose information when deletions occur. So, in general, the best idea is not to delete anything! Users should be deactivated in production systems, not deleted.

> If you accidently delete something, it may be found by navigating to **System Definition** > **Deleted Records**. The platform will even allow you to restore data that has been removed through a cascade delete. Check out the wiki for more information: `http://wiki.servicenow.com/?title=Restoring_Deleted_Records_and_References`.

This scenario also illustrates why the automatic fields are not reference fields, but instead copy information into the record. The **Created By** and **Updated By** fields store the text value of the user who performed the action, so they are not dependent upon the user record itself.

Many-to-many relationships

The other type of relationship between records is many-to-many. The relationship between siblings is many-to-many. I can have many brothers and sisters, as can they. But how can I store this? A reference field can only point to one record. Adding a lot of reference fields into a form is one way. Each reference field could point to another sibling. However, that's not great design. What if there were five populated reference fields and another brother or sister was born?

Instead, we could create another table that sits in between each target, acting as the "glue" that sticks the two together. A special many-to-many table can then have two reference fields, each pointing to a different side.

In the **Hotel** application, we want to take reservations for our guests. Each reservation might be for more than one person, and each person might have more than one reservation. This sounds like the perfect use for a many-to-many table:

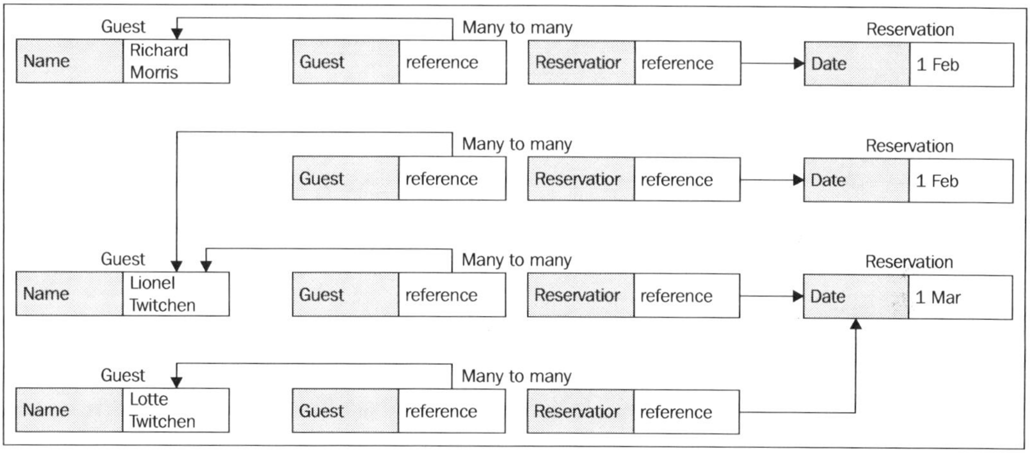

This diagram shows how this might work out. Richard is staying one night on 1 Feb. That's easy enough. Lionel is staying two nights, on 1 Feb and 1 Mar. He liked our hotel so much that he came back, and encouraged his wife Lotte to stay with him.

The ServiceNow platform makes this a little easier to visualize, since it hides the complexities of the many-to-many table in most situations. It focuses on the records in the two target tables.

Building a many-to-many table

Let's begin building a many-to-many table. To do this, perform the following steps:

1. Create a new table named **Reservation**:
    - **Label**: `Reservation`
    - **Name**: `u_reservation`
2. Add the first date field to the **Reservation** table:
    - **Column label**: `Arrival`
    - **Type:** `Date`

    Then add another as seen here:

    - **Column label**: `Departure`
    - **Type:** `Date`
3. Finally, since we want to reserve a room, let's also create a reference field called **Room**:
    - **Column label**: `Room`
    - **Type:** `Reference`
    - **Reference:** `Room`
4. Then navigate to the **Many to Many** table. The easiest way to do this is to enter `sys_m2m.list` in the filter text in the **Application Navigator**.

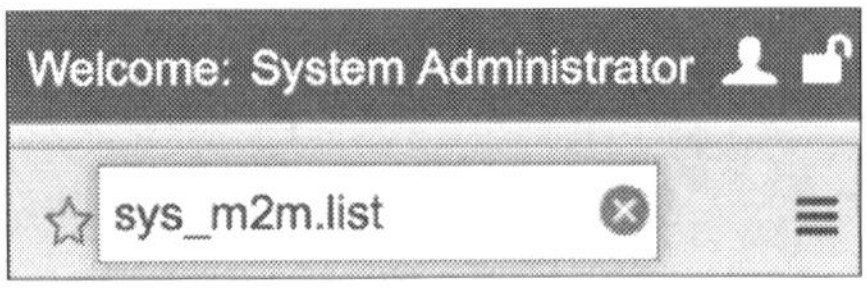

[The **Application Navigator** accepts a few shortcuts like this, `<table_name>.form`, will show the form of the table. For more information, refer to the following link:
`http://wiki.servicenow.com/?title=Navigating_Applications#Using_the_Navigation_Filter`]

5. Click on **New**. Use the following data:
   - **From table:** `Reservation [u_reservation]`
   - **To table:** `Guest [u_guest]`
   - **Type:** `Reference`
   - **Reference:** `Room`

   The **From** and **To** tables are where we want to point our reference fields. It doesn't matter which way round you do it:

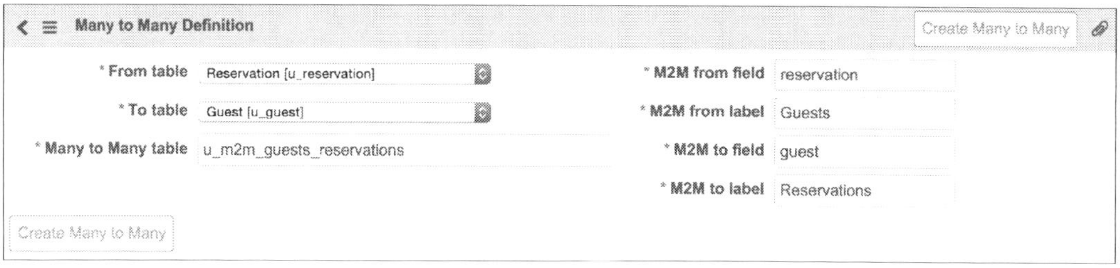

[You'll see the other fields populate automatically. Make sure the table name makes sense – but leave the `m2m` part in, so you know what it is. The default (`u_m2m_guests_reservations`) makes sense in this case and isn't too long.]

6. Click on **Create Many to Many**.
7. Go back to the **Guest** form. Navigate to **Personalize** > **Related Lists** and add in the new **Reservations** entry.

Adding fields to a many-to-many table

Sometimes, just having the two reference fields on the many-to-many table is enough. However, since it is a table, you can also add new fields to it. This technique is useful to identify something in particular about the relationship. Let's identify who the lead passenger in a reservation is:

1. Create a new field on the many-to-many table you created. You will find the table by going to **System Definition** > **Tables**.

   The table is called **M2m Guests Reservations**. Tidy it up to say **Guest Reservations**.

2. Add the following fields:
   - **Column label**: `Lead`
   - **Type**: `True/False`
3. Then go to the **Reservations** form and create a sample **Reservation** record.
4. Once done, add the **Guests** Related List to the form.
5. Once saved, right-click on the column headings of the Related List and go to **Personalize** > **List Layout**. Add in **Lead**.
6. Finally, right-click on the column headings again and navigate to **Personalize** > **List Control**. Once there, tick **List edit insert row**.

You can then use list editing on the Related List to record the information you want.

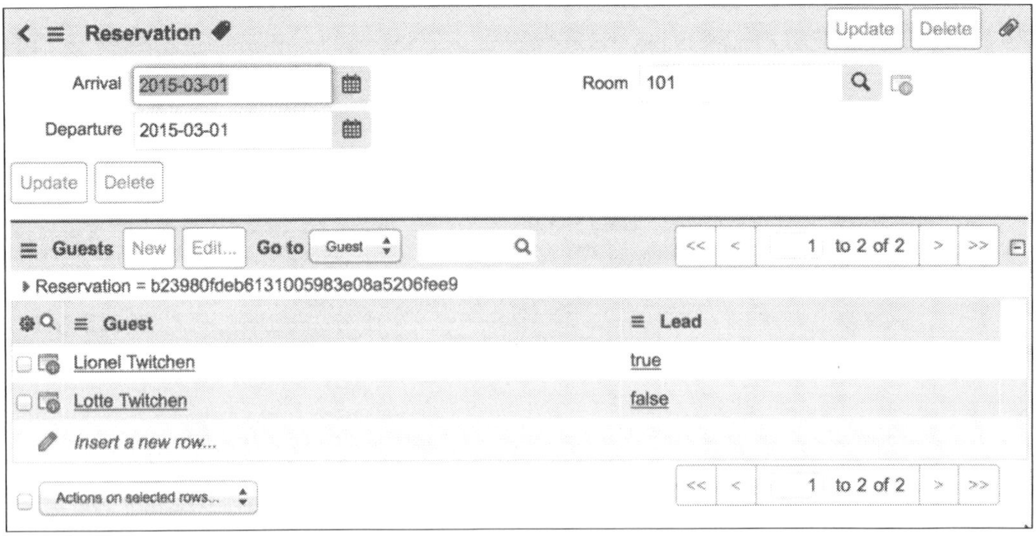

> The **Reservation** record currently has no field set as the display value. By default, a field called **Name** is used. If that doesn't exist, the `sys_id` is used, and that's the case here.

Many-to-many tables are very flexible, but by using them, you lose some advantages of simple reference fields. The biggest disadvantage is that you can't dot-walk in the same way. This makes scripting more challenging.

Also, on a simple list view, you can't easily identify related records. One way round this is through hierarchical list views, which we will discuss later.

We'll see further disadvantages of many-to-many tables as we progress.

Deleting a many-to-many table

Deleting a many-to-many table isn't straightforward. You need to do it in two parts: delete the table and then delete the entry from the `sys_m2m` table. However, there are security rules that prevent you from deleting records on this table. You will need to disable or modify those rules to proceed. But beware of what you are doing!

Glide Lists

Glide Lists store an array of `sys_id` values. That means that one field can reference multiple records. One field can work in a similar way to a many-to-many table. In our earlier example, a Glide List field could be added in to the **Reservations** form instead, pointing towards the **Guest** table.

> One disadvantage of Glide Lists is the interface. It is more difficult to interact with compared to other fields, both on the list and the forms. Since it contains multiple values, you can't dot-walk through it. Which one would you walk to?

When wanting to reference many records, consider the advantages of a Glide List against a many-to-many table:

- Glide Lists are represented as a field. They are more compact than many-to-many tables, and many built-in functions in ServiceNow accept the comma-separated reference fields as input. For example, a comma-separated list of users can easily be sent an e-mail. Glide Lists are usually simpler to deal with.

- Many-to-many relationships are represented as records in a table. This gives no limit to the amount of records stored, and you can easily extend the functionality. You can add extra fields (like the lead passenger representation). It also has better hooks for scripts and other functionalities. Many-to-many tables are generally more flexible.

Building the interface

We've already spent some time with the ServiceNow interface. But understanding some of the fundamentals of how the platform is used and what it provides deserves repeating.

If we rewind to our opening consideration that everything is in a database, ServiceNow provides two basic interfaces that we spend the majority of our time with: **forms** and **lists**. The form and the list are the two major views of data within ServiceNow. You can, of course, create custom user interfaces, and we'll cover those in *Chapter 10, Making ServiceNow Beautiful with CMS and Jelly*.

Lists

Lists show several records in a table, line by line. Pretty obvious, but let's break out of the frames and examine some URLs again. Remember how we navigated to a specific record in a field? Let's instead show a list of **Guest** records. The table name is suffixed with _list, with the usual .do. Here's an example: http://<instance>.service-now.com/u_guest_list.do

> You might be wondering what the .do is all about. This is the typical suffix that is used by Apache Struts, which has become the go-to framework for developing Java web applications like ServiceNow. This gives a hint as to the technologies used within the ServiceNow platform!

We've already seen that the sys_id can be used as a parameter to immediately jump to a record. There are other parameters that are useful too. Here's an example that shows how you can specify a database query through a URL: http://<instance>.service-now.com/sys_user_list.do?sysparm_query=user_name=fred.luddy.

If you navigate to this URL, you will be presented with a list of the records that match this query. If you remove the _list part from the URL, you will be presented with the first record that matches.

These URLs do not open up the familiar navigation frames, but simply show the content. You may want to have multiple browser tabs open, without the frameset. Edit the URL directly and get to where you want to go, fast. If you must have the frames, try `http://<instance>.service-now.com/nav_to.do?uri=u_guest_list.do`.

Choosing the fields to show

A list in ServiceNow can include any of the fields that are on the table. But a list works best when you show only the most relevant information. Adding in lots of columns takes longer to load (more data to get from the instance, to be sent across the Internet, and parsed by your browser) and often only adds to clutter and complexity.

Typically, this includes something that identifies the individual record (usually a name, number, and maybe a short description) and when the record was last updated. If there is a categorization field, that should be included too. It is very helpful to sort or group the records by these values. The **Go to** quick search option also allows you to search these fields.

The number of records that are shown on a list is configurable by the user. The System Administrator sets the choices they have in **UI Properties**. Keep the maximum number low, again to minimize the amount of data that needs to be worked with. Setting it to `1,000` is useful to be able to do mass deletion, but if everyone has it selected, it will impact performance.

Having reference fields on lists

Reference fields are treated slightly differently in a list view. The majority of fields are shown as simple text, but reference fields are always shown as a link to the referenced record. The first column in the list is also converted into a link, this time linking to the record itself.

Never put a reference field as the first column on a list. While the system will understand this, and consequently make the *second* column the link to the record, it is incredibly confusing to the user. People become very used to clicking on the first column and expect to see that record in the list.

You can always get to the record by clicking on the icon to the left of a particular column.

The varied capabilities of lists

Users of ServiceNow often forget about the extra functionality that lists provide. Functionality such as list editing and the powerful context menus (like **Show Matching** when you right-click on a list) should be thought about carefully and explained to users of the system to ensure they use the interface in an efficient manner.

A hierarchical list is not used that often, but is very powerful. It allows you to display the Related Lists of records on the list view. So even while looking at the **Reservations** list, the guests can still be inspected. You turn on this functionality in **List Control**.

Here are some tips to keep in mind when creating lists:

- Try not to include journal, HTML, or other multiline fields on the list. They just get big.
- Think carefully about **List Control**. Do you want **New** or **Edit** buttons? This especially matters on Related Lists.
- When running a query on a list, if you click on the **New** button, the values you searched for will be copied into the form.

Forms

In contrast to the simple concept of lists, a form generally contains more detailed information. It is where users usually interact with the data.

Try not to break away from the convention of having two columns of fields, with the labels to the left. Although it might be considered plain, it also means the forms are consistent, easy to read, and relatively uncluttered. The emphasis should therefore be on creating logic and process to control the data while keeping the interface simple.

> If you want to make things more exciting, CSS can be applied to the main interface using **Themes**. *Chapter 10, Making ServiceNow Beautiful with CMS and Jelly*, explores how completely custom interfaces can be made. Check out the wiki for more information: `http://wiki.servicenow.com/?title=CSS_Theme_Support`.

Annotations allow you to add text and even HTML to forms. They are especially useful to add simple work instructions, but be careful to ensure the forms don't get cluttered.

Finally, formatters allow you to include Jelly on your form. Rather than a sugary treat, Jelly is a scriptable language used to build the ServiceNow interface. *Chapter 10, Making ServiceNow Beautiful with CMS and Jelly*, discusses custom interfaces in more detail.

Creating useful forms

By following some best practices, you can make the ServiceNow interface a more pleasant place to be!

- Every table needs a form, even if it is basic.
- Forms should read top to bottom, with important fields at the top left.
- The reference name or number of the record is normally at the top left.
- Lay out the fields in the order you'd fill them in. Users can tab between fields.
- Mandatory fields should be obvious, again, usually towards the top.
- Keep to the standard layout for consistency – two columns at the top and full width at the bottom.
- Keep forms as short as possible. Don't include unnecessary fields. Views can be very useful to provide targeted designs.
- Use annotations to create **Section Separators** (not **Form Sections**) to separate out content on the page and provide a logical hierarchy or workflow of the data.
- For larger forms, use Form Sections. These are useful for creating tabs.
- Fields with multiple lines (such as descriptions or comments) should expand across the whole page, not half. This means they go at the bottom of the form.

Adding related and embedded lists

We've already seen Related Lists when discussing reference fields. But they come with a few disadvantages. Embedded lists remove some of their constraints:

- Embedded lists can be placed anywhere on the form, rather than just at the bottom.
- Since Related Lists show related records, they will only be displayed on a saved record. If it is unsaved, no records can be linked. Embedded lists will show at all times.

Let's use an embedded list to create **Guest** records at the same time as a reservation:

1. On the **Reservations** form, first remove the **Guests** Related List by going to **Personalize** > **Related Lists**.
2. Under **Personalize** > **Form Layout**, find the **Guests** embedded list. It'll show up in red in the **Available** column.

3. Once added and saved, a new **Reservations** record should look like the following screenshot. Guests can easily be added and removed from this interface by using list editing. Try it out!

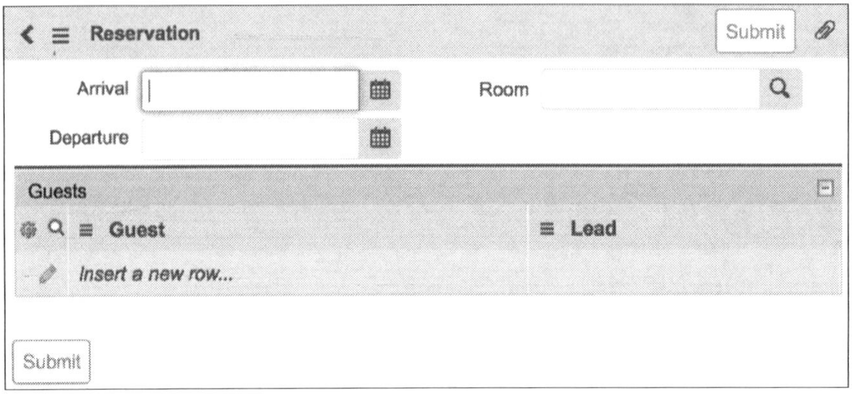

> Embedded Related Lists are not always appropriate. They are designed to have an interface where you often create new related records with a minimum amount of information. There is no way to disable the creation of new records, for instance.

Defining your own Related Lists

Defined Related Lists gives a list of any records you want at the bottom of the form. For example, a simple Defined Related List may be placed on the **Room** form that lists other rooms on the same floor. This helps you to quickly navigate to them.

> In order to create a Defined Related List, we'll need to use a little JavaScript. We'll work through this in more detail in the next chapter.

Navigate to **System Definition** > **Relationships** and click on **New**. Use the following details:

- **Name**: `Rooms on the same floor`
- **Applies to table**: `Room [u_room]`
- **Queries from table**: `Room [u_room]`
- **Query with**: `current.addQuery('u_floor', parent.u_floor);`

This code gets records where the `u_floor` field is the same as the record we are viewing. Two JavaScript variables are being used here, `current` is the table you are getting the records from and `parent` is the record that is being displayed in the form.

Navigate to the **Room** form and add the new Related List into the form. Now you'll see the other rooms listed as well. Useful!

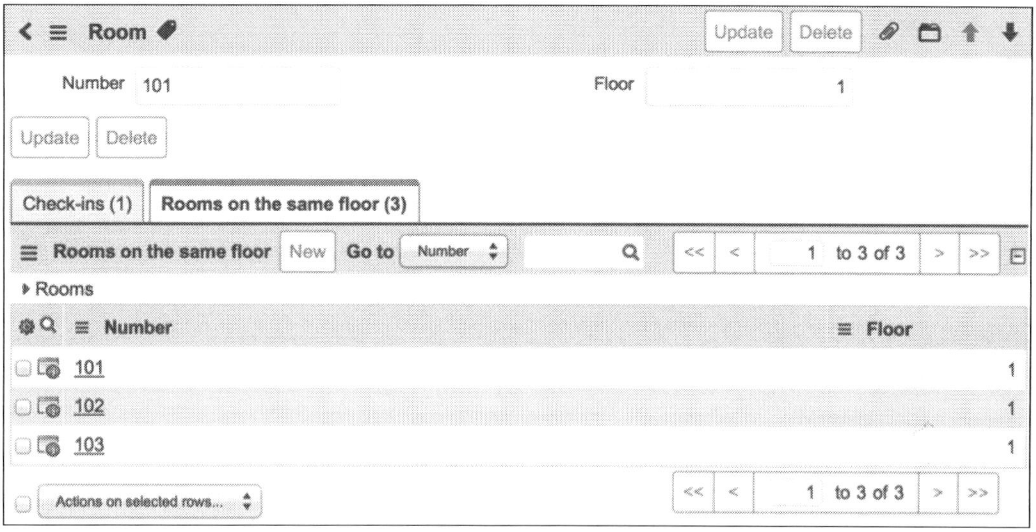

Creating tags and bookmarks

Do you lose things? Me too. I lose my hotel key all the time. Perhaps you are writing several difficult scripts that you want only a couple of clicks away, or you need to quickly navigate to a **User** record. Tags are a way to collect arbitrary records together, making them easy to find, while bookmarks give single-click access.

Adding a bookmark

A way to quickly access information is through bookmarks. To the left of the **Application Navigator** is the **Edge** toolbar, which lets you control your interface. Try dragging links to the bar, where they will be saved for one-click access.

Since ServiceNow is a real web application, you can obviously add bookmarks through your browser. You might need to break out of the frames first or use the **Copy URL** option on a link breadcrumb to get a navigable URL.

Defining a tag

Tags collect records together. To create one, go to a record form. Click on the Tags icon next to the table name or right-click on the context menu and go to **Assign Tag** > **New**. Type in a label and save.

Then find your records by clicking on **Tagged Documents** in the Edge toolbar on the left-most part of the user interface:

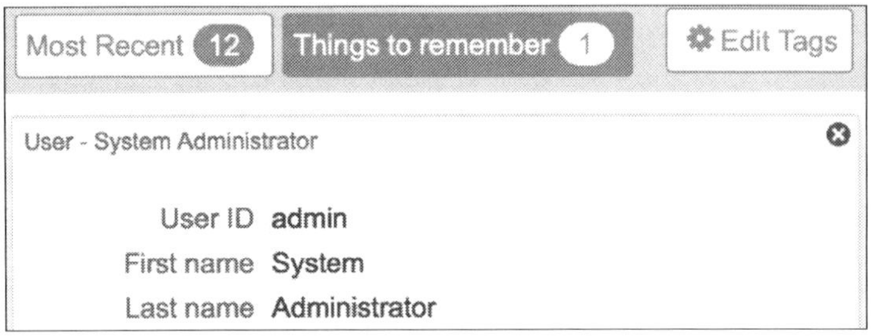

In older versions of ServiceNow, this functionality was called **labels**. You can inspect the different user interfaces available on the wiki: `http://wiki.servicenow.com/?title=Navigation_and_the_User_Interface`.

> You can also add tags to records from lists by selecting the items you want to add and then using **Assign Tag** from the **Actions on selected rows** choice list.

Tag configuration is possible by going to **System Definition** > **Tags**. This includes global tags (which show for every user) and dynamic tags (which try to automate the selection of labels for you; for example, the most recently used).

Enjoying views

If you find that you need to include lots of fields on a form or list, consider using views. They allow you to present a different set of elements that are specific to a situation. For example, in our hotel, a guest may be enrolled in our points program. In that case, we may want two views of user records: a simple uncluttered view for single-time guests (containing the minimum amount of information required to load quickly, and without extraneous data) and a more detailed view for frequent visitors (containing extra information to help serve them better).

Let's create a simple view of the **Guests** form.

1. Navigate to it now and then go to **Personalize** > **Form Design**.
2. On the **Default view** selection box, choose **New...** and enter **Simple** as the new view name.
3. Then remove all fields other than **First name**, **Last name**, and **Membership Number**, and click on **Save**.

A System Administrator (or a user with the `view_changer` role) can change views by clicking on the name of the table and choosing **View**. Otherwise, the view for the record is set through rules, through the view specified in the module link in the application menu to the left, or it is inherited.

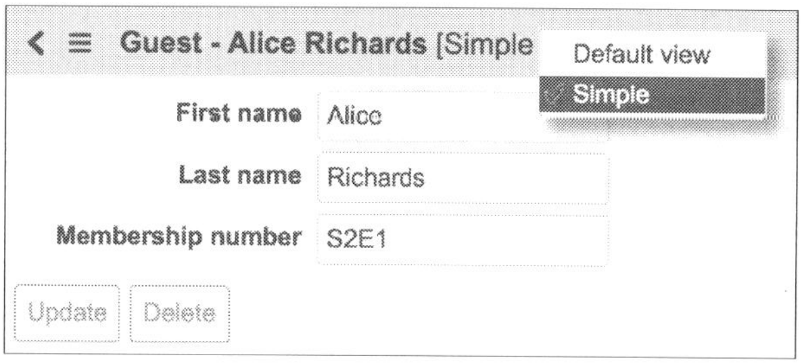

> The view of a record is inherited as you navigate through the interface. If you follow reference links, the system will attempt to be consistent and use the same view as before. If there isn't one with the same name, it will show the default one. Be aware of this behavior when you are naming and configuring forms.

Controlling views

View Rules (available under **System UI** > **View Rules**) are a great way to force the display of a particular view. They work with a condition that uses information on the record itself. For example, you may decide to create a VIP view that shows extra fields. The VIP view is then only shown when the VIP field is ticked.

If you need more control, then create a script that can use other information to make the correct choice. A great use case for this is selecting a view based on the role of the logged-in user. Learn how to do this by going through the *Special function calls* section in *Chapter 2, Server-side Control*.

> Learn more at the wiki: `http://wiki.servicenow.com/?title=View_Management`.

Views are often useful, but they can become frustrating. You end up managing several forms; for example, if you create a field and want it on all of them, you must repeat yourself several times and change the forms several times. And since the view you are using is kept as you navigate through the interface, be aware of which view you are editing: you may end up creating new views on forms unintentionally.

Menus and modules

To help you navigate the applications in ServiceNow, the interface provides you with the **Application Navigator**—or, as I like to call it, "the menu to the left". At its heart, this is a series of links to either forms or lists of data. They can specify a view name directly, and lists can include a filter, enabling you to decide exactly what the user sees when they click on it. This gives you a great deal of control.

> What is shown in the **Application Navigator** is only natively controlled by roles. However, modules, like all configurations, are stored in a database table - the `sys_app_module` table to be exact. This gives rise to the possibility of restricting who sees modules in other ways. One example is creating a query Business Rule on this table to filter modules by group. *Chapter 7, Securing Applications and Data*, explores how that is accomplished.

Specifying a view

Let's set the default view for **Guests** to be our simple one.

1. Navigate to **System Definition** > **Modules** > **Guests**.
2. Change the **View name** field to `Simple` and save.

Now, each time you follow this link, you'll see the three-field view.

Setting a filter

When providing links to lists, it is a good idea to include a filter. Not only does it let you find the data you are looking more quickly, but it also reduces the need to immediately create a filter yourself. Often, you aren't interested in records that are six months old, for instance, so filter them out of the link. If you always filter the list (such as to find guests who have recently checked in), why not create a new module so you can jump straight to them?

> Speak to the users of the system and understand what they are looking for. Not only will that make their interaction slightly easier, but you can also reduce the load on the instance by only displaying the appropriate information. Adding modules is really easy, and it can make a dramatic difference to usability.

Let's create a new module that shows **Reservations** for today. Navigate to **System Definition** > **Modules** and click on **New**. Use these details:

- **Title**: `Today's Reservations`
- **Application menu**: `Hotel`
- **Table**: `Reservation [u_reservation]`
- **Filter**: `Arrival - on - Today`

Building the right modules

Menus and modules should be appropriately named. The Navigation Filter at the top is incredibly useful for selecting from the enormous list available to you as an administrator. And it is also helpful to power users. But the filter only matches on the **Name parameter**. For example, one of the module names that really frustrates me is the name of the link to view all the items in the system error log: **All**. The text to find this precise entry will therefore be `all`. Using `log` or `error` or other strings will either produce a lot of or no results, which to me is quite unintuitive. If you do type `all` in, you see lots of completely irrelevant entries. Besides that, **All** is not very descriptive! Something like **All log entries** will help in every respect.

Summary

This chapter explored the key design principles that ServiceNow is built on, ensuring the foundations of the platform are well understood. A ServiceNow instance is a single-tenancy design, giving you a great deal of control and independence over how the platform works for you. The architecture of the system relies upon its database to store all configuration and data, so the hosting of ServiceNow gives a redundant pair for maintenance, disaster recovery, and performance reasons.

Creating tables and fields is a fundamental part of administrating ServiceNow. There are many field types available, from strings to URLs and journals fields. The dictionary stores information about each field and can make the values of the field unique, or act as the record's display value.

Hierarchical tables give a great deal of benefit. Inheritance allows the **Guest** table to take advantage of all the functionality provided by the out-of-the-box **User** table.

In a relational system, linking records together is a key part of data design. Reference fields provide links between two records and give a great deal of capability and configuration choice, such as dot-walking, dynamic creation, and handling deletion. In addition to these, there are other types of relationships, such as many-to-many tables and Glide Lists.

The ServiceNow interface is built on lists and forms. These relate to the database tables they are showing and give a great deal of functionality - from hierarchical lists to tags and from views to filtered modules.

The next chapter will build on this data structure. By adding logic to the ServiceNow platform, we go beyond just storing data and instead get control over it.

2
Server-side Control

ServiceNow gives you great control over your data; you can check it, change it, or censor it, but how? As we progress through ServiceNow, we'll see how information can be validated by a **Data Policy** or secured by an Access Control Rule. However, the most flexible way is through scripting. This chapter aims to give you a good understanding of how server-side scripting in ServiceNow works. In this chapter, we will be covering the following:

- Firstly, we explore how JavaScript works in ServiceNow by understanding the engine behind it.
- Then, we take a detailed look at `GlideRecord`, which is the most commonly written code in ServiceNow.
- Business Rules are the starting point for logic in ServiceNow. We explore the different flavors by running through a variety of scenarios.
- **Script Includes** provides a place for your code libraries. We look at how you can define classes, extend them, and run them.
- Finally, Data Policies and Advanced Reference Qualifiers show other ways of controlling data access and logic.

ServiceNow has over 30 places where you can write code to make the instance do what you want. Aside from a few exceptions, JavaScript is used in all. JavaScript is a very flexible and powerful language that is most commonly known for its inclusion in almost every web browser. This has made it almost mandatory for web development these days, with its simple syntax allowing many people to quickly add simple logic to web pages with minimum effort. Taking advantage of this familiarity, ServiceNow uses JavaScript both on the server and on the client.

A brief history of JavaScript

JavaScript doesn't have the greatest of reputations. The majority of code on the Web is simply copied and pasted with some of the popular tutorial sites not providing the most accurate of references. This results in JavaScript not really being developed, but simply "used". Especially frustrating are the browser incompatibilities, where earlier versions of Internet Explorer implemented support in different ways to the standard.

However, this is slowly changing. Libraries such as jQuery and Angular have had a remarkable impact, enabling you to quickly build more *real* applications by providing a higher abstraction level. They handle many of the common use cases easily and provide an interface to ensure all browsers work the same way. This means that more time can be spent realizing functional requirements rather than technical requirements. They have proven that JavaScript can solve real business needs.

The use of JavaScript is growing on the server side with platforms like node.js realizing the flexibility of the language and providing a modern event-driven framework. Also, browser makers are investing significant development time in reducing execution time and making the language more efficient. The competition between teams leads to innovation and is raising the profile of JavaScript.

Rather than being a niche scripting language only used for giving the modal "alert" messages, the future of JavaScript is promising.

Running background scripts

The simplest place to experiment with server-side scripting is perhaps the *Background Scripts* section in ServiceNow. This provides you with a large text box where you place your code and a button saying **Run Script**, without any fuss, formatting, or further complexity. Outputs from your session during execution (such as log statements) are captured and presented to the screen. This, therefore, provides an excellent place to run server-side code where you need to monitor the results, where you can experiment, or where you need to run one-off scripts, such as fix jobs.

Accessing the background scripts page requires you to have the `security_admin` role. The `security_admin` role is an **elevated privilege**, meaning that the role only applies to your current session. To start using it, ensure you've been given the `security_admin` role (and you need to log out and back in to get access to the role if you were just granted it), then click on the padlock next to your name to access the elevated privileges pop-up box. Activate it, and then click on **OK**:

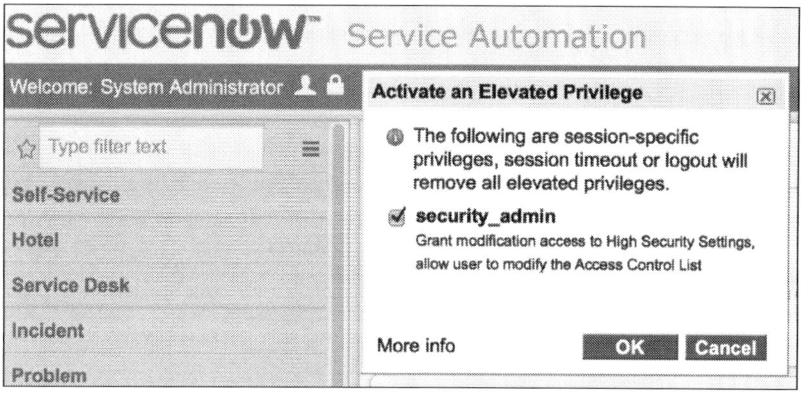

> We'll explore elevated privileges in *Chapter 7, Securing Applications and Data*.

Navigate to **Background Scripts** by going to **System Definition** > **Scripts (Background)**.

You will be presented with a large script box; however, before you get too enthusiastic, heed this warning. The reason that accessing Background Scripts requires an elevated privilege is to remind you that some badly written code really can delete all your data. Never experiment in a live production instance!

> Inefficient scripts get stuck in an infinite loop and can seriously impact performance or even cause outages or security breaches. Always test in a sandbox instance first.

Let's run the standard `Hello, World!` program as our first script:

```
gs.log('Hello, world!');
```

As the output, you should see the following:

```
*** Script: Hello, world!
```

The function used is not a standard JavaScript command. (`gs` stands for `GlideSystem`). It collects a bunch of useful functions and utilities, allowing you to control and instruct the ServiceNow platform more easily.

> The functions of `GlideSystem` are introduced throughout this book. For a detailed list of all its capabilities, see the wiki page: `http://wiki.servicenow.com/?title=GlideSystem`

You must be wondering why it's called `GlideSystem`. Originally, ServiceNow (the company) was called **GlideSoft**, and they produced a platform called **Glide**. As the company and platform grew, they were both renamed to the more familiar monikers used today. You may see other references to Glide and GlideSoft, particularly in the more original parts of the platform.

`gs` is one of the several objects that is instantiated before your script is run. These are often dependent upon the context that the code is running in. You will see many more as we journey through the ServiceNow platform. Generally, you do not instantiate these objects yourself; they are already available for your use.

The log function of `gs` is self-explanatory; it writes a message to the system log. In *Chapter 8, Diagnosing ServiceNow – Knowing What Is Going On*, we explore logging in ServiceNow in much more detail.

Let's try running some code that won't work:

```
alert('Hello, world!');
```

As the output, you should see the following:

```
Evaluator: org.mozilla.javascript.EcmaError: "alert" is not defined.
```

Interesting! This same simple snippet of JavaScript works in a browser, but not in ServiceNow. Why?

Rhino – the JavaScript engine powering ServiceNow

JavaScript needs to be interpreted and executed in order for it to do useful work. The functionality that does this in each web browser is the JavaScript engine; it understands the code written on the web page, and executes it to provide the functionality that the developer expects.

The speed and efficiency at which JavaScript engines do this has rapidly increased. Optimizations such as the *Just in Time* compilation and caching have meant that each browser reacts to events quicker and draws pages faster, providing a slicker, more interactive experience to the user. No one likes to click and wait! Each browser developer is battling to prove themselves as the fastest; at present, Chrome's V8 is the one to beat. Other client engines include SpiderMonkey, which is used in Firefox, and Internet Explorer uses Chakra. Until recently, the Internet Explorer JavaScript engine didn't have the best of reputations, being slow and not very standard-compliant. When we move into the client-side JavaScript, we'll explore this more. ServiceNow uses the Rhino JavaScript engine, which is managed by the Mozilla Foundation, the maintainers of Firefox. Rhino itself is written in Java, which provides a hint of what the backend platform code that ServiceNow is written in is. Rhino provides a full implementation of the language, with the exception of some objects that only make sense to the client. It's relatively complete and standard-compliant. ServiceNow includes a version of Rhino that supports up to version 1.5 of JavaScript.

Rhino is considered stable, and isn't developed at the same frenetic pace as the current crop of web browsers. In a moment, we'll run some very simple indicators that show that your desktop or laptop and its web browser can outperform the ServiceNow instance in some situations. Of course, the inefficiency of Rhino is slightly countered by the brute force of the powerful servers that the instances are running on, but it is worth considering if you are looking to build some very complex math-based scripts.

Accessing Java

The ServiceNow platform is written in Java using the Apache Struts framework. In earlier versions of ServiceNow, scripts could, through the support in Rhino, access Java code and execute calls to backend functions. For example, you might find examples that use the `ftp4che` FTP library. This is built into the platform to enable the Import Set functionality, which we'll explore in a later chapter. Since Java code is organized in classes and then into packages, Rhino normally provides a global variable called `Packages` that enables the scriptwriter to access any code they can find.

The benefit that this access brings—the ability to call any Java code distributed as part of the platform—has resulted in uncontrolled access. Scripters are finding classes, calling them, and then relying upon their specific behavior. Even if code wasn't supposed to be called in a script, it now is! This limits the platform developers, since they are unable to refractor and restructure perhaps as much as they would like. Any changes they make would have a dramatic impact on customer scripts. Some scripts even rely on bugs in the Java code!

In recent versions of ServiceNow, unfettered Java access has been curtailed and has been limited to a subset of classes and packages. Some Java functions are now marked as *Scriptable*, meaning that the JavaScript code can call it. There are several hundred classes currently accessible, but it is anticipated that this list will be reduced to enable the platform team to make more substantial changes to the API.

> For more information on scripting API changes, see `http://wiki.servicenow.com/?title=Scripting_API_Changes`.
>
> To make your scripts as future-proof as possible, ServiceNow recommends that you do not include code that is not documented on wiki. Any exceptions should be tested carefully and comprehensively after an upgrade. It might be that minor changes that you don't immediately notice could affect your code in surprising ways. This book focuses on the supported `GlideRecord`, `GlideSystem`, and other documented APIs, but there are some mentions of other functionalities. ServiceNow is built to be extended, but be careful how you are doing it.

Appreciating server-side code

It is important to understand the significance of writing JavaScript on the server. For the majority of the time, you can apply the same concepts to both the server and client contexts. You can create variables, iterate through arrays, and define functions in exactly the same way. However, some functions in JavaScript are designed to interact with the user or the browser; these are not supported. You can't, for example, use the `alert` function when writing a server-side script. In a web browser, `alert` pops up a dialog box in the browser. But if we remember that our code is actually running on the instance, perhaps in a scheduled job, on a server probably many hundreds of miles away, where would that alert box show?

The error that we got when running the code in Background Scripts occurred because Rhino can't pop up an alert dialog box. It doesn't have a screen it can display the message on. Instead, we need to use our first example, and use `gs.log` if we want to view our output.

Let's run some standard code that is almost obligatory in any scripting chapter, and see what the output is like:

```
function log (s) {
  typeof gs === 'object' ? gs.log(s) : console.log(s);
}
function fibonacci (n) {
```

```
    return n < 2 ? n : fibonacci(n - 1) + fibonacci(n - 2);
  }

  var s = new Date().getTime();
  for (var i = 0; i <= 30; i += 1) {
    log( i + ': ' + fibonacci(i));
  }
  var e = new Date().getTime();
  log('Execution time: ' + (e - s))
```

Firstly, note that it's a very simple logging function. This determines how to record the results using either the ServiceNow log system, or the console. It does this by simply inspecting whether `gs` is defined or not. This allows you to use exactly the same code in either your browser or background scripts.

The Fibonacci function is next. This calculates the Fibonacci number at a particular place, so we perform a simple loop calculating the first 30 Fibonacci numbers: 0, 1, 1, 2, 3, 5, 8, and so on. It uses simple math and recursive function calls to generate the number. It is a straightforward test of functional code speed.

Finally, Script Includes has a simple (and rather rough) execution timer. We grab the time, accurate to a millisecond, at the beginning and end of execution. The former is then subtracted from the latter to give a number.

Comparing engine speed

It is interesting to compare the different performances of browsers and their optimization techniques. In my tests, Chrome completes the script in 30 milliseconds. Firefox takes around a second, with the ServiceNow instance taking 5 seconds. All these are much faster than the older versions of Internet Explorer. In order to improve performance, the ServiceNow platform compiles scripts and stores them in its cache for future execution. However, it is not a panacea, as you can see.

> To try this yourself, execute the code in Background Scripts on your instance and compare it with the same code pasted into the console in your browser. This is typically accessible through a web developer menu.

These few tests show that the JavaScript used on the server in ServiceNow is standard, but has a few gotchas you need to be careful of. The fun really starts when you use function calls on the power of the ServiceNow platform.

Using GlideRecord (and its friends)

Chapter 1, ServiceNow Foundations, shows that ServiceNow is built around data. Background Scripts, and scripts in general, can use the excellent database connectivity capabilities built in ServiceNow to easily access whatever information we want. `GlideRecord` is instrumental in doing this.

`GlideRecord` is a class that represents a single entry in a database table. It is easy to use, but I recommend reviewing the basics from wiki or from a scripting course. There are some gotchas and some very interesting features that are misunderstood.

> For full details, investigate the documentation at `http://wiki.servicenow.com/?title=GlideRecord`.

Let's run some code in **Background Scripts** to allow us to understand how it works. We'll go through it line by line to get the details. The code is a little artificial, but the aim is to return at the most two **Check-in** records, and find out on which date they were created:

```
var results = [];
var gr = new GlideRecord('u_check_in');
gr.addQuery('u_guest.name', 'CONTAINS', 'Alice');
gr.setLimit(2);
gr.orderByDesc('sys_created_on');
gr.query();
while(gr.next()) {
  results.push(gr.sys_created_on + '');
}
gs.log(results.join(', '));
```

Now, let's look into the code in detail:

1. The very first line is a standard line of JavaScript. It creates a variable named `results`, making it an array. The output will be stored here.
2. A `GlideRecord` object is always instantiated by passing through the table. The resulting object is a representation of that table. However, it isn't usable until a function is called to either make a new record (`gr.newRecord()`) or perform a query (with `gr.query()`).

3. Perhaps it'd be useful to know when Alice is checking in to the hotel. In order to add a filter (which is simply adding a SQL `WHERE` clause), use `addQuery`.

> Note that the condition can use dot-walking to navigate through reference fields. In the background, ServiceNow performs a join on the referenced table, allowing it to filter the results. This is invisible to the scriptwriter since the resulting `GlideRecord` is exactly the same structure. This functionality is incredibly useful, and can save significant development effort. However, because you are performing a join, the database does need to expend more effort, so be smart about how you do it.

4. Generally, you either pass two or three parameters to `addQuery`. The first and last are the fieldname and the value you are searching for, respectively. The optional middle value is what type of clause you want, standard operations such as greater than, equal to, and as per this example, a pattern matching text search (equivalent to the SQL clause `LIKE '%<value>%'`). It is searching for a name that contains *Alice* anywhere in it; *Alice Cooper* will match, as will *Steve Doralice*.
5. Next, the script instructs ServiceNow to only return a maximum of two records no matter how many matching entries there might be in the database. When writing scripts, it is always a good idea to test them on a limited subset before unleashing your query on thousands of records.

> Once the query has been returned, you can use `getRowCount` to return the number of rows that actually have been found. However, only use this function if you are actually going to deal with the records anyway. For example, in a script that deletes records, use `getRowCount` to check how you will be deleting them. If you are expecting to delete five, but you see that you might be deleting 5,000! Stop!
>
> `GlideAggregate`, discussed later in this chapter, is a more efficient way of counting if you are only interested in the number of results.

6. The next step is to order the results. Choose any column to order the result set.
7. Once the query has been set up, it's time to execute it and ask the database to get the information. From now on, the `GlideRecord` object is the result set.

8. A `while` loop is then executed to deal with all the data. The `next` function will increment in the result set returning whether it was successful. This is a very common pattern for iterating around a result set.

> Sometimes you only want to get a single record in a table. On such an occasion, you can call the `get` function, which rolls several commands together: `setLimit(1)`, `query`, and `next`, skipping up to three lines. If you pass through a single parameter, `get` will assume it is a `sys_id`, allowing you to grab a record with little fuss. If you give two parameters, the first allows you to specify the field, the second the value. This is a real timesaver. Consider the following code snippet:

```
var gr = new GlideRecord('u_check_in');
gr.get('u_guest.name', 'Alice Richards');
gs.log(gr.sys_created_on + '');
```

9. Some standard JavaScript functions are used for each result, appending the information we are interested in (the built-in **Created On** field) to the array. The script ensures it is converted to an array. The next section talks about why in much more detail.
10. After the loop is closed, the result set is joined together. Finally, it is written to the system log using the `gs` function we've already seen.

Accessing data from GlideRecord

`GlideRecord` uses an unusual capability of JavaScript to redefine objects on the fly. Properties are created and changed whenever the database is worked with, such as calling the `newRecord` or `query` functions. Every time the `next` function is called, the ServiceNow platform iterates through all the fields on the table, and attaches them as properties to the `GlideRecord` object. These properties are stored as `GlideElement` objects, which represent the field in the database. They give you the value of the field, plus a few extra really useful features.

Wiki has more information on `GlideElement` objects at `http://wiki.servicenow.com/index.php?title=GlideElement`.

> Some of the most useful functions you can call on a `GlideElement` object are the `changes` and `changesTo` functions. These return `true` if the field value has been altered. As we'll see, this is invaluable for knowing what data is being altered, whether it be by the user or otherwise.

The GlideElement object in the property can be accessed in two ways, the typical dot notation (gr.sys_created_on) or through a bracket notation gr['sys_created_on']. This is very useful if you need to access fields programmatically:

```
var f = 'my_field';
gr[f] // is the same as:
gr.my_field
```

This allows you to quickly, for example, loop through several fields, clearing them in a fairly concise way:

```
var fields = ['u_field_1', 'u_field_2', 'u_field_3, u_field_4'];
for (var i = 0; i < fields.length; i++) {
  gr[fields[i]] = '';
}
```

Here, a for loop iterates through the array using the bracket notation to access the right property. The obvious alternative that just repeats code is not as elegant.

Walking through reference fields

Dot-walking lets you access information through reference fields by using the dot notation. Accessing the name of a guest from a GlideRecord object of **Check-in** is as simple as gr.u_guest.name.

The reference field has access to the fields of the table that it's pointing to. A reference field pointing to the **User** table will have access to the user fields and not to any fields on the **Guest** table, such as the **Membership number** field created in *Chapter 1, ServiceNow Foundations*.

> It is possible to access extended fields using a special notation: ref_<tablename>.<extended field>. So the **Membership number** field could be accessed through a **User** reference field such as gr.ref_u_guest.u_membership_number. This also works in conditions.

Converting data types

JavaScript is loosely typed. This means that it will convert values into different types wherever it can. If you are performing arithmetic, it will convert to a number according to the rules. GlideElement returns the value of the field when you access the object when you request a string; most of the time, that's great. In line 8 of the preceding script, it specifically converted the value into a string. This is important to do; if not, then you will get surprising results.

The surprising results of GlideElement

Consider this code. It is a very simplified version of our preceding script, running without any `GlideRecord` distractions or loops:

```
var obj = {};
var results = [];

obj.value = 1;
results[1] = obj;

obj.value = 2;
results[2] = obj;

gs.log(results[1].value);
gs.log(results[2].value);
```

The first couple of lines create an object and an array. Simple enough. The next command sets the `value` property of our object to `1`. The object is then pushed into the array. The next two commands do the same thing, but first they change the value property to `2`. Then the array is printed out.

If you run this in Background Scripts, you may be surprised to find that instead of printing out `1` and `2`, it prints out `2` twice. Why?

I must admit I was slightly untruthful in my description. When the object is pushed into the array, it actually puts an object *pointer* in the array. This means that the two elements of the array populated are actually pointing to the *same object*. Therefore, when the object is accessed through the two array elements, the same value is printed twice.

To return to the `GlideRecord` object, if `sys_created_on` was pushed into the array without converting it into a string, then that results in the pointer to `sys_created_on` of `GlideElement` being added to the array. It is not the *value* of the field. And of course, when `gr.next()` is called, the value of `sys_created_on` changes.

Sometimes this is exactly what you want. However, when you are manipulating a `GlideRecord`, this is often not the case. The way to avoid this is to get the value of the field. An easy way to do that is to ensure the data put into the array is a primitive like an integer, a floating-point number, or a string. So, if the fourth line of the preceding code was replaced with the following snippet, we would get the expected result:

```
results[1] = obj + '';
```

Getting the value another way

Of course, there are alternatives. There are some functions in `GlideRecord` and `GlideElement` that can help—specifically `getValue` and `toString`—which will do the conversions for you. You may want to always do this so you don't forget. Both these lines are drop in replacements for line 8:

```
results.push(gr.getValue(sys_created_on));
results.push(gr.sys_created_on.toString());
```

But programmers generally avoid keystrokes whenever necessary, and I certainly prefer manipulating `GlideElement` directly. Whatever you choose, it is always important to know why you follow certain conventions.

Dealing with dates

Dates and times are generally tricky to work with, since, while the idea of 60 minutes, 24 hours, 7 days, and 12 months are very normal to a person, the almost arbitrary nature of the amounts causes some consternation through code. Therefore, ServiceNow provides access to `GlideSystem` and `GlideDateTime`, both of which contain many functions to generate and deal with time.

> For more information, check out the wiki link here: `http://wiki.servicenow.com/?title=GlideDateTime`

Wiki provides many examples of how to perform date arithmetic. This is notoriously tricky to do manually so I suggest using them if possible. The most useful functions are available through `GlideDateTime`. On a date/time field you can extract the `GlideDateTime` object through a `GlideElement` object. For example, to increment a date by a day, you can use the following code:

```
gr.sys_created_on.getGlideObject().addDays(1);
```

If you get beyond simple situations (such as how many weeks in a month?), it can be advantageous to extract information in Unix time and work from there. (Unix time is the number of seconds since midnight 1 Jan 1970 UTC, which may be described as when time began for computers!) This then can be manipulated like any other number. The following line of code will give you the time in Unix time:

```
gr.sys_created_on.getGlideObject().getNumericValue();
```

Counting records with GlideAggregate

Earlier in this chapter, the `getRowCount` function of `GlideRecord` was introduced. It returns how many results have been found. However, this is only determined by getting all the information from the database, then counting it. Wouldn't it be more efficient if we could get just the total number? We can, with `GlideAggregate`!

> Wiki has more information available at `http://wiki.servicenow.com/?title=GlideAggregate`.

Run the following lines of code to get the total number:

```
var count = new GlideAggregate('u_check_in');
count.addQuery('sys_created_on', '>', gs.beginningOfYesterday());
count.addAggregate('count');
count.query();
var result = 0;
if (count.next())
  result = count.getAggregate('COUNT');
gs.log('Result: ' + result);
```

The style of working with `GlideAggregate` is very similar to `GlideRecord`. You can add filters, just like we do with `GlideRecord`, for example. Here, one of the functions of `GlideSystem` is used to return all records that are created after the beginning of yesterday (that is, yesterday midnight). The main difference is that the `addAggregate` function is used to ask for the desired information, and the query call then returns that instead of a list of fields.

The `addAggregate` function accepts two parameters: the first being the calculation (such as `min`, `max`, `count`, `sum`, or `avg` for average) and the second being the field to perform it on. The `groupBy` function is used to divide the result set up and return multiple entries that we loop over.

To get the last time that a guest has checked in, the following code could be used:

```
var gr = new GlideAggregate('u_check_in');
gr.addAggregate('max', 'sys_created_on');
gr.groupBy('u_guest');
gr.query();
while(gr.next()) {
  gs.log(gr.u_guest.name + ' ' + gr.getAggregate('max', 'sys_created_
on'));
}
```

Be aware that `GlideAggregate` only populates attributes in the object that are relevant. So you can only access the fields that you group by, or that you have an aggregate of. In the preceding example, `u_guest` is available since it is grouped by field. Other fields are not available.

Business Rules

The home of server-side scripts in ServiceNow may be known as **Business Rules**. They are so called because they allow you to apply business or process logic to the applications hosted on ServiceNow. Do you want to update a remote system through an integration? Perhaps check a date? Or populate some fields automatically? Business Rules are a great way to accomplish this.

> Business Rules have been simplified in the Eureka release of ServiceNow. Some common actions can now be performed without any code. However, ticking the **Advanced** checkbox enables the script and many other fields. For information on the simpler functions, check out the wiki link `http://wiki.servicenow.com/index.php?title=Business_Rules`.

Some like to think of Business Rules as database triggers since they perform a very similar function. Business Rules run whenever a record is inserted, updated, or deleted, or when a query is run against the table. Since ServiceNow is a data-driven platform, this allows great flexibility in manipulating and working with the information in the system.

Predefined variables

Whenever a Business Rule runs, it has access to several variables provided by the platform:

- `Current`: This is a `GlideRecord` object that represents the record in question. Any changes that the user (or a script) has performed on it are available for inspection.
- `previous`: This represents the record before any changes have been made.
- `g_scratchpad`: This is used as a temporary storage area for data; however, it's also available to client-side scripts. We'll explore this in more detail in the next chapter.
- `gs`: We've already met this; it contains several helpful functions for use in our scripts.

Setting the table

One of the first thoughts when creating a Business Rule is to set which table it will run on. Most of the time, this is obvious; if you want to affect the **Check-in** records, you need to place it on the **Check-in** table.

However, what makes Business Rules pretty special is that you can run them on any level of the table hierarchy.

In *Chapter 1, ServiceNow Foundations*, the **Guest** table was created, extending the **User** table. This means, it inherits the fields that **User** provides. This includes Business Rules too. So, if a Business Rule is created for the **Guest** table, it will run just for **Guest** records, but if it was placed against the **User** table, it would run for all **User** records, including **Guests**.

Displaying the right table

For a very simple example of this, let's create a Business Rule on the **User** table.

1. Navigate to **System Definition** > **Business Rules**. Click on **New**.
2. Use the following information:
    - **Table:** Display table on record creation
    - **Table:** User [sys_user]
    - **Insert**: <ticked>
    - **Advanced**: <ticked>
    - **Script**: gs.addInfoMessage ('You have created a ' + current.getTableName() + ' record');

    This code uses another of the GlideSystem function to output a message. Instead of it being visible in the log file, it is presented to the user that carried out the action. In the message, the table name of the current record is shown by utilizing the getTableName function of the current object of GlideRecord.

> It is always a good idea to give the Business Rule a meaningful name, so you can easily identify it later. There is also a description field that you can add to the form to allow you to better describe what the script does.

From now on, whenever you create a **User** or **Guest** record, you will receive a message telling you which table has been used.

For **Guest** records you get the following message:

For **User** records you get the following message:

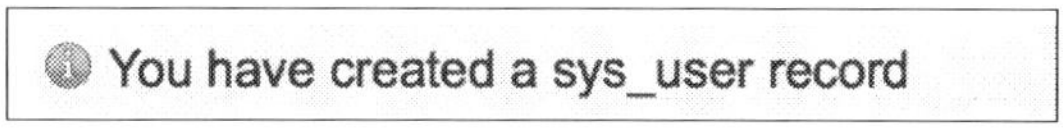

Conditioning your scripts

When records in a table are worked with, Business Rules are run. Each Business Rule has a condition that determines whether the script should run or not. The condition can be a JavaScript statement that is executed. If the result is `true`, then the main script is parsed and run, or the filter conditions and role conditions fields can be used.

It is good practice to always provide some sort of condition:

- Code should only be run when appropriate. Since the script field is only parsed if the statement passes, code that is not appropriate at that time is ignored, thus speeding up the execution.
- It provides easier debugging. Business Rule debugging tells you which scripts were run and when, and whether the condition was met or not. *Chapter 8, Diagnosing ServiceNow – Knowing What Is Going On*, discusses this in more detail.

The condition has access to the `current` object of `GlideRecord` and the other predefined variables, where appropriate. This lets you check what is happening to the record, ensuring the Business Rule is running only at the right time. For example, for a Business Rule on the **Check-in** table, a condition can be added to run the script only if the value of the **Guest** field has been altered:

```
current.u_guest.changes()
```

This line of code uses several elements we've already seen: `current`, our `GlideRecord` object representing the record we are dealing with; `u_guest`, the `GlideElement` object for the field, and a function we are calling on it that returns `true` if someone has altered the value of that field.

> In addition to always having a condition, it is good practice to always have a condition that includes a `changes` function call on a `GlideElement` object. It is common to see code like this:
>
> ```
> current.u_guest == 'Bob'
> ```
>
> This means that whenever `u_guest` is set to Bob, even if it hasn't changed, this Business Rule will run. For the majority of the time, you only want to run your rule when the value is first changed:
>
> ```
> current.u_guest.changesTo('Bob')
> ```

You may also want to use some of the other functions available in `GlideSystem` to limit Business Rules, such as the `hasRole` function. Roles and securities are explored in *Chapter 7, Securing Applications and Data*, but it is very common to show debugging information only to the System Administrator.

Having good conditions

When writing conditions, be careful with using the right JavaScript operators. Since the **Condition** field is a short line, the code can get quite compressed. If you have a very complex condition, consider:

- Splitting the Business Rule into parts. This is always good practice anyway. Instead of having lots of **OR** conditions and writing one big Business Rule, have several, more targeted Business Rules with smaller conditions.
- Putting the most important statements in the **Condition** field and placing the rest in an `if` block in the **Script** field.
- Writing a function and calling it from the condition. (The ideal place to store the function is in a Script Include, described later in this chapter.)
- Expanding the **Condition** field. It is possible to make the **Condition** field bigger by changing the dictionary settings. However, consider that this may just encourage you to write longer conditions, and longer conditions tend to go wrong!

> Finally, lay out your conditions carefully, and test thoroughly. The most common confusion I see is around negative *or* conditions. If you want to test that several values aren't `true`, you must use *and*. In English, we often say "I don't want a, b, or c", which is short for "I don't want a, I don't want b, and I don't want c". We need the long format! In JavaScript, that would be:
>
> ```
> current.u_field != 'a' && current.u_field != 'b' &&
>   current.u_field != 'c'
> ```

Controlling the database

Business Rules run when there is database access. So, if you try to delete 20 records, a delete Business Rule will run 20 times. It is most common for Business Rules to run on `insert` and `update`, but you can select a combination of the options relatively freely.

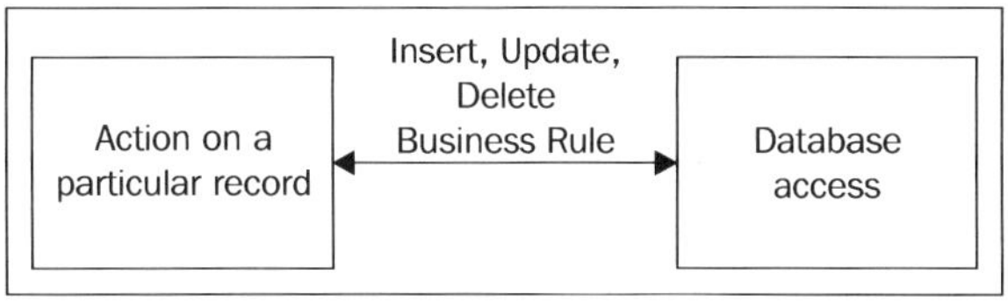

Controlling database queries with Business Rules

Query Business Rules are slightly different. These run before the user has a chance to interact with a particular record, and even before the database has got the results. In fact, they are designed to control exactly what the database returns. When a query Business Rule runs, the `current` object is still provided, but it is before the `query` function has been called. This gives you an opportunity to add conditions, like when we manipulated our first `GlideRecord` object.

A great example is the baseline Business Rule that means that inactive users are invisible to everyone bar System Administrators. Let's examine its contents:

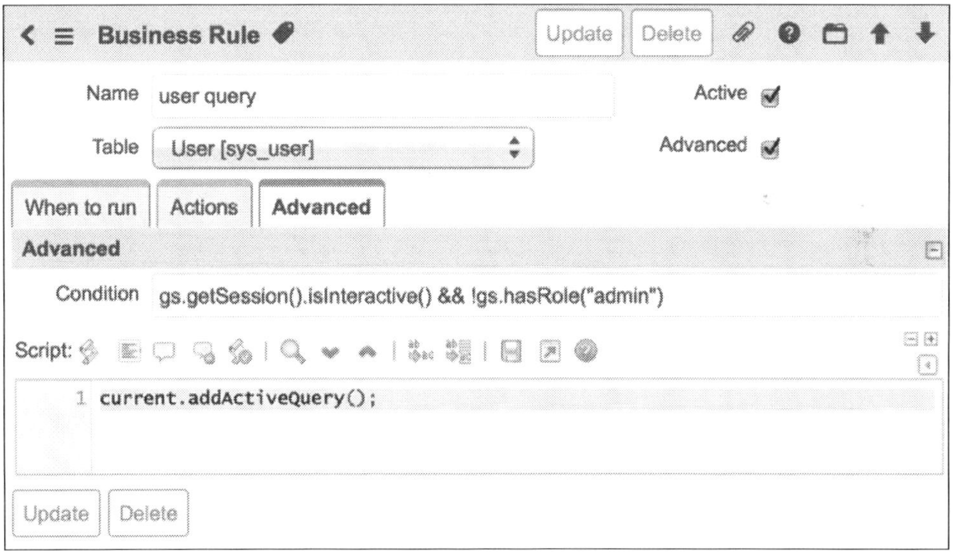

The first thing to look at is the following condition:

```
gs.getSession().isInteractive() && !gs.hasRole("admin")
```

The condition is split into two parts. First, it checks to see how the user is logged in. `GlideSystem` provides session details through the `getSession` function, and the `isInteractive` function returns `true` if the user is using the web interface. (Other alternatives include accessing the platform via Web Services, as discussed in *Chapter 6, Exchanging Data – Import Sets, Web Services, and Other Integrations.*)

Second, it determines whether the user has the admin role. So, if the user is accessing through the web interface, and they are not admin, the script will run.

If the condition matches, the one line script does the work:

```
current.addActiveQuery();
```

This is equivalent to running the `addQuery` function you may be more familiar with:

```
current.addQuery('active', true);
```

It uses slightly fewer keystrokes!

This Business Rule will always ensure that (subject to the condition) only active users are returned when accessing the **User** table. Once a user is marked as inactive, they will effectively "disappear". This technique is very useful to enforce particular security rules, but it is worth remembering if you wonder why you can't access some records. The following figure shows the work flow:

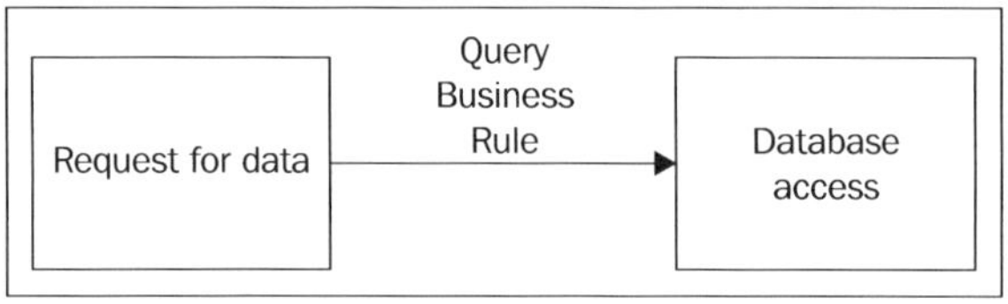

Choosing when to execute – before, after, and really after

In addition to the **Insert**, **Update**, **Delete**, and **Query** checkboxes, the **When to run** section on the Business Rules form also contains a dropdown list labelled **When** and an **Order** field. This controls exactly when your rule runs.

The **When** dropdown field controls at what point during the database operation the Business Rule runs: before it goes to the database, or afterwards. When inserting a record, you may want to programmatically set or alter default values. If this is done in or before the Business Rule runs, the additions to the record will be stored. The following figure shows the workflow of the three options:

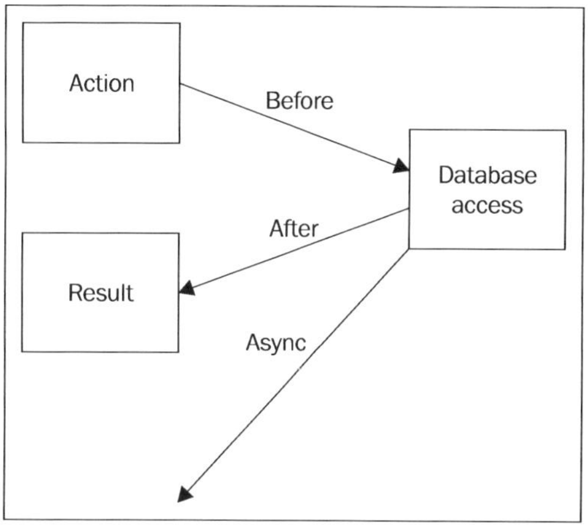

Defaulting data

Let's create a Business Rule that will automatically populate the floor number when you create or update a **Room** record. In most hotels, the first digit of the room number is the floor number. Let's automate this.

Create a new Business Rule, and set the following information:

- **Name**: `Set default floor number`
- **Table**: `Room [u_room]`
- **Advanced**: `<ticked>`
- **When**: `Before`
- **Insert**: `<ticked>`
- **Update**: `<ticked>`

- **Condition**: `(current.u_number.changes() || current.u_floor.changes()) && current.u_floor.isNil() && current.u_number.toString().length > 1`

  This fairly long condition checks several items. It'll only run when the **Number** or the Room field changes, that the floor field is not populated, and that the number field, when converted to a string, has a length of at least one character.

  > This condition could also be specified using the **Condition** builder.

- **Script**: `current.u_floor = current.u_number.substring(0, 1);`

  The script will take the first digit of the number value and assign it to the floor field.

> Notice that `current.update()` was not necessary. Since this is a `before` Business Rule, we are making changes before the record writes to the database. The Business Rule alters the current record but the reason that updated Business Rules are running is because something triggered the record to save. We don't need to try to save it again, and in fact, you may cause loops by doing so. However, the platform will detect and stop whenever this happens.

Now, try creating a room without the **Floor** field populated, but ensure **Number** is. When you save the record, the system will automatically give a value for the **Floor** field. This will also happen if you try to clear out the floor, effectively providing a rule that the system will ensure that a room number is generally always available.

As here, if you are providing default values or calculating new ones, it is a good idea to ensure you have the data and that the user hasn't overridden the system. When possible, you should trust the users of your system to know what they are doing. There are usually exceptions to policies, and if the system is too locked down and only caters for foreseen circumstances, frustration will arise!

> There are many other options for validation and checking data. In the next chapter, we'll explore client-side options, while later on in this chapter we'll look at Data Policy.

Validating information

Another use of `before` Business Rules is to validate data. If you find information that is wrong or missing, you can tell the platform not to commit the action to the database.

One of the big issues with our **Hotel** application is that you can check in to a room multiple times. There is nothing to prevent the allocation of the same room to several different people!

Let's expand the **Check-in** table slightly to include more information. Create a new field, and use the **Form Designer** to include it on the form. It represents the date on which the check-in happened:

- **Column label**: `Date`
- **Type**: `Date`

The **Check-in** table now appears as shown in the following screenshot:

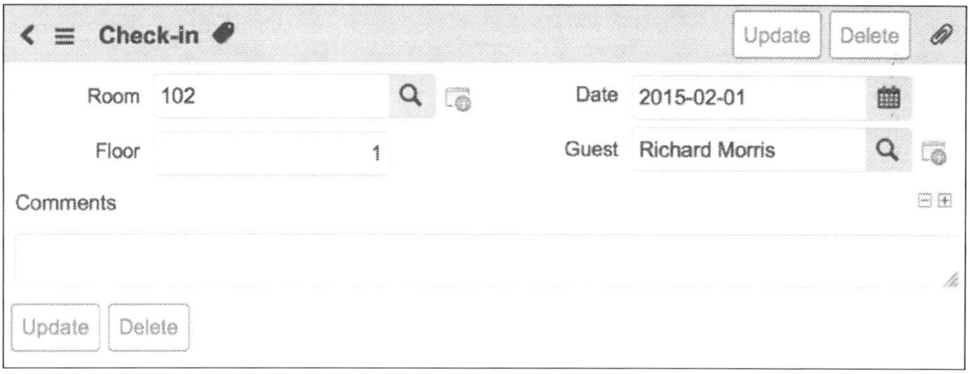

Now, let's create a Business Rule that uses this date and the **Room** field to ensure collisions don't occur:

- **Name**: `Stop duplicate check-ins`
- **Table**: `Check-in [u_check_in]`
- **Advanced:** `<ticked>`
- **Insert**: `<ticked>`
- **Update**: `<ticked>`

- **Condition**: `current.u_room.changes() || current.u_date.changes() || current.operation() == 'insert'`

  This condition is shorter. This rule will fire if the **Room** field changes or if the **Date** field changes. Also, there is an additional check to see if the record is being inserted. If you start with a completely blank record and insert it, then the **Date** and **Room** fields will both change (from nothing to something), but it is possible to "copy" a record (using **Insert and Stay**). In this edge case, you may end up with a record being inserted without any fields changing.

- **Script**: Use the following script:

```
var dup = new GlideRecord('u_check_in');
dup.addQuery('u_room', current.u_room);
dup.addQuery('u_date', current.u_date);
dup.setLimit(1);
dup.query();
if (dup.next()) {
  gs.addErrorMessage('This room is already checked in on this
date.');
  current.setAbortAction(true);
}
```

This script is longer than we've seen before, but it reuses much functionality we've already seen. The bulk of the code sets up a `GlideRecord` query to find any **Check-in** records that have the same room and date as the record we are dealing with. We are only interested if there is at least one record, so a limit is added—a simple optimization.

Then, we query the database. Instead of looping round the results, we just ask the database if there was a result. The next function of `GlideRecord` will return true if there is.

For this script, we then call two new functions. The `addErrorMessage` function of `GlideSystem` gives the user a red error message, and as the name suggests, `setAbortAction(true)` will stop the system in its tracks. This means the record is not inserted or updated.

Once the Business Rule is saved, you can test it by creating another **Room** record. If you choose a date and a room that is already recorded on a **Check-in** record, when you click **Submit**, you will be faced with the following error message:

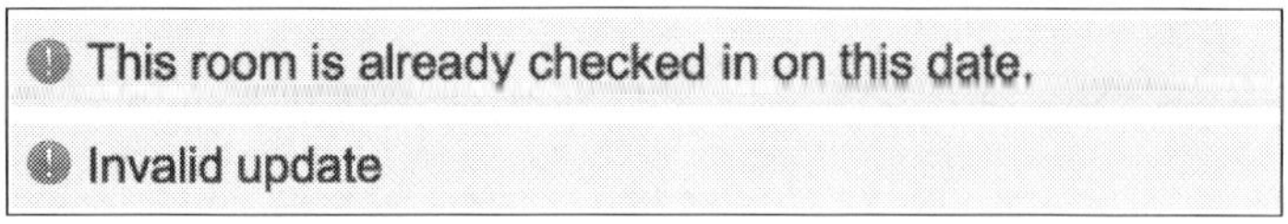

> `GlideAggregate` could have been used instead of `GlideRecord`. This lets the database do more of the counting.

Working with dates

A common requirement is ensuring dates make sense. Let's validate that the **Departure** field on the **Reservations** table is after the **Arrival** date. There are several ways to compare dates: ensure you check out all the functions available in `GlideSystem` to find the date a few days ago, or the beginning of the next quarter.

> A dedicated wiki page lists all the functions: `http://wiki.servicenow.com/?title=GlideSystem_Date_and_Time_Functions`

Create a new Business Rule, and set the following information:

- **Name:** `Stop duplicate check-ins`
- **Table:** `Reservation [u_reservation]`
- **Advanced:** `<ticked>`
- **Insert:** `<ticked>`
- **Update:** `<ticked>`
- **Condition:** `current.u_arrival > current.u_departure`

This very simple condition uses the power of coercion to compare two dates against each other. The script runs if `Arrival` is greater than `Departure`. Most of the time, you can work with the `GlideElement` objects as you expect them to, but ensure you always test thoroughly.

- **Script:** Add the following script:

```
gs.addErrorMessage('Departure date must be after arrival');
current.setAbortAction(true);
```

We've seen these two function calls before; we add an error message, and stop the record from being saved. Try out your script by entering an **Arrival** date that is after the **Departure** date.

Updating information

The other side to Business Rules is the after script. These rules will run after the record has been committed to the database. This means that you cannot use them to set field values or stop the database write, since it has already happened. Indeed, knowing that the record has successfully been saved means that it is the perfect place to update other records.

We can use this functionality to enforce another rule, ensuring there is only one lead passenger in a reservation.

Create a new Business Rule and set the following information:

- **Name**: Force single lead passenger
- **Table**: Guest Reservations [u_m2m_guests_reservations]
- **Advanced**: <ticked>
- **When**: After
- **Insert**: <ticked>
- **Update**: <ticked>
- **Condition**: Add the following condition:

  ```
  current.u_lead.changesTo(true) || (current.u_lead && current.
  action() == 'insert')
  ```

  This condition checks whether **Lead** has just been selected as true, or if it is a new record being inserted and the **Lead** field is true.

> A **True/False** field in ServiceNow will always be either true or false; it cannot be null. This means that current.u_lead === true is not necessary since it'll never be coerced.

- **Script**: Add the following script:

  ```
  var lead = new GlideRecord('u_m2m_guests_reservations');
  lead.addQuery('u_reservation', current.u_reservation);
  lead.addQuery('u_lead', true);
  lead.addQuery('sys_id', '!=', current.sys_id);
  lead.query();
  while(lead.next()) {
    lead.u_lead = false;
    lead.update();
  }
  ```

This is a fairly typical loop based on GlideRecord. It queries the many-to-many relationship table that relates guests to their reservations. It looks for the set of records that are for this reservation, and it finds every one that has the **Lead** field set to true. Of course, it should avoid finding the record being dealt with, so this is excluded.

The result set is looped around, with the script setting the **Lead** field of each to false, and finally it saves the record.

Try creating a new **Reservation** record, and set more than one of the guests to have **Lead** marked as true. You will find that the script will change the records so that only the last one to be updated will keep it. All the others will have **Lead** set to false.

Running things later with system scheduling

Another way to execute a Business Rule is to run it **async**, meaning asynchronous. This is similar to an after Business Rule, but instead of running the script immediately after the record is saved and before the results are presented to the user, it runs it at some time in the future. If the condition of an asynchronous Business Rule returns true, the platform records that some work needs to be done by creating a Scheduled Job.

> If you wish to see these jobs, navigate to **System Scheduler** > **Scheduled Jobs**. *Chapter 5, Events, Notifications, and Reporting,* explains these concepts in much more detail.

A Scheduled Job has a **Next Action** date that tells the platform when the record can be run. Jobs will be run after this date, but in order and only if the system has the capacity. If the instance is busy, perhaps serving interactive (user) requests, then the Scheduled Jobs may queue up. An asynchronous Business Rule will be scheduled to run immediately, but it is not guaranteed to run within a specific timeframe.

> Asynchronous Business Rules are not run within the user's current session. When a Scheduled Job is picked up, and it is assigned to a specific user account, the platform creates a new session and impersonates the user. This does have an impact on some session-specific functionality, like encrypted fields. However, most of the time, you won't notice it.

Asynchronous Business Rules are therefore perfect for jobs that may take some time to run, and don't need immediate feedback to the end user. For example, performing integrations such as **ebonding**, where ServiceNow connects to a remote system using web services and exchanges information after an update in ServiceNow. Another good example is sending an email notification. In general, you don't want to force the user to wait, blocking their browser session while this activity takes place.

Display Business Rules

We've discussed Business Rules that control queries, manipulate data on the way to the database, and react to events such as deletion, but there is a final, less common option available: the display Business Rule. Scripts marked to run on display will run after the record has been pulled from the database, but before is it displayed on a form. (Display Business Rules are not run for lists.)

Display Business Rules don't actually change the data that is stored, but only what is presented. So a script could, on every display, populate a field with a random number. The database change to the most recently generated number only if the record is saved.

However, the most important aspect of Display Business Rules is the ability to pass data to the client. A special variable called `g_scratchpad` is available, allowing calculated information to be passed to the browser, making it is instantly available. We'll discuss this capability in the next chapter.

Preventing colliding code

In ServiceNow, almost all JavaScript you write will be in the global scope by default. The scope of a variable refers to where it can be accessed, meaning that, by default, code in one Business Rule can affect another.

Consider the example of a Business Rule that runs at order 100. Any variables defined in this Business Rule will be available to one that runs at order 200. In fact, the platform relies upon this behavior: `current`, `previous`, `gs`, and the likes are defined as global variables, and are available everywhere. You may like to think that ServiceNow just concatenates all the code in the Business Rules together, and makes one huge script that runs when a record is updated.

If you search the Web, you will find many people that say that defining items in the global scope is a very bad thing, and should be avoided at all costs. This advice is also relevant to ServiceNow, it is a best practice to encapsulate variables, but you need to be aware that this does come at the cost of readability.

> Many issues can be avoided by properly initializing variables. Each time you want to use a new variable, ensure you define it by using the `var` keyword. Otherwise, JavaScript assumes you want to place it in the global scope, regardless.

The worst-case scenario is when two Business Rules collide. You may have a Business Rule on one table that triggers the update of another. This happens frequently in `after` Business Rules. Indeed, we've already seen it in our script that enforces a maximum of one lead passenger in the **Validating Information** section.

Consider the following script:

```
var count = 1;
var gr = new GlideRecord('u_check_in');
gr.query();
while(gr.next()) {
  gs.log('Record ' + count++);
  gr.setForceUpdate(true);
  gr.update();
}
```

This is a simple `GlideRecord` call that loops around every record in `u_check_in`. For each record, it logs the current value of `count`, increments it by one, and then saves the record. (The `setForceUpdate` function call will ensure the record is always written to the database even though we didn't change anything, thus setting the `sys_updated_on` fields, and more importantly to us, running the Business Rules.)

Try running the script in Background Scripts. You should get the following result if you have three **Check-in** records:

```
*** Script: Record 1
*** Script: Record 2
*** Script: Record 3
```

However, what happens if we put a Business Rule on the **Check-in** table with no condition and this simple one line script?

```
var count = 1;
```

This code should be fairly evident, but you may think it won't do much. It is just setting a variable and doesn't touch any field values. However, these two scripts combined don't work very well together. If you run the `GlideRecord` loop code again, you will get the following result:

```
*** Script: Record 1
*** Script: Record 1
*** Script: Record 1
```

What is happening? The Business Rule is setting the count variable to `1`, and since the count is already defined, it is just redefining it again and again. This shows that Business Rules can affect the variables and therefore the execution of code runs elsewhere.

> Think of the consequences of this. If unintended, it very difficult to debug; there may be hundreds of different code elements running against a record, and trying to find the right one can be tricky.

In order to stop this behavior, and ensure that our two count variables are independent, the code should be pushed into a function. This means that the script will initialize and keep a local copy of `count` separate and isolated from the single line Business Rule. For example, consider the following code snippet:

```
function counter() {
  var count = 1;
  var gr = new GlideRecord('u_check_in');
  gr.query();
  while(gr.next()) {
    gs.log('Record ' + count++);
    gr.setForceUpdate(true);
    gr.update();
  }
}
counter();
```

Run this code, and suddenly we return to printing **1, 2, 3,...** The variable that is being set in the Business Rule can't affect us any longer.

However, this still has one risk factor. You are defining the function name, `counter`, and still placing it in the global scope. So for full protection, use an anonymous function (also called an **Immediately Invoked Function Expression** or **IIFE**), where you define and run a function in a single step, without giving it a name:

```
(function (){
  var count = 1;
  var gr = new GlideRecord('u_check_in');
  gr.query();
  while(gr.next()) {
    gs.log('Record ' + count++);
    gr.setForceUpdate(true);
    gr.update();
  }
})();
```

These extra characters go against the philosophy of less keystrokes, but it is worth wrapping up code that may be run at the same time as other code. For more information on scoping, check out the multitude of information available on the web or in a good JavaScript book.

Global Business Rules

Sometimes, it is desirable to have code that runs all the time. You may have noticed that in a Business Rule you can change the **Table** field to say **Global**. You may think of this as "all tables", instead, since a script written in a global Business Rule is executed regardless of which table is being updated, queried, inserted, or deleted.

As they stand today, Global Business Rules have limited use due to the bluntness of their nature. If you wanted to run a script every time any record was deleted, then this is the way to achieve it. But this use case is not very frequent! In the past, a global Business Rule was the only way to define code that was always available, such as a utility function. However, Script Includes perform this job far more efficiently.

Instead, the rather large downside of a global Business Rule is that the code is parsed and executed very frequently—every transaction or interaction with the platform. A function defined in a global Business Rule, is parsed and stored in the memory, cluttering the namespace, even if it is not actually used. This therefore means that global Business Rules are generally only used in very specific circumstances.

You may see lots of legacy global Business Rules in the out-of-the-box platform. Over time, these will be removed, and replaced as Script Includes.

Script Includes

Business Rules are inherently tied to a database action. However, often you want to write code that is available in multiple places, perhaps creating utility functions, or even creating your own data structures. Script Includes are designed specifically for this situation. The big advantage, aside from the separation that encourages efficient reuse, is that the code is only accessed and parsed on demand, meaning that your scripts only run when they need to. This process is cached, optimized, and controlled, giving meaningful performance benefits.

When you create a Script Include, you give the record a **Name**. This is very different to the name of a Business Rule. The name in a Business Rule is purely descriptive, enabling you to find the script more easily. For a Script Include, the name field must be the same as the function or class you are defining, since it is used by the platform to identify the code when you try to call it. This means your Script Include names should contain no spaces, and in accordance with your convention. Use the **Description** field to document what the script is doing.

> When deciding upon names for your functions, it is a good idea to use CamelCase, as is the general convention, but `underscore_case` is also acceptable, except for classes. Always use CamelCase there. However, the most important thing is consistency!

Creating classes

This section goes heavily into JavaScript fundamentals. It is useful if you are interested in how ServiceNow allows you to work with classes and objects, but otherwise, you may want to skip the details. There are several great JavaScript books that focus on how you can simulate classes with JavaScript. John Resig, as always, has a very helpful article available, which uses the same methodology as ServiceNow. It can be read at `http://www.ejohn.org/blog/simple-class-instantiation/`.

A more detailed introduction to JavaScript object-oriented programming has been written by Dmitry Soshnikov:

`http://dmitrysoshnikov.com/ecmascript/chapter-7-2-oop-ecmascript-implementation`

JavaScript is an object-based language, but doesn't have a very strict class structure like Java. Using a variety of techniques, it allows you to simulate object-orientated behavior, such as inheritance. It is up to the coder to use a pattern that is appropriate. ServiceNow has a particular convention, which you should follow for the ease of upgrades and maintainability.

When you create a Script Include, and after you've populated the name field, the platform automatically fills in the script field with the beginnings of a class. If you are familiar with the various JavaScript libraries, you may recognize it as the style that jQuery and the Prototype JavaScript framework use. For example, consider the following lines of code:

```
var MyClass = Class.create();
MyClass.prototype = {
  initialize: function() {
```

```
    },

    type: 'MyClass'
}
```

There isn't a formal mechanism to specify classes in JavaScript. Instead, a class definition consists of setting functions and variables in the prototype property of a function. When the `new` keyword is used, it runs the prototype as a constructor, initializing the new object.

> The prototype is a pointer to another object. It inherits the properties of that object. The prototype chain is explained here: `https://developer.mozilla.org/en-US/docs/Web/JavaScript/Guide/Inheritance_and_the_prototype_chain`

ServiceNow includes some functionality to structure the definition of a class through the `Class` global variable. The `create` function returns a function. In ServiceNow, a class is therefore a function that creates an object. When the `new` operator is used on this function, it is executed, which in turn calls another function called `initialize`. This is defined in the class definition.

> To confirm the contents of the `Class` function, run this code that loops round every property and prints it out:
>
> ```
> for (var x in Class)
>   gs.print(x + Class[x])
> ```

After using the `Class.create` function, the next step is to define the prototype that is used as the class definition. It should contain the `initialize` function, and any other default variables and functions.

When `new` is called, an object is created that has had the `initialize` function run, and also contains the functions that are needed, with the appropriate values. Let's see how that works.

> The `new` operator is explained in this article `https://developer.mozilla.org/en-US/docs/Web/JavaScript/Reference/Operators/new`.

Coding a class

Create a new Script Include by navigating to **System Definition** > **Script Includes**, and clicking on **New**:

- **Name**: `SimpleAdd`
- **Script**: Add the following script:

```
var SimpleAdd = Class.create();
SimpleAdd.prototype = {
  initialize: function (n) {
    gs.log('Creating new object');
    this.number = (n - 0) || 0;
  },

  increment: function () {
    this.number++;
    gs.log(this.number);
    return this;
  },

  type: 'SimpleAdd'
}
```

The first line creates a variable called `SimpleAdd` and executes the `Class.create` function. This starts the definition of the object.

The second line is where the `prototype` is edited, to make the class to actually do something. The prototype consists of two functions: `initialize`, which is called when the object is created, and the `add` function.

The `initialize` function provides a variable called `number` that attaches itself to the object by using the `this` keyword. If you pass through a value when creating the object, the `number` will set to it, otherwise it will be zero. The double bar `or` function checks to see if the little expression in the brackets is `false`. If so, it provides a `0`. A little JavaScript trick is used to ensure that `number` is indeed a number; by subtracting zero, JavaScript will try turn `n` into a number. It will succeed for numbers as strings (such as '`100`') and fail for things it can make no sense of ('`foo`').

The end result of this ensures that when `initialize` runs, the `number` variable is indeed a number, or else it is set to zero.

Every time you call the `increment` function, it increases `number` by one, then displays it. The function then returns itself, which is useful for chaining.

Finally, the `type` variable at the end is a convention; it allows you to easily identify which object you are dealing with.

> The prototype definition has been accomplished by creating variables for every property. This includes defining the functions as *function expressions*, meaning `increment` is a variable with an anonymous function. The alternative *function declarations* (`function x() {}`) is a named function. See these articles if you are interested in learning more:
>
> - `http://javascriptweblog.wordpress.com/2010/07/06/function-declarations-vs-function-expressions/`
> - `http://kangax.github.io/nfe/`

Once the class has been defined, you can create it by using the following code. Run this in Background Scripts:

```
var sa = new SimpleAdd();
sa.increment().increment();
gs.log('Accessing the variable number ' + sa.number)
```

Together, this shows that the `sa` object is created from the class `SimpleAdd`, that the `increment` function is called twice in a chain, and how the `number` property can be accessed and logged.

> Note that it is generally considered bad form to rely on public variables. In this example, `number` is accessed directly. This breaks the idea of encapsulation, which means that anything outside the class shouldn't worry about what is happening on the inside. Provided functions that expose useful information (getters and setters) should be generally used. However, the theories that apply to formal programming languages may be less suitable to dynamic platforms such as ServiceNow.

Using classes to store and validate data

One of the judgments that is needed when designing a more complex ServiceNow application is whether to use a class to represent your data and provide validation and data manipulation, or to use the `GlideRecord` objects, Business Rules and other functionalities provided by ServiceNow. I suggest that in the majority of the situations, interacting directly with `GlideRecord` provides the most obvious, consistent and scalable solution; if you decide to start accessing your data via Web services for instance, Business Rules will need little alteration, while a custom class would need to have the access to it scripted. We've had to use several tricks in our initialize function to validate input, something that `GlideRecord` already does well. The overhead in maintaining a complex class is often not needed, it quickly gets frustrating to create getter and setter functions if you add a new field, for instance.

Extending classes

As with other object-orientated systems, extending a class allows you to take advantage of its defined functionality, while adding or altering it. Again, ServiceNow has a specific convention to do this simply. Extra functions have been added to the `Object` object: `extend`, `extendsObject`, and `clone`.

Extending the class example

Let's create a new Script Include:

- **Name**: `SimpleSubtract`
- **Script**: Add the following script:

```
var SimpleSubtract = Class.create();
SimpleSubtract.prototype = Object.extendsObject(SimpleAdd, {
  decrement: function () {
    this.number--;
    gs.log(this.number);
    return this;
  },

  type: 'SimpleSubtract'
});
```

The definition for this extended class begins in a similar way to `SimpleAdd`, by calling the `class.create` function and then defining its prototype. However, instead of providing the variables directly, it passes them through the `extendsObject` function of `Object`. This simulates inheritance by cloning the `SimpleAdd` class prototype, and then injecting all the new properties into the resulting object.

This results in all the functions of `SimpleAdd`, including `initialize`, being part of any `SimpleSubtract` object when `new` is called:

```
var ss = new SimpleSubtract(2);
ss.decrement().increment();
```

Utility classes

The classes defined so far have needed to be initialized with the `new` operator to perform their job as a data structure. Sometimes, however, this is not appropriate. Code could be packaged up in a utility library, which contains functions without creating a new object. In other programming languages, you can achieve this using static functions or classes. JavaScript doesn't have static functions, but to avoid calling the `new` operator, it's possible to define functions directly on the class, rather than in the prototype.

> ServiceNow provides several utility classes in the out of the box platform. Try searching for Script Includes that contain `Util` in the name. `JSUtil` and `ArrayUtil` are especially helpful.

Providing utility classes

Create a new class in a Script Include:

- **Name**: `SimpleMath`
- **Script**: Add the following script:

```
var SimpleMath = Class.create();
SimpleMath.square = function(x) {
    return x * x;
}
```

Note that the `square` function has been attached directly to `SimpleMath`, meaning that you don't need to use the `new` operator. Try this in Background Scripts:

```
gs.log(SimpleMath.square(10));
```

Because the prototype is used for the definition of object, if you do call `new`, the square function isn't accessible:

```
var sm = new SimpleMath();
gs.log(sm.square(10));
```

This will result in `undefined`.

Storing functions

Often, you don't need the full structure of a class if you just want to store a single function. There is a lot of overhead code in the `SimpleMath` class. Instead, let's create another implementation to simplify it.

Having functions in Script Includes

Create another new Script Include:

- **Name**: `square`
- **Script**: Add the following script:

```
function square (x) {
  return x * x;
}
```

> Note that `square` is written with an initial lower case letter, since it is a single function. `SimpleMath` started with an upper case letter, since it is a class.

You can then run this in Background Scripts very easily:

```
gs.log(square(10));
```

> The best style is to group similar functions together in a single utility class if possible. These can also be named using namespace—it means it is less likely there will be collisions or variables with the same name.

Client Callable Script Includes

While we've been making Script Includes, you may have noticed the **Client Callable** checkbox on the form. If this box remains unticked, then any request to run this code that is initiated from the client will not be served. Some function calls can be run from the client, for example, in Reference Qualifiers. Due to the damage that can be caused by calling code from the client, any such calls are made in a sandbox environment that prevents the modification of the database. For example, any attempt to delete records through `GlideRecord` will fail. This is discussed more in *Chapter 7, Securing Applications and Data*. The next chapter, discusses **GlideAjax**—a way of calling Script Includes from the browser.

Special function calls

One of the more legacy ways of configuring ServiceNow is to define specially named functions. The platform checks for the existence of these functions at particular times, such as when deciding which form view to show. While **View Rules** (explored in *Chapter 1, ServiceNow Foundations*) allows you to specify conditions, sometimes, you want more control.

There are several function calls like this in ServiceNow, especially in the older parts of the code base.

Specifying the view using code

Whenever ServiceNow displays a form, it needs to know what view to use. The simplest way to control this is through **View Rules**. These specify logic that depends on the record itself. However, you may want to use other data that has nothing to do with the record, such as the role of the logged in user.

To do this, you can create a new function (in a Script Include) that is called <tablename>GetViewName. This should set the global `answer` variable to the name of the view. For example, you may want administrators to always see the default view of the **Guest** form, and everyone else to see the **Simple** view:

- **Name:** `u_guestGetViewName`
- **Script**: Add the following:

```
function u_guestGetViewName() {
 if (gs.hasRole("admin"))
   answer = '';
 else
  answer = 'Simple';
}
```

Enforcing a Data Policy

Earlier in this chapter, we explored how a Business Rule can validate information, ensuring that data is consistent and appropriate. However, writing a script for every situation is an administration overhead. Reduce it by using Data Policy, which allows definitions to be made without writing a line of code.

> As is common with ServiceNow, there is a point and click method to accomplish something and a scripting method. It is good practice to use the point and click method if possible, since these can be optimized by the platform and will be upgraded proof. So, use Data Policy when possible, and use Business Rules otherwise.

Data Policy enables you to specify whether fields on a table should be mandatory or read-only under certain conditions. The conditions can only apply to the current record, which means the script checking for multiple lead passengers cannot easily be replicated with a Data Policy.

Forcing a comment using Data Policy

Let's create a Data Policy that means that you cannot change a **Check-in** record that is in the past, unless there is a comment. This will give us an explanation if we need to retroactively change someone's room.

Navigate to **System Policy** > **Rules** > **Data Policies**. Click on **New**.

- **Table**: `Check-in [u_check_in]`
- **Short description**: `Must have a comment if in past`
- **Use as UI Policy on client**: <unchecked>
- **Conditions**: `Date - before - Today`

  Once you save the rule, you can enter **Data Policy Rules**, which are the fields under control. Click **New** in the **Data Policy Rules** Related List and enter this information:

- **Field name**: `Comments`
- **Mandatory**: `True`

Then, to try it out, change or create a new reservation that has a date in the past. You should notice that if you try to save the record, you will get a message very similar to the `addErrorMessage` used before.

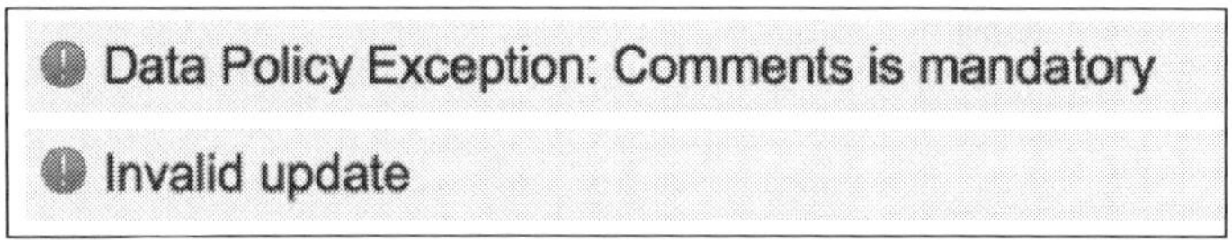

> In this example, we un-ticked the UI Policy option. This means the **Data Policy** will only be checked on the server. We'll explore UI Policy in *Chapter 3, Client-side Interaction*, and security in *Chapter 7, Securing Applications and Data.*

Specifying dynamic filters

Data Policy, like many areas of ServiceNow, uses condition fields as the basis for the logic. These are incredibly useful, but they don't solve every situation since they don't have context.

For example, if you wanted to have a Data Policy that allows only the guest themselves to change something on the **Check-in** record, you need to know who the current user is, and compare that with the **Guest** field.

In older versions of ServiceNow, you needed to embed JavaScript directly in the condition builder. In the example given, the condition would be: Guest - is - javascript:gs.getUserID().

> The JavaScript will show dotted red underlines while you enter the JavaScript code, indicating invalid data, but the system will let you save it.

Here, we are using the GlideSystem functions again, this time returning the sys_id of the currently logged in user. If the contents of the **Guest** field and this sys_id match, the condition will pass. Again, Script Includes is a great place to create your own function that can be embedded in the condition. Just remember to check the **Client Callable** box.

In the Dublin release of ServiceNow, this has become more user-friendly. You can use Dynamic Filters to provide with a simple dropdown option menu. Dynamic Filters can be where there is a condition filter, including lists. Let's create a Dynamic Filter for **Guests** now, to see how it works.

Showing Guests that are 'Me'

Navigate to **System Definition** > **Dynamic Filter Options**. Click on **New** and fill out the following information:

- **Label**: Me
- **Script**: gs.getUserID()
- **Field type**: Reference
- **Referenced Table**: Guest [u_guest]
- **Available for filter**: <ticked>

Once saved, navigate to the **Check-in** table list, and create a new filter. You should be able to create the following filter:

- Guest - is (dynamic) - Me

This will show the **Check-in** records made for the user you are currently logged in as.

Scripting Reference Qualifiers

Chapter 1, ServiceNow Foundations, looked at **Reference Qualifiers**. Reference Qualifiers filter the choices available in a referenced field. The three options (simple, dynamic, and advanced) all work in the same way, under the covers. They provide an encoded query, which is used by the platform to find the records that can be selected. Scripted Reference Qualifiers use JavaScript to accomplish this in a Script Include, in two broad ways:

- They dynamically create an encoded query. For example, you may wish to filter out inactive Guests if the currently logged in user is not a System Administrator.
- They dynamically create a list of multiple `sys_id`, which is used as an encoded query. The function typically uses a more complicated method to obtain a valid list of records, and passes the list to the reference field. Users then pick an entry from this list.

Showing only guests with reservations

Let's improve the reference qualifier on the **Guest** field on the **Check-in** table to only allow users who have a reservation to check-in.

Firstly, create a new Script Include. In this example, we'll create a single function for simplicity, but you could include it as part of a larger utility function:

- **Name**: `guestsWithReservations`
- **Script**: Use the following script:

```
function guestsWithReservations() {
  var result = [];
  var res = new GlideRecord('u_m2m_guests_reservations');
  res.query();
  while (res.next()) {
    result.push(res.u_guest + '');
  }
  var au = new ArrayUtil();
  return au.unique(result);
}
```

This script should be very familiar from the early part of the chapter. It does a `GlideRecord` lookup function call on the `u_m2m_guests_reservations` table, and loops round. Each result is put into an array, ensuring that it is converted into a string first. Then a new object of type `ArrayUtil` is made. This provides a function called `unique`, which removes any duplicates in the result. This is run, and then an array of the matching guest `sys_id` values are returned.

Next, create a **Dynamic Filter Option** using the following values. While it is not strictly necessary to do this (an **Advanced Reference Qualifier** could be used instead), it is a good idea for reusability and maintenance purposes:

- **Label**: `Guest has reservation`
- **Script**: `'sys_idIN'+guestsWithReservations()`
- **Field type**: `Reference`
- **Referenced table**: `Guest [u_guest]`
- **Reference script**: `Script Include: guestsWithReservations`

> It is not strictly necessary to populate this, but it does allow you to quickly find the script rather than searching for it!

- **Available for ref qual**: `<ticked>`

The **Script** field calls the function defined in the Script Include, and prefixes the result with `sys_idIN`. This reference qualifier still provides the platform with an encoded query, but is now dynamic. The `guestsWithReservations` function may return a different result each time. The `sys_idIN` string tells the platform that the **Guest** records must have a `sys_id` that matches one of these results.

> It is a good idea to have a generic function that returns data in a useful format, such as an array, so it can be reused elsewhere. In this example, JavaScript coerces the result into a comma-separated string.

Finally, we need to change the dictionary entry of the **Guest** field on the **Check-in** table:

- **Use reference qualifier**: `Dynamic`
- **Dynamic ref qual**: `Guest has reservation`

Now, when you use the **Guest** reference field on the **Check-in** table, you can only select guests that have a reservation.

Filtering using the current record, this function could be improved by further filtering the records. We probably only want to see guests who have a reservation for the date that the check-in is for. Rather wonderfully, the scripts has access to `current`, which contains the values that are filled out on the form at the moment, even if the form isn't saved.

> When you perform a type-ahead or use the magnifying glass on a reference field, the platform sends the current state of the form to the server to enable it to create the `current` object of `GlideRecord`.

Let's update the `guestsWithReservations` Script Include with a few more lines. Remove lines 3 and 4, and replace them with this snippet:

```
...
  var res = new GlideRecord('u_m2m_guests_reservations');
  if (current.u_date) {
    res.addQuery('u_reservation.u_arrival', current.u_date);
  }
  res.query();
...
```

The `GlideRecord` lookup now has an optional query added to it. If the **Date** field has been populated, then the arrival date of the reservation must match it. Notice that dot-walking has been used since we are querying the many-to-many table.

Try it out. Create a reservation for a particular date, and add a guest using the related list. Then create a **Check-in** record. Set the **Date** field to the same date, and notice that the **Guest** field is constrained.

Reference Qualifiers are incredibly useful and very powerful. They will help you show the right information in a reference field. But if you want to always constrain the results in a table, then a query Business Rule is a better fit.

Summary

ServiceNow provides a fantastic environment for scriptwriters. Rhino is embedded into the heart of ServiceNow and is used throughout the platform, enabling you to make the data work how you want.

Since ServiceNow is a very data-orientated platform, `GlideRecord` plays a critical role. This chapter explored how each field is represented by a `GlideElement` object, and what that means for dates and other areas of interest. `GlideAggregate` uses the database to perform calculations and so can perform much faster than alternative methods.

Business Rules are the home of scripting in ServiceNow. Since every item in ServiceNow is a database record and Business Rules allows you to alter queries and change the record itself, you get enormous power at your fingertips. We ran through several scenarios, including working with dates, validating data, and ensuring data integrity.

Script Includes are the perfect place to store commonly used code. By defining classes, you can create your own data structures, enabling you to extend ServiceNow in any way you require. The wide variety of Script Includes available out of the box should give you inspiration, but the background of each pattern and how it is used was explained.

Data Policies and Advanced Reference Qualifiers are another way to control data. Data Policies ensure that fields are mandatory and read-only according to predefined conditions, and Reference Qualifiers can be supercharged by using JavaScript.

The next chapter moves on to the way the user interacts with ServiceNow. It explores how the browser can improve the user experience through client-side scripting, buttons, and validation controls.

3
Client-side Interaction

In this chapter, we explore how we can control the way in which the user works with our application. We started with the groundwork for this in *Chapter 1, ServiceNow Foundations*, where we looked at how data is stored in ServiceNow and displayed it on the screen using forms and lists. More recently in *Chapter 2, Server-side Control*, we looked at how scripts and other server-side functions are used by the instance to control and manipulate data flow.

Since ServiceNow is a web application, the majority of the interactions happen on a user's web browser. This chapter focuses on what options you have to control user experience by understanding ServiceNow's capabilities for interaction through scripts, buttons, and data exchange. This includes:

- Using **Client Scripts** to manipulate forms dynamically, unleashing the power of the browser
- **UI Policy**, which gives simple functionality to guide the user without scripting
- Improving the user's experience of working with lists with **Context Menus** and list editing
- **UI Actions**, which enable you to add buttons that interact with the browser
- Communicating with the server using **GlideAjax**

Building a modern interface

There are two parts to a web-based platform such as ServiceNow: **the central server**, which is where most of the data is stored, and **the client machines** that ask for the data, display it, and then push information back to the server.

In ServiceNow, client interaction is almost always with a web browser. ServiceNow takes advantage of modern web browsers to provide a simple-to-use and feature-rich interface. This is built with JavaScript, the language of the Web.

Most ServiceNow System Administrators have had some experience working with client-side JavaScript. So, writing scripts that interact with the web browser is often very simple and familiar to them. They allow you to provide an improved experience to the users of your system by providing instant feedback and a faster way to interact. It is often much quicker to validate information using the browser than asking the instance to do the work, simply because it takes time to communicate with the server. The instance may be located many hundreds or thousands of miles away, across several internet links. While it should contain the definitive version of our data, we want to ensure we don't frustrate our users by forcing them to wait all the time.

A microsecond of Human Computer Interaction

When interacting with the Web and computers in general, users have expectations of how they will work. To a certain extent, they expect that when a link is clicked on, it will take a little time to bring up a new page. However, things like typing and scrolling should be smooth and interruption-free. Nothing is more annoying than a cursor that freezes or doesn't respond.

For example, when you scroll a modern mapping application, you don't want to wait for the whole page to refresh after dragging the mouse; you want the map to keep up with you. It is expected to be smooth and slick. If it takes longer than half a second, it is often noticed. The users of ServiceNow have the same expectations.

The power and pitfalls of AJAX

Asynchronous JavaScript and XML (AJAX) is a technique built by Microsoft but popularized by Google. It is a technique for loading data from a server, independent of page loading. The key to improving the user experience is that when this data is asked for, only the relevant information is returned and not the entire page. Normally, a HTML page might consist of data, some explanatory text, display information (such as CSS or links to style sheets), and often JavaScript code as well. When AJAX is used, the browser can ask for more data, keeping the rest of the page the same. This means that a web-based map can just return new map tiles when you zoom or scroll, and an e-mail application can check for new messages and keep the current ones on the screen.

In order to load the right information at the right time, JavaScript is called when particular events happen in the browser, for example, on a mouse click, or on a timer. This event may then request to connect to a server to get the required information. Originally, the data that was sent and received was XML, but it is getting more common to return JSON instead. The web application understands this data and updates part of the page layout.

JavaScript is single-threaded. It can only do one thing at time. So, when the browser runs scripts, it doesn't interact with the user. To stop the frustrating freezing that occurs when you click and nothing happens, the browser supports the use of **callback functions**. A callback function essentially provides a way to continue processing after a delay. Instead of just staying there and waiting, you provide a function and the browser will call it when it's got the data that it's been asked for.

> An analogy is simple. When you want to speak to someone in a telephone call center, do you want to hang on the line in a queue or do you want them to call you back while you get on with other things? Of course, you would prefer the latter. Likewise, the browser always keeps its promises, unlike many call centers!

As we explore the capabilities of ServiceNow for the client, we should keep in mind that application processing is best if it is invisible to the user. We don't want to frustrate them by forcing them to wait unnecessarily. We'll see different techniques that we can employ to provide a good experience to the user.

Choosing a UI Action

A **UI Action** is a rather grandiose name for a button. Using a button is possibly the simplest interaction that a user can make, and the UI Action performs some work after the click. (Or a tap, if the user is using a touch-screen device!)

There are several different representations of UI Actions, each displayed in a different way, available in both the form and list views.

- **Form button**: This is the most accessible one. It shows up as a more recognizable button and appears at two places: at the top right and the bottom left of the form. The context bar on which the buttons are located is fixed and will always display at the top of the screen, even as you scroll down the form. This accessibility and visibility makes Form buttons a great choice for important actions that will change the record that you are viewing. The Form button looks like the following screenshot:

> You can control some aspects of button display through properties, such as only displaying Form buttons on the context bar and not at the bottom.

- **Form link**: UI Actions are represented as links. These are presented underneath the form with a title named **Related Links**. It is possible to display more display text with a Form Links UI Action, making them helpful for less frequent actions that need more description. These UI Actions are also useful for navigating to other areas of the system, perhaps to launch a window or find a related record. Due to their disconnected nature when compared to the form data, they often do not alter the record.

- **Form context menu**: These show up when you right-click on the form header or use the Menu button. These are unobvious and should be reserved for real power users such as the System Administrator. The `Copy sys_id` UI Action, is a great example of a useful functionality that doesn't need to be easily available to everyone. The Form context menu looks like the following screenshot:

- **List link**: This is displayed in a similar way to a Form link. In addition to being a navigation link like the Form version, it is used to manipulate the list itself.
- **List banner button** and **List bottom button**: They show up at the top and bottom of a list and generally apply to selected records. They are not often used due to their visual separation from a record, though the **New** button is a List banner button. List bottom buttons are mostly used as a more obvious action on multiple records.
- **List choice**: This shows up in the drop-down menu at the bottom of the list. It is fairly obvious that this affects items that have been selected in the list, though the choices themselves are hidden in the selection box. The platform controls the visibility and display of the options depending upon the properties that are set on the UI Action. If the list choice will only affect 5 items in a list of 10, this will display **List choice (5 of 10)**. Due to the processing that occurs to check the conditions, the list can take some time to open. The List choice button is shown as follows:

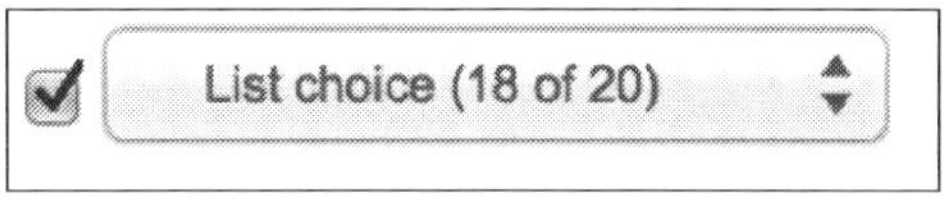

- **List context menu**: Just like the Form context menu, this adds an entry into a menu that appears when you right-click on a row. I recommend reserving this one for power users again due to its unobvious nature.

Finding the current table

In *Chapter 2, Server-side Control*, you saw how a simple Business Rule could display which table is being manipulated. Let's make a UI Action that will show up on every record that will find the current table, but on demand.

Navigate to **System Definition** > **UI Action**, then click on **New**, and use the following values:

- **Name**: `Show table name`
- **Table**: `Global [global]`

- **Form link**: `<ticked>`
- **Script**: `gs.addInfoMessage('The current table name is ' + current.getTableName())`

This script should be familiar. It uses `GlideSystem` to display a message and `current` is available too. This will output the table name whenever you click on a table. The code here is run on the server. Server side UI Actions can leverage all of the functionality explored in *Chapter 2, Server-side Control*.

Displaying UI Actions at the right time

There are several mechanisms that control if and where a UI Action will be displayed. They are as follows:

- The **Table** field works in a very similar way to the one in Business Rules. Table inheritance is supported (which means that when a UI Action is added to the **User** table, it'll show for **Guests** too), while choosing the **Global** table will mean that your UI Action will show on every record.
- The **Order** field, as expected, controls what sequence the buttons are put in. Lower numbers mean further to the left or top side of the window.

> Be consistent when you are ordering anything. It helps people to use your application when buttons are in logical places. Note how **Update** has been given an order of -100 to keep it always on the left side of the window, while the order of **Delete** is 1,000, so it is always on the right.

- **Action name** serves as a unique identifier across table extensions. If you create a UI Action for the User table, you can override it by creating a button with the same action name, which is against the **Guest** table.

> This is especially helpful to change how global buttons (such as **Save**) work. If you don't want **Insert and Stay** to show on your table, create a UI Action with an action name of `sysverb_insert_and_stay` and set the condition as `false`.

- The **Show insert** and **Show update** checkboxes are easy to control. Often, you only want to show buttons that are on already saved records, perhaps to control related records.
- The much-overlooked **UI Action Visibility** List controls the views on which your UI Action will be shown. You might, for example, have an advanced view that gives users extra functionality with more UI Actions. A UI Action can even be used to switch the views on demand.

Using the Condition field

Just like a Business Rule, a UI Action has a **Condition** field. The code is always run on the server. If it returns a `true` (after the code is subject to the other options controlling when and where), the button will be shown.

The `current` object of `GlideRecord` is available in the condition, as well as `gs` and the other global objects. List choices present a particular challenge because the condition must be evaluated for all the records that have been selected. If complex conditions are used on List choice UI Actions, this can cause considerable slowdown.

> Try to leverage Access Control Rules when you write conditions. Rather than creating a long string of conditions, checking roles, and recording values, use `current.canWrite()` as a base. In most situations, if a user can write to the record, they can use a button. This is discussed further in *Chapter 7, Securing Applications and Data*.

In general, the same advice that applies to Business Rules conditions also applies to UI Action conditions, keep them simple and maintainable so that you are never surprised when a UI Action is run.

Running client- or server-side code

What is quite special (and confusing!) about a UI Action is that the code that it runs can be either server- or client-side. In the definition of the UI Action, you can choose the **Client** checkbox, which will make an **Onclick** field appear. Any code that is entered here is placed directly in the HTML element on the rendered page, unsurprisingly in the `onclick` attribute. In the majority of cases, this should call a client-side function. A client-side button does not submit the form because `return false;` is appended to any contents of the **Onclick** field.

Additionally, when the **Client** checkbox is ticked, the content of the **Script** field is copied onto the page each time the button is shown and is enclosed in a `<script>` tag. This is often used to provide a client-side function for the button to use. The available client-side functions are explored later in this chapter.

A simple client-side UI Action example would involve populating the **Onclick** field with a function call:

```
sayHelloWorld()
```

Then, define the function in the **Script** field:

```
function sayHelloWorld() {
  alert('Hello, world!');
}
```

The following screenshot shows an example of a client side UI Action:

Client-side UI actions are commonly used to control pop-up interfaces, such as custom dialogs. Some of the ways to do this, one of which is `GlideDialogWindow`, are explored in *Chapter 10, Making ServiceNow Beautiful with CMS and Jelly*.

> Due to a quirk of how the platform works, you can combine code in the **Script** field that will be executed on the client and server. Even though different functions are available in each environment, you can detect the situation by checking the existence of objects in a way that is similar to the first code that we used in *Chapter 2, Server-side Control*. However, I strongly recommend that this technique is not used since it can be very difficult to debug when scripts are running on both the browser and the instance.

Saving and redirecting

If the **Client** checkbox is not ticked, the code in the **Script** field is executed on the instance, as a server-side JavaScript, just like a Business Rule. When the UI Action is clicked, the form submits, and the code is executed before the next page loads. In this case, the usual server-side variables are available, including `current`. In addition, any changes to the fields on the record are reflected in the updated `GlideRecord` object.

It is the job of the UI Action script to save these changes. The script of a simple Save UI Action would solely be `current.update()`. This would cause the database to be updated and trigger any Business Rule. Of course, you may want to change additional fields or perform other actions first. It's a good idea to leverage Business Rules for this.

> Server-side UI Actions should be there to help the user perform common actions by changing fields for them. For example, we could provide a button that extends all selected reservations by a day. The UI Action in this case would change the **Departure date** fields and then save the record. The Business Rules can then pick up the job of validating the data and aborting the update if it is not correct. This way the server-side checks will be consistent, regardless of how the data enters the system, through UI Action or field entry.

When a button is clicked, the platform default to return you to the previous screen. For example, if you chose a record from a list and then clicked on a UI Action, the default action would be to return you to that list. While this is probably the most efficient navigation exercise, users often want validation that the command was successful, and they would also like to see the updated record. Therefore, it is very common to see the following statement in a UI Action:

```
action.setRedirectURL(current);
```

Despite the name, `setRedirectURL` is rather flexible as it accepts a `GlideRecord` object as well as a string that should contain a URL.

> The `action` variable does contain other functions, including `setReturnURL`. This allows you to specify where the platform will redirect the user after another click of a button.

Converting a record from Reservation to Check-in

At the moment, our **Reservation** and **Check-in** tables are relatively unconnected. Let's address this with a UI Action that quickly makes a new **Check-in** record from **Reservation**.

Navigate to **System Definition** > **UI Action** and click on **New**. Then, fill in the following values:

- **Name:** `Check-in`
- **Table**: `Reservation [u_reservation]`
- **Form button**: `<ticked>`
- **Action name**: `checkin`
- **Condition**: `current.u_arrival > new GlideDate()`
- **Script**:

```
current.update();

// Get lead passenger
var m2m = new GlideRecord('u_m2m_guests_reservations');
m2m.addQuery('u_reservation', current.sys_id);
m2m.setLimit(1);
m2m.orderByDesc('u_lead');
m2m.query();

// Create the new check-in record
var gr = new GlideRecord('u_check_in');
gr.newRecord();
gr.u_date = current.u_arrival;
if (m2m.next())
  gr.u_guest = m2m.u_guest;
gr.insert();

action.setRedirectURL(gr);
```

Let's walk through this script.

After saving the current record, the script uses `GlideRecord` to query the **Many-to-Many** table. Since the aim is to find the lead passenger, and we know there will only ever be a maximum of one passenger (due to our Business Rule), the script sets a limit to reduce the load on the database and the instance. By ordering the result set, the script ensures that a record that is marked as lead will float to the top.

The next block of code concentrates on creating a new **Check-in** record. It copies over the **Date** field, and if a lead passenger is found, it sets the **Guest** field. The record is then committed.

Finally, it asks the platform to display the new record on the screen.

Running the client-side script

The client-side functionality in ServiceNow is very commonly misused. Its capabilities should be used in a targeted fashion to help the user to use the application more effectively by providing information and reducing mistakes. Almost every other objective can be better implemented in other ways:

- Security is most appropriately carried with Access Control Rules
- Data validation should be done with Business Rules and Data Policy
- Automation is accomplished with Workflow and Business Rules
- A custom look and feel can be built with UI Pages and the **Content Management System** (**CMS**)

> This chapter shows how client-side scripts and checks can easily be manipulated by malicious or mischievous users. Don't be lulled into a false sense of security.

The familiarity and capability of Client Scripts is alluring. The System Administrator has the full power of JavaScript coupled with the APIs that ServiceNow provides. During the rest of this chapter, I hope to help you to use this power effectively.

Proving the basics

It would be inappropriate to have any chapter on client-side JavaScript without having the "`Hello, world!`" example at the beginning.

ServiceNow has a very simple JavaScript executor that is the equivalent of Background Scripts, but this is for the browser. In almost any window, press *Ctrl* + *Shift* + *J* to launch the window. (You must be an administrator to launch the window.)

Let's run `Hello, World!`:

```
alert('Hello, world!');
```

Once you press the **Run my code** button, you should see the little pop-up alert box as shown in the following screenshot:

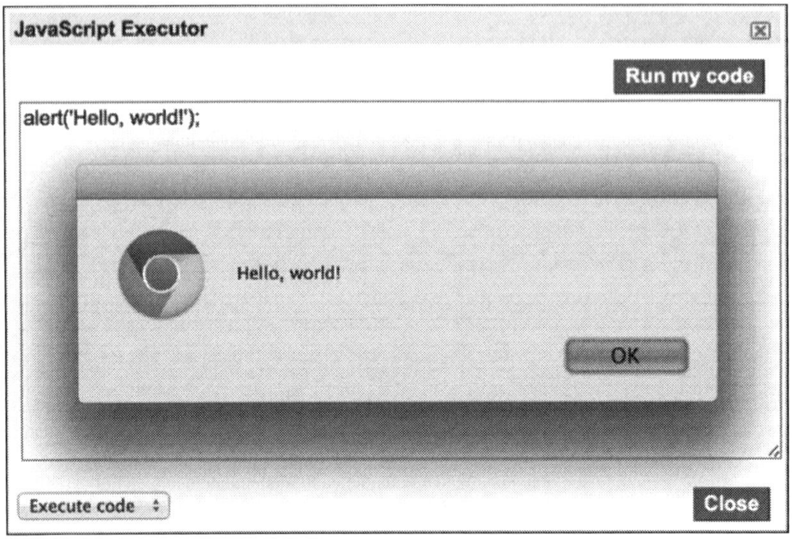

Your web browser executes the JavaScript that you put in the window. If you pasted the Fibonacci function used in *Chapter 1, Setting up the ServiceNow Architecture*, you would be able to see whether your browser can calculate the sequence faster than your instance, or you could use it to try out your client-side scripts. Most browsers have developer tools that include a console that provides this same functionality that you may already use and prefer, but it is helpful that ServiceNow gives you a simple alternative for every browser.

Meeting GlideRecord again

Perhaps you thought that we were finished with `GlideRecord`. Since `GlideRecord` connects to the database and returns records, how can it help us on the client? One of the rather wonderful aspects of the ServiceNow platform is the consistency between different areas of the system. However, beware! Due to the dramatic difference in environment, the usage of `GlideRecord` on the client would not be the same as that on the server.

Open the JavaScript executor as before and run the following code. You'll notice many similarities in the outputs of this script and the one from *Chapter 1, Setting Up the ServiceNow Architecture*:

```
var results = [];
var gr = new GlideRecord('u_check_in');
```

```
gr.addQuery('u_guest.name', 'CONTAINS', 'Bob');
gr.setLimit(2);
gr.orderByDesc('sys_created_on');
gr.query();
while(gr.next()) {
  results.push(gr.sys_created_on);
}
alert(results.join(', '));
```

The differences between this script and the one in *Chapter 1, Setting Up the ServiceNow Architecture*, are minimal, and can be found on only two lines:

- The results are not converted to a string since `GlideElement` does not exist on the client. Instead, `GlideRecord` returns strings.
- Instead of using `gs.log`, which is only available on the server, `alert` is used to pop up a message box.

> A new global function called `jslog` can capture client-side output. This and other debugging techniques are explored in *Chapter 8, Diagnosing ServiceNow – Knowing What Is Going On.*

By looking at this code, you might think that there are very few differences between client- and server-side `GlideRecord`. While the main capabilities are replicated, the similarity is quite superficial; on closer inspection, fewer functions are available for the user.

> It is probably easier to see what *is* available than seeing what *isn't* by going to `http://wiki.servicenow.com/?title=Client_Side_GlideRecord`.

The biggest obstacle to using `GlideRecord` on the client is latency, or the time taken to communicate between the database and the script, as discussed in the next few sections.

Making synchronous AJAX

The instance communicates with the database using a very fast and low latency network connection. Results are returned in microseconds. In contrast, the browser uses the internet connection of the user to communicate with the instance, which then goes to the database. If a user is on a low bandwidth connection, perhaps even using a satellite link, the communication could take seconds instead.

Client-side `GlideRecord` runs synchronously by default. This means that the browser will wait for a response before it continues. The key line is `gr.query();` this requests the data through the browser and asks it to connect to the server. As it waits, the function "locks" the browser, which means that it does not respond to the user input.

This is not user friendly. It is very frustrating when an application freezes. So, in the majority of occasions, control should be handed to the browser by providing a **callback** function.

> Callback behavior can be described as "tell me when you are done rather than making me wait".

To achieve this, create a new separate function, or use an inline anonymous function and pass it to `gr.query` as a parameter.

To trial it, take the following code snippet and use it to replace the last five lines of the previous example. They will work exactly as before but will allow the browser to do some work while waiting for the results.

The defined function

Perhaps the more obvious way to do this is to create a new function and pass the reference as a parameter to the `query` function:

```
gr.query(logCreatedOn);

function logCreatedOn(gr) {
  while(gr.next()) {
    results.push(gr.sys_created_on + '');
  }
  alert(results);
}
```

The results will be returned in the first parameter of your defined function.

The anonymous function

In the next example, an anonymous function is defined directly in the `query` method:

```
gr.query(function(gr) {
  while(gr.next()) {
    results.push(gr.sys_created_on + '');
  }
```

```
    alert(results);
});
```

While this form may not be a familiar one, it has the advantage of keeping all the code together in one place. This also reduces the risk of naming collisions, such as when two functions are called the same thing.

Using callbacks effectively

Client-side `GlideRecord`, and its alter ego `getReference`, should almost always have a callback function. If you do not provide one, the possibility of annoying your users is very high since this will cause their browser to be unresponsive for some time. Unfortunately, some out-of-the-box code doesn't follow this practice.

The only exception to using a callback function should be when you need an `onSubmit` client script to check the database. For example, when you click on a button, you may wish to proceed only after ensuring that the conditions are valid. An example of this is given in the *Checking when submitting* section later in this chapter.

Single set of data

The results from a client-side `GlideRecord` query are returned in a single JSON object, giving just the string data as it is stored in the database. The value of a reference field will be just the `sys_id`. This means that you cannot dot-walk on the client.

> This activity could be achieved by doing more `GlideRecord` lookups, but performing AJAX calls in a loop will quickly impact user experience, even if it is run asynchronously.

Additionally, the need to give a good condition using `addQuery` is even more important on the client. When `query` is called, the first 50 records are returned in a single dataset. On a large table with many columns, this can be a significant amount of data that's being transferred if you are only really interested in one or two records. Transferring tens or hundreds of kilobytes of data might be fine on a fast office machine, but in a remote location with a slow browser, this is not a pleasant experience!

Avoiding GlideRecord

In general, the use of `GlideRecord` on the client should be minimized. It is simple and familiar to ServiceNow scriptwriters and useful for quick solutions, but its inherent inefficiencies do not lend themselves to a good user experience. We'll explore more efficient methods of getting data from the instance by using `GlideAjax`, but it is still best that any logic is executed on the server through Business Rules or other techniques.

Managing fields with a UI Policy

In *Chapter 2*, *Server-side Control*, we looked at Data Policy. This forces a field to have a value by rejecting a database if it is necessary. The benefit of Data Policy is that it does not matter where the data came from. This will reject invalid updates from scripts through the browser, and even through Web Services, if the right options are set.

UI Policy has the same function, but it only works for the browser. It does have a good advantage; however, it works before the data is submitted to the instance, giving instant feedback to the user.

As discussed earlier, faster feedback to the user is often beneficial. However, UI Policy only requests the browser to perform the check. While the ServiceNow admin controls the instance, we must assume that the user controls the browser. Later in the chapter, we can see how a knowledgeable user can easily make the browser ignore any checks that you put in place.

Manipulating the form

In addition to making fields mandatory and read-only like Data Policy, a UI Policy Action can also hide a field. The **Form Design** functionality controls which fields are available in forms. Creating a UI Policy Action gives further control by hiding or removing fields on the form if a condition is met.

This power is often seized by inexperienced admins as an opportunity to make very large forms and make UI Policy control the visibility of a large proportion of the fields. This is almost always the wrong thing to do. Having lots of UI Policies can quickly slow down the browser, as they perform lots of page changes and a multitude of checks each time a form changes. In addition, the browser would still need to load data and functionality that may never be seen as the fields are hidden.

[A good rule of thumb is that you should not hide more than 20 percent of the fields on page load using UI Policy. Instead, use other ways to control visibility, such as views.]

Client-side conditioning

An immediate consequence of the client-side nature of UI Policy comes through its condition. Just like Data Policy, a UI Policy will fire when its condition is evaluated to be `true`. However, a UI Policy only has access to the fields on the form. If you create a UI Policy condition that references a field that isn't available on the client, the condition will never evaluate to `true`.

A common way around this is to place the required fields on the form and then have a UI Policy that always hides it. However, this compounds the problem; there is now an extra field that needs to be rendered and an extra UI Policy—all to hide some fields that should not show up!

Chapter 1, Setting Up the ServiceNow Architecture, showed you how views can be used to have different field layouts. You can use that instead.

Forcing a comment on reservations

In *Chapter 2, Server-side Control*, a Data Policy rule was created to make a comment mandatory if the date was before today. One drawback of server-side checks is that the data must be submitted to the instance and the new page must be loaded in order to get the results. Instead, let's optimize the user experience by making the checks on the client.

To do this, navigate to **System UI** > **UI Policy**. Then, click on **New** and use the following values:

- **Table**: `Check-in [u_check_in]`
- **Short description**: `Force comment if in the past`
- **Conditions**: `Date - before - Today`

Save this and create a new **UI Policy Action** in the Related List by setting the following values:

- **Mandatory**: `<checked>`
- **Visible**: `<checked>`
- **Field name**: `Comments`

Now try to create a new **Check-in** record. The **Comments** field will not be shown by default now. If you select a past date, it will appear almost instantly and be set as a mandatory field.

> This example also highlights one of the differences between the client and the server. Try submitting a completely blank **Check-in** record. The client-side checks will not fire (and thus not force you to enter a comment) while the Data Policy will. This is because a blank **Date** field on the server is considered to be the Unix epoch (1 Jan 1970) and so, it will be considered before now, while on the client, it is seen as not valid and will not be checked.

Controlling UI Policies

The majority of UI Policies do not use any of the options on the UI Policy form beyond the condition, the name, and the table to which they are assigned. The defaults are generally appropriate, and I especially recommend leaving the **Reverse if false** and **On Load** fields checked.

UI Policies are always evaluated when the field to which they are attached changes, and this normally happens when the form loads (the browser "changes" the field when it is first displayed). Having **On Load** checked means the condition will always be evaluated. Otherwise, it is terribly confusing if the UI Policy only kicks in sometimes.

Reverse if false means that when the condition is not `true`, the UI Policy Actions are applied but with the opposite action. This means that if you are displaying the **Comment** field when the date is before today, *it would be hidden at other times*. This is often what you want, but it can catch you unawares. This also makes conflicts much more likely since each UI Policy does two things: it makes changes when it's both `on` and `off`.

UI Policy conflicts occur when two actions for the same field are subjected to different conditions and the two conditions can both be `true` at the same time. The situation should be avoided to prevent unpredictable behavior, and the platform does a good job of warning you if this occurs. The simplest way to deal with this is to use the **Order** field; set more important UI Policies to have a higher number, and when they are run later, they will take precedence. Regardless, it is simplest to ensure that each field is only attached to one rule and make the condition very clear with multiple `OR` conditions if necessary to cover each situation.

The other options are straightforward. Perhaps the **Inherit** checkbox should be ticked by default, to be more similar with Business Rules, and allow UI Policies to apply to extended tables. A nice feature is that you can use views to only apply UI Policy to certain situations.

Manipulating the form with GlideForm

A UI Policy conditionally performs a limited set of actions on a form, such as making a field mandatory or hiding it from view. Internally, this uses a client-side class called `GlideForm`, which is also available for use by the System Administrator.

Just like Business Rules, ServiceNow also provides some global variables that smooth the interaction with the platform. On every form, you'll find a `g_form` object instantiated from `GlideForm`.

> For more information, check out the wiki at `http://wiki.servicenow.com/?title=GlideForm`.

Using GlideForm

`GlideForm` provides getter and setter methods that give access to the record as it is displayed on the screen. Let's run some code in the JavaScript executor in order to understand what options are available. Navigate to a new **Check-in** record and press *Ctrl* + *Shift* + *J* to launch the window.

Use the following code as an example; it is quite artificial, but it does show some of the important available functions:

```
var floor = g_form.getValue('u_room.u_floor');
if (floor > 2) {
  g_form.showFieldMsg('u_room.u_floor', 'This is a high floor!');
  g_form.setDisplay('u_comments', true);
  g_form.setValue('u_comments', 'Is the customer okay with high
floors?');
  g_form.flash('u_comments', 'lightyellow', 0);
}
```

Let's look at the code in more detail:

1. The very first line uses a getter method of `g_form`. You pass it the field that you are interested in, and it returns the value that it finds. Note that this will always return a string, and it will always return what would be saved in a particular field in the database. For a reference field, it will return a `sys_id`.

   Notice how we've used dot notation in this function. Since `u_floor` is a derived field, we needed to use the full path to the field to note that we access it through the **Room** field.

2. The next line is a standard JavaScript. It runs the provided statements if the room number is more than 2. We are rather afraid of heights at Gardiner Hotels, so we have chosen a low number here!
3. The `showFieldMsg` function is a useful part of `GlideForm`. It puts a little message underneath the field that you specify, which is really helpful for drawing attention to invalid values. The platform will scroll to the field if it can. While the native `alert` function is useful for getting attention, it is also annoying since it demands a response. A field message is a more gentle and persuasive method. There is also `showErrorBox` that presents a more ominous warning.
4. The `setDisplay` function is an echo of UI Policy. The first parameter specifies the field, while the second parameter lets you choose whether the field should be hidden or shown. If it is hidden, the function removes the field entirely from the form and fields move around to fill the gap. There is also a function called `setVisible` that is very similar, but instead of removing the field completely, it fills the gaps with whitespace.
5. The setter in `GlideForm` is `setValue`. Pass a string value. For fields with a label on a data item, such as choice fields, you must set the value. For reference fields, this means that you must provide the `sys_id`.

> Be aware that in order to provide the display value, the platform runs an AJAX call to find the display value. This may cause unexpected traffic if you are setting many reference fields. Instead, there is an optional third parameter to `setValue` that lets you specify the display value. Use this, if possible, to reduce network traffic.

6. The final line of significance uses the `flash` function. This draws even more attention to a field by performing a modicum of animation. The second parameter gives the color that the label should have, while the third parameter gives an indication of how many times it will flash.

> For a guide to what the numbers mean, go to `http://wiki.servicenow.com/?title=GlideForm_(g_form)#flash`.

The final **Check-in** table is shown in the following screenshot:

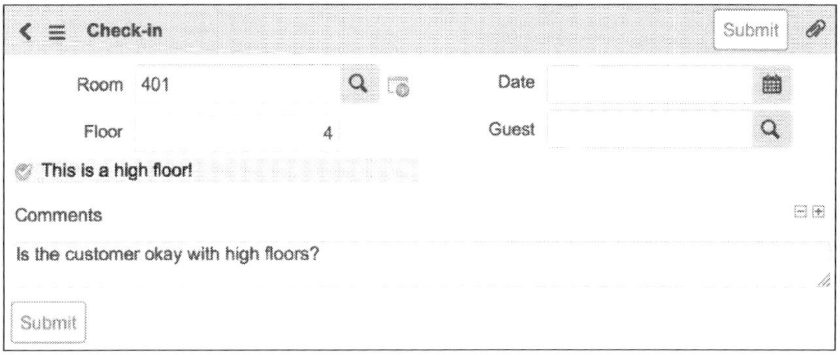

Choosing a UI Policy

`GlideForm` lets you to duplicate the functions of UI Policy exactly. In addition to the functions that we explored in the preceding section, `setMandatory` makes the platform check for population before submission, and `setReadOnly` prevents you from easily typing in the field. This means that there is the tendency to use `GlideForm` as the primary method for manipulating the field layout, but this is not a good idea. If possible, use UI Policy and then fall back to using `GlideForm` if you need to.

UI Policies have a number of advantages:

- They are optimized by the platform to be less resource-intensive by storing the details in a format that can be easily parsed by the Client Scripts.
- They are more likely to be upgrade safe. New versions of ServiceNow may include further benefits, and UI Policies will be easily transferred to the new version.
- Other interfaces such as mobile devices and tablets are much more likely to work. While the desktop interface is by far the most used, alternative device types should not be forgotten.

> There is another version of `GlideForm` for small-screened devices (such as smartphones). It has a reduced list of functions in comparison. For more information, refer to the link: `http://wiki.servicenow.com/?title=Mobile_GlideForm_%28g_form%29_API_Reference`.

Meeting Client Scripts

Business Rules may be more accurately named **Server Scripts**. In this sense, it is obvious what Client Scripts are: they let you run code in the browser as opposed to the server.

In many ways, Client Scripts are very similar to Business Rules. They run JavaScript against a specific table one record at a time. However, instead of running around a database access, Client Scripts add interactivity to a form. They attach to specific events that happen on the page: when a field changes, when the form loads, or when the form is submitted (when a UI Action is clicked on). This then causes JavaScript of your choice to run. In the majority of cases, this will use the `GlideForm` functions.

The **Global** Client Scripts run regardless of the view. If this checkbox is unticked, you should specify the view it should be run for.

If the **Inherited** checkbox is ticked, the Client Scripts will run on extended tables and not just the one in the **Table** field.

Sending alerts for VIP guests

When a guest is checked in, the system should flag whether they would need special attention. Start by adding the **VIP** flag on to the **Guest** form. Use **Form Design** to add it to the **Default** view and remove any superfluous fields while you are there. Ensure that some of the test **Guest** records have the **VIP** flag ticked:

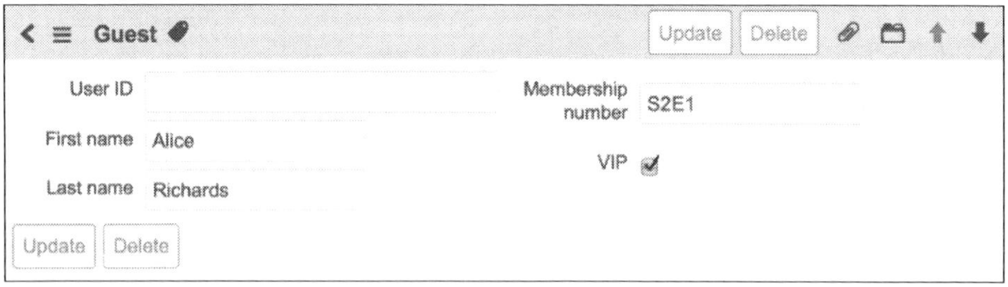

To show a message on the form, we need a Client Script. To create this, navigate to **System Definition** > **Client Scripts** and click on **New**. Then, use the following values:

- **Name**: `Alert for VIP`
- **Type**: `onChange`
- **Table**: `Check-in [u_check_in]`
- **Field name**: `Guest`

- **Script**:

```
function onChange(control, oldValue, newValue, isLoading,
isTemplate) {
  if (!isLoading) {
    g_form.hideFieldMsg('u_guest');
  }

  if (newValue == '') {
    return;
  }

  g_form.getReference('u_guest', function(guest) {
    if (guest.vip == 'true') {
      g_form.showFieldMsg('u_guest', 'Guest is a VIP!');
    }
  });
}
```

> This Client Script will be improved later in this chapter. It currently runs an AJAX call when a form loads, which is inefficient.

Client Scripts must have a function that depends on their type. When you create a new Client Script, a typical function template will be given to you; the `onLoad` Client Scripts must have an `onLoad` function. Don't ignore or remove this! Unlike Business Rules, the code must be wrapped in this pattern with the appropriate name, otherwise it will be ignored. Before the script is inserted onto the page, the platform renames the function so that it is unique and is run at the appropriate time.

Client Scripts do not have a condition field. Instead, you must include them in your script. The default template is quite typical, in that generally you do not have to run code if the user empties the field (represented by `newValue == ''`), or if the reason for the change in field value is that the form is loading.

> The `oldValue` variable is always the value that was in the database when the form was loaded. Perhaps it should be called `savedValue` instead!

Here, the script removes any messages that we've put up before, even for a blank field. It then returns immediately and stops further execution of the function. It does not remove messages when the script is loading, since there is no point in doing this.

> A useful function call for the `onSubmit` scripts is `getActionName` in the `g_form` object. This returns the action name of the button that was clicked. When we created the button for **Check-in**, we used `checkin`.

The final part of the script uses `getReference` to create a `GlideRecord` object for the client side. The `getReference` function uses the `sys_id` and the table from the reference field to get the data. An anonymous function is passed in as the second parameter, which then checks the value of the **VIP** field. Note that even though **VIP** is a Boolean field, `GlideRecord` only returns strings. Therefore, it must be checked as such.

> The only time it is appropriate to use a synchronous `GlideRecord` query is for an `onSubmit` script. In this scenario, the browser must be blocked, otherwise it will continue to submit the form. Alternatively, you must always provide a callback method!

Changing, submitting, loading, and more

The most common use of a Client Script is to run JavaScript when a field has changed. It allows the validation of fields as the form is being filled out. Alternatively, Client Scripts can validate fields, right before the form is submitted to the server. Returning `false` in an `onSubmit` script will cancel the button click.

Client Scripts that run when a page loads should be avoided. For the vast majority of use cases, a display Business Rule is more appropriate since it avoids the browser needing to parse and work with the form, right at the time when the user is waiting. Any AJAX that runs when a page loads is heretical and should be immediately changed due to its performance impact!

While every Client Script must keep the function that is provided in the template, it does not need to contain any code. Some `onLoad` functions are empty and have functions stored outside. For example, this `onLoad` client script is storing a function that is accessible from other client scripts on the same table. The `onLoad` function itself is empty and has no purpose other than to keep the platform happy:

```
function onLoad() { }

function ratherUseless() {
    alert("I don't do anything, but I can be accessed easily!");
}
```

> UI Scripts is a better place to store libraries, as discussed in the next section.

Client Scripts marked as `onCellEdit` are the only ones that are relevant to lists. They allow the validation of changes made via list editing, where the user double-clicks on a field to alter the value. To reject a change and keep the value of the field as it was earlier, the callback function should be passed `false`. You are provided an array of the `sys_id` strings of the records that are being changed, though the `g_form` object of `GlideForm` is not available.

Validating the contents of fields

One important use of client-side scripts is their ability to validate information before it is submitted to the server. While Client Scripts can be used on an individual field basis, there is also the option to write scripts that are dependent upon the field type. You may have already noticed this in action; if you write some syntactically incorrect JavaScript in a script field, the platform will notice it and show an error.

One common point of frustration is that **Date** fields are not validated client side. It is possible to enter any sort of text into a **Date** field and save the record. If it is nonsensical, the platform will ignore the value change with no error message.

Let's improve the situation with a few undocumented functions. To do this, navigate to **System Definition** > **Validation Scripts** and click on **New**. Then, use the following values:

- **Type**: `Date`
- **Validator**:

```
function validate(value) {
    if (!value) {
        return true;
    }
    if (getDateFromFormat(value, g_user_date_format) != 0)
        return true;
    return "Invalid date format.  Please use " + g_user_date_
format;
}
```

A validator script would return `true` if it determines that the entered value is appropriate. Otherwise, return `false` to display a generic error message or supply a custom one. This short script firstly accepts any blank values as appropriate ones since mandatory fields are handled separately. The `getDateFromFormat` function is an undocumented function that will return the number of milliseconds since the epoch, as long as it is passed a string that presents a date/time and the format of that date/time. If it cannot convert the time, it will return `0`. The default format is `yyyy-MM-dd` (for example, `2015-12-25` represents Christmas Day in 2015). ServiceNow stores the user's date/time preference in another undocumented variable called `g_user_date_format`.

> To validate Date/Time fields, use the `g_user_date_time_format` variable.

To try this out, navigate to a **Reservation** record and alter the **Arrival** date to a nonsensical date such as `'foo'`. If you try to save the record, a field error message will appear with the message stating that the date format is invalid. This will work on any other **Date** field, such as **Date** on **Check-in**. The following screenshot shows the output message that is displayed:

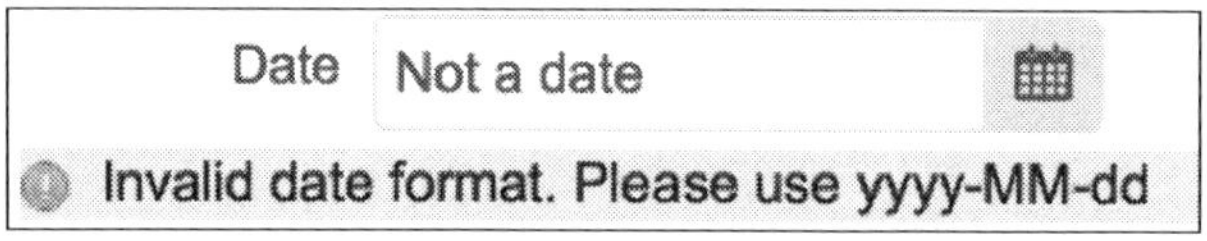

The disappearance of current

What confuses many new System Administrators is that `current` is not available on the client. They see the many similarities between the two environments and assume that their code will be completely portable. However, client-side code is often quite different, since it cannot assume that there is a fast link to the database.

On the server, the `current` object of `GlideRecord` is available in Business Rules, UI Actions, and many others. On the client, `g_form` is available as its closest functional equivalent; an object to manipulate the data with which the user is working. Since the two classes are focused on different things, there are quite a few differences; `GlideForm` focuses on the form, while `GlideRecord` is more about the data.

> Check out the ServiceNow wiki for all the details at `http://wiki.servicenow.com/?title=GlideForm`.

Unfortunately, the simple dot notation (`current.name = 'Bob'`) is not possible using `GlideForm`, and the longer getter and setter functions must be used (`g_form.setValue('name', 'Bob')`). Moreover, `g_form` can only change values that are on the form. In addition, to send the data to the instance and reload the window, `g_form.save()` is used instead of `current.update()` to commit to the database.

Translating client scripts

It is very common to store messages that are presented to users in Client Scripts. So, what happens if you want those messages translated into a different language? Business Rules have it easy; all you have to do is use `gs.getMessage`, pass a key to it, and the platform will find the appropriate translation by looking in the **Messages** table. Often, the key is the English phrase, such as the one found in this example:

```
gs.addInfoMessage(gs.getMessage('Hello, world!'));
```

If "Hello, world!" was translated into a different language, it would be returned in the language of the user. Otherwise, the `getMessage` function returns the key as the result by acting as the default.

This works great for the server, which has a fast link to the database where all the translations are stored. However, do you know what will happen on the client?

Try opening up the JavaScript executor and running the following code snippet. You should get a dialog box that says **'Questions? Comments? Send us your thoughts**!'

```
alert(getMessage('kb.comment.text'));
```

The `getMessage` function is a global client function that handles translations. If it doesn't have a translation at hand, it will perform an AJAX call to the server and find out. Since repeated AJAX calls are inefficient, a cache can be created by using the **Message** field on the client script form. Put a key on each line and the platform will find translations for each line, package them up, and send them to the client on page load.

> It is always a good idea to use `getMessage`, where possible. Translating the instance may not be your first priority, but when it becomes important, it is very difficult to find all the possible strings afterwards!

Additionally, the platform is smart and caches recent attempts for translations. You may spot the odd AJAX request that loads them on page load.

Efficiently transferring data to the client

The client-side version of `GlideRecord` is useful for situations where the dataset is limited and known. However, it doesn't give you total control over what is sent and received. This can lead to unnecessary data transfer and an application that seems to be slow.

`GlideAjax` is a technique that allows you to craft a specific communication interaction between the server and client, ensuring that only relevant data is transferred. At the moment, the VIP-alerting script returns the whole user record. Let's improve it by only returning a single field value.

Writing a Script Include for GlideAjax

`GlideAjax` comes in two parts: a client and a server script. A Script Include script should be written that extends `AbstractAjaxProcessor`. The following is a generic script that will return the contents of a single field. Create a new Script Include record by using the following values:

- **Name**: `QuickQuery`
- **Client callable**: `<ticked>`

> This flag means that the scriptwriter understands that this code can be executed from the browser. Unless you are careful, you could create a data leak and this is very possible with this script.

- **Script**:

```
var QuickQuery = Class.create();

QuickQuery.prototype = Object.extendsObject(AbstractAjaxProcessor,
{
  getField : function() {

     var table = this.getParameter('sysparm_table');
     var sys_id = this.getParameter('sysparm_sys_id');
     var field = this.getParameter('sysparm_field');
     var gr = new GlideRecordSecure(table);
     gr.setWorkflow(false);
     gr.get(sys_id);
     if (gr.isValidRecord()) return gr[field];
     else return null;
  },
```

```
    type: "QuickQuery"
  });
```

The script itself is relatively straightforward. `AbstractAjaxProcessor` provides several helpful functions to ease the creation of a script. The `getParameter` function will get data that was sent from the client, while `setParameter` will send data back. Alternatively, as here, simply return a value to populate the `answer` parameter.

> To send multiple values, you can use the `newItem` function. On the client side, you would use `getElementsByTagName` to create an array of the values. Alternatively, on the server, you could create a JSON object and embed it in a parameter.

`GlideRecordSecure` is an extension of `GlideRecord`, as you might expect. If it exists in the database, `GlideRecord` will generally find and return the data. It ignores all Access Control Rules and is only affected by Business Rules and Domain Separation. In contrast, `GlideRecordSecure` does respect Access Control Rules. This means that you must have the right role or some other condition must be met. Access Controls Rules are discussed in *Chapter 7, Securing Applications and Data.*

For scripts that are accessible by the client, by not using `GlideRecordSecure` you can open a security hold; if we had created a `setField` function that allowed the user to specify the table, the `sys_id`, the field, and the value, a malicious user would be able to virtually control the platform. However, it will not stop all malicious access; so, ensure that the Script Includes that delete records are well protected with appropriate conditions and checks.

Using GlideAjax

In order to take advantage of Script Includes, the **Alert for VIP** Client Script must be altered. Remove lines 10-14 of the Alert for VIP Client Script and the `getReference` function call, and replace them with this code snippet.

```
var ga = new GlideAjax('QuickQuery');
ga.addParam('sysparm_name', 'getField');
ga.addParam('sysparm_table', 'u_guest');
ga.addParam('sysparm_sys_id', newValue);
ga.addParam('sysparm_field', 'vip');
ga.getXMLAnswer(function(answer) {
  if (answer == 'true') {
    g_form.showFieldMsg('u_guest', 'Guest is a VIP!');
  }
});
```

The majority of the code sets the parameters that the Script Include will extract. Most are hardcoded, except for the parameter that contains the `sys_id` of the guest whose record we want to check.

There are several functions that will send the request and get the data. The `getXML` function of `GlideAjax` accepts a callback function in order to run the script asynchronously. It provides an unprocessed XML document to the function as its first parameter. The data can then be extracted using standard parsing methods such as `getElementsByTagName`.

Since the script is only getting a single data point from the instance, using `getXMLAnswer` saves us a few steps; it will unpack the XML document for us and give us a simple string from an attribute called `answer`. The script uses the result to determine whether the field message should be shown.

> Using `GlideAjax` in this simple example is 50 percent faster than using `getReference` of `GlideForm`, with a data reduction of 90 percent.

Passing data when the form loads

In *Chapter 2, Server-side Control*, we introduced `g_scratchpad`. This is a mechanism to include arbitrary data in the page as the form is rendered, giving Client Scripts easy access to it. At the moment, the Client Script runs an AJAX call when the form loads. The `g_scratchpad` object removes the need to contact the instance within milliseconds of the page being on screen.

Creating a Display Business Rule

Display Business Rules are run on the server just as the page loads. This gives us the opportunity to place our data on the page. Now, create a new Business Rule by using the following values:

- **Name**: `Get VIP flag`
- **Table**: `Check-in [u_check_in]`
- **Advanced**: `<ticked>`
- **When**: `display`
- **Script**: `g_scratchpad.vip = current.u_guest.vip;`

The `g_scratchpad` variable is a global object that is initially empty. The platform turns it into JSON and injects it right before any client scripts are included on the page.

One of the benefits of server-side code is the extra flexibility that you get. The VIP field is accessed via dot-walking through the **Guest** field. This is much more convenient than the equivalent `getReference`!

Using scratchpad on the client

The `g_scratchpad` object is reconstructed on the client side as a global variable. Edit the **Alert for VIP** Client Script again to take advantage of this data. The following reworked code includes the `GlideAjax` calls that we discussed previously.

- **Script**:

```
function onChange(control, oldValue, newValue, isLoading,
isTemplate) {
  var showVIP = function() {
    g_form.showFieldMsg('u_guest', 'Guest is a VIP!');
  }

  if (isLoading) {
    if (g_scratchpad.vip) {
      showVIP();
    }
    return;
  } else {
    g_form.hideFieldMsg('u_guest');
  }

  if (newValue == '') {
    return;
  }

  var ga = new GlideAjax('QuickQuery');
  ga.addParam('sysparm_name', 'getField');
  ga.addParam('sysparm_table', 'u_guest');
  ga.addParam('sysparm_sys_id', newValue);
  ga.addParam('sysparm_field', 'vip');
  ga.getXMLAnswer(function(answer) {
    if (answer == 'true') {
      showVIP();
    }
  });
}
```

The Client Script has changed a little. There are now two places that the system displays the message: one using the result of the scratchpad, when the form loads, and the other when the field changes. A `showVIP` function is used to reduce duplication. The code is otherwise largely the same.

Storing data in the session

When a Display Business Rule sets the `g_scratchpad` variable, the data is transferred to the client. However, it is not stored anywhere else. What if you had some data that you'd like to be available on every page? Rather wonderfully, ServiceNow allows you to add data to the currently logged in user's session, which means that it is accessible everywhere: on the client and on the server at any time.

To try this out, in Background Scripts, run the following code:

```
gs.getSession().putClientData('myData', 'Hello, world!');
```

Now, visit another page and open the client-side JavaScript executor. Then, run this code:

```
alert(g_user.getClientData('myData'));
```

Once you run the code, an alert box will appear on the screen that will show the text that we stored:

In addition to `putClientData`, the server can also access data with the `getClientData` function call. The client side `g_user` object does have a function called `setClientData` (note the difference in names!), but it does not update the information on the instance; so, it only lasts for that page load.

> The `g_user` object also contains other items of data in addition to the custom session data. Try the properties of `userName`, `userID`, and `lastName` as well as methods such as `hasRole`.

This technique is an excellent way to have information easily at hand. Any data that may be constantly used during the user's interaction with ServiceNow can easily be stored, meaning it does not need to be repetitively computed or pulled from the database. Indeed, it would be very useful even if it did not copy the data to the client.

Controlling lists with Context Menus

It is not common for lists to be controlled with Client Scripts. In the majority of applications, the user spends most of their time on a form and interacts with a single record. We've already discussed UI Actions, which can be placed onto a list to affect multiple records at once. In addition to these, the other options on a list are provided by Context Menus, a different type of control that runs solely on the client:

- **List title**: This provide filters for the table. This is visible when you click on a table's label at the top-left corner of the list. A list title generally affects the whole list in some way, perhaps by limiting the number of records on screen. The following screenshot shows an example of a List title:

- **List header**: This provides options for a particular field. It may include choosing a column to sort or to enable grouping. These are visible when you right-click on a column heading. In addition to affecting particular fields, they also provide options to import and export data. The following screenshot shows a **List header** example:

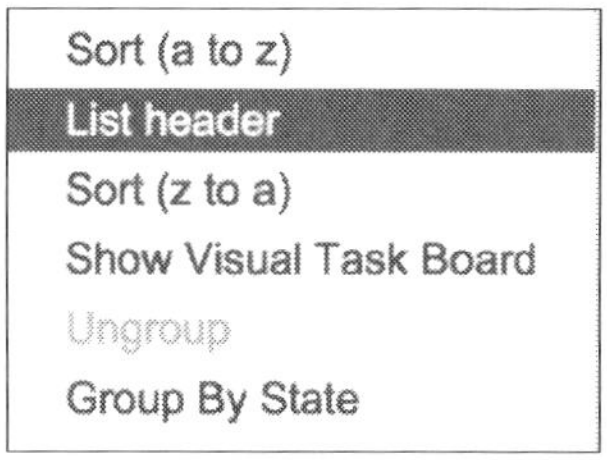

- **List row**: This is very similar to the **List context menu** UI Action. However, it provides more advanced functionality, such as submenus. These show up when you right-click on a row. The following screenshot shows an example of a List row:

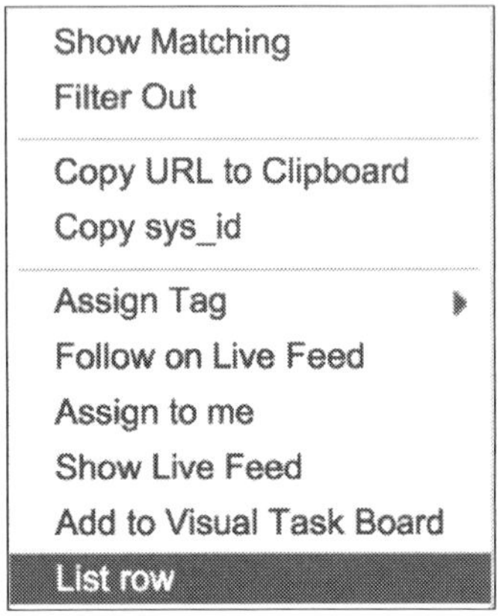

Context Menus provide a great deal of flexibility in terms of how the items are laid out. All these types can create submenus to nest information and prevent options that may create a long list. Labels and separators allow you to provide a slightly more controlled interface.

In addition to a standard condition field, Context Menus allow the use of dynamically controlled options. The platform allows you to add an arbitrary number of actions into each menu.

Finding out about the list

A Context Menu entry has access to several predefined variables. These are available everywhere a list can be found, even on Related Lists. The one that is most useful is `g_list`. The `g_list` variable is an instance of `GlideList2`, which is equivalent to `GlideForm`. It provides several help properties and methods. These are mainly used within the **Action** script field that defines what the item will do, but they are also available in other script boxes.

> GlideList2 shouldn't be confused with the Glide List field type. GlideList2 is a client-side list implementation that uses AJAX to only grab data but not formatting markup to improve navigation speed.

Some of the supported methods are as follows:

- `getQuery`: This provides the current encoded filter that the list displays. It accepts an object that uses flags to control what is returned. Use `g_list.getQuery({all : true });` to return `the group by`, `order by`, and `fixed` parameter fields.
- `setFilterAndRefresh`: This changes what query will be run and refreshes the list to show the records. It passes through an encoded query.
- `getChecked`: This returns a comma-separated list of the checked records.

Opening a new tab

Context Menus have a variety of uses, but they are not very common. Here are two simple examples to show the power that is available with it.

First, navigate to **System UI** > **UI Context Menus**. Then, click on **New** and use the following values:

- **Table**: `Global [global]`
- **Menu**: `List title`
- **Type**: `Action`
- **Name**: `Open in new tab`
- **Action script**: `window.open(window.location.href);`

To see the results of this addition, navigate to a list and then click on the table name at the top-left corner. The script doesn't use `GlideList2` at all; it simply uses standard JavaScript.

Now, create another **UI Context Menu** record for another example by using the following values:

- **Table**: `Global [global]`
- **Menu**: `List row`
- **Type**: `Action`
- **Name**: `Open in new tab`
- **Script**:

```
window.open('/' + g_list.getTableName() +
        '.do?sys_id=' + g_sysId);
```

When a user right-clicks on a record in a list, he or she will now get a new option to open the record in a new tab.

Customizing and extending the platform

Sometimes, there is a desire to perform manipulations that `GlideForm` cannot do. This might include supporting additional events, such as `onmouseover`, or altering the layout of the page. Although I'll tell you how you can achieve this, I'll recommend that you never do it.

> This section assumes that you have a basic understanding of Dynamic HTML.

Firing on more events

Client Scripts allow you to run the code when a field changes or when the form is loaded or submitted. However, the browser can tell JavaScript code about many more events, such as zooming on a tablet, moving a mouse, or dragging files.

One way is to create an `onLoad` client script that sets up these events manually. The following code uses some undocumented functions in the ServiceNow platform to run script when the mouse moves over the **Departure** field on the **Reservation** form. You can create a new Client Script on the **Reservation** table to try this out:

```
function onLoad() {
  var control = g_form.getControl('u_departure');
  Event.observe(control, 'mouseover', function() {
    g_form.hideFieldMsg(control);
    g_form.showFieldMsg(control, 'in');
  });
  Event.observe(control, 'mouseout', function() {
    g_form.hideFieldMsg(control);
    g_form.showFieldMsg(control, 'out');
  });
}
```

Firstly, `GlideForm` is used to get the field object by calling `getControl`. This is the HTML element that is displayed on the page. This is passed to a global function called `Event`, which accepts several parameters: the element in question, the event to react to, and the code that should run. Here, anonymous functions use some standard `g_form` functions.

Additionally, you can create your own events. These are more useful if you are building a large client-side application, but these events also give an indication of how ServiceNow works under the hood. Consider the following script:

```
CustomEvent.observe('sayHello', function() {
  alert('Hello, world!')
});
CustomEvent.fire('sayHello');
```

Custom events are a way of passing information between different scripts without using global variables. Of course, you can still have namespace collisions, but good naming practice can reduce this.

> This functionality is not documented on the ServiceNow wiki. It should be considered to be unsupported.

Using built-in libraries

ServiceNow has historically been built on the Prototype JavaScript library. It is used to provide helpful shortcuts and remove browser inconsistencies; therefore, it provides a much smoother base on which to build `GlideForm`. However, Prototype's method of achieving this helpful functionality is now generally agreed to be wrong as it extends object classes, thus changing their definition. This causes cross-browser incompatibilities, potential performance problems, and more. Other libraries, such as jQuery, wrap objects instead, which has been accepted as the better approach. In future releases of ServiceNow, other libraries like Angular will be utilized more frequently.

Nonetheless, Prototype gives quick access to the DOM: the hierarchy of elements that the browser uses to understand and display the page on the screen. It then allows you to manipulate them very easily.

Try running the following code in the JavaScript executor on a form and close the dialog window; then, move the mouse over some text fields, such as **Short description**, and see what happens:

```
$$('input').invoke('observe', 'mouseover', function(event) {
  this.setStyle({fontSize: '30px'});
});
```

This code is quite impenetrable to someone who isn't familiar with Prototype or other JavaScript libraries. First, the code searches for all input fields through the `$$` shortcut. It then runs a function called `observe` on each one. It passes through the `mouseover` event name and a function that will be called when that event occurs. This function then increases the size of the font of the element, so you will get a supersized text when the mouse hovers over it. This code could easily be made part of a Client Script.

While this example is just a nice trick, you can use similar techniques to really customize the way ServiceNow looks and feels. For example, you may want to change the background color of field labels dynamically or alter how the screen is laid out. However, this comes with some serious disadvantages, as mentioned in the next section.

What could go wrong

When you manipulate the layout of a document, you must make some assumptions about how that document will be laid out. An example is to alter the label of a field to include an icon. This is possible to achieve by setting a CSS style for the table cell. In order to do this, you need to know the way in which the text is oriented; is it right or left aligned? This will determine where the icon will fit best.

The ServiceNow development team is constantly looking to improve the look and feel of the interface. An upgrade of the ServiceNow platform may entail changes to assumptions that a script may be relying on. In the preceding example, the label's alignment may move from left to right.

Additionally, new techniques for accessing web applications are constantly being developed. Mobile devices are capturing an ever-increasing share of browsing habits. ServiceNow has a tablet- and mobile-phone-focused interface where different assumptions to the desktop environment are made.

Scripts will break when assumptions are wrong. Any scripts that go wrong may have unintended consequences and non-functional scripts normally need to be fixed. This means that scripts that alter the layout must be tested after an upgrade to ServiceNow or when a new method of accessing ServiceNow is introduced. Since many customers want seamless upgrades, with minimal testing and as little rework as possible, this means that scripts that alter the layout of a document though CSS, DOM manipulation, or otherwise, should be avoided.

Taking control of the browser

Client-side code is executed by the browser. This means that, in many respects, it should be considered to be a polite request only! A technical user can easily undo the setting of a mandatory field that was achieved through UI Policy or by `GlideForm`, as we'll see in this example:

1. Open the **Check-in** form in a new window. Do this by typing `u_check_in.FORM` in the **Application Navigator** filter text.
2. Populate the fields but ensure to set the **Date** field with a value in the past. This means the **Comments** field will be shown and made mandatory.

> If you try to submit the form without a comment, the platform will notice and present an alert box. It won't let you to send the data to the instance without filling in the comments.

3. Now, pretend to be a malicious user. In the address bar of your browser, enter the following online script and press enter:

```
javascript:g_form.setMandatory('u_comments', false);
```

> You may need to type this in rather than being able to copy and paste it. Some browsers attempt to protect against common attacks by removing the `javascript` prefix.

As you may expect, the Comments field loses its red mandatory indicator, and the form can now be submitted without a value.

Data Policy saves the day

Luckily, *Chapter 2, Server-side Control*, showed you a way to protect against this attack. We've already put a Data Policy in place that captures the error. The familiar red error message is displayed, and the record is not committed to the database. We've also been saved by a server-side check. Try disabling the Data Policy to prove that this is the only thing that is stopping the error from being shown.

This scenario is possible regardless of your role in the instance. You do not need to be an admin to disable mandatory fields in this way. With the right knowledge, a malicious user can instruct the browser to change the status of fields, setting read-only fields to writeable, or mandatory fields to optional. Code need not be used at all, since most browsers have developer tools that allow the manipulation of fields directly. This method even allows the population of fields that are not on the form, by changing the name of input fields in the DOM.

It once again underlines the importance of having strong server-side controls to properly validate client-side data.

Summary

Most ServiceNow System Administrators have had some experience working with client-side JavaScript. It is often very obvious and familiar to write scripts that interact with the web browser. Validating information using the browser will mean that your users can generally work quickly with the application rather than clicking and waiting.

However, client-side scripts do have significant drawbacks. They should not be used to guarantee data integrity and enforce security controls since a malicious user can easily manipulate the browser to disable the checks. Client-side scripts can easily start to slow the browser down in situations such as when there are dozens of fields that are being hidden by UI Policy.

However, there are many other ways to provide a great user experience. UI Actions are a great way to carry out complex actions in a single click. They can run code on the server, or in the browser, and can be placed on a form or in a list. Use them to simplify the interface for your users. In the same way, Context Menus let you manipulate lists and add additional buttons and functionality, mainly for power users.

If you need to communicate with the instance, `GlideRecord` is also available on the client. However, `GlideAjax` is a more efficient alternative and allows you to grab precisely what is needed and leverage the database processing power of the instance.

The next chapter focuses on the **Task** table. This important table begins our ascent out of the foundations of ServiceNow and into the building of a workflow-based solution that is designed to get stuff done.

4
Getting Things Done with Tasks

The first few chapters have focused heavily on the underpinnings of the ServiceNow platform: how data is stored, manipulated, processed, and displayed. With these tools, you can build almost any forms-based application. But starting from the beginning each time would be time-consuming and repetitive. To help with this, the ServiceNow platform provides baseline functionality that allows you to concentrate on the parts that matter.

If Business Rules, tables, Client Scripts, and fields are the foundations of ServiceNow, the **Task** table, approvals, and the **Service Catalog** are the ready-made lintels, elevator shafts, and staircases—the essential tried and tested components that make up the bulk of the building.

This chapter looks at the standard components behind many applications:

- The **Task** table is probably the most well-used and most important table in a ServiceNow instance. The functionality it provides is explored in this chapter, outlining several gotchas.
- How do you control these tasks? Business Rules is one way, but **Graphical Workflow** provides a drag-and-drop option to control your application.
- While you can bake in rules, you often need personal judgment. **Approval Workflow** lets you decide who to ask and lets them respond easily.
- The **Service Catalog** is the go-to place to work with the applications that are hosted in ServiceNow. It provides the main interface for end users to interact with your applications. We also briefly explore **Request Fulfillment**, which enables users to respond to the queries quickly and effectively.
- **Service Level Management** lets you monitor the effectiveness of your services by setting timers and controlling breaches.

Introducing tasks

ServiceNow is a forms-based workflow platform. The majority of applications running on ServiceNow can be reduced to a simple single concept: *the management of tasks*.

A task in ServiceNow is work that is assigned to someone. You may ask your colleague to make you a cup of tea, or you may need to fix a leaking tap in a hotel guest's bedroom. Both of these are tasks. There are several parts to each of these tasks:

- A **requester** is someone who specifies the work. This could be a guest or even yourself.
- A **fulfiller** is someone who completes the work. This may, less frequently, be the same as the requester.
- The fulfiller is often part of a **group** of people. Perhaps someone among them could work on the task.
- Information about the task itself. Perhaps a **description** or a **priority**, indicating how important the task is.
- The **status** of the task. Is it complete? Or is the fulfiller still working on it?
- A place to store **notes** to record what has happened.
- An **identifier** is a unique number to represent the task. The `sys_id` is an identifier which is very specific and unique, but not very friendly!
- Links, references, and **relationships** to other records. Is this task a subdivision of another task, or connected to others? Perhaps you are moving house—that's a big task! But this could be broken down into separate items.

Sometimes, the representation of a task is as simple as a Post-it note. Many of us have had something similar to, "Frank called, could you ring him back?" attached to our desk. But you often need something more permanent, reportable, automated, and which doesn't fall on the floor when someone walks by.

Looking at the Task table

The **Task** table in ServiceNow is designed to store, manage, and process tasks. It contains fields to capture all the details and a way to access them consistently and reliably. In addition, there is a whole host of functionality described in this chapter to automate and process tasks more efficiently.

> This wiki has an introductory article to the **Task** table: `http://wiki.servicenow.com/?title=Task_Table`. It also covers some of the lesser-used elements, such as the Task Interceptor.

To begin our journey, inspect the record representing the **Task** table. Navigate to **System Definition** > **Tables** and then find the entry named `task`.

In the Eureka version of ServiceNow, there are 62 fields on the **Task** table. There are also many other associated scripts, UI actions, and linked tables. What do they all do?

The important fields

It is often instructive to view the fields that have been placed on the form by default. Click on the **Show form** Related Link to check. In alignment with the design suggestions discussed in *Chapter 1, ServiceNow Foundations*, the big text fields are down the bottom, with the shorter fields (including reference fields) at the top.

- **Number**: A unique identifier, it's a 7-digit number prefixed by `task`. This is constructed using a script that is specified in the dictionary.

  > The script uses details in the `sys_number` table, accessible via **System Definition** > **Number Maintenance**.

- **Assigned to**: This field represents the fulfiller—the person who is working on the task. It is a reference field that points to the User table. It has a reference qualifier that lets only users with the `itil` role be selected. Roles are explored further in *Chapter 7, Securing Applications and Data*, but it will suffice to say that `itil` is usually necessary to work on tasks.

  The **Assigned to** field is also dependent on the **Assignment group** field. This means that if the **Assignment group** field is populated, you can only select users that belong to that particular group.

- **Assignment group**: This field is not on the form by default. You may want to add it by using the **Form Designer**. Groups and users are discussed further in the chapter, but in short, it shows the team of people who are responsible for the task.

[**Assignment group** has been made a tree picker field. The **Group** table has a parent field, which allows groups to be nested in a hierarchical structure. If you click on the Reference Lookup icon (the magnifying glass), it will present a different interface to the usual list. This is controlled via a property in the dictionary.]

The following screenshot shows a group hierarchical structure that is structured with the help of the **Assignment group** field:

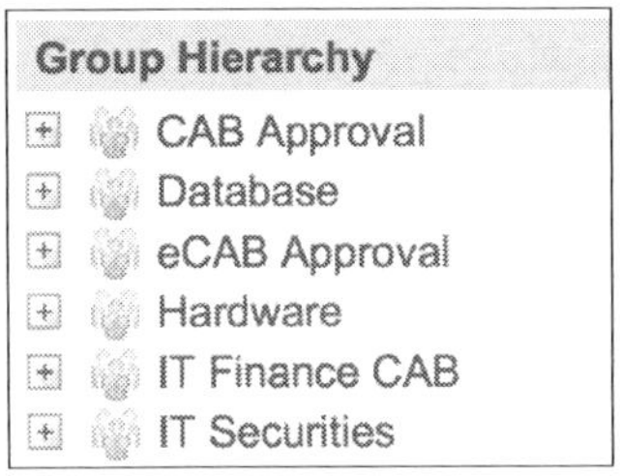

- **Active**: This field represents whether a task is "operational". Closed tickets are not active, neither are tasks that are due to start. Tasks that are being worked on are active. There is a direct correlation between the **State** of a task and whether it is active.

[If you change the choices available for the State field, you may be tempted to write Business Rules to control the Active flag. Don't. There is a script called `TaskStateUtil` that does just this. Try not to cause a fight between the Business Rules! Refer to the wiki for more information on this:

`http://wiki.servicenow.com/?title=TaskStateUtil`]

- **Priority**: a choice field designed to give the person working on the task some idea as to which task they should complete first. It has a default of 4.
- **State**: probably the most complex field on the table. So much so that it has its own section later in this chapter! It gives more details than the Active flag as to how the task is currently being processed.

- **Parent**: a reference field to another task record. A parent-to-child relationship is a one-to-many relationship. A child is generally taken to be a subdivision of a parent; a child task breaks down the parent task. A parent task may also represent a Master task if there are several related tasks that need to be grouped together.

> Breadcrumbs can be added to a form to represent the parent relationship more visually. You can read up more about this at:
> `http://wiki.servicenow.com/?title=Task_Parent_Breadcrumbs_Formatter`

- **Short description**: give a quick summary of the task here. It is free text, but should be kept short since it has an attribute in the dictionary that prevents it from being truncated in a list view. It is often used for reporting and e-mail notifications.

> Short description is a suggestion field. It will attempt to autocomplete when you begin typing; type in 'issue' as an example. While you are free to add your own suggestions, it is not commonly done. Check out this wiki article for more details:
> `http://wiki.servicenow.com/?title=Adding_Suggestion_Fields`

- **Description**: Here, you give a longer description of the task. It is a simple large text field.
- **Work notes**: This field is one of the most well-used fields on the form. It is a `journal_input` field that always presents an empty text box. When the form is saved, the contents of a journal field are saved in a separate table called `sys_journal_field`. The `journal_output` fields such as **Comments** and **Work notes** are used to display them. Strangely, this field isn't on the out-of-the-box form.

Populating fields automatically

The majority of the 62 fields that are on the **Task** table aren't on the form by default. Instead, many fields are autopopulated, through logic or Business Rules and as default values. Others are optional, available to be filled in if appropriate. All the data is then available for reporting or to drive processes.

Some of the more notable fields are explained here, but this list is not exhaustive!

- The **Approval** field is discussed in more detail later in the chapter. There are several automatic fields, such as **Approval set**, that represent when a decision was made.
- A Business Rule populates **Duration** when the task becomes inactive. It records how long the task took in "calendar" time. There is also a **Business Duration** field to perform the same calculation in working hours, but it uses calendars, which are depreciated.
- When a task is first created, a Business Rule records the logged-in user who performed the action and populates **Opened by**. When the task is set to inactive, it populates the **Closed by** field. **Opened at** and **Closed at** are date/time fields that also get populated.
- **Company** and **Location** are reference fields that provide extra detail about who the task is for and where it is. Location is dependent upon Company; if you populate the **Company** field, it will only show locations for that company. **Location** is also a tree picker field, like **Assignment group**.
- **Due date** is a date/time field to represent when a task should be completed.
- **Time worked** is a specialized duration field that records how long the form has been on the screen. If it is added to the form, a reverse countdown is shown. On save, a Business Rule then populates the **Time Worked** [`task_time_worked`] table with the current user, how long it took, and any added comments.
- A formatter is an element that is added to a form (like a field), but uses a custom interface to present information. The **Activity Formatter** uses the **Audit** tables to present the changes made to fields on the task: who changed something, what they changed, and when.

> *Chapter 8, Diagnosing ServiceNow – Knowing What Is Going On,* discusses the **Audit** tables in much more detail. The wiki also has more information on the Activity Formatter:
>
> `http://wiki.servicenow.com/?title=Activity_Formatter`

Recording Room Maintenance tasks

At Gardiner Hotels, we have the highest standards of quality. Rooms must be clean and tidy, with all the light bulbs working, and no dripping taps! Let's create a table that will contain jobs for our helpful staff to complete.

> This is an example of a **Custom App** in ServiceNow. ServiceNow is significantly enhancing the functionality of this area, and the Fuji version provides a more guided method. More details can be found here:
> `http://wiki.servicenow.com/?title=Creating_Custom_Applications`

The process for dealing with a maintenance issue at Gardiner Hotels is straightforward; the need gets recorded in ServiceNow and it gets assigned to the right team, who then work on it till the issue is resolved. Sometimes, a more complex issue will require the assistance of Cornell Hotel Services, a service company that will come equipped with the necessary tools. But to ensure that the team isn't used unnecessarily, management need to approve any of their assignments.

Have a look at the following figure, which represents what the process is:

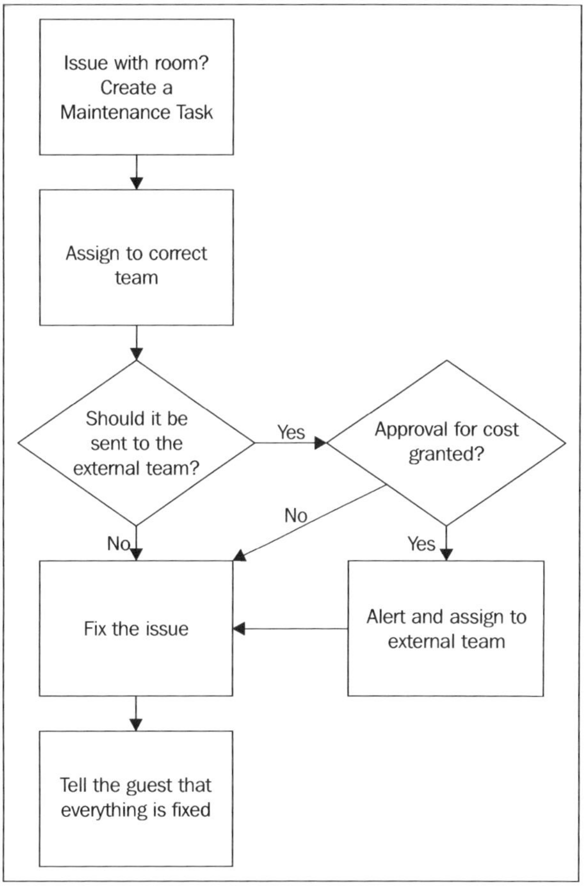

These requirements suggest the use of the **Task** table. In order to take advantage of its functionality, a new **Maintenance** table should be extended from it. All of the fields from **Task**, its Business Rules, and other functions will be available there. *Chapter 1, ServiceNow Foundations*, explains how table extension works.

> Any time that a record should be assigned to a person or a team, consider using the **Task** table. There are other indicators too, like the need for approvals.

Now, let's create the **Maintenance** table by performing the following steps:

1. Navigate to **System Definition** > **Tables** and create a new table with the following details:
    - **Label**: Maintenance
    - **Extends table**: Task
    - **Auto-number**: <ticked>
2. Then create a new field using this data:
    - **Column label**: Room
    - **Type**: Reference
    - **Reference**: Room
3. Click on **Design Form** and do the following:
    - Add the **Assignment Group**, **Approval**, and **Room** fields and the **Activities (Filtered)** Formatter
    - Remove the **Configuration Item**, **Parent**, and **Active** fields
    - Rearrange the form to make it look good!
4. Finally, make the **Approval** field read-only by editing the Dictionary record of the **Approval** field.

> Changing the settings on a field on the **Task** table will change it for tables extended from Task. This is often not what you want! Contrarily, a Dictionary Override will only affect the selected table. Read more about this here:
>
> http://wiki.servicenow.com/?title=Dictionary_Overrides

5. Now, create a new **Dictionary Override** entry with the following details . Navigate to the dictionary entry, and find the Dictionary Override Related List.
    - **Table**: `Maintenance [u_maintenance]`
    - **Override read only**: `<ticked>`
    - **Read only**: `<ticked>`

> There are better ways to make fields read-only. This checkbox setting won't be enforced through scripts or Web Services, and it can even be turned off with a Client Script. *Chapter 7, Securing Applications and Data*, shows how ACLs can make fields read-only.

The Maintenance table should now look something like this:

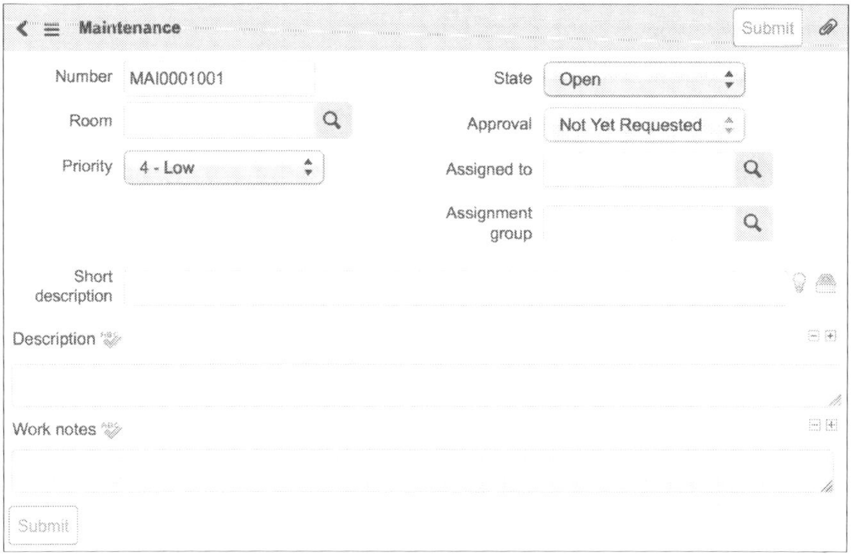

Working with tasks

You may be familiar with a work queue. It provides a list of items that you should complete, perhaps representing your work for the day. Often, this is achieved by assigning the item to a particular group. The members of that group then have access to the ticket and should do the necessary work to close it.

In ServiceNow, this concept is represented in the **Service Desk** application menu. Navigate to **Service Desk**. You will find the options: **My Work** and **My Groups Work**. The former is a simple List view of the **Task** table with the following filters.

- **Active** is `true`; this filters out **Closed** tasks
- **Assigned to** is the current user; so if you are logged in as the user called "System Administrator", you see tasks where the **Assigned to** field is set to **System Administrator**
- **State** is not Pending filters out tasks that should not be worked on right now

The entry **My Groups Work** is very similar, but shows tasks that haven't been given to a fulfiller and is still something that your group should deal with. It does this by showing tasks where the **Assigned to** field is empty and the **Assignment group** field is one of your groups. This means that when the **My Work** list is empty, you probably should get more work from **My Groups Work**.

The **My Work** list shows all records that are derived from the **Task** table. This means you will see a mixture of records in this table. It is incredibly useful to have a "single pane of glass", where all your activities are in a single place, with consistent fields and data values. They can be manipulated easily and effectively; assign all your tickets to your colleague when you go on leave with a couple of clicks!

Working without a queue

Some platforms make the use of a work queue mandatory; the only way to have the visibility of a task is through your work queue. It is important to realize that ServiceNow does not have this restriction. The **My Work** list is a filtered list like any other. You do not have to be "assigned" the work before you can update or comment on it.

> It may be a policy restriction in your organization that you must be assigned the ticket before you can update it. If you want to enforce this behavior in ServiceNow, it is possible through security rules and Business Rules. However, this often discourages collaborative working and information sharing.

There are many ways to find tasks to work on. This usually involves creating filters on lists. This may include tasks that have been marked as high priority or those that have been open for more than two weeks.

In many IT organizations, a central Service Desk team is the single point of contact. They have the responsibility to ensure tasks are completed quickly and effectively, regardless of who they are currently assigned to. ServiceNow makes this easy by ensuring tasks can be accessed in a variety of ways and not just through a work queue.

Working socially

Social media concepts are infiltrating many aspects of the IT industry, and ServiceNow is not immune. Some useful ideas have been pulled into the platform in an attempt to make working on tasks a more collaborative experience, ensuring the right people are involved. Two aspects to this in ServiceNow include Chat and Live Feed:

- **Chat** often focuses on helping requesters contact the Service Desk more effectively. It allows a Service Desk agent to have multiple chat sessions open at the same time, and also enables the conversation to be copied directly into a new incident. The system also allows two fulfillers to chat, but it requires both to have the Chat desktop open. Currently, there is no integration with a desktop chat client, meaning that the functionality is not often used. Turn on the Chat plugin to enable the functionality.
- **Live Feed** gives a Facebook wall interaction, where all types of users can read and add messages. This can be used as a self-service system, since the messages are searchable and referenceable by copying a link. It is a communication mechanism that allows users to be as involved as they'd like. Unlike e-mail, Live Feed is more of an optional choice to work with, so the right culture must be cultivated in a company for it to be most beneficial.

> ServiceNow is constantly improving its social capabilities. The new Collaboration interface in Fuji provides a new way to chat in the same interface.

Live Table Notification creates Chat and Live Feed messages automatically based on conditions and configurations. For example, during a service outage, the Service Desk may want an automatic communication to be sent out, alerting people proactively.

You may have noticed the **Live Feed** checkbox on the **Table** form (**System Definition** > **Tables**). If this is ticked, a Business Rule adds an attribute on the dictionary entry of the table, setting `livefeed` as `true`. The result of this is an icon on the context bar of the record. Clicking on it gives a pop-up window, allowing you to enter comments or work notes.

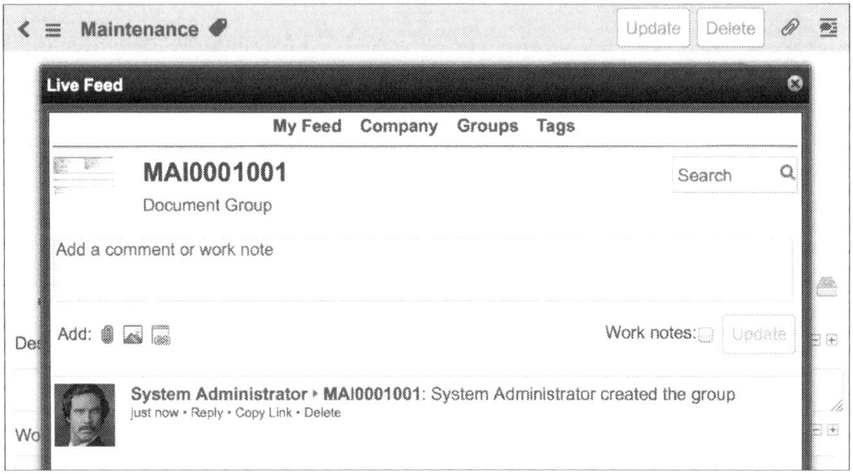

Organizing groups and users

In *Chapter 1, ServiceNow Foundations*, the **User** table was extended to create the home for the **Guest** records. It is generally a good idea to keep all your users in the **User** [`sys_user`] table, since it enables the built-in functionality such as **Additional comments** easily and effectively.

To organize users, put them into groups. Groups and users have a many-to-many relationship. One person can be a member of many groups, and a group can have many members.

> Groups are stored in the `sys_user_group` table. The relationship between groups is stored in the **Group Members** [`sys_user_grmember`] table

Groups are also hierarchical. A group has a reference field pointing to the group table, letting you build up a parent-child structure. A person in a child group is also treated as a member of the parent group in most circumstances.

There are many different uses for groups:

- **Assignment groups** will be completing tasks. You may want to ensure that only these groups will receive tasks by adding a reference qualifier to the **Assignment group** field on the **Task** table.
- The **organizational structure** of the company may be represented in groups. Departments and companies are mentioned in the next section.
- As discussed in the security-oriented *Chapter 7, Securing Applications and Data*, you may want groups designed to **distribute roles**—perhaps a Managers group that will have extra privileges.
- **Distributing reports** and **emails** via groups is very useful.
- Sending **approval requests** to a group rather than a user avoids making a process dependent on a single person.

There is a **Glide List** field on the **Group** table called **Types**, though it is not on the form by default. This points to the **Group Types** [`sys_user_group_type`] table, which allows you to identify what this group is being used for. The default configuration gives you a single group type, `catalog`, but you can add more.

> Another way to achieve this is just to add Boolean True/False fields on to the table, representing the different options. It is then very easy to check this in scripts and Reference Qualifiers.

Creating a room maintenance team

In order for our room maintenance system to be effective, we need some groups that will work on the tasks. Firstly, however, we need to create a new field in the **Group** [`sys_user_group`] table. Accomplish this through the **Form Designer** or your preferred method. Use the following data:

- **Type**: `True/False`
- **Label**: `Maintenance`

Navigate to **User Administration** > **Groups** and click on **New**. Use these details:

- **Name**: `Maintenance`
- **Manager**: `Howard Johnson`
- **Maintenance**: <ticked>

Once saved, the **Groups** Related List becomes available. Click on **New** to create a new child group with the following data:

- **Name**: `Housekeeping`
- **Parent**: `Maintenance` (should be populated already)
- **Maintenance:** `<ticked>`

Once saved, add some users into the **Group Members** Related List.

Finally, make another child group to **Maintenance** with these details:

- **Name**: `Cornell Hotel Services`
- **Parent**: `Maintenance` (should be populated already)
- **Maintenance:** `<ticked>`

The **Maintenance** group should look as follows:

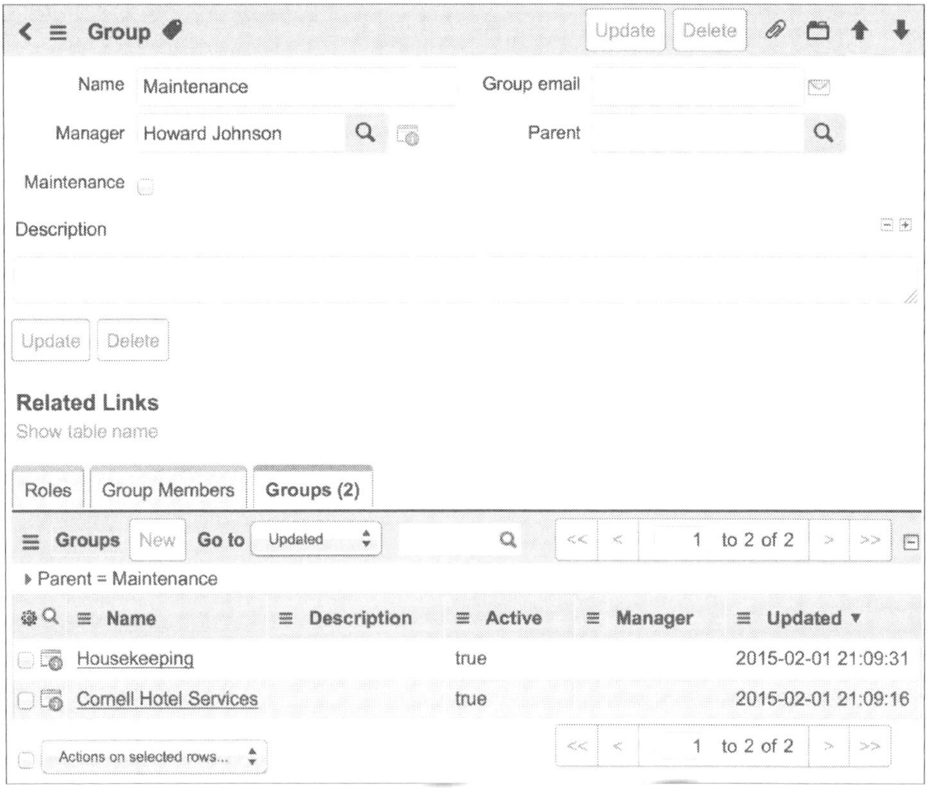

Creating a property

As seen in *Chapter 1, ServiceNow Foundations*, properties are used throughout ServiceNow. These provide a simple way to alter how the system works in a very controlled manner, without hardcoding choices. Let's make our own property to specify that Cornell Hotel Services is our external team.

As a first step, create a **System Properties Category** to group the items together.

1. Navigate to **System Properties** > **Categories** and click on **New**.
    - **Name**: `Room Maintenance`
2. The property is going to store the name of our external team. Click on **New** in the **Properties** Related List. Use these details:
    - **Name**: `maintenance.external_group`
    - **Description**: `The group that gets approved maintenance requests`

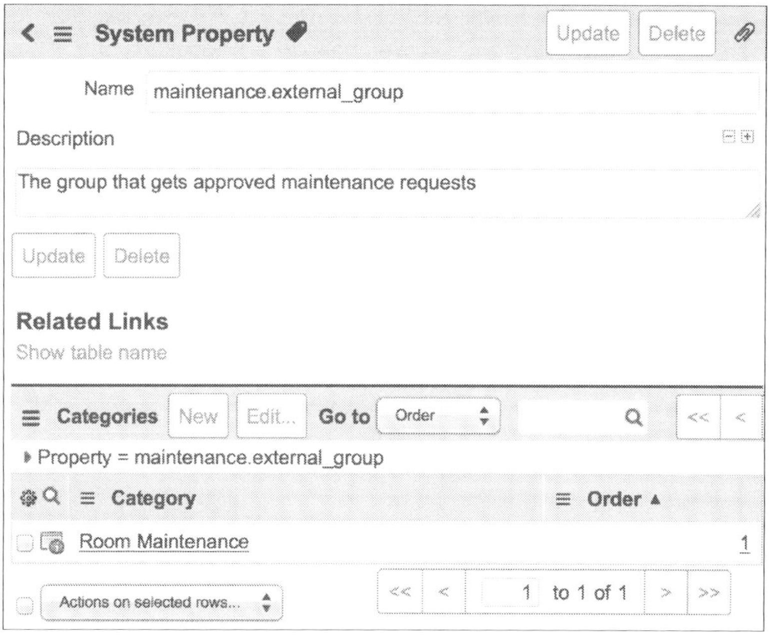

3. Now create a module that makes accessing the properties easy. Right-click on the **Hotel** application menu and choose **Edit Application Menu**.

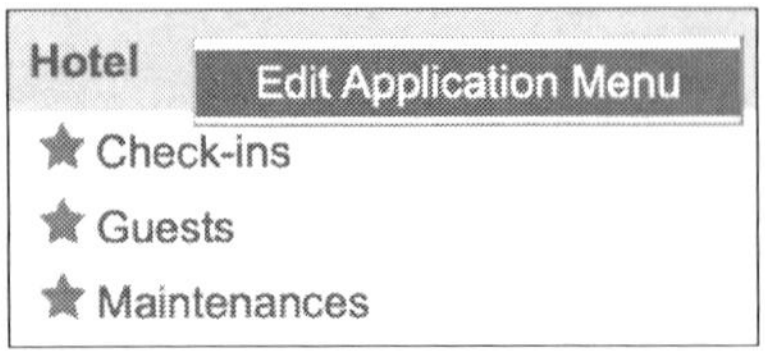

4. Create a new **Module** by clicking on **New** in the Related List. Use the following:
    - **Title**: `Room Maintenance Properties`
    - **Link type**: `URL (from Arguments:)`
    - **Arguments**: `/system_properties_ui.do?sysparm_title=Room Maintenance properties&sysparm_category=Room Maintenance`

    The URL points to a UI Page called `system_properties_ui`. It accepts two parameters: a category of the properties we are interested in and a title to display at the top of the page.

5. Once the module is saved, the Application Navigator will refresh. Click on the **New** link to see the simple interface, and populate the property as follows:
    - **The group that gets approved maintenance requests**: `Cornell Hotel Services`

    The **Room Maintenance properties** window is shown in the following screenshot:

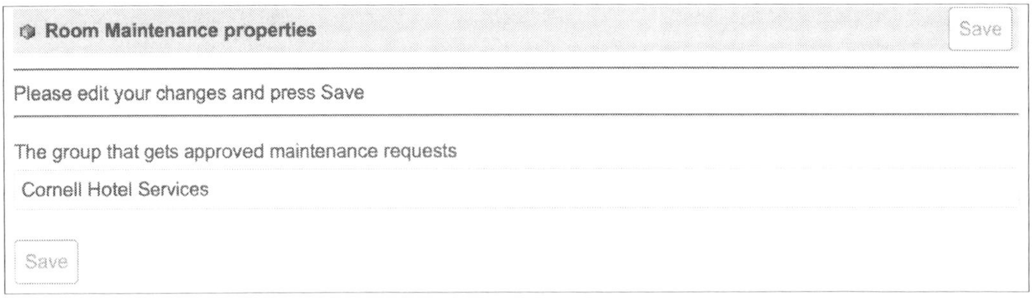

Using departments and companies

In addition to groups, ServiceNow also lets you associate users with departments and companies.

Departments and companies are slightly different to groups in that they have a one-to-many relationship with users; a user is only ever a member of a single department and one company.

Each of these tables records relevant information: a department has a cost-code and a manager and a company may be a vendor or a customer. Both are hierarchical and have a parent field.

Using Additional comments and Work notes

The central purpose of a **Task** record in ServiceNow is to record and communicate. The two journal fields on the **Task** table, **Additional comments** and **Work notes**, do just that. They provide an always-empty space to enter information that will be presented in the **Activity Formatter** or in a Journal Output field.

You may wonder why there are two fields.

- **Additional comments** is provided for communication with the requester. Often, they are status updates, giving the requester a progress report. They are made available to everyone.
- **Work notes** is targeted at notes for fulfillers. These are likely to be technical or sensitive in nature, and should not be shared with the requester.

As we'll explore later in *Chapter 7, Securing Applications and Data*, the **Work notes** field is protected by Access Control Rules, which means that requesters cannot see any of these entries.

There are two other fields not yet mentioned: the **Watch** and **Work notes** lists. These are often tied to the journal fields through notifications. When an entry is made in the Additional comments field, the requester and the users in the Watch list are sent an e-mail. When you save a record with **Work notes**, the contents get sent to the **Work notes** list and the user in the **Assigned to** field. This is discussed further in the e-mail notifications section in *Chapter 5, Events, Notifications, and Reporting*.

> The **Watch** and **Work notes** lists can contain e-mail addresses in addition to a `sys_id` representing a user record. This means you can send updates to people who do not have a record in the User table in ServiceNow.

Understanding the State field

The state of a task drives a tremendous amount of business logic in a typical ServiceNow application. It represents how a task is progressing - whether it should be worked on, whether it actually is being worked on, and when the task is done. This may drive e-mail notifications, be a trigger for service-level monitoring, and be a condition for a security rule, to name but a few.

The state field on the **Task** table is an integer choice field. This means a number is stored in the database, while the available options are given labels. In general, scripts use the number value, while the UI displays the label. This table shows the relationship between the two.

Label	Number	Description
Pending	-5	The task exists, but shouldn't be worked on yet. It may have been created for planning reasons. The convention is that any number less than 0 represents a state that hasn't yet started.
Open	1	The task has been created, but no one is yet working on it.
Work in Progress	2	The task is being worked on. This usually means the **Assigned to** and **Assignment group** fields have been populated. This indicates who is responsible for, or who currently owns, the work.
Closed Complete	3	The task was finished successfully, and no further work needs to be done.
Closed Incomplete	4	The work has been attempted, but it was not considered a success. It might be that the task was impossible, that this section of the work failed, or that it was only partially finished. It is no longer being worked on.
Closed Skipped	7	The task isn't complete, but it is no longer relevant. Perhaps it has been canceled or a predecessor task has failed, meaning this task will not be worked on.

One benefit of having the **State** field backed by an integer is that you can create a filter using greater than or less than conditions. For example, you could have **State ≥ Closed Complete** to get the closed states in one go.

Also, you know you are a ServiceNow master when you can remember all the state numbers!

Breaking down states

The progress of a task is stored in lots of fields, not just **State**. **State** is most often used for particular milestones, but other fields such as **Approval** also give information about what is happening.

Don't try to cram too much into the **State** field. Break down information into logical chunks, avoiding a cluttered, unorganized choice field. If necessary, create a **Substate** field that provides more options that is dependent upon **State**.

> There are three different closed states in the default configuration. I like to have been have a single **Closed** state and then a separate dependent **Substate** field that gives you the further options to refine.

Configuring different states

Many task-based applications add, remove, and re-label state choices in order to better represent the specific type of work that task represents. A very typical addition is **Awaiting Requester**. This usually means that the fulfiller, the user in the Assigned to field, is asking for clarification on the task. Perhaps not enough detail was provided, or there are multiple ways to complete the task and a choice should be given to the requester.

If the states are changed in an extended table, it is very important to align them correctly. For instance, if you remove **Closed Skipped** and add **Awaiting Requester**, do not give **Awaiting Requester** a number value of 7. Otherwise, it can be confusing when comparing different ticket types. Unfortunately, this is not well handled in some of the ServiceNow applications.

In order to see this, perform the following steps:

1. Navigate to **Service Desk** > **My Work**.
2. Alter the filter in such a way that all the provided conditions are removed and replaced with **State = Closed Complete**.

3. When you click on **Run**, you will ask the database to return all records where the State field is 3 for **Closed Complete**. You may therefore expect only to get closed records that are inactive. Unfortunately, you don't, as this screenshot shows:

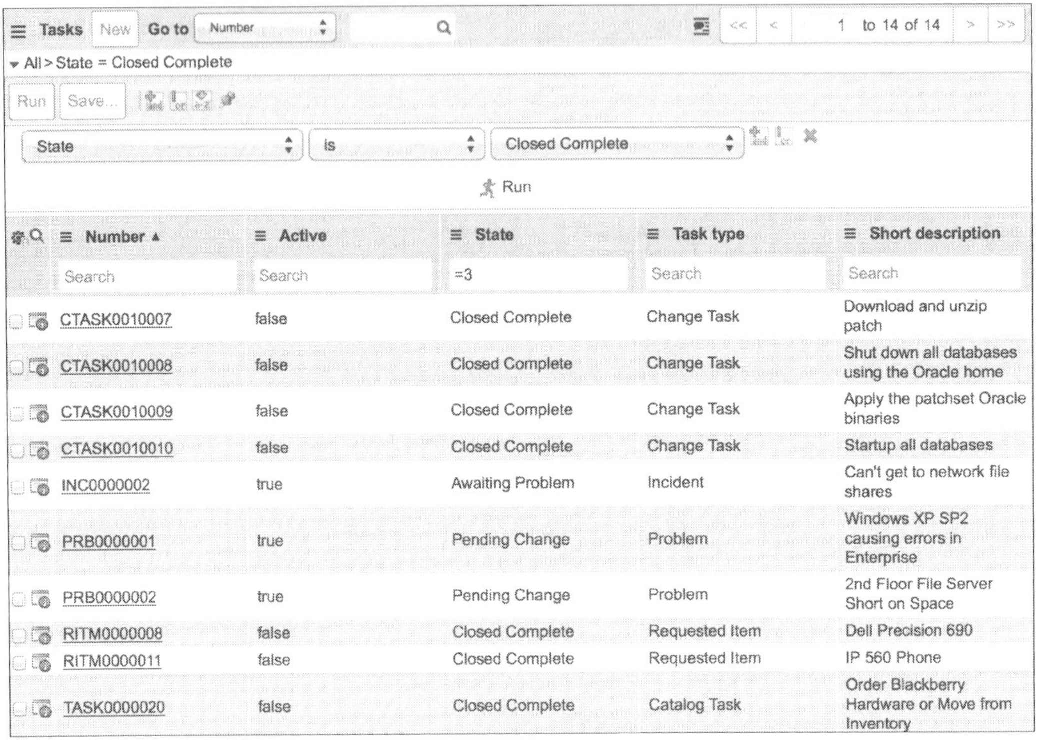

In order to highlight the impact, I've included the **Active** field in this list. As you can see, while many of the tasks (such as **Change Tasks**) and **Requested Items** have a state of **Closed Complete** and are inactive, tasks of type **Incident** and **Problem** are **Pending Change** and are Active. This is because the **Pending Change** state in these fields has a value of **3**. The **Closed** state of **Incident** has a value of **7**, the same as the task value of **Closed Skipped**!

[This can be a real problem if you heavily rely on the **Task** table to give an overview of all your tasks. You must create complex filters to achieve the result that you want.]

This is why this situation arises. Originally, ServiceNow did not allow table extensions to change the options in a choice field. This meant that if you extended the **Task** table, the states were fixed, unless you wanted to change them for every table. Therefore, some of the tables, such as **Incident** and **Problem**, have custom state fields such as `incident_state` and `problem_state`. This resulted in a situation where you then needed to synchronize `incident_state` to `state`, perhaps performing a translation, causing much confusion. Thankfully, having separate options is now possible, but it has left us with a heritage of frustratingly built applications.

Navigating between states

It is very frustrating when you want to do something, but inexplicably some system says **No**. Perhaps you are moving outside of the norm or are a power user - you know what you are doing is right, even if it is different. This is very often the case with states in a task. You may have a typical flow, moving from **New**, to **Open**, to **Closed Complete**, but are you allowed to move from **New** directly to **Closed Complete**?

> In order to get a more visual representation of the **State** field, you can add a Process Flow Formatter to the form. Find out more here:
> `http://wiki.servicenow.com/?title=Process_Flow_Formatter`

ServiceNow is a permissive platform by default. This extends to the states. It is a choice field that allows you to select whichever state you'd like. You simply choose the one you want from the drop-down selection list and click on **Save** or **Submit**.

However, sometimes this isn't quite right, for example, there may be a business decision that means that once you have closed the task, it should be completely read-only. Otherwise, it messes up reporting. If you reactivate tasks, your statistics may go backwards.

One way to fix this is to make the record read-only when the active flag is `false`. This is straightforward, as we'll find out when we discuss security in *Chapter 7, Securing Applications and Data*.

But what happens if you want to allow movement to **Closed Complete** only from the **Open** state? There are several ways to achieve this:

- Validate using a Business Rule with a script that uses `current.state.changes()` and check the `previous` and `current` values. This will work fine, but only works on the server side. It is frustrating to click on **Submit** and have the system tell you your previous update wasn't valid!
- Have a Client Script dynamically add and remove options from the state field. This is more user friendly, but as we've seen in the previous chapter, it can be overridden quite easily. We could combine this and the previous option, but it involves a fair amount of script. There are some solutions out there that involve a data-driven approach, letting you populate a table that gives each allowed combination, but this is a heavyweight option.
- My usual preference is to always make the state field read-only and then provide UI Actions to those which change the state for the user. This is secure, but does involve potentially quite a few buttons. I also believe it gives a more intuitive action, instead of clicking on the dropdown menu, selecting the option you want, and then clicking on **Save**, you just click on the relevant button.

  The biggest disadvantage is that UI Policy that makes a field mandatory on a state change is harder to implement since no fields are changing. One way is to create client scripts that detect which button you've clicked, use `g_form.setMandatory()` on the fields you want filled in, and then call `g_form.mandatoryCheck()` to determine if they are filled out.

> All of these options are achievable without scripting by using State Flows. It lets you specify which states are valid at each point and then create the Business Rules, UI Actions, and Client Scripts automatically. It will even make fields mandatory, visible or read-only, and add information to **Work notes**. Check out this wiki for more:
>
> `http://wiki.servicenow.com/?title=Using_State_Flows`

Ultimately, though, the design depends on how much freedom you wish to give the users of your application. If they need hand-holding, then a more controlled way to work is useful. But experienced users may become frustrated if they are prevented from achieving what they want in an efficient manner.

Creating room maintenance states

Let's change the default states to be a little more relevant for the Hotel application. It should represent when the outside repair team is required. Also, three different closed states are unnecessary.

1. Navigate to a **Maintenance** record and right-click on the **State** field. Choose **Personalize Choices**.

> You could use the **Show Choice List** option and do the work manually, but for extended tables, you need to be careful not to upset the default options. Use **Personalize Choices** to add and remove options, and **Show Choice List** if you need to change the value or labels of the options.

2. Remove **Closed Incomplete** and **Closed Skipped** and add a new option with the following details:
    - **New item text**: `External repair`
    - **Numeric value**: `10`

> It is a good idea to set numeric values above 10, since you then know they won't conflict with the default options. Be aware that the value is what is used to sort lists.

The choices should look as follows:

Although the team is trusted at Gardiner Hotels, some control is needed behind the **External repair** option. Since it will involve a financial outlay, this state should be tracked and controlled. So, setting values should only be possible after appropriate approvals.

> State Flows would remove the need for some of this scripting. But configuring this manually illustrates the steps.

Enforcing on the server

To make our server secure, create a new Business Rule with the following details:

- **Name**: `Secure External repair state`
- **Table**: `Maintenance [u_maintenance]`
- **Insert**: `<ticked>`
- **Update**: `<ticked>`
- **Filter condition**: Enter the following filter conditions:
    - `State - changes to - External repair`
    - `Approval - is not - Approved`
- **Abort action**: `<ticked>`

The condition means the Business Rule will run if a user tries to set the **State** to **External repair** without the **Approval** field being set to **Approved**. It simply stops the update and ensures the database remains unchanged, just like `current.setAbortAction(true)`.

Adding a Reference Qualifier

Right now, a user could manually select Cornell Hotel Services. To fix that, let's filter out the group entirely using a Reference Qualifier. And for extra validation, let's show only the **Maintenance** groups.

> A reference qualifier only controls the user interface. Client Scripts, for example, can still set whatever group they wish.

Go to the Dictionary entry for the **Assignment group** field on the **Maintenance** table and create a new **Dictionary Override**.

- **Table**: Maintenance [u_maintenance]
- **Override reference qualifier**: <ticked>
- **Reference qualifier**: javascript:'u_maintenance=true^name!='+gs.getProperty('maintenance.external_group')

This is an Advanced Reference Qualifier, as mentioned in *Chapter 1, ServiceNow Foundations*. It uses a short server-side JavaScript snippet to stop the user from picking a group with a name that is saved in the property. In addition, it only shows groups where the Maintenance field is ticked.

Test it out by trying to pick a group through the reference field. Only **Maintenance** and **Housekeeping** should be available. If you are having trouble, ensure the groups have the **Maintenance** field ticked. The following screenshot shows the reference field that contains only the two values, **Maintenance** and **Housekeeping**:

> The Reference Qualifier controls the **Assignment group** field via the user interface. However, it doesn't stop updates via web services, nor via a Client Script. Therefore, if the data or process is particularly sensitive, write a Business Rule, ACL, or Data Policy to protect the data. It is good practice to have multiple layers of security.

Removing states with Client Scripts

Next, make the option unavailable in the State choice list. Make a new Client Script with the following data:

- **Name**: Remove External Repair state
- **Type**: onLoad
- **Table**: Maintenance [u_maintenance]
- **Script**:

```
function onLoad() {
  if (g_form.getValue('state') != '10')
    g_form.removeOption('state', 10);
}
```

This script uses the `GlideForm` object to remove the **External repair** option from the choice list, but only if the state is not already selected.

> This will only take effect in the form view. List editing the State field will be unaffected. The state could also still be set with web services or other client scripts.

Automating an assignment based on state

There are several ways to set the **Assignment group** and **Assigned to** fields. We could use Business Rules or Workflow, for example. But there are built-in ways to do this without any scripting.

Using Data Lookup

Data Lookup is a way to populate information based on rules. It works by storing a matrix of several combinations in a Data Lookup table that you build. When a record or field is inserted or updated, the platform searches this table for matches. If one is found, data is set.

For example, a Data Lookup table could contain rules about the type of **Maintenance** request that has come in. If it is about a room that needs refreshing, then it could be assigned to Housekeeping. If the air conditioning was broken, it would go to Cornell Hotel Services.

Data Lookup works on whole field values and only on a single table. Inheritance is not supported, so rules on the **Task** table don't apply to **Maintenance**. However, one clever trick is that the matching and assignment is done both client and server side, so fields are immediately and dynamically populated, but it will also be enforced if necessary.

> For more information on Data Lookup, check out the wiki:
> `http://wiki.servicenow.com/?title=Data_Lookup_and_Record_Matching_Support`

Setting the Assignment group with Assignment Rules

There is a simpler method to set Assignment Rules to the Assignment group that doesn't involve creating a Data Lookup table. Assignment Rules uses a condition builder to specify when it should run. If it matches, then it'll either populate the **Assigned to** and **Assignment group** fields with a hardcoded value or you can use script. We have got the group we want to use in a property, so this option is perfect.

1. Navigate to **System Policy** > **Rules** > **Assignment** and click on **New**. Use the following:
    - **Name**: `Assign to External Team`
    - **Table**: `Maintenance [u_maintenance]`
    - **Conditions**: Add the following conditions:
        - `Approval - is - Approved`
        - `State - is - External repair`
    - **Script**: `gs.getProperty('maintenance.external_group');`

    Once saved, the Assignment Rule will be active. When the condition matches, the script will set the **Assignment group** field to the team specified in the property. Assignment Rules only work on the server, so the record will need to be saved before the change in assignment will take effect. Also, Assignment Rules only run if the **Assigned to** and **Assignment group** fields are empty - it won't overwrite an existing value.

2. Now, make a second Assignment rule to give a default value for the **Assignment group** field.
    - **Name**: `Default assignment`
    - **Table**: `Maintenance [u_maintenance]`
    - **Group**: `Maintenance`

> Assignment Rules will run in the sequence of the **Order** field, smallest first. The **Order** field is not on the form by default (though you can, of course, add it), but is shown on the list. Try list editing it.

Drag-and-drop automation with Graphical Workflow

Chapter 2, Server-side Control, discussed how Business Rules validate data and automate functionality. But as always in ServiceNow, there is another way. Graphical Workflow provides a drag-and-drop interface to quickly and easily run a series of automated steps, much like an automated flowchart. It is heavily used in Orchestration, reviewed in *Chapter 11, Automating Your Data Center*.

Workflows consist of blocks called **activities**. An activity has outputs, usually representing the result of the activity. The outputs then connect to the next activity. The connections are called **transitions**. More than one activity can be running at any point in time, as a single activity may have multiple output transitions. The outputs may be conditional; you often want a different path for failure than you want for success. You could then choose to retry or simply give up and send a notification.

A workflow uses **stages** to summarize progress. Each activity can be associated with a stage, and the value of the stage is copied into a field of your choice. A stage gives the user an indication of how the workflow is moving, letting them know what is happening at the moment. Most of the time, the stage of the workflow is copied into the state field.

> If you have several complex workflows, each following different paths, you may want to create a new field that has a type of Workflow. Use this as the output of your stage and it will dynamically contain the right options.
>
> To learn more about stages, visit the wiki: `http://wiki.servicenow.com/?title=Workflow_Stages`.

Running a workflow

Just like much of the other functionality in ServiceNow, a Workflow is set against a table with a condition. When the condition matches, the workflow runs against that record.

A workflow is in one of two states: **checked out** or **published**. For a workflow to run for everyone, it must be published, while if you wish to edit the activities or transitions, it must be checked out.

The majority of workflows last for some time, often as long as the record is active. The platform may run several activities and pause until a task is closed, an approval decision made, or a field changed.

Workflows are best suited for very controlled processes that step through activities in a linear, ordered manner, especially if there is automation. Tasks that jump from step to step, giving the users a lot of control with regard to what to do next, are not a great match. While you can have multiple branches and routing logic, it quickly becomes too complex to handle successfully, and your workflow becomes a nest of conditions and transitions. In such circumstances, you must consider carefully if a workflow is the right approach - you may want to use Business Rules to accomplish the same functionality with script.

It is also possible to run multiple workflows at the same time. This is appropriate for automating short, specific flows, but be careful not to have hundreds running against each record. Each workflow instance does consume resources, and is far more intensive than a simple Business Rule.

Exploring under the covers

When a workflow starts up, it creates a record in the **Workflow Contexts** table. This contains reference fields to the record that started it, what stage it is currently at, and which Workflow version it is using. Each time you check out a workflow, it creates a new version, stored in the **Workflow Version** table. Linked to this record are copies of all the activities and transitions that are used in this workflow.

> There is a good overview of Graphical Workflow on this wiki:
> `http://wiki.servicenow.com/?title=Workflow_Concepts`

By navigating to **Workflow** > **Active Contexts** you can see the running workflows. You get some helpful UI Actions, like **Show Timeline** and **Show Workflow**. The latter shows the workflow interface, but in a read-only fashion. The activity headers are color-coded: green for running and blue for finished, which gives you a great appreciation of how the workflow is progressing.

The activities themselves are stored in **Workflow** > **Activity Definitions**. They consist of a script that extends `WFActivityHandler` with functions such as `initialize` (which run when the workflow starts) and `onExecute` (which is called when the activity is run). The script has access to variables, which are displayed when you add the activity to the workflow. Perhaps the simplest activity is **Run Script**. It has a single variable, called `script`, and the workflow definition script simply runs `eval` on the contents.

> Sometimes, you may want to alter the activity definitions. Always copy the original before making your changes to ensure that upgrades are more successful.

Appreciating activities

The activities available to the workflow are listed on the extreme right pane of the Graphical Workflow editor. Some are dependent on which table the workflow is running against. For example, task activities are only available to a workflow on a table extended from **Task**.

> Some more useful activities are discussed next, but a full list is available on the ServiceNow wiki:
> `http://wiki.servicenow.com/?title=Using_Workflow_Activities#Adding_an_Activity_to_the_Workflow`

Useful activities that are available are given as follows:

- The **Approvals** group gives several activities that are mostly only available to **Task** tables. Workflow allows complex scenarios to be determined using the **Approval Coordinator**. The **Group Approvals** functionality allows us to involve multiple people easily. The next section dives into this topic in much more detail.
- The **Conditions** group allows logic to be made in the workflow through the **If** and **Switch** activities. By looking at the value of fields, the Workflow engine can go down different routes. Alternatively, you can add conditions that are based on the activities themselves by right-clicking on the activity and choosing **Add Condition**.
- **Wait for condition** will hold the flow until a field changes to a desired value. This is very useful in a branched workflow, perhaps to detect a canceled state.

> **Wait for Condition** will only check its condition after the record is updated in the database. Unless the record is saved, changing a field on a form will not trigger anything.

- Another way to hold up a workflow is through a **Timer**. It is very flexible, offering percentages, scripts, schedules, and time zones to work out how long it should wait. This activity is not dependent on the record updating.
- You can send out e-mail notifications with the **Create Event** notification. Don't use the **Notification** activity directly, since it is very confusing to try to find the right definition for an e-mail message when it is in a Workflow step.

> *Chapter 5, Events, Notifications, and Reporting*, discusses e-mail notifications in much more detail.

- **Create Task** is available for **Task** table workflows. It will create another task and link it to the current record through the parent field. If **Wait for completion** is ticked, the workflow will pause until the task is inactive. If you then add an exit condition, you can route on the success (or otherwise) of that task. The utilities section brings you **Script** activities, the ability to easily send **Rest** and **Soap** messages, and other helpful options like **Turnstiles**, **Branch**, and **Join**. These three options help with workflow branching, and having multiple activities valid at the same time. For example, Turnstiles is useful when retrying something several times while ensuring that the workflow doesn't enter an infinite loop.

> Workflow activities run just like the *before* Business Rule. You don't need to call `current.update()` in a script.

- **Sub-workflows** allows you to call other workflows. It can return values, letting you compartmentalize and separate functionality for easy reuse.

Using data-driven workflows

Since workflows are so powerful, with the ability to run scripts, any updates to them are usually part of the testing regime to ensure mistakes aren't made.

> The functionality and strategies used to manage testing is discussed in *Chapter 9, Moving Scripts with Clones, Update Sets, and Upgrades.*

To ensure that changes can be made quickly in production, a common strategy is to create data tables that are used by the Workflow or use platform functionality to drive the process. For example, what should the **Assignment group** be for a new task? If this information is hardcoded into the Workflow, it is difficult to change. Instead, store it in a property or use the Data Lookup functionality to populate the values.

Another common store of information is the CMDB. The Configuration Management Database (discussed in *Chapter 11, Automating Your Data Center*) is often used in implementations and **Assignment group** information could be stored there.

> Alternatively, a common and useful script for the **Create Task** activity is to copy the **Assignment group** from the parent task:

```
task.assignment_group = current.assignment_group;
```

Approving tasks

An important step in many applications is getting the approval to proceed. This may be due to a financial outlay, risk to the business, or simply getting the validation that you are doing the right thing.

There are several ways to get approval in ServiceNow. Workflow is the most powerful. For very simple scenarios, however, Approval Rules may be sufficient (available under **System Policy** > **Rules** > **Approval**). These allow you to hardcode a specific user or group or use a script to determine who will be asked to make a decision if the condition matches.

When an **Approval** record is generated, it is always associated with a single person. That person has a choice, to approve or reject. The decision of that person is taken into account when deciding what should happen next.

> It is common to want more options in an approval request, such as **Need more information** or **Defer decision**. This may stem from the language of **Reject**, which should mean 'I don't support this in its current form'. A rejection in an approval does not necessarily mean the whole request should be cancelled. It just gives an alternative option to **Approve**.

If you ask a group of people for approval, each person in that group will have an Approval record generated for them. A **Group Approval** activity in Workflow gives you several options to determine what happens during an approval request. This includes:

- **An approval from each group**: if there are several groups asked, we need a positive decision from every group. We should wait until we get that.
- **An approval from any group**: it is good enough that one person approves.
- **An approval from everyone**: it must be unanimous.
- **The first response from each group**: whoever answers first makes the decision for that group.
- **The first response from any group**: whoever answers first makes the decision for everyone.

If anyone rejects, you can decide what happens:

- Mark the overall decision as rejected.
- Wait to see what others say. Majority may rule.

Alternatively, by using an Approval Coordinator, you can even make the decision through script. Maybe you want a majority decision—first to 50 percent wins!

Making the decision

When an approval request is sent out, the approver is sent an e-mail. In the e-mail are several links: one to view the approval request, another to see the record that is being approved, and two further links that open up a new e-mail - one to approve and one to reject. The approver therefore has a choice to approve via the web interface or using e-mail.

> The next chapter, *Chapter 5, Events, Notifications, and Reporting*, which looks at notifications in more detail, explores how this is actually achieved.

The web interface contains two form UI actions: **Approve** and **Reject**. There is a client script that detects if you click on the **Reject** button and makes the comments field mandatory. However, a server-side script does not back this up. So, if you reject an approval request using an e-mail, you are not forced to leave a comment!

> This is a great example of how you must think about all the methods of interaction, not just the web interface.

Understanding what you are approving

Approval records are stored in the **Approvals** [`sysapproval_approver`] table. The table contains a special reference field that can point to any table. This means a workflow can create user approvals for any type of record.

This means that there is a single central store of all approval requests in ServiceNow. It may be an order for some new hardware or, as in our situation, a desire to bring in a team to fix a leaky tap in a hotel room.

This generic approach, although great for consistency and having convenience for the approval user, presents some challenges for the UI. If every approval request is handled the same, how can the approver know the specific details of the request? When you approve an order, you want to know how much it'll cost. When you approve a maintenance request, you need to know what's wrong. How do we show the relevant information?

In order to solve this conundrum, the Approval form has a formatter included, called **Approval Summarizer**. This pulls information from other tables to present relevant information in one place.

If you navigate to **System UI** > **UI Macros**, you can filter the list to show all the records that start with `approval_summarizer`. There is a specific UI Macro for each table that needs a custom summary. The name of the table adds a suffix to the name. If there is no specific UI Macro, the default is used instead, which embeds the pop-up summary window in the form instead.

> Type in `approval_summarizer%` into the **Go to Name** box on the UI Macro list. The percentage sign after the search term means **Starts With**, while as a prefix it means **Ends With**.

Asking for approval for the repair team

When a big maintenance job comes about, we need to call in the experts. In order to understand costs, we want to put a streamlined approval process in place. We'll do this using Graphical Workflow.

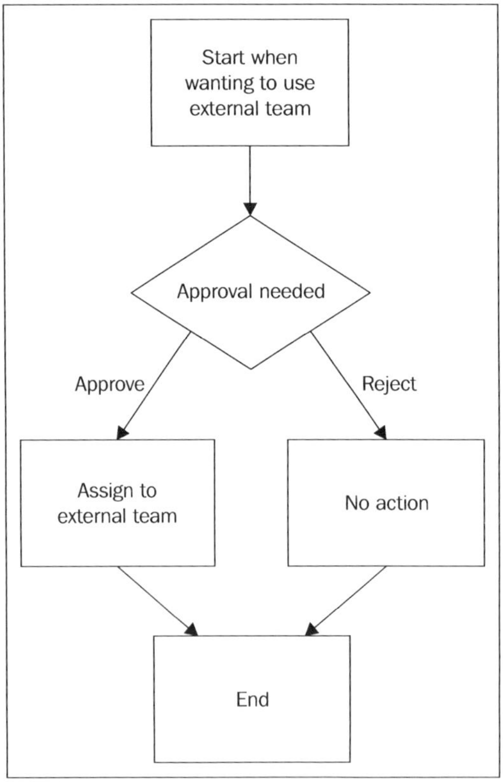

Performing the approval

Let's create the Workflow. The Workflow will create an approval request for the manager of the group, letting them decide whether a **Maintenance** task should be assigned to the external Cornell Hotel Services group.

Navigate to **Workflow** > **Workflow Editor** to launch the Graphical Workflow Editor. Click on **New**. Use these details:

- **Name**: `Ask approval for external team`
- **Table**: `Maintenance [u_maintenance]`
- **If condition matches**: `Run the workflow`

  Condition: `Approval - is - Requested`

> There are three options:
>
> - **-- None --** means the workflow will not automatically run, but will only be triggered through scripts or other workflows.
> - **Run if no other workflows matched yet** won't allow multiple running workflows. The order field is useful here.
> - The default **Run the workflow** simply starts the workflow when the condition matches.

When **Submit** is clicked on, an empty workflow canvas with the `Begin` and `End` activities is set out on the screen.

1. Firstly, add the **Approval – User** activity. Drag it from the **Approvals** group into the workflow or double-click to add it automatically. We want to send the request to the manager of the group:
   - **Name**: `Manager approval`
   - For **Users**, use the field selector to dot-walk to the manager of the Assignment group and the manager of the parent of the Assignment group.

> This strategy of adding the manager of the parent and the group works because we know that one of the three groups we added will be the Assignment group, and only one has a manager.

2. Add a **Set Values** activity from the **Utilities** group:
    - **Name**: `Rejected`
    - **Set these values**: `Approval - Rejected`
3. Add another **Set Values** activity:
    - **Name**: `Approved`
    - **Set these values**: Add the following conditions:

      `Approval - Approved`

      `State - External repair`

      `Assignment group - <blank>`

    The status fields of **Approval** and **State** are set to the correct values and the **Assignment group** field is blanked out. This forces the Assignment Rule to run.

4. Remove all the transitions between **Begin** and **End** and then create the transitions:
    - From **Begin** to **Approval - User**
    - From **Approval - User: Approved** to **Set Values: Approved**
    - From **Approval - User: Rejected** to **Set Values: Rejected**
    - From **Set Values: Rejected** to **End**
    - From **Set Values: Approved** to **End**
5. Arrange the activities so the diagram is clear and then click on **Publish** through the gear menu.

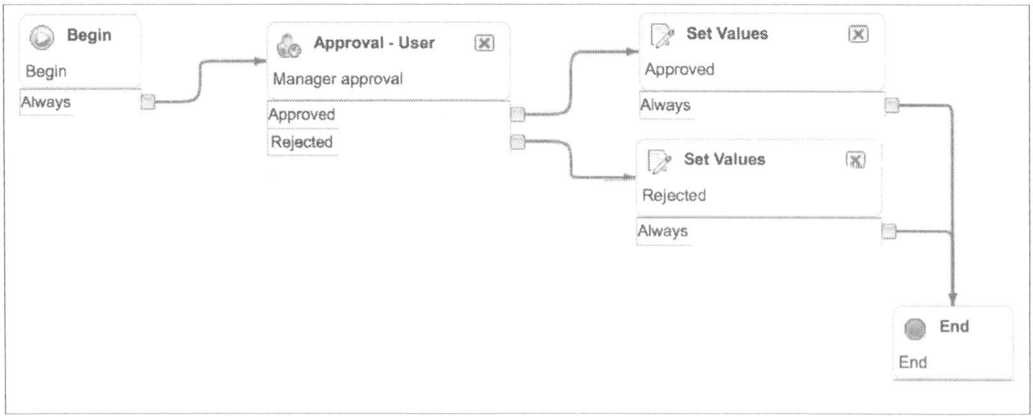

Starting up the workflow

The workflow starts when the **Approval** field is set to **Requested**. But the **Approval** field is read-only in the **Maintenance** form. Create a new UI Action to set the value:

- **Name**: Send to External
- **Table**: Maintenance [u_maintenance]
- **Form button**: <ticked>
- **Condition**: current.active && current.canWrite()

  The condition ensures the button only shows up when the task is active and the user has permission to write to the table.

- **Script**:

```
if (current.approval == 'approved') {
  current.assignment_group = '';
  current.state = 10;
} else {
  current.approval = 'requested';
}
current.update();
```

The script checks to see if approval has already been granted. If so, it doesn't run the workflow again, but instead sets the state and clears the **Assignment group** field, in the same way as the script in the workflow. Otherwise, it triggers the workflow to set by setting **Approval** to **Requested**.

> Of course, the **Assignment group** field could be set directly, using code like `current.assignment_group.setDisplayValue(gs.getProperty('maintenance.external_group'));`.
>
> But it is good practice to have a single place for setting fields like assignment. We are using Assignment Rules. Otherwise, it is confusing to determine which function is setting what and when!

Monitoring progress

When a Workflow is running, it creates an entry in the Workflow Contexts table, available under **Workflow** > **Live Workflows** > **Active Contexts**. This lets you visualize progress of the workflow. But this is hard to get to. Instead, the platform provides us a very useful UI Action that gives a one-click visualization.

1. Navigate to it by going to the UI Actions list and creating a filter to find the **Show Workflow** entry against the **Change Request** [`change_request`] table. Change the fields as shown here:
    - **Table**: `Global [global]`
2. Use **Insert and Stay** to make a copy.
3. Finally, add the **Approvers** Related List to the **Maintenance** form.
4. To test, create a **Maintenance** record and click on the **Send to External** button.

Use the **Show Workflow** link to visualize progress, and as an admin, approve it on Howard's behalf:

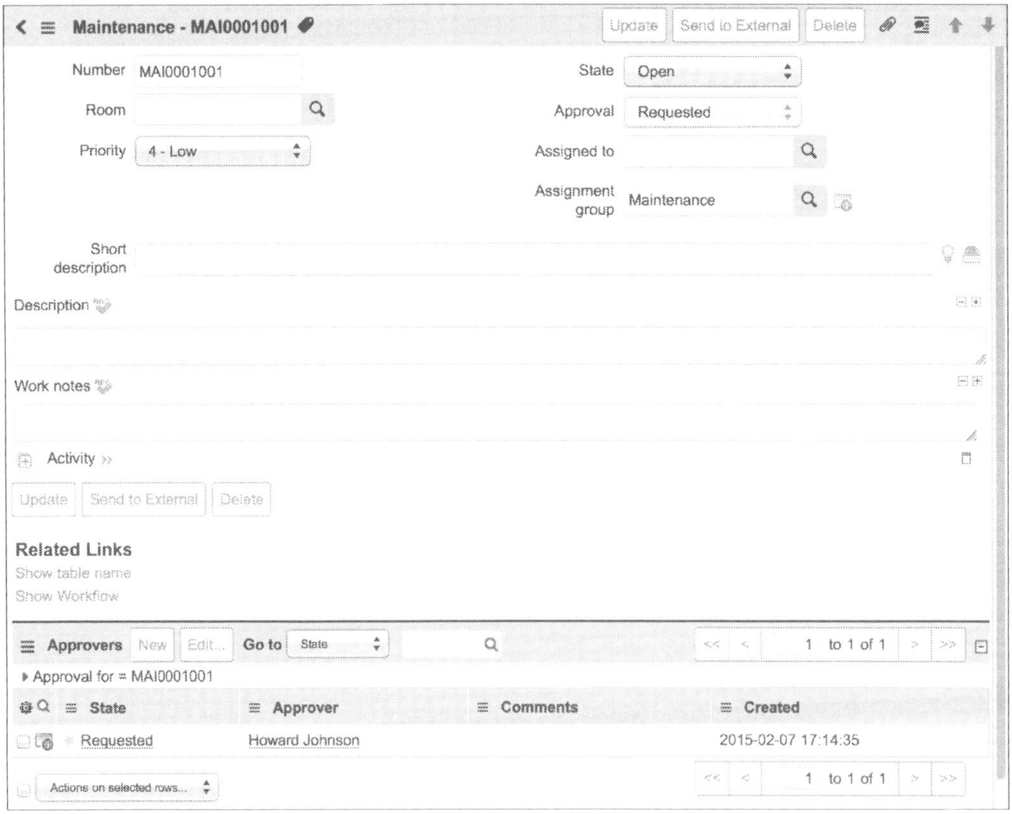

Using the Service Catalog

The **Service Catalog** in ServiceNow is often the backbone of an IT portal. It makes it easy for end users to submit requests to fulfillers by providing a one-stop shop for ordering new equipment, creating tasks, and monitoring their progress with a simple and straightforward interface. It is designed to reduce distraction and be similar to systems that they are already familiar with.

The **Service Catalog** is split into two main parts - a shopping style interface (with a cart, items to order, and a more graphical interface than we've seen so far) and a fulfillment backend that uses workflow to control how the orders are processed. Often, the two are conflated, even though they are aimed at two different audiences and achieve very different purposes.

The different types of Catalog Items

The **Service Catalog** frontend can do more than just create orders. When you navigate to **Self Service** > **Service Catalog**, you will see **Catalog Items** organized into categories. A Catalog Item is an item that provides some sort of service to the end user, and as such there are several different types:

- A standard **Catalog Item** is an item that has a workflow attached. It is often a mechanism to order something new—like a new keyboard or laptop—but may also be a request for a service. Once ordered, the items are processed using the Request Fulfillment tables. Unfortunately, there is no distinction in ServiceNow between an orderable Catalog Item and the more specialized alternatives listed here, so I will refer to these as **Catalog Request Items**.

> Catalog Request Items could use Execution Plans instead of Workflow, but this is an older, less powerful alternative. In almost every situation, Workflow is the better choice.

- A **Content Item** can be a simple HTML page or a link to a Knowledge Base article or any other URL. It cannot be ordered or manipulated by the end user but does give read-only information.
- An **Order Guide** is a mechanism to order multiple Catalog Request Items. By answering some initial questions, the order guide can bundle together several Catalog Request Items and put them all in the cart.

- A **Record Producer** creates a record in a table of your choice. It provides an alternative friendly interface, which means that end users do not need to see the standard form. Record Producers could create **Reservations**, **Guests**, **Maintenance** tasks, or any other record, which in ServiceNow means anything!

One of the defining features of a Catalog Item is that it is more graphical, with pictures and icons for each item, and HTML-formatted descriptions that allow the use of colors, fonts, and more. Together, these elements provide a more appealing interface than the typical stark form.

Creating a Record Producer

At Gardiner Hotels, it should be easy for our guests to communicate with us. Occasionally, there might be a problem, and it should be sorted out right away. Of course, our guests can pick up the phone and talk to someone at Reception, but we also want to give them the choice of doing it via the new Guest Portal we are designing. Let's build a Record Producer to make it easier to create a **Maintenance** task.

Navigate to **System Definition** > **Tables** and find the **Maintenance** table. Click on the **Add to Service Catalog** link at the bottom of the table definition. It gives an interface that quickly starts and does much of the manual work.

> It could be made manually through **Service Catalog** > **Record Producers**.

The values that need to be entered are as follows:

- **Name**: `Room Maintenance`
- **Short Description**: `Submit a Room Maintenance issue`
- **Category**: `Can We Help You?`

Pick **Short Description**, **Room**, and **Description** from the slush bucket.

> These fields have variables created with the same name as them. When a **Record Producer** creates a record, it copies the contents of variables into fields of the same name.

Click on **Save and Open** to see the final outcome:

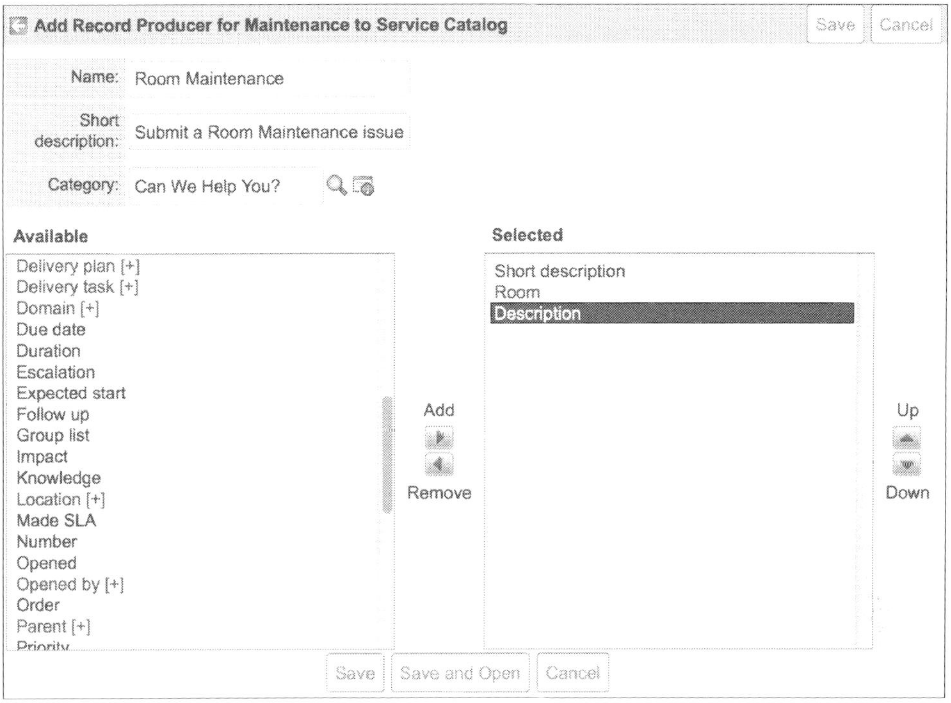

Adding more information

The Record Producer that has been created is ready to go. But a few changes could be made to make it friendlier:

- **Description**: `Are you having problems with your room? Please fill out this form, and click the Submit button to send through a maintenance alert. One of our team will be with you right away to fix the issue!`
- **Script**:

```
gs.addInfoMessage('Your maintenance request has been received.
The reference number is ' + current.number + '. A member of the
team will contact you shortly!');
```

This simple code has a single purpose; when the **Record Producer** is submitted, it will display an informational message on the screen, giving the user some feedback. The `current` object is available and references the record you are making. The `producer` object gives access to variables and other data, though that isn't used here.

Additionally, let's take full advantage of the layout to give better text for the variables. Click on each variable in turn in the **Variables** Related List. Use these details:

- **Short Description**:
    - **Question:** What issue are you facing? Please give a brief summary
    - **Mandatory**: <ticked>
- **Room**:
    - **Mandatory**: <ticked>
- **Description**:
    - **Question**: Please enter a longer description that outlines the issue you are having.
    - **Show help**: <ticked>
    - **Help text:** For example, which tap is leaking?

Routing the submitted request with templates

The next step is to tell the platform to route any of these requests to the Housekeeping team created earlier. An Assignment Rule sets the Maintenance team by default, but the majority of end user requests may be about cleaning. There are a number of ways to send the request to them instead, such as Workflow, more Assignment Rules, and other options, but we'll use a very simple template. This means it can be edited easily whenever necessary directly in a production instance instead of altering the script.

> A template is an easy way to fill out fields of a form, like a typing macro. If you have the template_editor role, you can right-click on a form header to see the **Templates** menu.

Navigate to **System Definition** > **Templates** and click on **New**. Use the following data:

- **Name**: Assign to Maintenance
- **Table**: Maintenance [u_maintenance]
- **Template**: Add the following value:
    - **Assignment group**: Maintenance

> The data in a template is actually stored in the database as a string, in the same format as an encoded query. This has the `field1=value1^field2=value2` format. This data is displayed in the user interface in a much more accessible manner.

To see what this will do, create a new **Maintenance** task. From the form header, select **Templates** > **Apply Template** > **Assign to Maintenance**. You'll see that the **Assignment group** field gets filled out. This is not very useful for a single field, but for lots of information that is commonly entered, this can be a real timesaver!

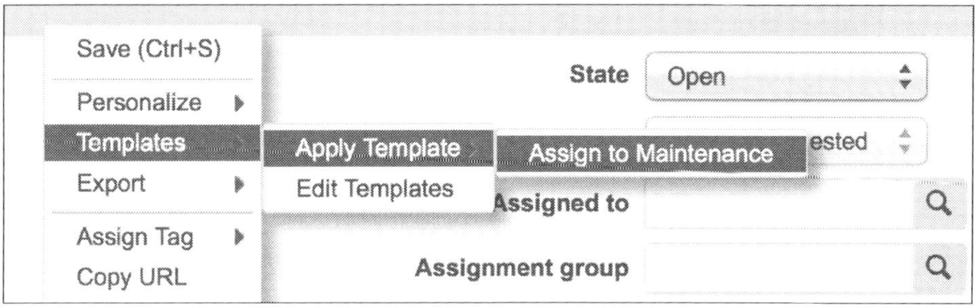

> A template is available to you if your user record is in the **User** field of the template, if one of your groups is in the template, or if the global checkbox is ticked.

Navigate back to the record producer by going to **Service Catalog** > **Record Producers**. Look for **Room Maintenance** and then, in the **Template** field, type in `Assign to Maintenance`.

Testing the Record Producer

Try out the Record Producer and report an issue about a room. You can do either of these:

- Click on the **Try It** button in the Record Producer
- Navigate to **Self-Service** > **Service Catalog** > **Can We Help You?** and then choose **Room Maintenance**

Fill out the form with any details you'd like and then click on **Submit**:

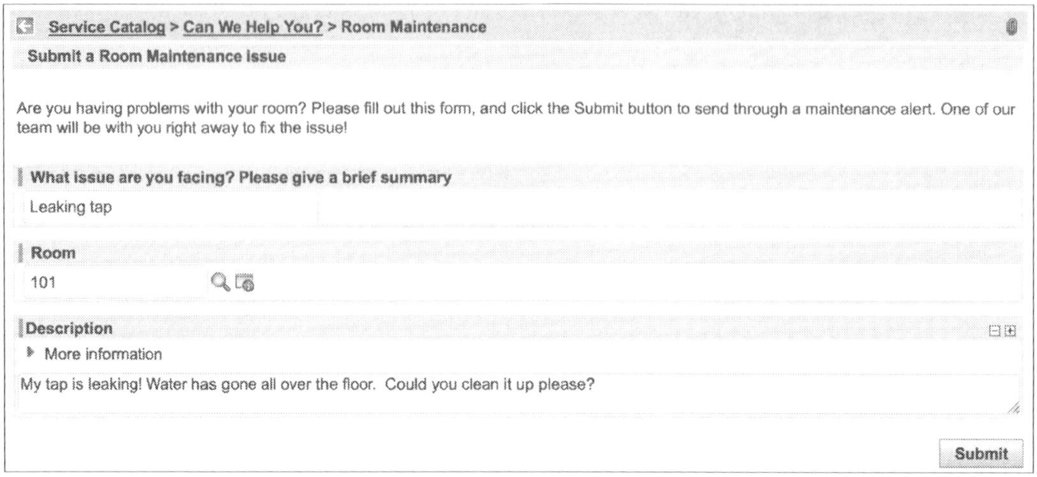

You will get an informational message while the record has been made in the background. It should be assigned to the **Housekeeping** team. If you impersonate a member of the **Maintenance** team, you will see that it shows when you click on **My Work**.

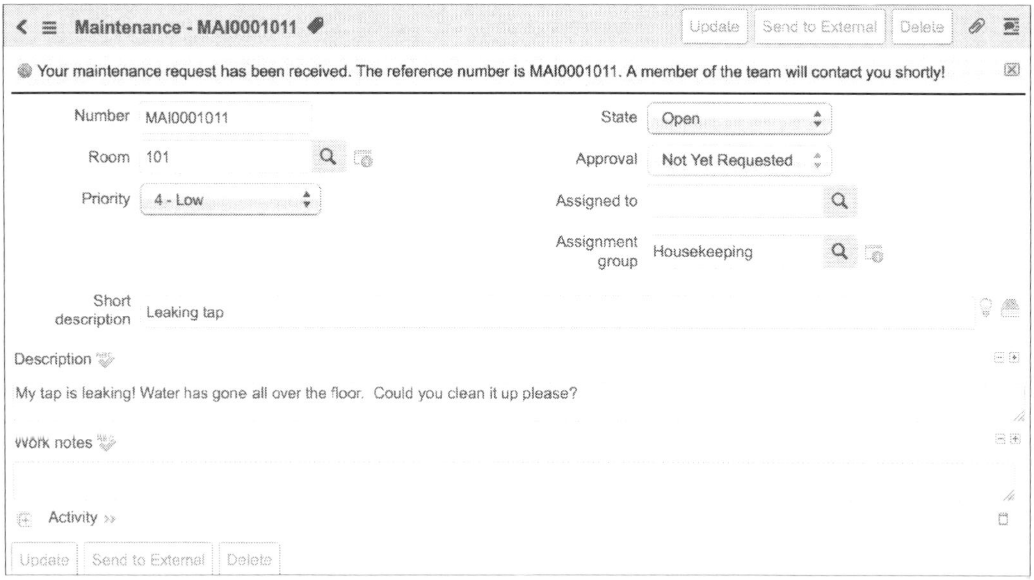

[A Record Producer does not have any option to use the shopping cart. The cart is only used for Request Fulfillment.]

Understanding the data behind the Service Catalog

Service Catalog items are stored in the `sc_cat_item` table. The other types, like Record Producers, extend this table. They all contain a description of the item, its title, and perhaps how much it costs. For **Service Request Items**, there is a reference field to a Workflow. The Workflow is started once the item is ordered to control its fulfillment.

A Catalog Item is almost always associated with **variables**. Variables are the questions that are presented to the user while they are using the **Service Catalog**. They give a means for the end user to provide extra information and choices. In that sense, they are similar to fields on a table, but their implementation is very different.

As we saw in *Chapter 1, ServiceNow Foundations*, ServiceNow is built on a foundation of data. The vast majority of applications are built on top of a table that stores its data, and to which the Business Rules, Client Scripts, and Security Rules are all associated. When viewing a form, you are seeing a database record. A list shows multiple records.

The **Service Catalog** does not use the same foundations. Instead, **Service Catalog** items are displayed much more dynamically, using multiple sources of information. Note that variables are stored in the **Variables** [`item_option_new`] table. Each variable has a **Name** (which is used in scripting), a label entitled **Question**, and a **Type** (which is similar to the one for fields). You can create reference variables that point to a record in a table, date variables, and more, including radio button choice variables that are not available as standard in a form.

Variables can either be associated with a single Catalog Item or with a **Variable Set**. A **Variable Set** is a reusable grouping of variables that has a many-to-many relationship with Variables and Catalog Items. Once in a **Variable Set**, a variable can then be associated with several Catalog Items.

When the Catalog Item is displayed in the **Service Catalog** interface, the system combines the information from these tables. Every Catalog Item, of which there may be hundreds or even thousands, may have different variables and thus different prompts for the end user, and different workflows to fulfill the request. Each Catalog Item can have its own distinct and unique visual identity.

Comparing records and Catalog Items

The difference in the data model means that many of the concepts explored in the first few chapters don't directly apply to the **Service Catalog**.

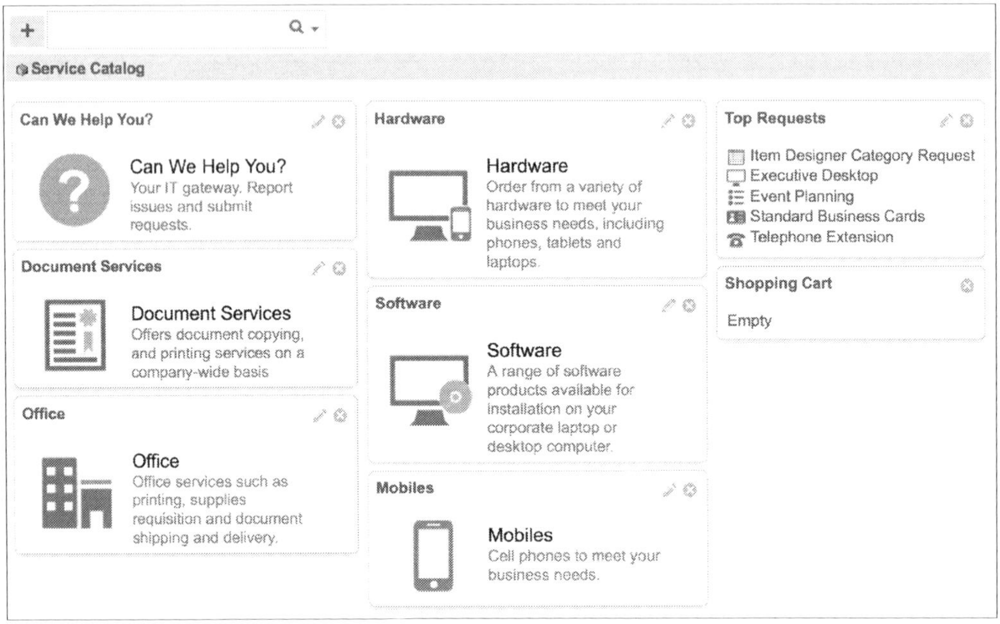

The following screenshot shows the **Catalog Request Item** page for **Google Nexus 7**:

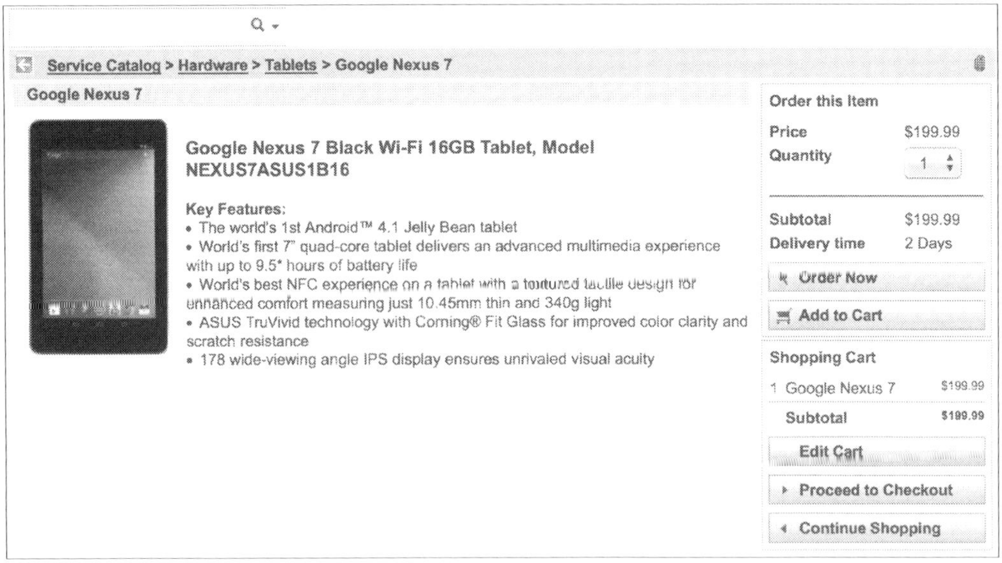

The following screenshot shows the next window that appears after an order is placed:

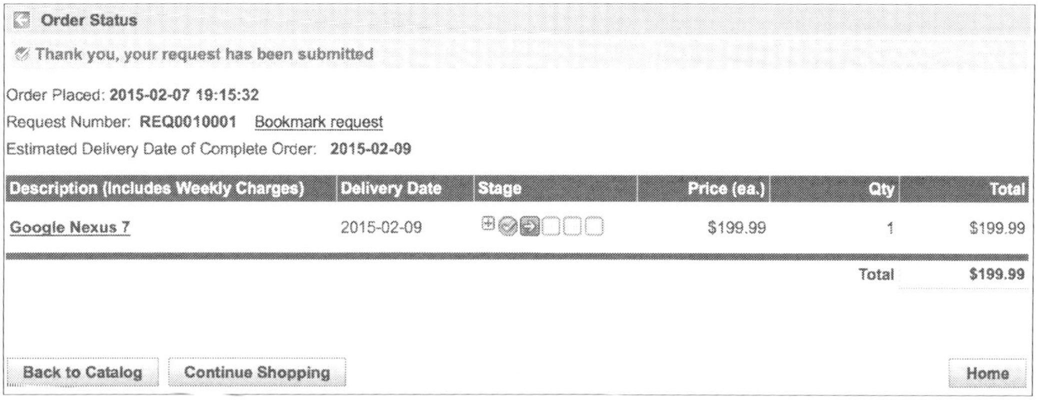

Immediately, you notice that the screen layout is not the same as a form, with the variables being organized and displayed in a different manner. The designers at ServiceNow often compare it to a shopping website like Amazon. There is a shopping cart that lets you collect items together.

Business Rules do not run against a Catalog Item, and Access Control Rules (explored in *Chapter 7, Securing Applications and Data*) are not applied. **Catalog Client Scripts** and **Catalog UI Policy** are similar to their form-based cousins, but are specially adapted. They are attached to a Catalog Item or a Variable Set instead of a table.

> Because of the structural differences of variables, reporting is much more challenging. This is one example of how the **Service Catalog** does not work quite the same as other areas. Nonetheless, the wiki gives some options:
>
> `http://wiki.servicenow.com/?title=Reporting_on_Service_Catalog_Variables`

Understanding Request Fulfilment

The Request Fulfillment functionality in ServiceNow is a way to deal with requests created from a Catalog Request Item submitted through the **Service Catalog**. This could be anything from a laptop order, to a facilities complaint, to asking HR a question. However, as we've already explored, the **Service Catalog** can provide an interface to any other table through a Record Producer, such as our **Maintenance** request. That allows us to build a more custom system.

So, which should we use?

- **Request Fulfillment**: Catalog Request Items are useful for lower volume, simpler requests, or for requests that are very aligned to orders. Workflow is used to create tasks or approvals.

> The **Catalog Item Designer** is a great way to quickly build out independent Catalog Request Items in a guided manner. Since it doesn't use Variable Sets or custom workflows, it doesn't allow reusability but instead allows teams of people to maintain hundreds or even thousands of Catalog Request Items directly in a production environment with minimal training. Check out this wiki article for more:
>
> `http://wiki.servicenow.com/?title=Catalog_Item_Designer`

- **Custom table**: Record Producers create a record in any table you specify. The use of a dedicated table gives more flexibility around custom fields, Business Rules, and other task functionalities. This gives the ability to implement the data structure that is most appropriate for the application. It is the more powerful option, but does require more configuration.

> The **App Creator** bundles together lots of technologies to create rich custom applications. The Maintenance functionality built out so far is a great example of a simple application, letting guests interact with staff quickly and easily. Check out the wiki for more:
>
> `http://wiki.servicenow.com/?title=Creating_Custom_Applications`

As your use of ServiceNow grows, you may decide to migrate from Request Fulfillment to a dedicated data table. If you start dealing with HR questions using Request Fulfillment, you may decide to use a dedicated table in the future, letting you categorize and manage your tickets in whatever way you'd prefer.

Checking out

As the user is browsing Catalog Request Items, they can decide to put them in a cart if they want order them. The checkout process takes this data and starts the Request Fulfillment process. The platform keeps a record of who is browsing the **Service Catalog** in the **Shopping Cart** [`sc_cart`] table. These records have a relationship to the **Item** [`sc_cart_item`] table, which references the answers the user has given to the variables and what the Catalog Item it is.

> There are quite a few system properties that control the **Service Catalog**. One includes having a two-stage checkout, which gives you a final opportunity to edit the variables and confirm any cost before submission. Have a look under **Service Catalog** > **Catalog Policy** > **Properties**.

Checking out is a conversion exercise for the instance, turning the cart into actionable tasks that can then get fulfilled. The three tables are the core of the Request Fulfillment process.

- A new record is created in the **Request** [`sc_request`] table. It acts as a container and a mirror for the cart - who ordered it, when, and what the total is.
- **Requested Item** [`sc_req_item`] records are made for each Catalog Item in the cart. It has reference fields to the **Request** table and to the **Catalog Request Item**. Through the **Variable Ownership** [`sc_item_option_mtom`] table, Requested Items are associated with the answers that the user gave to the variables.

- **Catalog Tasks** [`sc_task`] are generated according to the Catalog Request Item workflow. These drive the implementation process. Usually, the Catalog Tasks represent the individual steps that are necessary to deliver the service; they are often assigned to a variety of teams who each need to do their part.

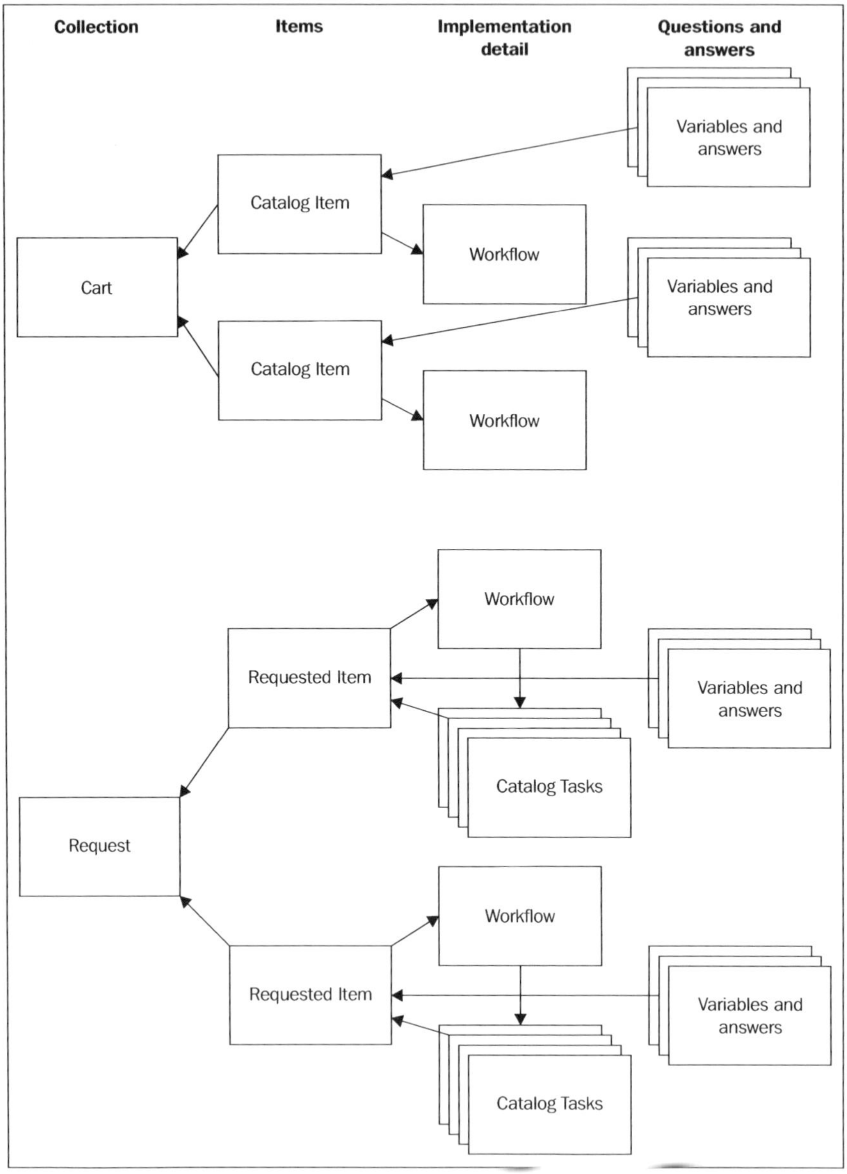

Using the request tables

All three of the **Request Fulfilment** tables extend the **Task** table. However, only **Catalog Tasks** are routinely assigned to fulfillers and their groups. A Service Desk may monitor the progress of Requested Items, while end users are most interested in the Request.

The three tables are generic. They always show the same fields no matter which Catalog Item has been selected. But the workflow allows per-item automation to occur. This may involve the creation of tasks and approval records. The progress of the workflow is recorded in a field on the Request Item table called **Stage**.

In order to see the information that the end user provides, the Requested Item form has a formatter called **Variable Editor**. This is a custom UI Macro that queries the **Variable Ownership** [`sc_item_option_mtom`] table to find the answers and the variables that were entered when the Catalog Item was ordered.

> The Variable Editor is relatively unsophisticated. The security is controlled by roles only, though client scripts and UI Policy can also run. If you want to have them as read-only, one way is to copy the variables into the **Work notes** field using a script to see them in the **Activity Formatter.**

Scripting variables

Business Rules and Client Scripts have access to variables once the Requested Item has been made. They are available through a global object called `variables`.

A Client Script can use the following script to hide a variable called `name`:

```
g_form.setDisplay("variables.name", false);
```

The `variables` property is also added to the current object for Business Rules to access, as follows:

```
gs.addInfoMessage(current.variables.name);
```

Service Level Management

When someone requests work, it needs to get done. The **Service Level Management** functionality specifies target times for how long a task should take and then uses Graphical Workflow to trigger notification reminders or perform automated actions. The results (success or failure) can also be reported or worked against.

The SLA (Service Level Agreement) engine in ServiceNow monitors effectiveness by comparing how long it takes to move between two conditions against a predefined goal. The main focus is on measuring time.

> There is a field on the SLA called Type, with the choices SLA, OLA, and Underpinning Contract. These are only for reference and selecting one does not impact how the system works.

This definition may be different to what you were expecting. In business terms, you may define a Service Level without a mention of times at all (such as reliability or uptime). These Service Levels would be implemented in ServiceNow using **Service Portfolio Management**.

In addition, there are other ways to measure time, including metrics and using Business Rules to populate date/time fields. Metrics are discussed in *Chapter 5, Events, Notifications, and Reporting*.

Exploring the SLA data structure

The definition of the SLA is done in the **SLA** [`contract_sla`] table. You can see the list by navigating to **Service Level Management** > **SLA** > **SLA definition**. This table provides the key information that the platform needs to perform the calculations - when to start, when to stop, when to pause, and what the target time is.

An SLA can only be registered against a table extended from a task, such as **Maintenance**. When an SLA starts, it creates a record in the **Task SLA** [`task_sla`] table, which has a reference field joining the SLA and the task. In addition, there are fields that contain estimated and actual times and information such as the percentage complete. It also has a state field that is controlled by the SLA engine.

Timing an SLA

While many options are in an SLA definition, probably the most important are the condition fields: **Start**, **Stop**, and **Pause**. These are used by the SLA engine to manipulate the elapsed duration timer that is on the **Task SLA** record.

It is common for the SLA timer to start when a task becomes active and stop when the task becomes inactive. This would be implemented by setting the **Start** condition to `Active - is - true` and the **Stop** condition to `Active - is - false`. The elapsed time would then be how long it took to transition between these two conditions.

In addition, the timer does not increment while the **Pause** condition is met. This means that often the SLA elapsed time is only part of the actual calendar elapsed time.

To illustrate this, consider this simple example, where the target time is 15 minutes:

Event	Calendar time	Current timer
Start condition becomes true	09:00	0 mins
Pause condition becomes true	09:05	5 mins
Pause condition is no longer true	09:10	5 mins
Stop condition becomes true	09:15	10 mins

This would result in a completed **Task SLA** record with an elapsed time of 10 minutes and an elapsed percentage of 66 percent.

> In the default SLA engine, it is more accurate to think of the **Start** condition as "valid while" instead. If, at any point, the start condition is evaluated to false, the state is set to **Cancelled**. This means that the start condition must continue to be true all the time that the SLA is running.

Finally, there is a **Reset** condition field that is not in the form by default. This will clear the elapsed time if the condition is met, meaning the timer starts from 0 again.

Travelling through time

There may be multiple SLAs registered against a single table. Priority-based SLAs are very common, where a high-priority task must be completed in a few hours, but a lower priority task may take several days. In this situation, the priority is included in the condition. If the priority changes, the start condition no longer matches, and the **Task SLA** is set to cancelled. Usually, another condition matches and it starts running.

Often, in this situation, the elapsed timer should not be 0. Ticking the **Retroactive start** checkbox allows the selection of a date/time field that will be used as the starting point. In this example, setting the start time to **Created** means the timer will be populated as if the SLA started from the creation of the task.

> The platform is clever enough to use the audit history of the record to factor in pause times, even if the SLA wasn't actually running at that point.

Enjoying relativity

The majority of SLAs have a specific, predetermined endpoint - maybe 4 hours or 4 days. But the platform also allows for durations to be calculated. For a promise to do 'next day delivery by 10 am', use a relative duration. The length of the timer will dependent on when the SLA started. Relative durations are defined by going to **System Scheduler** > **Schedules** > **Relative Durations** and running the script. There are several examples in the baseline build.

> A Relative Duration is only ever calculated once, at the start. Don't expect it to keep recalculating throughout the life of the SLA.

Scheduling and time zones

An SLA can also take working hours into account during calculations. By specifying a schedule (defined under **System Scheduler** > **Schedules** > **Schedules**), the timer will effectively be paused when appropriate. This is very useful for holiday periods. If a schedule isn't specified, the SLA runs all the time, 24/7.

Time zones are usually needed when a schedule is specified. When exactly 9 am - 5 pm occurs is dependent on the time zone.

Both of these items can be specified in the SLA itself, or they can be derived from other parts of the system. If a task has a location and the location is associated with a time zone, the SLA may use this for calculations.

These settings are specified in **SLA Properties**, available under **Service Level Management** > **Administration** > **SLA Properties**, along with several other useful options.

> There are two Script Includes that pick up this property: `SLASchedule` and `SLATimeZone`. It is possible to customize these scripts to provide more options, though be careful of reducing upgrade potential.

Customizing condition rules

The majority of SLAs run fine with the default condition rules; that is, they use the start condition to begin or cancel running, stop to finish, and so on. This logic is stored in a Script Include called `SLAConditionBase`.

A custom SLA Condition Rule will give you complete control over SLA runs. Most often, you create a Script Include that extends `SLAConditionBase` and change the functions that control how the **Task SLA** states are changed.

For example, in `SLAConditionBase`, there is a function called `cancel`. When this function returns true, the **Task SLA** has **State** changed to **Cancelled**. In `SLAConditionBase`, this occurs when the stop and pause conditions are both `true`.

This allows you to alter the logic and even add in extra fields on the SLA definition page. For example, you could add a new **Condition** field on the SLA definition page and label it **Cancel condition**. Then, in your Script Include, you could alter the `cancel` function to use this new field. Each time a record is updated, the `cancel` function will be called and the script would return the result.

Alternatively, you may want to create a more data-driven approach to starting the SLA rather than relying on the conditions. For example, you may want to have the SLA dependent on the **Assignment group** field. Another example is that when the **Service Portfolio Management** plugin is activated, it gives a different type of SLA that is activated via the **Configuration Item** field.

> You may wonder what is calling your new Script Include. There is another code block named `TaskSLAController` that is called by a series of Business Rules. I strongly recommend that you do not edit this script. It handles a variety of tricky situations, in order to prevent race conditions, collisions, and several other events. It is often updated by the ServiceNow development team. If you edit it, you won't take advantage of the improvements!

Once you have defined an SLA Condition Rule, you can make it the default rule through **SLA Properties** or use a field on the **SLA Definition** table called **Condition Type** that lets you specify it per record.

> This wiki has a very useful page on custom Condition Rules, including state diagrams:
>
> `https://wiki.servicenow.com/?title=Modifying_SLA_Condition_Rules`

Avoiding a breach

Having the **Task SLA** calculating the timer is very powerful, but what makes the system especially useful is the ability to run workflows. A workflow that is built against the `task_sla` table has an extra activity called SLA Percentage Timer. This activity will pause a workflow for a given percentage of the target time. This makes it very easy to have a generic workflow that can be attached to an SLA and makes it convenient to run commands at appropriate points. A reminder e-mail may be sent to the assignee of a task when the timer gets to 80 percent of the target time, and a manager may be informed in the case of a breach.

Workflow gives more options than just e-mailing, however. The task could be reassigned to the Service Desk or another team, or a message could be sent to another system—anything a workflow can do.

Working SLAs

Additionally, the baseline configuration provides modules under the Service Desk application menu for working SLAs. Navigate to them by going to **Service Desk** > **SLA's** > **My Work**. This view looks at the **Task SLA** table, with **Field Styles** being used to highlight records that are paused and near to breach. Since the list can show information that is dot-walked through the Task reference field, it can show any information on the **Task** table, such as **Short description** or **State**.

The **Task SLA** table can be used as an alternative to looking directly in the **Task** table. This slight shift in perspective may have a dramatic impact on how fulfillers work; instead of attempting to close the ticket, they would be trying to stop the SLA. This may give better service to the requesters.

Ensuring maintenance is quick

Let's create an SLA to monitor the performance of our room maintenance. We have high expectations for our staff, and we want to be able to prove how good a job they are doing.

Navigate to **Service Level Management** > **Administration** > **Workflow Editor**. This module provides exactly the same link as the one in the Workflow Editor. Click on **New**. Use the following:

- **Name**: `Notify and reassign`
- **Table**: `Task SLA [task_sla]`
- **If condition matches**: `-- None --`

Create the workflow as follows:

1. Add the **SLA Percentage Timer** activity in the **Timers** group to the canvas.
   - **Name**: `Wait for 75%`
   - **Percentage**: `75`
2. Add **Create Event** from **Notifications** to the canvas.
   - **Name**: `Give assignee a warning`
   - **Event name**: `sla.warning`

Events are covered in the next chapter, *Chapter 5, Events, Notifications, and Reporting*.

3. Add the **SLA Percentage Timer** activity in the **Timers** group to the canvas.
   - **Name**: `Wait for 25%`
   - **Percentage**: `25`

Note that the percentage timers are cumulative. Having 25 percent after 75 percent will be when the SLA breaches.

4. Drag **Create Event** from **Notifications** to the canvas.
   - **Name**: `Notify manager of breach`
   - **Event name**: `sla.warning.breach`
5. Finally, add a new **Run script** activity from **Utilities**.
   - **Name**: `Reassign to default team`
   - **Script**:

```
var tsk = current.task.getRefRecord();
tsk.assignment_group = '';
tsk.update();
```

   This code follows the **Task reference** field in the **Task SLA** table using `getRefRecord`. This returns a `GlideRecord`. Then the **Assignment group** field is blanked out and the record saved.

6. Connect up the activities as follows:
   - From **Begin** to **SLA Percentage Timer: Wait for 75%**
   - Then to **Create Event: Give assignee a warning**
   - Then to **SLA Percentage Timer: Wait 25%**
   - Then to **Create Event: Notify manager of breach**
   - Then to **Run Script: Reassign to default team**
   - Then to **End**

7. **Publish** the workflow through the gear menu and return to the normal interface:

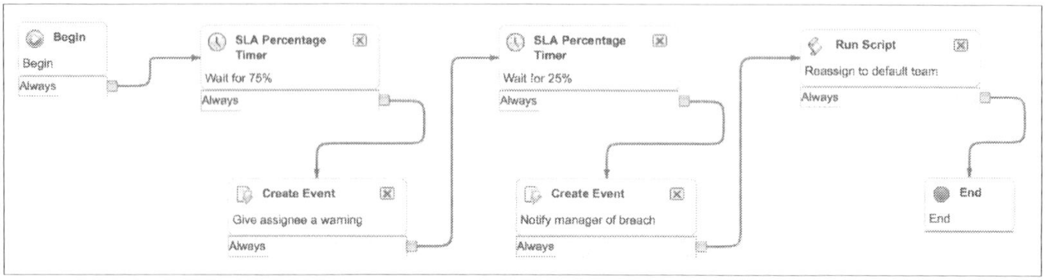

8. Navigate to **Service Level Management** > **SLA** > **SLA Definitions** and click on **New**. Use the following data:
    - **Name**: `Priority 1`
    - **Table:** `Maintenance [u_maintenance]`
    - **Workflow**: `Notify and reassign`
    - **Retroactive start**: `<ticked>`
    - **Set start to**: `Created`
    - **Duration**: `00 : 05 : 00` (5 minutes – just for our testing purposes!)
    - **Start condition**:

      `Active - is - true`

      `Priority - is - 1 - Critical`
    - **Stop condition**:

      `Active - is - false`

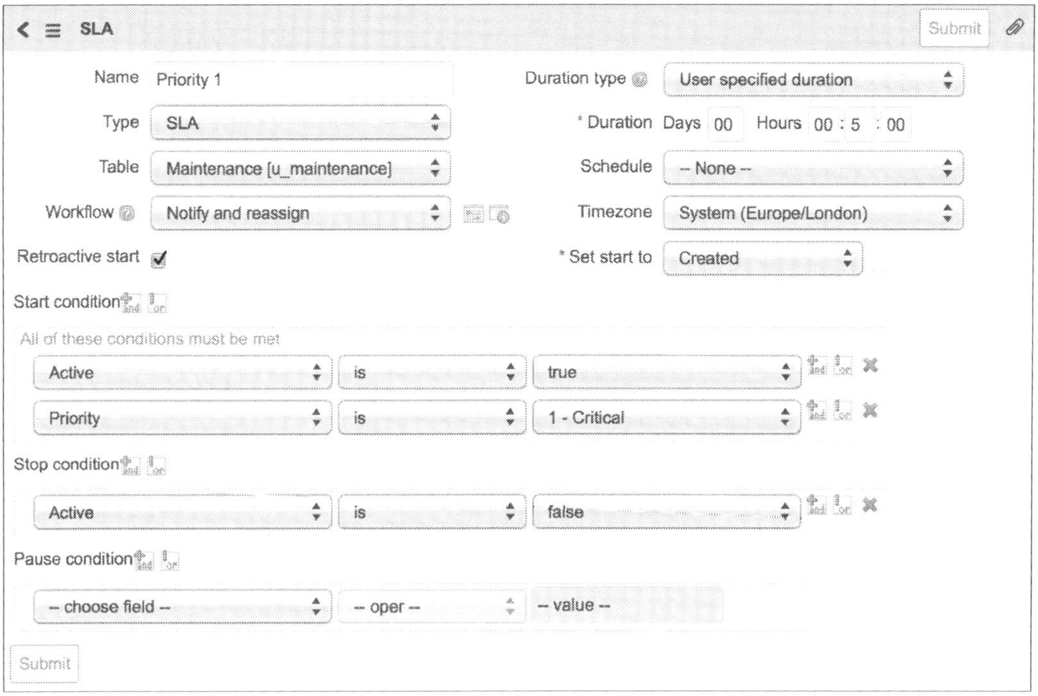

Once saved, make the following changes and use **Insert and Stay** in the context menu to create an altered copy:

- **Name**: `Other priorities`
- **Duration**: `00 : 10 : 00`
- **Start condition**:
    - `Active - is - true`
    - `Priority - is not - 1 - Critical`

To test this out, add the **Task SLA->Task** Related List in to the **Maintenance** form and create a new record (or update an existing one) with the **Priority** field set to **1 - Critical**. You should see the 5-minute SLA running against it. If you change the **Priority** field to **2 – High** and save, you will see the SLAs cancel and another one start. Keep refreshing the form using the **Reload form** context menu option to see the **Actual elapsed time** and percentage changing.

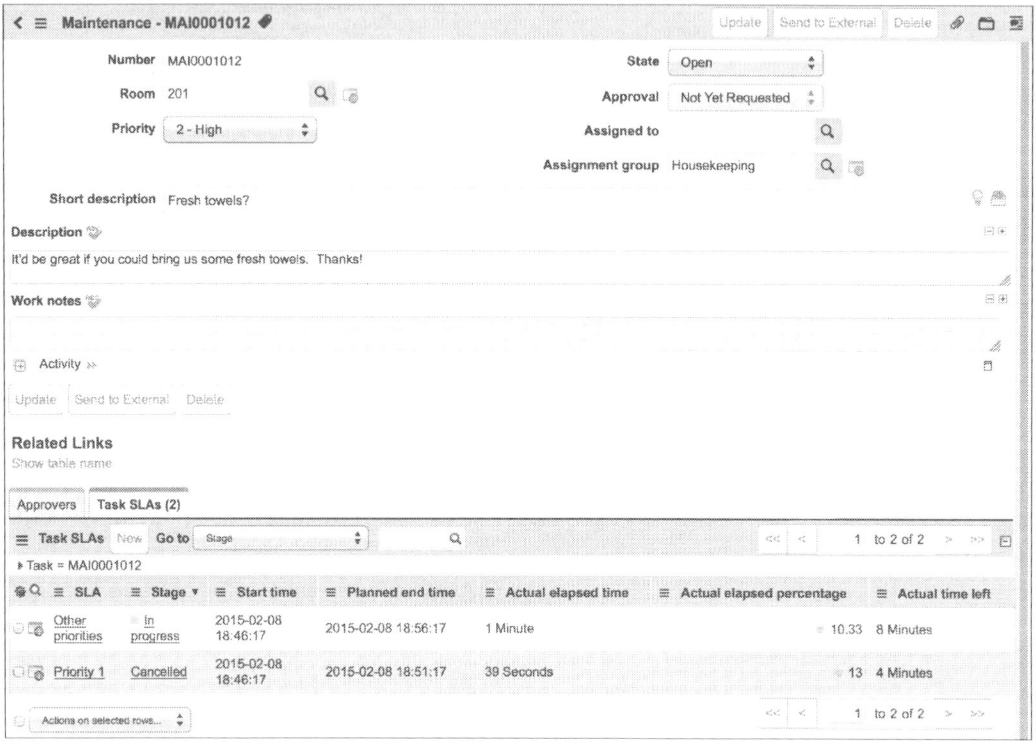

> The entries in the **Task SLAs** record are refreshed using a display Business Rule by default. This means that whenever you look at the form of a task, the Related List will be updated, but it does put a load on the platform. There are many different options in SLA Properties to control how they work.

Summary

This long chapter moved away from the foundations of ServiceNow and dealt with understanding how you can implement processes in more detail. The **Task** table is the basis of any work done in ServiceNow—it provides the single place that all tickets are stored in. Over 60 fields have already been created, with logic built around them. This means reporting is much easier, consistency is improved, and implementation time is reduced.

Graphical Workflow can control any table but is especially useful for tasks. It gives a drag-and-drop interface, allowing you to chain activities together. It is integrated into the SLA system and is the best way to deal with approvals. Users and groups can be asked for their opinion, which the workflow can then use to decide the course of a task.

The **Service Catalog** presents a different interface to end users. Record Producers can collect information that then gets turned into a task or any other record.

Some **Service Catalog** Items also make heavy use of Workflow. We touched on how to perform Request Fulfillment in ServiceNow, which uses three tables, all derived from Task. Together, it gives you a prebuilt application that can easily be used to implement a simple process.

SLAs are used to time the progress of a task. By defining start, stop, and pause conditions, it enables you to monitor how well the team is completing tasks.

Altogether, ServiceNow is a great place to build a task-focused application. The platform provides lots of helpful functionality to build a very powerful application in a very short amount of time. We built a fairly fully featured Maintenance application in the space of a chapter!

The next chapter, *Chapter 5, Events, Notifications, and Reporting*, looks at how to communicate from ServiceNow. This includes e-mails, reports, and explores some more of the automation features of the platform, including Scheduled Jobs and events.

5
Events, Notifications, and Reporting

Communication is a key part of any business application. Not only does the boss need to have an updated report by Monday, but your customers and users also want to be kept informed.

ServiceNow helps users who want to know what's going on. In this chapter, we'll explore the functionality available. The platform can notify and provide information to people in a variety of ways:

- Registering **events** and creating **Scheduled Jobs** to automate functionality
- Sending out informational **e-mails** when something happens
- Live dashboards and **homepages** showing the latest reports and statistics
- **Scheduled reports** that help with handover between shifts
- Capturing information with **metrics**
- Presenting a single set of consolidated data with **database views**

Dealing with events

Firing an **event** is a way to tell the platform that something happened. Since ServiceNow is a data-driven system, in many cases, this means that a record has been updated in some way. For instance, maybe a guest has been made a VIP, or has stayed for 20 nights. Several parts of the system may be listening for an event to happen. When it does, they perform an action. One of these actions may be sending an e-mail to thank our guest for their continued business.

> These days, e-mail notifications don't need to be triggered by events. However, it is an excellent example.

When you fire an event, you pass through a `GlideRecord` object and up to two string parameters. The item receiving this data can then use it as necessary, so if we wanted to send an e-mail confirming a hotel booking, we have those details to hand during processing.

Registering events

Before an event can be fired, it must be known to the system. We do this by adding it to **Event Registry** [`sysevent_register`], which can be accessed by navigating to **System Policy** > **Events** > **Registry**. It's a good idea to check whether there isn't one you can use before you add a new one.

An event registration record consists of several fields, but most importantly a string name. An event can be called anything, but by convention it is in a dotted namespace style format. Often, it is prefixed by the application or table name and then by the activity that occurred.

Since a `GlideRecord` object accompanies an event, the table that the record will come from should also be selected. It is also a good idea to describe your event and what will cause it in the **Description** and **Fired by** fields.

Finally, there is a field that is often left empty, called **Queue**. This gives us the functionality to categorize events and process them in a specific order or frequency.

Firing an event

Most often, a script in a Business Rule will notice that something happens and will add an event to the **Event** [`sysevent`] queue. This table stores all of the events that have been fired, if it has been processed, and what page the user was on when it happened.

As the events come in, the platform deals with them in a *first in, first out* order by default. It finds everything that is listening for this specific event and executes them. That may be an e-mail notification or a script. By navigating to **System Policy** > **Events** > **Event Log**, you can view the state of an event, when it was added to the queue, and when it was processed.

To add an event to the queue, use the `eventQueue` function of `GlideSystem`. It accepts four parameters: the name of the event, a `GlideRecord` object, and two run time parameters. These can be any text strings, but most often are related to the user that caused the event.

Sending an e-mail for new reservations

Let's create an event that will fire when a **Maintenance** task has been assigned to one of our teams. We'll pick this up later when we do e-mail processing.

1. Navigate to **System Policy** > **Events** > **Registry**. Click on **New** and set the following fields:
    - **Event name**: `maintenance.assigned`
    - **Table**: `Maintenance [u_maintenance]`
2. Next, we need to add the event to the Event Queue. This is easily done with a simple Business Rule:
    - **Name**: `Maintenance assignment events`
    - **Table**: `Maintenance [u_maintenance]`
    - **Advanced**: `<ticked>`
    - **When**: `after`

> Make sure to always fire events after the record has been written to the database. This stops the possibility of firing an event even though another script has aborted the action.

- **Insert**: `<ticked>`
- **Update**: `<ticked>`
- **Filter Conditions**:
    - `Assignment group - changes`
    - `Assignment group - is not empty`
    - `Assigned to - is empty`

  This filter represents when a task is sent to a new group but someone hasn't yet been identified to own the work.

- **Script**: `gs.eventQueue('maintenance.assigned', current, gs.getUserID(), gs.getUserName());`

  This script follows the standard convention when firing events—passing the event name, `current`, which contains the `GlideRecord` object the Business Rule is working with, and some details about the user who is logged in.

We'll pick this event up later and send an e-mail whenever it is fired.

> There are several events, such as `<table_name>.view`, that are fired automatically. A very useful one is the `login` event. Take a look at the **Event Log** to see what is happening.

Scheduling jobs

You may be wondering how the platform processes the event queue. What picks them up? How often are they processed? In order to make things happen automatically, ServiceNow has a **System Scheduler**. Processing the event queue is one job that is done on a repeated basis.

> ServiceNow can provide extra worker nodes that only process events. These shift the processing of things such as e-mails onto another system, enabling the other application nodes to better service user interactions.

To see what is going on, navigate to **System Scheduler** > **Scheduled Jobs** > **Today's Scheduled Jobs**. This is a link to the **Schedule Item** [`sys_trigger`] table, a list of everything the system is doing in the background. You will see a job that collects database statistics, another that upgrades the instance (if appropriate), and others that send and receive e-mails or SMS messages. You should also spot one called **events process**, which deals with the event queue.

A Schedule Item has a **Next action** date and time field. This is when the platform will next run the job. Exactly what will happen is specified through the **Job ID** field. This is a reference to the Java class in the platform that will actually do the work. The majority of the time, this is `RunScriptJob`, which will execute some JavaScript code.

The **Trigger type** field specifies how often the job will repeat. Most jobs are run repetitively, with `events process` set to run every 30 seconds. Others run when the instance is started—perhaps to preload the cache.

Another job that is run on a periodic basis is **SMTP Sender**. Once an e-mail has been generated and placed in the `sys_email` table, the SMTP Sender job performs the same function as many desktop e-mail clients: it connects to an e-mail server and asks it to deliver the message. It runs every minute by default.

> This schedule has a direct impact on how quickly our e-mail will be sent out. There may be a delay of up to 30 seconds in generating the e-mail from an event, and a further delay of up to a minute before the e-mail is actually sent.
>
> Other jobs may process a particular event queue differently. Events placed into the metric queue will be worked with after 5 seconds.

Adding your own jobs

The `sys_trigger` table is a backend data store. It is possible to add your own jobs and edit what is already there, but I don't recommend it. Instead, there is a more appropriate frontend: the **Scheduled Job** [`sysauto`] table.

The `sysauto` table is designed to be extended. There are many things that can be automated in ServiceNow, including data imports, sending reports, and creating records, and they each have a table extended from `sysauto`.

> Once you create an entry in the `sysauto` table, the platform creates the appropriate record in the `sys_trigger` table. This is done through a call in the automation synchronizer Business Rule.

Each table extended from `sysauto` contains fields that are relevant to its automation. For example, a **Scheduled Email of Report** [`sysauto_report`] requires e-mail addresses and reports to be specified.

Creating events every day

Navigate to **System Definition** > **Scheduled Jobs**.

> Unfortunately, the `sys_trigger` and `sysauto` tables have very similar module names. Be sure to pick the right one.

When you click on **New**, an interceptor will fire, asking you to choose what you want to automate. Let's write a simple script that will create a maintenance task at the end of a hotel stay, so choose **Automatically run a script of your choosing**. Our aim is to fire an event for each room that needs cleaning. We'll keep this for midday to give our guests plenty of time to check out. Set the following fields:

- **Name**: `Clean on end of reservation`
- **Time**: `12:00:00`
- **Run this script**:

```
var res = new GlideRecord('u_reservation');
res.addQuery('u_departure', gs.now());
res.addNotNullQuery('u_room');
res.query();
while (res.next()) {
  gs.eventQueue('room.reservation_end', res.u_room.
getRefRecord());
}
```

> Remember to enclose scripts in a function if they could cause other scripts to run. Most often, this is when records are updated, but it is not the case here.

Our reliable friend, `GlideRecord`, is employed to get reservation records. The first filter ensures that only reservations that are ending today will be returned, while the second filter ignores reservations that don't have a room.

Once the database has been queried, the records are looped round. For each one, the `eventQueue` function of `GlideSystem` is used to add in an event into the event queue. The record that is being passed into the event queue is actually the **Room** record. The `getRefRecord` function of `GlideElement` dot-walks through a reference field and returns a newly initialized `GlideRecord` object rather than more `GlideElement` objects.

Once the Scheduled Job has been saved, it'll generate the events at midday. But for testing, there is a handy **Execute Now** UI action. Ensure there is test data that fits the code and click on the button. Navigate to **System Policy** > **Events** > **Event Log** to see the entries.

> There is a **Conditional** checkbox with a separate **Condition script** field. However, I don't often use this; instead, I provide any conditions inline in the script that I'm writing, just like we did here. For anything more than a few lines, a Script Include should be used for modularity and efficiency.

Running scripts on events

The ServiceNow platform has several items that listen for events. **Email Notifications** are one, which we'll explore soon. Another is **Script Actions**.

Script Actions is server-side code that is associated with a table and runs against a record, just like a Business Rule. But instead of being triggered by a database action, a Script Action is started with an event.

> There are many similarities between a Script Action and an asynchronous Business Rule. They both run server-side, asynchronous code. Unless there is a particular reason, stick to Business Rules for ease and familiarity.

Just like a Business Rule, the `GlideRecord` variable called `current` is available. This is the same record that was passed into the second parameter when `gs.eventQueue` was called.

Additionally, another `GlideRecord` variable called `event` is provided. It is initialized against the appropriate Event record on the `sysevent` table. This gives you access to the other parameters (`event.param1` and `event.param2`) as well as who created the event, when, and more.

Creating tasks automatically

When creating a Script Action, the first step is to register or identify the event it will be associated with. Create another entry in **Event Registry**.

- **Event name:** `room.reservation_end`
- **Table:** `Room [u_room]`

In order to make the functionality more data driven, let's create another template. Either navigate to **System Definition** > **Templates** or create a new **Maintenance** task and use the **Save as Template** option in the context menu.

Regardless, set the following fields:

- **Name**: End of reservation room cleaning
- **Table**: Maintenance [u_maintenance]
- **Template**:
  - **Assignment group**: Housekeeping
  - **Short description**: End of reservation room cleaning
  - **Description**: Please perform the standard cleaning for the room listed above.

To create the Script Action, go to **System Policy** > **Events** > **Script Actions** and use the following details:

- **Name**: Produce maintenance tasks
- **Event name**: room.reservation_end
- **Active**: <ticked>
- **Script**:

```
var tsk = new GlideRecord('u_maintenance');
tsk.newRecord();
tsk.u_room = current.sys_id;
tsk.applyTemplate('End of reservation room cleaning');
tsk.insert();
```

This script is quite straightforward. It creates a new GlideRecord object that represents a record in the **Maintenance** table. The fields are initialized through newRecord, and the **Room** field is populated with the sys_id of current—which is the **Room** record that the event is associated with. The applyTemplate function is given the name of the template.

> It would be better to use a property here instead of hardcoding a template name.

Now, the following items should occur every day:

1. At midday, a **Scheduled Job** looks for any reservations that are ending today
2. For each one, the room.reservation_end event is fired
3. A Script Action will be called, which creates a new **Maintenance** task

4. The **Maintenance** task is assigned, through a template, to the **Housekeeping** group.

   But how does **Housekeeping** know that this task has been created? Let's send them an e-mail!

Sending e-mail notifications

E-mail is ubiquitous. It is often the primary form of communication in business, so it is important that ServiceNow has good support. It is easy to configure ServiceNow to send out communications to whoever needs to know.

There are a few general use cases for e-mail notifications:

- **Action**: Asking the receiver to do some work
- **Informational**: Giving the receiver an update or some data
- **Approval**: Asking for a decision

  While this is similar enough to an action e-mail, it is a common enough scenario to make it independent.

We'll work through these scenarios in order to understand how ServiceNow can help.

> There are obviously a lot more ways you can use e-mails. One of them is for a machine-to-machine integration, such as e-bonding. It is possible to do this in ServiceNow, but it is not the best solution. *Chapter 6, Exchanging Data – Import Sets, Web Services, and Other Integrations*, discusses integrations in more detail.

Setting e-mail properties

A ServiceNow instance uses standard protocols to send and receive e-mail. E-mails are sent by connecting to an SMTP server with a username and password, just like Outlook or any other e-mail client.

When an instance is provisioned, it also gets an e-mail account. If your instance is available at `instance.service-now.com` through the Web, it has an e-mail address of `instance@service-now.com`.

This e-mail account is not unusual. It is accessible via POP to receive mail, and uses SMTP to send it. Indeed, any standard e-mail account can be used with an instance.

Navigate to **System Properties** > **Email** to investigate the settings. The properties are unusually laid out in two columns, for sending and receiving for the SMTP and POP connections. When you reach the page, the settings will be tested, so you can immediately see if the platform is capable of sending or receiving e-mails. Before you spend time configuring Email Notifications, make sure the basics work!

> ServiceNow will only use one e-mail account to send out e-mails, and by default, will only check for new e-mails in one account too. This is discussed later in the chapter.

Tracking sent e-mails in the Activity Log

One important feature of **Email Notifications** is that they can show up in the **Activity Log** if configured. This means that all e-mails associated with a ticket are associated and kept together. This is useful when tracking correspondence with a **Requester**.

To configure the Activity Log, navigate to a **Maintenance** record. Right-click on the field and choose **Personalize Activities**. At the bottom of the **Available** list is **Sent/ Received Emails**. Add it to the **Selected** list and click on **Save**.

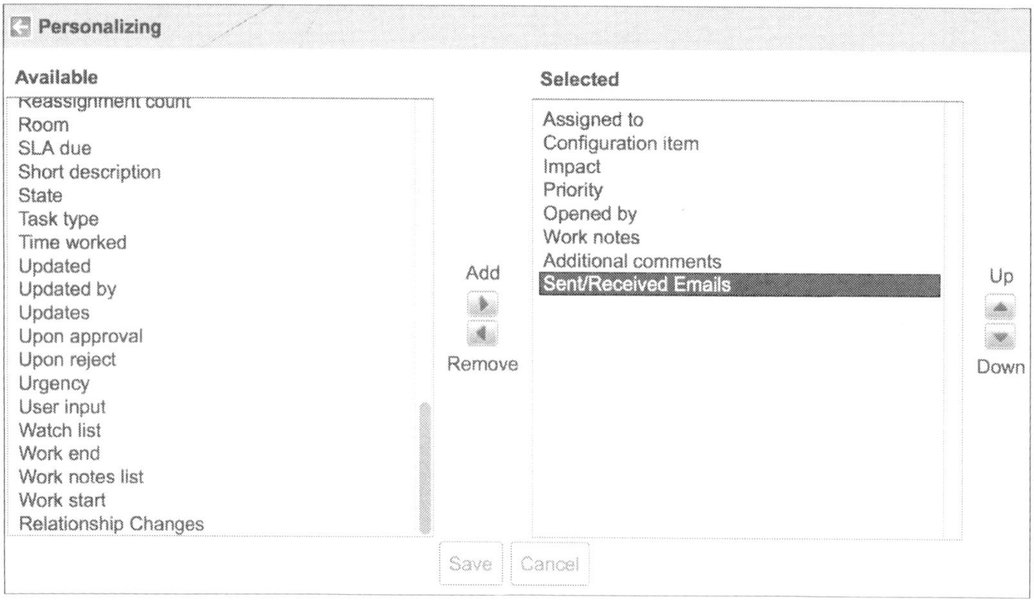

Once an e-mail has been sent out, check back to the **Activity Formatter** to see the results.

Assigning work

Our **Housekeeping** team is equipped with the most modern technology. Not only are they users of ServiceNow, but they have mobile phones that will send and receive e-mails. They have better things to do than constantly refresh the web interface, so let's ensure that ServiceNow will come to them.

One of the most common e-mail notifications is for ServiceNow to inform people when they have been assigned a task. It usually gives an overview and a link to view more details. This e-mail tells them that something needs to happen and that ServiceNow should be updated with the result.

Sending an e-mail notification on assignment

When our **Maintenance** tasks have the **Assignment group** field populated, we need the appropriate team members to be aware. We are going to achieve this by sending an e-mail to everyone in that group. At Gardiner Hotels, we empower our staff: they know that one member of the team should pick the task up and own it by setting the **Assigned to** field to themselves and then get it done.

Navigate to **System Policy** > **Email** > **Notifications**. You will see several examples that are useful to understand the basic configuration, but we'll create our own. Click on **New**.

The **Email Notifications** form is split into three main sections: **When to send**, **Who will receive**, and **What it will contain**. Some options are hidden in a different view, so click on **Advanced view** to see them all. Start off by giving the basic details:

- **Name**: `Group assignment`
- **Table**: `Maintenance [u_maintenance]`

Now, let's see each of the sections of **Email Notifications** form in detail, in the following sections.

When to send

This section gives you a choice of either using an event to determine which record should be worked with or for the e-mail notification system to monitor the table directly. Either way, **Conditions** and **Advanced conditions** lets you provide a filter or a script to ensure you only send e-mails at the right time. If you are using an event, the event must be fired and the condition fields satisfied for the e-mail to be sent.

The **Weight** field is often overlooked. A single event or record update may satisfy the condition of multiple **Email Notifications**. For example, a common scenario is to send an e-mail to the **Assignment group** when it is populated and to send an e-mail to the **Assigned to** person when that is populated. But what if they both happen at the same time? You probably don't want the **Assignment group** being told to pick up a task if it has already been assigned. One way is to give the **Assignment group** e-mail a higher weight: if two e-mails are being generated, only the lower weight will be sent. The other will be marked as skipped.

> Another way to achieve this scenario is through conditions. Only send the Assignment group e-mail if the **Assigned to** field is empty.

Since we've already created an event, let's use it. And because of the careful use of conditions in the Business Rule, it only sends out the event in the appropriate circumstances. That means no condition is necessary in this Email Notification.

- **Send when**: `Event is fired`
- **Event name**: `maintenance.assigned`

Who will receive

Once we've determined when an e-mail should be sent, we need to know who it will go to. The majority of the time, it'll be driven by data on the record. This scenario is exactly that: the people who will receive the e-mail are those in the **Assignment group** field on the **Maintenance** task. Of course, it is possible to hardcode recipients and the system can also deliver e-mails to **Users** and **Groups** that have been sent as a parameter when creating the event.

- **Users/Groups in fields**: **Assignment group**

> You can also use scripts to specify the From, To, CC, and BCC of an e-mail. The wiki here contains more information:
> `http://wiki.servicenow.com/?title=Scripting_for_Email_Notifications`

Send to event creator

When someone comes to me and says: "Martin, I've set up the e-mail notification, but it isn't working. Do you know why?", I like to put money on the reason. I very often win, and you can too. Just answer: "Ensure **Send to event creator** is ticked and try again".

The **Send to event creator** field is only visible on the **Advanced** view, but is the cause of this problem. So tick **Send to event creator**. Make sure this field is ticked, at least for now. If you do not, when you test your e-mail notifications, you will not receive your e-mail. Why?

By default, the system will not send confirmation e-mails. If you were the person to update a record and it causes e-mails to be sent, and it turns out that you are one of the recipients, it'll go to everyone other than you. The reasoning is straightforward: you carried out the action so why do you need to be informed that it happened? This cuts down on unnecessary e-mails and so is a good thing. But it confuses everyone who first comes across it.

> If there is one tip I can give to you in this book, it is this - tick the **Send to event creator** field when testing e-mails. Better still, test realistically!

What it will contain

The last section is probably the simplest to understand, but the one that takes most time: deciding what to send.

The standard view contains just a few fields: a space to enter your message, a subject line, and an SMS alternate field that is used for text messages. Additionally, there is an **Email template** field that isn't often used but is useful if you want to deliver the same content in multiple e-mail messages. View them by navigating to **System Policy** > **Email** > **Templates**.

These fields all support variable substitution. This is a special syntax that instructs the instance to insert data from the record that the e-mail is triggered for. This **Maintenance** e-mail can easily contain data from the **Maintenance** record.

This lets you create data-driven e-mails. I like to compare it to a mail-merge system; you have some fixed text, some placeholders, and some data, and the platform puts them all together to produce a personalized e-mail.

> By default, the message will be delivered as HTML. This means you can make your messages look more styled by using image tags and font controls, among other options.

Using variable substitution

The format for substitution is ${variable}. All of the fields on the record are available as variables, so to include the **Short description** field in an e-mail, use ${short_description}. Additionally, you can dot-walk. So by having ${assigned_to.email} in the message, you insert the e-mail address of the user that the task is assigned to.

Populate the fields with the following information and save:

- **Subject**: Maintenance task assigned to your group
- **Message HTML**:

```
Hello ${assignment_group}.
Maintenance task ${number} has been assigned to your group, for
room: ${u_room}.
Description: ${description}
Please assign to a team member here: ${URI}
Thanks!
```

To make this easier, there is a **Select variables** section on the **Message HTML** and **SMS alternate** fields that will create the syntax in a single click. But don't forget that variable substitution is available for the **Subject** field too.

In addition to adding the value of fields, variable substitution like the following ones also makes it easy to add HTML links.

- ${<reference field>.URI} will create an HTML link to the reference field, with the text LINK
- ${<reference field>.URI_REF} will create an HTML link, but with the display value of the record as the text
- Linking to CMS sites, explored in *Chapter 10, Making ServiceNow Beautiful with CMS and Jelly*, is possible through ${CMS_URI+<site>/<page>}

Running scripts in e-mail messages

If the variables aren't giving you enough control, like everywhere else in ServiceNow, you can add a script. To do so, create a new entry in the **Email Scripts** [sys_script_email] table, available under **System Policy** > **Email** > **Notification Email Scripts**. Typical server-side capability is present, including the current GlideRecord variable. To output text, use the print function of the template object. For example:

```
template.print('Hello, world!');
```

Like a Script Include, the **Name** field is important. Call the script by placing ${mail_script:<name>} in the **Message HTML** field in the e-mail.

> An object called email is also available. This gives much more control with the resulting e-mail, giving functions such as setImportance, addAddress, and setReplyTo.
>
> This wiki has more details: http://wiki.servicenow.com/?title=Scripting_for_Email_Notifications

Controlling the watermark

Every outbound mail contains a reference number embedded into the body of the message, in the format Ref:MSG0000100. This is very important for the inbound processing of e-mails, as discussed in a later section. Some options are available to hide or remove the watermark, but this may affect how the platform treats a reply.

Navigating to **System Mailboxes** > **Administration** > **Watermarks** shows a full list of every watermark and the associated record and e-mail.

Including attachments and other options

There are several other options to control how an e-mail is processed:

- **Include Attachments**: It will copy any attachments from the record into the e-mail. There is no selection available: it simply duplicates each one every time. You probably wouldn't want this option ticked on many e-mails, since otherwise you will fill up the recipient's inboxes quickly!

> The attach_links Email Script is a good alternative—it gives HTML links that will let an interested recipient download the file from the instance.

- **Importance**: This allows a Low or High priority flag to be set on an e-mail
- **From** and **Reply-To** fields: They'll let you configure who the e-mail purports to be from, on a per–e-mail basis. It is important to realize that this is **e-mail spoofing**: while the e-mail protocols accept this, it is often used by spam to forge a false address.

Sending informational updates

Many people rely on e-mails to know what is going on. In addition to telling users when they need to do work, ServiceNow can keep everyone informed as to the current situation.

This often takes the form of one of these scenarios:

- Automatic e-mails, often based on a change of the **State** field
- Completely freeform text, with or without a template
- A combination of the preceding two: a textual update given by a person, but in a structured template

Sending a custom e-mail

Sometimes, you need to send an e-mail that doesn't fit into a template. Perhaps you need to attach a file, copy in additional people, or want more control over formatting. In many cases, you would turn to the e-mail client on your desktop, such as Outlook or perhaps even Lotus Notes. But the big disadvantage is that the association between the e-mail and the record is lost. Of course, you could save the e-mail and upload it as an attachment, but that isn't as good as it being part of the audit history.

ServiceNow comes with a basic e-mail client built in. In fact, it is just shortcutting the process. When you use the e-mail client, you are doing exactly the same as the **Email Notifications** engine would, by generating an entry in the `sys_email` table.

Enabling the e-mail client

The Email Client is accessed by a little icon in the form header of a record. In order to show it, a property must be set in the **Dictionary Entry** of the table. Navigate to **System Definition** > **Dictionary** and find the entry for the `u_maintenance` table that does not have an entry in the **Column name** field.

> The value for the filter is `Table - is - u_maintenance` and `Column name - is - empty`

Click on **Advanced view**. Ensure the **Attributes** field contains `email_client`.

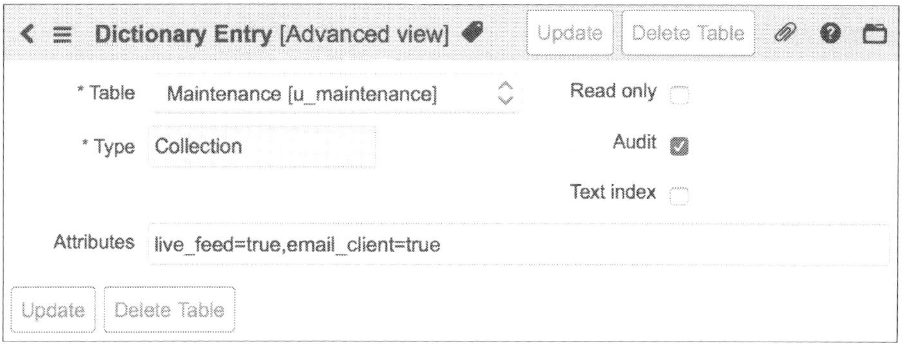

Navigate to an existing **Maintenance** record, and next to the attachments icon is the envelope icon. Click on it to open the e-mail client window.

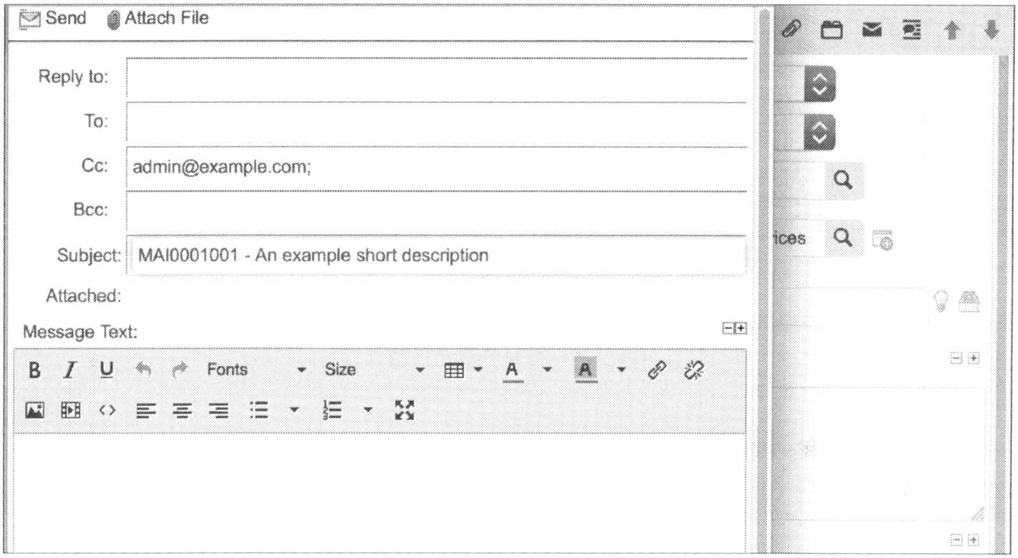

The Email Client is a simple window, and the fields should be obvious. Simply fill them out and click on **Send** to deliver the mail.

You may have noticed that some of the fields were prepopulated. You can control what each field initially contains by creating an Email Client Template. Navigate to **System Policy** > **Email** > **Client Templates**, click on **New**, and save a template for the appropriate table. You can use the variable substitution syntax to place the contents of fields in the e-mail. There is a **Conditions** field you can add to the form to have the right template used.

Quick Messages are a way to let the e-mail user populate Message Text, similar to a record template. Navigate to **System Policy** > **Email** > **Quick Messages** and define some text. These are then available in a dropdown selection field at the top of the e-mail client.

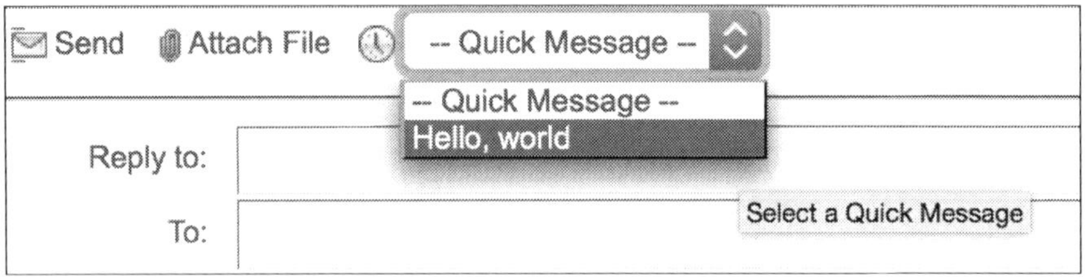

The e-mail client is often seized upon by customers who send a lot of e-mail. However, it is a simple solution and does not have a whole host of functionality that is often expected. I've found that this gap can be frustrating. For example, there isn't an easy way to include attachments from the parent record.

Instead, often a more automated way to send custom text is useful.

Sending e-mails with Additional comments and Work notes

The journal fields on the task table are useful enough, allowing you to record results that are then displayed on the Activity log in a *who, what, when* fashion. But sending out the contents via e-mail makes them especially helpful. This lets you combine two actions in one: documenting information against the ticket and also giving an update to interested parties. The **Task** table has two fields that let you specify who those people are: the **Watch list** and the **Work notes list**.

An e-mail notification can then use this information in a structured manner to send out the work note. It can include the contents of the work notes as well as images, styled text, and background information.

Sending out Work notes

The **Work notes** field should already be on the **Maintenance** form. Use **Form Design** to include the **Work notes list** field too, placing it somewhere appropriate, such as underneath the **Assignment group** field.

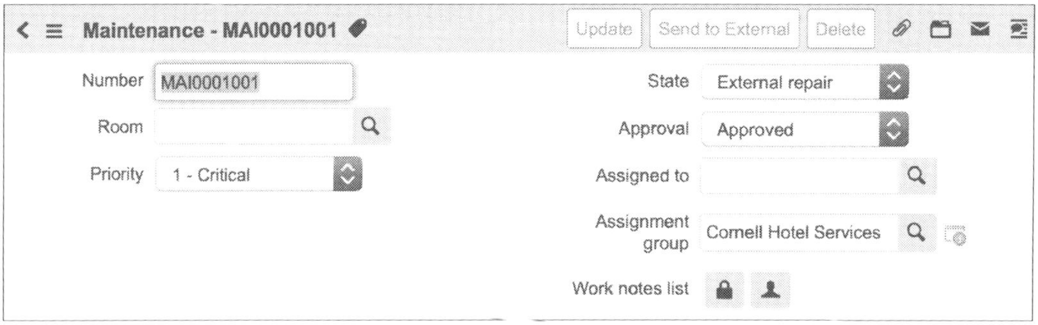

Both the **Watch list** and the **Work notes list** are List fields (often referred to as **Glide Lists**). These are reference fields that contain more than one `sys_id` from the `sys_user` table. This makes it is easy to add a requester or fulfiller who is interested in updates to the ticket. What is special about List fields is that although they point towards the `sys_user` table and store `sys_id` references, they also store e-mail addresses in the same database field. The e-mail notification system knows all about this. It will run through the following logic:

- If it is a `sys_id`, the user record is looked up. The e-mail address in the user record is used.
- If it is an e-mail address, the user record is searched for. If one is found, any notification settings they have are respected.

> A user may turn off e-mails, for example, by setting the Notification field to Disabled in their user record. More options are mentioned later.

- If a user record is not found, the e-mail is sent directly to the e-mail address.

Now create a new Email Notification and fill out the following fields:

- **Name**: `Work notes update`
- **Table**: `Maintenance [u_maintenance]`
- **Inserted**: `<ticked>`
- **Updated**: `<ticked>`

- **Conditions**: `Work notes - changes`
- **Users/Groups in fields**: `Work notes list`
- **Subject**: `New work notes update on ${number}`
- **Send to event creator**: `<ticked>`
- **Message**:

```
${number} - ${short_description} has a new work note added.

${work_notes}
```

> This simple message would normally be expanded and made to fit into the corporate style guidelines—use appropriate colors and styles. By default, the last three entries in the **Work notes** field would be included. If this wasn't appropriate, the `global` property could be updated or a mail script could use `getJournalEntry(1)` to grab the last one. Refer to this wiki article for more information: `http://wiki.servicenow.com/?title=Using_Journal_Fields#Restrict_the_Number_of_Entries_Sent_in_a_Notification`.

To test, add an e-mail address or a user into the **Work notes list**, enter something into the Work notes field, and save.

> Don't forget about **Send to event creator**! This is a typical example of how, normally, the person doing the action wouldn't need to receive the e-mail update, since they were the one doing it. But set it so it'll work with your own updates.

Approving via e-mail

Chapter 4, Getting Things Done with Tasks, spoke about approvals for tasks and how **Graphical Workflow** generates records that someone will need to evaluate and make a decision on. Most often, approvers will want to receive an e-mail notification to alert them to the situation.

There are two approaches to sending out an e-mail when an approval is needed. An e-mail is associated with a particular record; and with approvals, there are two records to choose from:

- The **Approval** record, asking for your decision. The response will be processed by the **Graphical Workflow**. The system will send out one e-mail to each person that is requested to approve it.

- The **Task** record that generated the **Approval** request. The system will send out one e-mail in total.

> Attaching notifications to the task is sometimes helpful, since it gives you access to all the fields on the record without dot-walking.

This section deals with how the **Approval** record itself uses e-mail notifications.

Using the Approval table

An e-mail that is sent out from the **Approval** table often contains the same elements:

- Some text describing what needs approving: perhaps the Short description or Priority. This is often achieved by dot-walking to the data through the **Approval for** reference field.
- A link to view the task that needs approval.
- A link to the approval record.
- Two `mailto` links that allow the user to approve or reject through e-mail.

This style is captured in the Email Template named `change.itil.approve.role` and is used in an Email Notification called **Approval Request** that is against the **Approval** [`sys_approver`] table.

The `mailto` links are generated through a special syntax: `${mailto:mailto.approval}` and `${mailto:mailto.rejection}`. These actually refer to Email Templates themselves (navigate to **System Policy** > **Email** > **Templates** and find the template called `mailto.approval`). Altogether, these generate HTML code in the e-mail message that looks something like this:

```
<a href="mailto:<instance>@service-now.com.com?subject=Re:MAI0001001 - approve&body=Ref:MSG0000001">Click here to approve MAI0001001</a>
```

> Normally, this URL would be encoded, but I've removed the characters for clarity.

When this link is clicked on in the receiver's e-mail client, it creates a new e-mail message addressed to the instance, with `Re:MAI0001001 - approve` in the subject line and `Ref:MSG0000001` in the body. If this e-mail was sent, the instance would process it and approve the approval record. A later section, on processing inbound e-mails, shows in detail how this happens.

Testing the default approval e-mail

In the baseline system, there is an Email Notification called **Approval Request**. It is sent when an approval event is fired, which happens in a Business Rule on the **Approval** table. It uses the e-mail template mentioned earlier, giving the recipient information and an opportunity to approve it either in their web browser, or using their e-mail client.

If Howard Johnson was set as the manager of the **Maintenance** group, he will be receiving any approval requests generated when the **Send to External** button is clicked on. Try changing the e-mail address in Howard's user account to your own, but ensure the **Notification** field is set to `Enable`. Then try creating some approval requests.

Specifying Notification Preferences

Every user that has access to the standard web interface can configure their own e-mail preferences through the **Subscription Notification** functionality. Navigate to **Self-Service** > **My profile** and click on **Notification Preferences** to explore what is available. It represents the **Notification Messages** [`cmn_notif_message`] table in a straightforward user interface.

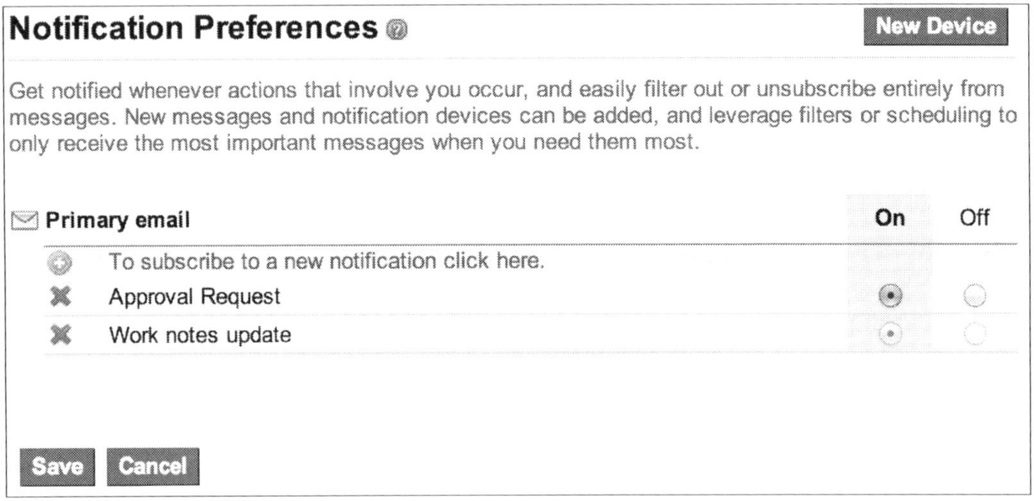

The **Notification Preferences** screen shows all the notifications that the user has received, such as the **Approval Request** and **Work notes update** configured earlier. They are organized by device. By default, every user has a primary e-mail device.

To never receive a notification again, just choose the **Off** selection and save. This is useful if you are bombarded by e-mails and would rather use the web interface to see updates!

> If you want to ensure a user cannot unsubscribe, check the **Mandatory** field in the **Email Notification** definition record. You may need to add it to the form. This disables the choice, as per the **Work notes update** notification in the screenshot.

Subscribing to Email Notifications

The **Email Notifications** table has a field labeled **Subscribable**. If this is checked, then users can choose to receive a message every time the **Email Notification** record's conditions are met. This offers a different way of working: someone can decide if they want more information, rather than the administrator deciding.

1. Edit the **Work notes update** Email Notification. Switch to the **Advanced** view, and using Form Design, add the **Subscribable** field to the **Who will receive** section on the form.
2. Now make the following changes. Once done, use **Insert and Stay** to make a copy.
    - **Name**: Work notes update (Subscribable)
    - **Users/Groups in fields**: <blank>
    - **Subscribable**: <ticked>

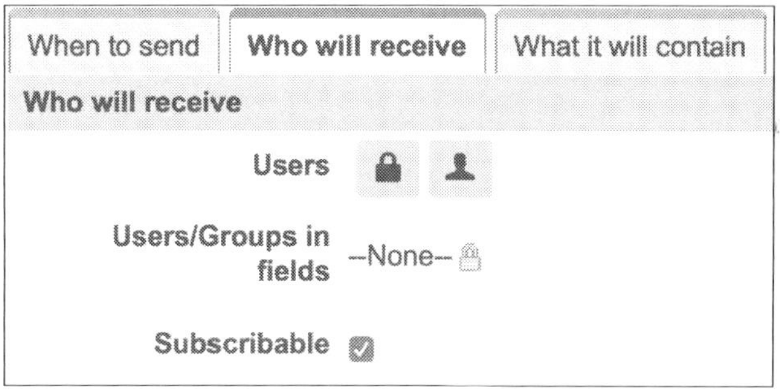

3. Go to **Notification Preferences** and click on **To subscribe to a new notification click here**. The new notification can be selected from the list. Now, every time a Work note is added to any **Maintenance** record, a notification will be sent to the subscriber.

> It is important to clear **Users/Groups in field** if **Subscribable** is ticked. Otherwise, everyone in the **Work notes** list will then become subscribed and receive every single subsequent notification for every record!

The user can also choose to only receive a subset of the messages. The **Schedule** field lets them choose when to receive notifications: perhaps only during working hours. The filter lets you define conditions, such as only receiving notifications for important issues. In this instance, a Notification Filter could be created for the **Maintenance** table, based upon the **Priority** field. Then, only **Work notes** for high-priority **Maintenance** tasks would be sent out.

Creating a new device

The **Notification Devices** [`cmn_notif_device`] table stores e-mail addresses for users. It allows every user to have multiple e-mail addresses, or even register mobile phones for text messages.

When a **User** record is created, a Business Rule named **Create primary email device** inserts a record in the **Notification Devices** table. The value in the **Email** field on the **User** table is just copied to this table by another Business Rule named **Update Email Devices**.

> A new device can be added from the **Notification Preferences** page, or a Related List can be added to the **User** form.

Navigate to **User Administration** > **Users** and create a new user. Once saved, you should receive a message saying **Primary email device created for** *user* (the username is displayed in place of *user*). Then add the **Notification Device->User** Related List to the form where the e-mail address record should be visible. Click on **New**.

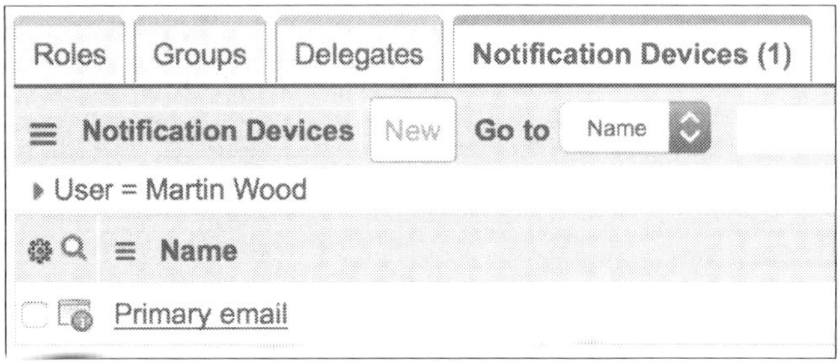

The **Notification Device** form allows you to enter the details of your e-mail- or SMS-capable device. Service provider is a reference field to the **Notification Service Provider** table, which specifies how an SMS message should be sent. If you have an account with one of the providers listed, enter your details.

> There are many hundreds of inactive providers in the **Notification Service Provider** [`cmn_notif_service_provider`] table. You may want to try enabling some, though many do not work for the reasons discussed soon.

Once a device has been added, they can be set up to receive messages through **Notification Preferences**. For example, a user can choose to receive approval requests via a text message by adding the **Approval Request Notification Message** and associating their SMS device. Alternatively, they could have two e-mail addresses, with one for an assistant.

> If a Notification is sent to a SMS device, the contents of the **SMS alternate** field are used. Remember that a text message can only be 160 characters at maximum.

The **Notification Device** table has a field called **Primary Email**. This determines which device is used for a notification that has not been sent to this user before. Despite the name, **Primary Email** can be ticked for an SMS device.

Sending text messages

Many mobile phone networks in the US supply e-mail-to-SMS gateways. AT&T gives every subscriber an e-mail address in the form of `5551234567@txt.att.net`. This allows the ServiceNow instance to actually send an e-mail and have the gateway convert it into an SMS. The **Notification Service Provider** form gives several options to construct the appropriate e-mail address. In this scheme, the recipient pays for the text message, so the sending of text messages is free.

Many European providers do not provide such functionality, since the sender is responsible for paying. Therefore, it is more common to use the Web to deliver the message to the gateway: perhaps using REST or SOAP. This gives an authenticated method of communication, which allows charging.

> *Chapter 6, Exchanging Data – Import Sets, Web Services, and Other Integrations*, discusses these integration techniques in more detail.

The **Notifications Service Provider** table also provides an **Advanced notification** checkbox that enables a script field. The code is run whenever the instance needs to send out an e-mail. This is a great place to call a Script Include that does the actual work, providing it with the appropriate parameters.

> Some global variables are present: `email.SMSText` contains the **SMS alternate** text and `device` is the `GlideRecord` of the Notification Device. This means `device.phone_number` and `device.user` are very useful values to access.

Delivering an e-mail

There are a great many steps that the instance goes through to send an e-mail. Some may be skipped or delivered as a shortcut, depending on the situation, but there are usually a great many steps that are processed. An e-mail may not be sent if any one of these steps goes wrong!

1. **A record is updated**: Most notifications are triggered when a task changes state or a comment is added. Use the debugging techniques discussed in *Chapter 8, Diagnosing ServiceNow – Knowing What Is Going On*, to determine what is changing.

> These next two steps may not be used if the Notification does not use events.

2. **An event is fired**: A Business Rule may fire an event. Look under **System Policy** > **Events** > **Event Log** to see if it was fired.
3. **The event is processed**: A Scheduled Job will process each event in turn. Look in the **Event Log** and ensure that all events have their state changed to **Processed**.
4. **An Email Notification is processed**: The event is associated with an Email Notification or the Email Notification uses the **Inserted** and **Updated** checkboxes to monitor a table directly.
5. **Conditions are evaluated**: The platform checks the associated record and ensures the conditions are met. If not, no further processing occurs.

6. **The receivers are evaluated**: The recipients are determined from the logic in the Email Notification.

> The use of **Send to event creator** makes a big impact on this step.

7. **The Notification Device is determined**: The Notification Messages table is queried. The appropriate Notification Device is then found. If the Notification Device is set to inactive, the recipient is dropped.

> The **Notification** field on the **User** record will control the Active flag of the **Notification Devices**.

8. **Any Notification Device filters are applied**: Any further conditions set in the **Notification Preferences** interface are evaluated, such as **Schedule** and **Filter**.
9. **An e-mail record is generated**: Variable substitution takes place on the Message Text and a record is saved into the `sys_email` table, with details of the messages in the Outbox. The Email Client starts at this point.
10. **The weight is evaluated**: If an Email Notification with a lower weight has already been generated for the same event, the e-mail has the **Mailbox** field set to **Skipped**.
11. **The email is sent**: The SMTP Sender Scheduled Job runs every minute. It picks up all messages in the Outbox, generates the message ID, and connects to the SMTP server specified in **Email** properties. This only occurs if **Mail sending** is enabled in the properties. Errors will be visible under **System Mailboxes** > **Outbound** > **Failed**.

> The generated e-mails can be monitored in the **System Mailboxes** Application Menu, or through **System Logs** > **Emails**. They are categorized into Mailboxes, just like an e-mail client. This should be considered a backend table, though some customers who want more control over e-mail notifications make this more accessible.

Knowing who the e-mail is from

ServiceNow uses one account when sending e-mails. This account is usually the one provided by ServiceNow, but it can be anything that supports SMTP: Exchange, Sendmail, NetMail, or even Gmail.

The SMTP protocol lets the sender specify who the mail is from. By default, no checks are done to ensure that the sender is allowed to send from that address. Every e-mail client lets you specify who the e-mail address is from, so I could change the settings in Outlook to say my e-mail address is `president@whitehouse.gov` or `primeminister@number10.gov.uk`.

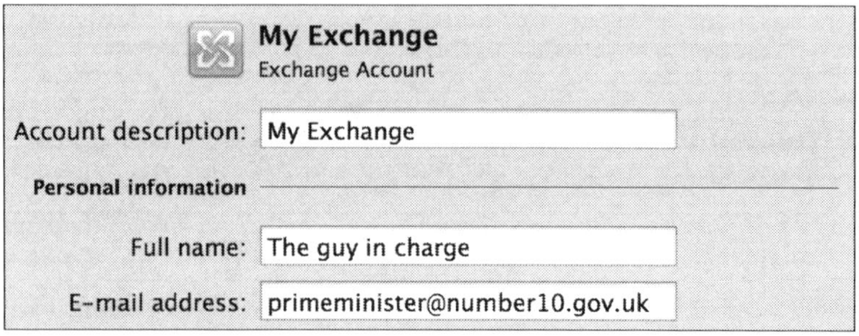

Spammers and virus writers have taken advantage of this situation to fill our mailboxes with unwanted e-mails. Therefore, e-mail systems are doing more authentication and checking of addresses when the message is received. You may have seen some e-mails from your client saying an e-mail has been delivered on behalf of another when this validation fails, or it even falling into the spam directly.

> ServiceNow uses SPF to specify which IP addresses can deliver service-now.com e-mails. Spam filters often use this to check if a sender is authorized. If you spoof the e-mail address, you may need to make an exception for ServiceNow. Read up more about it at:
>
> `http://en.wikipedia.org/wiki/Sender_Policy_Framework`

You may want to change the e-mail addresses on the instance to be your corporate domain. That means that your ServiceNow instance will send the message but will pretend that it is coming from another source. This runs the real risk of the e-mails being marked as spam. Instead, think about only changing the From display (not the e-mail address) or use your own e-mail account.

Receiving e-mails

Many systems can send e-mails. But isn't it annoying when they are broadcast only? When I get sent a message, I want to be able to reply to it. E-mail should be a conversation, not a fire-and-forget distribution mechanism.

So what happens when you reply to a ServiceNow e-mail? It gets categorized, and then processed according to the settings in **Inbound Email Actions**.

> Lots of information is available on the wiki: `http://wiki.servicenow.com/?title=Inbound_Email_Actions`.

Determining what an inbound e-mail is

Every two minutes, the platform runs the POP Reader scheduled job. It connects to the e-mail account specified in the properties and pulls them all into the **Email** table, setting the **Mailbox** to be **Inbox**.

> Despite the name, the POP Reader job also supports IMAP accounts.

This fires an event called `email.read`, which in turn starts the classification of the e-mail. It uses a series of logic decisions to determine how it should respond. The concept is that an inbound e-mail can be a *reply* to something that the platform has already sent out, is an e-mail that someone *forwarded*, or is part of an e-mail chain that the platform has not seen before; that is, it is a *new* e-mail. Each of these are handled differently, with different assumptions.

As the first step in processing the e-mail, the platform attempts to find the sender in the **User** table. It takes the address that the e-mail was sent from as the key to search for. If it cannot find a User, it either creates a new **User** record (if the property is set), or uses the **Guest** account.

1. Should this e-mail be processed at all? If either of the following conditions match, then the e-mail has the **Mailbox** set to skipped and no further processing takes place:
    - Does the subject line start with recognized text such as "out of office autoreply"?
    - Is the **User** account locked out?

2. Is this a *forward*? Both of the following conditions must match, else the e-mail will be checked as a reply:
    - Does the subject line start with a recognized prefix (such as `FW`)?
    - Does the string "From" appear anywhere in the body?
3. Is this a *reply*? One of the following conditions must match, else the e-mail will be processed as new:
    - Is there a valid, appropriate watermark that matches an existing record?
    - Is there an `In-Reply-To` header in the e-mail that references an e-mail sent by the instance?
    - Does the subject line start with a recognized prefix (such as `RE`) and contain a number prefix (such as `MAI000100`)?
4. If none of these are affirmative, the e-mail is treated as a new e-mail.

> The prefixes and recognized text are controlled with properties available under **System Properties** > **Email**.

This order of processing and logic cannot be changed. It is hardcoded into the platform. However, clever manipulation of the properties and prefixes allows great control over what will happen. One common request is to treat forwarded e-mails just like replies. To accomplish this, a nonsensical string should be added into the `forward_subject_prefix`, and the standard values added to the `reply_subject prefix`. property. For example, the following values could be used:

- Forward prefix: `xxxxxxxxxxx`
- Reply prefix: `re:, aw:, r:, fw:, fwd:...`

This will ensure that a match with the forwarding prefixes is very unlikely, while the reply logic checks will be met.

Creating Inbound Email Actions

Once an e-mail has been categorized, it will run through the appropriate **Inbound Email Action**. The main purpose of an Inbound Email Action is to run JavaScript code that manipulates a target record in some way. The target record depends upon what the e-mail has been classified as:

- A forwarded or new e-mail will create a new record
- A reply will update an existing record

Every Inbound Email Action is associated with a table and a condition, just like Business Rules. Since a reply must be associated with an existing record (usually found using the watermark), the platform will only look for Inbound Email Actions that are against the same table. The platform initializes the `GlideRecord` object `current` as the existing record.

> An e-mail classified as **Reply** must have an associated record, found via the watermark, the `In-Reply-To` header, or by running a search for a prefix stored in the `sys_number` table, or else it will not proceed.

Forwarded and new e-mails will create new records. They will use the first Inbound Email Action that meets the condition, regardless of the table. It will then initialize a new `GlideRecord` object called `current`, expecting it to be inserted into the table.

Accessing the e-mail information

In order to make the scripting easier, the platform parses the e-mail and populates the properties of an object called `email`. Some of the more helpful properties are listed here:

- `email.to` is a comma-separated list of e-mail addresses that the e-mail was sent to and was CC'ed to.
- `email.body_text` contains the full text of the e-mail, but does not include the previous entries in the e-mail message chain.

> This behavior is controlled by a property. For example, anything that appears underneath two empty lines plus `-----Original Message-----` is ignored.

- `email.subject` is the subject line of the e-mail.
- `email.from` contains the e-mail address of the **User** record that the platform thinks sent the e-mail.
- `email.origemail` uses the e-mail headers to get the e-mail address of the original sender.
- `email.body` contains the body of the e-mail, separated into `name:value` pairs. For instance, if a line of the body was `hello:world`, it would be equivalent to `email.body.hello = 'world'`.

Approving e-mails using Inbound Email Actions

The previous section looked at how the platform can generate `mailto` links, ready for a user to select. They generate an e-mail that has the word `approve` or `reject` in the subject line and watermark in the body.

This is a great example of how e-mail can be used to automate steps in ServiceNow. Approving via e-mail is often much quicker than logging in to the instance, especially if you are working remotely and are on the road. It means approvals happen faster, which in turn provides better service to the requesters and reduces the effort for our approvers. Win win!

The **Update Approval Request** Inbound Email Action uses the information in the inbound e-mail to update the **Approval** record appropriately. Navigate to **System Policy** > **Email** > **Inbound Actions** to see what it does. We'll inspect a few lines of the code to get a feel for what is possible when automating actions with incoming e-mails.

Understanding the code in Update Approval Request

One of the first steps within the function, `validUser`, performs a check to ensure the sender is allowed to update this Approval. They must either be a delegate or the user themselves. Some companies prefer to use an e-Signature method to perform approval, where a password must be entered. This check is not up to that level, but does go some way to helping.

> E-mail addresses (and **From** strings) can be spoofed in an e-mail client.

Assuming the validation is passed, the **Comments** field of the **Approval** record is updated with the body of the e-mail.

```
current.comments = "reply from: " + email.from + "\n\n" + email.body_
text;
```

In order to set the **State** field, and thus make the decision on the **Approval** request, the script simply runs a search for the existence of approve or reject within the subject line of the e-mail using the standard `indexOf` string function. If it is found, the state is set.

```
if (email.subject.indexOf("approve") >= 0)
  current.state = "approved";
if (email.subject.indexOf("reject") >= 0)
  current.state = "rejected";
```

Once the fields have been updated, it saves the record. This triggers the standard Business Rules and will run the Workflow as though this was done in the web interface.

Updating the Work notes of a Maintenance task

Most often, a reply to an e-mail is to add Additional comments or Work notes to a task. Using scripting, you could differentiate between the two scenarios by seeing who has sent the e-mail: a requester would provide Additional comments and a fulfiller may give either, but it is safer to assume Work notes.

Let's make a simple Inbound Email Action to process e-mails and populate the **Work notes** field.

Navigate to **System Policy** > **Email** > **Inbound Actions** and click on **New**. Use these details:

- **Name**: `Work notes for Maintenance task`
- **Target table**: `Maintenance [u_maintenance]`
- **Active**: `<ticked>`
- **Type**: `Reply`
- **Script**:

```
current.work_notes = "Reply from: " + email.origemail + "\n\n" +
email.body_text;
current.update();
```

This script is very simple: it just updates our task record after setting the Work notes field with the e-mail address of the sender and the text they sent. It is separated out with a few new lines. The platform impersonates the sender, so the Activity Log will show the update as though it was done in the web interface.

Once the record has been saved, the Business Rules run as normal. This includes ServiceNow sending out e-mails. Anyone who is in the **Work notes list** will receive the e-mail. If **Send to event creator** is ticked, it means the person who sent the e-mail may receive another in return, telling them they updated the task!

Having multiple incoming e-mail addresses

Many customers want to have logic based upon inbound e-mail addresses. For example, sending a new e-mail to `invoices@gardiner-hotels.com` would create a task for the Finance team, while `wifi@gardiner-hotels.com` creates a ticket for the Networking group. These are easy to remember and work with, and implementing ServiceNow should not mean that this simplicity should be removed.

ServiceNow provides a single e-mail account that is in the format `instance@service-now.com` and is not able to provide multiple or custom e-mail addresses. There are two broad options for meeting this requirement:

- Checking multiple accounts
- Redirecting e-mails

Using the Email Accounts plugin

While ServiceNow only provides a single e-mail address, it has the ability to pull in e-mails from multiple e-mail accounts through the `Email Accounts` plugin.

> The wiki has more information here: `http://wiki.servicenow.com/?title=Email_Accounts`.

Once the plugin has been activated, it converts the standard account information into a new **Email Account** [`sys_email_account`] record. There can be multiple Email Accounts for a particular instance, and the POP Reader job is repurposed to check each one. Once the e-mails have been brought into ServiceNow, they are treated as normal.

Since ServiceNow does not provide multiple e-mail accounts, it is the customer's responsibility to create, maintain, and configure the instance with the details, including the username and passwords. The instance will need to connect to the e-mail account, which is often hosted within the customer's datacenter. This means that firewall rules or other security methods may need to be considered.

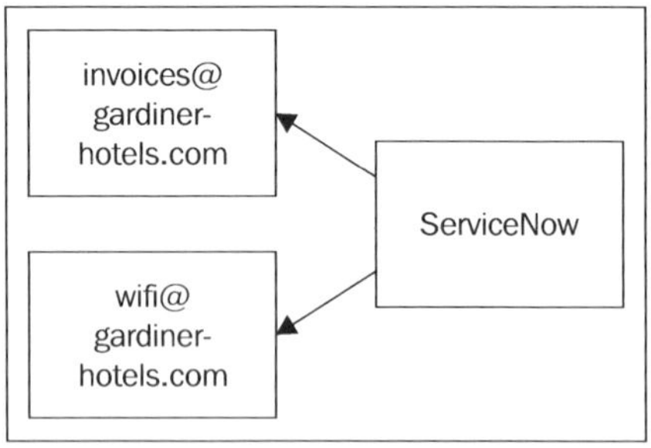

Redirecting e-mails

Instead of having the instance check multiple e-mail accounts, it is often preferable to continue to work with a single e-mail address. The additional e-mail addresses can be redirected to the one that ServiceNow provides.

The majority of e-mail platforms, such as Microsoft Exchange, make it possible to redirect e-mail accounts. When an e-mail is received by the e-mail system, it is resent to the ServiceNow account. This process differs from e-mail forwarding:

- **Forwarding** involves adding the FW: prefix to the subject line, altering the message body, and changing the *From* address.
- **Redirection** sends the message unaltered, with the original *To* address, to the new address. There is little indication that the message has not come directly from the original sender.

Redirection is often an easier method to work with than having multiple e-mail accounts. It gives more flexibility to the customer's IT team, since they do not need to provide account details to the instance, and enables them to change the redirection details easily. If a new e-mail address has to be added or an existing one decommissioned, only the e-mail platform needs to be involved. It also reduces the configuration on the ServiceNow instance; nothing needs to change.

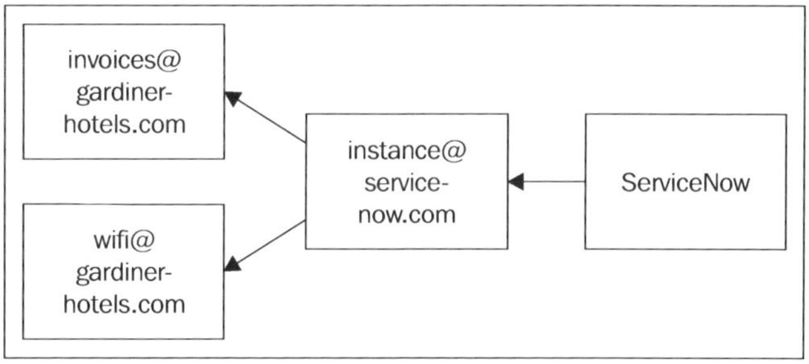

Processing multiple e-mail address

Once the e-mails have been brought into ServiceNow, the platform will need to examine who the e-mail was sent to and make some decisions. This will allow the e-mails sent to `wifi@gardiner-hotels.com` to be routed as tasks to the networking team.

There are several methods available for achieving this:

- A look-up table can be created, containing a list of e-mail addresses and a matching Group reference. The Inbound Email Script would use a `GlideRecord` query to find the right entry and populate the Assignment group on the new task.
- The e-mail address could be copied over into a new field on the task. Standard routing techniques, such as **Assignment Rules** and **Data Lookup**, could be used to examine the new field and populate the Assignment group.
- The Inbound Email Action could contain the addresses hardcoded in the script. While this is not a scalable or maintainable solution, it may be appropriate for a simple deployment.

Recording Metrics

ServiceNow provides several ways to monitor the progress of a task. These are often reported and e-mailed to the stakeholders, thus providing insight into the effectiveness of processes.

Metrics are a way to record information. It allows the analysis and improvement of a process by measuring statistics, based upon particular defined criteria. Most often, these are time based. One of the most common metrics is how long it takes to complete a task: from when the record was created to the moment the Active flag became false. The duration can then be averaged out and compared over time, helping to answer questions such as *Are we getting quicker at completing tasks?*

> Metrics provide a great alternative to creating lots of extra fields and Business Rules on a table.

Other metrics are more complex and may involve getting more than one result per task.

- How long does each Assignment group take to deal with the ticket?
- How long does an SLA get paused for?
- How many times does the incident get reassigned?

The difference between Metrics and SLAs

At first glance, a Metric appears to be very similar to an SLA, since they both record time.

> **Service Level Agreement (SLA)** is covered in *Chapter 4, Getting Things Done with Tasks.*

However, there are some key differences between Metrics and SLAs:

- There is no *target* or aim defined in a Metric. It cannot be breached; the duration is simply recorded.
- A Metric cannot be paused or made to work to a schedule.
- There is no Workflow associated with a Metric.

In general, a Metric is a more straightforward measurement, designed for collecting statistics rather than being in the forefront when processing a task.

Running Metrics

Every time the Task table gets updated, the `metrics events` Business Rule fires an event called `metric.update`. A Script Action named `Metric Update` is associated with the event and calls the appropriate Metric Definitions.

> If you define a metric on a non-task-based table, make sure you fire the `metric.update` event through a Business Rule

The **Metric Definition** [`metric_definition`] table specifies how a metric should be recorded, while the **Metric Instance** [`metric_instance`] table records the results. As ever, each **Metric Definition** is applied to a specific table.

The **Type** field of a Metric Definition refers to two situations:

- **Field value duration** is associated with a field on the table. Each time the field changes value, the platform creates a new Metric Instance. The duration for which that value was present is recorded. No code is required, but if some is given, it is used as a condition.
- **Script calculation** uses JavaScript to determine what the Metric Instance contains.

Scripting a Metric Definition

There are several predefined variables available to a Metric Definition: `current` refers to the `GlideRecord` under examination and `definition` is a `GlideRecord` of the Metric Definition.

The `MetricInstance` Script Include provides some helpful functions, including `startDuration` and `endDuration`, but it is really only relevant for time-based metrics. Metrics can be used to calculate many statistics (like the number of times a task is reopened), but code must be written to accomplish this.

Monitoring the duration of Maintenance tasks

Navigate to **Metrics** > **Definitions** and click on **New**. Set the following fields:

- **Name**: `Maintenance states`
- **Table**: `Maintenance [u_maintenance]`
- **Field**: `State`
- **Timeline**: `<ticked>`

Once saved, test it out by changing the **State** field on a **Maintenance** record to several different values. Make sure to wait 30 seconds or so between each **State** change, so that the Scheduled Job has time to fire. Right-click on the **Form header** and choose **Metrics Timeline** to visualize the changes in the **State** field.

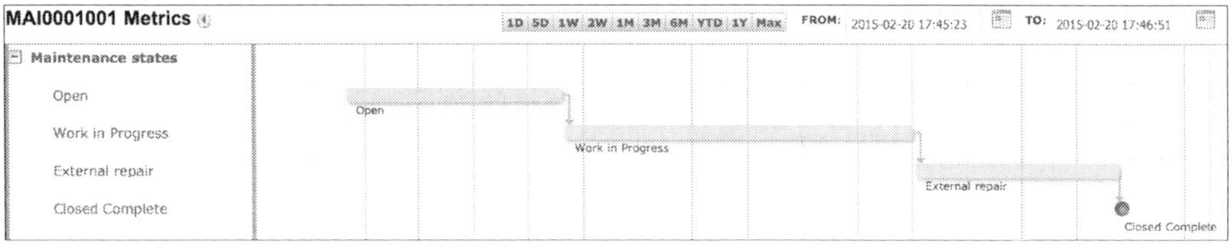

> Adding the **Metrics** Related List to the **Maintenance** form will display all the captured data. Another Related List is available on the **Maintenance Definition** form.

Flattening data with Database Views

The concept of a database view is easily understood. It takes information as it is stored in the database and presents it in a different way. In ServiceNow, **Database Views** are most often used to present a subset of useful information and to join tables together. It appears as a standard table to the user, albeit one that is read-only.

In many situations, Database Views are not strictly necessary. Dot-walking can achieve many requirements. In the background, ServiceNow performs the appropriate joins on the database tables, giving you the data that is needed. This means that you do not need to create a Database View to create a list of all the Maintenance tasks, what rooms they relate to, and what the phone numbers of the assigned people are.

Creating a Metric Instance Database View

Database Views are useful when working with Metric Instance records. A **Metrics Instances** table does not contain a regular **Reference** field, but instead a document **ID** and a **Table** field. Together, they can point to any record in any table in the system. This flexibility comes with a price; dot-walking is not possible.

Instead, a Database View can be used to present a single interface to the data.

Navigate to **System Definition** > **Database Views** and click on **New**. Use the following details:

- **Name**: `u_maintenance_metric`
- **Label**: `Maintenance Metric`
- **Plural**: `Maintenance Metrics`

Once saved, a Related List will be available. This specifies which tables to join together.

Click on **New** on the **View Table** Related List and set the following fields:

- **Table**: `Metric Definition [metric_definition]`
- **Variable prefix**: `md`

As you define each table, you have the opportunity to specify which fields you want from the table. If none are specified, all are used. Every field that is included will have their name prefixed with the variable prefix, followed by an underscore. Therefore, in this example, the fields will be `md_active`, `md_description`, `md_field`, and so on.

> Do not make the variable prefix too long – keep it to a couple of characters at most. It is easy to go over the maximum field length.

Create another new **View Table** record. Set the following fields:

- **Table**: `Metric [metric_instance]`
- **Variable prefix**: `mi`
- **Order**: `200`
- **Where clause**: `mi_definition = md_sys_id`

The **Where clause** is what joins the tables together. Two different tables, with different fields, will be combined together. Every row from one table will be joined to every row of the other. Then this combined set will have the `where` clause applied. Any combinations that match the clause will be kept.

> In general, you want to match the `sys_id` of one table with a reference field from the other table.

This example says that the **Definition** field from the **Metric Instance** table (the foreign key) will contain the same value as the `sys_id` unique identifier that is on the **Metric Definition** table. So we'll get a list of all Metric Instances with the appropriate **Metric Definition** fields alongside.

> The default join in ServiceNow is an inner join. A left join can be made by adding the Left join field to the form and checking it. In this instance, it will include entries where a Metric Definitions doesn't have any Metric Instances. This is not what we want.

Finally, we want to join the Metric information to our **Maintenance** table. Set the following fields on a new **View Table** record:

- **Table**: `Maintenance [u_maintenance]`
- **Variable prefix**: `m`
- **Order**: `300`
- **Where clause**: `m_sys_id = mi_id`

When you click on the **Try it** UI Action on the **Database View** form, you should see the result. We see every Metric Instance that is associated with a **Maintenance** task and a Metric Definition.

A Database View will behave in a similar fashion to normal tables. Each one can have a form designed, fields chosen for a list, and views for both. As we'll see in the next section, it gives us everything we need to create a report.

Reporting

You've already run reports in ServiceNow. Choosing what data you get, by picking the columns you want and adding the filters you need, is all part of using lists. Some times, this is all you need. Want to know how many Maintenance requests there have been today? Create the appropriate filter and then have a look at the record count. Easy!

Do you want to keep this data somewhere? From the standard list interface, right-click on the column headings and choose **Export**. You'll have a choice of **Excel**, **CSV**, **XML**, and several different PDF formats. The detailed versions of the PDF exports not only include the list, but also the forms of each record. There is even a **Print** icon on the top right of the interface, near the **Logout** button.

> The columns included in a download are the same as the list. Add in additional columns or use views to easily switch between what you export.

Many people like Excel documents or PDF files. But my advice is to right-click on the filter and choose **Copy URL**, and distribute that. That way, a recipient always gets the latest information just by clicking on the link. No out-of-date information!

> It is easy to save a list you particularly like. In the filter builder, there is a **Save** button that asks for a name as well as who can select it: just yourself, everyone, or a particular group. Access to these filters is controlled by role.

The functionality of a list

The list interface provides more than just a list. Right-clicking on the column headings displays several options. Some of them are as follows:

- **Group By ...** will collect all the records with the same field value together. Each grouping is expandable.

> The interface shows up to 100 groups at once, and inside each group is the number of rows you normally see (by default, 20). That means 2,000 records can be retrieved from the instance, and potentially many more. This can mean inefficient grouping is particularly slow.

- We've already seen the ability to export, but you can also easily import Excel or CSV documents. As long as the column headings match with the field names, it takes only a few clicks. *Chapter 6, Exchanging Data – Import Sets, Web Services, and Other Integrations*, has more about this.
- There are also two further self-explanatory options: **Pie chart** and **Bar chart**. Choosing either of these options on a column brings up the chart in the reporting interface. Using the option on choice list fields such as **State** usually work well.

Using reports elsewhere

A report can be created through a custom interface. Access it by going to **Reports** > **Create New**. It provides several chart types, with many of the options dependent on what you select.

> This wiki provides lots of detail about the options available for each report type: `http://wiki.servicenow.com/?title=Generating_Reports`

Once a report has been saved, quite a few buttons are made available. Most are obvious, but some are worthy of further explanation:

- **Publish** makes the report available via URL. When you click on the button, the URL is shown at the top of the page. This can be distributed to anyone, or perhaps embedded in a portal in an *iframe*. Anyone who visits the URL will not be prompted for a username or password, since the page has been declared public. The data itself is live and is subject to access control rules.

- Homepages are made from Widgets and Gauges. Clicking on the **Make Gauge** button makes the report available for selection on a Homepage. Homepages are discussed further in the next section.
- The **Add to homepage** button shortcuts the process by making a Gauge and adding it to the homepage in one step.
- **Schedule** will e-mail the contents of a report automatically in a scheduled manner.

> Note that the **Visible to** option only changes who can see the report, not what the report contains. The data is controlled by normal access control rules.

Sending a shift handover report

The **Scheduled Email of Report** [`sysauto_report`] table extends `sysauto`. Earlier in the chapter, we saw how the platform will run jobs automatically, given a time and something to do. A scheduled report has several options in order to make it easy to automate report distribution.

One common use of a Scheduled Report is to produce a report showing the activity of yesterday or last week. This is very easy with the relative time conditions. Let's build a list to show what **Maintenance** tasks were created yesterday, to give the incoming team a heads-up on what happened.

The quickest way is to create a report in the reporting interface. Set the following information:

- **Name**: `Shift handover`
- **Type**: `List`
- **Table**: `Maintenance [u_maintenance]`
- **Group by**: `State`
- **Header Footer Template**: `Default`

> A Header Footer Template is used when exporting to a PDF. It allows you to place titles and page numbers, and in various positions on the page.

- **Filter Condition**: `Created - on - Yesterday`

Once saved, click on the **Schedule** button.

The **Scheduled Email of Report** form should be straightforward. Set the following fields as an example. If you want to test it, save it and click on **Execute Now**.

- **Groups**: `Maintenance`
- **Subject**: `Daily handover report`
- **Run**: `Daily`
- **Time**: `05:00:00`
- **Omit if no records**: `<ticked>`

> There is little reason to send out an e-mail if there is nothing in it!

- **Introductory message**: `Enjoy the attached report!`

> The **Include with** field and Related List are useful. It allows several reports to be linked together, rather than having multiple e-mails with a single attachment each.

Analytics with ServiceNow

The basic reporting engine built in to ServiceNow is focused on transactional reporting. It reports on a single table at once, with little support for calculating values. The only way to get percentages in a report is a pie chart, for example. Since each report is focused on individual records, trending is difficult. Comparing data from two tables is not possible.

> The **Custom Charts** plugin does overcome some of these deficiencies. Using script, it gives control over the two main areas: generating the data and placing it into a **Summary Set** and then displaying it using `JFreeChart`, a Java library used to create a custom display. The following wiki article has more details on how this is achieved (but be warned - it is a considerable time sink!): `http://wiki.servicenow.com/?title=Custom_Chart_Definitions`.

Basic trending with Line Charts

One report that goes some way to determining how things change over time is the Line Chart. Create a new report on the **Maintenance** table by following these options:

- **Name**: `Tasks opened per day`
- **Type**: `Line chart`
- **Table**: `Maintenance [u_maintenance]`
- **Group by**: `-- None --`
- **Trend field**: `Opened - per - Date`

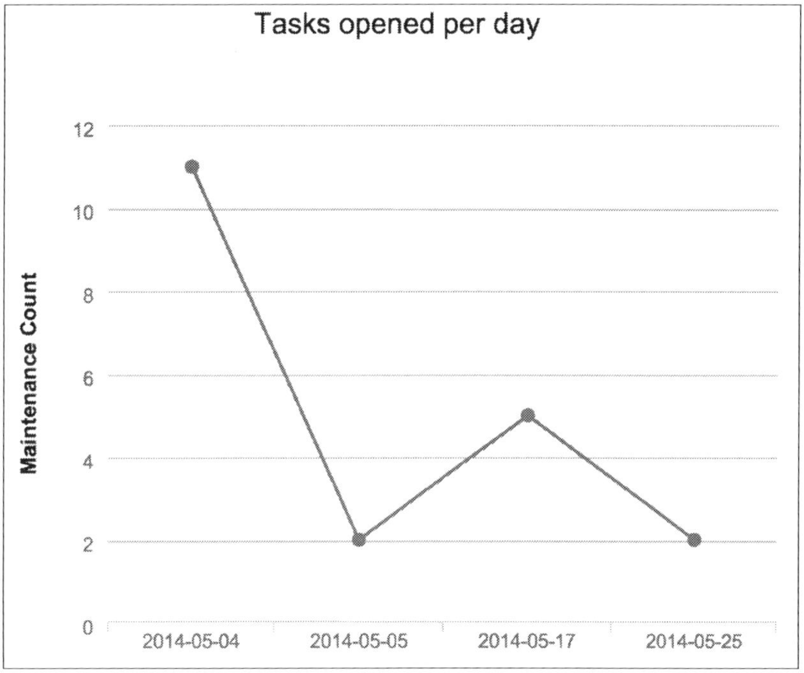

[This report gives a good indication of how demand for your service varies. However, the *x* axis is not consistent and will not render zero when there are no **Maintenance** tasks opened on that day.]

Performance Analytics

In order to provide a better reporting capability, ServiceNow offers Performance Analytics as an additional service. It provides a more capable system to define and report on Key Performance Indicators, especially around trend analysis.

- Data collection jobs run on a scheduled basis to pull information into the system. These include indicators such as the number of open tasks at any given moment.
- Formulas can be used to have indicators such as the average age of a ticket.
- A particular indicator can be broken down per assignment group or department.
- E-mail summaries can be sent when large changes in indicators occur.
- Targets can be given for indicators, such as having less than 10 percent of your tasks as high priority.

> This wiki has a great deal of information on **Performance Analytics**: `http://wiki.servicenow.com/?title=Performance_Analytics`.

Making sense of reports

ServiceNow makes easy reporting available to everyone. The reporting functionality is available to fulfillers, letting them pick any table they want to look at, and requesters can create a bar or pie chart from a list. However, that doesn't mean they get useful information from it!

> The Reports Application Menu is restricted to the `itil` and `asset` roles, but this can easily be changed. *Chapter 7, Securing Applications and Data,* talks more about roles and access.

As an example, consider a report that shows the number of tasks closed on a particular day, similar to how the example line chart we just saw shows opened tasks. What this report may do is count how many tasks have the same **Closed** date.

In this example, we'll start with the data set shown in this table:

Number	Closed
TSK001	1 May
TSK002	2 May
TSK003	1 May
TSK004	3 May

If a report on this data is run, it'll say that two tasks were closed on 1 May and one each on 2 and 3 May. Simple, right?

Now consider that **TSK003** was reopened on 3 May. It had its **State** changed from **Complete** to **Active**, since, in actual fact, the work had not been finished. Later that day, it was closed again. We now have a table like this:

Number	Closed
TSK001	1 May
TSK002	2 May
TSK003	3 May
TSK004	3 May

Now, if the same report was run again, it would give a different result. Only one task was closed on 1 May. This may surprise some people! Having a **Closed** date that has changed is a simple example, but one that commonly frustrates. Products such as **Performance Analytics** get round this by capturing the count and storing it for future comparison. Of course, it may be that logic and security rules in ServiceNow stops a task from being reopened, so this situation never arises. This is a common configuration, and we'll explore how to achieve this in *Chapter 7, Securing Applications and Data*.

Ensuring consistency

The example we just saw shows that reports need to be thought about carefully.

- Should you use the Active flag or **Closed** states?
- Which table should I start with to give me the right information?
- Will dot-walking give me the right information, or do I need a database view?

- Is reporting on the **Transaction** table on a busy instance a good idea, where only a **Contains** filter is applied on the URL field and then they are grouped by **Created**?

> The answer to that last question, by the way, is no. It will perform very badly!

ServiceNow offers several roles to control access, including `report_group` and `report_global`. These control the **Visible to** option when defining a report, and the `guage_maker` role specifies who can see the **Add to Homepage** and **Make Gauge** buttons. It is important to control these reports appropriately: not only do the reports need to make sense, but they should also be quick to run. Train report writers effectively, and make sure they understand the data they are producing.

I have often seen multiple reports, all answering the same question, but with different approaches and, therefore, results. Consistency is important, especially with items such as SLA reporting.

> Remember that 69.7 percent of statistics are made up on the spot. Are yours?

Using outside tools

As *Chapter 8, Diagnosing ServiceNow – Knowing What Is Going On*, ServiceNow has great support for integrating with external systems. Sometimes, therefore, it is most appropriate to use dedicated reporting tools. ServiceNow provides an **ODBC Driver** that allows tools such as **Crystal Reports**, **SQL Service Reporting Services (SSRS)**, or even Excel to connect to the instance and generate the reports. If an organization already uses a reporting tool, then it often makes sense to have ServiceNow feed into it. These often give more complex joins and calculated fields that just aren't possible in ServiceNow.

> The ODBC Driver uses Web Services to grab the data. ServiceNow does not allow direct connections to the underlining database for security reasons - all communication must go through the platform. This also means that all security rules, as we will discuss in *Chapter 7, Securing Applications and Data*, will be respected.

Other tools such as the **ServiceNow Data Mart Loader** (or **SnowMirror**) allow you to create a replica of all the ServiceNow data locally. This is useful for a data warehouse solution, where multiple systems all contribute data. Companies use this to compare and contrast data sets: does an increase in phone calls to the Service Desk result in slower resolution of tasks? Refer to these links for more information:

- `http://sourceforge.net/projects/servicenowpump/`
- `http://www.snow-mirror.com/`

Building homepages

When you log in to ServiceNow, the first thing you see is a homepage. These are built out of reports. They are often used as dashboards, giving a quick overview of the situation: perhaps showing high-priority tasks or SLAs that have been missed. It is the way to have multiple reports on the same page.

A homepage is organized through a layout. A homepage is made up of dropzones—areas that items can be added to. This can be seen in the following screenshot. The vast majority of homepages use the same layout, with a header, two columns, and a footer. This design uses HTML tables to position the elements.

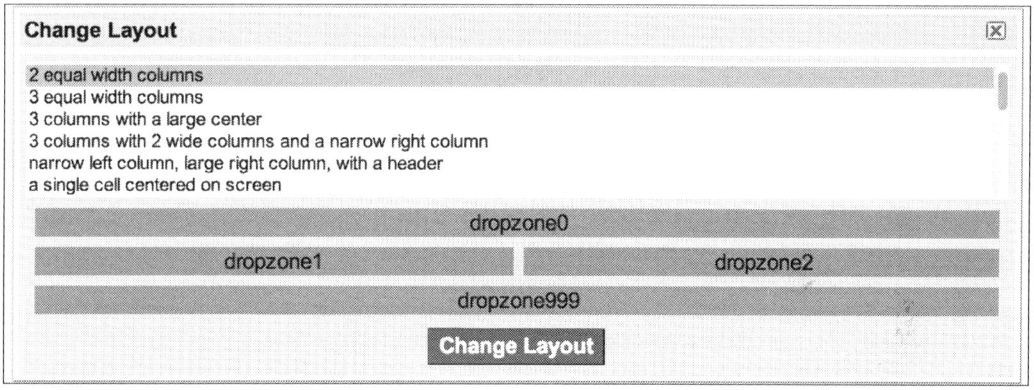

> Layouts are also used by the Content Management System, which is covered in *Chapter 10, Making ServiceNow Beautiful with CMS and Jelly*. Custom layouts are defined using Jelly. Check out this wiki for more: `http://wiki.servicenow.com/?title=Defining_a_Layout`.

Content in the form of widgets are added to each dropzone. The different types of widgets are listed under **System UI** > **Widgets**. A widget has to provide two things: a list of options, as selections, and how it should be rendered or displayed on the homepage. These are defined by making appropriately named functions, `sections` and `render` respectively.

It is unlikely that the widgets themselves will need to be edited or added, unless a particularly customized homepage is desired. The **Gadgets** and **Cool Clock** widgets serve as an example of how custom widgets are often made: make a UI Page that is then rendered when the homepage is displayed. UI Pages are discussed in *Chapter 10, Making ServiceNow Beautiful with CMS and Jelly*.

> The Gadgets widget is an example of how a homepage doesn't have to just have reports, but can also give useful navigation and other tools. It gives a little sticky note scratch pad, and a way to search the Knowledge Base - all from the homepage.

Creating a Maintenance homepage

Homepages are stored in the **Portal Pages** [`sys_portal_page`] table. Pages for CMS sites also live here, so there is a **Type** field that separates them. Navigate to **Homepage Admin** > **Pages** and click on **New** to create one. Use these details:

- **Title**: `Maintenance`
- **Selectable**: `<ticked>`

> The **Selectable** checkbox ensures that it is listed in the drop-down box on the homepage. If a homepage is not selectable, a link must be used to make it accessible.

- **User**: `System Administrator` (or whoever you are logged in as)

> To begin with, this homepage should be a personal homepage. The next section discusses this in more detail.

Once saved, navigate to the homepage. This is achieved either by navigating to **Self-Service** > **Homepage** or by clicking on the cog icon on the top right and then **Home**. In the **Switch to page...** selection, choose **Maintenance**. The page should be empty.

> The other way to create a new page is to select **New page** in this same selection box.

Let's add some content. Navigate to **Reports** > **View / Run** and find the **Shift Handover** report we made earlier. Click on the **Add to Homepage** button and choose somewhere in the layout to add it.

Now, when you navigate back to the **Maintenance** homepage, you should see the report. Try adding a few more.

Making global homepages

When a homepage is edited, the system makes a copy and turns it into a personal homepage. A personal homepage is directly associated with a user account. Editing could mean adding a new widget, repositioning a widget, or renaming the homepage by overtyping the title. You can often distinguish when a personal homepage has been created, since the platform adds the text *My* to the front of the title.

The majority of the time, this is desirable, since otherwise a user could ruin your carefully curated page with a single click! But how do you publish a standard homepage that everyone can see as a default?

To make the homepage global, navigate to the **Maintenance** homepage definition under **Homepage Admin** > **Pages** and make the following changes:

- **User**: <empty>
- **View**: maintenance

Once saved, an **Edit Homepage** link becomes available. This is because the **View** field has been populated. Use this link to edit the master copy of the homepage.

Because the **User** field has been cleared, other users can now select the homepage. If you wish to restrict who can see the homepage, use the **Read roles** field. Unless someone has made a personal homepage, they will see the homepage with the lowest order value that their roles allow.

Editing homepages

Accessing a homepage can either occur by using the **Switch to page...** field or through a link. There are two different types of links. Each handles the editing of pages slightly differently.

- A link that includes a `view` parameter will show and edit the master copy. This view uses **Write roles** to determine if a page can be edited. If the user doesn't have the role, they cannot change the page. This form is often used in modules, on the left-hand-side menu navigator. The format used is `/home.do?sysparm_view=<view name, like maintenance>`
- Otherwise, a link can be created that uses the `sys_id` of the homepage. Any edits to this page will create a personal homepage copy. The **Switch to page...** selection also uses this style: `/home.do?sysparm_userpref_homepage=<sys_id of homepage>`

Counting on a homepage

In addition to reports, **Count** Gauges give a quick insight into some important numbers. As with reports, the numbers are run on demand, so they are often used to say how many high-priority tasks are still open or the number of tasks assigned to you. They use a simple condition that is run against a table, from which the number of matching records are returned.

Navigate to **System UI** > **Gauges** and click on **New**. This record will be used to group the **Count** Gauges together. Use these details:

- **Name**: `Maintenance counts`
- **Type**: `Counts`
- **Table**: `Maintenance [u_maintenance]`

Once saved, click on **New** under **Count** Gauges. Let's return how many tasks are currently open and how many are higher priority. Use this data:

- **Name**: `Open Maintenance Tasks`
- **Table**: `Maintenance [u_maintenance]`
- **Short description**: `How many maintenance tasks still need to be closed`
- **Order**: `10`
- **Query**: `Active - is - true`

Once saved, create another with these options:

- **Name**: `High priority tasks`
- **Table**: `Maintenance [u_maintenance]`
- **Short description**: `Of those, how many are higher priority`
- **Order**: `20`
- **Omit line**: `<ticked>`

> If you tick this on the last entry, it makes the list look neater.

- **Query**:
    - `Active - is - true`
    - `Priority - greater than - 2 - High`

This gauge can then be added to the homepage. Ensure you navigate to **Homepage admin** > **Pages** and use the **Edit Homepage** link so that you don't create a personal copy. Use the **+** button and then select **Gauges**, **Maintenance**, and **Maintenance Count**.

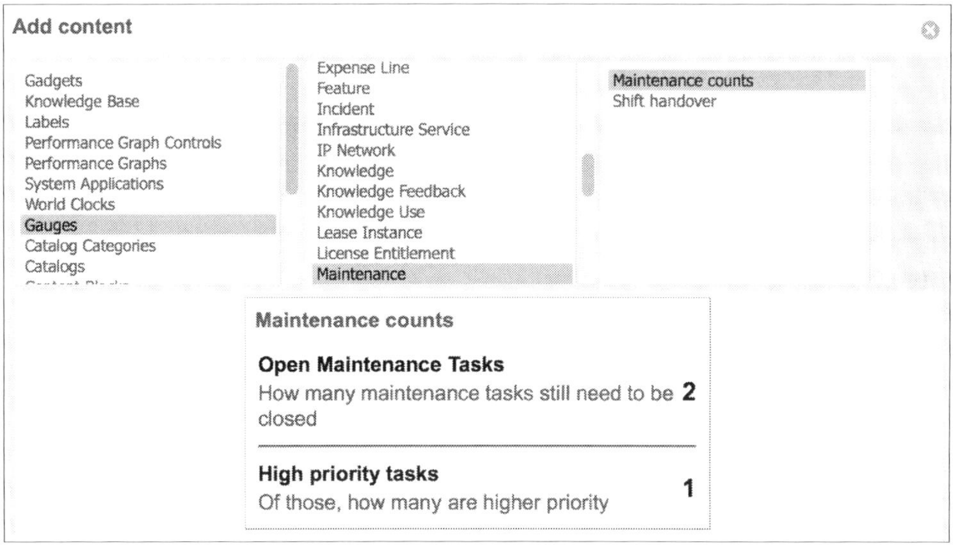

> Gauge counts can also use a script to determine a number. You can run any script in the provided field, with the return value providing what is displayed. It doesn't even need to be a number.

Optimizing homepages

Homepages seem innocuous. However, they frequently end up being a significant influencer on the overall performance of an instance. Consider the scenario:

- 50 people in the same team have the same homepage.
- The homepage contains 10 reports, with several using inefficient queries.
- Everyone logs in at the same time, at 9 a.m., when work starts.
- Even then, they all ignore the homepage, since they aren't relevant for them, and click on My Work. (Many of the reports actually aren't even seen, since they are beyond the 'fold', or only visible after scrolling.)

This gives the system a great deal of work to do: 500 graphs to show, all at the same time, but for no benefit! Again, a series of optimizing strategies is used by the instance, including caching, but it is most important to be considerate about the reports and the conditions they contain. Perhaps only show tasks that have been updated in the last month for example, instead of reporting on every record.

> Caching can be controlled by going to **Homepage Admin** > **Properties**.

Summary

This chapter showed how to deal with all the data collected in ServiceNow. The key to this is the automated processing of information. We started with exploring events. When things happen in ServiceNow, the platform can notice and set a flag for processing later. This keeps the system responsive for the user, while ensuring all the work that needs to get done, does get done.

Scheduled Jobs is the background for a variety of functions: scheduled reports, scripts, or even task generation. They run on a periodic basis, such as every day or every hour. They are often used for the automatic closure of tasks if the requester hasn't responded recently.

Email Notifications are a critical part of any business application. We explored how e-mails are used to let requesters know when they've got work to do, to give requesters a useful update, or when an approver must make a decision. We even saw how approvers can make that decision using only e-mail.

Every user has a great deal of control over how they receive these notifications. The **Notification Preferences** interface lets them add multiple devices, including mobile phones to receive text messages.

The **Email Client** in ServiceNow gives a simple, straightforward interface to send out e-mails, but the **Additional comments** and **Work notes** fields are often better and quicker to use. Every e-mail can include the contents of fields and even the output of scripts.

Every two minutes, ServiceNow checks for e-mails sent to its account. If it finds any, the e-mail is categorized into being a reply, forward, or new and runs **Inbound Email Actions** to update or create new records.

Metrics are useful to capture additional information about a particular record, such as how long it took to close. Reports can then use this information, especially if a **Database View** has been used to flatten the structure.

Finally, homepages were looked at. These display information for a user to see when they log in or any time they click on the home icon. Most often, they contain reports, but any **widget** can be made and added, giving great flexibility. You can even add some clocks!

The next chapter, *Chapter 6, Exchanging Data – Import Sets, Web Services, and Other Integrations*, explores how an instance can get data from other systems, synchronizing important information like who the users are, and also get them to pull updates from ServiceNow. Learn how to get the right data in the right place at the right time.

6

Exchanging Data – Import Sets, Web Services, and Other Integrations

The journey through ServiceNow has focused on configuring the platform, and creating a new application with scripts, data structures, and workflow functionality. However, an instance that doesn't exchange data; an instance that requires manual interaction every time an employee joins or leaves; or that needs task information copy-pasted into another system, is an instance not being used to its full capability.

This chapter explores how ServiceNow can make it easy to exchange data with almost any other system. There are quite a few ways to make this happen:

- Let others' system pull information using **Direct Web Services** with no configuration
- **Import** flat files like CSV, XML, or Excel spreadsheets on a manual or automatic basis
- Shape, control, and manage the flow of data with **Import Sets**
- Get user and group data from **Active Directory** or other **LDAP** servers
- Utilize the **MID Server** to easily communicate from behind firewalls and run custom scripts
- Use **Web Service Import Sets** to rapidly build your own interface
- Gain more control with **Scripted Web Services**
- Use **Processors** to create a completely custom-made communication interface
- Tighten up control with **WS-Security** and **Mutual Authentication**

Beginning the Web Service journey

ServiceNow was born in the cloud. Every instance has a native capability to share all its information in a variety of formats, without any configuration, directly over the Web.

People are often most comfortable browsing the Web when they see words, pictures, and some nice formatting. HTML provides a standard way to present this information to a user. A web server such as ServiceNow generates the page and a web browser (such as Chrome or Firefox), grabs it, and renders it on a screen. The person can then merrily click away, navigating their way through several billion pages.

But this data is not especially helpful to another computer. Pictures and free text are not easily understandable to a machine. While the Semantic Web (`http://www.w3.org/standards/semanticweb/`) is attempting to convert the currently unstructured data available into something more useful, ServiceNow can do this in a different way. It can present the same information stored in the database in a way that is more usable to a machine. It is your data; you can decide what to do with it.

Pulling data out of ServiceNow

ServiceNow provides this data in lots of different formats, all transferred via the Web. We'll explore each one of these, and more, in this chapter.

- Among file-based data, we will discuss CSV, XML, PDFs, and Excel documents
- Among Web-based data, we will cover RSS, JSON, and SOAP

Downloading file-based data

Chapter 5, Events, Notifications, and Reporting, explained how you could export any list in a variety of formats. You simply go to the list header, right-click, and choose Export. And *Chapter 1, Setting Up the ServiceNow Architecture*, explored how we could navigate to pages without using the frameset. Open up a new browser window and set the path as the table name suffixed by `_list.do`.

You may want a list of every **Maintenance** task in a format that Excel can use. Navigate to `http://<instance>.service-now.com/u_maintenance_list.do`. You will be presented with the **Maintenance** task list and you can choose **Export** > **Excel** to be prompted with a file to download.

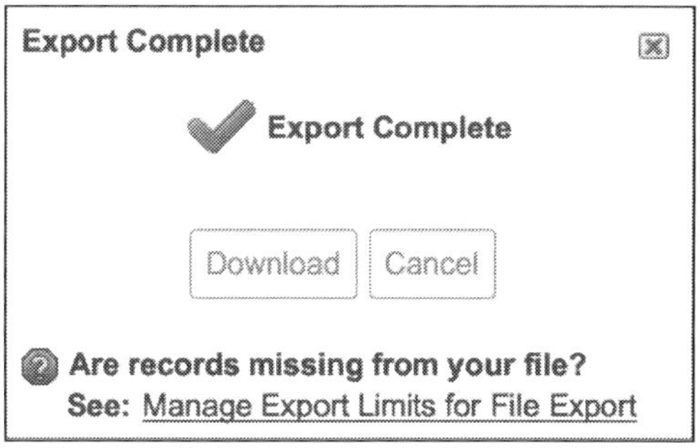

That's all very well, but it still takes a few clicks. By adding a URL parameter, we can skip those clicks. Add the suffix `?EXCEL` to the URL like this: `<instance>.service-now.com/u_maintenance_list.do?EXCEL`.

Now, without any clicking, the file is downloaded immediately. Of course, ServiceNow supports several URL parameters:

- **CSV**: **Comma Separated Values** (**CSV**) is a plain text file, with the field values separated by commas (as you'd expect!)
- **PDF**: **Portable Document Format** (**PDF**). This format is often associated with Adobe Acrobat and Reader. Since it is a more presentational format, it contains headers, footers, and even colors.
- **XML**: **Extensible Markup Language** (**XML**) is a ubiquitous and powerful format that many applications support. It has many powerful features, including the use of complex types that allow the grouping of elements, for example, street, city, and country may be part of a postal address. ServiceNow exports in a very flat structure, similar to a spreadsheet.
- **EXCEL**: A proprietary format used in Microsoft Excel, part of the Office suite. ServiceNow produces the original Excel Binary File Format (XLS), used primarily up until Excel 2007.

Automatically download data using cURL

ServiceNow is all about choice and flexibility. *Chapter 5, Events, Notifications, and Reporting*, looked at how Scheduled Reports could be used to send out an e-mail containing an Excel document on a periodic basis. But instead of filling everyone's mailbox, why not download it to a file-share instead?

cURL is a tool that downloads data from almost anything. It doesn't use a graphical interface; you just pass it a URL and it saves it to disk. Let's use it to download our Excel document without firing up our web browser.

Installing cURL

cURL is a free, open source software. It is available for almost every operating system. You can download it at `http://curl.haxx.se/download.html`.

- **Windows**: Download the binary from: http://curl.haxx.se/download.html under the **Win32** or **Win64 - generic**. The **Win64 2000/XP x86_64 MSI** version is probably the one you should pick for installing cURL.
- **Linux**: Most distributions include cURL in their package manager. It is most likely already installed.
- **OS X**: cURL is already installed.

Downloading the Excel spreadsheet

cURL is a command-line tool. Once it is installed, open the command prompt for your operating system. To test it out, type in `curl --version`. I get the following response:

```
curl 7.35.0 (x86_64-pc-linux-gnu) libcurl/7.35.0 OpenSSL/1.0.1f
zlib/1.2.8 libidn/1.28 librtmp/2.3
Protocols: dict file ftp ftps gopher http https imap imaps ldap ldaps
pop3 pop3s rtmp rtsp smtp smtps telnet tftp
Features: AsynchDNS GSS-Negotiate IDN IPv6 Largefile NTLM NTLM_WB SSL
libz TLS-SRP
```

To download the Excel document, use the following command:

```
curl --user <username> https://<instance>.service-now.com/u_maintenance_
list.do?EXCEL --output MaintenanceList.xls
```

Replace `<username>` and `<instance>` appropriately. You will be prompted for your password and the download will begin.

> The next chapter discusses authentication in more detail. For now, just use your normal username and password, as you would in a normal web interface.

This mechanism allows systems to grab whatever data they want to, without any configuration in ServiceNow. It is fairly straightforward to create a script and then combine it with a scheduler, such as Windows Task Scheduler or `cron`.

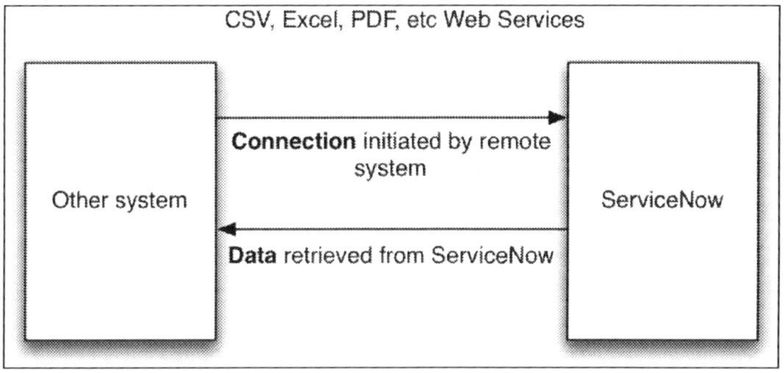

Using more URL parameters

Part of the appeal of the ServiceNow API is its simplicity. Nonetheless, the platform lets you specify more parameters in order to control what you see. Some of the Web Services, such as the JSON interface, support more parameters than the simpler CSV and XML interfaces. All, however, have a basic subset.

> The wiki provides more examples of how to jump directly to the data you want to: `http://wiki.servicenow.com/?title=Navigating_by_URL`.

Choosing the fields

The Excel files that are downloaded from the instance have the same columns that are shown in the web interface. Often, this is a limited subset of the total number available. To see more, or have more control, two options are available:

- Use a database view
- Create a list view

Database views were explored in *Chapter 5, Events, Notifications, and Reporting*. Their main purpose is to join multiple tables together, but they can be used to control which fields are shown for a single table. Then the URL would be constructed using the Database View, like so: `<instance>.service-now.com/u_maintenance_metric_list.do?CSV`.

Chapter 1, *Setting Up the ServiceNow Architecture*, saw how the views could be created for lists and forms. Try creating an All view for the list, and include every field. This also gives you control; if you don't select a view, the default one is used, which is more likely to be changed.

To select a view, use the sysparm_view URL parameter. An example URL would be: <instance>.service-now.com/u_maintenance_list.do?sysparm_view=all&CSV.

Specifying the records

As we saw in *Chapter 1*, *Setting Up the ServiceNow Architecture*, an encoded query lets you specify which records you are interested in. It is a simple field, operator, value notation, with "^" representing an AND. An encoded query can be presented to the list using the sysparm_query parameter. To see the higher priority tasks that are still active, you could use this example: <instance>.service-now.com/u_maintenance_list.do?sysparm_query=active=true^priority>2&CSV.

To get a filter, it is often easiest to copy it from the list. There are several operators such as LIKE, !=, NOT LIKE, IN, and others. The wiki has a section on creating encoded query strings: http://wiki.servicenow.com/?title=Encoded_Query_Strings.

> Rather than downloading all the data all the time, it is best to use the automatic fields to create deltas – just the fields that have changed since the last run. Pass through an encoded query, like the one shown in the next section using the sys_updated_on field like this:
>
> ```
> <instance>.service-now.com/u_maintenance_list.
> do?sysparm_query=sys_created_on><last run time>
> ```

Pulling data designed for the Web

In addition to the standard, more file-based formats of XML and CSV, ServiceNow lets you grab information that is often directly usable by applications. RSS and JSON are formats that are often only produced by web sites. SOAP is an industry standard interchange format for integrations:

- **RSS**: **Rich Site Summary (RSS)** is an XML file that has a specific schema to provide information about articles and items that are being frequently updated. It is often used on blogs or news websites.

- **SOAP**: Originally, **Simple Object Access Protocol** (**SOAP**), though it is now just a name. SOAP is a specification for requesting and receiving structured data, usually over the Web. It uses XML as its underlying format, so is relatively human readable. However, its power and capability often make it difficult to use.
- **JSON**: **JavaScript Object Notation** (**JSON**) is a lightweight name-value pair format. It uses the same notation as JavaScript, making it easy for web browsers to parse, though many other languages now offer support.
- **REST**: **Representational State Transfer** (**REST**) is a mechanism of transferring data, usually XML or JSON, over the web. It uses HTTP, taking advantage of the same methods (`GET`, `POST`, and so on) that web browsers use. While there is no official standard, it has rapidly gained popularity since it's a simpler, more efficient alternative to the rather more verbose, structured, and complex SOAP protocol.

Feeding tasks into an RSS reader

News aggregators take RSS feeds from multiple websites and present them in a single interface. They can run over the Web, such as Flipboard or Feedly, or as a desktop application such as Firefox, Outlook, or iTunes.

ServiceNow can provide an RSS feed to these applications. For example, some people may want a constantly updated list of tasks, available at their desktop without launching the ServiceNow web interface. By adding a specially crafted URL to your RSS reader, you can retrieve all of the **Maintenance** tasks assigned to yourself. This can be achieved in a multitude of ways:

> Prefix each with the instance domain name - `https://<instance>.service-now.com`. You will need to be logged into the instance; otherwise, you will be prompted to enter a password

- **Hardcoding a username in the URL**: This is dot-walking to the User ID on the **User** table through the **Assigned to** field.

```
/u_maintenance_list.do?sysparm_query=assigned_to.user_
name=System%20Administrator&RSS
```

- **Using a Dynamic Filter**, as discussed in *Chapter 2, Server-side Control*: This was created by using the query `Assigned to - is (dynamic) - Me`. The records that are returned depend on which username and password is used to log in.

```
/u_maintenance_list.do?sysparm_query=assigned_toDYNAMIC90d1921e5f5
10100a9ad2572f2b477fe&RSS
```

- **Using a scripted query**: Passing JavaScript to a filter is just like an Advanced Reference Qualifier. Again, it will depend on the username and password used to access the system to decide which user is taken.

  ```
  /u_maintenance_list.do?sysparm_query=assigned_to=javascript:gs.
  getUserID()&RSS
  ```

> You can change how the data is formatted in the response by editing the glide.rss.description_form property and passing the sysparm_format=true URL parameter, as per this wiki:
>
> http://wiki.servicenow.com/?title=RSS_Feed_Generator#Formatting_results

Cleaning up with SOAP Direct Web Services

SOAP is designed to be self-describing. A **WSDL (Web Services Description Language)** is an XML document that tells a system what data it can request, what data it can send, and what it will receive in return.

Armed with the WSDL, a system can create the right XML message and send it to the instance. The instance should understand it and respond with an XML message containing the results.

ServiceNow produces a WSDL for every table. You've probably guessed how you can access it; the URL parameter is WSDL. To view the data for the **Maintenance** table, navigate to <instance>.service-now.com/u_maintenance_list.do?WSDL.

> You will be presented with a big XML document. There are plenty of resources on the Web that will give you an understanding of what it all means! Some of the basics are listed in this chapter.

The WSDL describes the methods or operations that ServiceNow provides for each table. They are your typical **CRUD (Create, Read, Update, and Delete)** activities, letting you interact with the records in a fashion akin to database interaction.

- **insert** lets you create new records in the table. The parameters it accepts are fields, letting the calling system provide all the data necessary to create a record. No parameters are necessary. The sys_id of the created record is returned, as well as the field containing the display value.

> To add an additional `insertMultiple` method, activate the **Insert Multiple Web Service** plugin. It allows you to create multiple records at the same time, as you'd expect.

- **update** accepts all fields, but requires a `sys_id`. The matching record has its records set to the values provided. It returns the `sys_id` of the updated record.

> It is best practice to not use the `insert` and `update` methods on tables directly. Instead, use an Import Set, as we will explore in the upcoming sections.

- **get** accepts a `sys_id` and returns all the fields for that record.
- **deleteRecord** accepts only a `sys_id`. If it exists, it is deleted. It returns the number of records that have been deleted.
- **getKeys** accepts all fields and performs a query on the data. A list of `sys_id` values is returned, along with a count of how many records are present.
- **getRecords** combines `getKeys` and `get`. It accepts all fields and uses them to query the table. It returns all the records that match.

The instance provides these methods for every table. It allows a calling system to connect in to the instance, and create, read, update, and delete records in any table - as long as it has the right permissions:

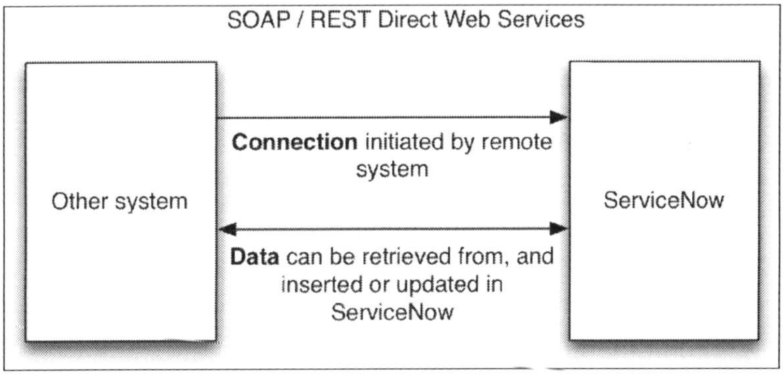

Using Direct Web Services

SoapUI is a great tool to test out Web Services in ServiceNow. It reads the WSDL, generates sample messages, and lets you send them to the instance in only a few clicks. SoapUI is open source and available for Windows, OS X, and Linux: http://www.soapui.org/.

Once installed, launch the program and create a new project, using https://<instance>.service-now.com/u_maintenance_list.do?WSDL as the URL. It will create a series of sample requests, one for each method. Expand **getRecords** and double-click on **Request 1**:

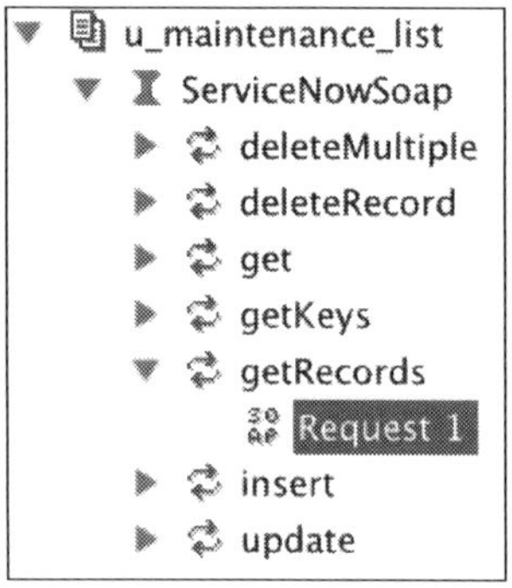

The request will open in another window, showing the XML message that will be sent to the instance. SoapUI provides an element for each field, as well as some extra parameters that we'll explore later. The majority of these elements should be removed, except for the ones you want to use as queries. As a simple example, remove all the elements other than those that are active. The resulting XML should look something like the following:

```
<soapenv:Envelope xmlns:soapenv=
  "http://schemas.xmlsoap.org/soap/envelope/"
    xmlns:u="http://www.service-now.com/u_maintenance">
  <soapenv:Header/>
  <soapenv:Body>
   <u:getRecords>
     <active>true</active>
   </u:getRecords>
  </soapenv:Body>
</soapenv:Envelope>
```

Before the message is sent to the instance, your username and password needs to be given to SoapUI. Click on the **Aut...** button at the bottom of the request window. In the **Authorization selection** field, choose **Add New Authorization**. Click on **OK** when **Authorization** is set to **Basic** and then fill out the **Username** and **Password** fields. Click on the green Play button on the window to send the message to the instance. The message should be posted to `https://<instance>.service-now.com/u_maintenance_list.do?SOAP`:

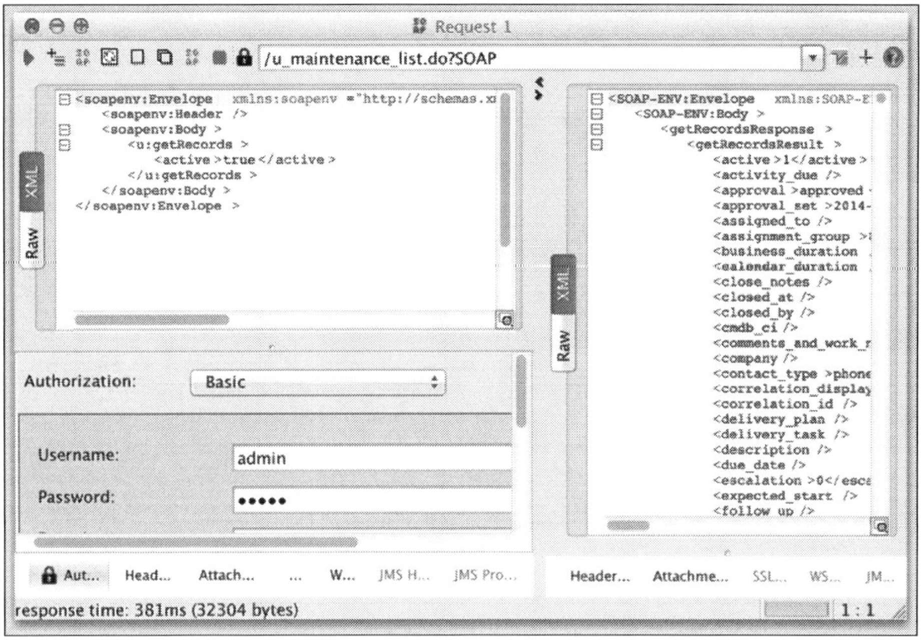

The right-hand-side pane will be populated with the response from the instance. In this case, it took 0.4 seconds to return a list of 20 records with the majority of their details.

Filtering the response

Creating AND-based queries is easy, by simply populating the nodes. The following XML snippet will look for high-priority **Maintenance** tasks for room 201:

```
<u_room>201</u_room>
<priority>1</priority>
```

As this example shows, you can query the display or database value of a field.

To perform more complex queries, and control how many results you return, there are several other parameters available, beyond those named after the fields. They all start with a double underscore (__) to keep them separate.

- `__encoded_query` lets you specify a more complex query, using conjunctions other than equal to. It does require an understanding of the ServiceNow query syntax, which means it is not self-describing.
- `__limit`, along with `__first_row`, is useful for paging through results. An alternative is `__last_row`. Only the data that you want is returned. If `__limit` is not specified, it defaults to 250. Use with `__order_by` for consistency.
- `__use_view` lets you restrict which fields are returned. By default, a view called `soap_response` is used. If it doesn't exist on the table, all available data is returned. A URL parameter of `sysparm_view` is also accepted.

> Specifying a view is a great way to include derived fields.

- `__order_by` and `__order_by_desc` lets you specify a comma-separated list of fields to sort the results.

Returning display values

By default, the content of the database column is returned for reference, choice, and other fields that have a display value. This means that a `sys_id` will be returned for the **Assignment group** field. The `displayvalue` parameter gives alternative options:

- To have the display value instead of the database value, set `displayvalue` to `true`.
- To have the display value as well as the database value, set `displayvalue` to `all`. This will cause an extra field to be added, prefixed with `dv_`. The **Assignment group** field would have two nodes in any response: `assignment_group` (containing the `sys_id`) and `dv_assignment_group` (containing the group name).

  The property can be set either as a URL parameter (for example, `u_maintenance_list.do?SOAP&displayevalue=all`)or we can set the `glide.soap.return_displayValue` property with either `false`, `true`, or `all`.

> Be consistent. If you grab the WSDL with `displayvalue=true` but send the SOAP message, because without it, the SOAP response will not confirm to the WSDL and some systems may reject it as invalid. I recommend setting the property to `all` if you like this feature, and leaving it.

Grabbing JSON

JSON is a standard lightweight method of encoding data. It is primarily used to transfer information between a server, such as ServiceNow, and a web-aware application. JSON is a simpler, less verbose format than XML, though it stores the data in a similar hierarchical fashion. Since the syntax of JSON is the same as the object, an array notation as JavaScript, it is easy to consume data in a web page.

The JSONv2 web service uses the typical ServiceNow URL format. To retrieve the data, use the `JSONv2` URL parameter, such as `/<table>_list.do?sysparm_query=<encoded query>&JSONv2`. In versions of ServiceNow earlier than Dublin, there is a slower version that uses the `JSON` URL parameter.

The JSONv2 method is not often used, as it is not aligned to REST integration conventions; for example, often, a typical HTTP status code is returned. Instead, wherever possible, the REST web service should be used.

Using REST

In the Eureka version of ServiceNow, a conventionally styled REST API is available. It provides the same functionality as SOAP, but uses the standard `GET`, `POST`, `PUT`, `PATCH`, and `DELETE` methods to manipulate data. REST uses the URL to specify the data element that should be affected by the method.

The API provides three endpoints: representing the direct table access, the ability to run Import Set, or to run aggregation commands against a table (such as determining average, minimum, or maximum values). The standard direct table access format is `https://<instance>.service-now.com/api/now/table/<table_name>`.

To get a specific record, the `sys_id` should be specified as another path. A single user record can be seen at `https://<instance>.service-now.com`.

Retrieving data

The instance will return the data in either XML or JSON format. Setting the `Cccept` header in the request to `application/json` will mean that the information needs to be returned in the JSON format. Use cURL to retrieve some data:

```
curl --user <username> --header "Accept: application/json"
http://<instance>.service-now.com/api/now/table/sys_user/
5137153cc611227c000bbd1bd8cd2005
```

> You can also use your browser to retrieve the data. It is likely that it will return in the XML format, due to the default headers that your browser sets.

Additionally, the REST API supports URL query parameters to control how the data is filtered, manipulated, and presented:

- `sysparm_query`: This accepts an encoded query, like in a standard URL
- `sysparm_display_value`: This works in the same manner as the `displayvalue` URL parameter in a SOAP endpoint
- `sysparm_view`: This is the same as the `__use_view` parameter
- `sysparm_fields`: This is a simpler method to directly specify a comma-separated list of fields
- `sysparm_limit`: This specifies the pagination limit, such as `__limit`, in the SOAP message
- `sysparm_exclude_reference_link`: This removes the normally generated URL that lets the calling system retrieve a record through a reference field easily

For example, this cURL command retrieves a single active maintenance record, while specifying the three fields, and the data should be in the XML format:

```
curl --user <username> --header "Accept: application/xml"
"https://<instance>.service-now.com/api/now/table/u_maintenance?sysparm_
fields=number,short_description,assignment_group&sysparm_display_
value=true&sysparm_limit=1&sysparm_query=active=true&sysparm_exclude_
reference_link=true"
```

This returns the following output from my instance:

```
<?xml version="1.0" encoding="UTF-8" ?>
<response>
    <result>
        <number>MAI0001001</number>
```

```
        <short_description>An example short description
            </short_description>
        <assignment_group>Cornell Hotel Services
            </assignment_group>
    </result>
</response>
```

Manipulating other data

The REST API is very powerful; in addition to retrieving data, it can update, create, and delete records, using SOAP.

> The following wiki articles provide more information about all the endpoints, parameters, and give sample messages and responses:
>
> - `http://wiki.servicenow.com/?title=REST_API`
> - `http://wiki.servicenow.com/?title=Table_API`

Bringing it in using Import Sets

SOAP and REST Direct Web Services allow you to insert or update data directly in a table. It is like having all the fields available in a form, without any UI Policy, Client Scripts, or other browser-based checks. This means it is very easy to create and edit data - but also uncontrolled and unchecked. Unlike in Easy Import, Business Rules are run, but the data format must still match that of ServiceNow. When populating the **Priority** field for a **Maintenance** task, one of the choice values must be supplied.

Import Sets is a set of technologies that work together to bring data into ServiceNow. It follows a particular pattern:

1. Importing from a **Data Source**, which specifies what the data is and where it is stored. This can be a file or information retrieved from a database or web server. After parsing, it is stored unaltered in a staging table.
2. The data is run through a **Transform Map**. This bridges the staging table and the target table. The target table can be any table in ServiceNow - anything from users, to tasks or even configuration. The Transform Map specifies how data should be copied from the staging table into the target table. A record in the staging table often results in a record in the target table, but the data can be checked or manipulated. Scripts can be run during the transform.

3. This process can be **scheduled**, running as often as necessary - or on demand.

> Easy Import gives you a predefined template that you fill out and upload to ServiceNow. If you don't want to bother with mapping fields and just want to get data in quick, use Easy Import. Read up on this further at: `http://wiki.servicenow.com/?title=Easy_Import`.

The diagrammatic representation of Import Sets is shown as follows:

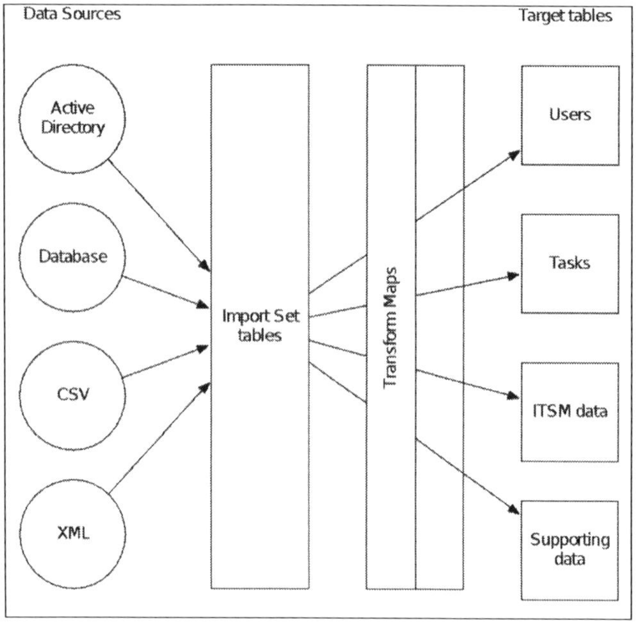

Specifying the Data Source

Each entry in the **Data Source** [`sys_data_source`] table contains the information that ServiceNow needs to pick the file up or connect to the server. Navigate to **System Import Sets** > **Administration** > **Data Sources** to see some example.

As you select the different types and options, UI Policies show or hide other fields. Some of the most important items are discussed in this section.

> This wiki explains all the options in more detail – files can be zipped up, deleted after collection, and much more: `http://wiki.servicenow.com/?title=Data_Sources`.

Several Data Sources such as the following are supported:

- **CSV, XML, or XLS Excel files**. Ensure the **Type** field in the Data Source has **File** selected and then select the type of data. Note that the Excel 2007 format (Office Open XML, suffixed as XLSX) is not supported.

> Custom separators can be used for CSV files. Just add the **CSV delimiter** field to the form. The pipe symbol (|) is quite common.

- Databases that can be accessed via **JDBC**.
- **LDAP servers, such as Active Directory**. They often store user and group information.

Once the data is retrieved from its source, it will be copied into a table in the instance, called an Import Set table. It is often referred to as a staging table. It is a standard database table, extended from **Import Set Rows** [`sys_import_set_row`]. Therefore, the data to be imported cannot be hierarchical and needs to be in a simple row-column format. Excel files shouldn't have merged cells, and the column headings must be on a single row.

Creating an Import Set Table

When creating a Data Source, populating the **Import set table label** field. It automatically fills out the **Import set table name** field. If the table doesn't already exist, it is created.

> I like to prefix all the **Import set table label** fields with **IMP**. Otherwise, it is difficult to know whether a table is a staging table or a standard table when creating reports or looking at the Dictionary.

The platform creates a field for each data point. For a CSV or Excel file, one is made for every column heading in the Data Source. By default, the column headings are assumed to be the first row. If the schema in the Data Source changes (such as a new column is added), the platform will create a new field in the table.

> This process can cause severe performance problems if the Import Set is very large. Set the `glide.import_set_row.dynamically_add_fields` property to `false` to prevent this. A second property, `com.glide.loader.verify_target_field_size`, will increase the size of a field if it is too small. It is `false` by default, but I find useful.

For CSV and Excel files, the **Load Data** module within **System Import Sets** will guide you through the process very easily. It creates a Data Source, attaches the file to the record, creates an **Import Set Table**, and brings in the data. It also creates an easy-to-access menu module to the table on the left-hand-side menu, under **System Import Sets** > **Import Set Tables**.

Cleaning up Import Set Tables

Import Set Tables can get pretty big very quickly. Each time an import runs, it stores more data. This is useful for debugging and testing, but can quickly slow the platform down during imports. There is a **Scheduled Job** that trims the data, removing records older than a week. The **Cleanup** module under **System Import Sets** > **Import Set Tables** lets you do this on demand.

> Make sure **Import Sets** are kept cleaned up. Since every **Import Set Table** is extended from the **Import Set Rows** table, the base table can easily contain millions of records. Performance issues will then impact all imports.

Dealing with XML files

XML files will be flattened, with the data found by using an XPath expression. XPath is used to define a particular set of nodes in an XML document. For instance, if the XML document was describing some rooms, it may look like this:

```
<xml>
  <produced_on>2014-07-01</produced_on>
  <room>
    <number>123</number>
    <location>
      <corridor>A5</corridor>
      <floor>1</floor>
    </location>
  </room>
  <room>
    <number>124</number>
    <location>
      <corridor>A5</corridor>
      <floor>1</floor>
    </location>
  </room>
</xml>
```

An XPath expression of `/xml/room` will return anything under an `xml` node and a `room` node. This effectively filters out the `produced_on` node.

> `//room` will give functionally the same result in this example, but searches the whole document for `room` nodes. It means the instance must keep a list of processed nodes, making the import vastly more inefficient. Test your XPath expressions at `http://www.xpathtester.com/`.

In this example, each `room` node will result in a new **Import Set Table** record. The `number` nodes will have a field created for it.

Many of the XML documents contain a hierarchical structure, like `location`. For these, the platform will create a field and populate it with the XML snippet:

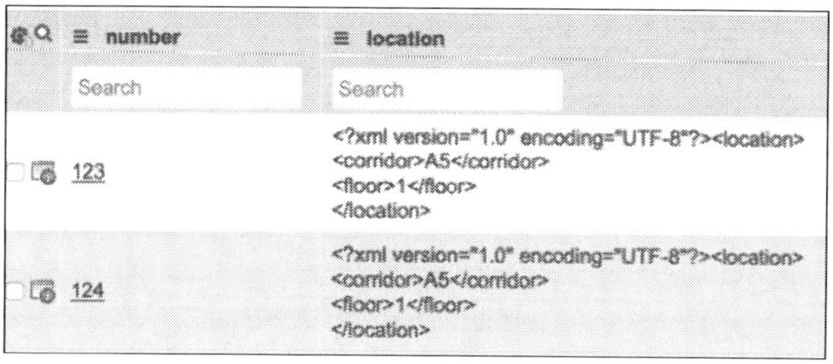

Ticking **Expand Node children** in the **Data Source** will create two more fields, **location/corridor** and **location/floor**.

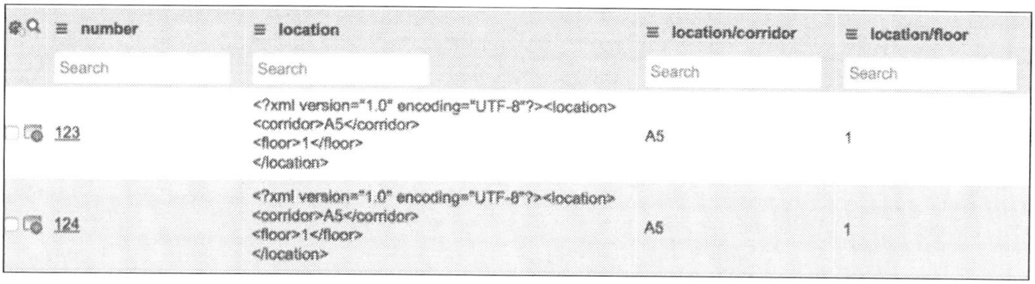

> If there are two nodes with the same name, then only the contents of one will be kept. In this instance, you may want to use a script to parse the XML and deal with the data manually. The **XMLDocument** Script Include is useful for this.

Getting data

CSV, XML, and XLS data can be retrieved from file servers, using the HTTP, SFTP, FTPS and SCP protocols. Data can also be retrieved from LDAP and database servers. Regardless of where it comes from, the data is always placed in an Import Set Table. Once configured, try grabbing data by clicking on the **Test Load 20 Records** Related Link to see if it works.

Every time the **Load All Records** (or the **Test Load 20 Records**) Related Link is clicked on, a new **Import Set** [`sys_import_set`] record is created. This records when the load happened, how long it took, which Data Source it came from, and what data was pulled in. Every entry in an **Import Set Table** will reference an Import Set, providing a link back to how it was originally brought into the system.

Navigate to **System Import Sets** > **Advanced** > **Import Sets** to see the list.

There are several Data Source options available:

- **Attachment** simply collects the file that is attached to the **Data Source** record. It is a good idea to build up an import in steps, and an attachment is often the place to begin.
- **FTP** is the easiest, though not secure. Try to avoid it when possible. It is useful for proof-of-concept purposes, however.
- **FTPS** and **SFTP** are secure file transfer protocols. Despite their similar names, they are quite different. Check carefully which protocol your server uses.

> It is very important to note that an FTP/SFTP/FTPS Data Source is tied to a single filename. You cannot use wildcards or expect the instance to find the latest file in a directory. When placing files on an FTP server for a scheduled pickup, it must always be in exactly the same location, with exactly the same filename. The instance can be configured to remove a file once imported. This is a useful option, and should be used if possible

- ServiceNow can also retrieve data over the web through **HTTP** and **HTTPS**.

> A ServiceNow-to-ServiceNow integration can take advantage of the XML generation capabilities of ServiceNow. If you want to import users from another instance, you can set the **File** path to be `/sys_user.do?XML`, with **Type** as **File** and **Format** as **XML**.

- The instance can also pull data in through a **JDBC** connection. Many databases are supported: **MySQL**, **SQL Server**, **Oracle**, **Sybase**, and **DB2**.

> The **Use last run datetime** option allows the SQL query to be filtered and only return the records that have changed—a delta. Use this if possible, since it will accelerate the import and the transformation dramatically.
>
> Since database connections are not encrypted, use either a MID server or a VPN tunnel. Both are discussed hereafter.

- **LDAP** is used to pull in users and groups from a corporate address list, like **Active Directory**. Importing data through a MID server is also possible. The next section explores LDAP servers in much more detail.

When importing data, ServiceNow initiates the connection and pulls back information from the source:

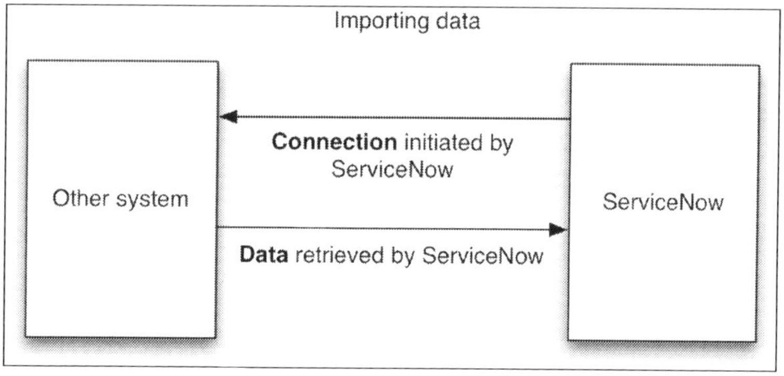

Transforming the data

Once the data has been brought into an Import Set Table, it needs to be transferred to its final destination. Transform Maps do exactly that. By creating field maps and scripts, Transform Maps will validate, check, and copy data to the appropriate place. A Transform Map is always associated with a source Import Set Table and a target table. The configuration is contained in a **Table Transform Map** [`sys_transform_map`] record, accessible under **System Import Sets** > **Administration** > **Transform Maps**.

The basic element of a Transform Map is a **Field Map**. It is an association between a particular field on an **Import Set Table** and one on the target table. There cannot be more than one Field Map for a particular field on a target table. When the Transform Map runs, each Field Map is looped through in order to populate the fields on the target table.

Field Maps can be created in three ways. The Related Links on a Transform Map link to the first two:

- Automatically, through **Auto map matching fields**. If a field with the same name or label exists on both the **Import Set Table** and the target table, a Field Map is created.
- **Mapping Assist** provides a drag-and-drop interface to create associations between the Import Set Table and the target table.
- **Field Map** records can be created manually. It allows full control of all the features of a Field Map.

Creating a Field Map

A Field Map created by either Auto map matching fields or Mapping Assist will have only the basic set of items. However, there are other options. **Coalesce** is one of the most important ones.

A Transform Map takes in data and attempts to apply it to a target table. Every row in the **Import Set Table** may become a new record in the target table. However, this isn't always desirable, especially for repeated or scheduled imports. Instead, you often want the platform to **update** existing records. Specifying if the platform will insert or update is the job of the **Coalesce** flag.

Any target field can be marked with the **Coalesce** flag. This means the field will be used as a unique key. If the value being imported matches an existing row, that record will be updated. Otherwise, an insert will happen. This is directly comparable to the `SQL MERGE` (sometimes referred to as `upsert`) statement.

If there are multiple field mappings that have the **Coalesce** flag set, then the platform will search for a record in the target table where *all* the field values match. For instance, matching on a person's name and address is more likely to find the right record to update than name alone.

> Almost every Transform Map should have at least one Field Map marked with **Coalesce**. Otherwise, it will create many duplicate records!

Once the **Coalesce** field is selected, you can refine how it works. Should it match only with case sensitivity? Should empty fields be matched?

Enabling Scripting in Transform Maps

The **Use source script** checkbox provides a **Source script** field that can be used instead of a field. This allows JavaScript to supply a value for the target field by setting the `answer` variable. There are several other global variables that are mentioned in the next section.

Creating new values

Reference and choice fields let you determine what happens if the source value doesn't exist:

- **create** will give a new option to choose from in the **Choice List** field

> I don't like that this is the default option. It is unlikely that you want to create lots of new entries in your Choice Lists.

- **ignore** will do nothing, and not set the field
- **reject** will stop the insertion of the entire row

Dealing with times

The data in an Import Set Table is stored as text. So, when importing date and time fields, the Transform Map will need to convert it. ServiceNow takes Java date formatting strings to tell the system how to deal with it. The **Date format** suggestion field gives several common patterns.

Importing into reference fields

Reference fields provide the option **Referenced value field name**. Normally, reference fields will find the right record using the display value, but any field on the table can be specified here. Use a unique value whenever possible.

> For example, if you were inserting **Maintenance** tasks, you may want to specify whom it is assigned to. But specifying the name of the person, the default display field, isn't likely to be successful. What if there are two people with the same name? Using something unique, like an e-mail address, will provide a better match. Specify the e-mail address in the **Reference value** field name field to do this.

The **Field Map** record is shown as follows:

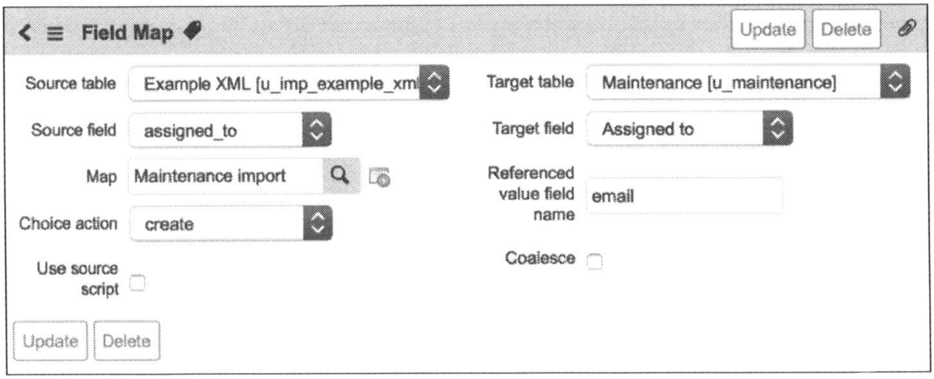

Scripting in Transform Maps

Transform Scripts are just like Business Rules, but simpler. There is no condition field, instead just a simple **Type** field that chooses when it should run:

- Before (**onBefore**) or after (**onAfter**) a record is inserted or updated in the target table
- When the Transform Map starts (**onStart**) processing or when it stops (**onComplete**)
- When choices or reference values are created (**onChoiceCreate**, **onForeignInsert**)

Create a new Transform Script by clicking on **New** in the Related List of the **Transform Map** record. There is also a **Script** field in the **Transform Map** table itself.

All the scripts in a Transform Map have access to these global variables:

- `source`: It's a `GlideRecord` object of the Import Set Table that is currently being processed
- `target`: It's the `GlideRecord` that is being inserted or updated in the target table
- `log`: It's a mechanism to add to the Import Log using the `info`, `warn`, and `error` functions
- `action`: It's a string that is either `insert` or `update`, depending on how the Coalesce has worked
- `ignore` and `error`: They will abort the current row or the whole import set, respectively, if set to `true`

> This wiki has examples and more information on each object: `http://wiki.servicenow.com/?title=Transform_Map_Scripts`.

Knowing when scripting will run

Since there are so many opportunities to run scripts, it is not immediately obvious when the code will be called. The list that follows shows the order that the scripts will be run every time a record in the **Table Transform Map** table is evaluated. Within each section, the **order** field of the Transform Script is respected. The following order will be performed:

1. The scripts in any Field Maps marked for **Coalesce**.

   > The platform will determine at this point whether it is an insert or an update.

2. The `onBefore` Transform Scripts.
3. The other Field Map scripts.
4. The `onForeignInsert` Transform Scripts.
5. The **Script** field on the Transform Map.

   > The write happens to the database between these steps.

6. The `onAfter` Transform Scripts.

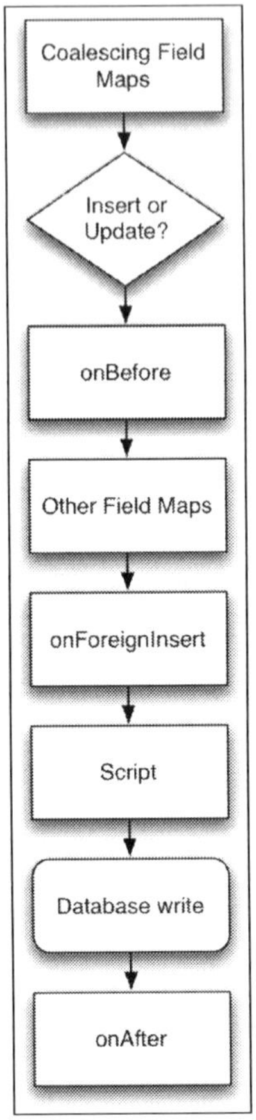

The **Script** field on the Transform Map is therefore a great place to do any error checking or validation. Every field should have been populated at this point.

> The user account that runs the transform will be recorded in the audit log when changes to the records are made. To impersonate another user, use `gs.getSession().impersonate(<username>);` in the **Script** field. The **Run As** field in a scheduled import can be used to specify which account is used.

Posting data to an Import Set

When interacting with a web server, you mostly use the `GET HTTP` method. This is designed to retrieve data. When you type in a URL into a browser and hit *Enter*, the browser goes to the resource and attempts to grab whatever data is there.

A browser can also `POST` data. When you have filled in a form on a website, perhaps registering your interest in the latest shiny gadget, you want to send that information to the web server and have it processed. The `POST` method should cause the web server to store or otherwise do something with that data.

ServiceNow accepts "POSTed" data into an Import Set. The `curl` command here will send CSV data to the special `sys_import` endpoint, where it will be automatically transformed:

```
curl "https://<instance>.service-now.com/sys_import.do? sysparm_import_
set_tablename=u_test_import&sysparm_transform_after_load=true" -u admin
--form "f=@upload.csv"
```

This functionality has a couple of tricks that aren't immediately obvious. The `sysparm_import_set_tablename` parameter doesn't actually need to be an Import Set Table. Instead, you could insert directly into any table, like Direct Web Services, as long as the first row of the CSV file matches the field names. If it is an Import Set Table, then any associated transform maps will run as normal.

The REST API accepts JSON and XML. The equivalent cURL command would be:

```
curl https:// <instance>.service-now.com /api/now/import/imp_notification
-XPOST --user admin:admin -H "Accept: application/json" -H "Content-Type:
application/json" --data "@upload.json"
```

Keeping Import Sets running

It is common to have Scheduled Imports running every day, processing hundreds of thousands of records. To ensure that the instance does more than just import data, make Transform Maps as efficient as possible. Their processing speed depends on a great deal of things, including how much data there is, what format it is in, and what the target table looks like.

> This wiki has an article on **Import Set Performance**. It provides some useful advice if things are getting slow: `http://wiki.servicenow.com/?title=Troubleshooting_Import_Set_Performance`.

One of the most important items is the checkbox on the Transform Map, labeled **Run business rules**. If it is unchecked, scripts and workflows won't be run for each inserted or imported record. It is often much quicker to turn this off, but be aware that you are then avoiding the automatic population and data-validation capabilities of Business Rules.

The platform can import data going up to many millions of records. Since it runs in the background, it'll crunch through the data, bringing in useful information. As long as the data is in a workable format, it is likely you'll be able to transform it.

> *Garbage in, garbage out* is still `true` for ServiceNow. Think carefully about where the best source of data is in your company.

Importing users and groups with LDAP

An **LDAP** (**Lightweight Directory Access Protocol**) server is just another Data Source. In theory, it could store any information, meaning an LDAP server can be used like a database. However, LDAP most commonly stores user data, including information such as their phone number, e-mail address, and location.

> Microsoft Active Directory is the most commonly used LDAP server that ServiceNow customers use, and is probably the most common integrations target. It is usually the most obvious source of user data in a company, but it's often badly maintained! Before integrating it without question, consider if you have a better source of user information, such as an HR database.

An LDAP server also has an extra capability for authentication. In ServiceNow, these two functions are distinct and operate independently of each other, though are obviously connected. Many LDAP servers, such as Active Directory, will have the capability for Single Sign-On (SSO)

> In this chapter, we focus on how the data is retrieved. *Chapter 7, Securing Applications and Data*, looks at authentication in more detail.

The structure of the data in an LDAP server is usually highly hierarchical. An object, such as a user, can be organized in many different ways. For example, users may be organized by location, team structure, or job role. Active Directory commonly uses the OU attribute, or Organizational Unit, to group objects together and apply Group Policy. In addition, users are very often organized into groups. This structure can easily be mirrored in ServiceNow.

> This section uses LDAP terminology. There isn't space to explain it in great detail, but there are many great tutorials and books available on LDAP technology.

Importing users from an LDAP server

Since connecting to an LDAP server is so common, ServiceNow provides a Record Producer to prompt you for the right information. Navigate to **System LDAP** > **Create New Server**.

- **Type of LDAP Server**: Other
- **Server name**: Forum Systems
- **Server URL**: `ldap://ldap.forumsys.com`

> This LDAP server provides a few test user records and a few groups. There are other example systems provided as a free service on the Internet.

- **Starting search directory**: `dc=example,dc=com`

> LDAP queries need a starting point, the top of the tree. Domain names like this are most commonly used, where `dc` stands for Domain Component.

Save the username and password on the LDAP Server record.

- **Login distinguished name**: `cn=read-only-admin,dc=example,dc=com`
- **Login password**: `password`

> ServiceNow will never update an LDAP server. It is often a good idea to create a user object that has read-only access to the objects you want.

Reviewing the configuration

The **Record Producers** create several different records necessary to pull in and process user and group information from this LDAP source. The default settings for these records are different depending on whether you choose **Active Directory** or **Other** in **Record Producers**.

- The **LDAP Server** record contains the information about which server to connect to and which username and password is needed.
- Linked to these are two **LDAP OU Definitions**, one for **Users** and another for **Groups**. These provide filters and further search criteria to select the appropriate objects.
- The object from the **LDAP OU Definitions** is linked to a Data Source. This provides the link to the **Import Set** functionality, specifying which **Import Set Table** the table should be placed in.

> In versions of ServiceNow from Dublin onwards, a MID server can be used as an intermediary. This is discussed later in the chapter. Otherwise, the LDAP server must be available over the Internet. The SSL tunnel version of LDAP or LDAPS is recommended to encrypt the data if you do not use an MID server.

- Finally, a **Scheduled Data Import** is made for the **Data Sources**. They are created inactive, so once tested, it is easy to turn them on to run every day.

> Some LDAP servers, such as Active Directory, support a persistent connection. In ServiceNow, this is termed as a **Listener**. This is essentially a search query imitated from the instance that is constantly open, reconnecting if it drops. The search query from the instance asks the LDAP server to return any changed information. This means that the creation or updation of a user record will be noticed within a few seconds and the updated data will be pulled directly into ServiceNow. A Scheduled Job is recommended to be run nightly anyway, to cover anything that has been missed.

For all these records, you may need to make some alterations; for example, mapping extra fields or altering search criteria depending on the schema of the data.

> If you are not familiar with LDAP, some of these terms may be confusing. Work with the appropriate LDAP technical contact to find the right configuration for each server.

When finding objects, the value of the **RDN** (Relative Distinguished Name) field is used along with the value of the **Starting search directory** field. (It can help to think about the RDN as the 'filename' of the item.)In our simple example here, the objects we are interested in are located at the top of the tree, so we need to blank it out.

Clear out the **RDN** field in the **LDAP OU Definition** of both **Users** and **Groups**.

Additionally, the groups in our Test LDAP server have a different object class to the default one in ServiceNow.

Set the **Filter** field in the **LDAP OU Definition** of **Groups** to `(objectClass=groupOfUniqueNames)`.

Once these changes are made, use the **Browse** button to explore what information the instance has access to.

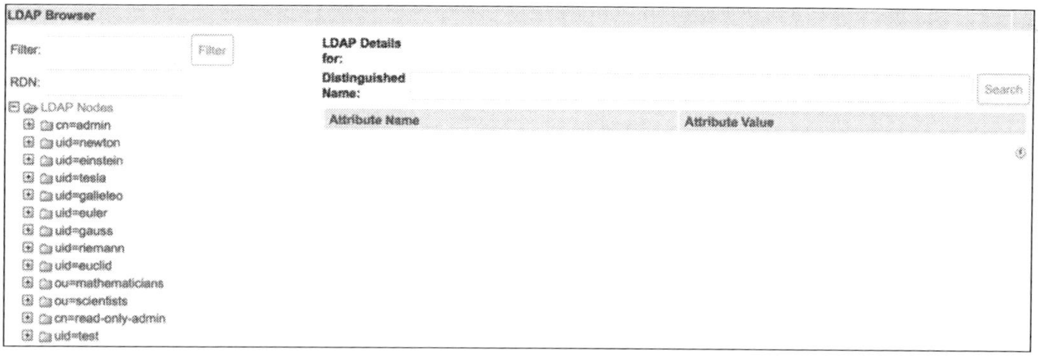

Altering the Transform Maps

As with a standard Import Set, a Transform Map is necessary to copy the data into the target tables. The provided Transform Maps are useful for Active Directory servers, but will need modification for anything else.

Firstly, load some data into the **Import Set** tables. Navigate to **System LDAP** > **Data Sources**. Find the `Forum Systems/Users` and `Forum Systems/Groups` **Data Sources**, then click on **Load All Records** for both. This will create the staging tables.

Then navigate to **System LDAP** > **Transform Maps**. Find the **LDAP User Import** Transform map. Ensure the configuration is as follows:

- **Source table**: `Forum Systems/Users [ldap_import]`
- **Target table**: **User** `[sys_user]`

Alter the Field Maps as follows. It may be easier to remove the existing ones, and use **Mapping Assist** to arrange them correctly.:

Source	Target
`cn`	Name
`mail`	Email
`source`	Source
`uid`	User ID

Now, set the Coalesce flag on the **u_uid / user_name** under **Field Maps**:

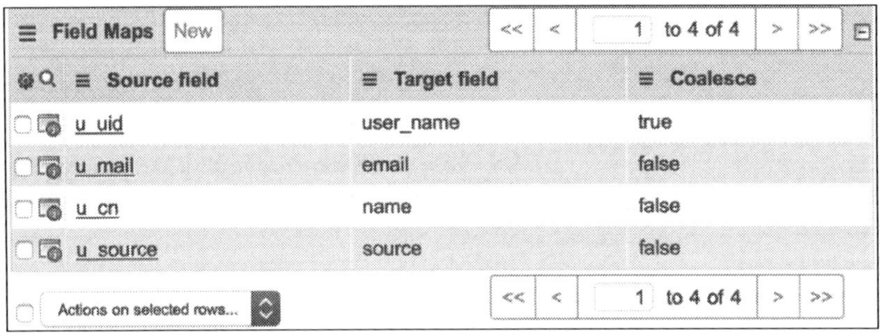

> The data structure used by the LDAP server has a big impact on what the Field Map should look like. An employee ID is often unique, and a good choice to coalesce against. Be cautious of values that change. A user name may be altered if a user changes their name.

Find the **LDAP Group Import** Transform Map, and again perform the following configuration:

- **Source table**: `Forum Systems/Groups [ldap_import]`
- **Target table**: **User** `[sys_user]`

- Set the values for **Field Maps** as follows, setting **Source** as **Coalesce**:

Source	Target
`cn`	Name
`source`	Source

Edit the `onAfter` Transform Script and edit the script as follows:

```
ldapUtils.setMemberField('u_uniquemember');
ldapUtils.addMembers(source, target);
```

As per the comment in the Transform Script, this uses a Script Include to parse the `u_uniquemember` field and create the **Group Member** records.

Once these modifications are done, use the Transform links in the Transform Maps and inspect the results. **Nikola Tesla** should be a member of the **Italians** group!

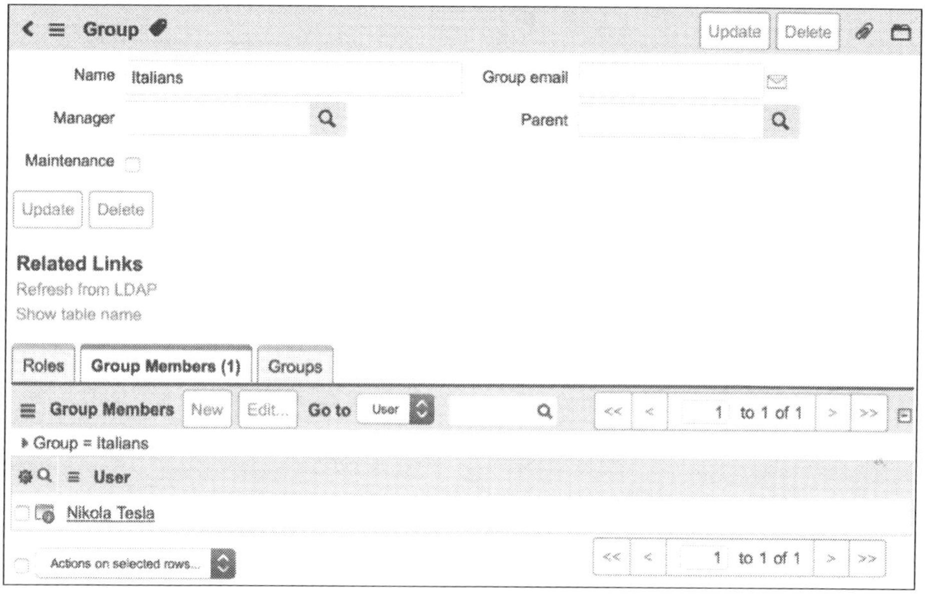

Building Web Service Import Sets

Web Service Import Sets, as the name suggests, attaches a SOAP or REST Web Service to the top of an **Import Set**. It therefore provides an interface to accept the data of your choice and a process to map that onto a table.

Navigate to **System Web Services** > **Inbound** > **Create New**. When the **Create** button is clicked on, the platform will generate a new Import Set Table, creating the fields listed in the **Web Service Fields** embedded Related List. To save ourselves the laborious task of recreating all the fields for a particular target table, tick the **Copy fields** checkbox and the platform will add them as well. Once the Web Service Import Set is saved, you are presented with a WSDL URL.

In a Web Service Import Set, the remote system pushes the data to ServiceNow, rather than as ServiceNow pulling the data as in a regular Scheduled Data Source Import Set:

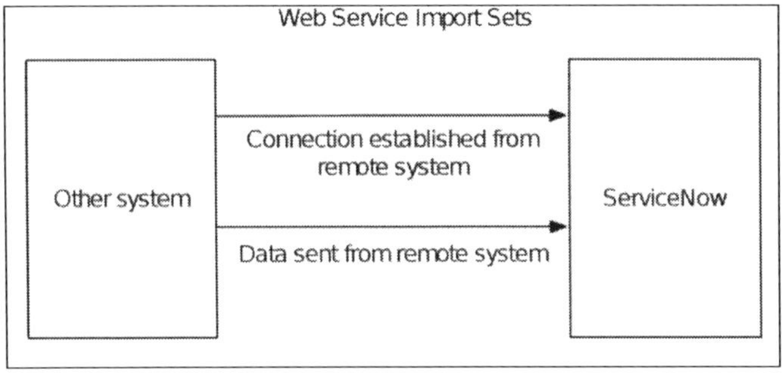

Using a Web Service Import Set WSDL

A WSDL generated from a Web Service Import Set contains all the methods of a Direct Web Service, but you only need one: **insert** (or **insertMultiple** if you have activated the **Insert Multiple Web Service** plugin). This creates the record in the **Import Set Table** triggering the Transform Map to process the data and copy it over to the target table.

> Always try to use a Web Service Import Set for creating records, instead of Direct Web Services. You get much more control with Import Sets.

The response back from an `insert` function is a little different to Direct Web Services. Instead of just the `sys_id`, it gives more information as follows:

- **table**: It's the table name (for example, **Maintenance**) that the record was created in. Note that this is the target table, not the **Web Service Import Set** table.
- **display_name**: It's the field that contains the display value. This will be `number` for a Task-derived record.
- **display_value**: It's the contents of that display value, for example, `MAI0001001`.
- **status**: It returns what happened: was the record created or updated?, was there an error?, and so on.
- **sys_id**: It's the `sys_id` of the record in the target table.

> Don't use other methods, such as **delete** or **update**. They will work on the **Import Set Table**, but not on the target table. You cannot return a record from the target table through Web Service Import Sets. Instead, it would return information from Import Set Table—probably not what you want!

Connecting to Web Services

So far, this chapter has concentrated on how other systems can connect to. In contrast, a SOAP or REST Message is the mechanism for ServiceNow to initiate the connection, and specify what data is sent or received.

Creating an outbound SOAP Message is achieved in just a few clicks. When the platform is provided with a WSDL, it scans it, automatically building out the relevant methods. This process of consuming the WSDL means that the configuration of a SOAP Message is very straightforward. To send a message, however, you must write some code, usually to include in a Business Rule. The platform will even generate a starting point for you!

Creating tasks after assignment

One common use of SOAP Web Services is to send information about a task to a remote system. This may occur if part of our support or business is outsourced, who use their own systems to manage their work. In Gardiner Hotels, we've outsourced work to Cornell Hotel Services and created an approval workflow to control it. But how do we send the work to our partners?

An easy way is to simply send an e-mail. This is a straightforward solution that can be quickly implemented by all parties. However, as is discussed in more detail later, e-mail should not be relied upon, since it is not a guaranteed protocol. There is no way of knowing when or even *if* an e-mail has reached its final destination. In addition, since the e-mail is unstructured, it is often difficult to send more complex data.

Instead, Cornell Hotel Services provide a very simple Web Service so that their customers can reliably submit information. Let's use this in our application.

Navigate to **System Web Services** > **Outbound** > **SOAP Message** and click on **New**.

- **Name**: `CHS`
- **WSDL**: `http://www.dasos.com/chs/tasks.php?wsdl`

> This Web Service is useful only for testing. Apart from some basic error checking, it randomly creates responses, and will not be consistent.

Click on **Generate sample SOAP messages**. This causes the platform to download the given WSDL, place it into the **WSDL XML** field, and parse it. If a WSDL is not available, you can paste the XML directly into the field and uncheck **Download WSDL**.

In the **SOAP Message Functions** Related List, two entries are shown. These are the methods that the Web Services supports: **create** and **status**. Click on **create** to see what parameters it takes.

In the SOAP Message Function, the Envelope contains what ServiceNow will send to the Web Service, just like the request in SoapUI. By inspecting the XML, we can see that ServiceNow has found three parameters, and for each one added variable placeholders:

```
<number>${number}</number>
<room>${room}</room>
<description>${description}</description>
```

When sending a message, you should specify the contents of these variables. This is typically done with the `setStringParameter` function, as shown later.

Testing the Web Service

Click on the **Test** Related Link to see what the Web Service does. A new **SOAP Message Test** record will be created and will show the results.

The **Request XML** Field contains the information that was sent to the Web Service, while the HTTP Status and Response XML fields give what was received. An HTTP Status of 500 is an error, and we can find out the reason for this by looking in the **Response** field.

Click on the orange XML button to format the XML nicely. You should see that the `faultstring` node contains the text `Task number and room are mandatory`, which gives a great hint as to what we need to do next.

```
- <SOAP-ENV:Envelope SOAP-ENV:encodingStyle="http://schemas.xmlsoap.org/soap/encoding/">
  - <SOAP-ENV:Body>
    - <SOAP-ENV:Fault>
        <faultcode xsi:type="xsd:string">Client</faultcode>
        <faultactor xsi:type="xsd:string"/>
        <faultstring xsi:type="xsd:string">Task number and room are mandatory</faultstring>
        <detail xsi:type="xsd:string"/>
      </SOAP-ENV:Fault>
    </SOAP-ENV:Body>
  </SOAP-ENV:Envelope>
```

> This Web Service doesn't indicate in the WSDL that some fields are mandatory. It is possible to do so using the `minOccurs` attribute. In many of the Direct Web Services methods, ServiceNow does the same; **insert** does not have any mandatory fields.

Changing the test parameters to the Web Service can be done in a couple of ways: editing the Request XML directly and clicking on **Rerun test** or by navigating back to the SOAP Function and entering test values in the **SOAP Message Parameters** Related List.

For now, do the latter, and for each of the **SOAP Message Parameters**, enter the name of the parameter and an example value you want to test with. Clicking on the **Test** Related Link will use these values.

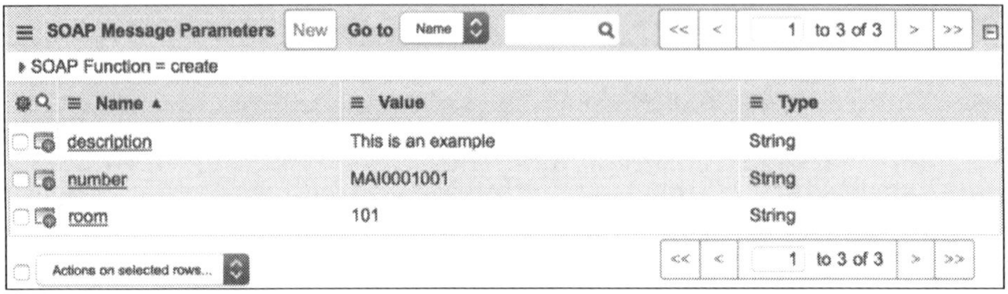

> The SOAP Message Parameters are only used for testing. They only provide example values for the variable substitution.

Once the Web Service receives the values it needs, it will generate a different response. The HTTP Status should be `200 (OK)` and the return result from the Web Service should say something along the lines of **Task accepted. Sending engineer to room 101**.

Sending the message

Once test messages are working, it is appropriate to integrate them into the application workflow. Once the **Maintenance** task is approved (which happens in a workflow), an Assignment Rule sets the **Assignment group** field to `Cornell Hotel Services`. That sounds like a good point to fire off the SOAP Message using a Business Rule.

First, however, click on **Preview SOAP message script usage** in the **SOAP Message Function** record. It will pop up a window with a code snippet that we'll use a basis, using examples provided by the SOAP Message Parameters. This code could be run as a Background Script as is:

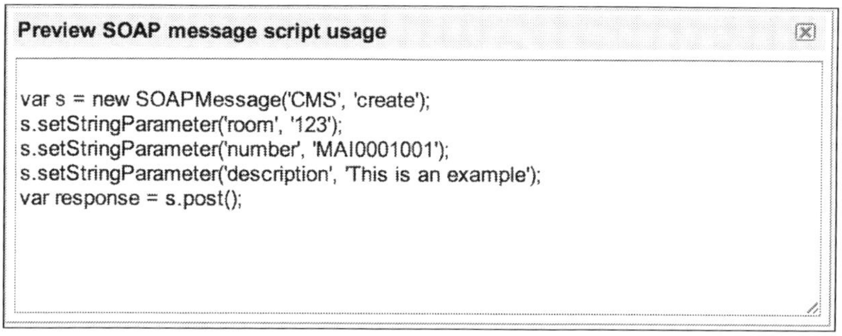

Create a new Business Rule that invokes the web service with the following data:

- **Name**: `Send to CHS Web Service`
- **Table**: `Maintenance [u_maintenance]`
- **Advanced**: `<ticked>`
- **Condition**:

```
!current.assignment_group.isNil() && current.assignment_group.
changesTo(gs.getProperty('maintenance.external_group'))
```

This Business Rule will run when the **Assignment group** field is not empty and when the **Assignment group** field changes its value to the same one in the `maintenance.external_group` property. Using properties, as described in *Chapter 2, Server-side Control*, is great for situations like this.

- **When**: `async`
- **Insert**: `<ticked>`
- **Update**: `<ticked>`
- **Script**:

```
var s = new SOAPMessage('CMS', 'create');
s.setStringParameter('room', current.u_room.getDisplayValue());
s.setStringParameter('number', current.number.getDisplayValue());
s.setStringParameter('description', current.description);
var response = s.post(true);

var xmldoc = new XMLDocument(response);

if (s.getHttpStatus() == 200) { // Success
  current.correlation_id = xmldoc.getNodeText("//data");
```

```
    current.work_notes = 'Successfully sent to external team';
  } else {
    current.work_notes = 'Did not successfully send to external
  team. ' + xmldoc.getNodeText("//soapfault");
  }
  current.update();
```

The script takes the code example and builds on it. First, a new `SOAPMessage` object is constructed, specifying the SOAP Message name and the required method. Then a series of parameters are set from the current `GlideRecord` object.

> `SOAPMessage` is discussed in more detail in the next section.

Once the parameters are set, the message is sent using the `post` method of `SOAPMessage`. As we have it here, the script blocks until the response is returned. It returns an XML string called `response`.

To find out if the message was successfully processed, the `getHttpStatus` method is used to see if the HTTP status code is `200`. If so, it is assumed that everything worked. A more robust check may search for the data that was returned.

The response variable is then used to create another object called `xmldoc`. This results from a class called `XMLDocument`, which provides several helpful functions for working with XML. The `getNodeText` function of `XMLDocument` is used to pull out the `data` node. This contains a reference number that the Web Service provides. It's saved in the **Correlation ID** field.

> The `XMLDocument` Script Include is documented in this wiki: `http://wiki.servicenow.com/?title=XMLDocument_Script_Object`.
>
> Another very helpful Script Include is `XMLHelper`. It has a function called `toObject` that converts XML to JSON. I recommend using JSON rather than XML if you need to iterate in loops or for manipulation.

Finally, regardless of whether the call was a success or not, an entry was made in Work notes and the record saved. If there was an error, the text is included as part of the note.

> When testing, ensure the **Room** field is populated. Otherwise, the Web Service will throw an error. It would be better to preclude this by adding another condition in the Business Rule or using a Data Policy to force the population of this field.

Using SOAPMessage effectively

The `SOAPMessage` Script Include simplifies the process of sending a SOAP message to a Web Service. But there are several options that will smooth the process of using it even further:

- When populating parameters, use either the `setStringParameter` or `setXMLParameter` functions. These give the data for the variable substitution of the message. Any values passed via `setStringParameter` will be escaped, otherwise the ampersand (`&`) and other invalid characters will cause errors. Data passed through `setXMLParameter` will be set as is. Use this if you are building XML directly. This is necessary for more complex structures, such as repeating nodes or complex types.
- `SOAPMessage` leverages other Script Includes such as `SOAPEnvelope` and `SOAPRequest`. If there is a particularly complex Web Service, you can use these classes directly and manipulate the XML yourself.
- In the example we saw earlier, a `post` function was called with the parameter `true`. This causes the message to be posted in the ECC Queue. The ECC Queue is examined in the next section, but if nothing else, it is very useful for logging purposes. Navigate to **ECC** > **Queue** to view the messages that were sent and received.
- All SOAP Messages sent by the instance are done so synchronously. This means the platform will block, waiting for the Web Service. To save the user waiting while this happens, use an async Business Rule as in the example we saw earlier. Nonetheless, even though it is happening in the background, the open connection is taking up resources on the instance. If the Web Service is very slow, or there is a lot of traffic, deploy a MID server and let it do the work. Specify the MID server that you'd like to send the message through in the function. Again, there will be more about the MID server in the next section.

Building REST Messages

Creating an outbound REST Message is almost as simple as using SOAP. Since REST does not have a schema like a WSDL, it is not autogenerating; however, it uses a very similar interface and concepts.

Each REST Message can have four functions: `PUT`, `DELETE`, `GET`, and `POST`. The latter two are most commonly used. While all four are created when a new REST Message is made, redundant ones, if any, can be removed.

Within each function, there are several Related Lists, which let you specify what data should be sent:

- The **REST endpoint** specifies the domain and path that the method should be sent to. It may contain variables in the typical form: `${variable_name}`
- **REST Message Function Headers** specify what is sent in the HTTP header. This may specify what output format you want (for example, JSON or XML).
- **REST Message Function Parameter Definitions** contain the parameters that the instance will append to the endpoint. For example, if the endpoint field was populated with `/endpoint/${number}`, and there were two parameters, the final URL generated by the platform could be `/endpoint/1?param1=hello&param2=world`.
- For `PUT` and `POST` methods, the platform will show another field, **Content**. This should contain whatever data you want to send to the system. As with all the fields, variable replacements will be made.

> If a parameter is defined, it is sent. Optional parameters are not easily dealt with, since the parameter name will be sent with a blank value, for example `name=;`.

Sending the REST message is very similar to SOAP, but uses an `execute` function instead:

```
var r = new RESTMessage('Test', 'put');
r.setStringParameter('param1', 'hello');
var response = r.execute();
```

Building custom interfaces

Web Service Import Sets and Direct Web Services provide a simple way to have a remote system send or retrieve data. However, beyond specifying the fields in Import Sets, the methods and schema are not configurable. What if you wanted a more flexible system?

Creating Scripted Web Services

A Scripted Web Service creates a Web Service with a single function. Two related lists let you specify the input and output parameters to generate a WSDL, and a single script field determines the processing. In it, the input parameters are represented with a global variable called `request`, while the output parameters is a variable called `response`.

Scripted Web Services are great when more processing needs to happen in ServiceNow, and especially when the data does not map directly on to a table. For example, ordering an item from the **Service Catalog** to initiate Request Fulfillment involves using variables and creating a number of records. This is a great candidate for a Scripted Web Service.

Doing multiplication with a Scripted Web Service

Navigate to **System Web Services** > **Scripted Web Services** and create a new record. Use these details:

- **Name**: `Multiply`
- **Function name**: `execute`
- **Script**: `response.answer = request.a * request.b;`

This one-line script looks at two input variables, multiplies them, and sends the response back.

Once the record is saved, use the Related Lists to create two Input Parameters called **a** and **b** and a single Output Parameter called **answer**.

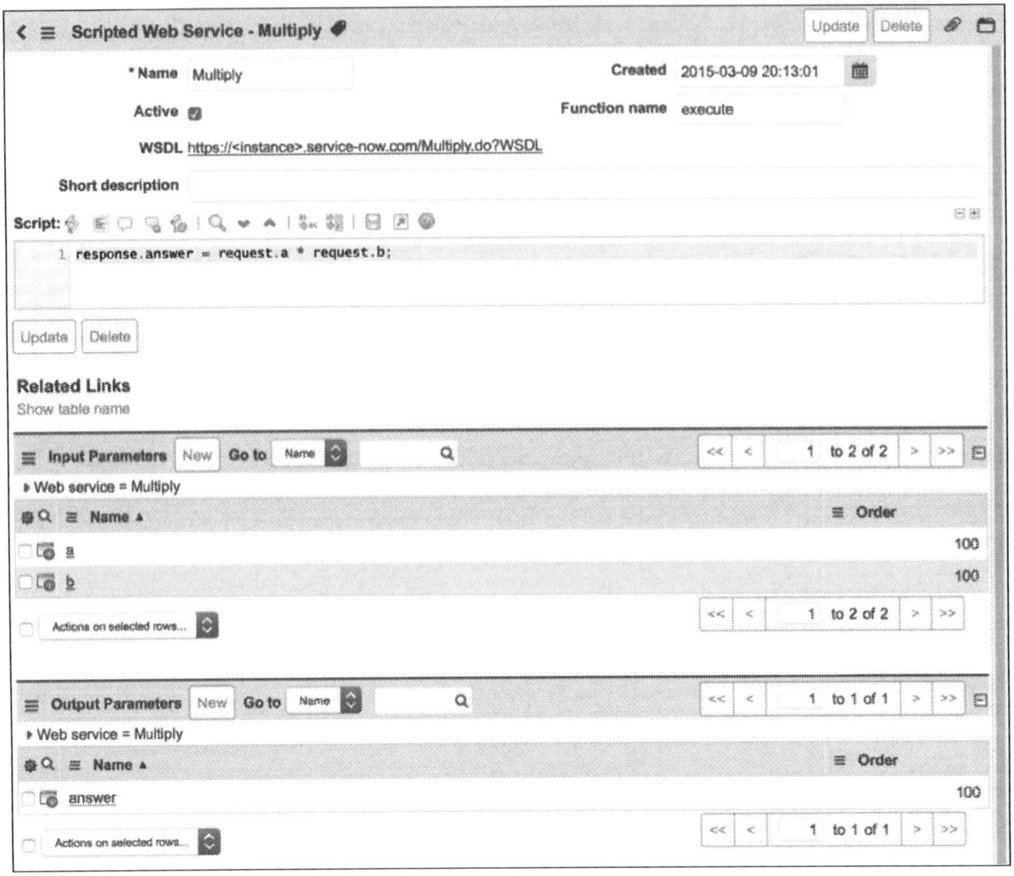

For more control, the `soapRequestXML` variable provides the full XML as sent by the client, while setting the `response.soapResponseElement` variable will accept a Node object from an XMLDocument.

The URL in the **WSDL** field can then be put into SoapUI for testing:

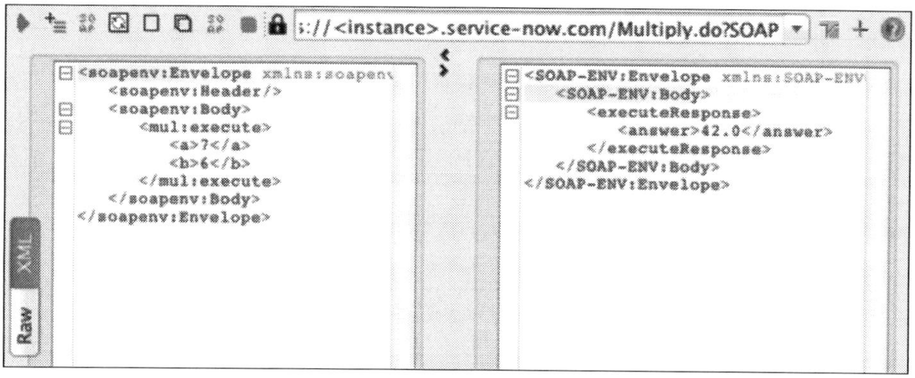

Introducing Processors – the ultimate in flexibility

Scripted Web Services give more control, but they only provide a single SOAP method. Processors let you hook into the backend of the ServiceNow platform, giving you direct access to the information sent over an HTTP session. Scripts can pick up parameters and "POSTed" data, letting you transfer information in any format you need.

> Having lower-level access is useful for building a custom interface. But it expects you to parse all the data yourself. Take advantage of the provided classes packaged as Script Includes when you can; this will save time.

Creating a custom processor interface

There are two types of Processors: Java-based and JavaScript-based. Java Processors call platform code, and so cannot be customized or changed. In contrast, JavaScript Processors provide a **Script** field to use. Navigate to **System Definition** > **Processors** and click on **New**. Use these details:

- **Name**: `Hello`
- **Type**: `script`
- **Path**: `hello`

- **Parameters**: `HELLO`
- **Script**: `g_processor.writeOutput('text/plain', 'Hello ' + g_request.getParameter('name') + '!');`

This one-line script introduces a couple of the global variables available. It uses `g_processor` to output some text. The first parameter of `writeOutput` is the mime type of the content, with the second parameter being the data. This is made up of some static text along with a URL parameter called `name`. This uses the `g_request` global variable.

To try it out, save the record and navigate to the new processor in your browser: `https://<instance>.service-now.com/hello.do?name=World`.

You should see `Hello World!` as the output. Change `World` in the URL to be whatever you'd like.

Building a processor

The platform provides access to the data sent by the browser in several global variables. Many are the raw Java objects, allowing you to call any of their functions:

- **g_processor** provides some helpful functions. `writeOutput` is an easy way to write out data rather than dealing with Java objects! The `redirect` function accepts a URL and will send the browser to the new location.
- **g_request** gives access to the data that the browser sent. The `getMethod` function returns it if it was `POST`, `GET`, or otherwise, while `getParameter` returns URL parameters.

> This is actually a Java object instantiated from the Tomcat Catalina `RequestFacade` class. It implements `HttpServletRequest`, which means `getRemoteAddr` will return the IP address of the request.

- **g_response** gives the mechanism to send the response to the browser. `setContentType` and others are available, but it is often more convenient to use the `g_processor` object.

  `g_response` is constructed from the `ResponseFacade` class.

- **g_target** gives a parsed representation of the path of the request. This is very often the processor name (`hello`, in this instance) or a table name.

> To run a processor on a table, populate the **Parameters** field in the Processor record. By convention, this is uppercase. Then call this as a parameter in a URL. If you navigate to the following URL, the processor will still be called, but `g_target` will be `u_maintenance`: `https://<instance>.service-now.com/u_maintenance.do?HELLO`.

Hosting a custom WSDL

If you create a Scripted Web Service, the platform makes a simple WSDL for you. The input and output parameters are listed against your single method. But what happens if you want to use complex types, nesting elements, and data in a hierarchy fashion?

The Static WSDL plugin lets you override any WSDL generated by the platform, or to host a new one, if you've built a custom processor. Essentially, it just provides a big XML box where you can paste your WSDL. Tools like Eclipse can generate WSDLs for you - or write it by hand!

A Static WSDL is in no way changed or updated by the instance, and no validation takes place at all. This means you need to change the endpoint information if you copy the WSDL between two instances.

> This wiki has a good article on how to combine Static WSDLs with a Scripted Web Service together in a stock quotes example: `http://wiki.servicenow.com/?title=Creating_a_Static_WSDL`.

Integrating with the ECC Queue

The **ECC Queue** [`ecc_queue`] table, where ECC stands for External Communications Channel, is designed to communicate with other systems. It has several fields that categorize the data, letting the right system pick it up and process it or post results back. The fields are generic, letting it be a storage area for any type of integration data, but their intended purpose is listed as follows:

- **Agent** is the external system that the instance is communicating with.
- **Topic**, **Name**, and **Source** depend on what the integration is. They can be used for anything, but often contain what the system should be doing and where it came from.

- **Response to** is used to relate two ECC Queue records together. Often, it is used in a reply to a particular command. The field itself is a reference field.
- **Queue** is either input or output. An input record is one received to the other system. Output is something designed to be sent.
- **State** tracks how the message is being processed. The value moves from the initial value of `ready`, optionally to `processing`, and then to either `processed` or `error`. This is typically controlled by a Business Rule.
- **Payload** contains the data itself.

Using the ECC Queue

Several parts of the ServiceNow platform use the ECC Queue as an integration point. A good example is `SOAPMessage`.

`SOAPMessage` utilizes the ECC Queue of the `post` function, if `true` is sent through as a parameter. The `SOAPMessage` object creates a new ECC Queue record and stores the XML message in the **Payload** field. Additionally, the endpoint is set in **Topic** and **Agent** contains the text `SOAPClient`. At this point, the message has not been sent, only recorded in the ECC Queue table.

This data is used by a Business Rule called `SOAPClient`, executing only when the **Agent** field is set to `SOAPClient`, among others. The script of the Business Rule uses the `SOAPRequest` class to perform the connection. It takes the response and uses it to create another entry in **ECC Queue**, sets the **Queue** field to `input`, and the **Payload** field to the `XML` it received. The original `SOAPMessage` object is then able to pick up this result.

> The **ECC Queue** table has a Business Rule in it that will decode and insert attachments that are sent to it using SOAP. Usage is explained in the following wiki, but the work is done in the `AttachmentCreatorSensor` Business Rule and `SoapAttachments` Script Include. Importing binary data can be tricky, but these scripts give a good indication of how it can be supported.
>
> `http://wiki.servicenow.com/?title=AttachmentCreator_SOAP_Web_Service`

Introducing the MID server

The **MID** server (**Management, Instrumentation, and Discovery**) is designed to ease communication with external systems. It is rather special, since it does not run on the instance; it is Java software that is installed in a customer's infrastructure. This gives the following advantages:

- The MID Server has direct communication with others systems, since it is in the customers network. This is very useful for communicating with unencrypted protocols, such as JDBC.
- Scripts that run on the MID server have access to the filesystem and can include custom Java code in JAR packages.
- The MID server only initiates connections. It does not accept inbound communication, and does not open any ports. This makes it more acceptable to security teams.
- It offloads work from the instance, enabling to scale out horizontally.

> The MID server is used heavily in Discovery. We'll meet it again in *Chapter 11, Automating Your Data Center.*

Picking up jobs

The MID server architecture is straightforward, though often misunderstood. It isn't a physical machine that ServiceNow provides, but should be installed on a customer's own hardware, or more likely in a virtual machine. Its design is such that it only ever connects outwards. The MID server opens no ports, and nothing connects in.

> You may argue, therefore, that the MID Server is not actually a server, in that a client does not connect to it!

In order to do work, the MID server relies upon the ECC Queue. It polls the instance, connecting to the ECC Queue every 15 seconds. It picks up jobs that are assigned to it, using the **Agent** field to find the right ones. It runs the script or worker job, and posts the result back to the ECC Queue. All communication with the instance is done securely over SOAP using HTTPS. It can even use a proxy server. The graphic representation of the process is shown as follows:

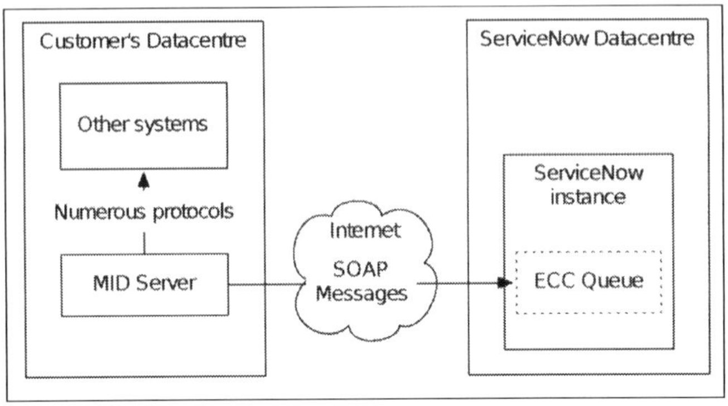

> We've mentioned one of the jobs it can do already. You can ask a MID server to send SOAP Messages for you; it's very useful if the SOAP endpoint is behind a firewall.

Installing the MID server

The MID server can be installed on either a Windows or Linux host, and in 32- or 64-bit versions. The MID server needs about 4 GB of RAM with a multicore 2+ GHZ CPU. It is often hosted in a virtual machine.

Setting up the server

To get the installation file, navigate to **MID Server** > **Downloads** and click on the required package. It is downloaded as a ZIP file from a ServiceNow web server. The instance will direct you to the right version.

Once downloaded, unzip it in a directory of your choice. The package includes the correct version of Java, so is relatively self-contained. No compilation required! The configuration file that matters is `config.conf`. Open it up and set the URL, username, and password values.

> It is a good idea to create a user dedicated to the MID server. Tick the **Web service access only** checkbox so the account cannot access the web interface, and tick **Internal Integration User** so it isn't affected by WS-Security if you plan to use it. Grant the `mid_server` role to the user account.

Note that the password will be encrypted on startup to ensure it isn't kept in plain text. If you'd like, you can also give a name. The examples later in the chapter use `test`. Otherwise, blank it out, and a name will be generated for you.

> More instructions are given in the wiki: `http://wiki.servicenow.com/?title=MID_Server_Installation`.

Run the `start.sh` or `start.bat` scripts to get the MID server working. Navigate to **MID Server** > **Servers**; after a few seconds, you should see a record indicating that the MID server has checked in and registered itself. If things have gone wrong, look at the MID Server log files and those on the instance.

Using the MID server

A MID server's job is to execute jobs that it collects. It constantly monitors the ECC Queue, picking up output commands and executing them. By using the **Topic** field on the ECC Queue record, the MID server knows what to do. The MID Server has several **probes**, one of which should be handling the job. More probes are discussed in *Chapter 11, Automating Your Data Center*.

Running a custom command

A simple example of this is running a shell script on the MID server. You will need to know the name of the MID server. Mine is called `test`. Navigate to **ECC** > **Queue** and click on **New**. Use these details:

- **Agent**: `mid.server.<name>` (for example, `mid.server.test`)
- **Topic**: `Command`
- **Name**: `whoami`
- **Queue**: `output`

This will run the `whoami` command on the MID server. It will return who the currently logged in user is. (This command is an easy example, since it works on both Windows and Linux hosts!)

Once saved, navigate back to the ECC Queue and set up a filter to look for all records where the value of **Topic** is `Command` and the value of **Queue** is `input`. Soon enough, a record will appear, though you may need to refresh a few times till you see it:

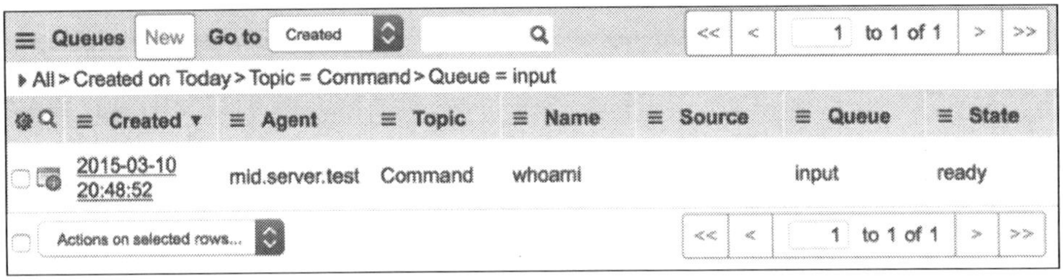

Open up the record and inspect the **Payload** field. Among some other items, there should be a result node, giving you what the command resulted in:

```
<result command="whoami">
  <stdout>martin</stdout>
  <stderr/>
</result>
```

In this example, the `whoami` command returned `martin`. This is the name of the user who is running the midserver agent.

This technique can be used to run whatever code you'd like on the MID server, whenever you'd like. It is therefore very simple to integrate with an esoteric system that can only be communicated with via a command prompt.

> To send longer commands, keep the **Name** field blank and instead use the **Payload** field with the information in a couple of XML tags as follows:

```
<parameters>
  <parameter name="name" value="./this_is_a_long_command
    with_quite_a_few parameters"/>
</parameters>
```

Running JavaScript on the MID server

In addition to running shell commands, the MID server can also run JavaScript, just like the instance. There are a couple of key differences, however:

- The MID server does not have direct access to the database and global variables (such as `gs`) are not defined. It also cannot access standard Script Includes.
- Instead, access to Java packages is allowed, enabling you to access lower-level functions within the extensive Java libraries.

Using MID server Background Scripts

Navigate to **MID Server** > **Background Scripts** > **Scripts**, select **Background**, to enter some code. You must also select the MID server you'd like to run the code.

The MID server uses the last JavaScript statement in a script as the return value. Therefore, to record "Hello, world!" is as simple as this statement:

```
"Hello, world!";
```

Of course, statements can be executed:

```
var user = "Martin";
"Hello, " + user + "!";
```

This will display the following screenshot:

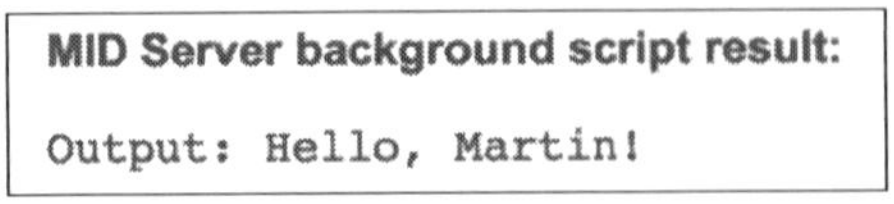

> When the **Run script** button is clicked, the instance prepares the job for the MID server and places it in the ECC Queue. There may well be a delay before it is picked up and processed, so be patient!

Interacting with the ECC Queue

To programmatically run JavaScript on the MID server, you can write a record to the **ECC Queue** table in the same way as you'd run a command. Use `JavascriptProbe` as **Topic** and use **Payload** to pass through an XML snippet with a script parameter. A full example would contain the following values:

- **Agent**: `mid.server.test`
- **Topic**: `JavascriptProbe`
- **Queue**: `output`
- **Payload**:

```
<parameters>
  <parameter name="script" value="'Hello, world!'"/>
</parameters>
```

However, it is easier to use a Script Include on the instance called `JavascriptProbe`. This wraps up the creation of the **ECC Queue** record in a few function calls.

To generate the same **ECC Queue** record as before, run this in the standard Background Scripts area:

```
var jsp = new JavascriptProbe('test');
jsp.setJavascript("'Hello, world!'");
jsp.create();
```

In this example, a new `JavascriptProbe` object, `jsp`, is created, passing through the name of the MID server. The **Payload** field is set by using the `setJavascript` function and the record is written to the database by calling `create`.

> It is a good idea to use the `setName` function to label your scripts, so you know where these ECC Queue records are coming from. It populates the **Name** field in the table.

To react to the results of the command, write a Business Rule for the ECC Queue that parses the XML and does what was necessary. Use the XMLDocument and XMLHelper Script Includes previously mentioned.

Working with parameters and MID server Script Includes

The payload XML can also contain more parameters than just script. Extra nodes with name-value attributes stores data that can be read using the `probe.getParameter` function call. The XML should look like this:

```
<parameters>
  <parameter name="script" value="'Hello ' + probe.getParameter(
    'yourName');"/>
  <parameter name="yourName" value="Bob"/>
</parameters>
```

The code passed to the script tag will run on the MID server. This example will return this:

```
Hello Bob
```

It is not good form to include lots of code as strings like this. If nothing else, the quotes quickly get very confusing! Instead, use the MID server Script Includes to contain the majority of your code, letting you write the code in a much saner environment. MID Server Script Includes work in much the same way as a typical Script Include; they can be functions (or more commonly classes) packing up code in a reusable fashion.

Creating a MID Server Script Include

Navigate to **MID Server** > **Script Includes**. Let's create a new record that mirrors the first Script Include in *Chapter 2, Server-side Control*.

- **Name**: `SimpleAdd`
- **Script**: Use the following script:

```
var SimpleAdd = Class.create();
SimpleAdd.prototype = {
  initialize: function (n) {
    ms.log('Creating new object');
    this.number = (n - 0) || 0;
  },

  increment: function () {
```

```
      this.number++;
      ms.log(this.number);
      return this;
    },

    type: 'SimpleAdd'
  }
```

This code is almost identical to a typical Script Include. The only difference is that, the logging is done with the `ms` global variable instead of `gs`.

The script has two functions. One is run when the object is created and sets the `number` variable. The second function, `increment`, adds `1` to `number` when it is called.

To try this simple code out, run the following code on the MID Server. You may choose to do this in the MID Server Background Scripts, which will give you the logging, or using the `JavascriptProbe` Script Include. Either way, you should receive a result of 2.0.

```
var sa = new SimpleAdd(1);
sa.increment();
sa.number;
```

> Note how the result has been represented as a decimal. The data will be translated into string anyway, so it is a good idea to convert it yourself to stop odd conversions. This could be done with last line being `sa.number + '';` instead.

Using Java on the MID Server

One exciting capability of the MID Server is that it lets you run Java commands. Just like the instance, the MID Server uses Rhino, a JavaScript interpreter written in Java, to execute your scripts. We've just been using this via the JavascriptProbe.

However, you may want to do things that JavaScript just can't provide. So Rhino also gives you access to the Java API and other libraries. Included with Java is a huge collection of programming tools, such as encryption algorithms, file and web access, math functions, and database control. It is easy to call these from the MID Server as follows:

```
var out = new Packages.java.io.FileWriter("file.txt");
out.write("Hello, world!");
out.close();
```

> Since the instance also uses Rhino, it can access the Java libraries too. However, this is considered bad form, and is being depreciated. It creates a big dependency on specific Java packages and also gives rise to security concerns. The MID Server isn't affected, since it is hosted on customers' own hardware and is under their control.

Java classes are organized into packages. To use a class, you must identify which package it belongs to, which is often easily achieved by searching the Java API documentation. These are hosted online at `http://docs.oracle.com/javase`. When referring to a Java class, use the package name, prefixed by `Packages`.

In the example we saw earlier, the `FileWriter` class is used. It opens up a file with the given name, and will output data using the `write` method. The `close` method writes it to disk. A file called `file.txt` will end up in the `agent` directory on the MID Server. Execute this script in the MID Server Background Scripts to test it out.

> Writing files is something the instance cannot do. This is incredibly useful if you wish to export data under the control of the instance. An interesting use would be to ask the MID Server to connect to the standard Direct Web Service APIs of the instance and save the result to disk. So, with the click of a button on the instance, you could create a file and save the data as a file!

Adding additional libraries

Many hundreds of classes are included in the MID Server. In addition to the Java API, other libraries are included in the `lib` directory. Many are focused around communication: `org.apache.commons.httpclient`, is helpful for downloading files, while `org.ftp4che` gives access to FTP servers.

You may want to add more. Rather than adding files into the `lib` directory, the platform provides a simpler way to distribute additional Java packages across all the connected MID servers. Navigate to **MID Server** > **JAR Files** and fill in the appropriate field. Once the file is added to the record, any restarting MID Servers will pick up the file and have it available for use.

> Tibco distributes packages as JAR files to connect to its **Enterprise Service Bus (ESB)**. Other vendors may also have integration points like this.

Authenticating and securing Web Services

Communication with a ServiceNow instance has two basic starting points:

- It happens over **HTTPS**. This provides encryption for the HTTP session and helps prevent man-in-the-middle attacks.
- **Authentication** is almost always required, usually in the form of a username and password. This ensures access is only granted to those deemed appropriate.

> This section focuses on machine-to-machine authentication. The next chapter, *Chapter 7, Securing Applications and Data*, explores user-based security in much more detail.

Designing integrations

How you connect other systems to ServiceNow requires considerable thought. Most of the time, the plumbing is fairly easy, but you need to know where to route the pipes. You don't want to get fresh and wastewater mixed up!

At a very high level, there are two points to consider when importing data or creating an integration:

- What data points am I transferring? For example, what fields should I match it with?
- When do I want to transfer it? Is it on a nightly basis, whenever a ticket is created, or even when the Work notes field is updated?

This information should feed into whatever mechanism you eventually use.

Transferring bulk data

In general, if you are exchanging data that represents more than one record at a time, ServiceNow uses a pull mechanism. This generally happens on a scheduled basis, usually nightly, to keep the two systems in loose synchronization.

Importing an XML or CSV file is easy with ServiceNow. Place the file on an FTP server and have ServiceNow check it periodically. Often, the only trick is finding a suitable FTP/FTPS/SFTP server, and scheduling the generation to always place it with the same filename.

Similarly, if you want to get multiple records out of ServiceNow, it expects the remote system to initiate the connection and ask for what it wants. Use the CSV and XML Web Services to retrieve what you need or use SOAP Direct Web Services to pull multiple records at once:

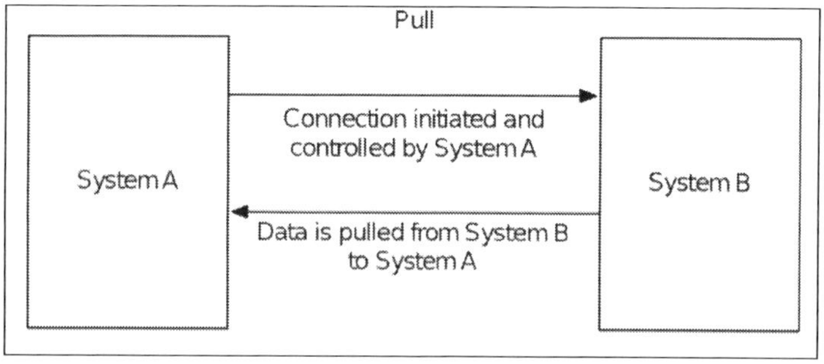

Real-time communication

In contrast, transferring single records often involves a push. This is most common if you want to transfer ticket data, so an outsourced team can be told within a few seconds that they've been assigned a task. This mechanism is far more efficient that polling for updates every few seconds.

eBonding is an extension of this mechanism, to allow tickets to be updated on either side at any point. Both sides will push data to the other upon any change. Serious logical challenges are raised through this, including race conditions, data synchronization, and reliability. For example, if a particular category is set on one side, it follows that it should be updated on the other. But what if the categorization structures don't match? Should user data be transferred alongside each ticket? What if two updates happen within seconds of each other?

> Think carefully about the impact that eBonding will have on your process and how you work with the resulting system. Often, compromises have to be made, such as aligning the systems so they are very similar (such as the fields and potential contents of those fields) or to have a looser bond and to transfer less information.

One mechanism that isn't recommended is integration via e-mail. This is often seen in legacy systems, since e-mail is so ubiquitous. However, the delivery and security of an e-mail can never be guaranteed and the data exchange format is often a free text field. Nonetheless, as explored in previous chapters, Inbound Email Scripts can process incoming e-mails just as easily from a machine as a person:

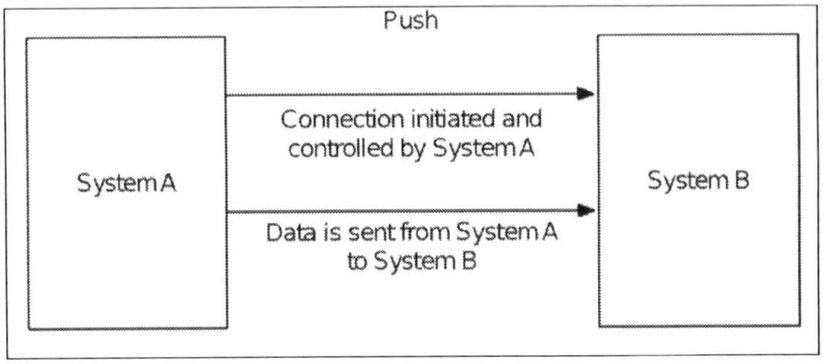

Communicating through the firewall

Perhaps the most important capability of the MID Server is that it can communicate to other systems from inside the firewall. This may be in a DMZ, or perimeter network, but often a MID Server has better access to systems than the instance does.

This is useful in several situations, but is not a cure-all. Due to the polling design of the MID server, there will be a latency of a few seconds at least. Nonetheless, a MID sever is very useful for grabbing data from sensitive systems, such as LDAP servers or databases:

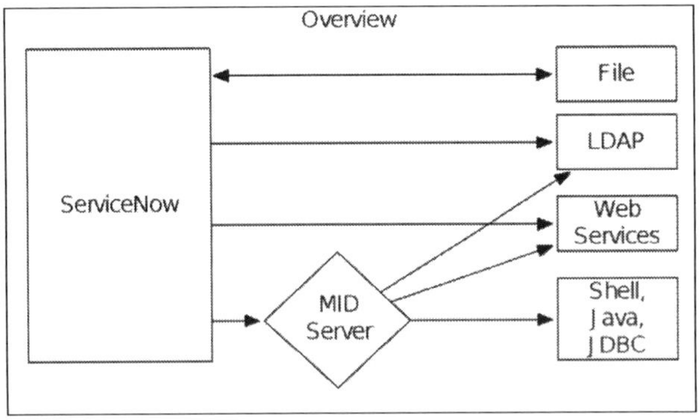

An alternative option is using a VPN tunnel. A secured, encrypted IPSEC link can be set up between the ServiceNow datacenter and a customer's infrastructure. ServiceNow recommends, however, that, whenever possible, secure protocols are to be used instead. For example, instead of using LDAP through a VPN tunnel, use LDAPS over the Internet. This allows greater flexibility and is often more efficient:

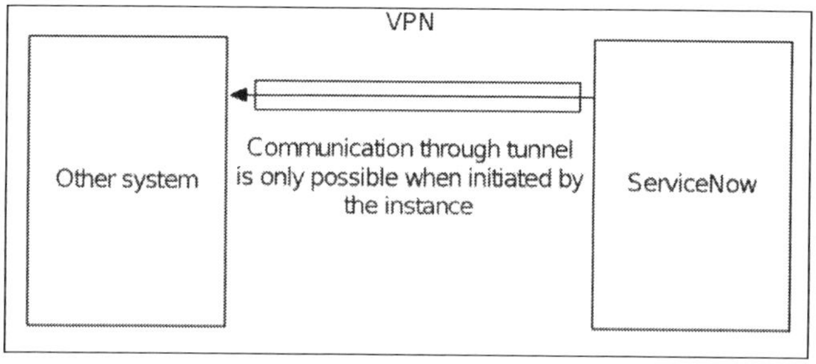

Summary

ServiceNow provides many different integration options. In this chapter, the majority of the mechanisms to get data in and out of the platform were discussed.

CSV and XML are universal file formats. Almost any system that can import or export data can use CSV and XML to store data, and ServiceNow is no different. The chapter started by exploring the ways to download data directly from the instance using specially crafted URLs. Use the optional parameters to filter and select the data you are interested in.

Import Sets are a very powerful way of pulling data into your instance. It again supports a variety of data formats and provides Transform Maps to translate the incoming information into the appropriate schema. Transform Scripts work like Business Rules to manipulate, check, and convert information.

LDAP is probably the most common integration. It pulls in users and groups, most often from Active Directory. ServiceNow provides a simple way to add an LDAP server in a wizard-style interface. Scripts are provided to keep the group membership information up to date, reducing the data administration necessary in the instance.

While Direct Web Services provides `insert` and `update` methods, I recommend using Web Service Import Sets. It allows the quick creation of a Web Service that is then tied to an Import Set, giving you much more flexibility and control.

When Web Service Import Sets are not enough, build Scripted Web Services or a custom Processor. These allow you to create any sort of Web Service, or indeed to support almost any data format whatsoever. Processors give you the capability to support your own formats.

The External Communications Channel is a mechanism to queue jobs. The MID Server is its most heavy user; commands are placed in the ECC Queue, which the MID Server (placed within a customer's datacenter) will pick up and process. This gives secure access to internal systems when you don't want to open up the firewall.

Finally, the security aspects and design challenges that integrations face were discussed. The next chapter, *Chapter 7, Securing Applications and Data*, provides much more detail on authentication and securing ServiceNow.

7
Securing Applications and Data

Data is often one of the most important assets of a business, and your ServiceNow instance is likely to contain a lot. The following list highlights some reasons why protecting data is important:

- Stolen **financial information** can create loss of revenue, customers and partners, as well as leading to fines or legal action
- **Personally Identifiable Information** (PII) must be protected to ensure that data privacy laws and the privacy of your employees are respected
- Information regarding the **separation of duties** and authority checking, such as during approvals and when updating other sensitive information
- **Knowledge-based information**, such as trade secrets and other intellectual property

Security should be included from the beginning. The ServiceNow platform provides a wide variety of functions and capabilities to protect against data loss and unauthorized manipulation. In this chapter, we will explore the main considerations to take into account when you build or configure an application:

- Understanding **roles** and how they get assigned to individuals
- Controlling data with **Contextual Security** (ACLs)
- Using **Domain Separation** to isolate fulfillers in a single instance
- Controlling the login process by choosing the right **authentication** process

Understanding roles

Some systems work very well as cooperative endeavours. For example, anyone can go and edit Wikipedia. This gives it a very low barrier for entry, letting anyone provide their knowledge and wisdom to others, by assuming that everyone is well-intentioned.

However, open access does have its issues, especially in the open Internet. Wikipedia often suffers from data "vandalism", and some editors have even introduced malware and malicious links. To combat this situation, some Wikipedia editors are tagged as administrators, which allows them to protect pages or block users that are dubious or behave inappropriately. Normal users cannot do this.

In a similar fashion, ServiceNow has different levels of access, which gives some people more control than others. For example, some users may be able to approve orders for a new tablet or mobile phone while others may be able to edit or update financial information. Controlling who can do what is incredibly important for an information security department.

The level of access is also tied in very closely with the licensing model. The essence of this closely-tied structure is that someone who uses ServiceNow frequently is a licensable user.

> The licensing model of ServiceNow is constantly under revision, and as such, different customers often have different terms. If there is any confusion as to how ServiceNow is licensed, you can contact your ServiceNow representative.

Defining a role

The starting point of controlling functions is a role. A role is essentially a tag or category that grants access to a particular function. Roles are associated with a user account, so someone using the particular account will have access to a particular function.

> Roles should always grant additional capability they don't subtract or take away access.

To explore the roles provided in the ServiceNow platform, navigate to **System Security > Users and Groups > Roles**. They are stored in the database as a record with a text name.

The name of a role often falls into one of the following two types:

- Job roles, such as team_leader, service_desk, or asset
- Functional, such as filter_global, soap, or view_changer

> In contrast to other areas of the system, roles are often referred to by name, especially in scripts. Therefore, it is the convention to keep the name short without spaces and in lowercase. The snake case form (where words are separated with underscore characters, like_this) is encouraged.

Assigning roles to users

Roles can be associated either to users directly or to a group. In the case of the latter, any members of the group will automatically be associated with a role. This even works with hierarchical groups: assign the role at the top and everyone underneath it will be granted the role.

> Roles are associated with users via a many-to-many table called **User Role** [sys_user_has_role]. The platform provides access to this via a virtual field called **Roles** on the **User** table, making it possible to create simple filters. For server-side scripting, the hasRole(<role>) function of GlideSystem and GlideUser will return true if the user has the desired role.

It is a good idea to use groups to assign roles to users whenever possible, since this makes their administration easier. Giving the itil role to the Service Desk group means that if you get added to the group, your access rights will be retained. The user administrator doesn't need to update both group membership and role membership for a new starter, as the role gets added automatically!

Nirvana occurs when another system, such as an Active Directory LDAP server, notifies ServiceNow about changes to a group's membership. This makes the process of assigning roles completely painless—associate the right roles with the right groups, and let import automation do the rest!

Differentiating between requesters and fulfillers

In *Chapter 4, Getting Things Done with Tasks*, the concept of a requester and fulfiller was introduced. A requester is someone who asks for the work to be done while a fulfiller is someone who does it. This ties in closely with roles, and how ServiceNow is licensed.

When someone uses the instance, such as loading a form or a list, the platform will either create or use an existing session. The session records information about the user, such as their name, whether they are using the HTML web interface or accessing the Web through Web Services and their roles. The roles that a session is associated with, has a dramatic effect on what these roles can see and do:

- Someone who has not logged in has **Public** access. This session is unauthenticated and the user has not entered a username or password. By default, in ServiceNow, access is extremely limited. In the majority of cases, the user will be redirected to the login page to enter their credentials.

> As noted in *Chapter 5, Events, Notifications, and Reporting*, some reports can be made public, but they will often be empty, since the data itself will be protected. There is an inactive module called Public Pages that points towards the `sys_public` table. Here, you can define exactly which pages you can see while you are unauthenticated.

- A **requester** is someone who has logged in but does not have any roles. The user cannot see or interact with anything that is not directly associated with them. A requester typically creates tasks.

> An extremely common request is for a requester to have access to their team's Incident tasks. This data is restricted by a query Business Rule. Since requesters should only have access to their own tickets, changing this may affect your licensing agreement.

- Someone who is logged in and has any role is a **fulfiller**. The most common role that is granted is the `itil` role, which gives a fulfiller the access to the ITSM applications and is key to many Contextual Security Rules. This gives the capability to see and potentially work with any task on the system.

> Note that although `itil` is the most common role, associating any role to a user will make them a fulfiller.

- The **admin** role is a special role. It grants almost unrestricted access to the instance. If a user has the admin role, then they have all the other roles too. In addition, most Contextual Security Rules apply to anyone other than admins.

> Think very carefully before assigning the admin role because an admin user has the power to do anything in the system.

Using impersonation

To verify what a particular user can see, use impersonation. A user with the `impersonator` role (including admins) has a small head/user icon next to his or her username. Clicking on it will launch the **Impersonate User** list where an account can be selected, and choosing one account will alter the session to enable you to do and see everything that the account can. The following screenshot shows the **Impersonate User** list:

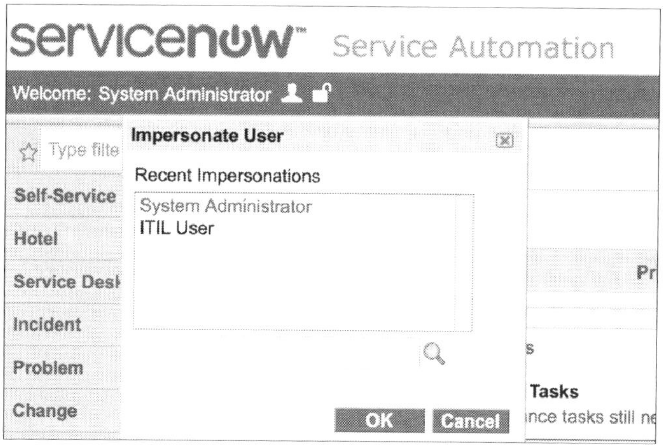

Impersonation is very useful when dealing with security and for testing in general. After you have created a security rule, consider using impersonation to validate that your rules work properly. To do this, keep some representative testing accounts ready for your use.

> There are several demo user accounts that you can use; ITIL User and Joe Employee are the most common, but the Beth Anglin account has several other roles, such as `catalog_manager` and `asset`. Having representative accounts that reflect real use cases gives a better test.

Impersonation in a production system is incredibly useful to validate and reproduce defects. However, it can also be a security concern because any updates or actions will appear to have been made by the impersonated user. Therefore, grant the privilege carefully.

> When someone uses impersonation, an entry is written in the logs. In addition, you may want to configure a Business Rule that sends an e-mail when impersonation starts. You could use the `impersonation.start` event to trigger the e-mail.

High Security Settings

All new instances have the High Security plugin enabled by default. This provides many of the functions, including Contextual Security, that are discussed in this chapter. Many of the capabilities are embedded into the platform but can be switched on or off, as desired, by navigating to **System Security > High Security Settings**. The options include:

- Enabling strict session cookie validation
- Rotating HTTP session identifiers
- Enabling escaping by default
- Checking security rules on inbound and outbound requests
- Requiring authorization for WSDLs, SOAP, and other requests

In general, the most secure settings are selected by default.

Elevating security

In order to change many security settings, including the creation of Contextual Security Rules, you need the `security_admin` role. Unlike most other roles, admins do not automatically inherit it, and you also need to activate it when you want to use it. This is designed to reduce mistakes. By elevating security, you confirm your responsibility each time!

To elevate security, use the padlock next to your name, which is alongside the impersonation key.

However, elevated privileges won't easily *stop* malicious admins from making security-related changes, since an admin can easily give themselves the `security_admin` role, just like any other role. So, instead of the elevated privileges, you may want to use logging or e-mail notifications.

Controlling access to applications and modules

The most immediate use of roles is to control the menus and modules in the Application Navigator. As we discussed in *Chapter 1, ServiceNow Foundations*, the menu on the left-hand side of the window contains links to forms and lists that often show filtered results. The definition for an Application Menu or Module contains a list field that lets you select a role. If the user has the role (remember that an admin has all roles), then the user will see the option. If they do not, then it will not be visible to them.

This does not control access to the data itself, only the link. A knowledgeable user can still navigate to the table list by entering `<table>_list.do` in the address bar of their browser.

> In *Chapter 9, Moving Scripts with Clones, Update Sets, and Upgrades*, we will discuss the creation of applications. The platform will automate the creation of roles and set up default Contextual Security Rules and module links.

Most of the time, this is good enough. However, what if you want to create an Application Menu and show it only to a subset of requesters? Perhaps, you want to let only some users see the option to create a new **Maintenance** request?

Controlling access to modules with groups

In *Chapter 2, Server-side Control*, we discussed the concept of query Business Rules. These scripts are executed by the instance when a user attempts to access a table. These are useful for controlling access to records. Let's create a new query Business Rule that checks what groups a user is in and uses that information to control access to modules.

1. Firstly, add a new field to the **Module** table. To do so, navigate to **System Definition > Tables**, then choose the **Module** [`sys_app_module`] entry in the list, and add the following fields with the given corresponding values:
    - **Column label**: `Group`
    - **Type**: `Reference`
    - **Reference**: `Group`
2. Arrange the form to include the new fields by using the **Form Designer**.
3. Then, edit the **Maintenances** module record as follows:
    - **Group**: `Maintenance`

> An easy way to navigate to the **Module** form is to right-click on the star icon and choose **Edit Module**.

The following screenshot shows the **Module** form with the preceding values:

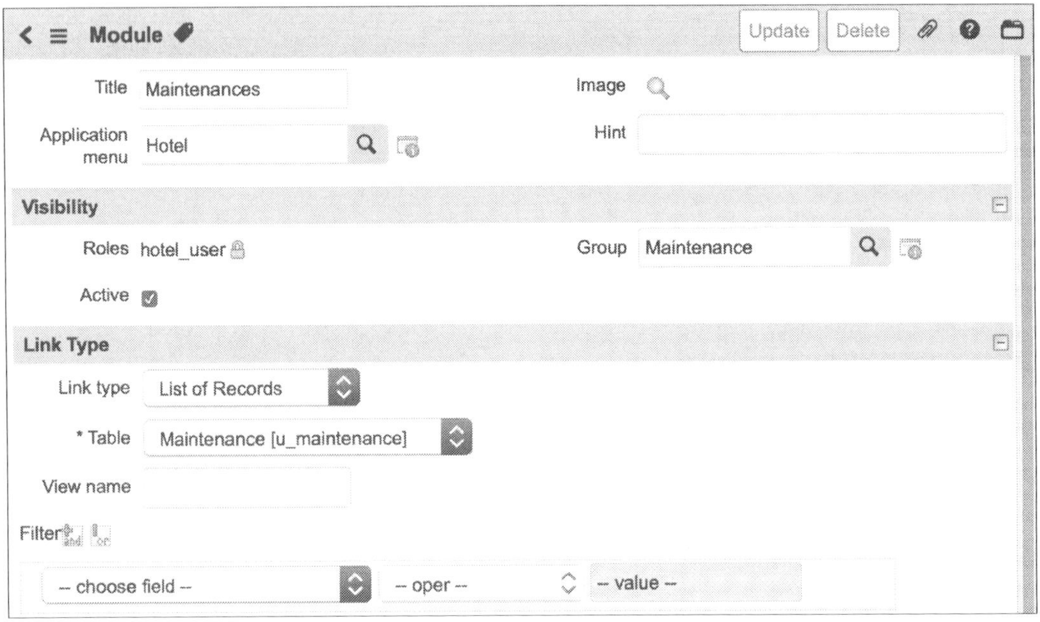

4. Now, create a new Business Rule by filling in the following values:
    - **Name**: `Control visibility via group`
    - **Table**: `Module [sys_app_module]`

- **Advanced**: `<ticked>`
- **When**: `before`
- **Query**: `<ticked>`
- **Condition**: `!gs.hasRole('admin')`

  This Business Rule will only run if the user does not have the admin role. Otherwise, the administrator will not be able to see the record, even to edit it!
- **Script**: `current.addQuery('u_group', '').addOrCondition('u_group', 'IN', getMyGroups());`

This script adds a condition when the **Module** table is queried. The records that are returned are those where the **Group** field is empty, or it contains one of the groups that the user belongs to.

To control visibility of modules, you can now use either a group or a role. To test this, grant the `u_hotel_user` role to two user accounts—one who is a member of the **Maintenance** group and one who is not. Use impersonation to validate that only the former can see the **Maintenances** module.

I've put the Albert Einstein user account, which was created by the LDAP integration in *Chapter 6, Exchanging Data – Import Sets, Web Services, and Other Integrations*, in the **Housekeeping** group, and given the user account the `u_hotel_user` role. This gives full visibility to the user account. In contrast, Issac Newton only has the `u_hotel_user` role and does not see the **Maintenances** module. In both cases, fewer applications and modules are available in the left-hand side menu. The Albert Einstein user account is shown as follows:

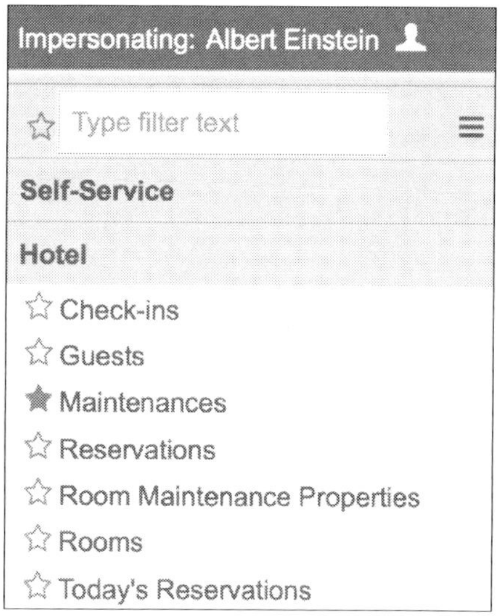

The Issac Newton user account is shown as follows:

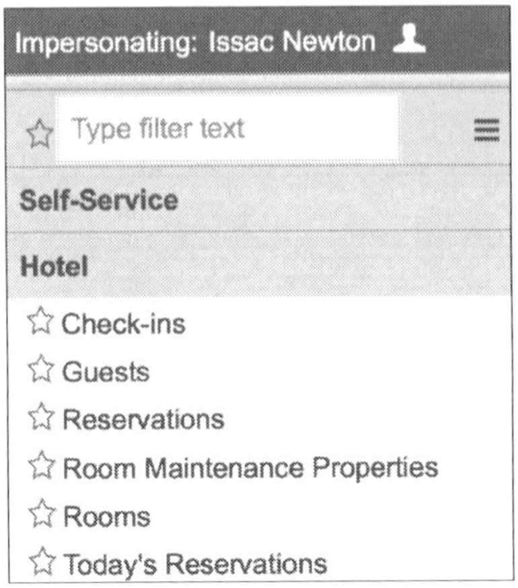

> Another way to achieve the same result is with a `read` Contextual Security Rule. The next section shows you how to do this.

This example is not only a useful configuration in itself, but it also affirms that roles are just one way to control visibility. Since virtually everything in ServiceNow is a record, the use of Business Rules and Contextual Security gives us many ways to achieve the same goal.

Protecting data with Contextual Security

The first few chapters showed how data could be protected using Business Rules and Data Policy, and that forms can be manipulated with Client Scripts and UI Policy. For example, a script can be used to ensure that you can write into a field only when the task is open. For a better experience, it'd be best to do it both on the server (to ensure that the browser didn't cheat) and the interface (to give feedback to the user). Therefore, it is easier to use Contextual Security that helps with both.

ServiceNow has two different security managers. These protect data as it leaves and enters the instance. The Simple Security Manager controls who can update a field through roles. The **Dictionary** entry for each field has several List fields where roles are selected: one for `create`, `read`, `write`, and `delete`. However, this doesn't give you any flexibility over when these actions can occur. If you have the role, you can perform the action at any time.

> CRUD, or Create, Read, Update (often substituted with Write), and Delete are the four actions that can happen to a data item. They map directly onto SQL commands (`INSERT`, `SELECT`, `UPDATE`, and `DELETE`).

In contrast, the Contextual Security Manager uses the *context* of the record. You have far more control over whether an action can occur through the use of conditions and scripts.

Understanding Contextual Security

The Security Managers are designed to stop data changing. If the scenario allows it, they provide the functionality to prevent a CRUD action from happening. They cannot force an action to happen, so security rules have no mechanism to make fields mandatory. Think of them as a guard on a building site. They check people as they come in or out, but they can't force people to enter the site—they can only stop them.

Contextual Security runs in two main places:

- As forms and lists are generated
- When data is submitted from a form

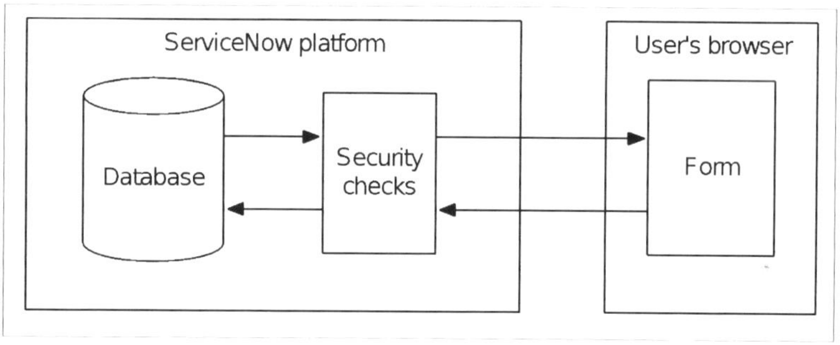

In this way, data is checked on the way out and on the way in. If a field cannot be read, it will not be shown. In fact, the data won't be included on the page at all. If a field cannot be written to, it is rendered as a text. Any attempts to manually alter a field by altering the browser's DOM, as shown in *Chapter 2, Server-side Control*, will fail. If a record cannot be created or deleted, the **New** and **Delete** buttons will not be shown.

This all means that Contextual Security should be your starting point when you think about access control.

Specifying rows and fields to secure

One of the most powerful items behind Contextual Security is that it can apply either to a particular field or an entire row. This also causes much confusion, since there is a delicate way to specify what you are trying to achieve.

Elevate your role to `security_admin` and navigate to **System Security > Access Control (ACL)**. Then, click on **New** to see the Access Control form and in particular, the **Name** field.

The **Name** field specifies what you are securing. There are two ways of looking at it—a text-only version and the one with drop-down menus. Use the blue arrow toggle to change between them. For the sake of clarity, I'll use the text-based form.

- To control a field, use the **<table>.<field>** structure.
- To control a whole row in a table, use **<table>** structure. (Note that this is rendered as **<table> --None --** in the drop-down menu.) No field is specified.

For example, if the **Priority** field on the **Maintenance** table would have to be secured, it would be specified as `u_maintenance.priority`.

Securing rows

When a user attempts to make a change to a record, the platform first checks the security rules that are listed against the table. If a write row rule prevents access, the record will be completely read-only. The fields cannot be written to or changed, and there is no **Update** or **Save** button on the form.

Similarly, if a create row rule prevents access, the **New** button will not show in a list; a delete row rule will control the **Delete** button.

> The UI Actions are not shown since they have conditions that check the `current` object of `GlideRecord` The `canWrite` and `canRead` functions of `GlideRecord` are far more preferable to use than building complex code using `gs.hasRole()` and other logic in the **Condition** field. It is a great idea to include `current.canWrite()` as part of the condition in a UI Action.

A read row rule will prevent access to the row entirely. This renders in ServiceNow in an frustrating manner, with a message at the bottom of a list that says **Number of rows removed from the list by Security constraints: <number>**.

This happens because security rules are evaluated after the data has been retrieved from the database. Each record in turn is analyzed by the security rules, and if necessary, the platform will not render it; instead, it presents this message in the list.

This has a big usability impact. Consider a scenario where there are 100 records in a table, and a user has set their page's size as 20. If the row read rules allowed access to all records, the user could happily page through 5 pages and see 20 at a time.

If the row read rule restricts access to, say, 80 of these records, then there will still be 5 pages. Depending on the sorting settings, the user may see 10 rows on the first page and a message saying that 10 rows are restricted. On the next page, they may see nothing aside from a message that says that all 20 rows are restricted and so on.

This is intensely frustrating for a user. In my experience, they will not understand this message, and they will not appreciate that you can page through to find the records they want.

I strongly recommend that a row read rule should be saved for situations when all rows need to be inaccessible. Instead, you can use Before Query Business Rules, as shown above. Its benefit is that it controls what the database actually returns, is more intuitive to use, and is just as secure.

> To try this out for yourself, create a table with no automatically created security rules. Make several test records. For your read rule, ensure that it is specified for the table and enter a script such as `answer = (Math.floor(Math.random() * 2) == 1);`. This will mean that on average half of the rows will be readable and the others won't.

Controlling fields

Most people intuitively understand the controls for a field, especially read and write. If a field is restricted for the create rule, it is read-only only when the record has not yet been saved. In the absence of a create field rule, the platform will use write rules for the field. This means that create field rules are often not used.

Even less relevant are delete field rules. They have no effect at all.

> Just like GlideRecord has canWrite and canRead functions, so does GlideElement. So, you can call current.<table>.canWrite() in server-side scripts to see whether the rules let the user edit a field.

When creating field rules, especially if there are many fields on the table, consider whether you will be generally permissive or restrictive. If more fields are going to be disallowed than allowed, it is a good idea to create a default <table>.* rule and make it always evaluate as false. Then, open up the fields that you want by using more specific rules.

The order of execution

Contextual Security rules are applied in a specific sequence. It can often be confusing to work out which rules are being applied if you aren't familiar with how they executed. However, once you are comfortable with the logic, Contextual Security rules let you control any CRUD situation!

Executing the row and then the field

For every record that is pulled from the database, row-based rules are determined first. They have priority over field rules. For instance, if the write row rules return false, then all the fields will be read-only. If the row rule returns true, then the field rules are considered.

Rules are searched for until one is found

The platform will work through the rule list in a specific order until it finds the best match. Once a relevant rule is found, it is taken into consideration. This level is then considered definitive. If the rule returns true, the action is allowed. If it returns false, the action is not allowed.

Defaults are possible

In addition to specifying field or table names, such as `priority`, `short_description`, or `u_maintenance`, an asterisk (`*`) can be used in either the table or field part of the Name field. This provides a default rule. If there are no other relevant rules, this default will be used instead.

The table hierarchy is understood

In our **Hotel** application, the **Maintenance** table is extended from the **Task** table. When looking for row rules, the platform firstly checks for any with the name of `u_maintenance`. If one is not found, it looks at `task`. If one is not found, it looks for `*`.

If no rules are found, the action is allowed. However, the Contextual Security baseline rule set includes a `*` row rule. By default, this rejects the action.

Multiple rules with the same name are both considered

It is perfectly possible (and encouraged) to have two rules with the same name and action. For instance, there could be two read row rules that have a name of `u_maintenance`. In this situation, both will be executed. If either returns `true`, then the action will be allowed.

Field rules check the table hierarchy twice

When looking for a field rule on an extended table, the platform checks each part of the rule in a term. First, the table gets less specific, and then, the field.

For instance, if the **Priority** field on the **Maintenance** table was being secured, then the platform will firstly look for rules with a name of `u_maintenance.priority`, then `task.priority`, and then `*.priority`. Then, looks for `u_maintenance.*`, then `task.*`, and finally `*.*`.

If a rule is found at any point, its decision is taken and the platform will stop searching. Two or more rules with the same name will result in being `true` if any are `true`. If all are `false`, the result will be `false`.

Summarizing the execution

Contextual Security analyses a great combination of rules. When a record is shown in a form, the row security rule is found first. If this returns `true`, then every single field on the form will trigger a rule check. Due to the great number of combinations, it is easy to lose track of what the platform is doing at each point. In the next chapter, we will look at how to debug security rules and watch the decisions that the platform takes.

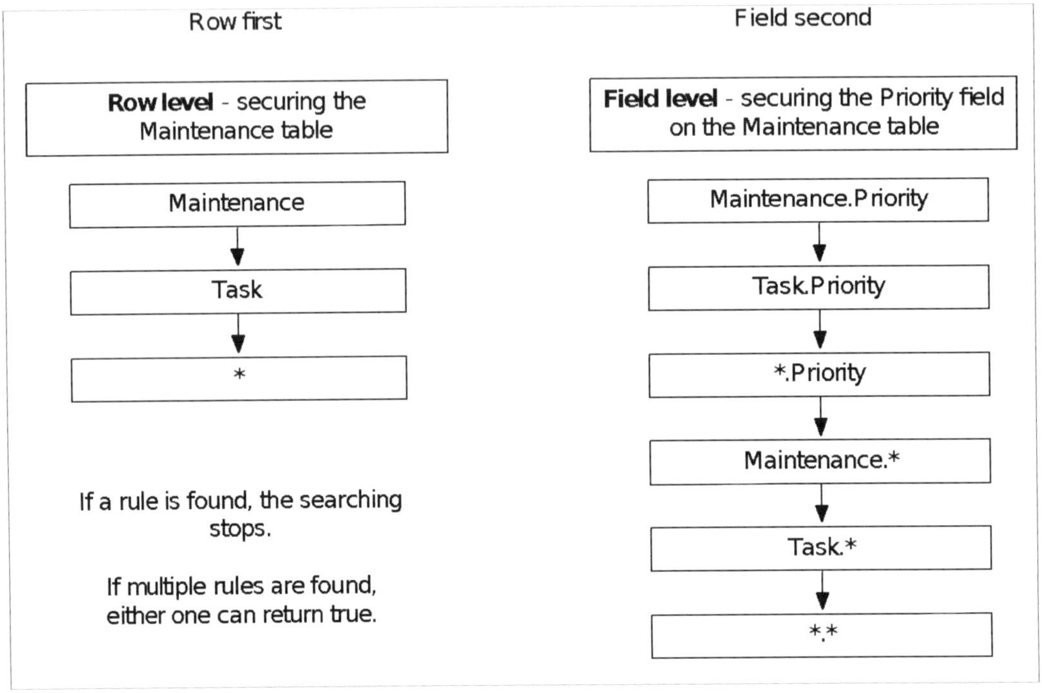

Scripting and Access Controls

The majority of JavaScript code that runs on the server, such as those in Business Rules and Workflows, is unaffected by Contextual Security. When `GlideRecord` accesses the database, it does so without regard for any rules. The majority of the time this is what you want—a UI Action script can change the state of a read only field. This means that it is the scriptwriter's responsibility to ensure that a user cannot do something that they shouldn't. Use the `canRead` and `canWrite` functions of `GlideRecord` to check whether the logged in user has the correct privileges to access the data.

Checking every record and field for access can be a bit frustrating and inefficient. Instead, consider using `GlideRecordSecure`. This extends the `GlideRecord` class, so it inherits all of its functions, but it will only perform actions that the user is allowed to do. For example, rows that are made read-only by Access Controls won't be available in `GlideRecordSecure`.

> One of the reasons why ServiceNow is so flexible and powerful is that you can accomplish almost anything with server-side scripting. You can add a role to a user, delete almost any record, and read all data. Treat scripting the same way as someone with the admin role – they have the keys to the instance!

The client can sometimes ask the server to execute a JavaScript. For example, in a filter, you can specify **User** – **is** – `javascript:gs.getUserID()`. This JavaScript command will be run on the server. Although it is very useful, it also opens up a large security hole; it is not a good idea to allow arbitrary JavaScript that is specified by the client to run!

> Consider the consequences if a user specified this filter as **User** – **is** – `javascript:(var g = new GlideRecord('sys_user'); g.query(); g.deleteMultiple())`. Don't try this at home!

To protect the database from a malicious user, the majority of code that is passed through from the browser is run in a sandbox. This takes it one step further than `GlideRecordSecure`, since it totally prevents any records from being written onto or deleted. So, the example code given in the preceding box will have no effect.

One notable exception to this policy is a Script Include that is marked as **Client callable**. By checking this box, which allows code to be called from the client, the scriptwriter confirms that they will handle any security checks themselves.

Securing other operations

In addition to the CRUD operations, ServiceNow lets you create Access Control rules to control access to several other parts of the system:

- To control visibility of UI Pages, set the **Type** field to `ui_page` and select **read** from **Operation**. Then, set **Name** to be that of the UI Page.
- Script Includes used by `GlideAJAX` can be prevented from running by setting **Type** to be `client_callable_script_include`. The **Operation** is automatically set to **execute**. Processors can similarly be restricted.

- The `report_on` operation very usefully restricts the table list that is available in the reporting interface. Since ServiceNow is very open and lets you report on almost any table, the list is by default quite cumbersome to sort through!
- To control the fields that can be set in a template, use `save_as_template`. Then, set **Name** to be the field you want to control. This prevents users from overwriting, for example, the **Approval** or **Number** fields from a template.

Outlining the scenarios

As we work through the rest of the chapter, we'll use the following scenarios to implement different security rules. They outline particular use cases. I find this very helpful to organize exactly what is necessary:

- Only authorized users are allowed to create or edit **Maintenance** tasks. The records become read-only when the tasks are closed.
- Only a team leader is allowed to edit the **Priority** field when any task is not closed.
- A user can only add to **Work notes** for a **Maintenance** task if they are on the **Work notes list** or in the **Assigned to** field.

Conditioning Contextual Security

A Contextual Security rule is made up of three elements; these are evaluated to determine if the user can carry out a particular action:

- A **condition** (if it applies)
- A **script** (that returns `true`)
- A **role** (specifies what the user must have)

A rule can have any combination of these elements. A rule could consist of a condition and a role, or it could just consist of a script. However, all must be satisfied for the rule to return `true`. A blank element will not be considered.

> More than one role can be listed against a security rule. In this situation, the user must have one of the roles. If the situation is such that the user must have multiple roles to carry out the action, then you must script it. Otherwise, better yet, create a new role!

By analyzing these statements, we can see that they split into conditions, scripts, and roles. Conditions can cater for the majority of scenarios, but occasionally, a script is necessary.

When a table is created, the Application Creator will automatically create a basic set of security rules. By default, the platform will create a read, write, create, and delete row rule for a new role, based on the table or the application that you have currently selected. Since we are working within an application called Hotel, a role called u_hotel_user has been created automatically.

> Applications are discussed further in *Chapter 9, Moving Scripts with Clones, Update Sets, and Upgrades*.

Item	Action	Condition	Role required	Script
1. Maintenance tasks	Write	State is not closed	Hotel user	-
2. Maintenance **Priority** field	Write	-	Maintenance team leader	-
3. Maintenance **Work notes** field	Write	-	-	Logged in user is in **Assigned to** OR Logged in user is in **Work notes**

Editing the automatic security rules

For the first requirement, which is to only allow Maintenance tasks to be edited if they are not closed, we must edit an automatically created row rule.

1. Firstly, ensure you have elevated security to have the security_admin role.
2. Then, navigate to **System Security** > **Access Control (ACL)** and find the rule with the name as u_maintenance and the operation as write.
3. Add the following values:
    - **Condition**: State - is not - Closed Complete
    - **Admin overrides**: <unticked>

> If the **Admin overrides** field is ticked, the security rule will be disabled for admins, regardless of the other conditions. This lets the admins override normal procedures to "fix" records, or deal with unforeseen circumstances. In this instance, we uncheck it to facilitate easier testing.

4. To test, set a **Maintenance** record to have a state of **Closed Complete**. Once you've saved the setting, you'll notice that the form is entirely read-only, and the **Update** and **Save** buttons have been removed.

Testing using impersonation

Although we've checked successfully with the admin user, the best practice is to use a real test account. The interplay of security rules can be complex.

1. To do this, impersonate a user with the right access. I've again used Albert Einstein.

> It is often helpful to use a second browser when using impersonation so that you can keep your admin user account open in one window and your test account in another. An alternative is to start a Private Browsing session or use the Incognito mode.

2. Navigate to a **Maintenance** record that *isn't* in a **Closed** state and review the available fields. Only the **Room** and **Assignment group** is writeable, and the **Work notes** field is not visible. The **Update** button is available. This is quite restricted. why?
    - Since the **Maintenance** table is inherited from **Task**, some default field rules have been included. Specifically, there are rules named `task.short_description`, `task.assigned_to`, and `task.description`. As an admin, try to create a filter that searches for security rules with names beginning with `task.` to see them all.
    - The majority of these security rules require the user to have the `task_editor` or `itil` roles. While you could create more specific rules, such as `u_maintenance.short_description`, to override these default rules, it is more sensible to include `task_editor` as part of the `u_hotel_user` role.
3. To do this, navigate to **User Administration** > **Roles** as an admin, find `u_hotel_user`, and include `task_editor` in the **Contains Role** related list.
    - This will automatically grant the `task_editor` role to anyone who has the `u_hotel_user` role. Verify this by looking at your test user—Albert Einstein in my case. In the **Roles** Related list on the **User** form, you should see both listed there, with `task_editor` as an *inherited* role, as shown in the following screenshot:

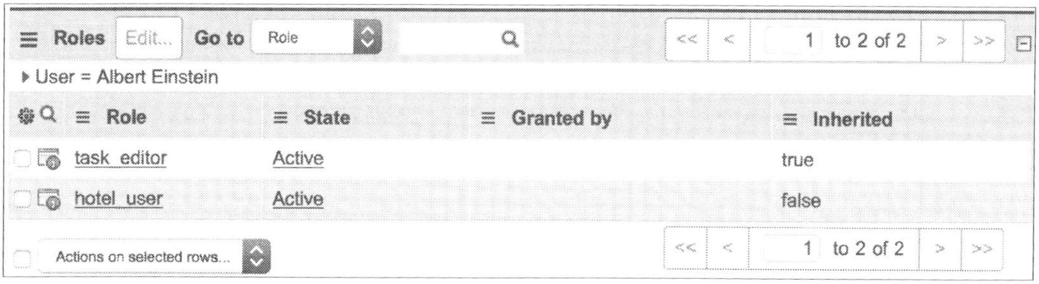

> Unfortunately, in the default configuration of ServiceNow, some security rules are entirely dependent on the `itil` role. However, using the `itil` role instead of `task_editor` would give you access to many more applications than what would probably be appropriate. We'll fix a particular issue with `read` access to the **Work notes** field for our third scenario.

4. Finally, in order to test, impersonate your test user again. Roles are only read after a user logs in, so the changes will be only seen if you select them again from the **Impersonation** dialog box. You should now also be able to edit the **Priority**, **State**, **Assigned to**, **Short Description**, and **Description** fields.

Setting security rules quickly

An often overlooked interface feature of ServiceNow is how you can create a security rule without using the Access Controls form. We'll use this method for our second security rule—only team leaders can edit the **Priority** field.

1. Firstly, create a new role by navigating to **User Administration > Roles**. Then, click on **New** and fill the following:
    - **Name**: `maintenance_team_leader`
2. Once created, make the `u_hotel_user` role a child by adding it to the **Contains Role** Related List.

3. Navigate to a **Maintenance** record as an admin and right-click on the **Priority** field label. Choose **Personalize Security**. Set the **Operation to Secure** field as **write** and set the `maintenance_team_leader` role. Finally, click on **OK** to save. The **Security Mechanic** window is shown as follows:

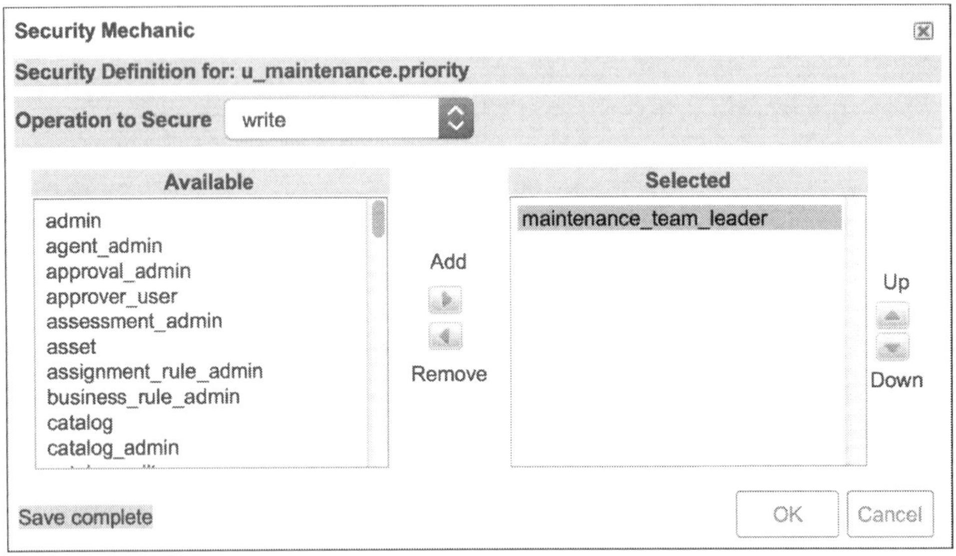

4. Click on **Cancel** to close the window. Don't worry! The rule would have been saved if a message displaying **Save complete** appears! You can confirm this by navigating to **System Security** > **Access Control (ACL)**. There, you should find a new entry with a name as `u_maintenance.priority`.

Scripting a security rule

Our final scenario is to control how Work notes are used. There is an existing read security rule named `task.work_notes` that only lets users with the `itil` role see the field or its output. This even extends to the Activity log. This ensures that requesters will not see anything entered in the **Work notes** field. However, to ensure that the hotel users get access, that should be extended to the `task_editor` role.

1. Create a new security rule to grant access by filling in the following values:
   - **Operation**: `read`
   - **Name**: `u_maintenance.work_notes`

> The more specific name of `u_maintenance.work_notes` will be evaluated before the original `task.work_notes` rule.

- **Requires role** related list: `task_editor`

> This rule can be created using the security mechanic form, which was used for the second rule.

The `write` security rule needs slightly more work. A script in a security rule needs to provide a binary answer—`true` or `false`—and set it in the provided answer variable. As we will discuss in the next section, you must ensure that the security rules are executed very quickly. They are called frequently, so avoid the temptation to do complex lookups or even log.

2. Set the following on a new security rule:
   - **Operation**: `write`
   - **Name**: `u_maintenance.work_notes`
   - **Admin overrides**: `<unchecked>` (for testing purposes)
   - **Script**: `answer = (current.assigned_to == gs.getUserID()) || (current.work_notes_list.indexOf(gs.getUserID()) > -1)`

   This one-line script runs two separate conditions. The answer variable will be set to `true` if either of the conditions are `true`. Firstly, the **Assigned to** field is checked. It succeeds if the contents of the reference field match the `sys_id` of the currently logged-in user. Secondly, the **Work Notes List** field is checked. This is a comma-separated string of `sys_id` values. This is searched to see if the `sys_id` of the current user is in it.

3. Try this out. Find or create a **Maintenance** record where the **Assigned to** and **Work notes** fields are empty, and note that the **Work Notes** textbox is not displayed. Then, add the System Administrator to the **Work notes** field (or whichever user you are logged in as), save it, and you'll now be able to see that it is visible.

> The rendering of a read-only journal field, such as **Work notes**, is different than a multiline text field, such as **Description**. With the former, the text area is completely removed, while for the latter, it is disabled.

Using security rules effectively

Contextual security rules can be confusing at first. To get used to how they work, it is critical to understand the order of execution. Even after this is understood, it is easy for you to slow the system down with inefficient security rules. While the platform does cache results and attempts to optimize, where possible, follow these key points to use security rules effectively:

- Read row rules are not user friendly. Query Business Rules are almost always more effective. They may also be quicker since they ask the database to filter out the records and prevent their processing.
- Read field rules can be very intensive for the system to process. Consider a <table>.* security rule that returns false for every field. This will mean that in a list of 10 columns and 20 records, the security rule will be executed 200 times.
- Scripts in general should be avoided wherever possible. It is very easy to write inefficient code. Always try to avoid querying the database by using GlideRecord. Instead, consider calculating it once using gs.getSession().getClientData(<key>, <value>); and putClientData(<key>);. An even better option is to avoid it entirely!
- Use the **Requires role** Related List wherever possible. The platform caches which roles a user has and can perform some smart optimization; for example, if a read field rule requires a role that the user doesn't have, then the whole column is disabled in a list. Don't use a script for this as gs.hasRole() won't be so clever!
- Try to keep **Admin overrides** ticked. A system administrator is responsible for the whole platform. It is inevitable that sometimes things will go wrong, and the admin may need to fix data, and change records in a way that was not initially envisaged.
- Security rules are designed for securing data. Always use them over UI Policy and the **Read only** checkbox in the dictionary. Since these only work on the client side, a malicious end user can easily override them.
- If a UI Policy or Client Script makes a field read-only, its value can still be changed through a client-side script, as you saw in *Chapter 2*, *Server-side Control*. If this happens, onChange Client Scripts associated with that field will fire. However, this will not happen for fields that are made read-only via access rules.
- Security rules can do more than protect records. They can also control the access of processors, UI pages, and Script Includes.

Encrypting data

ServiceNow provides support for two types of encryption. Both occur within the server, and the data is decrypted before it leaves the instance. Each provides a different form of **data-at-rest**-style encryption—it protects data that is not moving through a network. The two type of encryption are as follows:

- Full disc encryption protects a disk if it was physically stolen from the data center. The instance itself is unaware of any differences to a normal operating environment.
- Field and attachment encryption stores encrypted data in the database. This provides a level of protection against a malicious database administrator.

> All communication with the instance occurs over HTTPS. This means that all the data is protected in transit.

Many customers see field encryption as a highly desirable feature. Most security policies need personal or other protected data to be properly secured, and field-level encryption is a feature that may help in some circumstances. For example, an HR team may want to ensure that unauthorized people cannot see some specific private information. However, field-level encryption does suffer from some significant disadvantages, which are as follows:

- Only custom fields can be encrypted. Changing the type of an existing field is not supported.
- The only field type is a large multiline text field.
- Encrypted fields cannot be used in a list to filter or sort records.
- The data in an encrypted field is not exportable from a list.

> Encrypted fields are accessible through web services; this gives us an alternative data extraction technique.

- Since encrypted fields are tied to a role, they can only be used by licensed fulfillers.
- When impersonating a user, encryption contexts are not inherited. Impersonation is used by the platform when it runs a Transform Map; this means that encrypted fields cannot be used when importing.

- It does not protect from malicious administrators. It is simple to associate the security context with another role and let the administrator see the data.

> There are some enterprising workarounds to minimize some of these drawbacks. Since encrypted data is still accessible via web services, it is possible to write a Business Rule that moves the submitted data out of a field and saves it into another by connecting to the same instance via a SOAP or REST call.

- There are very few use cases where encrypted fields are truly useful. It is often far more useful to implement a well designed and tested set of Access Controls. They are more flexible and provide a similar level of protection since both rely on the system to control the data and only show it to the appropriate users.

Evaluating encryption gateways

Edge-based encryption gateways are a proxy-based technology. Several companies offer competing solutions, but all provide software that sits within the customer's infrastructure. Instead of connecting directly to ServiceNow, users would connect to the gateway. The gateway proxies all interaction to the instance, encrypting and decrypting specified fields as it passes through. This ensures that the encryption of data is fully under the customer's control. The general workflow is as follows:

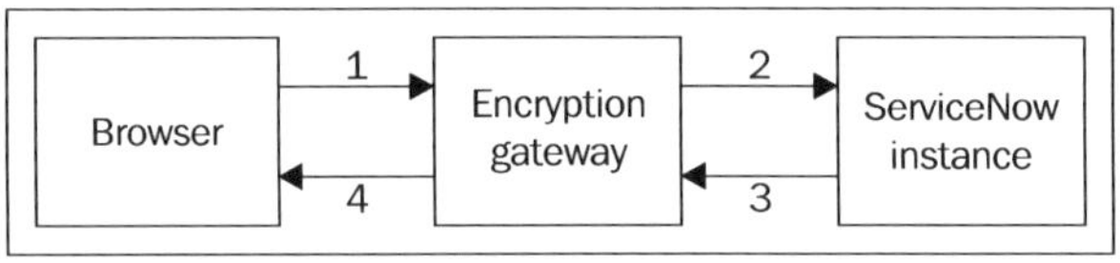

Now, let's walk through the process gradually:

1. The user's browser sends data to the encryption gateway. The encryption gateway encrypts any sensitive data.
2. The instance receives encrypted text and saves it in the database.
3. Encrypted data is sent to the gateway.
4. The encryption gateway decrypts the data for the user.

While these gateways effectively encrypt the data and provide extra security, careful evaluation is necessary. The design necessitates that all traffic flows through them, so functionality may be impacted, as follows:

- Importing and exporting data is usually difficult or not possible
- Manipulation of the encrypted text with server-side scripts may be difficult
- Searching and sorting will be impaired
- Certain user interface elements may be impacted if they need to use encrypted text
- Integrations, such as web services, will be more difficult
- It is important that all use cases (including administrative functions, such as importing) are fully evaluated when you select an encryption gateway

Introducing Domain Separation

Domain Separation is designed to control what fulfillers can see and do. ServiceNow applications have been typically designed so that a fulfiller has access to all the tasks in a particular application, and the application works consistently for each person. Domain Separation tags configuration and data so that the platform can choose what is relevant for a particular user at the appropriate time.

The design for Domain Separation is focused on the needs of **Managed Service Providers** (MSPs). These use ServiceNow for helpdesk and other services and sell their capabilities to their customers. This means that an MSP can provide a large call center, enjoying economies of scale, with a fulfiller who inputs incidents for multiple companies but in a single instance.

The instance should be configured with the MSP's standard processes as a baseline, but each customer of the MSP may have specific configuration requirements. Additionally, the MSP's customer may want to have their own users to log into the instance and work on tasks. Of course, the MSP would only want the users to see the data that they should. Therefore, Domain Separation helps to achieve three specific goals:

- **Process separation**: In process separation, configurations such as Business Rules or Client Scripts are selectively applied. A customer of an MSP may have different assignment rules to another.
- **UI separation**: In UI separation, different domains can have different forms and entries in related lists. This allows the customer of an MSP to have different categorization options.

Process and UI separation are both considered as configuration. When I refer to configuration separation, I'm referring to both process and UI separation.

- **Data separation**: In data separation, records such as other users, tasks, or locations are only available to the right people. This means that a user that works for an MSP's customer, perhaps even one with fulfiller rights such as the `itil` role, would only see records for their company.

The difference between configuration and data is discussed in much more detail in *Chapter 9, Moving Scripts with Clones, Update Sets, and Upgrades*.

Defining a domain

A domain is simply a logical grouping of configuration (or processes) or data. If a certain set of people need to have a configuration that applies just to them, or they want to be restricted from seeing certain records, then they may need a domain.

When you use the Domain Separation plugin, you need a table that will provide the domains. This table must have a reference field that refers to itself—the parent field. Most of the time, a dedicated table called **Domain** [`domain`] is used, but others, such as the **Group** table, are occasionally used.

The **Domain** table is created with the MSP Extensions Installer plugin. It also provides typical configurations and best practices.

In turn, every data or configuration record is associated with a domain. When the Domain Support plugin is turned on, it creates a reference field called **Domain** [`sys_domain`] on many hundreds of tables. This allows items, such as an Assignment Rule, to be associated with a particular domain. Users are also associated with a domain.

To add a domain field to a table, create a text field with a label called `sys_domain`. The platform will actually make a reference field called **Domain**.

Applying Domain Separation

At the most simple level, Domain Separation compares the domain of the user or the record, with that of the data or configuration.

If the domain of the logged-in user is the same as the domain of the data, it can be seen, as shown in the following figure:

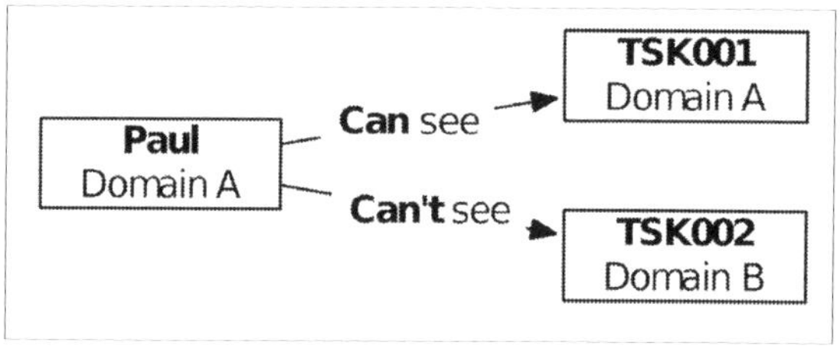

If the domain of the record is the same as the domain of the configuration, it is applied, as shown in the following figure:

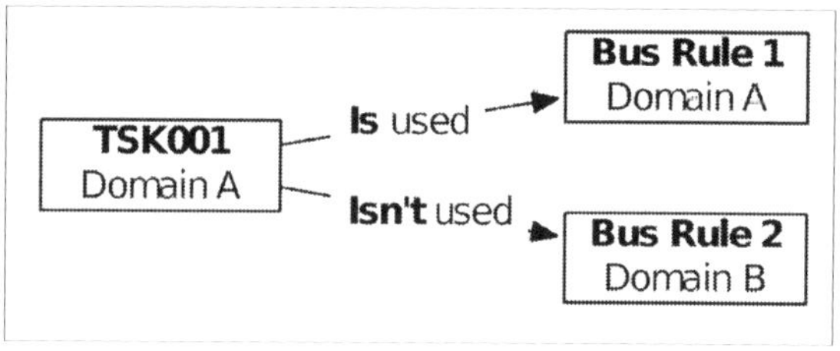

> At its most raw level, Domain Separation adds a `WHERE` clause to a database query. A highly simplified example is when a query for **User** records is modified to look like this:
>
> ```
> SELECT * FROM sys_user WHERE sys_domain = <domain of
> logged in user>
> ```

Organizing domains

A domain is typically related to another domain in a parent-child relationship. The domain hierarchy is the backbone of Domain Separation since it can have a great impact on how configuration is applied or what data can be seen. How the hierarchy is applied depends upon what item is being considered:

- The user's domain is used when viewing **data**. Any records that are associated with that domain or *lower* are visible.
- The record's domain is used when applying **configuration**. Any configuration that is associated with that domain or *higher* is applied.

Introducing global

Not all records in the instance will be tagged with a domain. Some tables, such as properties or Script Includes, do not have a **Domain** field. These items will be processed regardless of what domain is in use. For tables that are separated by domain, such as Business Rules, it is possible for the **Domain** field to be empty. In both these situations, the item is considered to be global.

Global is technically not a domain. Instead, it is the *absence* of a domain. If a record is global, then it is outside of domain processing. This means that if a Business Rule has no domain, it is always run. If a Group has no domain, everyone can see it, regardless of what domain the user is in.

If a user is not associated with a domain, they will again be outside of domain processing—they will see everything. If a record is global, then only global configuration will be applied to it.

Understanding domain inheritance

The following diagram shows a simple domain hierarchy. Domain A is the parent of both Domain B and Domain C. We'll use this structure to discover how inheritance works.

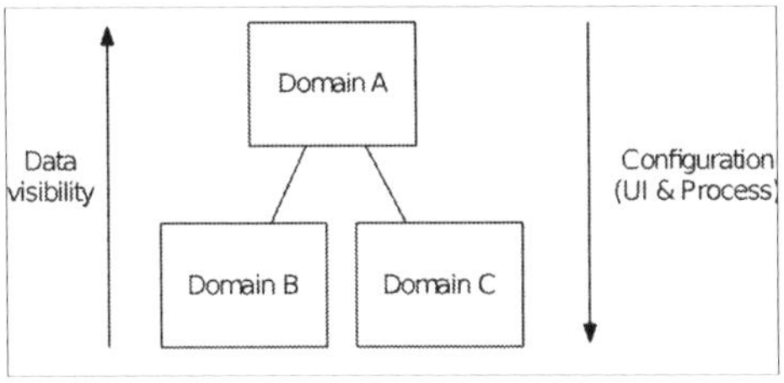

The table shows how the platform uses the domain structure to apply configuration and to control data visibility:

Domain being considered	Configuration applied	Data visibility
None (so global)	Global	Global, Domains A, B, and C
A	Global, Domain A	Global, Domains A, B, and C
B	Global, Domains A and B	Global, Domain B
C	Global, Domains A and C	Global, Domain C

The preceding table can be interpreted as follows:

- Since domains B and C are siblings, they have no impact on each other
- Global data is always visible, and global configuration is always applied
- A user in domain A will be able to see data associated with global and domains A, B, and C
- A record in domain A will only be affected by configuration that are associated with domain A (and global)
- Users in domain B will only see data that is associated with domain B (and global)
- Records in domain B will use configuration from both domains A and B (and global)

Turning on Domain Separation

In order to use Domain Separation, you must install the Domain Support plugin. I recommend starting with the MSP Extensions process pack that bundles the plugin, together with helpful scripts, demo data, and sensible default configuration.

> Once installed, Domain Separation cannot be removed from an instance. The functionality can be disabled, but the additional fields and options will still be available. Therefore, install this on a noncritical test instance only.

If you wish to activate the plugin, contact ServiceNow Technical Support. The plugin cannot be installed by an admin due to the complexities that it adds to administration. It may also affect licensing costs. Ask for **Domain Support - MSP Extensions Installer** to be activated.

Once installed, one of the mechanisms for switching domains should be enabled. This allows users to select which domain their user is associated with, if they have access to more than one user through the hierarchy. To enable it, navigate to **System UI > UI Macros** and activate `domain_select`. Then, refresh your entire browser window and click on the gear icon to access the system menu. A choice list will now be available to you to select the desired domain.

> The system menu is available in the Eureka version of ServiceNow. In earlier versions, the domain picker was placed in the banner frame.

The following screenshot shows the domain selected as **global**:

The MSP Extensions plugin contains a few example domains that are useful to understand how the system works. To see a list of these domains, navigate to **Domain Admin > Domains**, but a graphical representation can be found by navigating to **Domain Admin > Domain Map**. Unfortunately, this has been rotated, meaning the top parent domain is on the left, but it still gives a good idea of how the domains are related to one another.

Setting domains

Here, we present an example using this diagram:

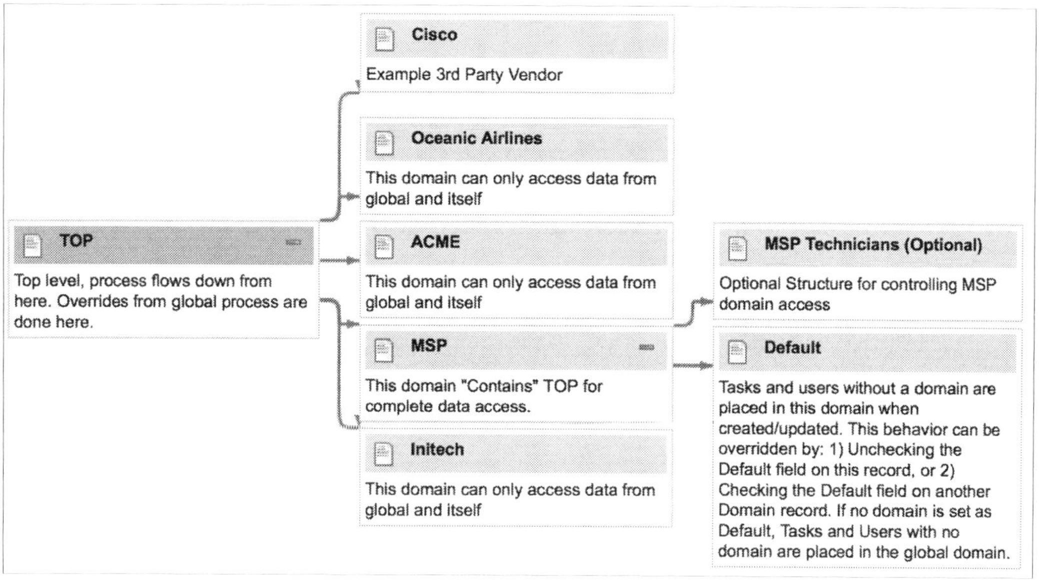

Most often, domains are related to companies. In this example, ACME, Oceanic Airlines, and Initech all buy services from the MSP. Cisco supports the MSP as a vendor. There are records in the both **Domain** table and the **Company** table to represent this.

The MSP Extensions plugin contains scripts that automatically set the domain when a company is set on a task or a user record. If a domain cannot be found, a Business Rule will move the tasks into a Domain called **Default**. This ensures that the tasks don't get put into the global domain by accident and are thus visible to everyone.

Exploring domain visibility

With the MSP Extensions plugin installed and the Domain Picker active, navigate to **User Administration** > **Users**. As you change the selection in the Domain Picker, the records that are visible will change. It is easiest to see the differences when you add the **Domain** field to the list and group by it.

If you pick the Initech domain, you will be subject to Initech's data visibility rules. This means that you will see the data tagged with no domain (that is, global), TOP, and Initech. In contrast, if you switch to the Cisco domain, you will see the Cisco users and not Initech's.

> Domains are usually represented with their hierarchical name in the interface. Since Initech is a child of TOP, it will be titled TOP/Initech. Note that once you have switched domains, there is no indication that you are not seeing the full dataset, beyond the domain picker. All queries, filters, and actions will be applied only to the limited list.

Understanding Delegated Administration

When discussing Domain Separation, the ServiceNow wiki talks about Delegated Administration. Many think that this allows a user to have a "sub-admin" capability—the ability of a user to change a part of the configuration in a certain domain. However, this is not the case.

Delegated Administration simply means that a configuration can be applied to a particular domain. In the example dataset, the configuration could be applied to the Initech domain, thus ensuring that it is only applied to Initech (and any subsequent children).

> A user with the admin role has control over the whole instance. The truth of this statement does not change with Domain Separation. An admin can choose which domain they are currently associated with and control which domain configuration and data it is associated with.

Overriding configuration

A configuration from a higher domain may be considered as a template. It will be applied to domains that are lower in the hierarchy unless it is overridden. In a domain-separated instance, all configuration will have a field called **Overrides** [`sys_overrides`] in addition to **Domain** [`sys_domain`]. The **Overrides** field is a reference field to the table on which it is created. For example, the **Overrides** field on the **Business Rule** table will refer to the **Business Rule** table.

> The definition of a configuration in a domain-separated instance may be considered as a table that has both the **Domain** and **Overrides** fields.

When altering configuration that is inherited from a higher domain, the platform will automatically use this field to create copies. This ensures the right domain receives the right version.

Displaying different messages for different domains

To show how a configuration can be overridden at a particular domain, let's create a simple Business Rule and then override it at a lower domain level.

1. Firstly, use the domain picker to switch to the TOP domain. It is good practice to put all the configuration into a domain rather than use global.
2. Then, create a Business Rule by using the following values:
    - **Name**: Display message (TOP)
    - **Table**: User [sys_user]
    - **Advanced**: <ticked>
    - **When**: display
    - **Add message**: <ticked>
    - **Message**: TOP domain
3. Once the setting is saved, change into the Initech domain using the **Domain Picker**. Find the Business Rule that you created and change the values in the following items:
    - **Name**: Display message (Initech)
    - **Message**: Initech domain
4. Ensure that you click on the **Submit** (or **Save**) button to *update* the current record. (Do not use **Insert and Stay**.)

    A message will appear letting you know that the platform has not actually overwritten the Business Rule, but it has created a copy and set the **Overrides** field:

5. To see what has happened, switch to global in the **Domain Picker** and look at the **Business Rules** table. I've added the **Domain** and **Overrides** field to the list to be to see what has happened.

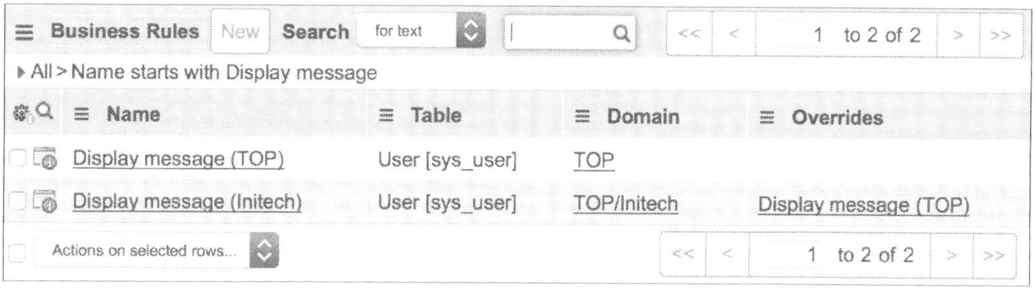

The **Domain** field specifies which domains will run the script. Any domain underneath TOP will run the `Display message (TOP)` Business Rule, except for records associated with the Initech domain. This has its own Business Rule that will run instead and specify this with the **Overrides** field.

To try this out, navigate to the **User** table and open up a variety of users. The message that will appear will be dependent upon the domain of the user:

- When you view user records in the Global domain (such as Joe Employee in the following screenshot) you will not receive a message:

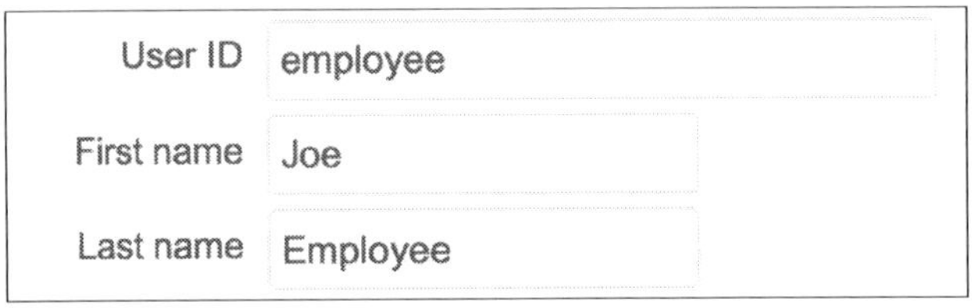

- User records in the Initech Domain (such as Initech Employee in the following screenshot) will show **Initech Domain** due to the specific Business Rule associated with this domain:

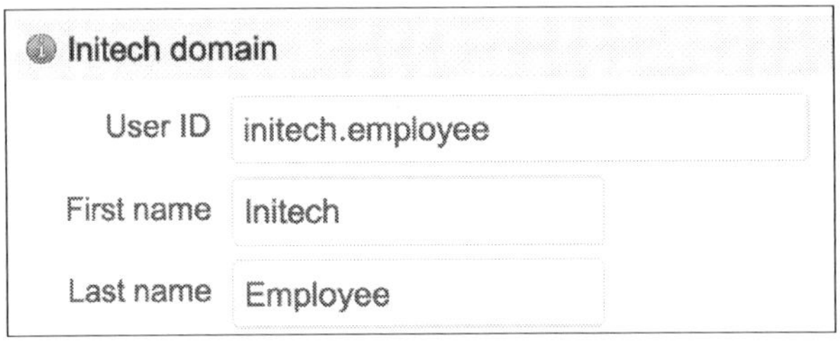

- User records in the ACME Domain (such as ACME Employee in the following screenshot) will show **TOP Domain** since they inherit the configuration from the TOP domain:

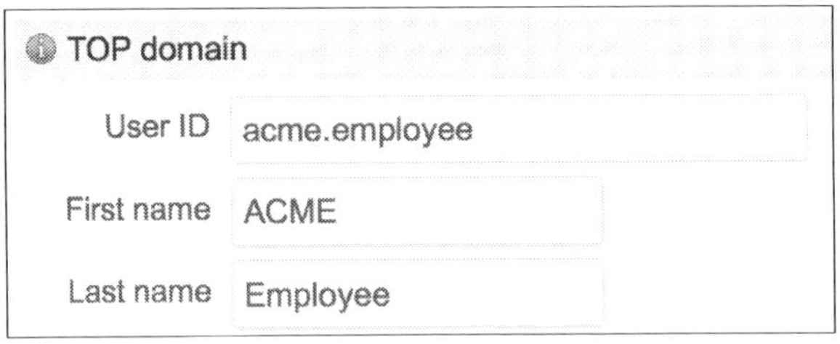

Creating more domain relationships

In addition to the hierarchical relationships, a domain can **contain** other domains. This can be accomplished by using a related list on the Domains form and populating the **Contained Domains** (`domain_contains`) table.

When containing a domain, you should indicate that you want to see all the data that the domain can. Since data flows up, you effectively specify another parent.

In the example data, the MSP domain contains TOP. This means that a user in the MSP domain can see all of the data that TOP can see, and since TOP is at the top of the hierarchy, this means that the user can see everything. Even though MSP is a sibling of Initech, because MSP contains Initech's parent, which is TOP, MSP can see all of Initech's data. The graphical representation is shown as follows:

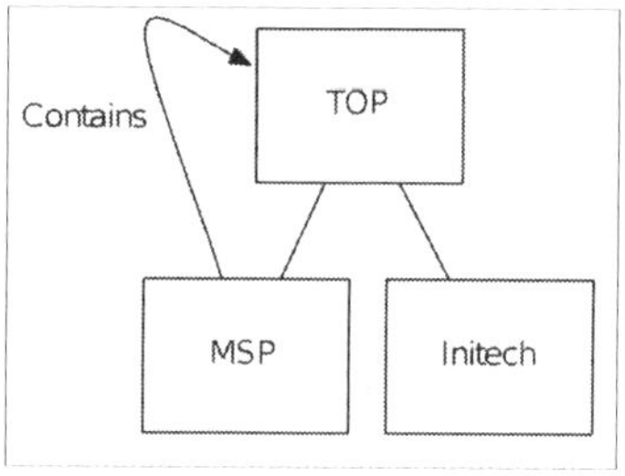

One reason to do this is to allow tasks associated with the MSP domain to have special domain-specific processing rules, but its users can also have a wider domain visibility. They can work on Initech tasks, while Initech users cannot see them.

> Another way to access more data is through a Visibility group; a specific group can be given the privilege to see another domain's data.

To try this out, switch to the MSP domain, where you can see every user—even those in a sibling domain.

Using Domain Separation appropriately

Domain Separation is sometimes seen as the cure for all separation needs. Although it is a powerful feature, it isn't always the right choice. It is a complex technology, and there are simpler alternatives to each of its features:

- For UI Separation, you can use views with view rules and dependent fields to drive choice lists
- For Process Separation, you can use conditions on Business Rules and other functionality such as Assignment Rules and add conditions into Client Scripts
- For Data Separation, you can use access controls and before query Business Rules

> It may also be more appropriate to create a custom app for a particular situation, perhaps by using table inheritance. For instance, consider creating a dedicated app for the grounds maintenance team instead of trying to break up a hotel room maintenance system. Two tables are often much easier to deal with than one that is domain separated.

However, for MSPs, it provides a great way to provide a global template that allows processes to be overridden at appropriate levels.

Take the following items into consideration when implementing Domain Separation:

- Ensure that the hierarchy is well thought out. Are some domains similar? Do they have to share a common parent?
- There should be a good common ground to consider process separation, since it cannot overcome very diverse ways of working.
- Domain Separation gives more options, which leads to complexity. When changing form layouts, you must consider each domain in addition to each view.
- Tables and fields are global. If you create a field, it will be available to all domains. (It may not be on the form, but it is still reportable and accessible on a list.) Access Control Rules can stop visibility, if necessary.
- System properties are global. Domain Separation will likely lead to further configuration and customization to control this.
- Someone with the admin role has control over all domains. For example, Update Sets (which will be discussed in *Chapter 9, Moving Scripts with Clones, Update Sets, and Upgrades*) are global.

Authenticating users

Most of the content in a ServiceNow instance is private and not available to the public Internet. To control what users can see and do, you need to know who they are, and to do so with some proof. There are many different authentication mechanisms in ServiceNow, ranging from a simple username and password to complex industry standard protocols such as SAML and OpenID.

Using internal authentication

The standard way to log into an instance is with a username and password. The **User** table contains User ID and password fields. When an unauthenticated user accesses the instance, a login form is provided to them. Their entered values are compared, and if they match, a session is created, the roles associated with that user are recognized, and the user can begin their work. If the optional **Remember me** checkbox is checked, a longer life cookie is stored in the browser during the login process. This cookie will be used, instead of prompting the user for a username and password again if the session expires.

Controlling authentication

Installation Exits contain the logic to deal with authentication requests. They contain the code that is called whenever a user wants to log in or out, and when a password change is necessary during login. The platform looks for Installation Exits that override `Login`, `Logout`, or `ValidatePassword`. If one is found, it is executed. Otherwise, the default behavior is used.

For instance, as with most other areas of the system, ServiceNow starts with an unconstricted, simple approach. A password has no complex requirements and could even be a single letter. Many customers wish to change this if they are using internal authentication!

> When the **Password needs reset** checkbox is ticked on the **User** record, the instance will display a prompt. To enforce a minimum of 8 characters and a mixture of character types, navigate to **System Definition** > **Installation Exits** and activate the `ValidatePasswordStronger` record. This overrides the default `ValidatePassword` behavior.

Installation Exits also provide you with the opportunity to add further controls. Do you only want admins to log into ServiceNow when they are on your internal network? Otherwise, do you want to restrict what time of the day ServiceNow can be logged into? These are achievable with an Installation Exit. Indeed, custom authentication methods can be written to receive a token and check it for validity. SAML and other Single Sign On mechanisms all use Installation Exits as their hook into the ServiceNow login process.

> Additionally, once a user is logged in, an event named `session established` is fired, letting you log the usage or perform further session processing.

Using an LDAP server for authentication

In *Chapter 6, Exchanging Data – Import Sets, Web Services, and Other Integrations*, we explored how an LDAP server can be used as the source for user data. ServiceNow connects to it on a regular basis and synchronizes the data with the **User** table.

LDAP servers can also perform authentication, with Microsoft Active Directory being almost ubiquitous in enterprise environments. Therefore, it is common to use it and offload the decision whether a user should have access to the instance. This can be accomplished by connecting to the LDAP server with the username and password that the user gave. If the credentials are accepted, a session is created.

A User record contains two fields that are not visible on the form but are populated during the import of user records. The **LDAP Server** is a reference field to the record specifying a particular server, as set up in *Chapter 6, Exchanging Data – Import Sets, Web Services, and Other Integrations*, and **Source** contains an identifier can uniquely specifies a particular object – the **Distinguished Name** (**DN**). Along with some details supplied by the user, these elements give the platform everything that it needs.

ServiceNow follows these steps when you are using LDAP authentication:

1. A user seeks authentication by entering a username and password.
2. The username is matched against a **User** record.
3. If the **User** record contains an LDAP server, then a connection is opened.
4. The instance uses the **DN** in the **Source** field and the password supplied by the user.
5. The LDAP server signals whether the credentials are valid.
6. If so, the platform creates a session and the user can start their work.

A graphic representation of the preceding process is shown in the following figure:

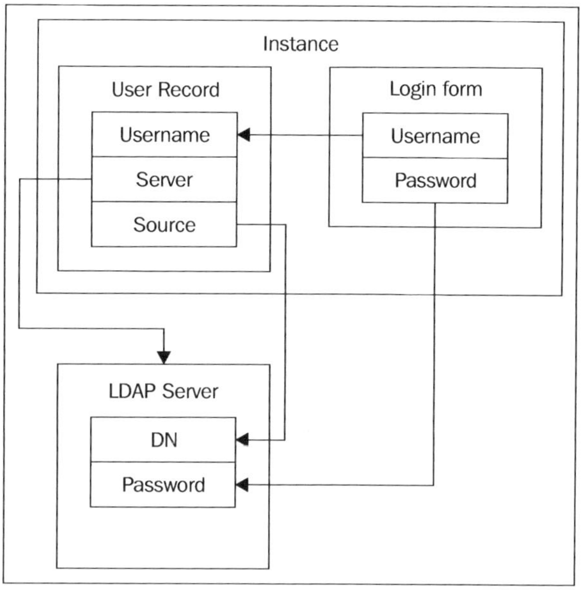

Typically, this process happens in only a few seconds and lets users log in quickly and easily. Using an LDAP server is an easy way to improve the authentication experience due to the following reasons:

- Users do not need to remember another username and password. Familiar credentials can be reused, reducing the risk of "password fatigue".
- The passwords are never stored within ServiceNow, meaning password changes don't need to synchronize, and are kept securely in the LDAP server.
- Password policies are unnecessary in ServiceNow as the LDAP server controls the authentication.
- If the LDAP user account is disabled, then the authentication will fail. This means that lockout policies and inactive accounts will automatically apply to ServiceNow.

The mechanism that ServiceNow uses relies on the continuous availability of the LDAP server. Any downtime will mean that ServiceNow will be inaccessible. Additionally, many companies prefer not to expose their LDAP server over the Internet even with the use of a secure protocol such as LDAPS. In this instance, other external authentication protocols such as SAML can be used, which provide further advantages.

> LDAP authentication is sometimes considered to be almost like a Single Sign On. It provides many of the same advantages, such as a single authentication mechanism, but it also means that a user must type their private authentication details into a website. The security policies of many companies do not like this.

Enabling Single Sign On through SAML

The use of **Single Sign On** or SSO has exploded in the past few years. **Active Directory Federation Services (ADFS)** has contributed to this growth by providing a mechanism to which many companies can easily hook in. ADFS provides a SAML 2 endpoint with which cloud-based solutions such as ServiceNow can authenticate.

> SAML is by far the most common SSO solution (mainly because of ADFS), so it is discussed in this section. Other technologies such as OpenID get very similar results.

SAML (short for, Security Assertion Markup Language) is a relatively complex XML-based protocol that provides many different ways to exchange authentication data securely. ServiceNow supports the browser post profile. This means that when it is accessed, the instance will redirect the user's web browser to the identity provider—the system that can prove identity. This can happen in many different ways, such as a simple username and password or a more complex multifactor authentication involving smart cards or physical dongles.

> SSO integrations are referred to as external authentication since ServiceNow offloads the decision to another system.

Once authenticated, the identity provider generates a token—an XML document that is base64 encoded. It returns this to the user's web browser, which in turn sends it to the instance. This happens through a series of form submissions. The identity provider never directly communicates with the instance, which means that it is possible (and common) for it to reside on an internal network. Only the user's web browser needs to communicate with both sides.

The token contains a reference, such as a username, that the instance can use to match with a **User** record. Once this has been found, a session is made, in just the same way as any other method. A graphic representation of the process is shown in the following figure:

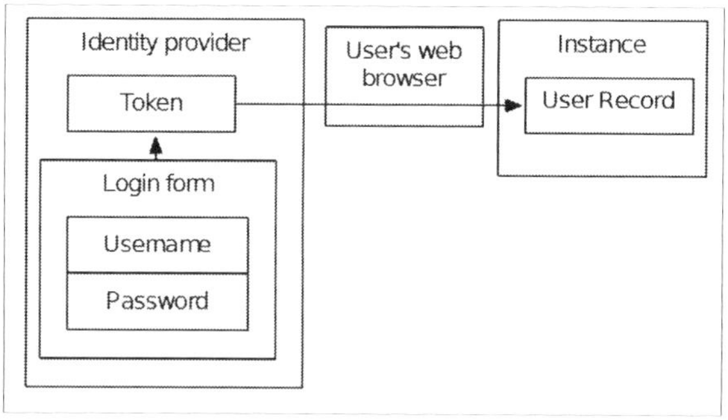

The instance must be able to trust the token. In order to know that the right identity provider created the token (and therefore isn't a fake), the token must be signed using a certificate. ServiceNow needs the public key of the certificate, and it uses this to ensure that the identity provider has the private key. Any certificate will do; it can be self-signed or from a certificate authority.

Logging out

Once the user is finished with their work, they may decide to log out of ServiceNow. Doing so will end the session for ServiceNow, and if it is configured, ServiceNow will ask the identity provider to end its session too. Some identity providers, such as ADFS, require that this request should also be signed. To achieve this, ServiceNow must have the private key of a certificate. This must be stored in a Java key store in order to protect it.

> Java key stores need a password for access. Private keys need more protection than public keys.

Configuring Single Sign On

Enabling SAML is a multistep process. The wiki at `http://wiki.servicenow.com/?title=SAML_2.0_Web_Browser_SSO_Profile` has a long article that describes in detail how to achieve this. In the majority of cases, enabling SAML is not hard; you just require to know the appropriate configuration settings, and you must upload the right certificate. Be sure that you turn on SAML debugging and inspect the logs.

If you wish to experiment, SSOCircle (https://www.ssocircle.com/) provides a free identity provider. Indeed, the example configuration in ServiceNow is aimed at this service. In *Chapter 8, Diagnosing ServiceNow – Knowing What Is Going On*, we will discuss debugging in more detail.

> SSOCircle gives a wide variety of authentication methods. Aside from username and password, you can see how a client certificate, a hardware token, or even mobile provider, could be used.

Some systems will attempt to self-configure based on the metadata supplied by another system. ServiceNow does generate metadata, but I have found that it is more reliable to add the configuration manually.

Navigating to the side door

What happens if your identity provider isn't available or refuses to log anyone in? The instance will keep attempting to redirect your browser to it, without knowing that it is not working. In order to use internal authentication, a special URL is made available at https://<instance>.service-now.com/side_door.do. If you navigate to this URL, the instance will ignore all Installation Exits and present the standard username and password login form. You may want to keep an additional admin account with a strong password to ensure that you can login to debug any problems.

Preventing access to the instance

Sometimes you may want to go one step further than an authentication involving a username and password, and make it impossible for users outside your company's network to access the instance at all. With IP address access control, the administrator can specify a range of IP addresses and specify whether or not they can access the instance.

Navigate to **System Security** > **IP Address Access Control** to add a range. Typically, the configuration involves adding the IP ranges that should access the platform with a Type of `Allow`, and then specify a blanket `0.0.0.0` to `255.255.255.255` range with a Type of `Deny`. The IP addresses will need to be the public IP addresses that servers on the Internet will see. There are many websites that will tell you what your external IP address is.

> The platform will try to stop you from locking yourself out! You must have an allow range that includes your current IP address before setting a blank deny.

If the IP address is not in one of the allowed ranges, a **HTTP 403** error will be generated, with a minimalistic error message that will say "Access restricted". This control is checked at a very early point when connecting to the instance, so it is effective for either the standard web interface or any Web Services.

IP address authentication works well for companies that have well-defined exits from their networks to the Internet. This may involve a proxy server or a NAT solution. These tend to give a single IP address for many users. This means only a few IP ranges need to be configured; therefore, it is easily managed.

For a more distributed workforce, IP address authentication is not so useful due to the following reasons:

- Any partners or suppliers that access the instance must have their networks added as IP ranges
- Remote working (such as from a coffee shop) is not possible directly, though stopping this is often desirable
- Accessing the instance through a mobile network (such as through a 3G or 4G phone or a tablet) is not feasible since IP addresses are often dynamic and shared through NAT
- Disaster recovery locations must be considered or else your instance will be unavailable when you may need it most!

To help with these scenarios, many companies ask their employees to use a VPN tunnel, which gives them access to the internal network. However, it does introduce another step into the connection process and may affect response times. ServiceNow is a web platform and making it inaccessible to the majority of the Web must be considered carefully.

Securing Web Services

As explored in *Chapter 6, Exchanging Data – Import Sets, Web Services, and Other Integrations*, the Web Services hosted by ServiceNow use Basic Authentication as the primary means for proving identity. A username and password should be used by the remote system when it connects to the instance. This is commonly referred to as a system account.

> Basic Authentication is HTTP-level authentication. The calling system must provide a base64 encoded value of `username:password` to the Authorization header. The connection is refused if this is not present, making it fast and efficient. In addition, since headers are protected by HTTPS, malicious users cannot intercept this in transit.

When creating a user account for use in Web Services, it is a good idea to consider the following points:

- Create a new user account for each integration target. Don't use the same one each time, in case you need to disable it!

> Note that integrations cannot use External Authentication (such as LDAP or SSO)

- Tick the **Web Service Access Only** checkbox. This means that someone with the user account cannot enter the web interface.
- Grant the right roles since Access Control Rules should still be applied. You may want to create a role specifically for integration to your application; `hotel_integration`, with access to only certain fields, might be useful in our application.

In addition to the roles that are needed to pass Access Control Rules that you may have, you must also grant your system accounts extra privileges. Typically, this is just the `soap` role, which gives the holder of the role access to perform any CRUD role via SOAP Web Services.

However, there are other more specific roles too. The `soap_create`, `soap_update`, and `soap_delete` roles should be obvious! More roles are listed in the wiki at `http://wiki.servicenow.com/?title=SOAP_Web_Service`.

> In *Chapter 6, Exchanging Data – Import Sets, Web Services, and Other Integrations*, we used an admin account to access web services. Since the admin role has access to all the roles, we did not have to grant these specifically. However, it would be a bad idea to give a third party system an admin account!

In the rest of this section, we will discuss some advanced options to authenticate Web Services. The wiki article `http://wiki.servicenow.com/?title=Web_Services_Security` that lists the necessary configuration steps. The majority of integrations do not need Mutual Authentication or WS-Security.

Using WS-Security

In addition to Basic Authentication, the instance can also insist that all SOAP messages should be signed. The WS-Security standard provides a mechanism to ensure that messages are trustworthy and not tampered with.

ServiceNow can verify the identity of a remote system in two ways—through a certificate or with a username and password. In both cases, it is usually an addition to Basic Authentication; however, by navigating to **System Security** > **High Security Settings**, you can turn this setting off.

Improving security with signatures

If the message is signed, then the platform will validate that the data hasn't been changed or tampered with. In order to do this, the public certificate must be uploaded. The instance will compare it to the certificate embedded in the message and ensure that it matches.

SOAP messages that conform to the WS-Security standard contain a timestamp. If the timestamp varies too much from the current time on the server, the message is rejected. This can help to reduce replay attacks.

The instance can also impersonate a user once the message has been deemed valid. The user can either be chosen upfront, or the user can be contained as part of the message.

ServiceNow uses a **Java keystore (JKS)** to hold the credentials needed to verify a signed SOAP message. A keystore holds a collection of certificates and keys, and is itself protected by a password. They are stored in the instance under **System Definition** > **Certificates** as attachments.

WS-Security can be used for both incoming and outgoing messages.

- For outbound messages from ServiceNow, specify the keystore containing the private key, and its password, in the SOAP Message Function.
- Inbound SOAP messages can be validated with a WS Security Profile. It will be applied to all messages, except for those marked as Internal Integration Users on the User table. Specify the certificate you want to validate with.

> More information on WS-Security is available on this wiki: `http://wiki.servicenow.com/?title=Web_Services_Security#WS-Security`.

Mutual authentication

The vast majority of HTTPS sessions rely only on one certificate, which is provided by the server when the client connects. This provides two fundamental benefits:

- The identity of the server is correct, which means that the client is not connecting to a 'man-in-the-middle'
- The communications are secured and encrypted

However, the server has no idea who the client is. By accepting all connections, the server needs another way to find out who the client is; as this chapter has shown, this is often done by the application layer (by creating a session) or through Basic Authentication.

However, ServiceNow also supports Mutual Authentication for outbound messages. When an SSL connection is set up, the instance provides proof of its identity to the systems that it is connecting to. Both sides then swap certificates, letting the remote system verify the ServiceNow instance.

> Mutual Authentication is outbound only. ServiceNow will not validate or check any certificates that are presented to it in a HTTPS connection. In fact, ServiceNow does not validate any certificates anywhere.

Setting up outbound Mutual Authentication

Enabling Mutual Authentication involves uploading a Java key store. The key store should contain the client certificate with the private keys and any root certificates that provide trust. Once the required certificates are in place, a new URL scheme can be registered in ServiceNow to enable its use.

The URL scheme of SSL/TLS over HTTP is HTTPS. This means that all URLs that start as https are assumed to use SSL/TLS over HTTP. For example, this means that a client will connect to the server on port 443 instead of port 80.

To register a URL scheme in ServiceNow, you must make two properties. Create them in the **Properties** table by populating **Name**: **Value** as follows:

- `glide.httpclient.protocol.mauth.class`: `com.glide.certificates.DBKeyStoreSocketFactory`
- `glide.httpclient.protocol.mauth.port`: `443`

> This has been made much simpler in the Fuji version of ServiceNow with Protocol Profiles. For more details on this, refer to: `http://wiki.servicenow.com/?title=Outbound_Web_Services_Mutual_Authentication`.

In this example, I've made the URL scheme of `mauth`. It uses a ServiceNow class called `DBKeyStoreSocketFactory` to handle the request. Now, every time I want the instance to use Mutual Authentication, I would alter the URL to read `mauth://<target>` instead of `https://<target>`. This URL could be used anywhere: not just for SOAP requests but also in an Import Set Data Source.

Summary

The security aspects of a cloud solution are always under great scrutiny. Many companies consider data to be their greatest asset, so they demand that it is well protected. The ServiceNow platform has a range of functionality to address this concern. Of course, this must be coupled with assurances that the ServiceNow security team can give on physical security, penetration tests, and code reviews of the platform itself.

The chapter started with a discussion of roles. **Roles** are an immediate way to classify users, and ServiceNow slices the population into requesters, fulfillers, and admins. As such, the use of roles is closely tied to the licensing module. It is important that an administrator understands the impact of adding a role to a user; this may mean a financial commitment for their company. A ServiceNow representative should be consulted if there is any uncertainty.

Roles are used to control access to application menus and modules in the Application Navigator. However, with some additional configuration, a `before` query Business Rule can be used to control via groups.

Contextual Security uses Access Control Rules to control access to records. Create, read, update, and delete actions are either allowed or rejected by the evaluation of roles, scripts, or conditions. Since almost all configuration and data items are stored in records, Access Controls provide a powerful way to determine what a user can do and see. They provide an alternative, for example, to control who can see each application menu and module, just as a before query Business Rule. The ways in which rules are evaluated seem complicated when you see them for the first time!

Domain Separation is a method to partition data and configuration, again to ensure that the right person can see and do the right thing. By allocating users and configuration into a domain, the platform will use hierarchical rules as the basis of control. Data flows up, meaning a user in a domain at the top of tree can see data associated with its descendants. Configuration flows down, with domains at the bottom of the tree being affected by those further up. Configuration, such as a Business Rule, can be overridden at a particular level. Other relationships, such as contains, can also be used.

A key part of security is **authentication**. To ensure the right people are logging into the system, internal or LDAP passwords can be typed into the instance and checked in the appropriate lace, or SSO can be used to hand off the decision entirely. **Installation Exits** contain scripts that are called to log in users, sign them out, and change passwords.

Finally, the **Web Services** provided by the platform can utilize advanced methods to control access. WS-Security is an industry standard that allows ServiceNow to check timestamps and signed messages on incoming messages. Mutual authentication uses certificates from both sides when it sets up a HTTPS session, allowing systems to check that a client who connects is valid.

In the next chapter, we will look in detail at how to debug and determine what is happening when things don't work as you expect—and that includes security!

8

Diagnosing ServiceNow – Knowing What Is Going On

Have you ever written code that is longer than a few lines and it worked the very first time? Has a script always worked perfectly? Probably, the answer will be a no. Things don't always go according to plan during a complex implementation. Functionality doesn't quite work as you or someone else expects. Therefore, the tools and techniques needed to investigate the issue, come up with a diagnosis, and hopefully find a solution is a critical part of any administrator's toolkit.

ServiceNow provides a wide variety of ways to understand what is happening in the system. This chapter covers many of the ways through which the instance can tell you what's going on:

- The typical **System Log** where the system records messages while it processes
- Using the interactive **JavaScript debugger** to help you solve server-side JavaScript problems
- The database records its activity in the **SQL Log**, giving you an insight into slow queries
- Every request is stored in the **Transaction Log**, indicating where performance problems may lie
- **Versions** that track how configuration has changed
- The **Audit Log** that keeps detailed information on who did what and when

Building a methodology

ServiceNow can support itself. As you build your ServiceNow instance, consider using the software development applications to track features and functionality requests. Then, as people start using the instance, you can track their success (and failure) within the platform. This makes it easy to identify areas that need improvement and track progress effectively. Use the reporting functionality within ServiceNow to track your efforts so that you can avoid going back to using spreadsheets!

> The ServiceNow Scrum plugin gives a fully featured development application that users submit feature requests, allow stakeholders to prioritize functionality, and developers to track progress. Find out about it in the ServiceNow wiki: `http://wiki.servicenow.com/?title=SDLC_Scrum_Process`

Identifying the issue

When an issue is reported, you must get a good bug report before any investigation can begin. Understanding what happened is fundamental since this will help you determine what steps should be taken next. This typically requires the following information as a minimum:

- **What was done?** What buttons were clicked and which fields were filled out? Who was the user, what was the time, and what was the record number on which the action was carried out?
- **What happened**? Were any error messages shown? What fields were changed (or not changed)? A full browser screenshot is often very useful.
- **What was expected**? The system didn't work as the user thought it would. What should have happened? Did they expect it to produce a different output?

Once this information has been collected, it is much more straightforward to replicate the issue. The system administrator can then use impersonation to verify the issue, check the logging functions, and subsequently simply ensure that any fix works.

Looking at the System Log

The majority of the diagnosis starts with the System Log. This is the place where most of the applications in the platform display their warnings and errors, generating entries that can fall under these three levels: **Information**, **Warning**, or **Error**. You can view them all at **System Logs** > **System Log** > **All**. There are also modules for individual levels. Add the **Created by** field to the list to show which user generated the entry.

> The System Log can become pretty huge. Each of the modules contains a filter that only shows items that are `Created - on - Today`. If you build your own filter, keep a date filter in place, even if it is modified.

The platform and applications will record any scripting or internal errors in the System Log. If things aren't working quite right, the System Log will give you an indication. For example, if the instance can't connect to an FTP server that is used while importing data, this will be registered in the system log. If the platform itself fails, then often a Java stack trace will be recorded. Additionally, some normal usage is also included, such as when records are deleted. This is useful when you want to understand why a table that once contained data is empty now!

> Keep an eye on the system log. Aim for zero errors; to achieve this, you may need a scheduled report or a homepage that helps you understand what is happening in the instance. Try looking at how many messages are logged over time. A sudden spike might indicate trouble. Try making a trend chart, for instance, to spot the increase.

Writing to the System Log

Use the `log` function of `GlideSystem` to add your own messages when you are writing scripts. This takes two parameters; the first should be a text string with whatever message you'd like. The second optional parameter should be copied into the **Source** field on the System Log. If you'd like to see an example, try running the following script in Background Scripts and check the output by navigating to **System Logs** > **System Log** > **All**:

```
gs.log('Hello, world!', 'Test');
```

> In the Fuji release of ServiceNow some of the API calls have changed for scoped apps. Use `gs.info()`, `gs.warn()`, `gs.error()` and `gs.debug()` instead.
>
> The `log` function generates an entry with a level of **Information**. You can also try `logWarning` and `logError`, to log a warning and error, respectively.
>
> It is a good idea to use the source parameter. This lets you filter the messages in the list very easily.

The `JSUtil` class has an incredibly useful function to investigate the contents of a JavaScript object. `JSUtil.describeObject` returns a string while `JSUtil` adds it to the system log.

The following line gives an example of how `describeObject` could be used:

```
JSUtil.logObject({'str': 'value', 'num': 1});
```

It is logged like this:

```
*** Script: Log Object
  Object
    str: string = value
    num: number = 1
```

> If you want to use a much more comprehensive logging function, investigate the GSLog Script Include. This provides a more finely grained BSD or Log4j-style interface.

Using the file log

The System Log is stored in the database in the `syslog` table. Therefore, this is accessible from any node and could be manipulated like any other record. There is also a slight overhead when you write to the database, so writing many entries in a tight loop will slow down the instance.

Instead, consider using the file log. This is a simple text file that is stored in the instance and contains more detailed debugging information. It is around 10 times faster to use `gs.print`, which writes to the file log, than `gs.log`. Anything that is written to the System Log will also be written to the file log.

The file log can be accessed through several different interfaces, which are as follows:

- The `logtail` interface presents the log file in a continually updating text window. It is great to keep this open in another browser tab, enabling you to easily monitor the system. Access it by navigating to `https://<instance>.service-now.com/channel.do?sysparm_channel=logtail`
- The file log is saved on the server with a name: `localhost_log.yyyy-mm-dd.txt`. Every day, a new file log is generated and the instance keeps log files for about a month. You can download the one you want by navigating to **System Logs** > **Utilities** > **Log File Download**.

> Note that a busy instance might have a multigigabyte log file, and even though it is delivered zipped, it can still be rather big. Therefore, try to use cURL to download it.

- To **search** through the log file, use the Log File Browser that is available by navigating to **System Logs** > **Utilities** > **Log File Browser**. This lets you specify a date and time along with some other parameters to filter. The session ID is very useful to only look at the entries for a particular user.

> The file log is time-stamped with US Pacific time, reflecting ServiceNow's San Diego's roots. This can become immensely confusing, but the Log File Browser filter does convert the time for you when you are searching.

The file log and System Log are intrinsically linked together. There is a Related Link UI Action on the System Log form that creates a filter for the file log. It often shows a little bit more information about a request.

Logging appropriately

The `log` and `print` functions of `GlideSystem` are incredibly useful. They provide a permanent and central store of runtime information. However, there is a performance impact from logging, and especially for the System Log, since the database must be engaged. Having lots of logs can also be overwhelming when it is difficult to identify what is important and what is not.

It is good practice to not record superfluous information. Logging is very helpful for difficult to replicate or rare errors, so reserve it for when it is necessary. Another strategy is to only log information if a property is set, meaning you can easily enable more detailed information, if necessary. Consider the following example:

```
if (gs.getProperty('debug.hello', false))
  gs.log('Hello, world!', 'Test');
```

This only writes the message to the log when the `debug.hello` property is set to `true`.

In the rest of this chapter, we will show you many additional ways to find out what is going on instead of just filling the logs.

Using the debugging tools

If the reason for an error is not immediately obvious, then it is time to use debuggers. Debuggers provide an insight into what the platform processes and the decisions it takes. This can even include watching all the database activity with a SQL debugger. There are many other tools too!

The session debuggers can be found by navigating to **System Diagnostics** > **Session Debug**. Once activated, they will continue throughout your session and provide you with feedback until you choose to stop (by navigating to **System Diagnostics** > **Session Debug** > **Disable all**), log out, or your session times out. This means that you can enable debugging and then impersonate a user; the debugging will continue. This is critically helpful when you debug security or any other permission issues since an admin account is often treated very differently.

Debugging Business Rules

Let's turn on debugging to investigate some of the server-side scripts that we wrote earlier.

1. After you've navigated to **System Diagnostics** > **Session Debug** > **Debug Business Rules (Details)**, extra output will appear at the bottom of the screen, showing the rules that have been evaluated. Since **Debug Business Rules (Details)** has been clicked, the platform will also show the fields that were changed by the Business Rule.

> Business Rules are evaluated is several places. On Display Rules will fire whenever you pull up a record and On Query Business Rules are fired when you issue a database query. This means that you will often see lots of output once these rules are turned on.

2. Earlier, we made a simple Business Rule called `Maintenance assignment events` on the **Maintenance** table. It logs an event when the **Assignment group** field changes. Try to create a new **Maintenance** record, set the **Assignment group** field, and then save the record. The platform will show an output that is similar to following one somewhere at the bottom of the screen:

```
19:56:49.143: ==> 'Maintenance assignment events' on u_
maintenance:MAI0001010
19:56:49.145: <== 'Maintenance assignment events' on u_
maintenance:MAI0001010
```

Let's analyze the preceding output:

- The first elements (`19:56:49.143` and `19:56:49.145`) are the exact times when the Business Rule started and finished. The arrow pointing to the right means the start of Business Rule, and the arrow to the left means that it finished. In total, this Business Rule took 2 milliseconds to run.
- In this case, nothing happened inside the Business Rule, beyond the logging of a message on the screen. If the rule had changed a field, a message noting which and how the field changed would have been included between these two lines. The output from `gs.log` or `gs.print` would also have be shown here.

> If the Business Rule affects another record, such as performing an update of a `GlideRecord` object, this itself would cause a series of Business Rules to run. The output of the Business Rules would be indented and included inline.

- The name of the Business Rule is given and is rendered as a link. To see the code, click on the link. The table and the display name of the Business Rule is also given.

3. If the **Assignment group** value doesn't change, then some different output will be given:

```
20:07:33.94: === Skipping 'Maintenance assignment events' on u_
maintenance:MAI0001010; condition not satisfied: Filter Condition:
assignment_groupVALCHANGES^assignment_groupISNOTEMPTY^assigned_
toISEMPTY^EQ
```

Much of the output here is similar, except that the condition is shown Since the condition did not return true, the script in the Business Rule was not executed.

Debugging Contextual Security Rules

Besides Debug Business Rules, Debug Security Rules is probably the most frequently used option. Without it, it can be rather difficult to understand what the Contextual Security Manager is doing. Let's start by performing the following steps:

1. Activate the option by navigating to **System Diagnostics** > **Session Debug** > **Debug Security**. This will cause the platform to do two things: place little bug icons on all the fields and add lots of logs at the end of every page.

2. Once enabled, impersonate a user that has the `hotel_user` role; I'll use Albert Einstein again, like I did in *Chapter 7, Securing Applications and Data*.
3. Open an existing **Maintenance** record and then click on the green bug on the **Priority** label. This gives the result of the security rules, which are color coded appropriately:

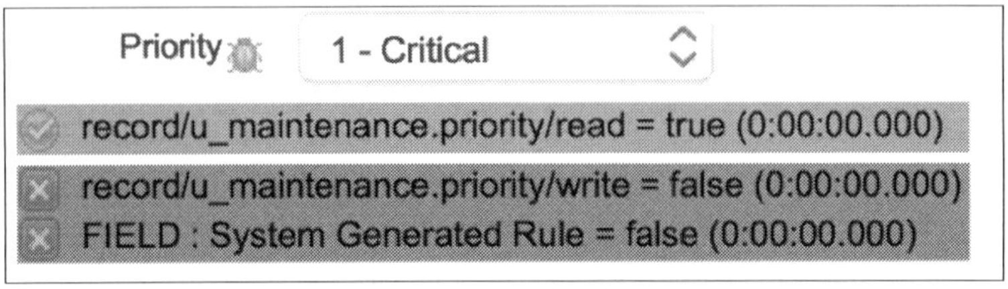

The message comes in two parts: the first message, (here in green) is the result for read access and the second (in orange) is for write access. We can see both the parts were evaluated for the **Priority** field on the **Maintenance** [`u_maintenance`] table.

The colors and icons indicate success or failure. The read access was successfully granted, but the permission to write to the field was denied. Why did this happen? This happened because a rule with the description of **System Generated Rule** was evaluated as `false`. This shows how important good descriptions are!

> The description of **System Generated Rule** is given to the rules that are created via the **Personalize Security** dialog box that is available on forms. Since this option is not helpful when debugging, it is a good idea to update this with something more meaningful.

If multiple rules are evaluated, then the success of each is shown. This is invaluable for knowing which rule failed.

The text at the bottom of a form contains the details of every rule that has been run. There are three icons for each of the elements that make up a security rule: roles, conditions, and scripts. These icons are as follows:

- A green tick (✓) represents a successfully evaluated element. It means that the element either returns `true`, or it is blank.
- A red cross (**x**) represents an element that was returned `false`. This will prevent access.
- A blue tick (✓) or cross (**x**) is a cached result. This is often seen on rules with `*` in the name.

The following screenshot shows the details of the rules that have been run:

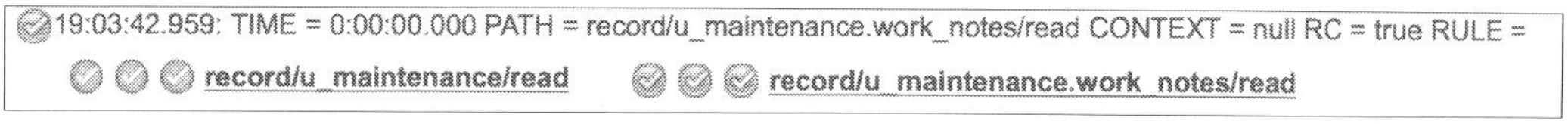

In the output of a **Maintenance** record, the `maintenance.work_notes/read` rule has given three green ticks. The `maintenance/read` rule is also checked, but the results of that are cached.

The following screenshot shows another set of rules that gave the output of the **Maintenance** record:

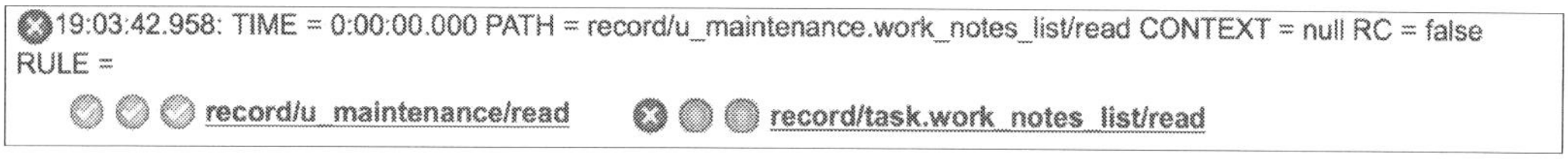

The **Work notes list** field is not shown on the form. The red cross (**x**) symbol shows that the roles' check failed. Hovering over the icon shows that the `itil` role is necessary for the check to be successful.

> Permission issues are very quickly evident. If an administrator can carry out an action but another user cannot, it is very likely that a security rule is preventing the user. Use impersonation to replicate and confirm.

Scrolling through the output will show you how much work the Contextual Security Manager performs. All the Related Lists and their fields along with the tables pointed to in reference fields are also checked. This reinforces how important it is to have security rules that execute quickly.

> Each rule shows how long the security rule took to execute. Be cautious of any rule that takes more than a few milliseconds.

Enabling the JavaScript Debugger

The debug log that shows the output of Business Rules is very useful to display what Business Rules are running and when. However, the JavaScript debugger also allows you to *interact* with the Business Rules, letting you set breakpoints and edit code on the fly. In addition, it shows the output of client-side JavaScript and features functionality that would enable you to see what is controlling the value of a field—on both the client side and the server side!

Controlling Business Rules on the fly

Let's use the JavaScript debugger to find the `Maintenance assignment events` Business Rule that we started looking at earlier:

1. Activate the JavaScript debugger by clicking on the green bug icon in the system menu. This is accessible through the cog, which is at top-right corner of the window. In versions other than Eureka, the icon may be put in a different location:

2. A new section will be presented at the bottom of the page. On the first tab, the JavaScript Debugger lets you choose the scripts that you are interested in and set the breakpoints that you like:

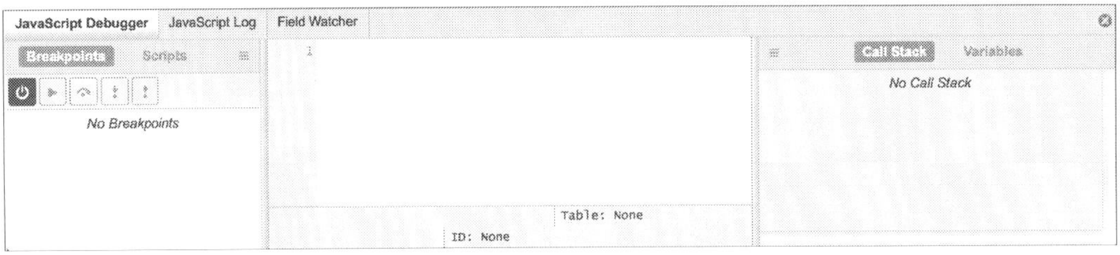

3. To find `Maintenance assignment events`, click on **Scripts**. Then, either use the search option or filter the results using the **Type** and **Table** dropdown menus. Finally, click on the script to load it into the script editor.

> The script editor is live. You can edit the script as per your need, and a **Save** button will appear immediately after that. It is best to refrain from doing this in the production system though.

4. Once it is loaded, switch back to **Breakpoints**. This brings the controls to handle script execution.

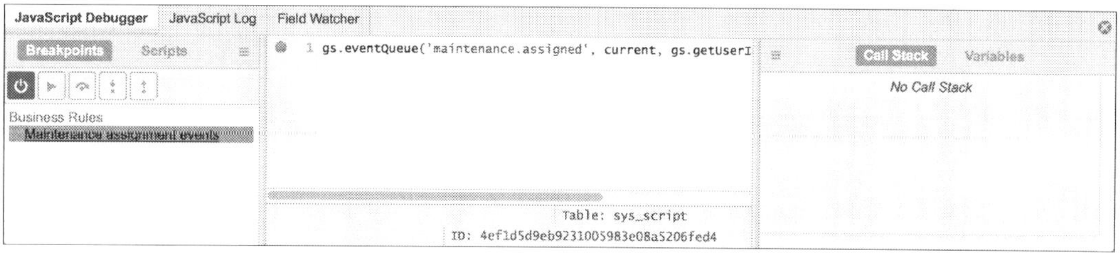

5. By clicking next to the line number, you can set **breakpoints**. When the Business Rule is run, the execution will stop at the breakpoint.

> The line that is being executed is highlighted in blue.

The following screenshot shows the controls available during script execution.

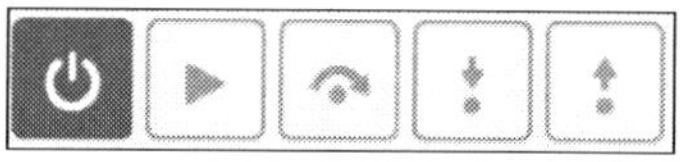

The icons are activated when a script is being debugged. Working from left to right, they are as follows:

- The **On/Off** (power icon) button will enable or disable the functionality
- The **Next Breakpoint** (Play) button moves the execution to the next breakpoint

- The **Step Over** button will execute the next line of code. If the current line is on a function call, it will be executed, but the debugger will not step through it. This keeps your focus on the code that you see on the screen.
- The **Step Into** button will follow the code to the next line, wherever it may lead. This will descend into functions.
- The **Step Out Of** button will skip all the lines on the screen and leave the function. (Pressing **Step Into** and then **Step Out Of** is the same as pressing **Step Over**.)

When the execution is paused, the **Variables** table will be populated. This lets you explore the `GlideRecord` objects: `current` and `previous`, as well as any that have been set in the script.

> Try to use the **Variables** section instead of scattering your code with logging statements. Save those logging statements for errors or when a property enables them.

6. As you go about executing the code, step-wise, the **Call Stack** tab will show you where you are, which Business Rule or script you are executing, and the function in which you are. If there is recursive or otherwise nested code, the **Call Stack** tab lets you trace back who called what.

> The name of the Business Rule, the table it is on, and the `sys_id` is listed. If you explore code that exists on the server, then some of these items won't be listed or will be misleading.

7. Clicking on the **Menu** button lets you choose how exceptions should be handled. The default is to capture uncaught exceptions. This will then pause the execution, letting you explore the **Call Stack** and **Variables** tabs. You can pause execution on undefined methods, which are otherwise ignored. It can be very difficult to find typos in method names, so this option is of importance.

Seeing client-side messages

The alert box is probably the most often used way to display information. It's probably also the worst! It interrupts and distracts the user and isn't stored or logged. In addition, for a user, it can be difficult to cancel multiple invasive pop ups.

> It is especially important not to use alert boxes when you are diagnosing an issue in production. It can really affect user experience. If you must log, use `jslog`, which is discussed next.

All modern browsers provide client-side debugging tools. These allow you to see client-side JavaScript errors in a client-side log and the majority of these tools give you the same variable exploration, Call Stack, and Breakpoints that ServiceNow provides for the server.

> Access the tools in Chrome by clicking on the Menu icon and navigate to **Tools** > **JavaScript Console** or **Developer Tools**. In Firefox, go to the Menu icon, first select **Developer**, and then **Debugger** or **Web Console**.

The **JavaScript Log** tab is a simpler alternative to these. It will display some debugging information that is otherwise displayed in the browser's console, such as the Client Scripts that have run.

Logging to the JavaScript Log

A global client-side function is used to populate the JavaScript log: `jslog`. This will output to both the JavaScript Log and the browser's console. Perform the following set of steps:

1. To try it, open **JavaScript Debugger** and then choose the **JavaScript Log**.
2. Then, in the main interface, navigate to a form or a list and invoke the JavaScript Executor that we first explored in *Chapter 3, Client-side Interaction*.
3. Press *Control* + *Shift* + *J* to bring up the dialog box.

> The JavaScript Executor also allows you explore variables. Change the drop-down selection to **Browse vars**.

4. In the dialog window, enter the following example and click on **Run my code**:

   ```
   jslog('Hello, world!');
   ```

5. At the bottom of the **JavaScript Log** window, you'll notice an entry like the following one:

   ```
   08:06:25 (696)  u_maintenance_list.do  Hello, world!
   ```

   This shows the time of execution with the milliseconds in brackets. The page from which the message came is also listed.

6. Close the **JavaScript Executor** option and navigate around lists and pages. The debug output will be displayed, showing how and which client-side JavaScript is executed. The square brackets contain the information about how long the script took to execute. For example, the `Remove External Repair state` Client Script created in *Chapter 3, Client-side Interaction*, was executed rather quickly!

```
08:10:55 (905)  u_maintenance.do  [00:00:00.000]  onLoad Remove
External Repair state
```

> In the next section, we'll discuss the **Response Time Indicator**—an alternative and more detailed way of knowing how quickly every element was rendered on the page.

Watching fields

There are many ways to manipulate and control data in ServiceNow, from Business Rules to Graphical Workflow, and from UI Policy to Contextual Security. If a field changes, to know what brought about the change can sometimes be a challenge! The **Field Watcher** functionality is designed to help you with this investigation.

Finding out what set the Assignment group

As an example, let's use the **Field Watcher** functionality to see how the **Assignment group** field is set:

1. Navigate to the new **Maintenance** record form.
2. Right-click on the **Assignment group** label. Then, click on **Watch – 'assignment_group'**.

   This provides the now familiar pane and shows a little bug symbol on the **Assignment group** field. Whenever something interacts with this field, it is displayed in the **Field Watcher** page. The section also shows some information from the Dictionary, such as the Reference Qualifier. You'll see the following screenshot under the **Field Watcher** tab content:

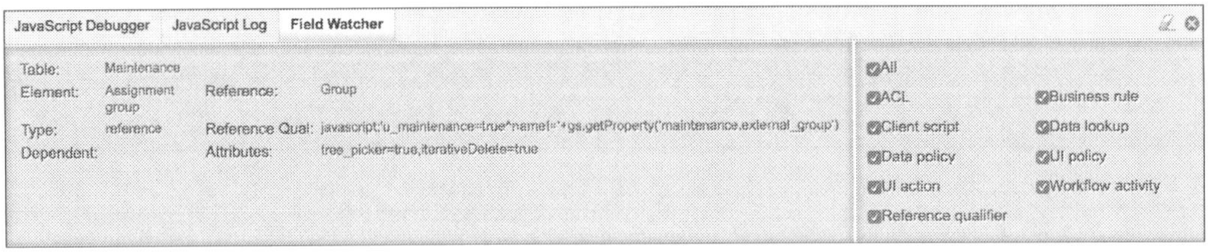

> To watch a field that is not on the form, run the following code in Background Scripts: `gs.getSession().setWatchField('<field_name>');`

3. To see the **Field Watcher** at work, type two asterisks (`**`) into the **Assignment group** field. This will show all the available choices in the drop-down selection window.

   The **Field Watcher** logs the query string that the Reference Qualifier used to filter the results. The exact time is also shown in the same fashion as the JavaScript Log:

```
09:06:12 (139)   REFERENCE QUALIFIER QUERY
  u_maintenance=true^name!=Cornell Hotel Services^ORDERBYname
```

4. Now, choose the **Maintenance** group and save the record. This will give you more entries, which will list the button that you clicked and note that the browser sent back a new value for the field:

```
09:09:50 (329)   REQUEST ACTION - Save  Value received from client
is: Maintenance
```

> Interspersed with this are the results from the security rules, showing that you can read from and write on this field. This can become a bit overwhelming. Deselect the ACL checkbox to remove the clutter. The dedicated ACL debugger gives necessary additional information.

5. Click on the **Send to External** button and perform the approval. This puts in motion a series of actions that can be examined by clicking on the expand icon **[+]** to the left of the log messages. The following dropdown menu appears after expanding:

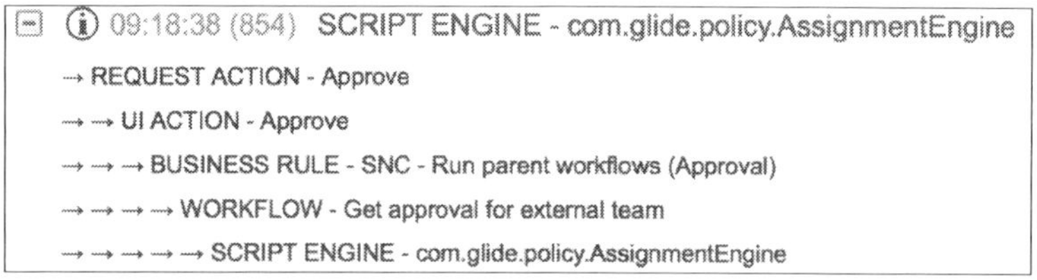

   This shows the flow of actions that lead to the setting of Cornell Hotel Services. First, the **Approve** button is clicked, which updates the **Approval** record. This then fires a Business Rule that notifies the workflow engine. This in turn causes the Assignment Rules to fire. This sets the **Assignment group** field appropriately.

Tracking each page request

Each time that a user attempts to access something in ServiceNow—a list, a form, or anything else—the request is logged along with several useful data points:

- The exact date and time at which the request was managed
- The type of item, which includes Form, List, Scheduler, Report, SOAP, and so on

> Although the majority of events are logged in the transaction log, some are not and AJAX requests are a notable exception.

- The URL that often includes the query or record that was being accessed. For example, `/u_maintenance_list.do?sysparm_query=active=true`

> If the request is an update to a record, this will most likely occur through a UI Action. The Action Name of the UI Action is recorded in a URL parameter called `sys_action`.

- The username that made the request
- The IP address from which the user is connecting
- The node that served the request

This information is incredibly useful in narrowing down exactly what a user performed a particular action for. It is easy to verify and replicate their experience, just by copying the URL in the transaction log and pasting it into your browser.

The **Transaction Log** is accessible by navigating to **System Logs** > **Transactions**. The **All user** and **Background** modules provide extra filters to users to focus on interactive and non-interactive transactions respectively.

> You can access several very useful reports by navigating to **Reports** > **View / Run** and then filtering by **Transaction**.

Recording the time taken

Performance is important. So, the platform records many statistics to help you understand why things might be slowing down.

Every request into the instance follows the same pattern and involves three key groups of systems:

- The **instance** must work with the database to get the data and turn it into something useful for the user.
- The **network** must deliver this data to the user. The instance administrator typically has the least control over this step.
- The **browser** must understand the information and display it on the screen.

The instance records lots of time-based statistics for every request. This includes for how long the database was busy, the time taken by the network to send and receive data, and it also records how long the browser took to understand the form. Each of these statistics is broken down in granularity of milliseconds, letting you identify areas where things are working well or not so well.

The following diagram breaks down a page request transaction into these groups:

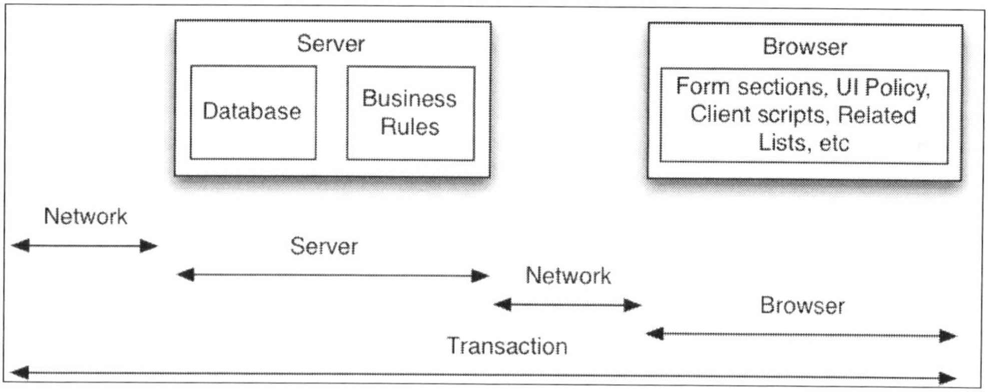

Monitoring the instance's performance

Once a request for some data is received by the instance, the platform will start timing how long it takes to produce the page. The Transaction Log contains the results of the following timings, which are listed here:

- The **server time** is saved in the Transaction Log in the **Response time** field. This is a summation of the many activities that the instance carried out, indicating how long it took to process the whole transaction. This will be more than the addition of SQL time and Business Rule time since it also includes the time taken for form generation and other processing.

- **SQL time** and **SQL count** record how long the database took to deal with a request and how many SQL queries were executed. The SQL time is usually less than one second, though for complex home pages, reports, and global searches in particular, it may be more.
- **Business Rule time** and **Business Rule count** show the time that any associated scripts take to process the record. If these are particularly high, then it means there might be an opportunity for optimization, such as moving scripts to an asynchronous operation.

Recording the browser's perspective

On the majority of web pages delivered by the instance, some JavaScript is included that asks the browser to run some timings of its own. Once the page has finished loading, as long as it is within the frameset, the statistics are returned and stored on the server in the Transaction Log. This gives a holistic view about the experience that the user is receiving.

The **transaction time** is stored in the **Client response time** field. It's a simple summation of the factors that contribute to the loading of the web page. This number is obtained when the following three points are added together:

- **The network time**: This is the time it takes to deliver the response from the server to the browser.
- **The server time (from the perspective of a client)**: This is how long it takes for the server to respond, from the moment the request was sent to the first response back. (This will very closely match the response time discussed in the preceding point, but it will not exactly match it due to timing inaccuracies.) This is not saved in the Transaction Log.
- **The browser time**: A web browser needs to interpret the HTML that the instance provides. This will include building the DOM and displaying the page. A faster browser, such as Chrome, will accomplish this much more quickly than an old version of Internet Explorer.

This information can be viewed on the delivered web page. At the bottom-right corner, a small clock icon called the **Response Time Indicator** can be clicked to show the details on demand:

In this example, the user had to wait 877 milliseconds (or 0.9 seconds) for the page to be displayed. This is made up of 192 milliseconds of network transmission time, and the server spent 264 milliseconds to generate the page. The browser also spent 421 milliseconds to render the page.

Breaking down the browser's time

You may wonder what the browser was doing for almost half a second; that was the biggest part of the transaction. The **browser: 421** in the preceding screenshot is actually a clickable link. This expands to show where the browser is spending the time:

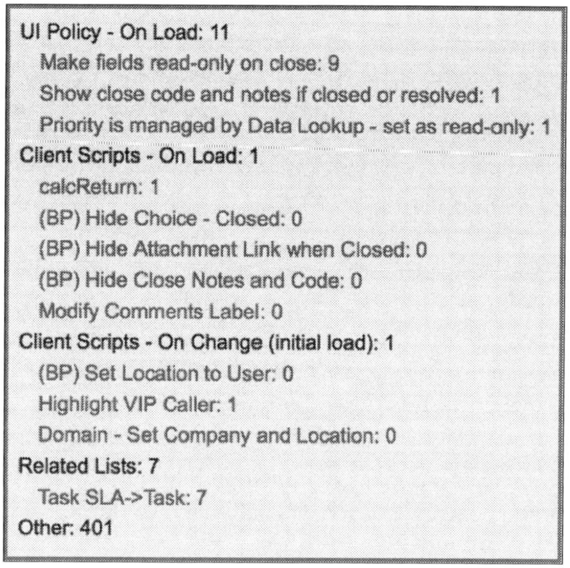

Each section (aside from **Other**) is expandable, giving an incredible amount of detail about how long the page took to load.

- The **Other** section times how long the browser took to render the form. In this example, the majority of the time was spent manipulating the DOM and laying out the page. The number of fields that are placed on the form has a dramatic impact on how long the form takes to load.
- All the sections can be expanded to show how long each particular item took to load. In particular, the On Load **UI Policies** and **Client Scripts** should be examined closely and kept as minimal as possible. The Display Business Rules is often a very close replacement for these sorts of activities.

- **Related Lists** can sometimes take the majority of time that is used to render. Therefore, enough thought should be put in before you add more to the form.

> These items can be easily reported on to find problem areas. Try the **Browser Timings by Table (Form)** report as an example.

Going through other logs

In our journey through ServiceNow, we've already used several tables that are useful for developing a diagnosis. Since ServiceNow is a very data-oriented system, it is easy to use these tables. Create Scheduled Reports or put useful filters on a home page so that you are aware of issues quickly. Some of the logs are as follows:

- The **Event Log** (which can be found by navigating to **System Policy** > **Events** > **Event Log**), which was first discussed in *Chapter 5, Events, Notifications, and Reporting*, stores data about deferred transactions. This lets the platform react to a particular situation, asynchronously or in a decoupled manner. Events often send emails or run Script Actions to run arbitrary code. The time taken to run these actions is recorded in the **Processing duration** field. If this is very short (under a few tens of milliseconds), then it is likely that the system did nothing and something has gone wrong.

> Try not to fire too many events that do nothing. The platform will diligently check to see what is listening each time, which is a waste of time if nothing is!

- The Transaction Log also contains Scheduled Jobs. A filter can be found by navigating to **System Scheduler** > **Scheduled Jobs** > **Slow Job Log**.
- **E-mail** communication, both inbound and outbound, is stored in the **Email** [`sys_email`] table. This is accessible by using filters in the **System Mailbox** application. Different views are used for each situation, with outbound e-mails showing the events that caused them and inbound e-mails recording the details of the user it was from. If you need to track exactly when an email was processed, the relevant timestamps allow you to match it up with other mail servers.

> If you aren't receiving emails check the infamous **Send to event creator** checkbox, which was discussed in *Chapter 5, Events, Notifications, and Reporting*.

- Several integrations, including the ones involving the MID server, utilize the **ECC Queue**. It is can be found by navigating to **ECC** > **Queue**, as discussed in detail in *Chapter 6, Exchanging Data – Import Sets, Web Services, and Other Integrations*. It again stores outbound and inbound messages and lets you understand exactly what was sent and received. By sending SOAP messages via the ECC queue, you can keep a detailed record of the messages that were sent through the Web Service Consumer plugin.

> To log all the SOAP messages that are received by the platform, create a new property called `glide.processor.debug.SOAPProcessor` and set its value to `true`. The messages will quickly fill the system log, and impact performance, so switch off the property when done.

Finding slow database transactions

The transaction log shows an aggregated performance metric for how long the database is involved. So, how would you know whether the database is struggling for a particular query, or your reports and lists have inappropriate filters? The Slow Query log gives you valuable insights into how the platform is used. You can access it by navigating to **System Diagnostics** > **Stats** > **Slow Queries**.

The instance uses a concept of total execution time. This is calculated by adding together all the execution times of similar individual transactions. Two transactions are considered similar if their SQL queries are the same, except for the values of the `WHERE` clause.

> As a very simple example, these queries are considered similar since only the value of the `WHERE` clause changes:
>
> ```
> SELECT * FROM task WHERE state = 5;
> SELECT * FROM task WHERE state = 3;
> ```
>
> In contrast, the following queries are not similar since they select different information and have dissimilar conditions:
>
> ```
> SELECT number FROM task WHERE state = 5;
> SELECT * FROM task WHERE state = 3 AND active =
> TRUE;
> ```

Classifying slow queries

By determining the total execution time, you can see where the database spends its time. Any query with a total execution time of more than 5 seconds is recorded. In order to provide a representation of what queries are, example SQL queries, URLs, and stack traces are provided. They often break down into a couple of categories.

> A stack trace indicates what the Java platform is doing at that moment. Each line from the bottom up lists which classes and methods are being stepped through. As one method calls another, another line is added.

You can break down the entries in the slow query log into several categories I've listed here:

- **Very frequent and very fast queries**: These will have a high execution count, but a low average execution time. These tend to be internal platform queries or from other scripts like those in calculated fields. I've seen instances where a "simultaneous update" AJAX script is run after the record is saved. This attempts to avoid one user "overwriting another". Although this check may only take 5-10 milliseconds to complete, it would have been done hundreds of millions of times. This means that, in total, the database would have spent a long time on this!

> This particular script is often a hangover from older systems that performed record locking, which only allowed one user to work on a ticket at one time. In a more modern system such as ServiceNow, this becomes a process question—anyone can add **Work notes**, but only the **Assigned to** user is in charge of changing the ticket.

- **Very slow queries that only happen occasionally**: These will have a low execution count. Often, these will be scheduled jobs or reports. If an example stack trace begins with `glide.scheduler.work`, then this is probably happening on a worker node. This means it is still taking up database time, but it'll not put extra load on the application server. Stack traces that begin with `http` or have an example URL that starts with a forward slash (/) have been initiated by a user. If these slow queries happen when the instance is not busy, then they may not impact many users.

- **Slow queries that happen often**: These should be avoided and are often great candidates for optimization. Check the scripts associated with **Scheduled Imports** and look at the queries provided in URLs. You will often see `/home.do` as the example URL; this indicates a slow report on a home page. You can make it better!

Examining the Slow Query log

> A development instance is unlikely to contain the same sort of results as a heavily utilized production system. On my development instance, the instance spends the vast majority of its time on scheduled jobs. In fact, there are no user-initiated transactions that have taken a total execution time of more than 5 seconds.

To examine the Slow Query log, navigate to **System Diagnostics** > **Slow Queries** and create the following filters:

- **Average execution time (ms) - greater than - 1000**
- **Example URL - starts with - /**
- Order by **Total execution time (ms)**, with the condition: **z to a**, so the largest is at the top:

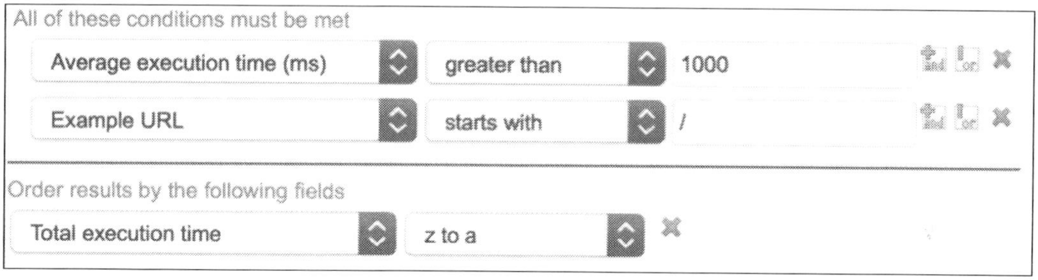

This setting will return a list of database queries that have been somehow initiated by the user. On average, the database takes over a second to return this data to the user, thereby suggesting that the query is inefficient. You are likely to return several examples of either lists or a home page.

Choose a record and investigate the **Example URL** field. For a list, you'll see the query that was given to the instance. One example I found gives the **Example URL** simply `/task_list.do, sysparm_query=GROUPBYassigned_to`. In this scenario, the instance was asked to group by the **Assigned to** field for every task in the instance, which is a big job. This task took the database over 10 seconds to return the data, which is still not bad considering that there are half a million records, but this is still something to be avoided. Here, the database is spending a long time returning data that is not necessary. No one will page through 500,000 records!

Understanding behavior

Most users use the modules in the Application Navigator as the starting point for queries. To perform the inefficient query example above, there may be a module called **All tasks** in the Application Navigator that returns all the 500,000 task records and then users simply perform the grouping.

> Understanding what users are doing is often very instructive. For example, why did they perform this query? What are they trying to achieve? You may want to review the transaction log to get the answers but simply interviewing them can be most useful.

Providing efficient modules that show relevant, filtered data is a good way to nudge the user into making more efficient queries. An optimization would be to add a time-based filter to the module and just show active tasks. This means that when the user does the grouping, it'll do it on a smaller set of records, hopefully making it faster.

> Of course, education is critical too. Helping the users to use the platform efficiently will speed up their interactions and make it easier for the instance!

Seeing the plan

The **Slow Query** log also includes a field labelled Example that contains an SQL statement. This will show you exactly what the database was asked to do and gives an insight into how more efficient queries can be made. This includes what data has been asked for and what joins have been made.

To get more information, the **Explain Plan** UI Action asks the database how this query would be carried out. Then, a Related List containing the data appears, showing which database indexes would be used (if any) and how the data would be selected. If the **Key** field is empty and the transactions are taking a long time, the queries may benefit from an index. Contact the ServiceNow Customer Support team to discuss options if you want to add an index.

> The one way you can add an index yourself is by making the field unique. However, this has its own disadvantages, which were discussed in *Chapter 1, ServiceNow Foundations*.

Dealing with other performance issues

The hints and tips in this book try to give the best possible experience of a ServiceNow instance to its users: administrators, fulfillers, and requesters alike. Tricks such as using client-side code to check a form before submission can really help the system *feel* faster.

However, performance issues can occur. An out-of-date browser, running on a slow terminal server, whose virus-checking tools are checking Client Scripts can quickly frustrate a user. Most of the time, there is no single issue that causes performance problems, but there will be a combination of multiple factors, such as these:

- The Transaction Log has a **GZipped** column. Research the circumstances of any user where this is `false`—this is a red flag! The instance compresses the HTML that is generated before sending it out, but it only does so for browsers that support it. All modern browsers do support it, but inefficient proxy servers or older browsers don't. These users will typically receive a poor experience.
- If there is a time period that is consistently slow—perhaps Monday morning between 09:00 and 09:30—where all transactions are slow, this may indicate there is **a scheduled job** that is sucking resources. This is often an import, but it can potentially be an extract that is initiated from another tool.
- Every **field on the form** will increase the amount of data that the instance needs to prepare, how long it will take to send this data across the network, and the amount of effort the browser needs to render it. This is applicable for Related Lists, or anything else on the form.

> Having large sections of the form hidden by UI Policy is a common configuration. However, this means much work will be done that'll not be used!

- **On Load Client Scripts** are usually unnecessary and the ones that use AJAX should never be used. They require the browser to change the form just as the page is loading. Instead, you must ensure that the form renders that way to begin with. Display Business Rules are very useful for this.
- **Reference fields** search through the Display values of records. Normally, this uses a `startswith` operator, but it can be configured to use a `contains` search instead. This query is much more complex for the database to perform. For 5,000 records, this'll probably be okay. However, for 500,000 records, it will likely be much slower.

> Consider tweaking the autocomplete settings to search others columns instead. Check this wiki for more information: `http://wiki.servicenow.com/?title=Auto-Complete_for_Reference_Fields`.

- Use **Client Scripts** effectively. If it does not impact on the user experience, do it on the server. For example, routing a ticket is probably best done by the server, especially if there are lots of rules to consider. It is best to do this in a Business Rule, but unless it is absolutely necessary, `GlideAJAX` may be an alternative.

> In general, excessive configuration can cause problems. If there are large numbers of fields, Client Scripts, Business Rules, sections, workflows, SLAs, and so on, these can combine to create issues. There are very few hard limits in ServiceNow, so the platform won't stop you from creating and adding 200 fields to a form. However, it will be slower to use than 20 fields. Use the logging capabilities and test them thoroughly to find out what is acceptable for you.

Managing large tables

Large tables, such as **Task** or **System Log**, can become slow to query and work with. It is often preferable to keep data the way you need it, as it is difficult to remove once it is gone. However, you also don't want to keep unnecessary data. Moreover, a task has a very different profile to an information entry in the System Log. Correspondingly, there are several functions in the platform that are employed for large tables.

Archiving data

It is best to never delete a task. ServiceNow acts as the store of all requests, and it is very useful to have a full audit trail of information. However, closed tasks that are more than a year old are less important, and you don't need them in a shift handover report.

The **Data Archiving** plugin lets you set a condition for a particular table. Specify them by navigating to **System Archiving** > **Archive Rules** once the plugin is activated. Once the set condition is met, matching records will be moved into a separate table. This data is flattened and denormalized. This means that the archived record will only consist of strings; all references will be replaced with their display values.

For example, consider an archived **Maintenance** record. Instead of having a reference to a **Room** or an **Assignment group**, the archived record just stores the number of the room and the name of the group. (In instances where there are multiple languages, only the system language is used.)

There are some considerations that should be kept in mind when you set up the Data Archiving plugin:

- The archival and primary tables are not connected. Searching or filtering in one will not show the records in the other. An archived record can be restored, which will recreate it in the primary table. The instance keeps a separate store of the original data in the Archive Log table.
- When defining the Archive Rules, there is an option to archive related records. For example, child tasks may need to be archived along with their parents. This is similar to the situation when you delete a record but the archiving functionality lets you choose different actions for different fields. You can choose from **Archive** (to archive the related record), **Clear** (to clear the reference field), or **Delete** (to entirely remove the record). Most of the time, **Archive** is the best, though it can result in a cascade effect.
- Any references to an archived record will be left as is, unless there is an action in the **Archive Related Records** list. This may mean that a reference field that pointed towards a record contains a `sys_id` that no longer exists. This group has been archived without altering the reference field.

- Restoring an archived record will not affect reference fields. If you clear or delete, the association is gone permanently.

Rotating and extending through sharding

Some other large tables, such as the System Log, are managed in a different way. Rather than moving records into a single other table that is based on a condition, the platform chooses which table should receive new records depending upon the date. The table changes every 1 to 30 days or so, depending upon the configuration.

- **Table rotation** has a preset number of tables over which the data is spread. If the last is exhausted, it starts at the beginning again overwriting the contents of the first table.
- **Table extension** has an ever-growing number of tables. When a new table is needed, the platform simply creates another table.

Either method will break up a very large set of data into more manageable chunks that will be easier for the database to deal with. These chunks are known as shards. The use of a rotated or extended table is transparent to the user since the platform will decide which shards need to be queried in order to find the relevant data.

When a user looks at a rotated table, the platform joins (actually unions) all the underlying shards tables together, as necessary. If a date is specified, it makes the queries quicker since the database has to look at a much smaller dataset. Inserting new records is also quick. However, general search must involve many shards, giving things considerably. For this reason, always use a **Created on** date filter on large log tables. The following screenshot shows that a query which is for two months data involves searching two database tables. If there was no date filter, it could search many more:

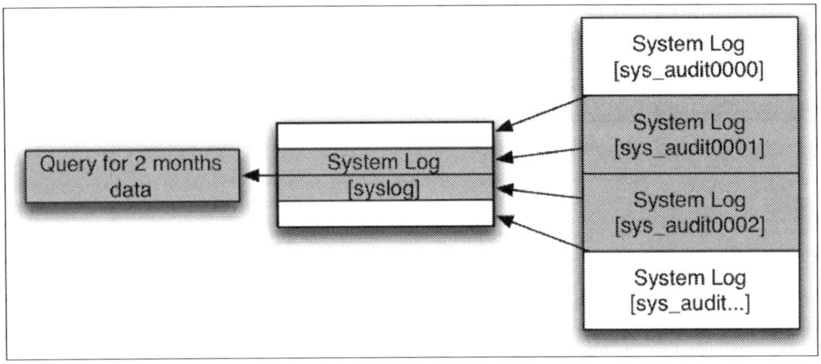

Choosing table extension

Tables that need to keep large amounts of data indefinitely but will not be subject to searching are great candidates for extension. The Email table is a good example of this; all the sent and received e-mails are kept, but it won't perform well if a `contains` query is performed across a wide date range. Another example is the Audit log, which we will explore next.

Selecting table rotation

Information that doesn't need to be kept, such as logs, are best suited to table rotation. This means that data can be written to it quickly, and the most recent information can be accessed easily, but it is self-limiting. For example, after 8 weeks, the oldest System Log shard will be removed. This keeps the table smaller and more manageable.

> The Database Rotation plugin is activated by default, but it is worth checking with ServiceNow Customer Support if you wish to make any changes or additions. For more information, refer to `http://wiki.servicenow.com/?title=Database_Rotation`

Auditing and versioning

Some tables, such as the Task table, are audited. Every time a record is updated, the platform records what was changed, when it was changed, and who changed it by recording an entry in the **Audit** [`sys_audit`] table. Every entry in the Audit table represents a change to a field. This is tremendously helpful when you diagnose issues since you can clearly see how a record was manipulated over time.

Turning on auditing

To make the platform audit a table, go into the Dictionary entry of the table and check the Audit flag. I almost always enable it on the User table since it is very useful to see how the records are changing over time. Note that you need to enable it for every extension, so turn it on for a guest too!

Viewing audit

You've already seen the output of the Audit table. The Activity Log presents the data that is captured by the auditing process and presents it in a filterable, more attractive way. However, it is possible to see all the data using the History Calendar view. If you've turned it on for the User table, navigate to **History** > **Calendar** from the context menu. This gives you a breakdown per change and can highlight them on a calendar-style interface. The **Use History Detail** window is shown in the following screenshot:

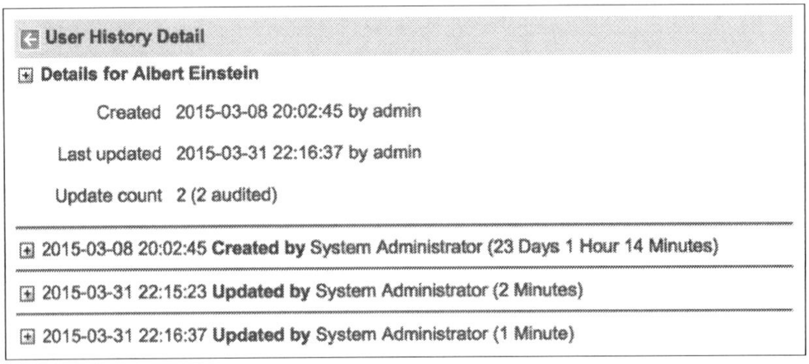

Using auditing responsibly

There is some impact from turning auditing on, but its advantages often outweigh the negatives. Consider the following points to get the maximum benefit:

- To prevent some very frequent updates from swamping the system, you can add the `no_audit` attribute to the dictionary entry of a field. A good candidate for this is the **Last Login time element** on the **User** table, which is very frequently updated.
- Never report or even query the **Audit** table. Not only is its size likely to be in several gigabytes since it is sharded (using the extension mechanism), but the queries over a date range are also likely to be incredibly slow. I have seen some instances getting overwhelmed with scripts that scan the **Audit** table; so, don't do it!
- Don't try to change the contents of the **Audit** table. This is designed to be a permanent storage of the changes. To improve performance, the **Audit** table works in conjunction with the **History Set** [`sys_history_set`] table. The platform works in the background to keep them synchronized and it is very difficult and quite risky to alter this behavior.

Versioning configuration

While the audit log is available for every table, **versioning** provides richer functionality for configurations such as Business Rules and Client Scripts. It takes advantage of the way in which Team Development captures changes to give an easy way to compare differences and restore unwelcome alterations.

> Team Development is discussed in the next chapter, *Chapter 9, Moving Scripts with Clones, Update Sets, and Upgrades*, where more detail is given about how this data is stored and which records are considered a configuration.

You may have already spotted the **Versions** Related List at the bottom of many forms. Whenever you save a record that is considered to be a configuration, the platform automatically creates an entry in the **Update Versions** [`sys_update_version`] table. This stores the details such as who made the change and when they were made. In contrast to the **Audit** table, the entire contents of the record are stored here and not just the changes.

Reviewing the changes

Since every attribute about the record is stored, the platform can easily show the differences between any previous versions and the current one.

In order to see this at work, find a Business Rule to which you've made multiple changes. Then, right-click on an earlier version in the Related List and click on **Compare to Current**. This will produce a dialog window that will list the differences between the two versions. Any fields that are identical will not be shown, and those that have will be shown in orange, as shown in the following screenshot:

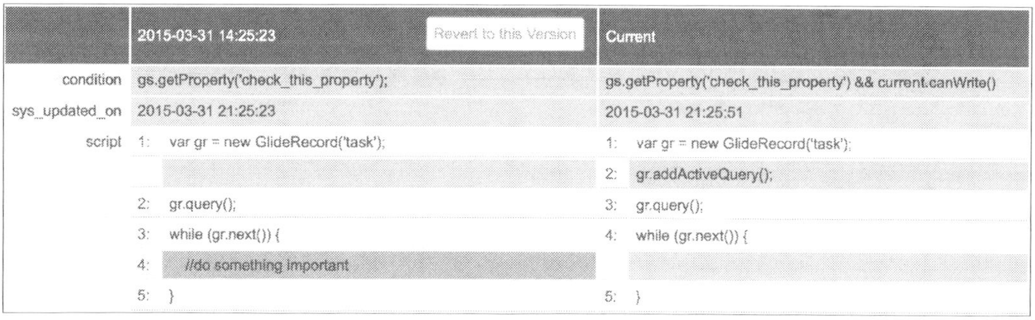

What makes versioning particularly useful for scripts is that it also performs a line-by-line difference comparison. Any lines that have been added are highlighted in green, while those that are removed are listed in red. This makes it very easy to identify the changes that have occurred over time.

In addition to the changes that the system administrators have made, the platform will also record the changes that are made by system upgrades. The source field of the **Version** record will list in which version of ServiceNow the configuration was included.

If you wish to go back in time, you can revert to an older version through the dialog box. This also helps if you want to restore an out-of-the-box version of a script or if you determine that things were better the way they used to be.

> There are also List Actions to compare two records and you don't have to use the current version. The list context menu also contains the commands to revert.

Optimizing hardware resources

ServiceNow provides dedicated resources for each instance. As discussed in *Chapter 1, ServiceNow Foundations*, an instance is independent, and a high load in one will not impact another instance.

Nonetheless, users do share resources with all those who use the same instance. To ensure that the platform can serve their request, the following strategies are employed by the ServiceNow Cloud Operations team:

- **Horizontal scaling** by giving busier instances more nodes. The load balancer distributes users over the nodes. Read replicas are used to help fully loaded databases.
- **Vertical scaling** includes providing the right level of memory and database connections.

  > These parameters are controlled by the ServiceNow Cloud Infrastructure team. You can work with your ServiceNow representatives if you feel these are inadequate.

- **Preventing long running transactions** and terminating those that exceed a preset time. By default, UI transactions that last more than 298 seconds will be automatically canceled. This is slightly less than the 5-minute time out that the load balancer enforces.

> Transactions that last more than 15 seconds will prompt a message and give the user the option to cancel it. If you are not working within the frameset, visiting `/cancel_my_transaction.do` will attempt to cancel any running transaction.

- Other transactions are subject to different **quotas**. The `typeahead` functionality on a reference field won't run for more than 15 seconds. These are defined in the **Transaction Quota Rule** [`sysrule_quota`] table.
- **Limiting session concurrency**, which means that one session cannot run more than one transaction at one time. This can be experienced by opening up multiple browser tabs at once; note that each will be served in turn.

> To start a new session, start your browser in the "private browsing mode" or open a new browser.
>
> Some transactions may be marked as "cancelable" (using the `sysparm_cancelable=true` parameter). These will be automatically canceled if another such transaction comes through.

- **Gating access** with semaphores to ensure that a running transaction has reasonable access to shared resources.

Controlling resources with semaphores

The ServiceNow platform uses a semaphore gating system to control access to system resources. The aim is to prevent one user from monopolizing resources and to even out access in times of heavy contention.

Whenever a node receives a request, it is classified into a set; the request may be a SOAP or REST message, when someone's using the UI, or a debug transaction. Then, the platform sees whether there are any available semaphores in that set. If there are none, the transaction is forced to wait until one is free. This will, paradoxically, help the overall responsiveness of the platform since the platform does not need to switch between threads frequently. The transactions in progress have resources they can rely on.

> Sometimes you just need to concentrate on something to get it done. Semaphores work just like this, as would-be distractions are queued up in a to-do list!

On a smaller instance, you may have eight semaphores in the default set, which is the classification for UI transactions. This means that a maximum of eight transactions can be carried out simultaneously on a single node. The consequence of this is that if 10 users tried to access the instance at precisely the same time, 2 would need to wait. In reality, it is very unlikely that 10 users would need server time at the same instant since there would be some natural variations in the experienced cadence. In addition, the load balancer will spread out transactions across nodes, providing a natural scaling system.

Accessing the system internals

The system logs tend to focus on what is happening inside the application layer. ServiceNow also lets you dig deeper into the nuts and bolts of the server. Lots of statistics are available, including summaries of performance indicators, thread statistics, and more database information.

Understanding the ServiceNow Performance homepage

System Administrators can access the Performance home page by navigating to **Self-Service** > **Homepage** and then selecting **ServiceNow Performance** in the **Switch to page...** selection box.

The top controls specify the time range and the size of the graph. (I always select **Extra Large**!)

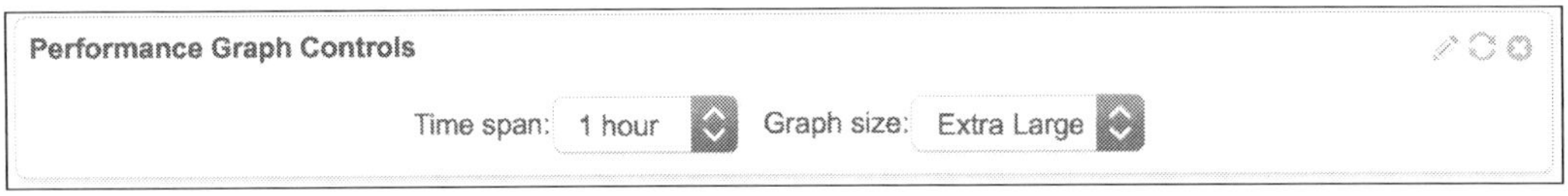

The other controls let you drill into a particular node, focusing on particular attributes. Choose the node that you want to view by selecting it in the CI selection list.

> The typical naming convention is `<hostname>.<datacenter>.service-now.com`

As noted in *Chapter 1, ServiceNow Foundations*, an instance is made up of several nodes. Every instance typically has two nodes, but an instance that is sized for a large number of users will have many more. In particular, a production system will have redundant nodes across two data centers, so the CI selection list of a busy instance may contain eight or more choices.

> Since the nodes are redundant, the nodes from one data center are likely to be very quiet, and with very little work being done.

The full set of data is very comprehensive and often not relevant to a typical system administrator. However, the ServiceNow Servlet set provides several interesting graphs that give you an indication of performance.

The **System Overview** graph indicates how busy the instance is and on what it spends its time. Every second, it looks to see what each thread is doing and categorizes it appropriately:

- The `business_rule_mean` category indicates that a thread is executing Business Rules. This shouldn't be a significant part of the platform's work. If it becomes overwhelming, investigate the causes of this.
- The `concurrency_mean` category should be low, unless the server is very busy. If a thread is in this state, it is waiting for a semaphore or some other access. Semaphores are explained further in the next section.
- The `cpu_mean` category represents other processing that cannot be categorized as Business Rules. Typically, this is the Java platform that is processing transactions. This is the bedrock of a standard graph.
- The `db_mean` category shows that the platform is waiting for the database. If a Business Rule is currently causing database work, it will be recorded in this state.

- The `network_mean` category is usually very low. This is when the platform is writing data to the network.

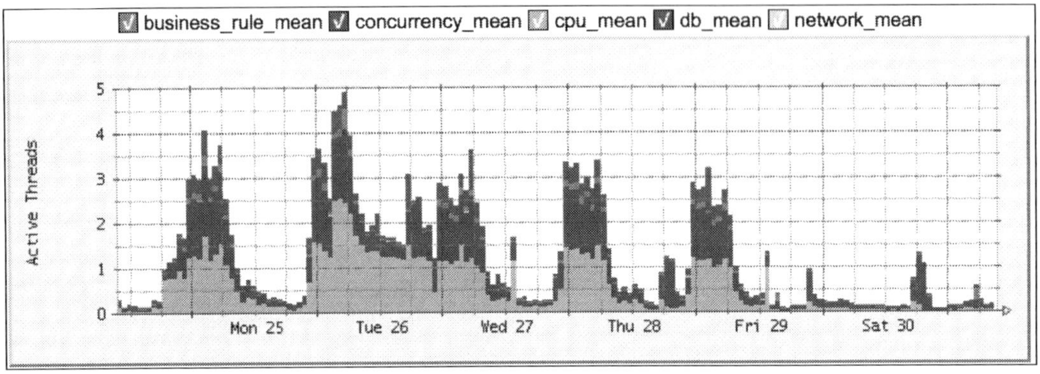

The number of **Sessions** gives an indication of how many users are logged in. There are often many more sessions than users since a single user might have opened multiple browsers. If an integration user doesn't reuse sessions and logs in afresh for each transaction, this will climb very high. This can potentially be an issue since the platform uses resources maintaining information that will never be used again. Instead, you can make the integration present the session ID authentication cookie to make things much faster.

> To see which users are logged in on your node, navigate to **User Administration** > **Logged in Users**. The session can be ended if desired. Eventually, if there is no activity, each session will timeout. The default is 30 minutes. `http://wiki.servicenow.com/?title=Modifying_Session_Timeout`

The **Session Wait Queue** is how many of the sessions are unable to progress with their transactions because the platform is gating their requests. Typically, this is due to a thread waiting for a semaphore or a mutex. If this is a high number, it means that these sessions are waiting for a scarce resource or perhaps, the database is very busy, slowing things down.

> A mutex is a way to stop two threads from changing the same thing. For example, some code may attempt to create an object if it doesn't already exist. If two threads at exactly the same time try to make this decision independently, you will very likely end up with two objects since when each one would check, the object wouldn't have existed.

The **Transactions** count is a simple graph showing the number of transactions per minute. This is a great way to understand when your peak times are – most likely during working hours.

Response time graphs the maximum, median, and minimum time that a transaction takes. The median often hovers around 1 second.

The next few graphs focus on how Java handles **memory**. These are generally less relevant to the system administrator. However, if you are creating lots of custom Jelly pages, you may wish to keep an eye on the PermGen levels. Writing inefficient Jelly depletes PermGen memory and leads to performance issues and even outages.

[Jelly is touched on in *Chapter 10, Making ServiceNow Beautiful with CMS and Jelly*. It is a mechanism to create custom user interfaces.]

The **CPU Usage** graph is reported by the operating system. It shows how much processing is happening. The platform is not often CPU-bound, so the graph should show user and system usage at a low level.

Finally, the **Scheduler** shows how many jobs are being processed. If the instance is busy, jobs will begin to queue. For example, this will cause e-mail delays and slower asynchronous processing of web service calls. If lots of jobs are scheduled at the same time, try to spread them out.

[The wiki at `http://wiki.servicenow.com/?title=Performance_Metrics`, explains many of these items in more detail.]

Flushing the system cache

In order to improve performance, the platform employs caching. Instead of continuously loading the same data from the database, the platform just grabs it once, stores it in memory, and then reloads it from the cache when it is needed the next time. Some of the items that the cache stores are as follows:

- The Business Rules and UI Policies that are associated with each table
- Contextual Security Rules
- The layout of a form
- Choice lists
- System properties

- GlideUser objects, such as the one retrieved with gs.getUser()
- The colors used in some graphs

When the underlying records change, the platform should clear the cache appropriately in order to allow the use of the new configurations. For example, there is a Business Rule that flushes part of the cache when a UI Policy is updated. The next time that information is asked for, the platform gets it directly from the database and stores it in the cache again.

Sometimes, this does not work effectively and the values are not removed when they should be. This causes the use of old ("stale") configuration to be continued. When performing development work, you may find that you need to empty the cache completely to force the platform to reread the configuration.

To perform a cache flash, navigate to <instance>.service-now.com/cache.do. You will see that the platform gives you some before and after figures for memory usage.

> Avoid performing cache flushes on your production instance unless it is strictly necessary. This has a big impact on performance!

The performance impact is considerable. Some example timings suggest that a cached form can be displayed in 150 milliseconds of server time, while just after a cache flush, it could take over 1500 milliseconds. This 10-fold difference underlines how important caching is and why any clearing of the cache should be done with caution.

Accessing system stats

Sometimes, an instance can be unresponsive and it wouldn't be possible to view the system log, the performance graphs, or even any standard page in the interface. One scenario may be when the database is totally overwhelmed. Since every standard page requires records from a database, severe contention may mean you can't see or do anything.

To enable you to see what is happening to the instance at a glance, even in times of stress, a page is accessible at <instance>.service-now.com/stats.do. You will always see the information of the node that you are currently allocated to. Therefore, this may not reflect everyone's experience.

> There is no deterministic way to choose which node you are on. The ServiceNow load balancers make the decision. In order to continue your session on the same node, a cookie is set by the load balancers. Therefore, clearing your cookies and connecting again will force the load balancer to route you anew. If you try it several times, you may get lucky!

The **Stats** page provides a great deal of useful data:

- The **build information** displays exactly what version of the ServiceNow platform is running. The build tag contains which release (Dublin, Eureka, Fuji, and so on) and which hotfixes and patches are included (patch1, hotfix2, and so on). It also shows the node that you are using.
- The same **memory information** that is displayed when you clear the cache is also shown.
- **Servlet statistics** gives counter-based information about uptime, the number of transactions, errors, sessions, and handled requests. This gives a little insight into the demands on the system.
- The **Semaphore Sets** section shows the current groupings in which the transactions are bundled. The number of semaphores is a big factor in the number of users that a node, and consequently an instance, can support. If users are awaiting session synchronizers, they are listed here too.

> Most transactions get bundled into the Default set. If the instance is busy and you must absolutely see a result without queuing, try adding `sysparm_debug_transaction=true` as a parameter. For example, try `/u_maintenance_list.do?sysparm_debug_transaction=true`. This will cause the transaction to use the debug semaphore set (reserved for the JavaScript Debugger), which will be much less congested.

- The familiar **Server**, **Network**, and **Client** times are averaged over several time periods; from 1 minute to 1 day. This gives a better idea as to how the system is performing over time. To reduce outliers, a 90 percent statistic is produced too. This prevents very slow transactions, such as a difficult report, from overly influencing the numbers.
- In a similar way to semaphores, the **Database Connection Pool** controls access to the database. Some transactions may be held until the others are completed. Any slave databases are also listed here, letting you see if the redundant systems are up to date.

> Full text searching is very intensive for the database. While the platform has an optimized search engine called Zing, it requires many queries to find the relevant information. A separate database pool is often used to prevent these from swamping other requests.

- The background scheduler works through jobs in the `sys_trigger` table, as discussed in *Chapter 5, Events, Notifications, and Reporting*. E-mails, events, SLA updates, and so on, all use scheduled jobs to perform work at the most appropriate time. The queue length is listed, as well as how long, on average, jobs are waiting, and how long each is taking.

Some customers want to feed their own monitoring systems with information that is provided by the instance. To grab all this data and a whole load more, use the XML data available at `<instance>.service-now.com/xmlstats.do`.

Summary

In a complex system such as ServiceNow, there are many elements that work together to provide the functionality that you need. Consequently, there are many ways to find out what really is going on.

The **System Log** is the primary source for platform and application messages. It is especially useful for working out what just happened when you weren't able to see it in person. Use it to diagnose issues on the production system. Everything in the System Log and much more is also stored in the **file log**. It is a more detailed read-only store of information. You can download it for forensic analysis. Additionally, the **Transaction Log** records all access to the platform and stores who did what and when. Timings are also saved, breaking down how long things took on both the server and the client.

For more interactive debugging, use the **session debugging** tools to see which Business Rules are being executed and the decision of the Contextual Security Rules manager. The latter is an excellent way to determine permission issues. The server-side **JavaScript debugger** provides three tabs: to control, edit, and step through Business Rules; to see client-side messages; and to track how fields are being altered at almost every part of the platform.

Performance is critical for enterprise applications. If the speed of database access isn't quite what it might be, the **Slow Query** log will help you to identify what is happening. In addition, you can take into consideration whether archiving and rotating large tables will help, though this does impact on how the tables can be queried.

The **auditing** and **versioning** capabilities of ServiceNow let you record the changes on a record-by-record basis. If a Business Rule doesn't work out, then you can revert to an earlier version or find out who edited the user record.

ServiceNow provides a great deal of information about how the server and the platform are running. **Semaphores** are used by the platform to controls resources such as CPU time and the database. They stop one user from monopolizing the platform. They can also be monitored, along with many other elements, on the **System Performance home pages** and statistics pages.

In *Chapter 9, Moving Scripts with Clones, Update Sets, and Upgrades*, we will look at how to make the most effective use of your instances, how to share configuration, and what moving to production means.

9

Moving Scripts with Clones, Update Sets, and Upgrades

A ServiceNow instance is independent. Making changes to one instance will not affect another one. But, how could you move your carefully developed and tested scripts from one instance to another? Obviously, you wouldn't want to repeat the configuration over and over again and copying and pasting is time-consuming and fraught with mistakes.

This chapter explores the mechanisms that will help you to implement an effective development methodology, letting you release good quality configurations in a consistent manner; these are as follows:

- **Update Sets** record configuration into groupings, bundling code and other items together.
- **Team Development** provides the functionality to push and pull the configuration to a parent instance, building a more Git-style mechanism.
- The **App Creator** provides another way to bundle work together, but it also gives a quick and easy way to start building your own custom app.
- All data and configuration can be exported and imported to **XML files** to make portable, self-contained stores of data.
- **Cloning** copies an instance, replacing the destination with a perfect replica of the source. This is the best way to ensure that two systems are exactly alike.
- ServiceNow releases regular **platform upgrades** than can range from minor fixes and improvements to new applications and user interfaces. The upgrades are carefully designed to be as safe as possible.

Using your instances

ServiceNow provides at least two instances to every customer. One is a production system that is used for live data and is used by requesters and fulfillers to do useful work. In the case of Gardiner Hotels, the production instance would manage guest reservations and maintenance issues. The other instance is sub-production. This is, in the vast majority of ways, identical to a production instance; it differs only with the resources that are allocated to it. Sub-production systems tend to be only used by System Administrators and testers. Many more people use the production instance; so, it needs extra hardware.

It is more common for a customer to have three instances. The instance names are often the name of the company and the sub-production instances are suffixed with their intended functions, which are typically a development environment and a testing environment. In the case of Gardiner Hotels, the instances may be called as follows:

- `gardinerhotels.service-now.com` is the production system. It is used by all the requesters and fulfillers.
- `gardinerhotelstest.service-now.com` is the testing system. It is used to validate new or updated functionality before it is released into production.
- `gardinerhotelsdev.service-now.com` is the development system. It is used by System Administrators to create new functionality.

> These options do vary, so contact your ServiceNow representative for more information.

This chapter explores several ways to move information from one instance into another instance, combining these instances to produce an effective implementation cycle. Towards the end, we will discuss a common methodology for managing the instances.

Serializing records to XML

As we saw in *Chapter 1, Setting Up the ServiceNow Architecture*, virtually everything in ServiceNow is a record. The database stores all configurations, such as Business Rules, UI Policies, and Contextual Security Rules, in addition to all the data, such as users, groups, and tasks. We also saw in *Chapter 6, Exchanging Data – Import Sets, Web Services, and Other Integrations*, how data can be exported to CSV and Excel from a list or via a URL parameter. However, ensuring that every part of the record is stored so that it can be reconstructed perfectly is difficult using just these methods. What if you want to move data between instances even keeping the `sys_id` the same?

In order to get an exact representation of a database record, the platform can store data in a slightly augmented XML schema called the **unload** format. This stores the entire contents of a record in a serialized manner, but with a few added instructions. Each field in the record is represented as an element, and the action attribute specifies what should happen when the data is read. As a truncated example, a Business Rule may be serialized as follows:

```
<unload unload_date="2014-09-09 07:46:52">
  <sys_script action="INSERT_OR_UPDATE">
    <name>My Business Rule</name>
    <when>before</when>
    <insert>true</insert>
    <update>true</update>
    <script>
      var gr = new GlideRecord('incident');
      ...
    </script>
    <sys_id>62b8d8abebf21100be5be08a5206fe1a</sys_id>
    <sys_updated_on>2014-09-04 19:43:33</sys_updated_on>
  </sys_script>
</unload>
```

This data provides the platform with enough information to completely restore the record, exactly as it was. The instance can be provided with this data, and the record will be created or updated. All the fields will be identical like the XML document, including the `sys_id` and the date and time on which the record was last updated.

However, if the action parameter in the second line were replaced with `DELETE`, the platform would not update the record; it would be completely removed.

Exporting and importing serialized XML

All records can be exported to an XML file. Simply navigate to a list, right-click on the column headings, and choose **Export** > **XML** or add the URL parameter of `UNL`.

> A maximum of 10,000 records are exportable via XML at one time. Think it over carefully before you raise the limit because this can cause performance issues. Instead, you can use filters to get them in chunks.

Importing an XML file is powerful. The platform blindly follows the instructions given to it, and there is little trace of what's happened. Therefore, to carry out this action you must use the elevated `security_admin` role. Try this out:

1. Export data from the **Maintenance** table using **Export** > **XML**.
2. Open the file in a text editor, such as Notepad or TextEdit.
3. Replace any field values, such as the **Short description** field, or change the **action** attribute to `DELETE`.
4. Elevate to the `security_admin` role using the padlock in the banner frame.
5. Navigate to a list, right-click on the column headings, and choose **Import XML**. The platform will ensure that the database reflects the data in the XML file.

This import will not trigger any Business Rules, apply any validation, or even leave much trace, which makes the import very powerful but also rather dangerous. Since the audit log is not updated, you cannot see who altered the data. Additionally, invalid information can be entered; you can change the `sys_id` field to anything you wish and potentially breaking references. You must be extremely careful with this functionality.

> Using the Import XML functionality on a list is very different from importing XML via an Import Set. The latter, as described in *Chapter 6, Exchanging Data – Import Sets, Web Services, and Other Integrations*, uses Transform Maps to validate and check data before it is put into the target table.

Transporting data via XML

Since the **Import XML** menu uses a precise extract of data from any table, this is a useful mechanism for copying information from one instance to another instance. For example, to move the groups configured in the production instance to development, it is easy to export the data to XML and then import it in the appropriate instances. This ensures that the two instances have identical data in each instance, including the `sys_id`.

> Some configuration, such as Assignment Rules, relies upon data, such as groups, and needs their `sys_id` values to remain constant. As discussed later in the next section, Assignment Rules can be captured in Update Sets, but groups cannot be captured

For more varied data, this process quickly becomes more difficult. Since an extract to XML only contains the data from a single table, you may need to repeat the extraction process several times. For instance, a useful UI Policy is made up of at least two records—one in the **UI Policy** [`sys_ui_policy`] table and at least one in the **UI Policy Actions** [`sys_ui_policy_action`] table. Each of the records would need to be extracted individually and uploaded.

> The file can be uploaded using **Import XML** menu choice from any table. This is because the XML element contains the table name into which the data should go. This means that even multiple XML files can be merged together.

Recording configuration in Update Sets

Moving data via XML is useful, but what if the platform automated the process for you? In fact, what if the platform watched what you were doing and recorded the changes that you made to the records that matter? This is essentially a description of Update Sets.

An Update Set is a container for configuration. By navigating to **System Update Sets** > **Local Update Sets**, you can create a new Update Set or choose an existing one. By ticking the **My Current Set** checkbox or selecting it from the **Update Set** picker that is available in the **System** menu, you set a user property to tell the platform what container you want to use:

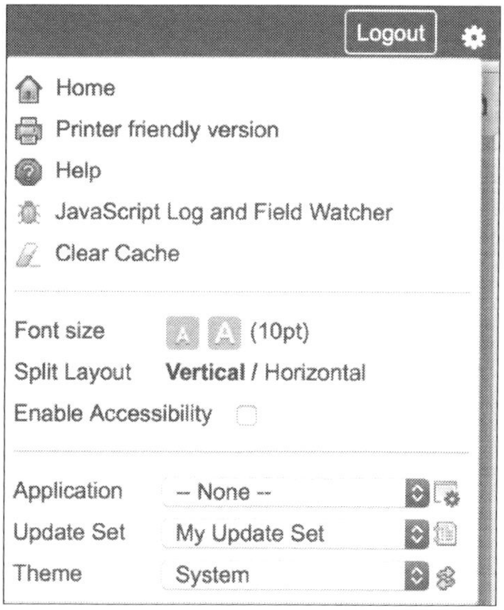

Then, whenever you make a configuration change in ServiceNow, the platform will create an entry in the **Customer Update** [`sys_update_xml`] table. This stores some information such as the table, who made the change, and the Update Set to which the change is associated. However, the most important field on the **Customer Update** table is the **Payload** field. This contains the serialized XML data that represents the entire altered record.

> Whenever you perform the configuration of an item, its current state is recorded in its entirety—it does not just record the delta. Update Sets capture the changes if records are deleted (such as the removal of a script), if a field is created, or a form is reorganized.

In this way, the Customer Update table keeps a list of the configuration that is made on an instance.

Capturing configuration

Update Sets only record changes to **configuration** and not **data**.

- **Configuration** is something that affects how the system works. For example, Scripts, Workflows, and so on. Configuration is generally performed in the **development** instance.
- **Data** is typically what the configuration acts upon, for example, Users, groups, and tasks. Data is maintained in the **production** instance.

This distinction is done for a good reason. Imagine that you built some new functionality, perhaps a Hotel application, in the development instance. At some point, after it is tested, it should be moved into production where everyone can use it, including the Workflows, fields, and forms that you designed. However, you don't want your test user accounts and example **Maintenance** tasks to be copied too.

So, if a Business Rule is created or a Client Script is updated, the system will record the event. However, if a user is edited or a group is updated, the platform will not create an entry in the Update Set for it. So, how does the platform know what to do?

The dictionary entries of both the Business Rule and Client Script tables contain an attribute called `update_synch`. This defines the table as one that contains configuration and is used by the Update Set handler to know what to record.

> Do not add the `update_synch` attribute yourself. The platform attempts to stop you since adding it on a very busy table, such as the **Task** table, will cause significant performance problems. Update Sets are not designed to transfer data. Instead, consider using the the 'Add to Update Set' utility available on Share.

Some configurations are handled more intelligently than just recording a single change at a time. The records that make up lists and forms are shared across several tables and they interact with each other. This means that when you alter a form section, the position of every element is recorded.

> To see exactly which tables are recorded, run a query on the **Dictionary** table:
>
> ```
> Attributes - contains - update_synch
> ```
>
> Many hundreds of tables are listed, which shows the vast array of configuration options in ServiceNow!

Transferring an Update Set

Once the **State** value of an Update Set is set to **Complete**, no further configuration will be recorded against it. Anyone who is using that Update Set will be warned that any further configuration that they perform will be placed into the Default Update Set.

> Even though there is a warning, get into the habit of regularly checking your Update Set. Mistakes happen, but try to minimize them!

A complete Update Set is then ready to be moved. This can be done in a couple of ways:

- **Using the UI Action**: **Export to XML**. This will give an XML file that contains the Customer Updates, with each file containing a payload that contains the record that has changed. Update Sets can be imported using the **Import Update Set from XML** UI action on the **Retrieved Update Set** table.

> Moving an Update Set via XML is a great way to share code. The ServiceNow Share platform, which is discussed later, lets you submit Update Sets to the community.

- One instance can retrieve Update Sets directly from other. Create a new **Remote Instance** record at **System Update Sets** > **Update Sources**. Provide a username and password to an account with the admin role on the remote instance. Then, use the **Retrieve Completed Update Sets** UI Action, and the platform will pull in all the complete Update Sets.

> Once an Update Set is set to **Complete**, don't reopen it and add any more entries. The **Retrieve Completed Update Set** functionality won't detect additional entries in an Update Set that it has already seen.

Applying an Update Set

Once an Update Set has moved into an instance, the configuration stored within it can be replayed. This will alter the instance as you require by deleting records, adding fields, and altering forms. The instance to which the Update Set is applied is known as the **target** system, while the instance from which the Update Set comes is the **source**.

> Update Sets will not drop tables or change field types. This will need to be done manually. The aim of this process is to minimize any accidental data loss.

The whole process is diagrammatically depicted in the following figure:

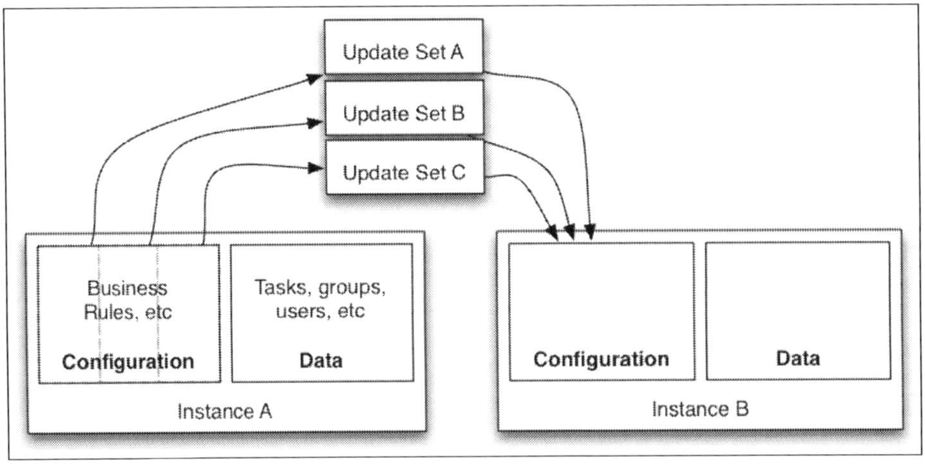

Before the changes occur, the Update Set is **previewed** first. This attempts to minimize issues by checking for **problems**. If any problems are discovered, action must be taken. The following screenshot shows one such problem:

Some of the problems that might occur are as follows:

- **Collisions** happen when the record on the target instance is updated after the one recorded in the Update Set. For example, imagine that a Business Rule is edited and captured in an Update Set in the source instance. Five minutes later, the Business Rule with the same `sys_id` is edited in the target instance as well. The item in the Update Set is now out of date, and the instance will not apply it without further instruction.

> Once you use Update Sets, you must always use them. Collisions often happen when manual changes are made to the target system. Don't change the same record twice in two instances, instead use Update Sets or another controlled method to synchronize the changes.

- **Missing object** problems occur when two changes depend on each other. If, for whatever reason, a UI Policy Action is included in an Update Set, but the UI Policy itself is not, then the platform will notice this and produce a problem.
- **Uncommitted update** problems occur when Update Sets are applied out of order. Perhaps a field that has been created in an Update Set is included on a form. This is discussed further in the upcoming sections.

Understanding multiple Update Sets

There are often multiple active Update Sets. While a single System Administrator can only use one Update Set at a time, another administrator may be using a different one. This can cause significant challenges.

Consider a situation where two administrators have their own Update Sets. As each one works, their changes are captured in their individual Update Set. If they both edit one record, such as a Client Script, then the state of the record as it was when saved will be recorded in their respective Update Sets. This means that there are now two versions of the same record that are stored in two Update Sets.

> There cannot be multiple copies of the same record within a single Update Set. If changes are made to the same record, only the latest change is saved.

The diagrammatic representation of the preceding process is explained in the following figure:

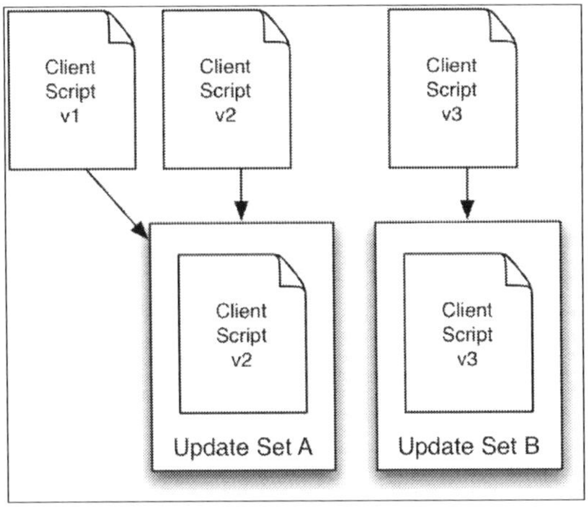

If the Update Sets are applied out of order (for example, based on the preceding figure, **Update Set A** is applied after **Update Set B**), then a collision problem will occur during the Update Set preview. The System Administrator who applies the Update Set will need to decide which version to keep.

Relying upon other updates

Some dependencies can be detected. If a UI Policy Action is missing the UI Policy or if an `onChange` Client Script is registered against a field that does not exist, then the platform will produce a record of the problem. However, this is not always successful, especially when the dependency is in code. The diagrammatic representation of the situation is depicted in the following figure:

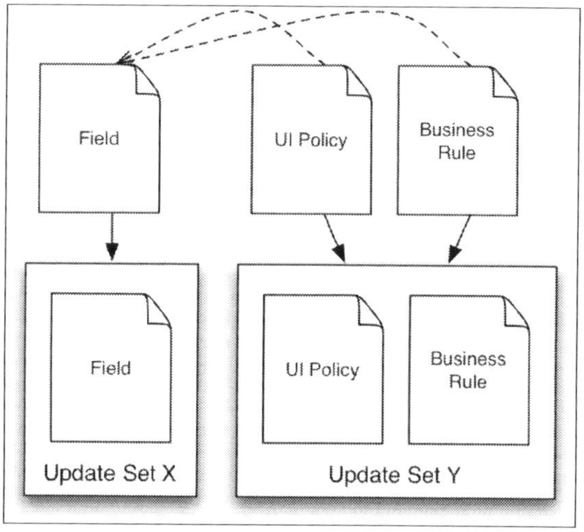

In the preceding example, both the UI Policy and the Business Rule rely on the new field. The UI Policy makes the field mandatory in some circumstances while the Business Rule script will validate the data.

If only Update Set Y is applied to the target instance and Update Set X is forgotten, then the configuration will not be valid. UI Policies and Business Rules cannot affect a field that does not exist.

In this circumstance, an Update Set problem will be raised against the UI Policy. The missing field can be detected in the structured data, and the administrator will need to resolve the error.

However, the platform will not be able to detect that the script in the Business Rule is referring to a missing field. The Update Set could still be applied, but the script simply would not work.

Managing Update Sets

In order to reduce potential problems, Update Sets must be managed very carefully. When multiple administrators have several Update Sets open, it is critical that they use and apply the right ones. There are several strategies to manage this situation.

- Using a **single Update Set** for all administrators: This is the simplest solution where all the configurations for a particular development period are made in a single Update Set. However, if a staggered development cycle is in progress, some partially finished functionality is likely to be captured in the Update Set and promoted through the environment. This can cause unexpected behavior.

- Applying the Update Sets in the **correct order** and fixing problems as they are presented in the Update Set preview: This provides the most flexibility but is time consuming and error-prone. This procedure may miss out some dependencies.
- **Merging all Update Sets** before moving on: The Update Set merge tool will take multiple Update Sets and pick the latest version of each record from each. The resulting new Update Set can then be transferred to the next environment. The correct Update Sets must be picked for this strategy to be successful and this is not always obvious.

Using the wrong Update Set

The success of Update Sets relies upon the administrator using the correct Update Set. Do you want that configuration to be moved now or later to another instance?

It is common to see a configuration recorded in the wrong Update Set. Perhaps the administrator didn't notice that another administrator closed the Update Set on which he or she was working, or he or she was doing two tasks at once and forgot to switch to the correct Update Set. If this happens, how can you move the configuration to another Update Set?

> While it is possible to edit the **Customer Update** record and change the **Update Set** field manually, this is not recommended. It will cause issues, for example, if there is an entry already recorded against that record. In addition, never attempt to commit the **Default** Update Set.

You can switch to the correct Update Set and make a non-destructive change to the record. For example, you can add a comment into a script or alter the Updated date. Any change to the record will force a new version of the record into the Update Set.

> This concept is similar to the `touch` command-line program on Unix-derived systems.

However, this process is fraught with difficulties because all the records must be touched, including any related records. For example, all the UI Policy Actions must be recorded as well as the UI Policy record itself. This is very often a long and error-prone process.

Working with Workflows

Update Sets and Graphical Workflow don't work well together. A Workflow uses many records to store all the relevant information. Therefore, Workflows only touch Update Sets when they are published.

There are several situations where the Workflows won't be properly transferred to the target instance:

- When the main workflow is published subflows are not recorded. Each Workflow must be published separately to ensure that it is recorded in the Update Set.
- Update Sets will capture all the versions of the current Workflow, but in some circumstances, it is possible to have the wrong version active.
- Variables are written to Update Set upon their creation rather than when the Workflow is published.

> The best practice is to merge and transfer all Update Sets when you are dealing with Workflows. There is more detail on these scenarios on the wiki at `http://wiki.servicenow.com/?title=Moving_Workflows_with_Update_Sets`.

Having the wrong IDs

Update Sets work with the unique identifier of a record—the `sys_id`. They assume that the `sys_id` values of records are consistent between the target and source environments. Reference fields use `sys_id` values to record links between records. If the `sys-id` values change, the relationship breaks.

This often has an impact when the configuration relies upon data. Assignment Rules are a good example of this; the Assignment Rule itself is tracked in an Update Set, but the **Group** reference field contains the `sys_id` of a group record, which is not tracked.

Consider a scenario where a new group is created, and a rule is made to assign tasks when specific criteria are met. Both the Assignment Rule and Group are made in the development system, but only the Assignment Rule is tracked in the Update Set since only that is required in the configuration.

If the Update Set is committed to the production instance, the **Group reference** field of the Assignment Rule will contain the `sys_id` of a group record that does not exist on the target instance. Creating a group with the same name will not fix the issue since creating a new record will generate a new `sys_id`.

One way to resolve this is to export data such as groups from the source instance as XML. This can then be imported on the target system, which will help to maintain the same `sys_id` values. The following screenshot shows how the **Assignment group** field is populated, but with the **sys_id** of a group that does not exist on the target system:

Alternatively, you can force the platform to add dependent data like this to the Update Set. Use a utility such as **Add to Update Set** available on Share, and use it to include the group in the Update Set.

> In some circumstances, a new instance may contain different `sys_id` values but refer to the same record. Some records are automatically generated the first time the instance is started. These include some security rules, fields, choice lists, and some reports. The way to deal with this is through a clone, which is discussed next.

Backing out Update Sets

It is unusual for things to work first time in all situations even if thorough testing has taken place. A completed Update Set has a **Back Out** UI Action, which reverses the configuration that it contains.

> Clicking on the **Back Out** button will delete any tables that have been created, remove added fields, and restore changed records. The Update Set itself will also be removed, so you may want to export the Update Set first.

Backing out an Update Set will restore a record to its most recent entry in the **Customer Updates** table. This means that it will be reverted to the latest update from another Update Set. For instance, if a record has been created and edited five times in a single Update Set, the record would be removed since it does not exist in another Update Set. It does not just undo the last work.

However, if a record was created in one Update Set and edited in another, backing out that final Update Set would restore the record to how it was first made.

Update Sets are, therefore, sometimes used as a fallback to allow the administrator to "restore from backup". However, unless Update Sets are created very frequently, backing out an Update Set often undoes too much work. Instead, it is often more appropriate to "fix forward" and make the changes that are needed to make it work, or even just deactivate broken Business Rules and other configuration.

> Use versions, which we will explore later, instead of backing out Update Sets. This is much more targeted since you only roll back the single record rather than many items. Reserve the Back Out process for the worst case scenario.

Moving away from Update Sets

Since Update Sets are difficult to work with, ServiceNow has layered on further functionality to make the process more robust. Both the Application Creator and Team Development use Update Sets as a core platform feature. The App Store in the Fuji release is another mechanism to share apps. Consider using them to abstract away the details. The Application Creator and Team Development are discussed in more detail in later sections.

Cloning instances

Update Sets are designed to move some configuration from one instance to another instance. They allow administrators to push new functionality—or bug fixes—to another instance, thereby migrating only the configuration that has changed.

In contrast, a clone is much more complete. It shifts almost the entire database from one instance to another instance. Since ServiceNow stores pretty much everything in the database, this results in everything being copied from the source to the target. This includes all the configuration and the data. It could even include the **System Log** and **Audit** tables. The following figure shows the diagrammatic representation of the cloning process:

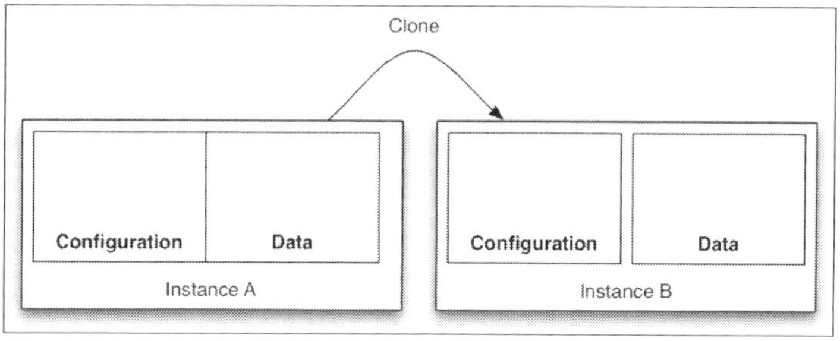

> A clone results in an almost identical copy of an instance. The target system will be wiped, including any in-progress work. All the tasks will also be overwritten. A clone cannot be undone.

Cloning is performed through the **System Clone** menu in the Application Navigator. Since it is so absolute, it works in conjunction with the ServiceNow Customer Support system, which records and schedules the work appropriately. This gives an opportunity to stop the cloning before it happens. It also ensures that the two instances run the same version of ServiceNow and perform any adjustments appropriately.

> Cloning is accomplished by copying the database using a JDBC connection between the instances. This means that the instances must be able to communicate, so ensure that the IP address restrictions do not block traffic.

Preserving and excluding data

Copying every record without exception between two instances is probably not desirable. Some items, such as email accounts or some properties, are necessarily specific to an instance. In addition, copying email logs to the target instance won't be helpful. So, ServiceNow allows some flexibility regarding which items are copied and what all is preserved, as follows:

- The clone **Exclude Tables** list gives a short list of records that won't be copied from the source to the target. This normally tends to be logging information, but if a table is identified as holding sensitive information, it can be added to this list.
- The clone **Data Preservers** work on the target system. Typically, all tables on the target instance are dropped and emptied before cloning, but if some items should be retained, a Data Preserver will keep them. Items that match a conditional criterion will be kept. For example, CSS colors are often used to identify an instance and this is a way to keep them.

> Unfortunately, hierarchical tables cannot be preserved. This means that **Task** tables cannot be protected against a clone. For this reason, a clone cannot be used as a release technique.

- **Cleanup Scripts** are the final item that run on the target system. These prepare the newly cloned instance for use. This is a great place for any obfuscation to take place. For instance, **Personally Identifiable Information (PII)** could be removed or changed from the Location or User tables.

> A script always disables emails after cloning. Otherwise, scheduled jobs may send out notifications, resulting in mass confusion! Always check the email outbox before enabling emails again.

Using clones effectively

Cloning ensures that two environments are identical, so it is a good idea to make a clone before any configuration work. This ensures that the development instance uses fresh, realistic data for testing and development purposes.

The process to do so is as follows:

1. Clone from production to development.
2. Perform the configuration work.
3. Use Update Sets (or another method, such as Team Development) to migrate the configuration to production.

Using this technique provides us with several great benefits, which are as follows:

- Data used by configuration will be properly synchronized. This ensures that items such as Assignment Rules will reference the data using a `sys_id` that is the same in development and production.
- Testing is more complete and accurate. Using dummy data often doesn't give realistic scenarios as it is often shorter and simpler than real life. For instance, have you tested your new Client Script against a 30-character description or a more realistic 30 KB error log that has been pasted in?
- Development work is focused on real use cases and includes outliers and edge cases. If we consider certain real-world examples, is it right to assume that all users have a first name followed by last name? What about Asian cultures that are often the other way round?
- Optimization strategies can be found through in-depth analysis. Rather than focusing on every scenario, focus on the most used scenario. For example, which Catalog Items are ordered most often? How can they be improved?

> Sometimes it may not be appropriate to use all production data in development. ServiceNow does not typically hold consumer information, but if so, privacy laws may only allow data to be used for the purpose it was supplied. Testing may be excluded from this. In this scenario, consider obfuscating the data to remove sensitive information.

Packaging with the App Creator

The App Creator provides a faster, simpler way to build applications quickly, easily, and with useful defaults. It also gives us a mechanism to package it up, with any associated configuration, possibly to be exported as an Update Set.

> When an application is created, a new entry is made in the Application Picker in the System Menu. This works like an Update Set; when you do a configuration, it gets recorded against that application.

ServiceNow also divides all out-of-the-box functionality into applications, making it easy for you to identify where a record came from. Navigating to **System Applications** > **ServiceNow Applications** lets you view the breakdown.

> Plugins are used to define an out-of-the-box ServiceNow application. They are discussed in more detail later in the chapter.

At the beginning of the book, the App Creator was used to create a container for the Hotel application. However, we only used its capabilities to kick-start part of our application, meaning we created many things (such as tables) manually. Let's review a basic app to see how quickly it can be stood up.

Creating applications quickly

Gardiner Hotels has decided to branch out into gourmet dining. The in-house restaurant is widely acclaimed and is getting busy. Therefore, management has decided that a ServiceNow app will help to manage bookings.

Let's start by creating an application:

1. Navigate to **System Applications** > **Create Application** to start and use the following value:
    - **Name**: `Restaurant`

    When you click outside the **Name** field, the **Menu** and **User** role fields will be automatically populated. The green background means the field has a dynamic creation script, which was first mentioned in *Chapter 1, ServiceNow Foundations*. This means that the reference field will create the **Menu** and the role automatically when the new **Application** record is saved.

2. Click on **Submit** to create the application record:

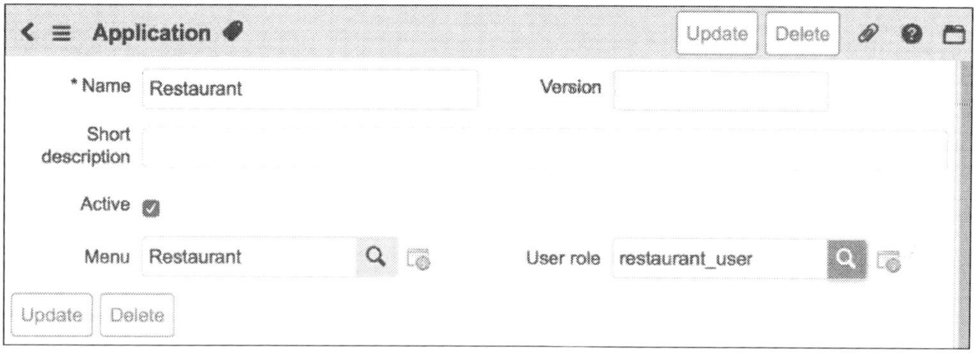

    The form provides a series of Related Lists that make it very easy to add something to this application.

3. Next, click on **New** that is next to the **Table** Related List and use the following value:
    - **Label**: `Booking`

    The **Name**, **User role**, and the **Add module to menu** field should be auto-populated.

    Before saving, note the **Table Columns** embedded Related List. This provides a very fast way to create fields. The only required entry in a Table Column is the **Column label** field. All the other fields will be defaulted: **Type** will be a string and **Max length** will be 40 characters. Try this out by entering the following values in the specific fields:
    - **Column label**: `Guest`; **Type**: `Reference`; **Reference**: `Guest`
    - **Column label**: `When`; **Type**: `Date/Time`

- **Column label**: `Party size`; **Type**: `Integer`
- **Column label**: `Special requests`; **Max length**: `100`

After putting in the preceding values, you will see something in the following lines:

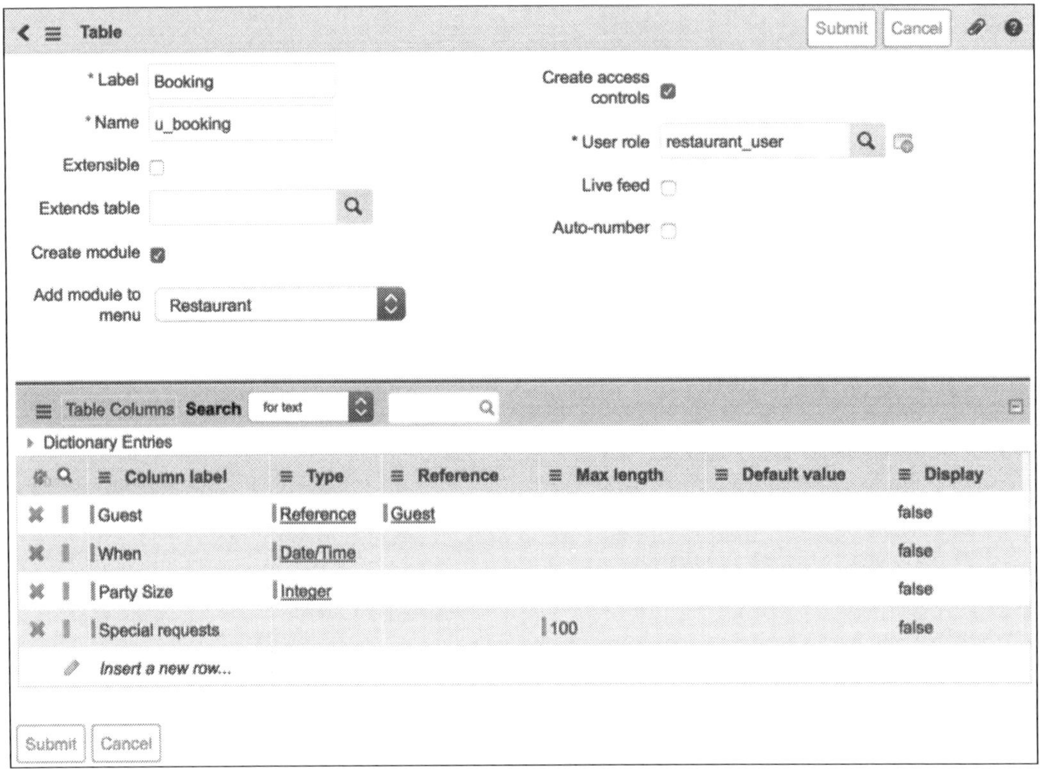

4. Click on **Submit**; the table and the fields will be created.

> At the bottom of the **Table** record, note the automatically created Access Control Rules that give the default roles of create, read, write, and delete access to the record. These can be easily edited.

5. Finally, navigate to **Restaurant** > **Bookings** to see the list and click on **New** to see the form, and enter a record into it as follows:

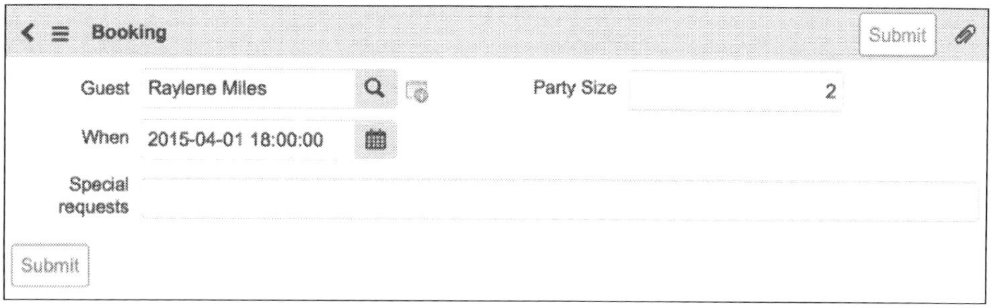

In only a few moments, a new, functioning application has been created that is virtually ready for use. The restaurant manager can record all his or her bookings in a single place. In addition, since this is on the ServiceNow platform, its powerful list features make the creation of filters and initiating searches very easy!

Exporting an application to an Update Set

Once an application is built, it is likely that you will want to move it to another instance. To do this, the platform can export it to an Update Set. This copies all the configuration associated with the application and, optionally, the data in the tables too. The **Publish to Update Set...** UI Action starts the process.

- The configuration associated with an Application is listed in the **All Files** Related list. The latest version of these files is exported.

> Exporting an application at regular intervals is a good idea because this gives a snapshot of the configuration at that time.

- If the **Include data** checkbox is ticked, then any records in the tables that are associated with the application (up to a maximum of 1,000) are also copied into the Update Set. This is really useful for providing test or example data, and it is a lot like the out-of-the-box data that is provided with many ServiceNow applications. In the preceding example, any records in the **Booking** table would be included into the Update Set.

> Note that the referenced data won't be included. If a Booking record contains a reference to the Guest table, then the Guest record will not be included.

Versioning records

Whenever a change is made, ServiceNow records it in two places: the **Customer Updates** [`sys_update_xml`] table, which stores it for Update Sets and the **Update Versions** [`sys_update_version`] table, which stores it for the App Creator and Team Development. Both are superficially similar; they contain the entire contents of the record, which is serialized in XML. This allows you to see who made a change, when it was done, and what they did, much like the **Audit** table. However, the way each table handles multiple changes is very different.

> The **Customer Updates** table used to be the only place where the configuration was stored. The Update Versions table is a more recent interpretation of the functionality. Update Sets are widely used, and they indeed dovetail with the App Creator; so, the Customer Updates table continues to serve its original function.

The following actions are performed when changes are introduced in a record:

- The latest version of a record is stored in an Update Set. When a record is changed, the currently selected Update Set is updated with the new version. Only one entry per Update Set is assumed in the **Customer Updates** table.
- Every change to a record is stored in the **Update Versions** table. This makes it more similar to the **Audit** table. This allows a script to be restored to an earlier version, without the need to rollback an entire Update Set. The **Audit** table is described in more detail in *Chapter 8, Diagnosing ServiceNow – Knowing What Is Going On*.

Capturing configuration

Both Update Sets and the App Creator capture configurations. As an administrator makes the changes, each one monitors records of the work and saves them for analysis and transportation to another instance.

However, there are differences in how each of the functionalities react and where and how the data is stored. In the following table, a container refers to either an Update Set or an app.

Functionality	**Update Sets**	**App Creator**
Stores a copy of the record each time it is altered	Yes, in serialized XML, in the **Customer Update** [`sys_update_xml`] table.	Yes, in serialized XML, in the **Update Versions** [`sys_update_version`] table.

Functionality	Update Sets	App Creator
Stores metadata for the record	No.	Yes, in the **Application File** [sys_app_file] table.
Contains information about relationships between tables (such that UI Policy Actions are related to UI Policy)	No.	Yes, in the **Application File Types** [sys_app_file_type] table. The platform will prompt a user to associate a record with the correct application, if possible. Note that this table should not be modified.
Stores different versions of the same record in different containers	Yes. Two versions of the same record can be stored in two Update Sets.	No. A record can only be associated with a single Application via **Application File**.
Moving the configuration between containers	Yes. The correct Update Set must be selected and the record "touched". Editing **Customer Update** is not recommended.	Yes. The Application File may be altered to move it to a different Application. The context menu of every record contains a link to **Application File**.
Captures changes to an application	Yes. But only the specific configuration changes.	Yes. All associated configurations are exported every time. This can also include data.

> In the Fuji release of ServiceNow, the Application File table has been moved to `sys_metadata`. Fuji contains many more functions that are related to applications, such as protection policies and scoping.

Synchronizing with Team Development

Update Sets and the App Creator rely on the administrator to identify a container that holds the configuration. In contrast, Team Development compares the current instance with another and determines the differences between them. Changes from the remote system can be pulled down and applied, or your changes can be pushed to it, making it similar to source control systems such as Git or **Concurrent Versions System** (**CVS**).

Having a parent

The first step in Team Development is to identify the parent instance.

Typically, the instances are organized into a hierarchy. Every instance is set to have a single parent, with production at the top of the tree. A particular instance may have multiple children.

This hierarchy, or promotion chain, shows where the configuration is moved. Most customers have the following three instances, and Team Development is typically configured to reflect these relationships:

- **Prod** (short for production) contains the currently in use functionality. This is the stable version.
- **Test** contains the next version, undergoing testing. This may be called a beta.
- **Dev** (short for development) contains a future version. This is often of alpha quality, and it's incomplete.

This workflow of these instances is diagrammatically represented in the following figure:

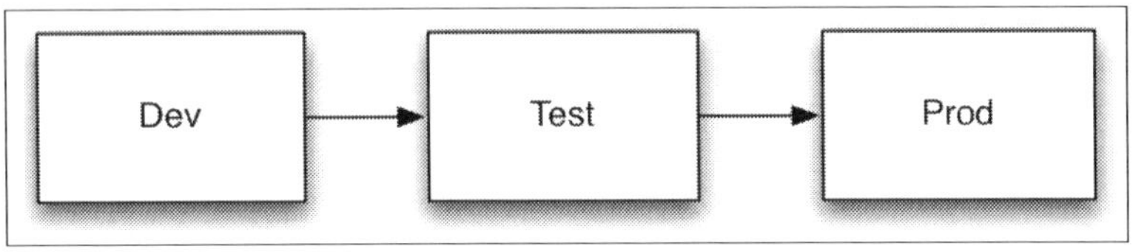

> The typical instance hierarchy is described in more detail later in this chapter. The development instance is the child of the testing system, which in turn is the child of production.

Comparing instances

The core of Team Development is **Instance Comparison**. At its heart, it compares the **Update Versions** table of two instances. Most often, this action occurs with the parent, but you can choose to compare your instance with any other instance.

You can do this by navigating to **Team Development** > **Remote Instance** as shown in the following screenshot. Then, populate the instance URL and the credentials of an admin account. The **Compare to Local Instance** UI Action will start the process.

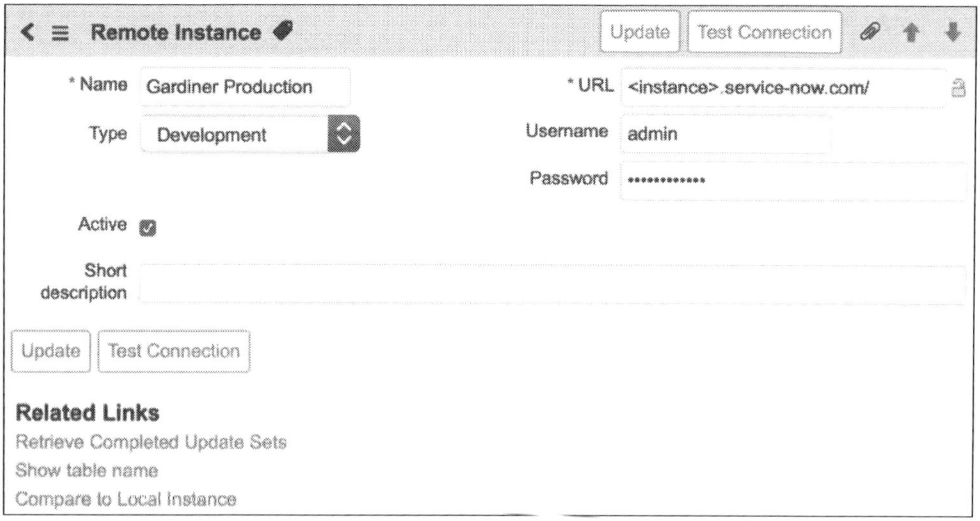

Once the two systems have been compared, any differences are flagged up in two lists: **On Remote and not on Local** and **On Local and not on Remote**.

> The local instance refers to the one you are currently working on, while remote is the one you are comparing with, typically the parent.

The **Instance Comparison** record is shown in the following screenshot:

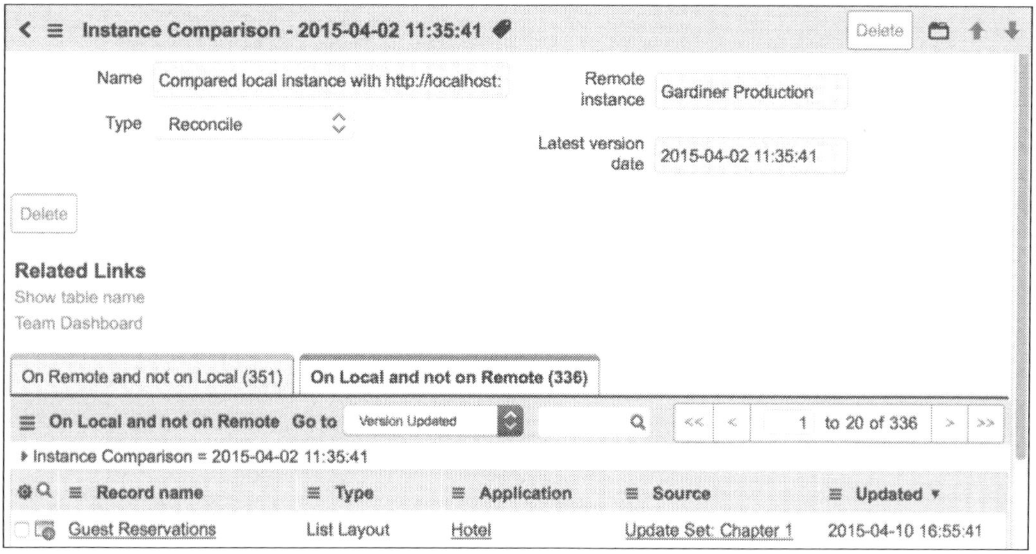

In this example, the local instance has made 336 configuration changes, as shown in the **On Local and not on Remote** Related List. These could be pushed to the remote instance.

The remote instance has 351 configuration changes. These can be pulled down into the local instance.

The Related Lists provide two UI Actions that are accessible through the context and list menus; these are as follows:

- **Load This Change**: This will bring the single record into the local instance. It will work for new records that have not yet been seen on the local instance or for a record that has already been shared between the two instances.
- **Compare to Current**: This will show the field-by-field differences between the remote and local instances in the same way as when you compare two local versions.

> If Update Sets go wrong, performing an instance comparison is a great way to investigate the reason for it. Looking at the differences between a working test instance and a production instance that has a few issues can be very instructive.

Using the Team Dashboard

The Team Dashboard wraps instance comparison in an interface that makes it easier to understand where changes are being made and how they are being migrated through the instance hierarchy. The custom page, as shown in the following screenshot, can be found by navigating to **Team Development** > **Team Dashboard**:

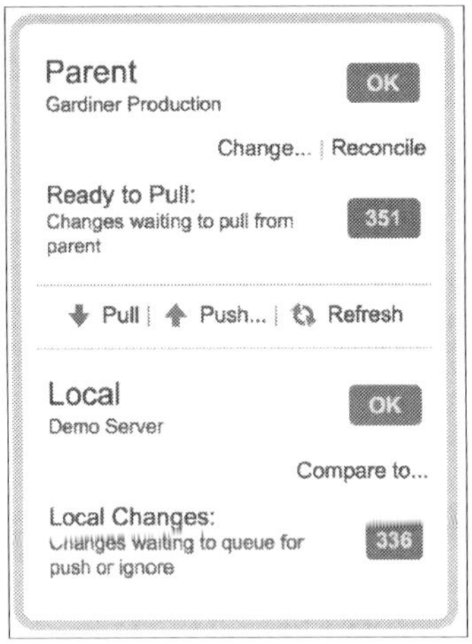

The control panel shows the status of the local and the parent (remote) instances.

When the parent of an instance is changed, the platform will download the remote Update Versions table and compare it with the Update Versions table on the local instance. This instance comparison is used to know which configuration records are different between the parent and the local instance.

A reconciliation can be done manually at any time, but it is normally only needed if the instance loses track of the parent's changes (for instance, if the parent is cloned over) since it can put a high load on both instances.

The control panel contains the actions—**Push**, and **Pull**—that can occur once the differences have been identified. Each action is logged and the results are recorded in the Pushes and Pulls module in the Team Development Application Menu.

Pulling changes

If the parent has changes that the child does not, the **Pull** action will update the child. This ensures that the child is working on the latest version of any scripts, security rules, or other configurations.

[A Pull action must always be done before a Push action.]

Team Development assumes that the parent instance is controlled, that is, all the configuration there is supposed to be present. Since the child instance should contain the latest version of the configuration, items that can be pulled must have been built elsewhere and should be incorporated within it immediately to maintain a consistent environment.

Therefore, pulling changes in Team Development is similar to pulling an Update Set, but it will involve all changes, and is more aggressive in applying them. The updates will be applied immediately, and presents the errors afterwards. The diagrammatic representation of the workflow is shown in the following figure:

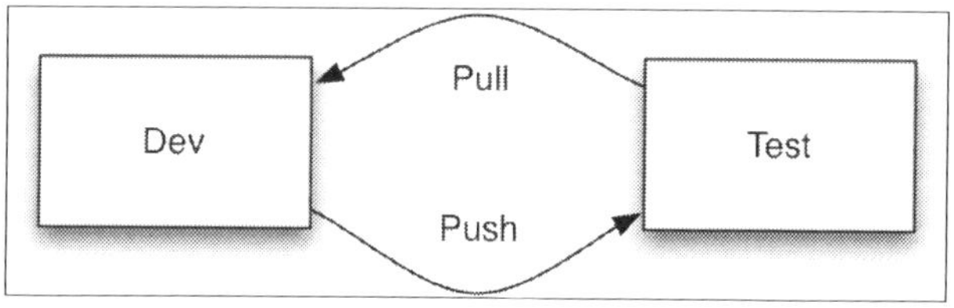

> As discussed in the next section, you must choose what should be pushed, but you'll get everything in a pull. This is because you only want to push a configuration that is ready. However, the Test instance should not contain anything that Dev does not have, so a pull will grab it all.

Dealing with collisions

A collision occurs when both the local and the parent instances have changed the same record in different ways.

The System Administrators of the local instance must determine which version they should keep. This can be achieved through the **Collisions** Related List on the **Team Dashboard**. Everything must be resolved with a decision before a Push (or another Pull) can occur. This puts the onus on the local instance to make the right decision about whether to keep their configuration or have it overwritten by the parent's version.

The **Resolve Collision** Related List in the Team Dashboard contains a **Resolve Collision** UI Action that is available in the context menu to compare the differences. Alternatively, the **Use Pulled Version** or **Use Local Version** options in the **Actions** menu can be used to make a bulk choice.

> If collisions are detected, a decision must be made before any further pushes or pulls can occur.

Pushing updates

Team Development assumes that configuration work will happen in the local instance. A push will send this configuration to the parent instance. For example, a bug in a Business Rule may have been fixed in the local instance, but pushing the change will alter the Business Rule in the parent too.

A pull is always performed before a push. This ensures that conflicts are resolved locally, in contrast to Update Sets where the target instance manages any collisions.

The **Local Changes** list, as shown in the following screenshot, gives all the records that could be pushed to the parent, just like the **On Local and not on Remote** Related List after an instance comparison:

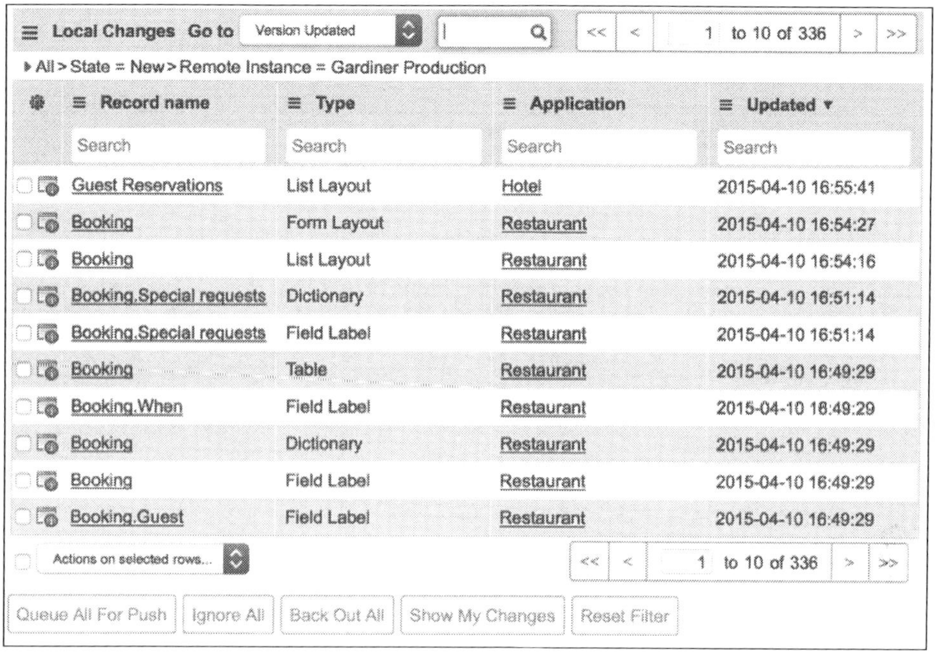

For each record, a decision must be made: **Push** or **Ignore**. If a decision is not made, the **Local Change** will stay in the queue.

Push will queue it up for transfer so that it is ready to overwrite the parent instance. Most often, the majority will be pushed up stream, so the **Queue All For Push** UI Action will act on the entire list of filtered records.

> Use the filtering capabilities built into ServiceNow to select exactly what you want to change. The **Source** and **Application** fields are useful to select the right records.

Ignore marks the Application File appropriately, noting this as a local change only. This may be an experimentation or a configuration that only applies to the local instance. Once it is marked as such, further updates to this record will not trigger a Local Change entry.

Working with multiple development instances

In a typical three-level hierarchy, where there is a maximum of one child and parent for each instance, it should never, in theory, be necessary to pull changes. All configuration work should be undertaken in the child instance, and only pushing should be used to promote new configuration through the chain. (Theory often does not work out though!)

However, in a multichild environment, there may be parallel working where administrators (or teams of administrators) have their own instance. This scenario is represented in the following figure:

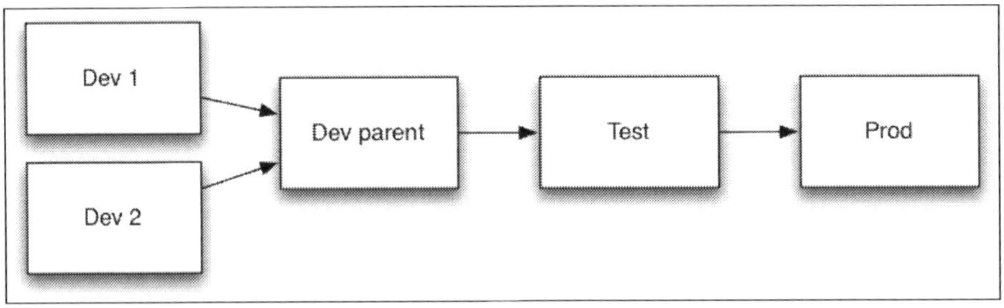

In the preceding figure, there are five instances, two of which are dedicated to doing configuration work (**Dev 1** and **Dev 2**). **Dev parent** is the parent of both; so it contains the amalgamation of **Dev 1** and **Dev 2**.

In practice, if **Dev 1** pushes new configuration to **Dev parent**, **Dev 2** will see those changes as items that must be pulled. This ensures that both the configuration instances work on the same code base.

Regular pushes and pulls will reduce the number of conflicts that could occur. Conflicts are more likely to happen if **Dev 1** and **Dev 2** work on exactly the same configuration, such as a single Business Rule or Script Include. It is good practice to push and pull regularly to keep this manageable.

> Having two teams working on the same items will cause extra work. So, ensure that all the teams are aware of what each team is doing!

Deciding between Update Sets and Team Development

Team Development works on a comparison process rather than packaging up configuration. This makes it more reliable than Update Sets since it avoids the possibility of having the wrong configuration item in the wrong package.

However, this means that the configuration is less reusable. Update Sets are often used to transport the configuration between multiple instances, which is something that Team Development cannot do easily.

Instead, you can leverage the strength of both, by doing the following:

- Use Update Sets when a single, self-contained package of configurations is desired, and you want to share it across many instances
- Use Team Development as part of a release strategy across a series of consistent, well understood hierarchical instances.

Sharing with Share

ServiceNow customers are rather creative. The platform has been used to build some amazing custom apps, useful tweaks, and powerful utilities. To help everyone benefit from ideas from the platform, the ServiceNow Share portal is designed to bring them all together in a very accessible manner. You can visit the ServiceNow Share portal at: `https://share.servicenow.com/`.

Any customer can submit an Update Set (which is possibly exported from the App Creator) to be stored on the **Share** portal. This is then available for other customers to download and use as they wish. Some of the more popular items on Share are as follows:

- **Facility4U** is a facilities management system
- **Dynamic Knowledge Search** gives a means to automatically search the Knowledge Base
- **PDF Document Generator** allows you to create more custom PDF documents from a record by using a HTML template
- **File Builder FTP** exports data from the instance and uses a MID server to save it on an FTP server
- **UAT Application** manages the users and their tasks when it tests your ServiceNow application

Content that is shared this way is not supported or vetted by ServiceNow. Some basic scans of the content do take place to encourage good practice, but any applications that are installed should be understood, especially if they are to be relied on.

Adding more with plugins

Every ServiceNow instance includes many hundreds of plugins. Each contains a different part of the ServiceNow system; some provide licensable functionality, some provide integrations or additional add-ons, and some give core platform capabilities. Together, they provide all of the native functionality that ServiceNow provides.

There is a wide variety of capabilities contained within plugins. This short selection gives an indication of what is available:

- **Coaching Loops** let your staff review how a task has been completed by using an automated framework
- **Email Filters** help you to delete spam automatically and sort the rest into separate mailboxes
- **Insert Multiple Web Service** gives you an extra method in SOAP messages to insert more than one record in a single call
- **Restore Deleted Records** stores deleted records as serialized XML, letting you undo some mistakes
- **Self Service Password Reset** allows users to reset their ServiceNow password if they forget it

To see the available plugins, navigate to **System Definition** > **Plugins**.

> The ServiceNow wiki maintains a full list of plugins at `https://wiki.servicenow.com/?title=List_of_Plugins`.

Activating plugins

Some of the plugins are activated by default when the platform is first started. Some include the ITSM applications or contain the core capabilities of the platform, while others require activation. Of these, a System Administrator can activate some plugins, while others must be turned on using an account with the `maint` role—a privilege that is generally reserved for ServiceNow personnel. It could be possible that one of these plugins will enable functionality that is licensable separately, or the plugin may cause functionality changes that need to be controlled. To enable the plugins, contact ServiceNow's Customer Support team.

> The activation of a plugin is not recorded within an Update Set. If a plugin is necessary for some configuration, ensure that it is manually enabled before any Update Sets are applied.

Plugins can be considered very similar to Update Sets. They consist of a package of serialized XML data files that are stored on the filesystem of the instance. Once a plugin is activated, the data is copied into the appropriate records of the instance database. A plugin may contain additional tables and fields, Business Rules, application menus, or any other record, just like the applications that a System Administrator can make. A diagrammatic representation of the plugin files and the database records is shown in the following figure:

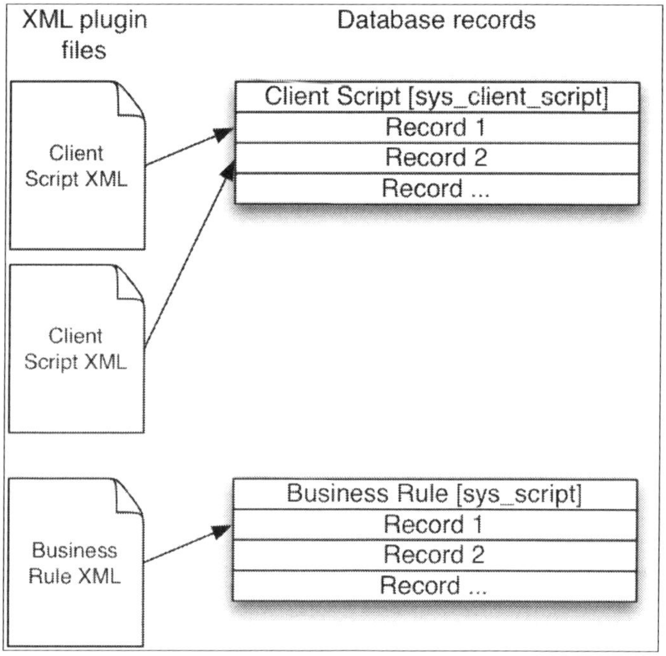

> Activating a plugin creates database records. They do not alter what the core Java platform can do. However, a plugin may activate latent functionality that is not otherwise exposed.

Choosing the right plugin

Since there are so many plugins, it can be difficult to know which are useful. It is tempting to turn them all on, just like that, but there are some disadvantages with this:

- Once a plugin is enabled, it cannot be turned off. It is a decision that cannot be reversed.
- Some plugins affect existing functionality. This may be an upgrade to an existing app, but you cannot rollback if you don't like the changes.

> Often you can set a property to deactivate functionality, but you won't be able to remove it entirely.

- Plugins often have demo data. This is very helpful to understand what the plugin does, but it may create data that you weren't expecting.
- Enabling lots of plugins may make areas cluttered, such as the Application Navigator. It is difficult to navigate through lots of options that you don't actually need.

The only way to reverse the effects of a plugin activation is to arrange a clone or ask **Customer Support** to restore the instance from the previous night's backup. Be cautious about what plugins you activate.

Instead, try out new plugins in a sandpit environment or be prepared to clone over your instance if it doesn't work out.

Upgrading ServiceNow

ServiceNow has a quite unique upgrade capability due to its cloud-based, single-tenant architecture. Releases happen more frequently in ServiceNow than boxed software, with new functionality being released around once or twice a year. However, unlike multitenancy architectures, the customer is more in control of when and how often each upgrade occurs.

The release roadmap and methodology that ServiceNow follows is constantly being refined, but as of 2015, the following strategy applies:

Category	Example name	Contains	Frequency
Feature release	Calgary, Dublin, Eureka, Fuji, Geneva	This contain new functionality and many fixes	Twice a year
Patch release	Patch 1	This contains a bundle of bug fixes.	As needed
Hotfixes	Hotfix 1	This solves a specific bug or issue.	As needed

> The wiki at `http://wiki.servicenow.com/?title=Release_Notes` contains a list of all the versions of ServiceNow, but you will need to create a free account to view the information.

Customers can schedule an upgrade by using the self-service functionality in the Hi Customer Service system, or customer support can recommend a particular patch or hotfix to solve an issue. Some releases need to be authorized by ServiceNow to ensure that they are appropriate, but otherwise a customer has the choice about when to select an upgrade.

ServiceNow does reserve the right to force instances to upgrade, primarily if there is a security issue.

> Starting up an instance for the first time will enable many default plugins, and these plugins may change between instances. Upgrading an instance does not typically enable any feature plugins. This means that an instance upgraded from Calgary to Dublin will have a different set of enabled plugins to one that starts on Dublin.

Understanding upgrades

Since ServiceNow is a Java application, it is compiled in a WAR file. This is essentially a large compressed file that contains all of the resources that are necessary to run the ServiceNow platform. Upgrading or patching involves applying a new WAR file to the instance in question. This updates the two core areas that make up a ServiceNow instance:

- The Java class files that are the bedrock of the platform
- The XML files that make up the plugins

Once the WAR file has been expanded, the XML files are parsed. Each of these XML files represents at least one database record. So, the platform copies the information into the database. For example, if a ServiceNow developer has changed or updated a Business Rule, the XML file will contain the new code and upon upgrade, the platform will update the record in the Business Rule table, only if the customer has not edited it.

> The upgrade process, and how it affects configuration, is discussed in much more detail over the next few sections.

ServiceNow has automated the upgrade process, embedding it into the instance itself. Every hour, a Scheduled Job contacts an upgrade controller and asks it whether there is a new version of the software for the instance. If there is, the WAR file is identified, downloaded, unzipped, and applied. These items are monitored in **System Diagnostics** > **Upgrade Monitor**, and also under the **Upgrade History** and **Upgrade Log** modules.

Configuration and Customization

ServiceNow provides a great deal of functionality. However, the platform is also designed to be adaptable to specific requirements that are not available out of the box. The platform and any ServiceNow apps can be configured or customized to make them work as desired. These functionalities have been explained as follows:

- **Configuration** is generally defined as the addition of new records. It's a new Business Rule that updates a new field, which in turn triggers a new Graphical Workflow.
- **Customization** is accepted to be the alteration of existing, out-of-the-box records or those provided through an upgrade. For example, if the way in which SLAs are calculated is not the same as your business, then the Script Include can be edited.

> Both configuration and customization happen in the same way through the standard interface. The only difference is if you are creating new, or editing something provided by ServiceNow.

During an upgrade, the platform will avoid changing any configuration or customization. This is by design because simply overwriting all the changes may undo your hard work and mean that the platform no longer meets your needs.

Knowing areas of risk

ServiceNow provides enormous flexibility. Almost everything about the platform can be edited and changed. However, it is recommended that you avoid customizations when it is possible. An upgrade will avoid overwriting them, but you may miss out on improvements and bug fixes. The customization of a particular record is, therefore, referred to as the System Administrator **owning** the record. This refers to how the System Administrator, rather than ServiceNow, is responsible for the maintenance of this item.

> Some configuration and customization will result in disadvantages, such as maintenance or performance, as mentioned throughout the book. There is no single rule to follow, other than understanding how the platform works so that decisions can be taken with all the available facts.

Owning some areas are very low risk. It is expected that the System Administrator would want to control these items by performing the following steps:

- Data, such as users and groups. It would not be appropriate to keep the demo user data, such as Fred Luddy, in your instance.
- Adding fields, forms, lists, and UI Actions. Within reasonable limits, you can add as many fields to a form as you wish and name them as you like. Adding many hundreds though will result in slower rendering times, both on the server and on the client browser.
- Adding scripts, such as Business Rules and Client Scripts, is a very common activity. However, inefficient scripting, such as performing synchronous calls from the client to the instance, will result in performance issues.

Other areas involve more risk. Consider these actions carefully:

- Editing existing scripts. Any scripts edited by the System Administrator will be kept after an upgrade; however, other areas of the platform may assume that a script works in a particular way or a function returns a particular range of values. After any upgrade, be sure to test it carefully.
- Performing DOM manipulation in Client Scripts assumes that the DOM will remain the same after an upgrade. Ensure that code is written in such a way that a script will "fail safe" if it does not.
- Editing existing UI Macros and UI Pages is not recommended since it changes how the platform renders the interface. UI Macros and UI Pages are discussed further in *Chapter 10, Making ServiceNow Beautiful with CMS and Jelly*.

- Using package calls on the instance. *Chapter 6, Exchanging Data – Import Sets, Web Services, and Other Integrations*, discussed how MID server scripts could use Java packages. It is currently possible to access Java classes on the instance, depending on the version, but this is strongly discouraged.
- Later versions of ServiceNow, starting with Fuji, make it harder or impossible to perform some customizations to better protect the platform and ensure upgrades are seamless.

Applying upgrades

When an instance receives a new WAR file, it starts to upgrade. It looks in each XML file to find what record it represents and checks it against the **Customer Updates** [`sys_update_xml`] table.

> The **Customer Updates** table is discussed in more detail in the Update Sets section. An entry is made in this table each time you perform a configuration, such as editing a Business Rule or changing a form.

If there is no entry in the **Customer Updates** table, then the action in the upgrade is applied. This could be an **insert**, **update**, or **delete**. No entry means ServiceNow owns the record, and it will be kept 'out of the box' even if the upgrade means 'out of the box' is changing.

If an entry does exist, the upgrade process will do a little more work. In most cases, the platform will **skip** the update: no changes will be made to the record, and things will carry on working as they were.

However, the platform will still determine what has been changed by the System Administrator. If only excluded fields have changed, then the upgrade process will still change the record. The **Active** field is an excluded field.

For example, consider a System Administrator editing an out-of-the-box Business Rule:

- If the **Script** field was changed, the platform will keep it as the System Administrator configured it.
- If the **Active** field was unchecked on the Business Rule (and that was the only field that was changed by the System Administrator), then the Business Rule will be updated in the upgrade. The Active flag will remain unchecked, but the **Script** field (and the other fields) will be changed to represent the upgrade.

> For more information about this, check out the wiki at `http://wiki.servicenow.com/?title=Administering_Update_Sets`.

Most of the time, this is exactly what you want. Consider that you have edited a form's layout to make it look the way you want. You'd be rather annoyed if the upgrade undid your hard work! However, if you didn't use a certain Business Rule, you could deactivate it and still be certain that the code is of the latest version; you could always reactivate it later.

> Checking the **Replace on upgrade** checkbox in the **Application File** will create an entry in the **Customer Updates** table if one did not already exist. However, unchecking it will not change how the platform upgrades.

Reverting customizations and restoring out of the box

To get the latest out of the box updates for a record, the following two methods are available:

- Delete all entries for that record in the **Customer Updates** table. These can be seen as a Related List in the Application File. Navigate to it by using the **Show Application File** option in the menu of the record. This will ensure that on the next and subsequent upgrades, the record will be upgraded. A message will be displayed to confirm your action:

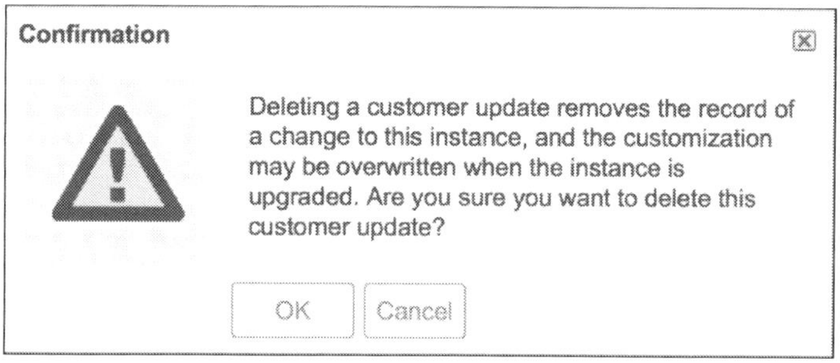

- If the upgrade has already happened, navigate to **System Diagnostics** > **Upgrade History**, select the appropriate upgrade, and in the **Upgrade Details** Related List, find the record that you dealing with. The **Revert to Out-of-the-box** UI Action will be available if the **Disposition** was **Skipped**.

> The **Reapply Changes** button will let you toggle between the customized and out-of-the-boxes versions.

Upgrading instances automatically

It is recommended to be on the latest feature release, or at least within two versions. Each new release contains bug fixes, performance improvements, and new capabilities, and since each new functionality tends to be enabled through plugins and properties, there are few disadvantages.

Without other instructions, ServiceNow upgrades subproduction instances, then production instances automatically after a new version has been released. This happens in a phased rollout basis, with the Customer Support team sending out email notifications to their technical contacts ahead of time.

Of course, as with any complex software, changes must be carefully controlled. Many customers want to specify a particular date and time for an upgrade and to only upgrade when they are ready. The ServiceNow terminology for stopping automatic upgrades is **pinning** by which the instance is pinned to a specific version. You can contact Customer Support to pin your instance.

> Even if your instance is pinned, it may be upgraded if ServiceNow deems it necessary, such as for security or other reasons. However, the Customer Support team will contact you before this happens.

Managing instances

Making the most effective use of your allocated instances means understanding and implementing an effective plan. Following a simple set of rules will ensure that the configuration and data is in the right place at the right time. The following diagram shows the typical actions to a customer's instances.

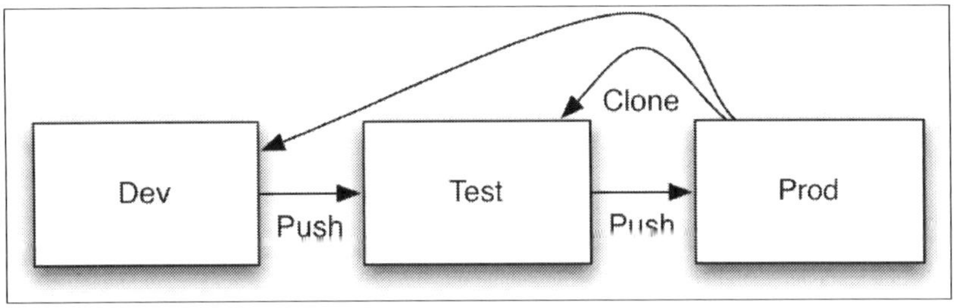

Managing a complex system with multiple stakeholders and business critical applications is challenging. However, by leveraging the platform in the right way, it can be made easier to deal with ServiceNow. These tips will help:

- Use a three-tier hierarchy. Ensure that you know what activities will be carried out on each instance and who will be carrying them out.
    - **Prod** is the production system. The Requesters submit work while Fulfillers carry out the process to get it done. There's no tester access and very limited System Administrator access to ensure stability.
    - **Test** tries out new functionality before it is put into production. The instance is used by a testing team. They carry out regression and new functional testing. There's limited System Administrator access.
    - **Dev** is where new functionality is configured. This is used by the System Administrators.
- Limit customizations, and test thoroughly if any are needed.
- Use ServiceNow to manage ServiceNow. Software Release applications such as Scrum let you document requirements and manage their implementation within the platform.
- Be nimble. Release new functionality frequently rather than storing it up for months.
- Clone as frequently as possible from Prod to Dev and Test. This should proceed any development cycle. This ensures that you have great testing and development data.
- Use Team Development to push configuration upstream.
- Upgrade frequently and take advantage of the fixes and new features in the products.

Summary

Configuration is independent. It only affects a single instance, unless you decide to copy it elsewhere. ServiceNow provides many tools to let a System Administrator share configuration (and customization) and data with other instances.

Data can be exported and imported from a list into an **XML** container. This is often very useful when moving small, discrete data chunks from one instance to another instance. No validation or automation occurs when you import XML.

Update Sets take the same thought and automates it. An Update Set collects the configuration that you do and stores it in a named collection. This can be exported or transferred to another system, where the configuration will be replayed, applying the same changes automatically. **Team Development** provides a more structured way to push and pull the configuration to a predefined parent instance.

The **App Creator** provides a quick starting point for new configurations. It also provides another neat way to bundle your work together, giving you a single, manageable place to understand what is happening. The configuration can also be exported out to an Update Set, which will act as a portable, self-contained store of your work.

In addition to the configuration work that a System Administrators does, ServiceNow provides regular **platform upgrades**. These can range from minor fixes and improvements to new applications and a brand new user interface. In many ways, upgrading an instance is straightforward, but it still needs thought and consideration to be successful.

In addition to these targeted changes to an instance, ServiceNow can arrange a complete overwrite of the database with a copy from another instance. **Cloning** is an effective technique to ensure that two systems are exactly alike.

The next chapter describes how the interface can be altered to make it work the way you want. The **Content Management System** (**CMS**) can create a portal, but UI Pages and UI Macros underpin the way the platform displays records throughout the platform. So, configure away!

10

Making ServiceNow Beautiful with CMS and Jelly

ServiceNow is a great platform to manage data. Tools such as Graphical Workflow, Business Rules, and Client Scripts make it easy for you to create a service-management-oriented application that processes information quickly and efficiently. However, function without form makes for an unappealing experience! Many companies have design patterns that their users understand. Taking advantage of this will make your applications much more trustworthy, accessible, and easy to use.

In this chapter, we will examine some of the capabilities in ServiceNow to change the look and feel of ServiceNow and make it work the way you want it to. These include:

- The **Content Management System (CMS)**, which wraps a skin over the logic and data, which is already built into the instance, adding user-friendly menus and extra navigation elements
- Using standard web design technologies, such as **CSS**, to change colors, control text size, and add images
- Adding custom design elements to the ServiceNow interface, such as **GlideDialog** boxes, **decorations** and **contribution** reference icons
- Creating completely custom interfaces with **UI Pages** and **UI Macros**, giving you complete creative freedom

Designing a portal

The CMS in ServiceNow is a custom interface that builds over existing data and logic. All of the chapters so far have concentrated on building the application; the CMS allows you to change how it looks so that you move away from plain forms and lists.

This means that a CMS should not bring any new functionality to your application. Instead, this is intended to provide a new way for requesters to access capability that has already been built. The Hotel application for Gardiner Hotels includes a way to raise Maintenance tasks and create reservations. Wouldn't it be great if the requesters (the hotel guests) could do this themselves?

Giving self-service access

Technology has been used to improve the accessibility of many services. ATMs let you withdraw cash whenever you want, and telephone calls no longer need to go through an operator. Similarly, we want to let our hotel guests communicate with us anytime, day or night. Of course, Gardiner Hotels has some of the best reception staff in the business, but we want to make it easy to reserve a room while being in the middle of a conference call.

Understanding the options

As discussed in *Chapters 4* and *7*, a requester is someone without a role that asks for some work to be done on their behalf. Having a **Self-Service** interface lets those requesters browse the **Service Catalog**, see the status of existing tasks, or create new requests in their own time.

There are two interfaces built into the platform to allow a requester to submit new tasks:

- The first is the standard user interface, with the Application Navigator, lists, and forms. To submit a request, navigate to `https://<instance>.service-now.com/`, substitute `<instance>` with your instance name, and log in using a user account with no roles. Alternatively, you can use impersonation to view a requester account—Joe Employee is the out-of-the-box example shown in the following screenshot:

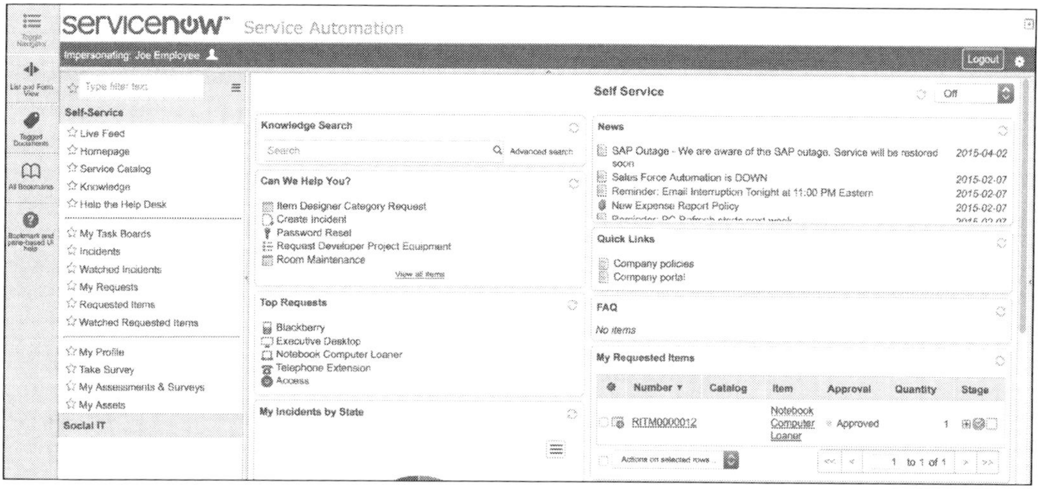

- The second is the CMS interface that uses a more graphic, user-friendly interface. To submit a request, navigate to `https://<instance>.service-now.com/ess/`. If you are already using impersonation, simply change the URL to include `/ess/`. The following screenshot shows the CMS interface:

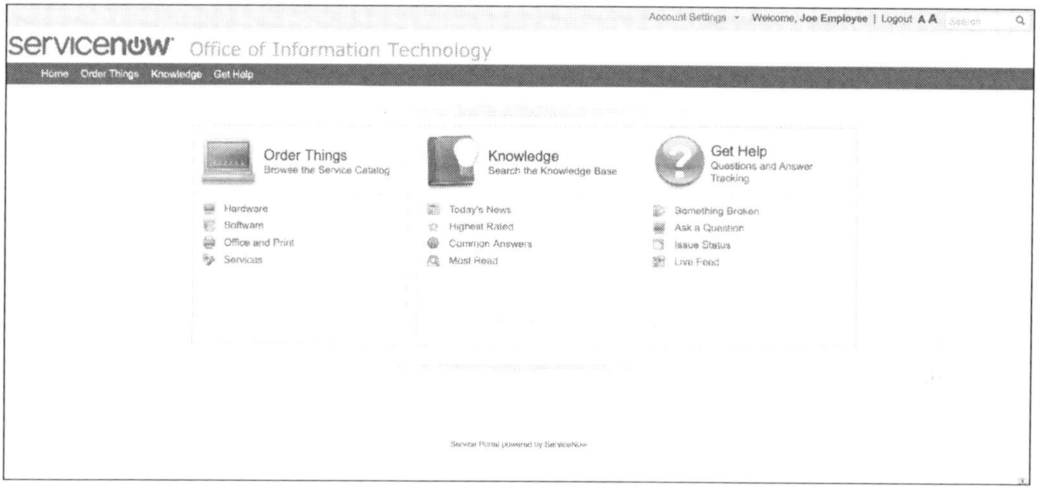

Although the two look quite different, they have several common threads:

- The **Service Catalog** can be accessed by navigating to **Self Service** > **Service Catalog** in the standard interface or through **Order Things** in the CMS layout
- Open Incidents can be viewed, either by navigating to **Self Service** > **Incidents** or **Issue Status** below the **Get Help** menu
- **Knowledge Base** articles can be accessed by navigating to **Self Service** > **Knowledge** or the **Knowledge** link in the middle of the CMS page
- Items such as the user's name, the logout button, and even the global search field are present in both interfaces

Things look more familiar when you navigate into these items. Try to navigate to the **Hardware** category within the **Service Catalog** in both interfaces. Alternatively, try viewing the list of open Incidents. Although the information surrounding the data is different, the items to be ordered and the Incident list look identical.

> Since the CMS portal is aimed at non-technical users, its language is simpler and friendly. The **Service Catalog** and **Incident** ITIL terms have been replaced with **Order Things** and **Get Help**. However, the functionality that they refer to is the same.

All users can use either interface. A user with the admin role can log into the CMS portal and use the functionality that is visible to them. However, the user is still an admin. Since there are no separate security policies for a CMS portal, an admin user will be able to view any record they wish, while a requester would be able to view only their own record. While the CMS might change the look and feel of your application, everything else will stay the same—from Business Rules to Access Controls.

> The portal does understand roles. If you log into the portal with the admin role, a hidden option will become available in the Account Settings menu next to your name in the top-right corner. The CMS Administration pages give some extra hints and tips on how to create a CMS site.
>
> In theory, you could build a complex portal in this manner that would allow your fulfillers to do their work in a CMS interface. However, it would involve a lot of work!

Choosing a portal

Building a Self-Service portal does not necessitate the use of the CMS. While it provides a more graphic interface, with the ability to create a custom look and feel, the standard interface is quicker to configure. Your decision to use the CMS or just rely upon the standard interface generally rests upon who the target audience is.

If your **Requester** user base is **relatively technical**, they may appreciate the **standard interface**. Power users often want lots of options and an interface that lets them find them without fuss. For example, using the filter text in the Application Navigator means that modules can be found quickly by a user. Additionally, often little effort is required to configure the standard interface, beyond creating a few modules and validating the security rules.

Since a **CMS** can create almost any look and feel, it is often more appropriate for **non-technical users** who have no training. The language and layout should be obvious and easy to follow, and it should focus on the most common use cases. Using style guidelines from an intranet or a corporate website will make the portal more familiar and easier to use.

If a CMS is desired, the next step is to decide how to approach it. Do you want to take the example site and change it according to your needs? Or, do you want to build a completely customized interface, beginning from a blank sheet of paper? Consider both the options carefully:

- Changing the out of the box portal is useful if you want a simple, menu-driven system with the three basic ITSM functions. Alternatively, consider using the numerous examples on ServiceNow Share to kick-start your project.

> While it may be appealing to use the example site, it will quickly become frustrating if you do more than the basics of changing colors, logos, and Service Catalog categories.

- Beginning with a clean slate enables you to build the design that you need. While this involves more upfront work, it often becomes easier than constantly editing another design. You may also want to use more modern design techniques such as Angular or Bootstrap, which become possible when you build it your self.

This chapter concentrates on creating a new CMS portal. The concepts and techniques are still relevant if you decide to base your design on the example site.

Building a portal with CMS

The CMS uses standard web technologies to create a user-friendly and accessible interface. HTML and CSS are used to define layouts, style content, and display information.

> This chapter assumes that you have a working knowledge of CSS and HTML. There are many resources on the Internet that will teach the basics.
>
> The **Mozilla Developer Network** (**MDN**), which can be found at `https://developer.mozilla.org/`, is a great place to start.

A CMS implementation is approached slightly differently than other configurations. Building a portal involves more graphic design than a ServiceNow development. So, the first step often involves building wireframe diagrams that mock up what the site might look like on paper. This generally includes at least two items:

- Deciding what pages are needed and how they will link together
- Deciding what should be on the pages and how they should be laid out

> The adage that *paper is cheap* is helpful when building CMS. Spending time upfront to determine what should be built is a good investment.

Getting the assets

Creating a visually attractive portal usually means that logos and graphics will be required. We asked the design team at Gardiner Hotels for the company logo as well as some icons for the menus. They provided us with a `.zip` file that contained these items, and also informed us that their corporate font is Lucida Grande.

> You can download the example asset pack from `http://www.dasos.com/chs/assets.zip`.

Structuring a site hierarchy

The structure of a CMS portal begins with an entry in the **Site** [`content_site`] table, which is accessible by navigating to **Content Management** > **Sites**. A site defines the URL suffix (like the out-of-the-box `/ess/` extension) and collects a number of **Pages** [`content_page`]. Each page contains an activity, showing a clear organizational strategy. The desired structure for our site is shown in the following figure:

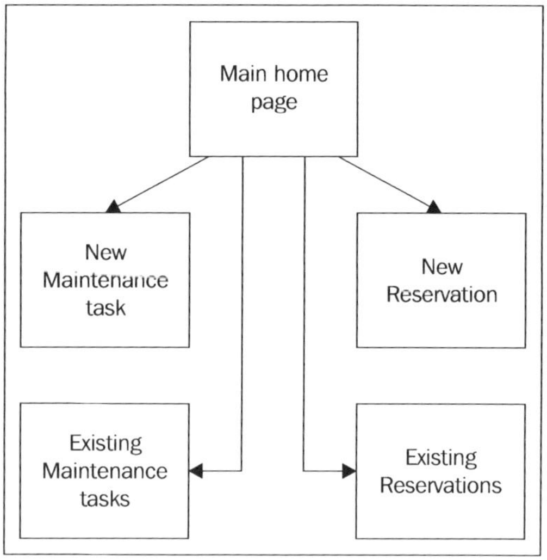

In this example, Hotel is the Site, with the blocks inside representing the Pages. As the connections show, after logging in, the **Main Page** will be shown. A menu allows a user to access more Pages, enabling them to create or view **Reservations** or **Maintenance** tasks.

Designing the Pages

The CMS is a template system at heart. Pages are made up of **blocks**, which can be considered as reusable chunks of functionality. ServiceNow provides many different blocks, such as several types of menus, headers, lists, and areas for content. Of course, you can also create your own! Combining these blocks together is a key element of designing each page.

In order to reduce complexity and keep the portal simple and straightforward, three main blocks are going to be used for each page on Gardiner Hotel's portal: a **header**, containing the Gardiner Hotel's logo and a menu; the **page title**; and the main **content** of the page, which may be the new **Reservation** form or a list of outstanding Maintenance requests. The main page will be a little different, with a large welcome image.

> The blocks that ServiceNow provides can be quite complex. Often, they combine several other blocks or functions to reduce what you need to include. A header block, for instance, can provide a search bar, two menus, a logo, some text, and more!

These blocks must then be arranged on the screen. When creating a page, the System Administrator must choose a **layout**. Each layout contains several **dropzones** where blocks can be put. This process is very similar to how home pages are constructed—choose the desired items and then arrange them on the page.

Gardiner Hotels has a concept of clean efficiency, so a simple layout will suffice. A layout of three sequential blocks on each page will give the structure.

Finalizing the mock-ups

When creating a CMS portal, pictures may be worth more than a thousand words. Create a quick sketch to get a better understanding of what the pages will look like. Putting pen to paper often provides a much clearer idea of what needs to happen. The CMS portal we will create is as follows:

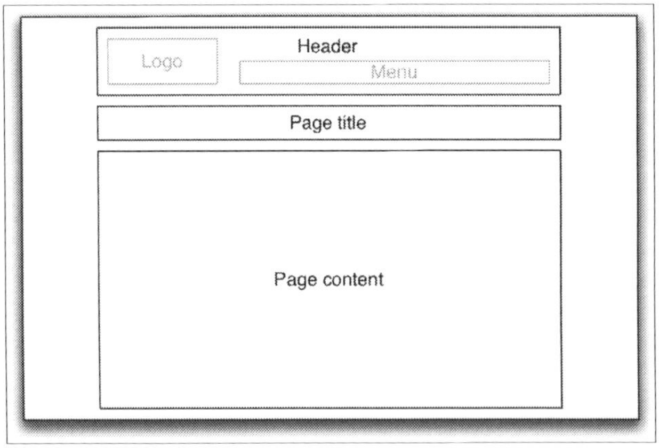

The majority of pages have a header along with a logo and a menu. The page's title sits above the page's content.

The main page provides the same previous header, but with a large, friendly central image instead of a title. The menu block provides quick access to the main functions by using some large icons. The following image shows you want the home page should look like.

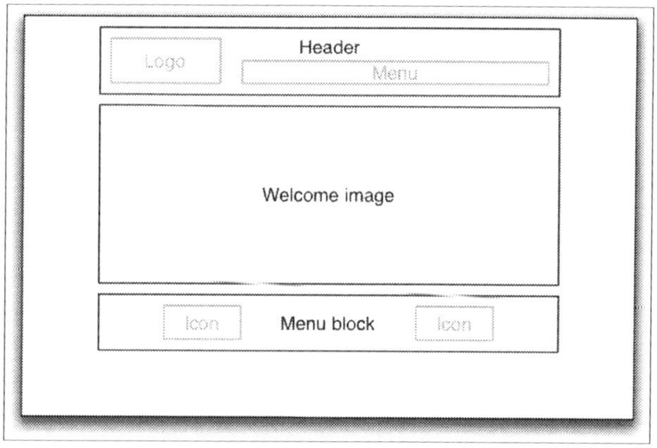

Configuring the pages

The mock-ups show that the CMS site needs a layout that supports three blocks, all of the same width, that are placed sequentially in the middle of the page. This is the same for both the front and content pages. Most ServiceNow customers have a more complex layout, for example, a menu in a column on the side of the screen.

There are several out of the box layouts that are suitable for many scenarios, but it is of course possible to create custom ones. Navigate to **Content Management** > **Design** > **Layouts** to see what is provided.

> To see a visual representation of how the dropzones are arranged, use the **Change Layout** link when you use the **Edit Page** UI Action on a **Page** record.

Making a div-based layout

Many of the ServiceNow layouts use tables to position items. Modern web design techniques recommend reserving tables to display data, rather than layouts. So, let's define a very simple block structure to allow CSS to position the elements. Adding the `class` and `id` attributes will make the application of CSS much easier.

To create a layout, navigate to **Content Management** > **Design** > **Layouts** and click on **New**. Then, fill in the following data:

- **Name**: `column_layout`
- **XML**:

```
<?xml version="1.0" encoding="utf-8" ?>
<j:jelly trim="true" xmlns:j="jelly:core" xmlns:g="glide"
  xmlns:j2="null" xmlns:g2="null">
    <div id="${jvar_name}" class="layout_container">
        <!-- Header -->
        <div class="cms_header_container container">
            <div id="header" class="cms_header dropzone"
              dropzone="true" />
        </div>
        <!-- Title -->
        <div class="cms_title_container container">
            <div id="title" class="cms_title dropzone"
              dropzone="true" />
        </div>
        <!-- Content -->
        <div class="cms_content_container container">
            <div id="content" class="cms_content dropzone"
              dropzone="true" />
        </div>
    </div>
</j:jelly>
```

Most of the layout is a straightforward HTML. There are three `div` elements, one for each block, with a container round them all and some classes that have been added for styling later. Setting the custom `dropzone` to the `true` attribute indicates the place where the content can be added later. In addition, there are also some strange XML tags, which are native to Jelly XML documents. These will be discussed in more detail later in the chapter.

Setting the Site

The Site is the core of a CMS portal. It relates pages to each other, providing their default settings. Create a new **Site** record by navigating to **Content Management** > **Sites** and clicking on **New**; then, fill the following values:

- **Name**: `Gardiner Hotels`
- **URL suffix**: `self-service`

  This provides the path in the URL. It is the suffix to the URL and the prefix for the page.

- **Default layout**: `column_layout`

This layout is the one that was created in the previous step. This provides the layout for all the pages unless they specify a different one.

We'll populate more of these fields later once we have done more configuration.

Creating a Page

A page holds the relationship between the blocks and the layout. Let's create the main page first.

Under the **Pages** Related List on the **Site** form, click on **New** and fill in the following values:

- **Name**: `GH - Main`

  GH is short for Gardiner Hotels here. The prefix is used here simply to separate these pages from the out of the box pages.

- **URL Suffix**: `main`

> Alongside the Site URL, the Page URL Suffix defines how this page can be accessed. In this example, the page is accessible at https://<instance>.service-now.com/self-service/main.do.

- **Title**: `Welcome to Gardiner Hotels`

  This text populates the **<title>** element on the HTML page. It is often shown in the browser tab or as the window text.

Finding the right page

The URL suffixes for the site and the page are important for the instance to serve the right page. When a browser attempts to access a page, the platform will look in the CMS configuration to find a match, but it will fall back to the standard interface if nothing is found.

In the preceding case, if a user attempts to access `https://<instance>.service-now.com/self-service/main.do`, then this newly created CMS page will be displayed. In contrast, accessing `https://<instance>.service-now.com/self-service/task.do` will show the Task form from the standard interface. However, accessing the page in this manner through an IFrame makes it possible to apply styles.

> The platform looks in quite a few places before it displays the standard interface, including UI Pages. In this manner, you can override what the platform will do in response to a URL.

Including the content

Now that a Page is defined, we should add some content to it. The **Edit Page** UI Action gives the same interface when adding gauges to a homepage. Click on it and then on **Add content** to see the available out of the box blocks.

> The generic out-of-the-box dynamic blocks are all prefixed with `*New` to make them easy to find in the list.

The following screenshot shows how to add content to a Page:

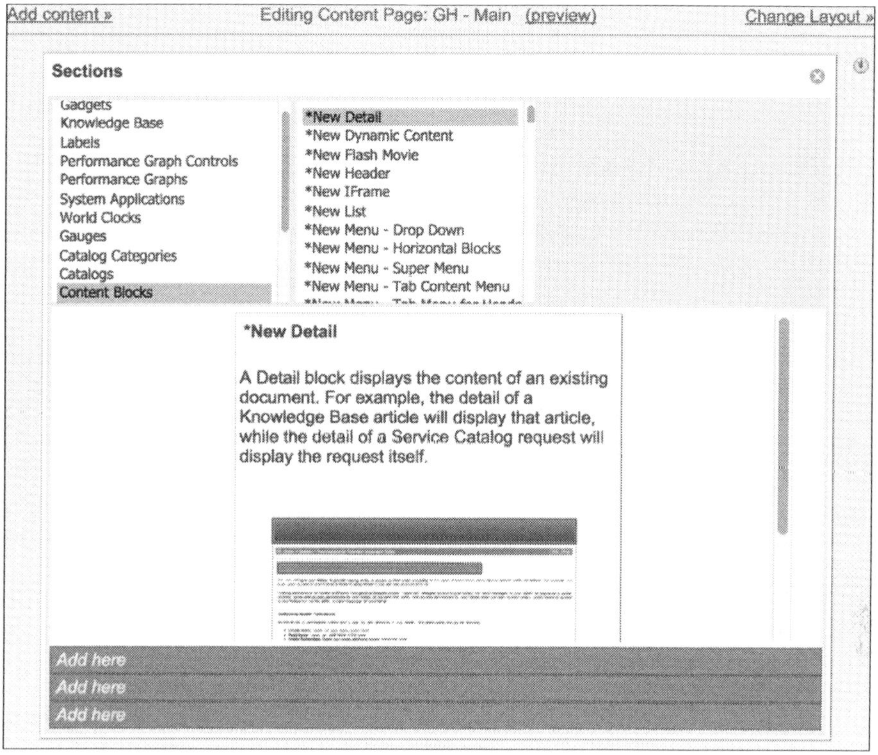

Perform the following set of actions:

1. Choose the ***New Header** Content Block and then click on the *top* **Add here** dropzone. This will provide the logo and top menu by using a definition in the **Header** [`content_block_header`] table.
2. Choose ***New Static HTML** and click on the *middle* **Add here** dropzone. This will turn into the welcome image, which is defined in the **Static Content** [`content_block_static`] table.
3. Choose ***New Menu – Horizontal Blocks** and click on the *bottom* **Add here** dropzone. This will become the icon-based menu in the **Navigation Menu** [`content_block_menu`] table.

Once these have been added, close the dialog box to see your new blocks shown in the following screenshot:

Helpfully, each of the blocks has a link that lets us easily configure the content for the block. Click on the link in the header block and enter the following information:

- **Name**: `GH - Header`
- **Logo**: upload the `logo.png` file from the `asset` pack.
- **Search**: `<unchecked>`
- **Font sizer**: `<unchecked>`

Once this is saved, return to the edit screen of the **GH - Main Content** page and create the Static HTML block and fill the following values:

- **Name**: `GH - Welcome image`
- **Static content**: click on the Insert image icon in the HTML field and ensure that **Image Library** is selected in **Type**. Next, click on **New** to create a new record and upload the `welcome.jpg` image from the asset pack.

> Using an attachment instead of the image library may cause Access Control issues. Therefore, store images for the CMS in the **Image** [`db_image`] table. Then, navigate to **Content Management** > **Design** > **Images** to see them.

For the bottom block, create the **Navigation** menu by filling the following value:

- **Name**: `GH - Main menu`

  Much more will be set in this block later.

Finally, to set this page as the default, find **Gardiner Hotels** by navigating to **Content Management** > **Sites** and populate this field:

- **Home page**: `GH - Main`

  This ensures that the main page is shown when you click on the logo in the header; this also ensures that the page of `main.do` is not needed in the URL.

To see the results so far, click on **View page** in the `GH - Main` Content Page or navigate to `https://<instance>.service-now.com/self-service/`. The main page of Gardiner Hotels should be as follows:

Source: https://www.flickr.com/photos/prayitnophotography/7049818919/

While this is a good start, it certainly isn't complete! There are no menus and the styling is very wrong. All the items are aligned to the left and are very jumbled, giving a rather displeasing result. To create menus, we need content, which means more pages, but the styling can be fixed with some CSS. Let's do this now.

Adding some style

A **Content Theme** [`content_theme`] table is a collection of **Style Sheets** [`content_css`]. A CSS style sheet gives the browser instructions on where the items should be positioned on the page and how they should be rendered. Associating multiple style sheets to a theme allows you to quickly swap in and out the CSS, and reuse records across multiple themes or sites. The CSS can be stored in the ServiceNow database, or a style sheet can be an URL that references an external file, making it possible to simply reuse data from a website.

> Some of the styles applied to elements are included since ServiceNow sets some standard styles on all CMS and UI Pages. You may need to use the inspection tools in your browser to find the right elements to style.

Create a new Content Theme by navigating to **Content Management** > **Design** > **Themes** and click on **New**; then, fill in the following values:

- **Name**: `Gardiner Hotels`
- **Active**: `<checked>`

Once the record is saved, create a new style sheet by using the Related List; then, fill in the following data:

- **Name**: `GH - Basic`
- **Style**:

```
body {
    font-family: Lucida Grande, Verdana, 'Lucida Sans Unicode',
sans-serif;
}
/*
The corporate font is used throughout the page.
*/

.dropzone {
    width: 900px;
    margin: 0 auto;
}
.cms_title img {
    margin: 0 auto;
    display: block;
}
/*
Center the content areas, making them 900 pixels wide.  The large
image in the content block is also centralized.
*/

#title {
    font-size: xx-large;
    padding: 10px 10px 10px 20px;
}
/*
```

```
This alters the title text, enlarging the size of the characters
and adding some padding.
*/

.cms_header_container {
    padding: 20px
}
/*
This rule ensures the header has some space around it.
*/

.cms_header_logo img {
    width: 200px;
}
/*
The logo in the header is resized, and some padding is added at
the top and bottom.
*/

.cms_header_container,
.cms_header table,
.cms_header_login a,
.cms_menu_dropdown a {
    background-color: #CC6600;
    color: white !important;
}
/*
The text in the header is made white, and the header background is
made a burnt orange.
*/

.cms_content>div {
    width: 700px;
    margin: 0px auto
}
.cms_menu_section_blocks_image_left img {
    width: 100px;
    float: right
}
.cms_menu_section_blocks {
    width: 350px;
    float: left;
    margin: 0 auto
}
.cms_menu_section_blocks_image_left {
    width: 120px
}
.menu_bullet {
    margin-left: 110px;
```

```
    width: 25px;
}
/*
This series of styles aligns the block menu, rearranging it to fit
in the middle of the screen.  It ensures that two blocks can float
in the middle of the page, with the elements lining up nicely.
*/

.cms_menu_dropdown_container {
    float: right;
    height: 0px;
    margin-top: -20px
}
/*
The header menu is moved to the right, and realigned to the bottom
of the banner.
*/

.cms_menu_dropdown li {
    float: right;
    margin: 0 5px 0 50px;
    font-size: large
}
/*
The items in the header menu are arranged beside each other, with
a margin, and the text made bigger.
*/

.cms_header_login {
    float: right;
    height: 0px;
}
/*
The welcome message is floated to the right, and reduced in height
to align it with the logo.
*/
```

Once this is saved, go back to the Gardiner Hotels site (which can be found by navigating to **Content Management** > **Sites**) and populate the following field as follows:

- **Default theme**: `Gardiner Hotels`

Copying pages

Once you have created one page, duplicates can quickly be made through the use of the **Copy** UI Action.

Follow these steps to create the next page:

1. Go to the **GH - Main** Page (by navigating to **Content Management** > **Pages** > **GH - Main**).
2. Click on **Copy**.
3. In the resulting entry, change these items with the following values:
   - **Name**: `GH - New Reservation`
   - **URL suffix**: `new_reservation`
   - **Title**: `New reservation`
4. Once this is saved, click on **Edit Page**.
5. Remove the bottom two blocks that contain the large image, and what will be the main menu, by clicking on the little circular x at the top right of each block.
6. Click on **Add Content** and include the following two blocks:
   - Choose the ***New Dynamic Content** content block and click on the *middle* **Add here** dropzone.

     This will be a reminder of the page that's being viewed, which will be defined in the **Dynamic Content** [`content_block_programmatic`] table.
   - Choose the ***New IFrame** and click on the *bottom* **Add here** dropzone.

     This will be the actual content of the page. This will be defined in the **IFrame** [`content_block_iframe`] table.
7. Next, configure the middle Dynamic Content block and set the following fields:
   - **Name**: `GH - Page title`
   - **Dynamic content**:

```
<?xml version="1.0" encoding="utf-8" ?>
<j:jelly trim="false" xmlns:j="jelly:core" xmlns:g="glide"
xmlns:j2="null" xmlns:g2="null">
<span class="title">${current_page.getTitle()}</span>
</j:jelly>
```

This slight foray into Jelly uses a JEXL expression, similar to the one used in e-mail notifications. The code accesses the `current_page` object, which provides a `getTitle` function. This returns the title as specified on the page. We'll see more information on this in detail later, in the *Using Jelly in the CMS* section.

8. For the IFrame, set these fields:
    - **Name:** `GH - New reservation`
    - **Sizing:** `Expand to fit content (internal content only)`
    - **URL:** `u_reservation.do?sys_id=-1&sysparm_view=ess`

> Note that the URL does not have a slash. This is important to ensure that it stays within the Self-Service site that is already defined. The `ess` view has also been specified, which is used later to create a specific form layout.

9. Navigate back to the Page and click on **View Page** to see what you have made:

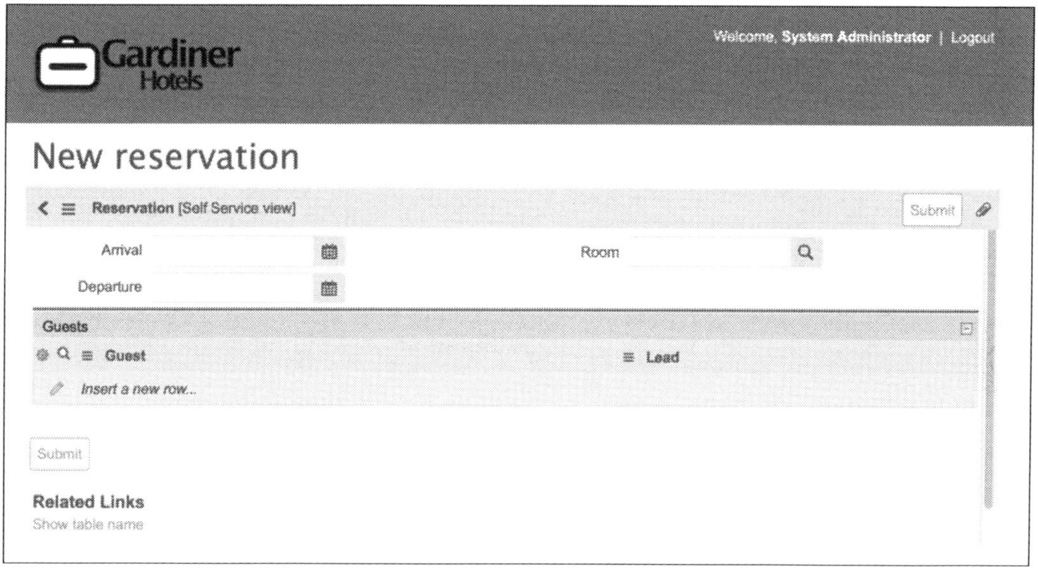

This is looking good! The layout is much better, the colors make the title pop, and everything looks a little cleaner and more aligned. The title makes it more obvious as to what is happening, and the IFrame allows a guest to submit a new **Reservation** record.

However, the style of the form is a little plain. This is fine for fulfillers, but it is not very attractive for non-technical requesters. Let's create a new Style Sheet to make the form a little better-looking.

Styling the form

Navigate to **Content Management** > **Design** > **Themes** and then choose **Gardiner Hotels**. In the **Style Sheet** Related List, click on **New** and fill out the form as follows:

- **Name**: `GH - Forms and Lists`
- **Style**:

```
.header, #page_timing_div, .related_links_container  {
    display: none;
}
/*
Remove the header, page timer and any related links
*/
button {
    font-size: large;
}
/*
Make the text on the buttons bigger.
*/
```

In this manner, the form can be completely reworked and restyled in whatever way you wish. However, ServiceNow often changes the styling of elements during an upgrade, so be careful to check it after.

It is often a good idea to create a new view for the form that will be used in a Self-Service portal, by focusing on the fields that a requester will be interested in. This means that custom text and action can be used to make things a little friendlier.

Creating a Self-Service form

Let's create a new view for the **Reservation** form. To do this, perform the following steps:

1. Navigate to the **Reservation** form and then navigate to **Personalize** > **Form Design**
2. Create a new View called `ess`. Remove the Guests-embedded Related List and the Room reference field.

> A view called ess with a label of Self Service is already specified within the system. The platform will match them up.

3. Create a new UI Action (by navigating to **System Definition** > **UI Actions**) and set the following fields:
   - **Name**: Create reservation
   - **Table**: Reservation [u_reservation]
   - **Action name**: sysverb_insert

   By specifying sysverb_insert as the Action name, we override the default Insert button.
   - **Form button**: <checked>
   - **Show update**: <unchecked>
   - **Condition**: current.canCreate()

- **Script**:

```
action.setRedirectURL(current);
current.insert();

var m2m = new GlideRecord('u_m2m_guests_reservations');
m2m.newRecord();
m2m.u_reservation = current.sys_id;
m2m.u_guest = gs.getUserID();
m2m.u_lead = true;
m2m.insert();
```

The first part of this script ensures that when the button is clicked, the platform shows the newly created record and then commits it to the database, as most people like to see the reaction to their action. Next, a record is added to the many-to-many table that lies between the **Guest** and the **Reservation** tables. The currently logged-in user will be added as the lead guest. This button automates the potentially fiddly and error-prone mechanism of adding Guests with the Related List.

4. Once the settings are saved, use the **UI Action Visibility** Related List to include only the Self-Service view.

   This means that the button will be visible only for those who access the form with the view selected as Self-Service, such as those through the CMS portal.

Creating this UI Action has a cascading effect. Our new button overrides the default Submit button, but it will only be displayed on the Self Service view. If you now try to create a new **Reservation** record in the standard interface, you will find that there is no Submit button.

To counter this, create another new button. The easiest way to do this is to find the original UI Action.

1. Navigate to **System Definition** > **UI Actions**.
2. Search for the entry where the value for **Name** is `Submit`, **Action name** is `sysverb_insert`, and the **Table** is `Global`. The entry can be seen in the following screenshot:

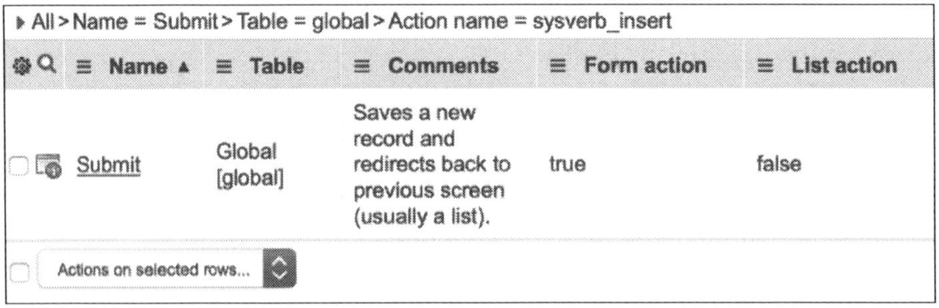

3. Once it is found, use **Insert and Stay** to copy the UI Action.
4. Change the **Table** field as follows and click on **Save**:
    - **Table**: `Reservation`

Use the **UI Action Visibility** Related List, select Self-Service again, and then use List Editing to set the **Visibility** field as **Exclude**. This can be seen in the following screenshot:

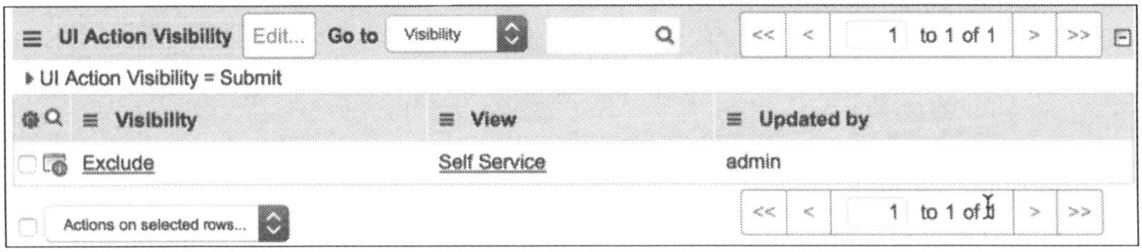

This now means that there are two UI Actions on the **Reservations** table: one that will be shown in the Self-Service view and one that will not. Try from both perspectives.

Adding more pages

The **New Reservation** page is good enough for now, but more pages are needed. The site map calls for four content pages. They should be similar to the **New Reservation** Page, so use it as a template:

1. Navigate to **Content Management** > **Pages** and find the `GH - New Reservation` page.
2. Click on the **Copy** button.
3. On the new record, use the following details: These three steps should be performed three times in total.

Name	URL suffix	Title
`GH - Existing Reservation`	`existing_reservation`	`Existing reservations`
`GH - New Maintenance`	`new_maintenance`	`Request cleaning or tell us about things that aren't working`
`GH - Existing Maintenance`	`existing_maintenance`	`Status of cleaning or repairs`

4. For each new page, use the **Edit Page** link.
5. Remove the bottom IFrame and add a new IFrame block by using the **Add Content** link.

6. To configure each block, use the following details: These three steps should also be repeated three times.

Name	Sizing	URL
`GH - Existing Reservation`	`Expand to fit content`	`u_reservation_list.do?sysparm_view=ess`
`GH - New Maintenance`	`Expand to fit content`	`u_maintenance.do?sys_id=-1&sysparm_view=ess`
`GH - Existing Maintenance`	`Expand to fit content`	`u_maintenance_list.do?sysparm_view=ess`

For each of the IFrame URLs, the Self-Service view has been specified. This gives the user the option to specify a specific set of fields on the list of the form later, if desired.

Populating the menus

All the pages are now created; however, there is no way to get to them. We've built the main menu block, but the pages aren't related to them. In addition, the header that's included on every page has a space for a menu, but it hasn't also been created yet. Let's fix this now.

Configuring the main menu

Let's begin with the steps to perform the configuration of the main menu:

1. Find the main menu block by navigating **to Content Management** > **Blocks** > **Navigation Menus**; then, find **GH - Main menu**.
2. In the **Menu Section** Related List click on **New** and fill out the form as follows:
    - **Name**: `Reservation`
    - **Left image**: upload the `reservation.png` file from the asset pack.
    - **Second level text**: `We'd love to have you again!`

3. Once saved, use the **Menu Items** Related List to create two entries with the following details:

Name	Redirect to	Detail page	Image	Order
`Create a new reservation`	`A content page`	`GH - New Reservation`	Upload `bullet.png`	`10`
`See upcoming and past stays`	`A content page`	`GH - Existing Reservation`	Upload `bullet.png`	`20`

4. Return to the **GH - Main menu** record and add another **Menu Section** value using the following details:
   - **Name**: `Cleaning and maintenance`
   - **Left image**: upload the `maintenance.png` file from the asset pack
   - **Second level text**: `We'll keep your room spic and span!`

5. Use the **Menu Items** Related List to create two entries with the following details:

Name	Redirect to	Detail page	Image	Order
`Alert us to something that's wrong!`	`A content page`	`GH - New Maintenance`	Upload `bullet.png`	`10`
`Monitor existing requests`	`A content page`	`GH - Existing Maintenance`	Upload `bullet.png`	`20`

> In this example, the same image has been uploaded four times. This is wasteful. Instead, the UI Macro called `cms_menu_section_blocks` that defines the menu could be duplicated and altered, or the image stored in **Content Management** > **Design** > **Images** could be altered.

To test this out, navigate to the main page that is available at https://<instance>.service-now.com/self-service/. Remember to replace <instance> with your instance name. You should see something like this:

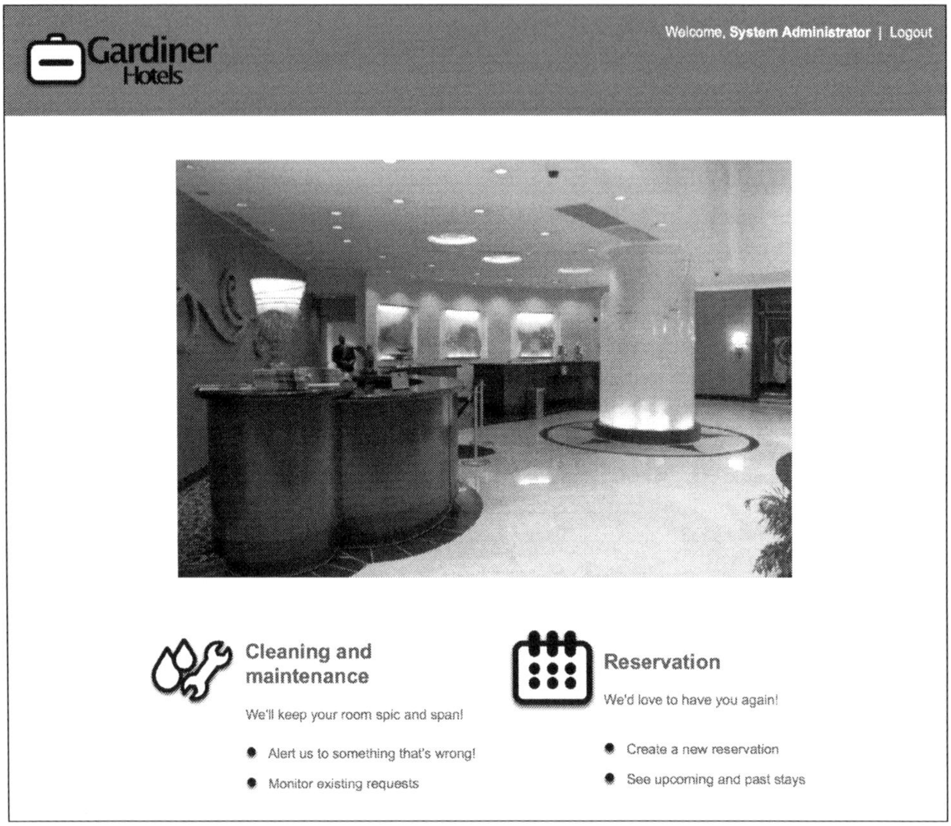

Making the header menu

The main menu now gives easy access to the defined pages. However, once you are on the **New reservation** page, for example, access to the other pages is not possible. Let's make the navigation a little more efficient by adding a menu in the header. To do this, perform the following steps:

1. Navigate to **Content Management** > **Blocks** > **Navigation Menus** and click on **New**.
2. Click on **Drop Down Menu for Headers**.
3. Set the value for the following field:
    - **Name**: GH - Navigation menu

4. Once saved, populate the menu with the same Menu Sections and Menu Items as those for the block menu, but without the images and the second-level text.
    - **Menu Section** > **Name**: `Reservation`
    - **Reservation** > **Menu Items**:

Name	Redirect to	Detail page	Order
`Create a new reservation`	`A content page`	`GH - New Reservation`	`10`
`See upcoming and past stays`	`A content page`	`GH - Existing Reservation`	`20`

    - **Menu Section** > **Name**: `Cleaning and Maintenance`
    - **Cleaning and Maintenance** > **Menu Items**:

Name	Redirect to	Detail page	Order
`Alert us to something that's wrong!`	`A content page`	`GH - New Maintenance`	`10`
`Monitor existing requests`	`A content page`	`GH - Existing Maintenance`	`20`

5. Navigate to **Content Management** > **Blocks** > **Headers** and then click on the **GH - Header** block.
6. Set the value for the following field:
    - **Bottom menu**: `GH - Navigation menu`

Locking down the data

With the menus in place, the blocks are now finally configured. However, the data that's being returned is not what is expected. The **Existing Reservation** and **Existing Maintenance** pages show a list of all records and not just the ones that are relevant to the current user.

There are several ways to rectify this, but one of the cleanest options is through a query Business Rule, which was discussed in *Chapter 7, Securing Applications and Data*. However, to filter the results correctly, we need to know the hotel room in which a Guest checked in. To do this, we can combine the techniques that we have used in the book so far, including storing the data in the session to speed up queries, as mentioned in *Chapter 3, Client-side Interaction*.

> In this section, we revisit the techniques that were mentioned in other chapters. Since a CMS portal sits on top of the standard functionality, most implementations will need to address these topics. The items are addressed here but in less detail.

Checking the room

Let's create a Script Include (by navigating to **System Definition** > **Script Includes**) with the following values in the given fields:

- **Name**: `findReservations`
- **Script**:

```
function findReservations() {
  var res = gs.getSession().getClientData('guest.reservation');
  if (res)
    return res;

  var m2m = new GlideRecord('u_m2m_guests_reservations');
  m2m.addQuery('u_guest', gs.getUserID());
  m2m.query();
  var res_arr = [];
  while (m2m.next()) {
    res_arr.push(m2m.u_reservation + '');
  }
  res = (new ArrayUtil()).unique(res_arr).join();
  gs.getSession().putClientData('guest.reservation', res);
  return res;
}
```

The aim of this function is to find the user's logged-in reservations.

Firstly, the script checks whether the answer is already stored in the session. This is a useful way to avoid accessing the database more than necessary. Otherwise, the script queries the many-to-many tables that store the relationship between the guests and the reservations. Only entries where the user is in the **Guest** field are returned. All of the matching records are looped through, and the results are put into an array, being sure to convert the `GlideElement` objects into a string. The array is then processed using an out-of-the-box Script Includes called `ArrayUtil`, which removes any duplicate entries. The result is converted into a comma-separated string. This data is then stored in the session for later reuse, and the session value is returned.

> Storing data in the session will speed up access, but this also means that the database will only be looked at once per login. The user will need to log out and back in again if a new reservation is made. You should strive to balance performance with usability!

To use this data, create a new Business Rule by using the following values:

- **Name**: `Filter reservations`
- **Table**: `Reservation [u_reservation]`
- **Advanced**: `<checked>`
- **Query**: `<checked>`
- **Condition**: `!gs.hasRole('u_hotel_user')`
- **Script**: `current.addQuery('sys_id', 'IN', findReservations());`

This simple Business Rule alters the query that will be sent to the database whenever the Reservations table is looked at. This runs when the user does not have the `u_hotel_role` role and asks the database to return records only when the `sys_id` matches the array that is returned by `findReservations`.

Filtering Maintenance tasks

To control visibility to the **Maintenance** requests, a different approach is possible. Instead of using a script, a filter can be used to show only records that are opened by the current user. Let's start by creating filters for **Maintenance** tasks:

1. Navigate to the **Maintenance** list and create a filter with the following conditions:

   ```
   Active - is - true
   Opened by - is (dynamic) - Me
   ```

2. Click on **Run** to perform the query.
3. Right-click on the rightmost breadcrumb and choose **Copy Query**. You will get an encoded query string such as `active=true^opened_byDYNAMIC90d1921e5f510100a9ad2572f2b477fe`.

4. Navigate to **Content Management** > **Specialty Content** > **IFrames** and edit the **GH - Existing Maintenance** record.
5. Alter the URL to have another parameter called `sysparm_query` with a value of the encoded query. The full URL should look like this:

```
u_maintenance_list.do?sysparm_
view=ess&sysparm_query=active=true^opened_
byDYNAMIC90d1921e5f510100a9ad2572f2b477fe
```

Altering Access Controls

In addition to query Business Rules, Access Controls need to be altered. Currently, only users with the `u_hotel_user` role will be able to create, read, write, or delete records, and requesters should be able to do the first two items at least.

There are two tables that need to be controlled—**Maintenance** and **Reservations**. Both need `create` and `read` rules at the field and row levels. This means that eight Access Controls need to be made in total. Since the aim of the rules is to allow access, simply creating the rule with the right name and operation will suffice. The description is given here for documentation purposes:

Name	Operation	Description
`u_maintenance`	`read`	Allows everyone to read every **Maintenance** record
`u_maintenance.*`	`read`	By default, allows everyone to read every field on the **Maintenance** table
`u_maintenance`	`create`	Allows everyone to create a **Maintenance** record
`u_maintenance.*`	`create`	Allows everyone to write on every field when they create a **Maintenance** record
`u_reservation`	`read`	Allows everyone to read every **Reservation** record (subject to query Business Rules)
`u_reservation.*`	`read`	By default, allows everyone to read every field on the **Reservation** table
`u_reservation`	`create`	Allows everyone to create a **Reservation** record
`u_reservation.*`	`create`	Allows everyone to write on every field when they create a **Reservation** record

We rely on query Business Rules and filters to restrict views of the data, and we don't control which fields can be written into on creation. (For instance, a requester could, in this scenario, create **Maintenance** tasks for rooms other than their own.) In a more fully featured implementation, it is likely that these would be locked down more.

Testing the site

Let's try out all this new functionality. Perform the following set of steps:

1. Impersonate a guest with no roles. I'm using **Alice Richards**, which we created in *Chapter 1, ServiceNow Foundations*. Impersonation requires the user to have a User ID. Populate the field if you haven't already.
2. Navigate to `https://<instance>.service-now.com/self-service/`
3. Verify that you can create a **New Reservation**.
4. Check that you can only see your own records in **Existing Reservations**.
5. Check whether you can create new **Maintenance** tasks.
6. Validate whether you can only see the **Maintenance** tasks that you created.

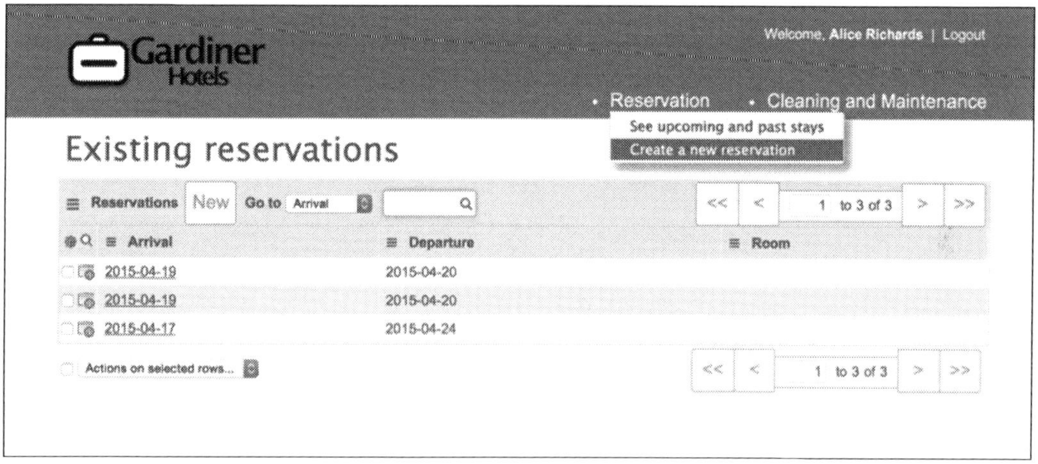

The site is pretty usable. However, there are some areas of improvement that could be made:

- For implementation speed, forms were used for the **New Reservation** and **New Maintenance** pages. Instead, **Service Catalog Record Producers** are often a better fit. They provide more options for friendly help text, the inclusion of images and description, and require fewer security rules. Use an IFrame to embed the catalog home page (`catalog_home.do`) or a specific page with a Detail block.
- A filter was used to control the maintenance tasks that the requester could see. Having the right Access Controls is also important because a malicious user could inspect the HTML of the page, see the filter, and manipulate it to have access to everything.

- Further work on the fields shown on the forms and lists would give the right level of information. The removal of UI Actions (such as **Send to External**) on the Self Service view and the actions of these buttons will likely need adjustment. The fields on the **Maintenance** view should be minimized too.
- The lists and forms themselves are not very attractive. **List Definitions** and **Content Types** can be used to create entirely new pages. You'll see how these are made after a foray into Jelly.

Creating truly custom pages

The web's language is HTML. Every page rendered by a web browser has some HTML content. Therefore, the ultimate job of any website is to generate the HTML that contains data formatted in the desired manner. The browser then renders it and hopefully displays something beautiful, informative, and useful.

> Knowledge of HTML is ubiquitous in the Web Design world. There are many resources, including books, online courses, and other tutorials, that will teach you the basics of building a web page.
>
> The **Mozilla Developer Network** (**MDN**), which can be found at `https://developer.mozilla.org/`, is a great place to start.

ServiceNow uses Jelly to generate HTML. The Jelly processor in ServiceNow takes in an XML template and produces HTML. There are a variety of Jelly elements, including variables, loops, and conditions, which means that the produced HTML is dependent upon the data that the processor is fed. In addition, ServiceNow has extended beyond the standard Jelly tags, allowing JavaScript to be used inside a Jelly XML document while also building in caching. This makes it powerful and fast!

> The name Jelly is a short form of Java Elements. You can find more information about it on the Web at `http://commons.apache.org/jelly`. It is not something to eat!

Since Jelly is critical to ServiceNow's presentation layer, CMS uses it heavily. However, it extends further out into the platform. All of the elements that you see in ServiceNow have been generated using Jelly; these include forms, lists, and all the interfaces, such as the Service Catalog and the Application Navigator. Most of the XML documents that produce the most common interface sections are file-based and are stored on the instance, but there are some items such as UI Macros and UI Pages where the XML is stored in the database, just like how JavaScript is stored in records in the Business Rules table.

Creating a UI Page

As with everything else, we need to create a Hello World page. To do this, navigate to **System UI** > **UI Pages** and click on **New**. Then, fill in the following fields with the given values:

- **Name**: `hello_world`
- **HTML**:

```
<?xml version="1.0" encoding="utf-8" ?>
<j:jelly trim="false" xmlns:j="jelly:core" xmlns:g="glide"
xmlns:j2="null" xmlns:g2="null">
  <b>Hello</b>, <i>world</i>!
</j:jelly>
```

When you create a new **UI Page** [`sys_ui_page`] record, a template is used by default. In the third line, some standard HTML has been inserted. Click on the **Try It** button to display your first Jelly page.

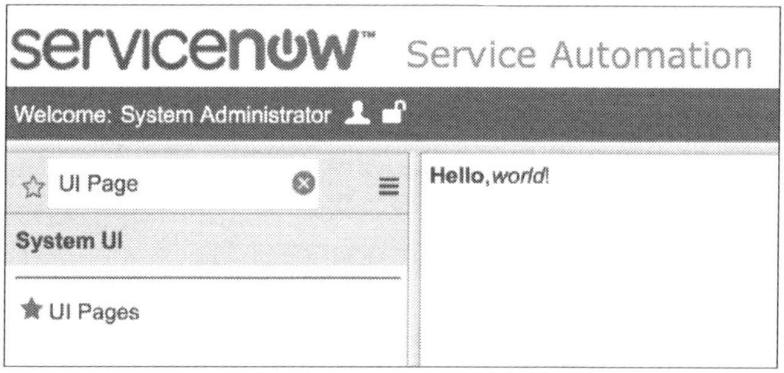

Try to navigate to `https://<instance>.service-now.com/hello_world.do`, by replacing `<instance>` with your instance name. The new page will be displayed. As you can see, the UI Page can be accessed via its the name in the URL.

Adding interactivity to UI Pages

You've probably noticed the Client Script and Processing Script fields. Let's update our test record with some more code:

- **HTML**:

  ```
  <?xml version="1.0" encoding="utf-8" ?>
  <j:jelly trim="false" xmlns:j="jelly:core" xmlns:g="glide"
  xmlns:j2="null" xmlns:g2="null">
    <form action="ui_page_process.do" onsubmit="return check();">
      <input type="hidden" name="name" value="hello_world"/>
      Name: <input name="user_name" id="user_field"/>
      <input type="submit" value="Submit"/>
    </form>
  </j:jelly>
  ```

  The **HTML** field is not HTML, but Jelly! However, HTML can also be used. Tables, forms, images—any tags can be used. The data is passed to your browser to render, like a normal web page, but is only part of the data. In this case, a form is used that provides a simple input field and submit button. When the form is submitted, the browser runs the check function. Everything is standard HTML here!

- **Client script**:

  ```
  function check() {
    if ($('user_field').value == '') {
      alert('Please enter your name');
      return false;
    }
  }
  ```

  The **Client script** field is JavaScript. Any code that is placed here is placed in a script tag, directly after the HTML.

> Note the use of the Protoyype library, which checks to see whether the input field is empty. While it isn't perfectly safe to use these core libraries due to the changes that may happen during upgrades (as discussed in *Chapter 3, Client-side Interaction*), since you are more in control of the DOM that you are making, the risk is reduced.

- **Processing script**: `gs.addInfoMessage('Hello ' + user_name);`

  The **Processing script** field is server-side JavaScript. It is run when `ui_page_process` is called and handles forms that have been sent via POST or GET. As shown in this example, parameters are automatically copied into JavaScript variables, allowing easy access to data that is sent from the client.

Click on **Try It** to see your new interactive page. With a few lines, we have produced a little interactive form that shows off quite a few features of UI Pages!

Including UI Macros

Jelly is a template system. It allows you to create a HTML structure and control its output through loops and conditions. However, you can also create reusable components by using UI Macros. These are little blocks of Jelly that you can call from other Jelly elements to build more complex structures. Let's begin by creating a UI Macro:

1. To create a new UI Macro, navigate to **System UI > UI Macros**, click on **New**, and fill in the following values in the fields:
   - **Name**: `instructions`
   - **XML**: Add the following script:

     ```
     <?xml version="1.0" encoding="utf-8" ?>
     <j:jelly trim="false" xmlns:j="jelly:core" xmlns:g="glide"
     xmlns:j2="null" xmlns:g2="null">
       Please type in your name below.
     </j:jelly>
     ```

2. Then, edit the `hello_world` UI Page and place the following tag on a new line, right above the `<form ...>` tag:

   ```
   <g:instructions />
   ```

   The first four lines of the UI Page will look like this:

   ```
   <?xml version="1.0" encoding="utf-8" ?>
   <j:jelly trim="false" xmlns:j="jelly:core" xmlns:g="glide"
     xmlns:j2="null" xmlns:g2="null">
     <g:instructions />
     <form action="ui_page_process.do" onsubmit="return check();">
   ```

3. Click on the **Try It** button on the `hello_world` UI Page to view the results.

> It is likely that you will need to clear the cache to see the changes. To do this, navigate to `https://<instance>.service-now.com/cache.do` by replacing `<instance>` with your instance name as always. Note that clearing the cache, as discussed in *Chapter 8, Diagnosing ServiceNow – Knowing What Is Going On*, will impact performance until the cache reloads.

Now, when you look at the output UI Page, you'll see that the content that gives some instruction would have been inserted from the UI Macro.

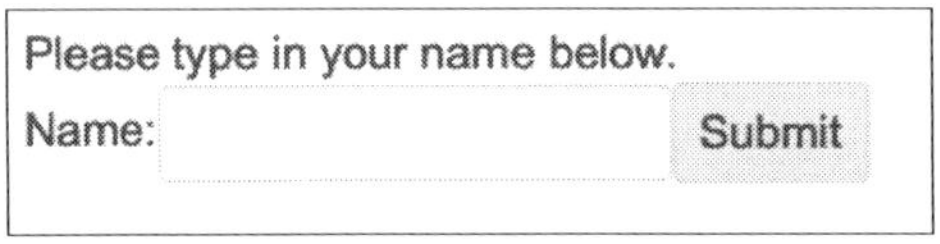

The name of the tag is the name of the UI Macro, and UI Macros can call other UI Macros. This means that you can quickly build a library of Jelly snippets. It is best practice to create lots of smaller blocks of code that can be easily debugged.

> Setting attributes in the tag will pass variables to the UI Macro; the `<g:instruct jvar_test="hello" />` will set the test variable to `hello`. In addition, content that is entered between opening and closing tags (such as `<g:instruct>hello</g:instruct>`) can be accessed with the `<g:insert/>` tag in the UI Macro.

There are lots of UI Macros that you can leverage when you build Jelly. The ones prefixed with `ui_` are rather useful; in addition to other uses, they also help to create references, date/time fields, forms, and tables.

Dynamically creating content with Jelly

Even if UI Pages only used HTML, UI Pages would be very powerful. However, UI Pages really come alive when the HTML is dynamically generated by using Jelly.

To see how this works, edit the `hello_world` UI Page again. Remove the HTML tag that renders the `input` field:

```
<input name="user_name" id="user_field"/>
```

In its place, add the following line:

```
<input name="user_name" id="user_field" value="${gs.getUserName()}" />
```

When you refresh the page, you'll see that the input field has been populated with the User ID of the currently logged-in user. This is a JEXL expression that evaluates some JavaScript. What's all this? Let's find out!

Touching on XML

Jelly must always be syntactically valid XML. HTML is a subset of XML, but most people are used to HTML not being perfectly valid. For example, web browsers can often work without closing tags. However, the Jelly parser in ServiceNow will not accept this. To help you, there is a Client Script that will check the syntax of your Jelly before saving the UI Page or UI Macro.

In addition, the first couple of lines and the last line will almost always be the same. The XML declaration (`<?xml ... ?>`) signifies that it is an XML document, and the Jelly tag (`<j:jelly ... />`) shows how the document will be processed. The namespaces used will be discussed in just a moment.

> The XML descriptor must be the first thing on an XML document. There can be no whitespace or anything else before it!

For brevity, I won't include the XML declaration or the Jelly tag in the rest of the examples. Just work with the rest of the document, but remember that these three lines must always be there.

Looping with Jelly

Even on its own, Jelly can do some great things. As we'll see, it can deal with variables, loops, conditions, and more. When the processor runs, it'll find the tags and evaluate them. The content of the tag could contain other tags, either Jelly or HTML. Consider them like functions or commands.

> Since Jelly tags are XML, they'll have attributes that work as parameters for the command. The contents of a tag are typically the body of a command.

To see an example, create a new UI Page and try out this Jelly:

- **Name**: `LoopWorld`
- **HTML**:

```
<j:forEach indexVar="i" begin="1" end="3">
  <p>Hello, world!</p>
</j:forEach>
```

This simple example shows the `forEach` tag. This is supplied with three parameters: `indexVar`, `begin`, and `end`. When it is executed, it'll take these parameters to execute something very similar to a JavaScript `for` loop. In this example, it will repeat "Hello, world!" three times.

To set a variable in Jelly, use the set tag. To write out a variable, use the curly braces' syntax. The following couple of lines contains a JEXL expression, which works in a way similar to a macro—the contents is evaluated and is replaced.

```
<j:set var="jvar_message" value="Hello, world!"/>
<p>${jvar_message}</p>
```

> **JEXL** is **Java EXpression Language**, which is another Apache project that is hosted at `http://commons.apache.org/proper/commons-jexl/index.html`. For our purposes, we can consider that it just runs JavaScript.

In essence, Jelly does two things: it makes decisions on what HTML should be rendered using conditions and loops, and it programmatically generates the HTML with JEXL expressions. There are several more core tags, including a very common `if` tag. Often, the `evaluate` attribute has a JEXL expression in it to determine whether the contents of the tag should be output.

> There is a full listing on the Apache Commons site at `https://commons.apache.org/proper/commons-jelly/tags.html`.
>
> The ServiceNow wiki at `http://wiki.servicenow.com/index.php?title=Jelly_Tags#Jelly_Tags` shows a more limited set, but it has more realistic examples.

Expanding on Jelly

While Jelly is pretty useful on its own, ServiceNow has supercharged it. Before we are in too deep, let's look at some attributes of the `jelly` tag again:

```
<jelly xmlns:j="jelly:core" xmlns:g="glide" ...>
```

For those who are intimate with XML, this will be familiar. It specifies that `j` will be the namespace for Jelly tags, and `g` is the namespace for Glide. ServiceNow has extended Jelly and made its own tags to provide the desired functionality.

[There are around a hundred additional tags, with more added-in plugins. In fact, you'll never encounter the vast majority of them!]

So, when you see the `g:` and `j:` namespace prefixes on elements, you'll know whether you are using the core Jelly tags or the Glide extensions.

One of the most important tags that ServiceNow has added is the evaluate tag. It runs server-side JavaScript. If you create a JavaScript variable, it can be accessed by using JEXL.

```
<g:evaluate>
  var roll = Math.round(Math.random()*5) + 1 + "";
</g:evaluate>
${roll}
```

This code creates a variable called `roll`; by using some standard JavaScript, it generates a random number between 0 and 5, rounds it down, adds 1 (so that it can be between 1 and 6), and finally turns it into a string. The JEXL expression then simply outputs it.

[Never put a JEXL expression into an evaluate tag! This will contribute to the instance node to restart! This is discussed later in this chapter.]

Accessing Jelly and JavaScript variables

You may have noticed something interesting in our variable naming. When we used the Jelly set tag, the variable was prefixed with `jvar_`. Why did I do this? Jelly, JEXL, and JavaScript all have different rules about variables and how they access them:

- Jelly only knows about Jelly variables. It has no concept of JavaScript variables.
- JEXL has been extended, so that it knows about JavaScript. In fact, it will think that every expression is a JavaScript expression unless it is passed a string that is prefixed with `jvar_`. Then, it will switch to using Jelly variables.
- JavaScript, when it uses the `evaluate` tag, can access Jelly variables by copying them into a new JavaScript variable. This only happens if the `jelly` attribute is set to true, as shown here:

  ```
  <g:evaluate jelly="true">...</g:evaluate>
  ```

This probably makes no sense, so let's work through a series of examples.

Mixing variables

If you removed the `jvar_` prefix when you set a variable through the Jelly set tag and then tried to access it through JEXL, nothing would be displayed.

```
<j:set var="jvar_hello" value="Hello"/>
<j:set var="jelly_name" value="Jelly"/>
<p>${jvar_hello} ${jelly_name}</p>
```

This will output just "Hello". JEXL has no access to a variable set by Jelly unless it begins with `jvar_`. Create a new UI Page by using the following values to see this in action:

- **Name**: `HelloBelly`
- **HTML**:

  ```
  <j:set var="jvar_hello" value="Hello"/>
  <j:set var="jelly_name" value="Jelly"/>
  <g:evaluate jelly="true">
    var script_name = jelly.jelly_name + "Belly";
  </g:evaluate>
  <p>${jvar_hello} ${script_name}</p>
  ```

The `evaluate` tag can access the Jelly variables since the `jelly` attribute is set. These are copied into a JavaScript object called `jelly`. A JavaScript variable is then set after a little string concatenation. JEXL is then used to output the text, and it has access to the JavaScript variable.

> If you want to access a Jelly variable in the evaluate tag, then ensure that you use this method. Do not use a JEXL expression, as noted below, since the instance will eventually restart!
>
> You can also set Jelly variables by passing parameters through the URL. The variable names will be the same as the parameters—just remember the `jvar_` prefix!

Using JEXL and escaping

JEXL is one of the first things to be evaluated when Jelly is parsed. This means that it can be included in almost every tag, and a typical Jelly script can contain many different tags— even client-side scripts. For instance, it is relatively common to output messages using JEXL expressions, as shown in this simple example:

```
<script>
  alert('Hello, ${gs.getUserName()}');
</script>
```

This will create a client-side JavaScript that has been created dynamically using server-side JavaScript and executed as part of a JEXL expression!

The only place where one can avoid using JEXL is in an `evaluate` tag. Due to the way that ServiceNow (and the Jelly and JEXL parsers) work with the data, this depletes a Java resource called PermGen memory. If it runs out, the instance will restart! (This occurs because the JEXL expressions cannot be de-allocated, so the garbage collector will never clean them up.)

The exception to this is the use of static JEXL expressions. Since the ampersand (`&`) is a reserved character in XML, it cannot be used; this causes some problems when you create conditions. Indeed, the greater than and less than characters (`>` and `<`) are also reserved. So, ServiceNow has ensured that JEXL can be used for outputting these characters and a few others:

- `${AMP}` will produce the ampsersand (`&`)
- `${AND}` creates a double ampersand (`&&`)
- `${GT}` makes the greater than symbol (`>`)
- `${LT}` makes the less than symbol (`<`)
- `${SP}` creates a nonbreaking space (` `)

These can be used directly within evaluate tags. So, to create a simple condition, the following Jelly is valid by using `&{AND}` instead of `&&`:

```
if (a == b ${AND} b == c) {...}
```

And, for a loop, the following Jelly is valid:

```
for (var x = 0; x ${LT} 10; x++) {...}
```

However, this is quite difficult to read. Instead, try to rewrite the query for readability, as follows:

```
for (var x = 0; x != 10; x++) {...}
```

> Even after you rewrite it, it quickly turns into a painful exercise and becomes very unreadable. Try calling Script Includes instead to retain your sanity. Client-side scripts can be created as UI Scripts and included on the page with the <g:requires name="MyUIScript.jsdbx" /> syntax.

Setting Jelly variables

One of the most common things to do in a UI Page is to use JavaScript to get or generate some data and then use Jelly to loop through it. The typical use case involves accessing some database records through GlideRecord and then iterate over each one. We'll see some examples of this later.

There are several ways to get JavaScript variables into Jelly. The easiest is just to use a set tag and a JEXL expression:

```
<g:evaluate>
  var test = "Hello, world!";
</g:evaluate>
<j:set var="jvar_test" value="${test}"/>
```

However, this takes another line. Instead, the evaluate tag can set a Jelly variable directly. The return value of the tag will be set in the variable specified in the var attribute. Since you are setting a Jelly variable, be sure to use the jvar_ prefix.

```
<g:evaluate var="jvar_test">
  "Hello, world!";
</g:evaluate>
```

This will produce the same result as the Jelly variable called jvar_test. However, this will also coerce the variable into a string. So, set the object attribute to true to keep it as an object if you want to return a GlideRecord or an array.

Try out this example as a new UI Page:

- **Name**: `Flintstones`
- **Code**:

```
<g:evaluate var="jvar_names" object="true">
  ["Betty", "Wilma"];
</g:evaluate>

<j:forEach items="${jvar_names}" var="jvar_name">
  <p>${jvar_name}</p>
</j:forEach>
```

This uses all Jelly variables in order to iterate over an array. However, JavaScript variables can be piped directly into the `forEach` tag with a JEXL expression. Note that the `forEach` tag sets a Jelly variable on each loop's iteration, so ensure to prefix it with `jvar`.

```
<g:evaluate>
  var names = ["Betty", "Wilma"];
</g:evaluate>

<j:forEach items="${names}" var="jvar_name">
  <p>${jvar_name}</p>
</j:forEach>
```

> The Jelly in ServiceNow uses both these techniques; often, it uses both at the same time. This allows data to be accessed from everywhere!
>
> ```
> <g:evaluate var="jvar_names" object="true">
>   var names = ["Betty", "Wilma"];
>   names;
> </g:evaluate>
> ```
>
> In this example, both the Jelly variable `jvar_names` and the JavaScript variable names can be used.

Caching Jelly

The different namespaces and processors in Jelly make it quite difficult to get your head a round them. What makes this even harder is the idea of caching. You might have already seen the use of the `j2` and `g2` namespaces and the JEXL expressions with square brackets (`$[]`). These are used in the second phase of Jelly evaluation.

All Jelly is parsed twice. Everything that we've created so far has been for Phase 1. All of the generated output is cached in memory so that it can be retrieved and shown really fast. However, sometimes you don't want to cache output, since you want it to be dynamically generated each time; perhaps based on parameters or information in the database.

So, every tag is also defined in a second namespace: `j2` and `g2`.

```
<j:set var='jvar_hello' value='Hello'/>
```

In addition, JEXL is executed in phase 2 when square brackets are used:

```
$[jvar_hello]
```

To understand how this works, consider the following Jelly and how it looks after each phase.

- **Original Jelly**:

```
<j:set var='jvar_hello' value='Hello'/>
<g2:evaluate>
    var user = gs.getUser();
</g2:evaluate>
<p>${jvar_hello} $[user]</p>
```

- **After phase 1**:

```
<g2:evaluate>
    var user = gs.getUser();
</g2:evaluate>
<p>Hello $[user]</p>
```

- **After phase 2**:

```
<p>Hello admin</p>
```

Each phase performs the replacement of the tags in the relevant namespace. In addition, each phase is independent, so the variables aren't automatically shared. While there is an attribute of the `evaluate` tag to copy variables to phase 2 (the aptly named `copyToPhase2` attribute!), you need to use the `set` tag to copy Jelly variables between phases as shown here:

```
<j2:set var="jvar_phase1" value="${jvar_phase1}" />
```

Mixing your phases

Getting your phases wrong, along with mixing up Jelly and JavaScript variables, is probably the most common problem you'll encounter. However, it's worth understanding since caching makes a vast improvement in the speed of parsing.

A simple example may be obvious, but it is worth emphasizing that this will not work:

```
<j:set var="jvar_test" value="true" />
<j:if test="$[jvar_test]">hello</j:if>
<j:if test="!$[jvar_test]">world</j:if>
```

Both the `if` tags in this example run in phase 1 and expect to see something valid in the `test` attribute. However, these JEXL expressions are only replaced in phase 2. In this example, nothing would be output. There would be no errors, which means that it will be difficult to debug. Ensuring that your phases are correct (perhaps even keeping everything in a single phase until everything works) is important.

> The `breakpoint` tag is helpful to output the current state of variables into the System Log.

Using Jelly in the CMS

All this Jelly is rather interesting, but how can we use it to enhance our portal? The layout of the portal is all custom, but we rely on the standard forms and lists layout. Although they are functional, they are not very attractive. So, how can we make them better?

Some Jelly has already been used to build the page's title. So, let's review our first foray into more advanced CMS implementations to see what can be leveraged.

Using Dynamic Blocks

The `GH - Page title` Dynamic Block is very simple. It contains a single JEXL expression:

```
${current_page.getTitle()}
```

This uses a global variable called `current_page`, and the `getTitle` function is called to return. We also know that it's done in phase 1. The `current_page` variable gives access to the items in the Page record, which is perfect for the use we have here. Of course, Jelly and the `evaluate` tag could be used to make a much more complicated entry.

In this way, custom pages can be created, and they can generate content through database access. In addition, the Jelly in CMS has access to a global variable called `RP`, which stands for `RenderProperties`. This is a Java class that has a useful method called `getParameterValue`. This allows a CMS page to work with the information that is provided to it as parameters. For example, the following information that is passed in a URL:

```
https://<instance>.service-now.com/self-service/page.do?sysparm_
parameter=test
```

This can set a Jelly variable using the following Jelly:

```
<g2:evaluate var="jvar_sysparm_parameter">
RP.getParameterValue('sysparm_parameter');
<g2:evaluate/>
```

This means you could create a page that accepts a parameter, such as a `sys_id`, and use this to find and display the desired content—like a search engine.

However, creating lots of Dynamic Blocks and making lots of custom pages would be tiresome. Instead, we can have ServiceNow do some of the work with Content Types.

Specifying Content Types

In a similar fashion to MIME types (such as `text/html`), ServiceNow Content Types tell the platform how the data should be rendered. By defining a Content Type for the Maintenance table, Jelly can be used to create a custom look and feel every time a Maintenance record is accessed.

First, let's create a **Content Type** for the list of **Maintenance** records.

1. Navigate to **Content Management** > **Configuration** > **Content Types** and click on **New**. Then, fill in the following values:

    - **Type**: `Maintenance [u maintenance]`
    - **Content site**: `Gardiner Hotels`
    - **Summary template**:

    ```
    <g:content_link>
    ${HTML:current.number.getDisplayValue()} - ${HTML:current.
    short_description.getDisplayValue()}
    </g:content_link>
    ```

There are a couple of new things here:

- The `getDisplayValue()` function is called on the fields, the `GlideElements`. Rather than returning whatever is in the database, `getDisplayValue` properly formats the text, making sure dates and times are in the correct time zone, perform any language translation as necessary.
- The `HTML:` prefix tells ServiceNow what content you are expecting and to escape any characters. So, if the **Short description** contains angle brackets (<, >), this will ensure that they are turned into the correct entities (`<`, `>`).

> Make sure you always escape text from the database or else you will introduce security vulnerabilities into your site. A malicious guest could try to insert JavaScript within the Short description!

- There is also the inclusion of a UI Macro called `content_link`. This produces a clickable link, which we will explore further in a moment.

The next step is to create a list to utilize this definition.

Creating CMS Lists

Let's start by creating a CMS list:

1. Navigate to **Content Management** > **Blocks** > **Lists** and click on **New**.
    - **Name**: `GH - Maintenance list`
    - **Table**: `Maintenance [u_maintenance]`
    - **Type**: `list_simple`
    - **Maximum entries**: `20`
    - **Order**: `Opened`
    - **Title**: `Check outstanding items here`
    - **Query**:

      `Opened by - is (dynamic) - Me` and `Active - is - true`
2. Now, add the block. Navigate to the `GH - Existing Maintenance` Page and choose **Edit Page**.
3. Remove the `GH - Existing Maintenance` IFrame.
4. Add the block called `Check outstanding items here`.

Now, when you navigate to the Maintenance task list in the CMS portal (perhaps, using the **Monitor existing requests** menu item), you'll get a very simple listing of records.

> If you can't see any tasks, ensure that you have some tasks open and with the **Opened by** field set right. You can change the **Opened by** field through list editing.

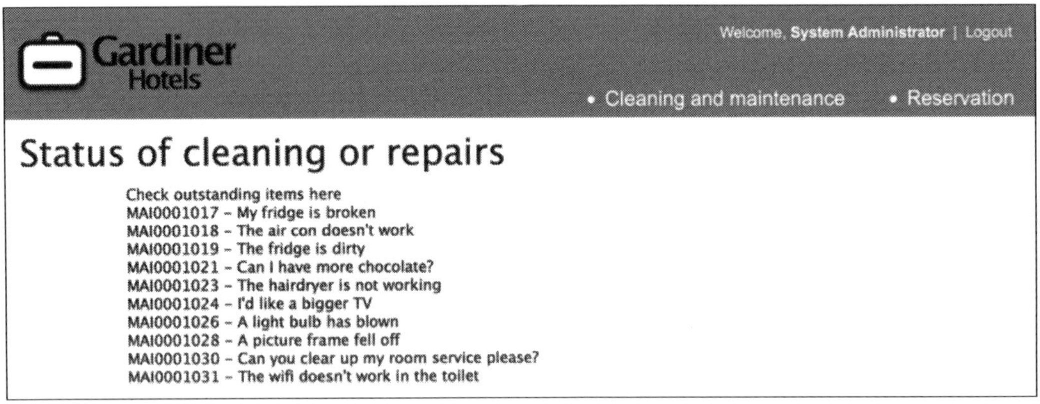

This pulls together several of the elements that we have discussed so far.

- The List record specifies which and how many records to get along with the order in which they should be collected. Together, these parameters create a GlideRecord object that queries the database.
- The result is passed to the List type. This is a UI Macro that has a `for` loop, which iterates over each record.
- For each entry, it uses the Jelly in the **Summary Template** field in the **Content Type** to output some text.

This example produces a clear but quite plain list. We'll see later how this can be styled to be a little better.

First, let's deal with the issue about the links not working.

Building Detail Content

Just as the **List block** uses the **Summary Template** in the **Content Type**, **Detailed Content** uses the **Detail** Template. However, while we could just change the block on the existing **Maintenance** List, a new page is needed for the detail page. Previously, the detail content just loaded in the IFrame and couldn't have its own page but specifying the Content Type gives it extra flexibility.

1. As a first step, navigate to the `GH - Existing Maintenance` page and click on the **Copy** button.

   Fill the following fields:

   Name: `GH - Maintenance Detail`

   URL suffix: `detail_maintenance`

   Title: `Details of the outstanding job`
2. Once saved, click on the **Edit Page** link and remove the `Check outstanding items here` list.
3. Using **Add content**, add a ***New Detail** block. Configure it as follows:

   Name: `GH - Maintenance content`

   Type: `Show the page's current document`

Now, let's alter the Content Type to show the information that we want.

1. Navigate to **Content Management** > **Configuration** > **Content Types** and choose the one for the Maintenance records. Then, add these fields:
   - **Default detail page**: `GH - Maintenance Detail`
   - **Detail template**: Add the following scripts:

     ```
     <p>${HTML:current.number.getDisplayValue()}
     <br/>${HTML:current.short_description.getDisplayValue()}
     <br/>${HTML:current.state.getDisplayValue()}</p>
     ```
2. Try it out! Open up the portal and look at the **Status of cleaning or repairs** page. Now, all the links should work on the list. When we click on a Maintenance record, we are presented with a very short summary of the maintenance issue. This is great!

Understanding the link structure

Try to examine one of the links on the **Status of cleaning or repairs** page. This looks quite different to the standard URLs:

```
https://<instance>.service-now.com/self-service/detail_maintenance.
do?sysparm_document_key=u_maintenance,97b09770eb2331005983e08a5206fe
3f
```

As you can see, it uses a parameter in the URL called the document key, which is the unique identifier for any record in ServiceNow. Its structure is quite simple: the table name and `sys_id` of the record, separated by a comma. A link to a CMS detail page must use this structure.

To help with this, there is a UI Macro called `content_link`. It creates the relevant HTML for you, but it expects the existence of JavaScript `GlideRecord` variable called `current`.

Improving lists and forms

Since everything is working, let's delve into some more Jelly to make things a little more attractive. Let's add some extra HTML elements that can be styled better:

1. Navigate to **Content Management** > **Configuration** > **Content Types** and find the one for `u_maintenance`.
2. Update the following fields:
    - **Summary Template**:

    ```
    <div class="content_summary maintenance">
    <span class="updates">
        <j:set var="jvar_updates" value="${current.
            sys_mod_count.getDisplayValue()}"/>
        <div class="value">${jvar_updates}</div>
        <div>
            <j:if test="${jvar_updates == 1}">${gs.
                getMessage('Update')}</j:if>
            <j:if test="${jvar_updates != 1}">${gs.
                getMessage('Updates')}</j:if>
        </div>
    </span>
    ```

```
<span class="summary_info">
    <g:content_link>
        <h3>${current.short_description.
            getDisplayValue()}</h3>
    </g:content_link>
<span class="summary_meta">
    <label>${gs.getMessage('Reference:')}</label>
    ${HTML:current.number.getDisplayValue()}
    <label>${gs.getMessage('Last updated:')}</label>
    ${current.sys_updated_on.getDisplayValue()}
    </span>
  </span>
</div>
```

- **Detail Template**:

```
<div class="detail">
    <span class="detail_summary">
    <p><label>${gs.getMessage('Reference:')}</label>
        ${HTML:current.number.getDisplayValue()}</p>
    <p><label>${gs.getMessage('Last updated:')}</label>
        ${current.sys_updated_on.getDisplayValue()}</p>
    </span>
    <span class="detail_detail">
        <h2>${gs.getMessage('You said:')}</h2>
        <label>${HTML:current.short_description.
            getDisplayValue()}</label>
        <p>${HTML:current.description.getDisplayValue()}</p>
        <h2>${gs.getMessage('What we are doing:')}</h2>
    <span class="newline">
        ${HTML:current.comments_and_work_notes.
            getJournalEntry(-1);}</span>
    </span>
</div>
```

The preceding edits provide several benefits:

- More information is pulled from the `current` object of `GlideRecord`. This represents either the current list item or the subject matter of the detail record. This gives more detail to the user.
- Several `span` and `div` tags are added, making styling much easier.

- Throughout, the `getMessage` function from `GlideSystem` is used, which is first mentioned in *Chapter 3, Client-side Interaction*. This provides a simple translation system: if the specified text is available in the user's language, it is shown; otherwise, the same text is returned.
- The `getJournalEntry` function of `GlideElement` is called on the `comments_and_work_notes` field, allowing all of the entries of both to be visible. Note that this function respects Access Control Rules—since the requester does not have access to the **Work Notes** field, only Additional comments will actually be shown.

3. To make it a little more attractive, let's create a new style sheet. Find the **Gardiner Hotels** theme by navigating to **Content Management** > **Design** > **Themes** and create a new record by filling the following details in the fields:
   - **Name**: `GH - Content Type`
   - **Style**:

```
.content_summary .updates{
    float: left;
    margin-right: 10px;
    textalign: center;
    background: #fff;
    border: 1px solid #e0e0e0;
    fontsize: smaller; padding: 4px;
    min-width: 24px;}
.content_summary .updates .value { font-size: large; }
/* Put the number of updates in a bordered box, and style it */

.content_summary .summary_info h3 { margin-bottom: 5px}
.content_summary .summary_meta {font-size: 0.9em}
/* Align the list information and size the text appropriately */

.cms_content label {font-weight: bold}
.cms_content { padding-left: 10px}
.cms_content .detail .newline { white-space:pre-line; }
/* Arrange and align the text in the detail text properly */
```

Final testing

Let's take a look at what our configuration has achieved:

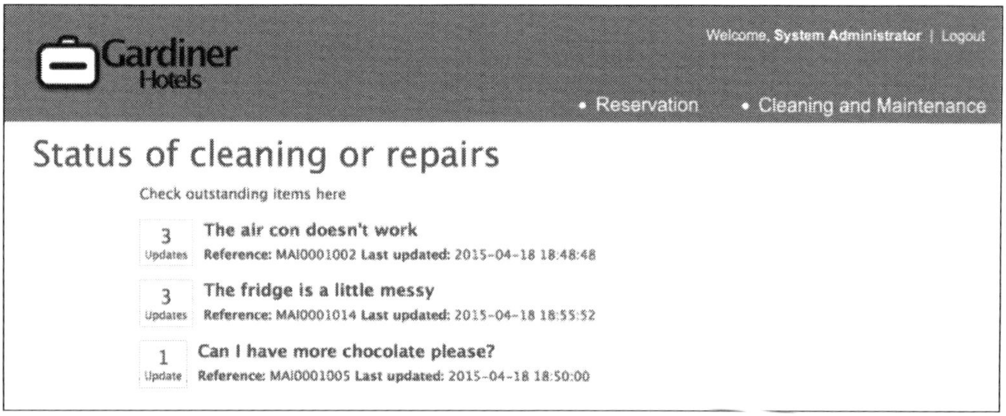

The list and layout looks very clean. The layout is simple and fits much more easily into the style of the rest of the site:

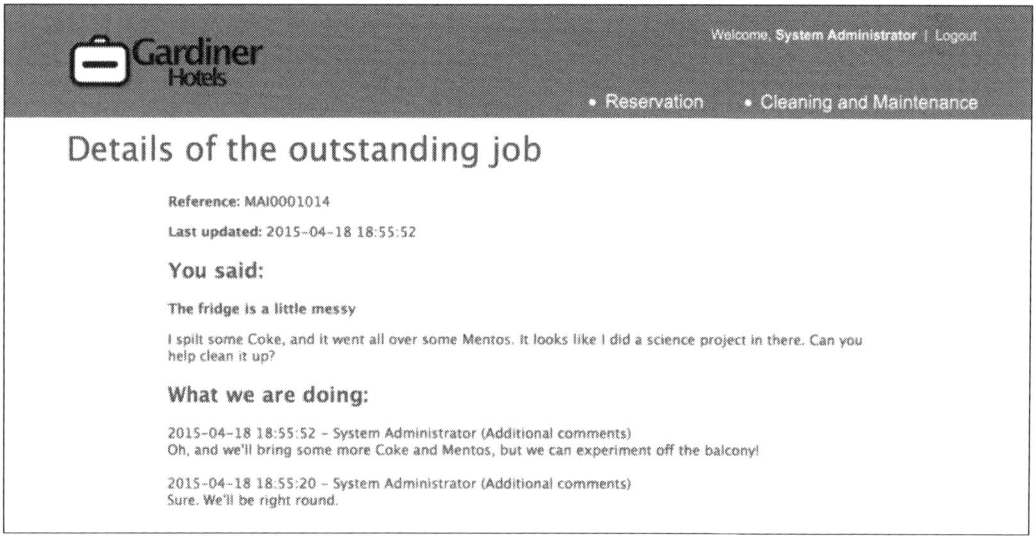

The detailed view uses friendly text and removes all the field boxes, giving a simple look.

Of course, there is much more that can be done to the site:

- A **Content Type** could be created for the **Reservations** table, making the list and detail of the record more usable.
- The detail view of the **Maintenance** record could be further improved with more styling—parsing and editing the Additional comments output would help.
- A new List definition could be made, which would perhaps allow the manipulation of the list. The **Script** field that is made available when the **Advanced** checkbox is ticked has access to the `RP.getParameterValue` function, which means that you can pass and process parameters between pages.

While **Content Types** and their associated Lists and Detail Blocks provide much more capability than styling forms, they do have their limitations and considerations:

- It is not straightforward to have an editable form. Since there is no equivalent to the Processing script on a UI Page, any form would need to be dealt with in a custom way—perhaps through GlideAJAX and Script Includes or even a custom Processor that takes submissions and redirects to the appropriate CMS page. Again, the RP `RenderProperties` variable, even those sent via POST, could be used to process incoming parameters. However, there is no clean solution!
- The amount of work (and thought) necessary to build a completely custom site is significant. Since you control all elements of the page, elements such as security must be carefully considered. When you use the standard forms and lists, for instance, the platform automatically escapes the data for you to prevent cross-site scripting and other attacks. However, there is less protection in custom Jelly-based pages.
- Building a CMS site is a mixture of science and art. Having a strong design upfront is important. Ensure that the desired pages are clearly defined and that the blocks that are required to build the page are identified. Then, build each item by being clear about how you will achieve it in the style that you want. It can be very tiresome to change the same thing in multiple pages, so using pen and paper will save time.

Including Jelly in the standard interface

Jelly is not reserved just for CMS. Since the ServiceNow platform is built using the language, there are several places where you can inject your own code to further control your instance.

Adding Formatters

One of the simplest ways to do so is with a Formatter. This item provides a mechanism to include a UI Macro onto a form. Navigate to **System UI** > **Formatters** to see the out of the box items. There are several examples, including the Process Flow formatter, the Activity Log, and the variable editor placed on the ITSM tables, that show what is possible.

Let's cover a simple but useful example. This will run on the Maintenance form, making it more obvious when an SLA has breached.

Navigate to **System UI** > **UI Macros** and click on **New**.

- **Name**: `check_breached_sla`
- **XML**:

```
<j2:if test="$[!current.isNewRecord()]">
    <g2:evaluate>
        //get real glide record
        var gr = new GlideAggregate("task_sla");
        gr.addActiveQuery();
        gr.addQuery('breached', true);
        gr.addQuery('task', current.sys_id);
        gr.addAggregate('count');
        gr.query();
        gr.next();
    </g2:evaluate>
    <j2:if test="$[gr.getAggregate('COUNT') > 0]">
      <h3 style="color:red; padding: 5px">There are
         breached SLAs</h3>
    </j2:if>
</j2:if>
```

> Don't forget to keep the XML declaration and the `jelly` tag.

This Jelly mostly consists of a `GlideAggregate` count, which was introduced in *Chapter 2, Server-side Control*. It uses the `current` global variable to know which Maintenance task is being viewed and accesses the **Task SLA** table. If any records meet the criteria of being breached, active and matching the current record, then a red warning message is displayed. All the logic only runs if the current object has been saved, and thus `isNewRecord` is false.

> Note that all the Jelly takes place in phase 2. Since it changes record by record, it should not be cached.

To include the UI Macro on the form, create a new Formatter by navigating to **System UI > Formatters**:

- **Name**: `Check breached SLA`
- **Formatter**: `check_breached_sla.xml`
- **Table**: `Maintenance [u_maintenance]`

> The Formatter value is made up of the UI Macro name, which is suffixed with `.xml`. This shows how some formatters are actually stored on the instance server as XML files.

Once the settings are saved, configure the **Form Layout** of the **Maintenance** form. It will contain an extra entry called **Check breached SLAs**. Include this onto your form, probably at the top, to give a very obvious warning to your Maintenance team!

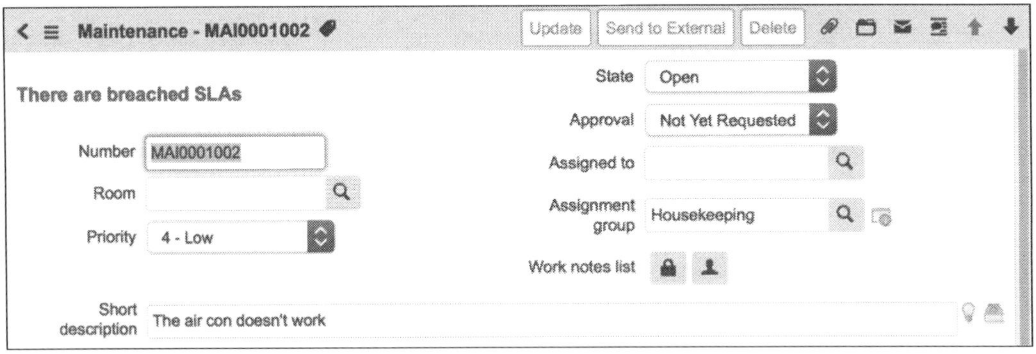

> UI Macros can also be included on the **Service Catalog**. There is a variable type that lets you select the one that you want.

Decorating and contributing to fields

Reference fields often have icons to the right of the input field. For example, on the **Task** table, the **Configuration Item** field has a little icon that is shown when the field is populated. Clicking on it will show the Business Service Map. In addition, the **Planned Task** table has several fields that are calculated from the child fields. These "rollup" fields then have a little icon next to them to indicate this situation.

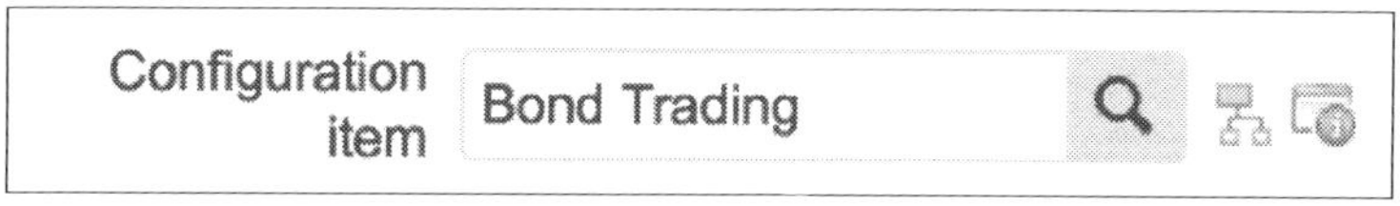

The mechanism to create a Decoration and Contribution is straightforward:

1. Create a UI Macro with the desired functionality. The `ref` JavaScript variable stores the name of the field, while `__ref__` is a JavaScript `GlideRecord` object to which the reference field points.
2. Edit the **Dictionary** entry for the field to which you want to add it.
3. Set an attribute called `field_decorations` or `ref_contributions`. Either will work.
4. List the name of the UI Macro as the attribute value.

For example, there is a UI Macro with a name of `show_related_records`. This contains some Jelly that provides a button, and launches a dialog box that shows other active tasks that are related to the same CI. The Dictionary entry for this field contains the `ref_contributions=task_show_ci_map;show_related_records` attribute.

[In this example, there are actually two UI Macros that are separated by semicolons.]

The `show_related_records` UI Macro itself is relatively complicated. It creates an icon that is positioned on the page next to the reference field. It performs a `GlideAggregate` query, similar to the one above, and shows the icon if there are other active tasks.

It then includes client-side JavaScript that uses the ServiceNow event handlers to register a function for the on change event of the **Configuration Item** field. When the field is changed, a function is run to determine whether or not to show the icon. This logic uses a `GlideAJAX` call to a Script Include to make the determination. Finally, if the icon is shown, it launches the dialog box when clicked.

> Creating a new `GlideEventHandler` function provides the structure for the platform to call a function if an `onchange` event occurs. The parameters for a `GlideEventHandler` are a unique identifier, the function, and what field should be watched. This object should be pushed into the `g_event_handlers` array. Note that this function is undocumented, so it is unsupported.

Quite a few admins try to duplicate this UI Macro to provide similar functionality to other fields. While this is achievable, care must be taken to make unique JavaScript function names so that there are not namespace collisions.

Launching a dialog box

Modal dialog boxes are quite common in user interfaces. They provide a very direct and visual way to prompt the user, usually to provide input. ServiceNow provides several ways to do this. Often, these dialog boxes are presented after a client-side UI Action click.

> All these techniques are undocumented; so, although some baseline apps use the functionality, they are not supported.

Launching UI Pages with GlideDialogWindow

If you've built a cool UI Page, you can easily display it using `GlideDialogWindow`. To start things off, let's just launch the dialog box using the JavaScript Executor:

1. Navigate to a form or a list.
2. Press *Ctrl* + *Shift* + *J* to launch the window and use this code to launch the window:

   ```
   var dialog = new GlideDialogWindow('hello_world');
   dialog.setTitle('Hello, world!');
   dialog.render();
   ```

The script initializes a new `GlideDialogWindow` object, passing through the name of the UI Page. One of the example pages that we made earlier is used here. The `setTitle` function gives the title of the window. The UI Page is created in a floating `div`, submitting the form will affect the whole page.

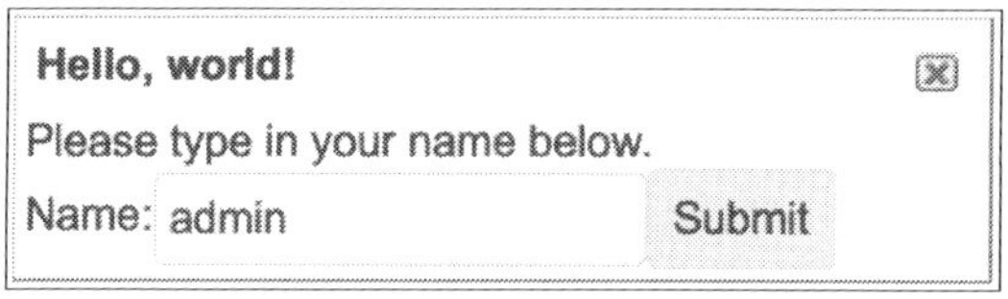

Use the `setWidth()` function of `GlideDialogWindow` to adjust the size and pass parameters with the `setPreference('sysparm_name', 'value')` function. The `destroy` function closes the window. This is useful if you have a **Cancel** button on the UI Page.

Fitting in a form

The UI Page is the ultimate in flexibility. However, you don't always want to write Jelly. Instead, you may want to create a new record or show an existing one. With GlideDialogForm, which is an extension of GlideDialogWindow, you can do just that.

Create a new **UI Action** on the **Room** table to easily create a Reservation record for that room. To do this, navigate to **System Definition** > **UI Actions** and click on **New**.

- **Name**: `Create Reservation`
- **Table**: `Room [u_room]`
- **Client**: `<checked>`
- **Form link**: `<checked>`
- **Onclick**: `launchReservationDialogForm();`
- **Script**: :

```
function launchReservationDialogForm () {
    var dialog = new GlideDialogForm('Create Reservation',
      'u_reservation', function() { alert('Reservation created!') });
   dialog.addParm('sysparm_view', 'ess');
    dialog.render();
}
```

This script is slightly more complex, but it is still not very long. The `GlideDialogForm` object requires three parameters: the title, the table, and a callback function. This is called when the form is submitted. In this script, the callback function doesn't accept any parameters, but it could with four: the action, the `sys_id` of the record, the table, and the display value of the record. This is very useful to populate fields on the original form from the dialog box.

The `addParm` function sets parameters similar to `setPreference`. This button ensures that the simple Self Service view that we created earlier is used.

Note that when the dialog is submitted, only the dialog closes and not the whole page.

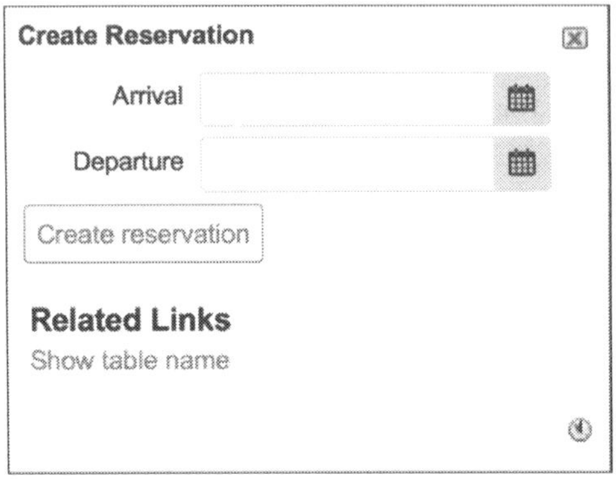

Displaying any page with GlideBox

If a form is not flexible enough, then GlideBox is available. It accepts a URL and displays it in an IFrame, letting you show anything you want—perhaps a map or a complex page.

Let's use GlideBox to show the CMS interface of the Maintenance record even in the normal interface. To do this, create another UI Action by populating these fields:

- **Name**: `Show Self Service view`
- **Table**: `Maintenance [u_maintenance]`
- **Client**: `<checked>`
- **Form link**: `<checked>`
- **Onclick**: `launchSelfServiceMaintenanceView();`
- **Script**:

```
function launchSelfServiceMaintenanceView() {
    var box = new GlideBox({
        iframe: '/self-service/detail_maintenance.do?
          sysparm_document_key=' + g_form.getTableName()
            + ',' + g_form.getUniqueValue(),
        width: '95%',
        height: 500,
        title: "Self Service view",
```

```
            fadeOutTime: 1000
        });
        box.render();
    }
```

The style to create a GlideBox object differs somewhat from GlideDialogWindow. It accepts a single object with name-value property pairs. Here, the `iframe` property is set by building up the URL programmatically. The `width`, `height`, and `title` are set along with the time in milliseconds for a gradual fade out.

> GlideBox supports many options. Instead of an IFrame, HTML could be supplied with the `body` parameter. Lots of events, such as `onHeightAdjust`, and `onBeforeClose`, will notify a callback function, if you pass one.

Summary

One of the benefits of a web-based application is that anyone can access it. Web browsers are built into phones and tablets. This accessibility means that ServiceNow is great for building a self-service interface; something that allows guests of Hotel Gardiner to see and submit information.

The easiest way to providing a **self-service portal** is to use the standard interface, with requesters logging in and accessing the platform with no roles. This provides a very quick setup, with only security rules to think about.

However, the look and feel of the standard interface could be considered quite restrictive and plain. On the form, the fields are in two columns with the label on the left. The lists provide lots of functions, with checkboxes, menus, and icons. This is great for power users, but it is perhaps intimidating to casual users.

> As noted in *Chapter 1, ServiceNow Foundations*, these plain forms do provide a consistent and clear experience. There is a great deal of benefit to this.

To provide a more attractive interface, usually for requesters, the **Content Management System** (**CMS**) is employed. This allows you to build up content on a page-by-page basis building block-by-block. The blocks provide lots of different functions—from simple HTML blocks to complex menus and headers. To display content, an IFrame is normally employed, to place standard forms and lists in the page. The contents of an IFrame—and everything else—can be styled by using CSS, which gives a great deal of power.

To get a really customized interface, you need to use **Jelly**. Jelly is an executable XML format, and while it can be difficult to work with, it provides a powerful way to conditionally output HTML.

ServiceNow has supercharged Jelly. With the addition of the `evaluate` tag, the platform can run JavaScript to perform database lookups and complex manipulation in the page itself. To ensure that the output is rendered quickly, a two-phased approach caches the initial run through; while the second phase is executed on each page view.

Jelly can also be included in the main interface. Custom **UI Pages** can deliver a new interface, while **UI Macros** can be embedded on forms using **Formatters** and next to fields using **decorations** or **contributions**.

With these elements in place, ServiceNow provides many ways to build an interface that is right for your needs. In the next chapter, we will look at ways to stretch out of the web and get deeper into your data center.

11

Automating Your Data Center

Our ServiceNow project for Gardiner Hotels has so far concentrated on business-focused process functionality. This included creating simple data structures for storing information about our guests, then we moved on to task-based workflows, and most recently, we looked at building complex, custom user interfaces. While *Chapter 6, Exchanging Data – Import Sets, Web Services, and Other Integrations*, did explore some of the ways in which two systems could integrate together, there is more capability in ServiceNow. In addition to automating your business, ServiceNow can automate your IT infrastructure.

In this chapter, we will look into the following areas:

- ServiceNow **Discovery** is an agentless method of collecting information about your IT estate. Working through your MID server, Discovery will communicate with the switches, routers, and servers that underpin the services that the business relies on to find out the information that you need.
- The **Graphical Workflow** engine can be extended with **Orchestration**, which enables ServiceNow to even start changing these services. It allows you to make new user accounts in Active Directory with the click of a button or deploy a software change quickly and automatically. Of course, you can use this building block to create your own automated actions.
- **Cloud Provisioning** goes one step further to give you a complete process to spin-up, manage, and destroy new virtual machines in your own VMWare cloud—or use Amazon Web Services.
- **Configuration Automation** can then apply templates to these new resources, changing and updating each one in only a few clicks.

> This chapter has few examples since the configuration is very dependent on your infrastructure. However, the foundations are explored to give you a grounding of the functionalities.

Servicing the business

ServiceNow is often positioned as an IT Service Management (ITSM) platform. It allows the IT department to define, deliver, and direct the services that they provide to the rest of the business. Most organizations rely on IT, and Gardiner Hotels is no different. Our fictional organization depends on a variety of systems to deliver a world-class service:

- The **door lock security** uses a contactless keycard, written by a computer sitting at reception.
- The finance department uses an ERP suite to manage **payments and expenses**.
- The guest TV hooks into a **video-on-demand** system that gives them the choice of thousands of movies.
- The Research and Development team always look for new ways to improve our guest's experience, so their **test lab** needs a flexible virtual machine environment.
- The facilities team, as we've seen in earlier chapters, needs to send **maintenance jobs** to an external contractor. They use ServiceNow to accept and store jobs.
- Human Resources manage **recruitment and payroll** through a SaaS application.

These business functions all rely on IT infrastructure: servers (virtual or physical), hosted platforms, or SaaS. Moreover, the IT infrastructure is interconnected, with systems relying on each other too. The video-on-demand system needs to bill the customer for their viewing pleasure and requires a very large file storage system for all the videos.

The IT staff work hard to ensure that the servers are well maintained, with the operating systems patched and replacing disks quickly when they fail. To do this, they need an accurate inventory of what is out there, so that no operating system is missed and the right replacement disk is easily known.

Discovering devices

The primary purpose of Discovery is to find what is out there. ServiceNow Discovery is **agentless**. This means that it does not rely on the software installed on individual machines.

Instead, ServiceNow will communicate with the devices on your network. Everything with an IP address is connected to, interrogated, and the results are recorded. This means that your servers, disks, network routers and switches, and even printers can be automatically found and saved.

> Other systems rely on the software that is installed on the device to communicate back to a central service. This is very useful for mobile devices, such as laptops, which may often change networks or simply turn off. However, the roll out of the agent software is often problematic and for some systems, such as network routers, it is simply not possible.

Getting a list of hardware is an incredibly valuable part of Discovery. Many companies leverage Discovery simply to understand what devices are out there counting servers via Excel is not a robust solution.

However, wouldn't it be better if the system could be even more proactive? Imagine the benefits if the platform could tell you the impact of a disk failure, in a business sense? Or that changing a critical item during peak time is ill-advised? You can achieve this by having a relationship-based CMDB where the Business Services are related to the IT infrastructure that underpins it.

Building relationships

One of the fundamental items of a good CMDB is a trustworthy set of relationships. This shows how all the items in the CMDB work with one another.

If we extend some of the examples that we have used so far, we can represent the information in the following diagram:

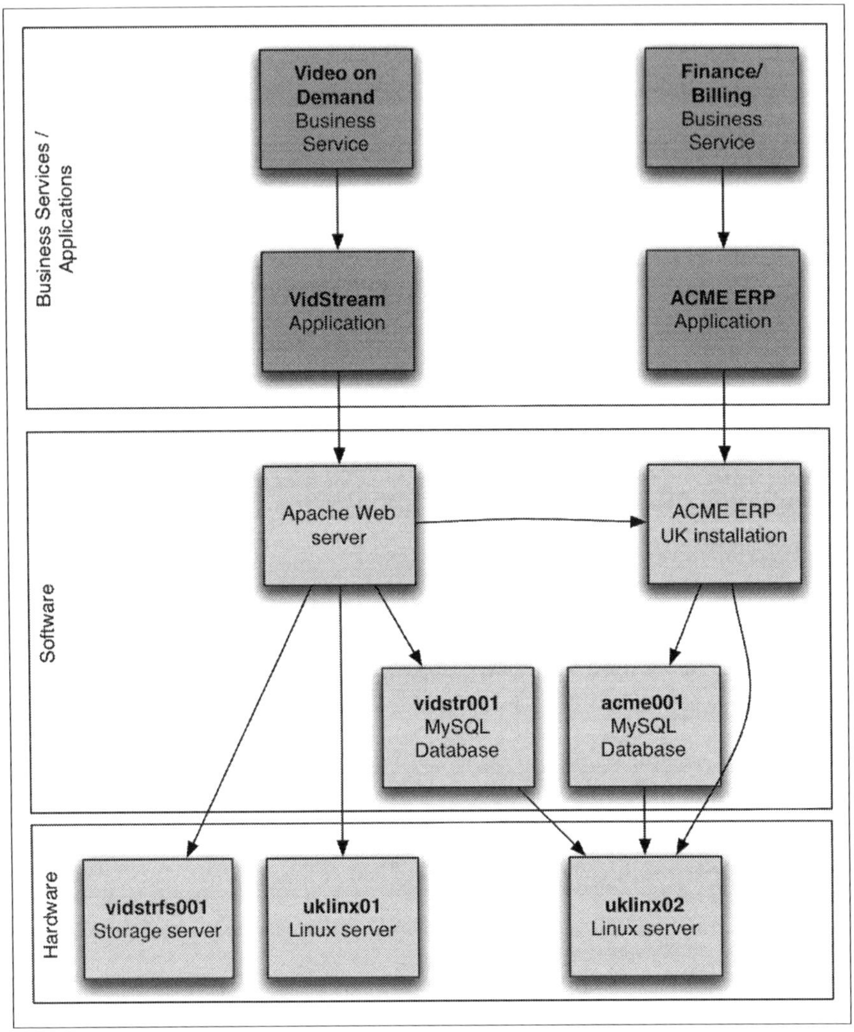

Each box in the diagram is a Configuration Item. This is a component in a service that is provided to the business. As you work down the diagram, from the top to the bottom, it becomes less recognizable to the business.

> A Configuration Item has a specific meaning in ITIL. This is an element of a service that needs to be controlled, supported, and managed.

The diagram shows three main sections, as follows:

Services and applications

- The top layer contains the Business Services we've been talking about. This represents the items that the hotel needs to do their normal activities.
- The applications represent a system that will provide the services. This may be a SaaS service (such as ServiceNow) or some other system. Note that it isn't a program or an executable—that comes next.

Software

- The third layer is the running software. It represents executable code, something that uses resources. The `VidStream` application uses an Apache Web Server to host the functionality.
- The next layer represents databases. Databases are used by software to store data, and in turn, they utilize hardware.

Hardware

- The bottom layer shows things that you can kick. The software and hardware is installed on physical machines. Here, the databases use a couple of servers, as well as some storage.

> Each item has more attributes than just its name. For instance, the database CIs should indicate the version of MySQL they are running and the port on which it is listening on.

Each layer depends on the layer below, in the direction of the arrows. For instance, at the bottom of the diagram, the two databases, `vidstr001` and `acme001`, are both hosted on the `uklinx02` physical server. In turn, the Apache Web Server connects to and depends on multiple systems; it runs on the `uklinx01` server, stores data on the `vidstrfs001` storage server, and connects to the ACME ERP UK installation. This latter relationship represents the need for the video-on-demand system to connect to the billing system.

This dependency diagram immediately shows the single point of failure. If the `uklinx02` server has a problem, then it is likely that both the Business Services are going to be impacted. If the billing system cannot work, video-on-demand may not work properly.

Using the BSM in ServiceNow

The **Business Service Map (BSM)** is a type of diagram that is available in ServiceNow. The BSM shows the relationship between CIs. Some examples are included with the demo data. Let's start with it by performing the following set of steps:

1. Navigate to **BSM** > **View Map**.
2. In the reference field at the top-left corner, enter and select **Email**. This will display the Email Business Service as shown in the following screenshot:

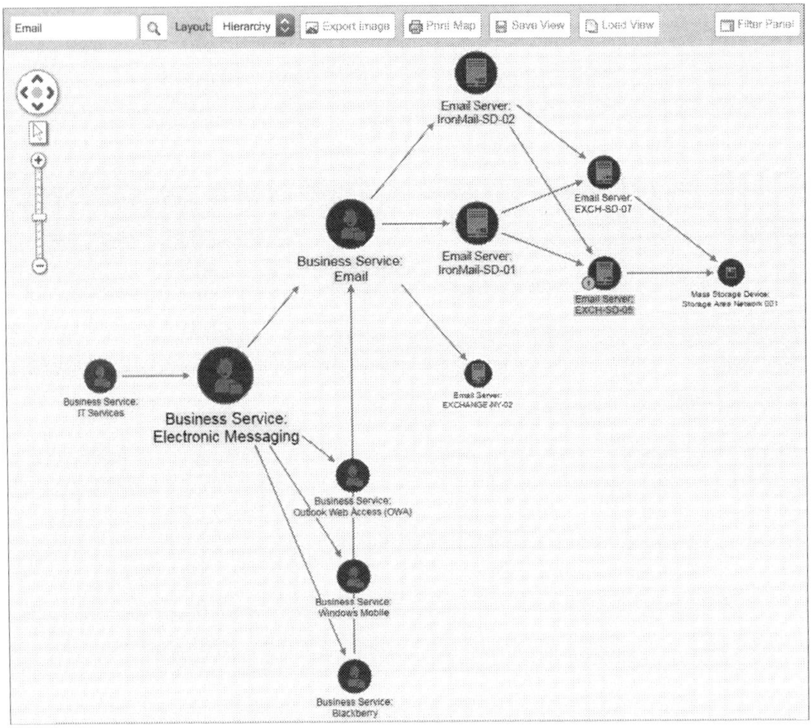

This diagram shows how many Business Services (such as the BlackBerry service) rely on e-mail. In turn, this is supplied by some e-mail servers, which use a SAN.

> The BSM is powerful. It integrates closely with the ITSM functionality. Tasks such as Incidents can be associated with CIs, letting others know that there is an issue with the item.

Of course, there is more detail to a CI than this. Double-clicking on a CI will open a new window. This allows us to see additional details, for example, the Storage Area Network 001 is a CyberRAID system with 10 disks and 1.8 TB of storage space.

The BSM displays the CIs in the ServiceNow CMDB. A CMDB populated by Discovery can give you a multitude of benefits:

- You can find all the resources that are connected to your network
- You can know what software is running on each server
- You can understand how each item is connected to and dependent upon each another
- You can link everything to a Business Service, giving better visibility and outage impacts

So, where is all this data kept in ServiceNow?

Storing relationships and CIs

The ServiceNow CMDB is stored, like all other data, in a series of database tables. The base table is **Configuration Item** [`cmdb_ci`]. This has many fields on it, such as Manufacturer, Description, and IP address, which represent the attributes of the CI. The basic aim of Discovery is to populate these and many other fields.

> Tables are often referred to as classes in the CMDB. It is an object-oriented data structure. *Chapter 1, ServiceNow Foundations* discusses how tables can be extended from each other.

The Configuration Item table is heavily extended and very hierarchical. Around 60 other tables extend it, such as **Software** [`cmdb_ci_spkg`], **Hardware** [`cmdb_ci_hardware`], and **Business Service** [`cmdb_ci_service`]. In turn, these tables are themselves extended.

- The Hardware table is the base for the **Network Gear** [`cmdb_ci_netgear`] and **Computer** [`cmdb_ci_computer`] tables
- The **Server** [`cmdb_ci_server`] is itself extended from Computer
- In addition, there are many extensions from Server, such as **Linux Server** [`cmdb_ci_linux_server`] and **Windows Server** [`cmdb_ci_windows_server`]

> By convention, all the names of the CMDB tables that contain CIs are prefixed with `cmdb_ci`. If you create new tables, then ensure that the table name starts with `u_cmdb_ci`.

Creating a new table to store new types of devices is easy. New fields can be added that are specific to the type of item that it is. It also allows Discovery to be more specific when it is collecting data. For example, Windows servers use a different mechanism to grab information than Linux servers do.

However, there is sometimes a tendency to create many new classes when there is no real need. Think carefully whether you need a new class or an attribute that describes the data better.

For example, there is little point in creating two classes, one for servers running Windows 2003 and another for Windows 2008. There will be very few differences between both, but there will be more maintenance overhead. It would be better to use an attribute such as the OS field to differentiate between the two different types of CIs.

Visualizing the extensions

Understanding how tables are extended is made easier with the Schema Map, which was first noted in *Chapter 1, ServiceNow Foundations*.

1. Navigate to **System Definition** > **Tables** and choose the table, such as **Windows Server**, that you want to explore.
2. Click on the **Show Schema Map** Related Link.
3. Deselect all the checkboxes except **Show extended tables** (and optionally **Show extending tables**).

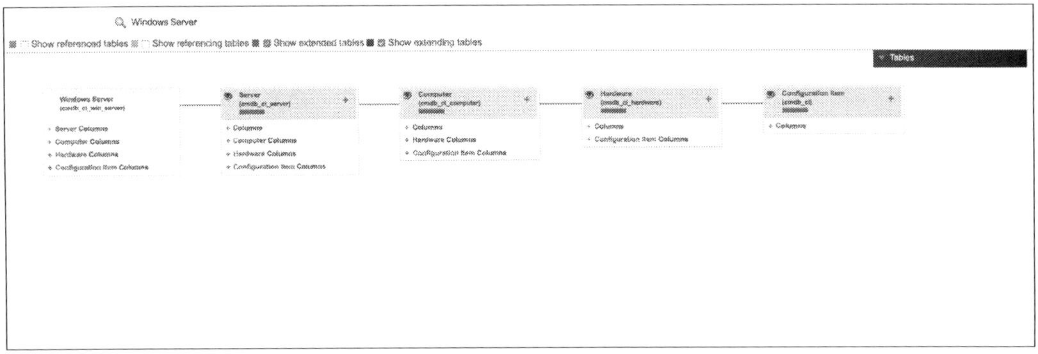

Linking the CIs together

The BSM shows two main elements—the CIs and the links between the CIs. The **CI Relationships** [`cmdb_rel_ci`] are stored in another table. This is effectively a many-to-many table with two reference fields (one is called the parent and the other is called the child), each pointing to the **Configuration Item** base table. This allows any two CIs, no matter what class, to be related together. To describe what the relationship is, the **CI Relationship Type** [`cmdb_rel_type`] table is also referenced.

Relationship Types have two parts, which can be seen from different angles. The parent may have a **Depends on** relationship with the child while the child would have a **Used by** relationship with the parent. This would be displayed as **Depends on::Used by**.

[Relating some CIs together just wouldn't make sense. For example, relating a software package to a rack that physically holds servers doesn't make sense. Suggested Relationships will help someone who is maintaining the CMDB to pick the right type of relationship, but it is not mandatory to follow this.]

Separating relationships and classes

Often, there is confusion between the definitions of a Configuration Item, its relationships, and what class it is in. Let's take an example of a cat called Sylvester, and consider what would happen if Sylvester was represented in a CMDB:

- Sylvester the character is a **CI**. This is a specific representation of a particular item. It has some attributes, such as that Sylvester has black and white hair and a name that immediately identifies who he is, that is stored in fields.
- Sylvester is a cat. Therefore, `cat` is his **class**. Sylvester is also a `mammal`, and more generally, an `animal`. If a class hierarchy was set up, you will have `animal` as the base class, which will be extended by `mammal` and extended again by `cat`.
- Sylvester has **relationships** with other CIs. For instance, he may have a **Tries to catch::Runs away** relationship with Tweety Bird and another with Speedy Gonzales. Perhaps, the relationship exists in the other direction between Sylvester and Hector the Bulldog.

[Note that relationships exist between CIs and not between classes. While it may be very common for cats to try to catch birds (and thus, it would be a Suggested Relationship), it is not always the case. I do not believe that Sylvester attempts to catch Daffy Duck.]

Building your own BSM with Discovery

ServiceNow Discovery gives you the ability to create relationships between CIs, build connections between applications, and even create and link to Business Services with Application Profile Discovery.

Discovery is a very feature-rich and incredibly customizable application. It allows you to tweak and change exactly what the system does at almost every point, meaning that it can quickly seem complex. Due to this, there is little need for customization since there are plenty of opportunities to add custom scripts and logic without creating or editing Business Rules and Script Includes.

Since many of the default options are very sensible, it is eminently possible to start finding devices in only a few minutes. In the next few sections, we will walk you through how these default options work.

Unlike most applications hosted on the ServiceNow platform, Discovery does not typically interact with users. Instead, it creates jobs on a scheduled basis, which is designed to populate data in the instance that other functions rely on. Most of the work that Discovery does happens through the MID server.

> Discovery is a separately licensable product. Other systems, such as Microsoft SCCM or HP uCMDB, may already have much of the data that Discovery will need to find. You may find that integrating with these products will achieve the same result.
>
> ServiceNow also offers a product called ServiceWatch. This was acquired through the acquisition of Neebula. As of the Fuji release of ServiceNow, it is not integrated into the ServiceNow platform. ServiceWatch also builds a relationship-based CMDB, but it does this at the application layer rather than by detecting infrastructure.

Remembering the MID server

The MID server, which was first found in *Chapter 6, Exchanging Data – Import Sets, Web Services, and Other Integrations* is a lightweight Java application that picks up jobs from the MID server, runs them, and then posts the results back to the instance. It does this locally by sitting inside the network and behind the firewall. This gives it far more access to the corporate devices than the instance, making it a critical part of Discovery.

> Corporate networks are set up to prevent external systems from probing and connecting to their business critical systems. Unfortunately, this prevents the ServiceNow instance too.

The graphic representation of the MID Server is given as follows:

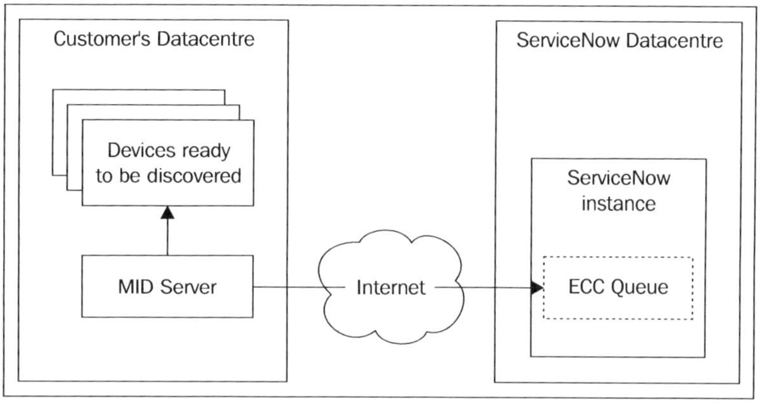

In general, you will need a MID server for each network that you wish to discover. Firewalls will stop the probes that a MID server uses, so, in a highly segmented network, you may need several. Additionally, if you have a large network and find that one MID server takes too long to deal with all the devices, you can scale out horizontally and add more copies for load balancing. Extra MID servers can also be added for redundancy.

> Not all MID servers are equal. For example, a Linux-based MID server is unable to use PowerShell to communicate with Windows servers. Discovery and Orchestration use the information on the **IP Ranges and Capabilities** Related Lists of the MID server record (**MID Server** > **Servers**) to determine which MID server can communicate with which device. More information on this is available at `http://wiki.servicenow.com/?title=MID_Server_Autofinder_for_Orchestration`.

Much of the MID Server terminology stems from its use in Discovery. A job given to the MID server to execute is called a **probe**; this attempts to find out more about the target by running commands. The response is acted on by a **sensor**—a script that attempts to make sense of the data. Both of these use the ECC queue to coordinate the processing that happens on the instance and the data collection run by the MID server. These probes are grouped together and collect information at various levels of detail.

Performing the Disco steps

Discovery follows a step-by-step process to find and link together the items that live in a network. These steps are methodical, predictable, and entirely configurable, giving you control over what Discovery does and subsequently sees. Each step consists of at least one probe and its equivalent sensor, cascading into the next.

- **Shazzam** (a port scan): ServiceNow scans the network and detects systems.
- **Classification** (connection): The open port is connected to and information is gathered about what the system is.
- **Identification** (find unique identifiers): Once the type of device is found, more appropriate commands can be run to extract unique identifiers, such as serial numbers, IP addresses, and hostnames.
- **Exploration** and **Process Classification** (get further information): These pick up as much information as possible, such as what software is running.

Finding devices with Shazzam

The vast majority of devices on a corporate network will have an IP address. Even if the device speaks multiple protocols (such as a SAN communicating over Fibre Channel), a management IP is likely to be available. Each IP address should be unique within the network, much like a phone number.

A port scan is much like someone deciding to ring every phone number in a town, one after another. If someone picks up, then the assumption is that the phone number is valid.

However, imagine if all the phones had extensions on them, which were mandatory to use. Then, in addition to knowing what phone number to dial, you would also have to give the extension number when you called it. However, to be helpful, suppose everyone agreed to work the same way, so that every sales team was on extension 10 and the support team was on extension 20. In this situation, the extension number is similar to a port.

When you visit a website, you will likely instruct your browser to connect to a server that is listening on either port 80 or port 443 (for a secure HTTPS connection) at a particular address. You need the Web Server to be waiting for your connection, ready to respond to your request.

> The ports used for an application are controlled by convention. The IANA maintains an official list of assignments, but this does not technically need to be followed.

Many systems in a network have open ports. Windows servers listen on port 135, while Unix-style devices listen on port 22, which is SSH. Other devices, such as routers, switches, and printers, listen on port 161.

All these three protocols are generally used for configuration and control. Just knowing whether the port is open is useful information. So, to continue our analogy, if we phoned extension 135 and someone picked up, then we are likely to speak to someone who knows WMI.

Configuring IP addresses for Shazzam

One of the first things that Discovery needs to know is where it should scan. In theory, you could ask Discovery the equivalent of ringing every phone number in the world, by starting at number 1. However, this is likely to take a while.

Instead, you should let Discovery know the IP addresses that it should scan for. This may be a private address range (such as 192.168.x.x) or a public range (such as 25.x.x.x). The main requirement is that the MID server should be able to connect to it.

If the networks are known, then a Discovery Schedule is the first configuration step. This specifies when and how often the scan should take place. The minimum information is simply a name, a time, and a MID server; the rest will take defaults.

Navigate to **Discovery** > **Discovery Schedules** to find the list. Use the **Quick ranges** Related Link to enter a network and the IP addresses in a simple format. Just entering the start and end IP addresses separated by a dash is a quick way to enter the information without needing to understand subnets. Of course, you can use the CIDR notation if you wish:

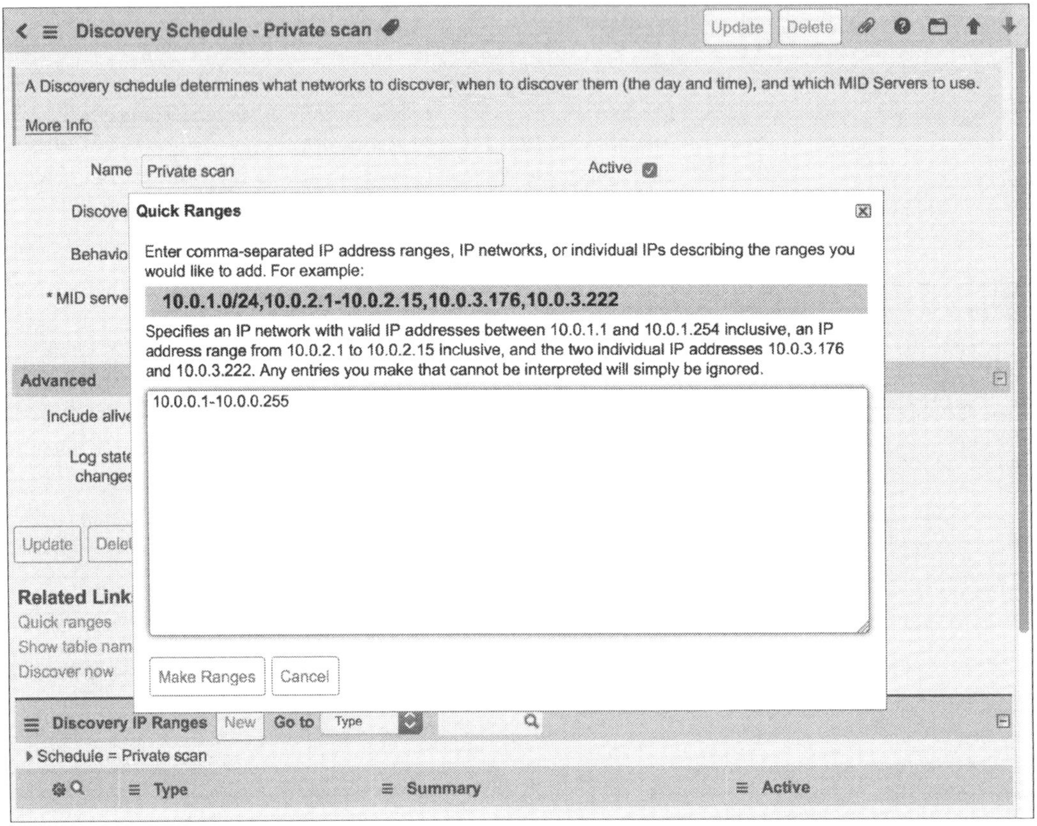

> Discovery Range Sets allow you to create a reusable bundle of IP ranges, meaning you don't need to repeat your entries. This is especially useful if you have a series of small subnets rather than a large network.

Automatically finding IP addresses

Wonderfully, Discovery can even find IP ranges from the network itself. A Network Discovery can be set up to query the routers that the MID server is connected to and find out what is accessible. To do this, create a Discovery Schedule, set the **Discover** field to Networks, and choose the **Network Discovery auto-starting routers** Related Link.

Once it has started, the MID server uses SNMP to connect to its default router, asking it for the list of networks that it supports. The router will tell the MID server about other routers, enabling it to fan out across the whole network. For more information on this feature, go to `http://wiki.servicenow.com/?title=Network_Discovery`.

> Most firewalls will prevent the MID server from jumping into another network. Ensure that you understand where the MID server logically sits compared to the items you want to discover.

Shouting out Shazzam

CI Discovery starts with a brute force scan. When the schedule starts, the instance places a message on the ECC queue, asking the MID server to connect to all the IP addresses in the IP range and connect to a series of ports to determine whether a device exists.

By default, the instance tries the active CI Discovery Ports. Each port is attempted using the **Classification** priority order and it usually stops when a connection is successful. If a port can be connected to, the MID server captures the response and then places it back in the ECC queue. This information is then used for the next stage—classification.

The **Discovery Port Probe** [`discovery_port_probe`] table defines each port and how it is dealt with. It is a critical part of Discovery since it is the starting point for the cascade of information. You can investigate the list by navigating to **Discovery Definition** > **Port Probes**.

Configuring Shazzam

There are many options available to control the scanning. A **Discovery Behavior** record can be associated with a schedule, which lets you choose the ports that will be scanned. For instance, if you know that only Linux servers exist in a particular network, it is a waste of time checking whether a Windows-only WMI port can be opened. It can also be used for load balancing and in devices that need special configuration.

A lot of logic can be added to the Discovery Behavior record. Groupings of ports are possible through **Functionality Definition** records, which can be made conditional with **Functionality Criteria**. These can use the `equality`, `contains`, and `start` operators—and even regular expressions—to determine what should happen.

Again, the wiki (`http://wiki.servicenow.com/?title=Discovery_Behavior`) has a great deal of detail on the available options.

> This is a good example of the high level of configurability that is available in Discovery. However, it is optional. By default, the platform will simply try all active CI Discovery Port Probes.

The Discovery Port Probe itself contains multiple options. For example, the **Scanner** field on the **Discovery Port Probe** record makes a note of how the port will be connected, and the choice made here selects which Java class will be used on the MID server to perform the connection. If the existence of an open port is enough, then the Generic TCP scanner will suffice. Others, such as HTTP and DNS, are more complex and will return more information on the initial connection than just on their existence. The **Script** field can take this information and use it to start to populate the CI.

Classifying CIs

An open port gives a certain amount of information. An open SSH port suggests a Unix-style server. So, when the instance detects a system where port 22 can be connected, it launches the **UNIX - Classify** probe. This is again defined on the Discovery Port Probe record.

However, many operating systems are Unix-based: Linux, Solaris, BSD, and even Apple's Mac OS X. How do we know which one it is?

To find out, you can run the `uname -a` command. When it is executed, it returns the name of the OS, its version, and lots of other details. For example, on a Linux system, the first item will be `Linux`; for an Apple MacBook running OS X, it will return `Darwin`. This provides us with just the information that is needed.

In fact, when faced with a system that allows a SSH connection, Discovery will run this exact command to find out what the device is.

- The **Unix - Classify** probe is a MultiProbe. This is a collection of two individual probes. Both are run at the same time.

> There are many probes that are provided in the out-of-the-box system and are stored in the **Probe** [`discovery_probes`] table. They can be found by navigating to **Discovery Definition** > **Probes**.

- First, the **UNIX - OS** Probe runs `uname -a`, the MID server simply executes this command on the remote system. The **Type** field on the Probe shows that it will be run using the `SSHCommand` Java class on the MID server.

> You may remember the **Topic** field on the ECC Queue table. It was used in *Chapter 6, Exchanging Data – Import Sets, Web Services, and Other Integrations,* to run JavaScript and other executables on the MID server (using JavascriptProbe and Command respectively).

- The other probe, **ESX - OS**, executes a script that is designed to extract information from a VMWare ESX server.
- The MID server executes the commands and places the results on the ECC queue. These are then processed by the relevant sensor.

> You can see all the sensors by navigating to **Discovery Definition** > **Sensors**.

- Since **Unix - Classify** is a MultiProbe, the **UNIX - Classify** MultiSensor provides two sensors, one for each probe.
- The **UNIX - OS** sensor parses the data that is returned from `uname`. In addition, another script field is available for further processing, if it is needed. In general, these sensors will start processing more, as we'll see next.

Sensing the classification

The results of the initial classification typically set properties. These properties are then used as an input for **Classification Criteria** that will examine the information and determine the type of device.

The **UNIX - OS** sensor understands the results of our command to find the OS that is running. The script in the sensor takes the first item in the returned string and stores it in the `name` variable of the `ciData` object. This is the most important item obtained from the Probe at this stage since it represents exactly what OS the device is running.

Once the sensors have collected and parsed the information, the instance must decide what to do with it next. The **Classifications** [`discovery_classy`] table is used to provide the information. Each Classification record has **Classification Criteria** associated with it. The Classification Criteria looks at the data stored in the `ciData` object. If the conditions evaluate to `true`, then the Classification is run.

> Find the Classifications by navigating to **Discovery Definition** > **CI Classification** > **All**.

- The Mac OS X Classification has a Classification Criteria of `name - equals - Darwin`.
- Unsurprisingly, the Linux Classification is `name - equals - Linux`.
- A Windows 2012 Server will need to have `name - contains - 2012` to be `true`.
- Some servers are slightly more complicated. An old Windows 2000 server must have a name containing `Windows 2000`, but it must not contain the word `Professional` in it. This indicates the desktop version of the Operating System that should be classified differently.

> To save time, the Classifications table is extended. The SSH Discovery Port Probe references the **Unix Classification** [`discovery_classy_unix`] table so that the irrelevant Windows records won't even be checked.

Once selected, the Classification will typically run a script. This can set some early properties of the CI, but it is often blank. In addition, many more probes will be launched. The instance knows what device it is dealing with, so it can ask the most appropriate questions. This information starts the Identification and Exploration phases.

> There are many opportunities to script in Discovery. There are lots of predefined Script Includes that are ready for reuse. These range from defining a MultiSensors structure to parsing manufacturer names. Over 100 scripts are listed and can be found by navigating to **Discovery Definition** > **Script Includes**.

Classifying other devices

The technique of using `uname` to classify the device is unique for devices with an open SSH port, but the process is common to all. The Classification probe that runs is dependent upon which port was found open through Shazzam.

For routers, switches, printers, and similar devices, SNMP is used, and WMI is, by default, used for Windows machines. If port 135 is open, then WMI is used to connect to and extract information from the Windows device (A property allows the use of PowerShell instead, which is generally recommended.) To see which Classification Probe is used for a particular port, look at the **Triggers probe field** in the Discovery Port Probe record.

Dealing with credentials

The majority of systems require authentication during the connection process. Just like how you need to give a username and password to access your computer, the MID server needs the appropriate credentials to access the devices that it has found. The details are stored in the instance in the **Credentials** [`discovery_credentials`] table, which is accessed by navigating to **Discovery** > **Credentials**.

> Several different types of authentication mechanisms can be stored in the table, which align with different scanner and connection mechanisms. A password can be given for SNMP devices and a username and password for Windows. For SSH, you can give a private key.

Some of the probes, or actions, that the MID server carries out may need superuser privileges. For example, understanding which processes are running on a Linux machine requires the use of `sudo`. Windows machines require access to sensitive information too. The provided credentials are encrypted inside the instance and transferred to the MID server when it is necessary.

Much more information, including what sort of permissions that the credentials require, is available at the wiki: `http://wiki.servicenow.com/?title=Credentials`.

Additionally, if desired, the information does not need to be sent to the instance at all. Instead, the credentials could be stored on the MID server or even in another database. This involves creating a Java class that retrieves the necessary details in the desired manner. Exactly how this is achieved is detailed in the wiki at `http://wiki.servicenow.com/?title=External_Credential_Storage`.

> As we've seen, a MultiProbe is a collection of other probes. The MID server authenticates once before running each element of a MultiProbe and seriously speeds things up.

Identifying the CI

When Discovery knows the type of device it is dealing with, the next step is to work out exactly which CI it is. For instance, you may know that the device is a Linux or Windows server, but how would you determine which one it is, out of the many hundreds or even thousands of devices in your network?

In a corporate network, you may use the domain name or the IP address of a server to identify it. Although they are useful, IP addresses may change. Additionally, a server often has multiple IP addresses, which would cause duplicate CIs to be created. A more unique item is a manufacturer-issued identifier, such as a serial number. However, not every device is issued with one or is simply unable to return a serial number. In addition, some devices may have multiple serial numbers!

Getting the right information

The identity probes try to collect as much information as possible. Many of the identification MultiProbes include at least two probes— network and hardware—to get the right information. The former collects the IP and MAC addresses of the device, while the latter grabs the serial numbers. These may come from the motherboard, the chassis, or something similar. The sensors for these probes populate the `ciData` object with the information.

> The ways to gather this information are OS dependent, but like the classification mechanism, they tend to be WMI focused for Windows devices and executable commands such as `dmidecode` and `system_profiler` for Linux and Mac OS X devices.

The Identification sensors are associated with the Classification record. Very often, they are reused. For instance, the **DNS** probe is associated with the both Windows and Linux servers, as well printer and switch Classifications. Others such as the **Windows - Identity** MultiProbe are more specific. Each one will interact with the device to extract a unique identifier, wherever it is possible.

> The **DNS** probe asks the operating system to reverse the IP address that it is using, in an attempt to find the fully qualified domain name and its hostname. This can be used as an identifier.

Performing identification

The data collected and parsed is then run through a series of **CI Identifier** [`ci_identifier`] scripts. Navigate to **Discovery Definition** > **CI Identification** > **Identifiers** to see them.

The aim of identification is to search the CMDB to see whether this device has been seen before. These scripts will result in one of following three actions:

- If an existing CI cannot be found, Discovery will create a new one
- If a single CI is found, then Discovery will update it with whatever information it has and can find
- If multiple matches are found and there are no other ways to differentiate between them, Discovery will log the information and stop.

The CI Identifier scripts take the information they have and perform lookups and queries to find matching CIs. Each CI Identifier has an order field and, as usual, lower numbers are processed first. More specific and more unique mechanisms are treated first.

For example, Discovery can find VMWare ESX virtual machines. Each virtual machine is given a unique identifier (UUID) by VMWare, and this is consistent and unique. This, therefore, goes first if the device has been classified as an ESX Server.

Afterwards, CI Identifiers that search for serial numbers are run and then the name of the device (usually the hostname) is used; this is followed by the IP and MAC addresses of the network.

If a single CI is found, then the execution stops. Otherwise, the platform will keep stepping through each one and try to make sense of the data to find the right CI.

> There are other deactivated identification scripts that are available in the base system. Activate them or create your own. The scripts must define a function that accepts the `ciData` object, a log variable, and the `GlideRecord` of the CI Identification record itself. In turn, they will all create an object that is instantiated from the `CIIdentifierResult` class. This contains the list of the matching CIs. It can also ask for the identification process to cease, if necessary.

Exploring the CI

In addition to initiating the identification of the device, the Classification record also launches several Exploration probes. For a Linux machine, this consists of 11 probes, while for a Windows Server 2012, up to 14 probes may be launched.

Some of these probes have conditions. For instance, Discovery may have detected in the Classification stage that the Windows machine is a HyperV host. This will cause the MID server to look for virtual machines and their associated networking.

Understanding exploration probes

Exploration probes are relatively straightforward since they follow the typical pattern that we've seen so far. The probes may run commands on the machine, perhaps by using an API to get information, pulling in a file, or asking for data using SNMP or WMI.

Then, the sensor parses the information. The majority of the sensors use JavaScript to understand the data returned from the MID server, but some probes will return an XML document. A sensor may then interpret the XML file directly.

In either case, the sensor has access to the `current` object of `GlideRecord`. Since the identification process has found the appropriate CI record, exploration sensors can set fields directly.

Creating custom probes and sensors

When dealing with issues on a server, it can be very useful if its resources, such as the amount of memory installed and the amount of free disk space, are at its disposal. The `Linux - Memory` and `Linux - Disks` exploration probes do just this. They are great examples of how your own custom probes can work.

`Linux - Memory` is a simple example. The probe runs a single command: `cat /proc/meminfo`. The `cat` command outputs the contents of the given file, which in this case is `/proc/meminfo`. On an UNIX-like operating system such as Linux, this virtual file contains a great deal of information about the current memory usage. The probe simply grabs it all and returns it back to the instance. The output may look something like this:

```
MemTotal:         3933000 kB
MemFree:           103004 kB
Buffers:            56092 kB
Cached:           2652648 kB
SwapCached:         70688 kB
Active:           1594160 kB
Inactive:         2059044 kB
...
```

The `Linux - Memory` sensor has a script that parses this information. First, it grabs the contents of the output, then it iterates over it line by line. Almost all of the information is thrown away, apart from the `MemTotal` line. This value is manipulated to be a value in megabytes, and then it is rounded up and stored in the **RAM (MB)** field of the `current` object of `GlideRecord`.

Each sensor instantiates a new object using the `DiscoverySensor` class. The object overrides its own properties on creation by using the functions that have been passed to it. The whole Script Include is relatively complex, but for simple situations, you only need to create the process function. A very simple example would be to just use the `output` variable from `result` and set the description field, as follows:

```
new DiscoverySensor({
    process: function(result) {
        current.short_description = result.output;
    },
    type: "DiscoverySensor"
});
```

> One way to simplify sensor scripts is to create a more involved command-line tool to get the data from the device. Using standard tools, output can be cut and "grepped" to find just the item that you are interested in. It is a judgment call as to whether processing in the command line or on the instance is preferable.

Relating CIs together

The **Linux - Disks** sensor is more complicated but shows how detected information can be made into child CIs. For example, a storage device such as an SSD or HDD is an independent unit that can be replaced or removed. Recording what drives are inserted into a machine can be useful to help with the diagnosis of out of space errors!

Discovery will create a new CI for every drive that it finds in a particular machine. It then creates a relationship and uses a Reference field.

The `addToRelatedList` function in `DiscoverSensor` is used to do this. Call it from the `process` function that we discussed previously:

```
var disks = [{
    'name': 'disk0s2',
    'disk_space': '250.01'
}]
this.addToRelatedList('cmdb_ci_disk', disks, 'computer', 'name');
```

The first parameter is the CI class or its table. The second parameter is an array of objects that contain information about what fields should be populated—in this case: `name` and `disk_space`. The third parameter is the reference field pointing to the CI, while the fourth parameter is the value that should be taken from the parent CI to relate the CIs together.

> The same process is used to discover and then relate software. In this case, the process runs a command (or looks at the installed software in the registry). Discovery also looks at open connections on the machine with the hope of finding two CIs that are communicating with each other. This will cause a relationship to form.

Ensuring high-quality data

Discovery relies upon the information that the device returns. It will record data, such as how much memory is installed on the machine, what the operating system is, and much more, in the CMDB.

However, inconsistencies in the way the information is presented to the instance can have an impact on how useful it would be. For instance, some devices may return the manufacturer as HP, while others may return Hewlett-Packard, HP Company, or a multitude of other combinations. Otherwise, some may count disk space using base 10 and others with base 2.

To deal with this problem the Field Normalization plugin is often used with Discovery. It provides two great features to get the data into the right format:

- **Normalization** changes different forms that mean the same into a consistent value. Xeon, Intel(R) Xeon(TM), and Intel Xeon 3GHZ can all be normalized into a single string, Intel Xeon. Regular expressions can be used to detect the strings that you want to replace. For more information on this refer to the wiki at `http://wiki.servicenow.com/?title=Normalizing_a_Field`.
- **Transformation** alters the value using rules. For instance, the prefix `Inc` could be removed from all company names, as well as rounding numbers, for example, from `4112` to `4000`. For more information on this refer to the wiki at `http://wiki.servicenow.com/?title=Field_Transformations`.

Associating CIs to Business Services

Since Discovery finds information from the device up, it cannot figure out what it is actually used for. For example, while it may discover that a web server is running on a Linux machine, it wouldn't know what that web server was actually hosting; the intranet, a public portal, or a web application.

> ServiceWatch is specifically designed to provide a top-down approach so that it has a much better idea of what the installed software is doing.

In order to help you, Discovery can use a series of probes and sensors called Application Profile Discovery, or APD. This requires two XML files to be placed into the system:

- The **environment** file describes the application, what Business Service it belongs to, and any other services that it relies on. (In our previous example, you may want to connect the VidStream application with the billing systems.)
- The **version** file is typically bundled with the software. If the software, and thus the service, is updated, then the version file should be altered and incremented.

> Note that I'm distinguishing between software, which is executable, and an application, which gives the user the functionality. For example, ServiceNow is an application, and it uses MySQL and Tomcat software to do what it does.

Using APD

When APD is activated in the Discovery properties, the MID server will scan a particular directory to get the environment's XML file. In this example, the following file would be placed at the default location: `/etc/opt/APD/vod.xml`. It contains information on what Business Service the application is related to—in this case, the Video On Demand Business Service:

```
<?xml version="1.0" encoding="UTF-8"?>
<apd>
<config version="1.0" application="VidStream" type="environment"
system="uklinx01">
  <environment>
    <label>Production</label>
    <business_service>Video on Demand</business_service>
    <application_version_path path="/usr/local/vidstream/vidstream.
xml"/>
    </environment>
</config>
</apd>
```

The location of the version file and the system is specified in the environment file. In this case, the `/usr/local/vidstream/vidstream.xml` file is searched on `uklinx01`.

> The `system` attribute is optional. Discovery defaults to the current device. In addition, there are several other optional parameters, such as those relating to other Business Services. The `<label>` tag describes the information that is placed onto the Environment-related list on the Application CI. You can find more information on the wiki at `http://wiki.servicenow.com/?title=Application_Profile_Discovery`.

The version file describes the application a little more, giving details such as the description, which group owns the application, and the version number:

```
<?xml version="1.0" encoding="UTF-8"?>
<apd>
  <config version="1.0" application="VidStream" type="version">
    <version>
        <label>VidStream</label>
        <description>Custom build application to stream video to
whoever wants it</description>
        <ownership>Development</ownership>
    </version>
  </config>
</apd>
```

Finally, since this information will cause Discovery to find a new CI, we need to classify it. A new **Application Classification** record should be created in **Application** by navigating to **Discovery Definition** > **CI Classification** > **Application**. This specifies the relationship type (such as **Runs on::Runs**). To ensure that Discovery matches this information to the Application, a **Classification Criteria** name should be made with, for example, `name - equals - VidStream`.

When Discovery is run now, it should make a great looking BSM!

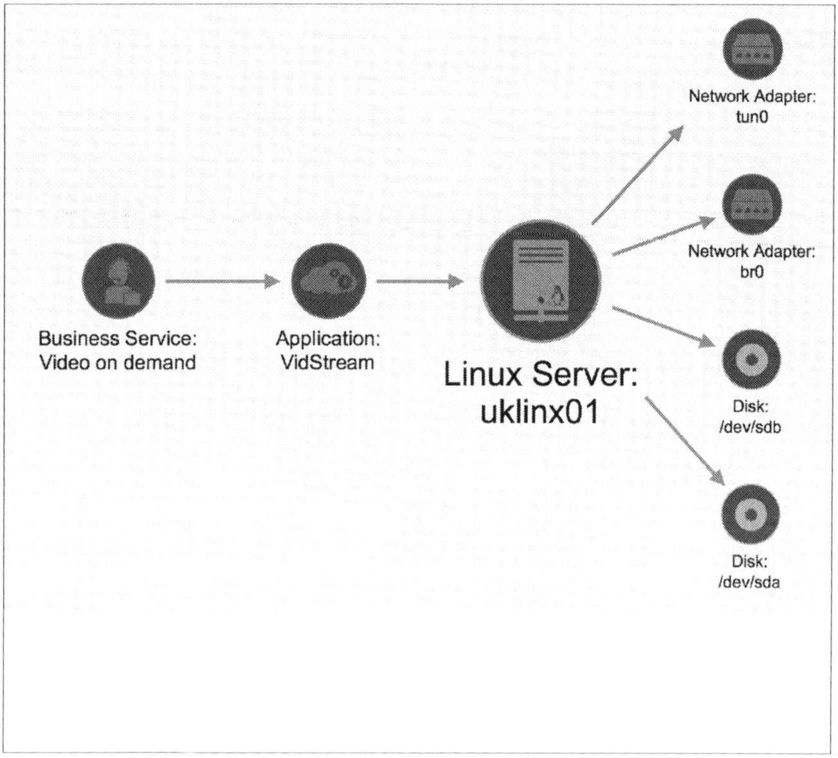

Summing up Discovery

The process that Discovery follows is very iterative; the instance uses probes that ask the MID server to connect to devices, and sensors deal with the response.

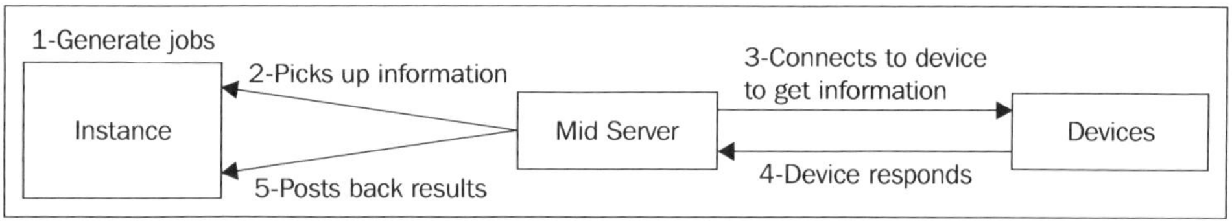

The purpose of the probes differs, depending on the stage in the process in which Discovery is:

- **Shazzam** connects to an IP range and tries the ports that are defined in the Discovery Port Probe record
- **Classification** is given a hint about what port it is successfully connected to. It runs commands or extracts information through that port. The credentials are used at this step.
- **Identification** occurs so that Discovery knows exactly which device is being dealt with. It uses serial numbers and network information to try to uniquely identify the device.
- **Exploration** updates (or creates) a new CI with all the information that Discovery can find. This includes resource information such as disks and memory, what software is running on the machine, what connections are open to other machines, and what applications are reliant upon this machine using APD:

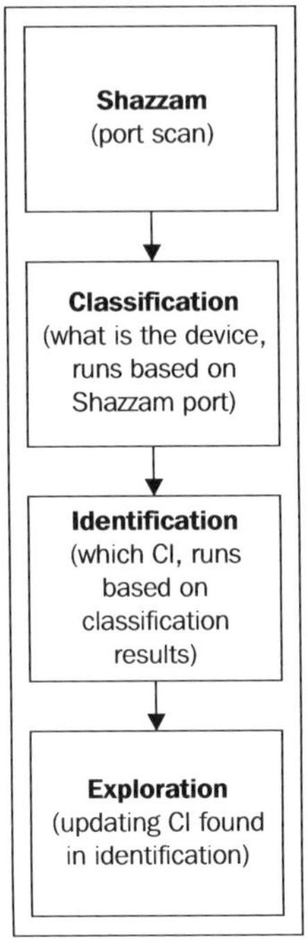

Together, these elements extract information from your devices and place it in the ServiceNow CMDB. This data then allows you to understand the relationship between items, giving impact analysis capabilities. Of course, this information can be used in the Orchestration and Configuration Automation capabilities of ServiceNow.

Automating services with Orchestration

The idea behind Orchestration is a simple one. ServiceNow automatically performs jobs on servers that would otherwise be done manually. Some of these tasks may be subject to automation because they are complex and error prone, but most often because they are repetitive. For example, it is probable that the most common use of an IT help desk is to reset passwords. This has a high cost to the business in terms of time spent by the requester and the staff manning the help desk. By using Orchestration, an analyst could reset an Active Directory password through the click of a button, save everyone's time, and provide a much better service.

> ServiceNow also has a dedicated **Password Reset** application. It uses some of the technologies in Orchestration to provide a Self-Service application that allows anyone to reset their password with a few clicks. You can find more information on the wiki at `http://wiki.servicenow.com/?title=Password_Reset`.

Orchestration is essentially an extension to the Graphical Workflow engine. This was first discussed in *Chapter 4, Getting Things Done with Tasks*. Graphical Workflow will run through a string of predefined activities– it may perhaps perform an approval, followed by the creation of a task, and then send an e-mail. However, instead of performing actions that affect tasks inside ServiceNow, the activities provided by Orchestration run on remote systems.

> Orchestration is a separately licensable part of ServiceNow. All of the functionality that the plugin provides could be replicated using scripts and Business Rules on the ECC queue, as described in *Chapter 6, Exchanging Data – Import Sets, Web Services, and Other Integrations*. Orchestration makes automation easy.

Over 30 new activities are provided by Orchestration, and they cover a wide variety of administrative topics. Some of these are as follows:

- **Install Windows App** targets a Windows machine and installs an MSI package. This could be used to automate software delivery through a Service Catalog request.
- **Run SCP** copies a file from one system into another. This activity could automate a software release—perhaps, the movement of a configuration file.
- **Change Service State** connects to a Windows machine and starts or stops a service running on it. This could be part of a failover activity.

- **Test Server Alive** checks whether a machine responds on a specific port. This simply performs the Shazzam Discovery step on demand and gives vital clues about the health of a server.

> For a full list, check out the wiki at `http://wiki.servicenow.com/?title=Orchestration_Activities`.

All of the activities work in the same way; they place jobs on the ECC Queue, which the MID server runs. We've already seen how this works in *Chapter 6, Exchanging Data – Import Sets, Web Services, and Other Integrations*.

Automating password resets with Orchestration

The drag and drop nature of the Graphical Workflow makes it very easy to build an automated Password Rest activity. A very simple workflow can reset a password with only one activity.

1. Create a Workflow with the name **Reset password** on the **User** [`sys_user`] table.
2. Ensure that **If condition matches** is set to **-- None --** since it must be triggered manually.
3. Include an activity, either **Reset AD User Password** or **Reset Linux User Password**. Within the activity, set the server that should be targeted and specify the username as `${current.user_name}` and a temporary password.
4. To complete the configuration of this very simple workflow, join all the activities with transitions:

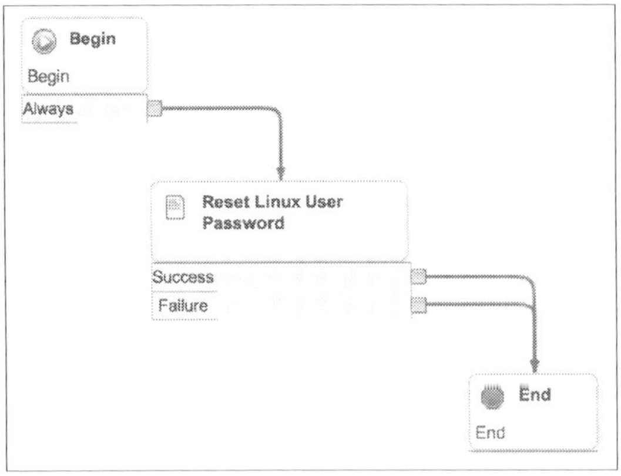

Running the Automation workflow

This workflow needs to be run on demand. This can be done through a script.

Create a UI Action by using the following details:

- **Name**: `Reset Password`
- **Table**: `User [sys_user]`
- **Form link**: `<checked>`
- **Script**:

```
var w = new Workflow();
var flowId = w.getWorkflowFromName("Reset password");
w.startFlow(flowId, current, current.operation());
```

> This script could be run through a Business Rule or on any other of the multitude of places in ServiceNow where a script can run.

The code uses the Workflow Script Include. Firstly, it finds the `sys_id` of the Workflow through the `getWorkflowFromName` function and passes it into the `startFlow` function. This also takes the the `current` object of `GlideRecord` that the workflow runs against.

When the UI Action is clicked, a stream of actions happen:

1. The script in the UI Action finds the Workflow and starts it.
2. The Workflow starts and runs the **Reset User Password** Activity.
3. This places a job (a probe) on the ECC Queue.
4. The MID server picks up the job and executes it.
5. This instructs the MID server to initiate a connection to the target server.
6. The appropriate command is run (such as `passwd` on a Linux target).
7. The response is collected through the connection.
8. The MID server places the information on the ECC Queue.
9. The **Sensor** script reads the ECC Queue and processes the response.
10. The running workflow is triggered and the activity is completed.
11. The workflow ends.

> This process could be made much better. At the moment, there is little error handling, no feedback is given to the user, and the same password is used each time. One way to improve the workflow is to generate a random password and e-mail it to the user upon success. At the very least, a little logging should be included!

Running custom commands

While the built-in activities cover many common situations, such as creating new user accounts, you may want to do something that isn't covered by these activities. The generic activities included in the Orchestration plugin are a great way to achieve this:

- **Run Powershell** asks a Window-based MID server to run a PowerShell command. PowerShell is an interface that allows commands and scripts to configure and interact with Windows systems. Almost any activity that can be achieved through the Windows GUI can be accomplished with a PowerShell command or script, and many Microsoft products provide cmdlets for extra functionality. For instance, System Center will control virtual machines through a PowerShell script. The Run PowerShell activity will often reference a PowerShell script that is stored on the MID server or a remote drive. The sensor script allows you to parse the output that is stored in the `activity.output` variable in case Workflow branching is required.

> The Exchange activities run predefined PowerShell commands. They make it easy to do common activities such as deleting mailboxes and creating mailing lists.

- **Run Command** executes a script or executable on a target machine that is accessible through SSH. The MID server makes a connection, then runs the commands, using `sudo` if specified, and returns any output. This allows you to communicate with a daemon or run shell commands, just as you would if you were remotely connected to it.
- **Run Probe** is the base activity for Orchestration activities. The others extend this in an object-oriented fashion. The Run Probe activity requires the name of a probe from the **Probes** [`discovery_probes`] table. You can make your own activities in this way and build a library of predefined commands and templates that you can string together, as necessary.

There are also **SOAP Message** and **REST Message** activities that are included in the ServiceNow platform. These allow you to connect to remote systems in a Workflow, just like the other activities that Orchestration provides, but they do not provide any additional functionality beyond this. Instead, they provide a wrapper around the standard functionality that was shown in *Chapter 6, Exchanging Data – Import Sets, Web Services, and Other Integrations*.

ServiceNow Cloud Provisioning

Orchestration gives you the tools to build your own automated workflows. However, if you are looking for a full end-to-end lifecycle system for virtual machines, then Cloud Provisioning may fit the bill. It pulls together many elements from almost every chapter in this book to provide a full application to manage VMWare and Amazon EC2-based virtual machines.

> If you'd like to create your own workflows, then the **Orchestration Activities - VMware** and **Orchestration Activities - EC2** plugins will provide you with the appropriate activities. Otherwise, the **Orchestration - VMWare Support** and **Orchestration - Amazon EC2** plugins will provide all the functionality.

Introducing virtual machines

Virtual machines provide a way for one physical machine to host many instances of a computer system. The most common implementations fully virtualize an entire machine, so the virtual environments may not realize that they do not have full control of the hardware. Several operating systems, known as guests, are run on one host machine. The Hypervisor is the software that runs on the host and manages the virtual machines.

> Virtualization provides many benefits, including enormous flexibility, cost savings, and the faster provisioning of systems.

Requesting a virtual machine with Cloud Provisioning

A ServiceNow instance that runs Cloud Provisioning will send commands to the Hypervisor on behalf of the requester. It will connect to the APIs provided by VMWare ESX or Amazon EC2 to create virtual machines, alter settings, or terminate instances that are no longer required. Although installing the desired OS from the beginning is possible, images built by the IT department are often preferable as they contain the right software that is already installed.

1. The requester uses the Service Catalog in ServiceNow, which was first seen in *Chapter 4, Getting Things Done with Tasks*, to browse and search for the virtual machine image that they want. The Service Catalog provides information, such as the expected delivery time of the virtual machine, and asks the requester about the resources that they need—the disk space or processor requirements.
2. As the requester changes the options, such as asking for more memory, the price may change. This is reflected in the interface and is made visible in any approvals.
3. Once the selection is made, a provisioning workflow can either be fully automatic, only pausing for the necessary approvals, or a fulfiller can intervene and make decisions about where the machine will be hosted. Notifications, such as those described in *Chapter 5, Events, Notifications, and Reporting*, are leveraged throughout the process.
4. The MID server is used to communicate with the VMWare ESX systems, which was first set up in *Chapter 6, Exchanging Data – Import Sets, Web Services, and Other Integrations*. The instance communicates "cloud to cloud" with Amazon EC2 Web Services using REST.
5. Virtual machines running on ESX can be collected and used to populate the CMDB. This ensures that virtual infrastructure can be visualized through the BSM, which was discussed in the first sections of this chapter.
6. Once the virtual machines are established, they can be controlled through UI Actions on the CMDB record. A user with the appropriate permissions can stop, start, and pause virtual machines.
7. In order to save costs and remove virtual machines when they are no longer needed, virtual machines can be automatically started and stopped, freeing up resources for other uses. The instance uses scheduled jobs to ensure this happens at the right time, which was covered in *Chapter 5, Events, Notifications, and Reporting*.

8. Reporting, which was also discussed in *Chapter 5, Events, Notifications, and Reporting*, is a part of the Cloud Provisioning feature set. Three home pages provide lists of which machines are running, and they also give an overview by using a variety of graphs and lists. These are accessible in the interface by navigating to **Cloud Provisioning** > **Management** > **Service Monitoring Portal** and **Cloud Operations Portal**.

Configuration Automation

Cloud Provisioning is a quick and easy way to generate new virtual machines. With a few clicks, a requester can select the image they want, and ServiceNow will work with the host's API to get it running. The virtual machines may be used to add extra resources to a live system, or perhaps, for testing new versions. In either case, they will need to be configured to meet the needs of what they are hosting:

- An application server may need a specific version of Java installed
- A secure web server will need certificates to be installed and maintained
- A database will need the right user access permissions and security settings

While a recent image may provide the basic configuration, it is not feasible to create a completely comprehensive library that will meet all needs. Additionally, servers need to be maintained as certificates will expire and security patches will need to be applied.

Configuration Automation utilities help with these activities. They provide a host of benefits:

- **Speed**: An automated system can configure many targets much quicker than a person can
- **Consistency**: Each target will be prepared in exactly the desired manner each time
- **Time**: Automation frees up a developer or System Administrator to work on other projects

ServiceNow provides pre-built integrations with two Configuration Automation systems— Puppet and Chef—to enable them to prepare systems as needed. The plugins extend the CMDB, so the devices will follow the configuration that is set on the CI.

> The **Puppet Configuration Management** and **Chef Configuration Management** plugins contain all the functionality, while the **Orchestration Activities - Puppet** and **Orchestration Activities - Chef** plugins just contain the Workflow Activities.

Controlling servers with Puppet

Puppet is an open source system that is designed for System Administrators to manage servers automatically. It uses an agent that is installed on the node, which can be running Windows or Linux. The Puppet agent will regularly check in with a server called the Puppet Master.

> The Puppet agent is often installed as part of a base image of the virtual machine.

The Puppet Master creates catalogs; each contains the desired system state for a particular node. The Puppet Master will use a variety of information sources to develop this catalog, specifying exactly what should be installed and set. One of these sources can include ServiceNow.

Creating the catalogs

Each catalog is made up of Puppet resources, such as files and packages, which need to be controlled on the node. It is written in a device-independent language and gives a cross platform element. For example, if two nodes were running different operating systems, they can be commonly specified to install a web service module. This may result in Apache on a Linux node or IIS on Windows.

> The Puppet resources must be maintained on the Puppet Master. ServiceNow communicates with the Puppet Master to collect the resources and populate them in the instance.

From these resources, the Node Definition can be created within ServiceNow. This represents the contribution of the ServiceNow instance for the desired configuration. To create a Node Definition, navigate to **Puppet** > **Resources** > **Node Definitions** and combine the resources that are provided by the Puppet Master.

Configuring Puppet and ServiceNow

The communication between the Puppet Master and ServiceNow occurs in both directions. The MID server runs commands through SSH to update the Puppet Master, while scripts installed on the Puppet Service can pull information from the instance on demand.

To achieve this integration, the Puppet plugin provides several components:

- A sample External Node Classifier script that contacts the ServiceNow instance whenever the Puppet Master needs to build a new catalog. This must be installed on the Puppet Master.
- A Scripted Web Service that runs on the ServiceNow instance. This accepts the domain name of the node and returns a YAML-formatted response that the Puppet Master understands.
- An extended CMDB, allowing a CI to be associated with Puppet resources and attributes. A Linux Server CI may be associated with a web server module through the Node Definition record. This may instruct Puppet to install software or alter files.
- Workflows and activities that extract information from the Puppet Master and the nodes it is communicating with. These are implemented as probes and sensors; the MID server uses SSH to connect with the Puppet Master and runs queries to return the desired information. For instance, the Get Modules Workflow Activity asks the Puppet Master what modules are installed on a particular node.

> The Workflow Activities included with the Puppet plugin are described in detail on the wiki at `http://wiki.servicenow.com/?title=Puppet_Activities`.

- Scheduled extraction of the resources from the Puppet Master. This uses the workflows to update the Puppet resource tables in ServiceNow that need to be mixed into a Node Definition.

Cooking with Chef

Chef provides a very similar functionality to Puppet and works in a similar way. It also has nodes that run client software and check into a central server. However, rather than the agent comparing the configuration to a provided list, Chef runs a more procedural approach where a list of conditional activities is executed line by line. These sets of activities, in line with the culinary theme, are called recipes. A recipe describes the state in which resources should be, such as installing packages, running services, or editing files.

Chef uses the Ruby programming language to define its recipes. This makes it much more powerful, with the possibility of more control, but it makes it more complicated to use, especially for non-programmers.

This has resulted in Chef being used more by developers, and especially for code deployments. It enables developers to write and test a deployment script that will quickly ensure that the target system is set up in just the right way.

Folding Chef into ServiceNow

Chef does not have the concept of an External Node Classifier such as Puppet. Instead, ServiceNow is more proactive, and you have to push changes to the Chef central server when necessary. No scripts need to be installed on the Chef server. It nonetheless uses the same base functionalities as Puppet:

- Certain CMDB classes, such as Server, can be associated with a Node Definition. When the Node Definition changes, a Workflow is run to update the Chef server.
- Chef recipes often use the attributes of the node to decide what needs to be done. This can be listed against each CI in an extension of the CMDB model.
- Several new Workflows and Activity Definitions are included. These communicate with Chef's server using SSH via the MID server.

> The Workflow Activities included with the Chef plugin are described in detail on the wiki at `http://wiki.servicenow.com/?title=Orchestration_Chef_Activities`.

- Just like Puppet, the instance extracts the appropriate information from the central server. All the recipes and components are pulled from the server on demand.

> While there is no built-in extraction like there is in the Puppet plugin, this can easily be configured by using a Scheduled Workflow.

Running Configuration Automation

Using ServiceNow as a component of Puppet or the Chef Configuration Management system brings great advantages. The ServiceNow instance becomes the place where servers are managed and controlled, giving a tight integration to the ITSM Change Management process. This gives a chain of automated actions:

1. A user with the appropriate permissions may want to update or change a CI—perhaps, repurpose it or move it to a newer software version. This is done by creating a **Configuration Automation Change** [`cfg_auto_change`] record, which is visible as a Related List on the **Computer** [`cmdb_ci_computer`] form.
2. Once the appropriate settings have been made, a **Request Change** Related List UI Action is available to create a **Change Request** record.
3. Upon the approval of the Change Request, a UI Action is available on the **Configuration Automation Change** record to proceed further. This updates the CI record itself.
4. If the node is managed by Puppet, it will contact the Puppet Master on a scheduled basis. In turn, this will connect to the web service in ServiceNow and pull down the desired configuration.
5. For nodes managed by Chef, the instance will, using an Orchestration Workflow, connect to Chef's server via the MID server and update the desired configuration.
6. The node will make the appropriate configuration changes by installing, removing, and modifying files and packages as necessary.

Summary

In this chapter, we've seen how Gardiner Hotels can represent Business Services within ServiceNow. IT systems underpin almost all activities within a modern business, and the Business Service Map shows how a multitude of devices support each service.

Often, it can be a challenge to find out just which devices are out there in the network. **Discovery** is designed to do just this and more. In conjunction with the MID server, Discovery runs an agentless scan to find everything that can respond. A step-by-step process then classifies, identifies, and explores each device. The resultant information is stored in the ServiceNow CMDB.

Any servers that have been found can be automated with **Orchestration**. This plugin provides extra activities for the Graphical Workflow engine and allows interaction with corporate systems to perform activities such as the creation of e-mail accounts and users automatically.

Additionally, the Chef and Puppet plugins provide even more capability with **Configuration Automation**. These automatically ensure that a server is set up in just the right way by applying a Node Definition template. **Cloud Provisioning** works with Amazon EC2 and VMWare ESX to provide a complete end-to-end lifecycle. New systems can be created or destroyed on demand or automatically, providing flexibility and responsiveness to virtual infrastructure.

ServiceNow is focused on Service Automation. Being a task-based workflow platform, it enables requests to be managed from conception to completion. These requests may be for IT services or for other parts of the business. This book started with the foundations of the platform and ramped up, explaining how a ServiceNow master can configure, control, and customize their instance.

Together, these tools enable ServiceNow to manage, monitor, and maintain all Business Services. Better visibility of information and more automation enables a service-centric approach, ensuring that the business's critical systems are deployed quickly and kept running reliably. Everyone can get a great night sleep, not just the guests at Gardiner Hotels.

Index

A

B

D

F

G

H

I

J

L

M

N

O

P

S

T

U

V

W

X

[PACKT] enterprise
PUBLISHING professional expertise distilled

Heroku Cloud Application Development

ISBN: 978-1-78355-097-5 Paperback: 336 pages

A comprehensive guide to help you build, deploy, and troubleshoot cloud applications seamlessly using Heroku

1. Understand the concepts of the Heroku platform: how it works, the application development stack, and security features.
2. Learn how to build, deploy, and troubleshoot a cloud application in the most popular programming languages easily and quickly using Heroku.
3. Leverage the book's practical examples to build your own "real" Heroku cloud applications in no time.

Salesforce CRM: The Definitive Admin Handbook

Second Edition

ISBN: 978-1-78217-052-5 Paperback: 426 pages

A comprehensive guide for the setup, configuration, and customization of Salesforce CRM

1. Updated for Spring '13, this book covers best practice administration principles, real-world experience, and critical design considerations for setting up and customizing Salesforce CRM.
2. Analyze data within Salesforce by using reports, dashboards, custom reports, and report builder.

Please check **www.PacktPub.com** for information on our titles

[PACKT] enterprise
professional expertise distilled
PUBLISHING

QlikView for Developers Cookbook

ISBN: 978-1-78217-973-3 Paperback: 290 pages

Discover the strategies needed to tackle the most challenging tasks facing the QlikView developer

1. Learn beyond QlikView training.
2. Discover QlikView Advanced GUI development, advanced scripting, complex data modelling issues, and much more.
3. Accelerate the growth of your QlikView developer ability.
4. Based on over 7 years' experience of QlikView development.

Visual Studio 2013 Cookbook

ISBN: 978-1-78217-196-6 Paperback: 332 pages

Over 50 simple but incredibly effective recipes to get you up and running with the powerful features of Visual Studio 2013

1. Provides you with coverage of all the new Visual Studio 2013 features regardless of your programming language preference.
2. Recipes describe how to apply Visual Studio to all areas of development: writing, debugging, and application lifecycle maintenance.
3. Straightforward examples of building apps for Windows 8.1.

Please check **www.PacktPub.com** for information on our titles

43920519R00335

Made in the USA
Lexington, KY
17 August 2015